intel®

U.S. and CANADA LITERATURE ORDER FORM

NAME: ______________________

COMPANY: ______________________

ADDRESS: ______________________

CITY: ______________________ STATE: ______

COUNTRY: ______________________

PHONE NO.: ( ) ______________________

AF710030

ORDER NO.	TITLE	QTY.		PRICE		TOTAL
			×		=	
			×		=	
			×		=	
			×		=	
			×		=	
			×		=	
			×		=	
			×		=	
			×		=	
			×		=	

Subtotal ______

Must Add Your Local Sales Tax ______

Include postage: Must add 15% of Subtotal to cover U.S. and Canada postage. (20% all other.) → Postage ______

Total ______

Pay by check, money order, or include company purchase order with this form ($200 minimum). We also accept VISA, MasterCard or American Express. Make payment to Intel Literature Sales. Allow 2-3 weeks for delivery.

☐ VISA ☐ MasterCard ☐ American Express Expiration Date ______________________

Account No. ______________________

Signature ______________________

Mail To: Intel Literature Sales
P.O. Box 7641
Mt. Prospect, IL 60056-7641

International Customers outside the U.S. and Canada should use the International order form on the next page or contact their local Sales Office or Distributor.

For phone orders in the U.S. and Canada
Call Toll Free: (800) 548-4725

Prices good until 12/31/93.
Source HB

CG/LOF1/103092

intel.

INTERNATIONAL LITERATURE ORDER FORM

NAME: ____________________

COMPANY: ____________________

ADDRESS: ____________________

CITY: ____________ STATE: ________ ZIP: ________

COUNTRY: ____________________

PHONE NO.: ( )

ORDER NO.	TITLE	QTY.		PRICE		TOTAL
			×		=	
			×		=	
			×		=	
			×		=	
			×		=	
			×		=	
			×		=	
			×		=	
			×		=	
			×		=	

Subtotal ________

Must Add Your Local Sales Tax ________

Total ________

PAYMENT

Cheques should be made payable to your *local* Intel Sales Office (see inside back cover).

Other forms of payment may be available in your country. Please contact the Literature Coordinator at your *local* Intel Sales Office for details.

The completed form should be marked to the attention of the LITERATURE COORDINATOR and returned to your *local* Intel Sales Office.

CG/092792

8086/8088 USER'S MANUAL PROGRAMMER'S AND HARDWARE REFERENCE

1989

Additional copies of this manual or other Intel literature may be obtained from:

Intel Corporation
Literature Sales
P.O. Box 7641
Mt. Prospect, IL 60056-7641

CG-110392

PREFACE

This manual describes the Intel® 8086/8088 Family of Microprocessors.

The information is divided into two sections.

Section One, "Programming," is a general introduction. It contains an overview of the Central Processing Units (CPUs) of the 8086/8088 family, and gives some general design information. This section also includes a general description of the programming design of the 8087 Numeric Processor Extension (NPX).

Section Two, "Hardware," is a reference source. It contains specific hardware design information on the operation of the CPUs in the 8086/8088 family. This section also includes specific hardware design information on the operation and functions of the 8087 NPX.

This manual contains the following chapters and appendices:

SECTION ONE, PROGRAMMING

- Chapter 1, "Introduction to Microcomputers." It introduces microcomputer concepts and terminology.
- Chapter 2, "The 8086/8088 Family Overview." It provides an overview of the key features of the 8086/8088 family. It also contains a brief overview of the 8087 NPX.
- Chapter 3, "The 8086/8088 Architecture and Instructions." It discusses in detail the programming architecture of the 8086/8088 family, including the execution unit (EU) and bus interface unit (BIU), register structure, memory structure, I/O port organization, addressing modes, and instruction set. This chapter contains several programming examples.
- Chapter 4, "8086/8088 Hardware Design Overview." It contains block-diagram-level information that the programmer can use when incorporating the basic 8086/8088 microprocessors into microcomputer systems. This chapter also describes the bus structures, multiprocessing, and processor control of the 8086/8088 family.
- Chapter 5, "8087 Numeric Processor Extension (NPX) Programming Design." It includes an overview of the 8087 NPX. This chapter describes the architecture, computational fundamentals, and instruction set of the 8087 NPX. It also contains several programming examples.

SECTION TWO, HARDWARE

- Chapter 6, "The 8086/8088 CPU." It contains specific hardware design information on the operation of the CPU in the 8086/8088 family. This chapter presents architectural and software considerations, pin functional and electrical signal definitions, operating modes, address and data bus operation, protocols for bus transfers, and interrupt operation. This chapter also describes the functions of the circuits that support the 8086/8088 family.

- Chapter 7, "8087 Numeric Processor Extension (NPX) Hardware Design." It provides general information on the NPX coprocessor and its operations, including a component overview of the architectural and software considerations, and pin functional signal definitions.

  This chapter also describes the operating modes, bus operation, and timing of the NPX, along with its general operation with 8086/8088 host CPUs. In addition, this chapter explains the NPX protocols for bus transfers to the host CPUs, and the interrupt operation of the NPX.

TABLE OF CONTENTS

PAGE

CHAPTER 1
INTRODUCTION TO MICROCOMPUTERS

CHAPTER 2
THE 8086, 8088 FAMILY OVERVIEW

CHAPTER 3
THE 8086/8088 ARCHITECTURE AND INSTRUCTIONS

CHAPTER 4
8086/8088 HARDWARE DESIGN OVERVIEW

CHAPTER 6
THE 8086/8088 CPU

CHAPTER 7
8087 NUMERIC PROCESSOR EXTENSION (NPX) HARDWARE DESIGN

Figure

Figure

Figure

Figure

Figure

Tables

Tables

Tables

CUSTOMER SUPPORT

INTEL'S COMPLETE SUPPORT SOLUTION WORLDWIDE

Customer Support is Intel's complete support service that provides Intel customers with hardware support, software support, customer training, consulting services and network management services. For detailed information contact your local sales offices.

After a customer purchases any system hardware or software product, service and support become major factors in determining whether that product will continue to meet a customer's expectations. Such support requires an international support organization and a breadth of programs to meet a variety of customer needs. As you might expect, Intel's customer support is quite extensive. It can start with assistance during your development effort to network management. 100 Intel sales and service offices are located worldwide — in the U.S., Canada, Europe and the Far East. So wherever you're using Intel technology, our professional staff is within close reach.

HARDWARE SUPPORT SERVICES

Intel's hardware maintenance service, starting with complete on-site installation will boost your productivity from the start and keep you running at maximum efficiency. Support for system or board level products can be tailored to match your needs, from complete on-site repair and maintenance support economical carry-in or mail-in factory service.

Intel can provide support service for not only Intel systems and emulators, but also support for equipment in your development lab or provide service on your product to your end-user/customer.

SOFTWARE SUPPORT SERVICES

Software products are supported by our Technical Information Phone Service (TIPS) that has a special toll free number to provide you with direct, ready information on known, documented problems and deficiencies, as well as work-arounds, patches and other solutions.

Intel's software support consists of two levels of contracts. Standard support includes TIPS (Technical Information Phone Service), updates and subscription service (product-specific troubleshooting guides and; *COMMENTS Magazine*). Basic support consists of updates and the subscription service. Contracts are sold in environments which represent product groupings (e.g., iRMX® environment).

CONSULTING SERVICES

Intel provides field system engineering consulting services for any phase of your development or application effort. You can use our system engineers in a variety of ways ranging from assistance in using a new product, developing an application, personalizing training and customizing an Intel product to providing technical and management consulting. Systems Engineers are well versed in technical areas such as microcommunications, real-time applications, embedded microcontrollers, and network services. You know your application needs; we know our products. Working together we can help you get a successful product to market in the least possible time.

CUSTOMER TRAINING

Intel offers a wide range of instructional programs covering various aspects of system design and implementation. In just three to ten days a limited number of individuals learn more in a single workshop than in weeks of self-study. For optimum convenience, workshops are scheduled regularly at Training Centers worldwide or we can take our workshops to you for on-site instruction. Covering a wide variety of topics, Intel's major course categories include: architecture and assembly language, programming and operating systems, BITBUS™ and LAN applications.

NETWORK MANAGEMENT SERVICES

Today's networking products are powerful and extremely flexible. The return they can provide on your investment via increased productivity and reduced costs can be very substantial.

Intel offers complete network support, from definition of your network's physical and functional design, to implementation, installation and maintenance. Whether installing your first network or adding to an existing one, Intel's Networking Specialists can optimize network performance for you.

Introduction to Microcomputers

1

CHAPTER 1
INTRODUCTION TO MICROCOMPUTERS

WHAT IS A MICROCOMPUTER?

A microcomputer is a system of one or more integrated circuit devices that use semiconductor technology and digital logic to implement large computer functions on a smaller scale.

The Intel® 8086 and 8088 family of microprocessors and other closely related Intel processors described in this manual are essential functional blocks of microcomputers.

A microcomputer contains three main elements. These elements and their functions parallel those found in all computers. Each element has a special role to play in the overall operation of the computer system. The block diagram in Figure 1-1 shows these three elements: the *central processing unit* (CPU), the *memory*, and the *input/output* (I/O) devices or ports.

THE CPU

The heart of the microcomputer system is the CPU. It performs the numerical processing (additions, subtractions, etc.), logical operations, and timing functions.

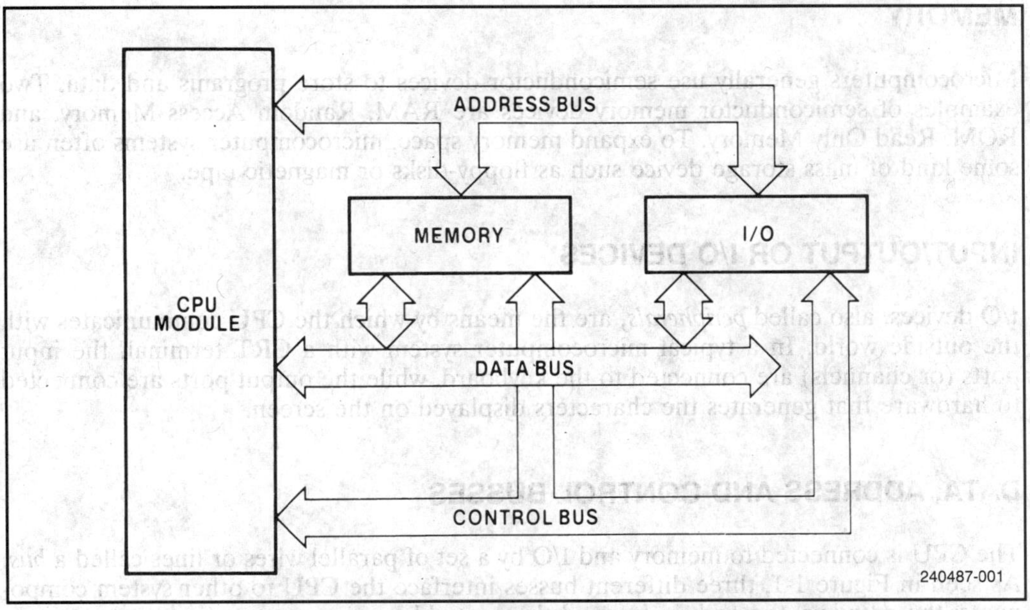

Figure 1-1. Microcomputer Block Diagram

CPU operations are controlled by a set of *instructions*, called a *program*. Programs are stored in the memory. Data is also kept in the memory, where it is processed according to programmed instructions. The CPU reads in data and control signals (instructions) through the input ports, executes one instruction at a time, and sends data and control signals to the outside world through the output ports.

A typical CPU consists of the following three functional units: the *registers*, the *arithmetic/logic unit* (ALU), and the *control circuitry*.

Registers provide temporary storage within the CPU for memory addresses, status codes, and other information useful during program execution. Different microprocessors have different numbers and sizes of registers. The Intel 8086 and 8088 family of microprocessors has 16-bit registers.

All CPUs contain an *arithmetic/logic unit* or *ALU*. The ALU contains an adder to perform binary arithmetic operations on the data obtained from memory, the registers or other inputs. Some ALUs perform more complex operations such as multiplication and division. ALUs provide other functions as well, including Boolean logic and data shifting.

The ALU also contains flag bits that signal the results of arithmetic and logical manipulations such as sign, zero, carry, and parity information.

The *control circuitry* coordinates all microprocessor activity. Using clock inputs, the control circuitry maintains the proper sequence of events required for any processing task. The control circuitry decodes the instruction bits and issues control signals to units both internal and external to the CPU so the CPU can perform the proper processing action.

MEMORY

Microcomputers generally use semiconductor devices to store programs and data. Two examples of semiconductor memory devices are RAM, Random Access Memory, and ROM, Read Only Memory. To expand memory space, microcomputer systems often use some kind of mass storage device such as floppy-disks or magnetic tape.

INPUT/OUTPUT OR I/O DEVICES

I/O devices, also called *peripherals*, are the means by which the CPU communicates with the outside world. In a typical microcomputer system with a CRT terminal, the input ports (or channels) are connected to the keyboard, while the output ports are connected to hardware that generates the characters displayed on the screen.

DATA, ADDRESS AND CONTROL BUSSES

The CPU is connected to memory and I/O by a set of parallel wires or lines called a *bus*. As seen in Figure 1-1, three different busses interface the CPU to other system components: the *data bus*, the *address bus* and the *control bus*.

Data travels between the CPU, memory, and I/O over the *data bus*. This data can either be instructions for the CPU, or information the CPU is passing to or from I/O ports. In the 8088, the data bus is 8 bits wide; in the 8086, the data bus is 16 bits wide.

The CPU uses the *address bus* to select the desired memory or I/O device by providing a unique address that corresponds to one of the memory or I/O elements of the system.

The *control bus* carries control signals to the memory and I/O devices, specifying whether data is to go into or out of the CPU, and specifying exactly when the data is being transferred.

BUS CYCLES

As the microcomputer program executes, data is transferred to and from memory and I/O devices. Each instance of data transfer from one part of the system to another is called a *bus cycle* (or *machine cycle*). The timing of these cycles is done by the CPU clock signal. Operations like instruction fetch, memory read, memory write, read from an input port, or write to an output port are operations taking place in one or more bus cycles.

The length of bus cycles is determined relative to the frequency of a clock signal. Typical clock rates at which microcomputers operate are 5, 8 and 10 MHz. The 8 MHz versions of the Intel 8086 have clock cycles of 125 nanoseconds (or .125 microseconds).

At the beginning of a bus cycle, the CPU issues a code to the address bus to identify the memory location or I/O device to be accessed. Then, the CPU issues an activity command on the control bus. Next, the CPU either receives or transmits data over the data bus.

The CPU then performs the logical, arithmetic, or I/O operations as required by the instructions.

The CPU keeps track of the instruction sequence with the *program counter* register, which contains the address of the next instruction in memory. In more recent Intel CPUs, the term 'program counter' has been replaced by the term 'instruction pointer.'

Normally, the instruction pointer is incremented after a given instruction is executed. The CPU automatically fetches instructions from memory, decodes them, and executes them in sequence until the program ends, or until special instructions tell it to execute instructions in other parts of program memory.

Certain situations can interrupt the normal sequential flow of instruction execution. For example, a *wait state* may be imposed in a given bus cycle to provide more time for memory or an I/O device to communicate with the CPU. Wait states are needed when the rate of data transfer from memory is slower than the rate at which the CPU requests it. In such cases, the memory must request a wait state when it receives the CPU signal that a memory read or write operation has commenced. After the memory responds, it signals the CPU to leave the wait state and continue processing.

INTERRUPTS

Another situation that alters sequential instruction execution is an *interrupt*. For example, consider a computer that is processing a large volume of data, portions of which are to be output to a printer. The CPU can send a given amount of data to the printer in a single bus cycle, but the printer may take several bus cycles to print the characters specified by that data. Thus, the CPU must remain idle until the printer can accept the next data. The interrupt capability permits the CPU to output to the printer and then return to other data processing.

When the printer is ready to accept the next data byte, it signals the CPU via a special interrupt control line. When the CPU receives the interrupt signal, it suspends the main program execution and automatically switches to the instructions that output to the printer. Once this switch occurs, the CPU continues main program execution at the point where processing was suspended.

Several interrupting devices often share the same CPU. In order to service all of them, interrupts can be prioritized. When two or more interrupts occur simultaneously, the one with the higher priority is serviced first.

DIRECT MEMORY ACCESS

Another feature that improves microprocessor efficiency is *direct memory access*, also called DMA.

In ordinary input/output operations, the CPU supervises the entire data transfer as it executes I/O instructions that transfer data from the input device to the CPU, and then from the CPU to a specified memory location. Similarly, data going from memory to an output device goes by way of the CPU.

Some peripheral devices transfer information to and from memory faster than the CPU can accomplish the transfer under program control. By using DMA, the CPU allows the peripheral device to hold and control the bus, transferring the data directly to and from memory without involving the CPU itself. When the DMA transfer is done, the peripheral releases the hold request signal. The CPU then resumes processing instructions where it left off.

ADDRESSING MODES

The address that the CPU provides on the address bus selects one specific memory or I/O device from all of those available. This address can be generated in different ways depending on the operation being performed. The ways of generating these addresses are called *addressing modes*.

In the simplest addressing mode, the desired data item is contained within the instruction being executed. In a more complex addressing mode, the instruction contains the memory address of the data. Or, the instruction may reference a CPU register that contains the memory address of the data.

Finally, within some microprocessors, the instruction may tell the control circuitry to generate a complex address that is the sum of several address components, such as multiple registers plus data contained in the instruction itself.

Generally, the most powerful microprocessors are the ones with the widest variety of addressing modes available.

INTEL® MICROCOMPUTER COMPONENTS

Intel manufactures a complete line of microcomputer components. These components constitute building blocks that can be tailored to precisely fit the performance needs of a particular application. This manual describes the following components: the 8086 CPU, the 8088 CPU, and the 8087 Numeric Processor Extension (NPX).

The 8086, 8088 Family Overview

2

CHAPTER 2
THE 8086, 8088 FAMILY OVERVIEW

INTRODUCTION

The 8086 and 8088 family consists of advanced, high-performance microprocessors. The family includes general data processors (8086 and 8088), and specialized coprocessors such as the 8087 numeric processor extension (NPX).

Four key architectural concepts shaped the microprocessor designs. All four reflect the family's role as vehicles for modular, high-level language programming (in addition to assembly language programming).

The concepts are:

- Memory segmentation,
- Operand addressing structure,
- Operation register set, and
- Instruction encoding scheme.

The 8086/8088 memory segmentation scheme is optimized for the reference needs of computer programs, and is separate from the operand addressing structure.

The structure for addressing operands within segments directly supports the various data types found in high level programming languages.

An operation register set is provided to support general computation requirements. It also provides for optimized operation register sets to do specialized data processing functions with its inherent multiprocessor and coprocessor support.

The family uses optimized instruction encoding for high performance and memory efficiency.

High-level languages using modular programming have become the norm on large software development projects in the last decade. The 8086, 8088 microprocessor family with its memory segmentation scheme is designed for modular programs. It supports the static and dynamic memory requirements of program modules, as well as their communication needs. The register scheme employs specialized registers and implicit register usage.

These CPUs are substantially more powerful than microprocessors previously offered by Intel. High performance is realized by combining a 16-bit internal data path with a pipelined architecture that allows instructions to be prefetched during spare bus cycles. A compact instruction format that enables more instructions to be fetched in a given amount of time also contributes to the performance.

Software need not be written in assembly language. These CPUs are designed to provide direct hardware support for programs written in high-level languages such as Pascal-86 and Intel's PL/M-86. However, routines with critical performance requirements that cannot be met with a high-level language may be written in ASM-86 (the 8086 assembly language) and linked with Pascal-86 or PL/M-86 code.

While these CPUs are totally new designs, they make the most of the user's existing investments in systems designed around the 8080/8085 microprocessor. Many of the standard Intel memory, peripheral control, and communication chips are compatible with the 8086 and 8088.

Other important features of the 8086 and 8088 CPUs are dual operating modes (minimum and maximum) and built-in multiprocessing capability.

These characteristics, as well as others to be described in following chapters, make the 8086/8088 family suitable for uniprocessor, minimal-memory designs implemented with a handful of chips (Figure 2-1).

THE CPU ARCHITECTURE

The following sections of this chapter describe the mainstays of the microprocessor family: the central processing units. The internal operation of the CPU and the interaction of the processors with other devices are discussed in functional terms. Electrical characteristics, timing, and other hardware related information may be found in Chapter 6.

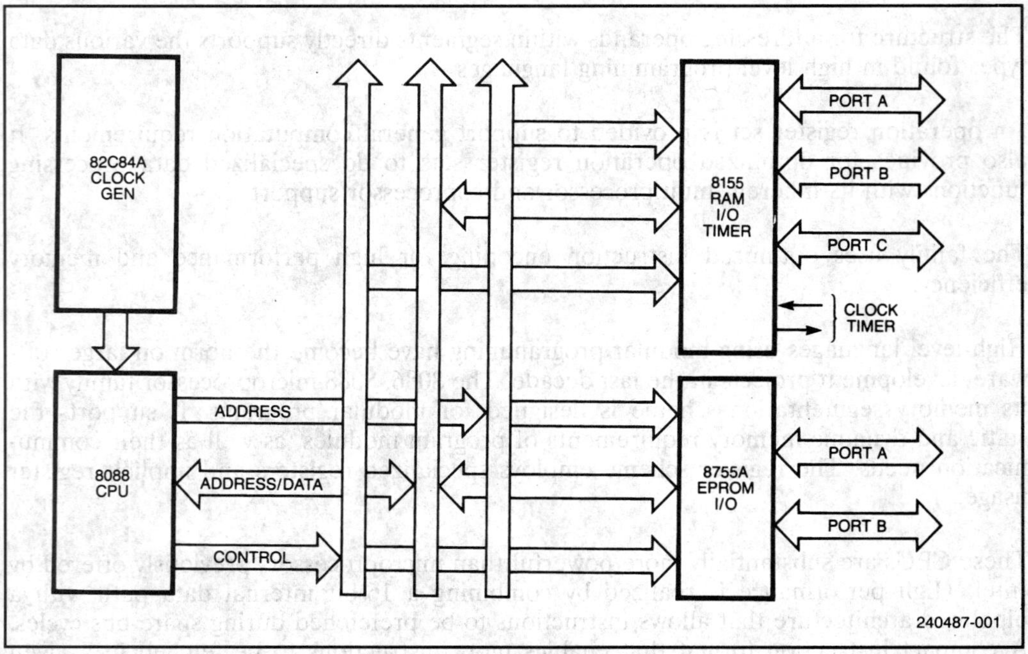

Figure 2-1. Small 8088-Based System

Functional Units

Standard microprocessors execute a program by repeatedly cycling through the steps shown in Figure 2-2. First, the microprocessor must fetch the instruction to be performed, then it executes the instruction. Only after the execution is complete is the CPU ready to fetch the next instruction, execute that instruction, etc.

The CPU hardware that executes instructions must obviously wait until the instruction is fetched and decoded before execution begins. Therefore, in standard microprocessors, the execution hardware (primarily the control circuitry and the arithmetic and logic unit) spends a lot of time waiting for instructions to be fetched. The 8086 and 8088 microprocessors eliminate this wasted time by dividing the internal CPU into two independent functional units (see Figure 2-3).

The BIU and EU – Pipelined Architecture

The CPUs have a separate bus interface unit (BIU), whose only job is to fetch instructions from memory and pass data to and from the execution hardware and the outside world. Since the execution unit and the bus interface unit are independent, the bus interface unit fetches additional instructions while the execution unit (sometimes called the EU) executes a previously fetched instruction. This is made possible by the instruction pipeline (or queue) between the bus interface unit and the execution unit. The BIU fills this pipeline with instructions awaiting execution. Thus, whenever the execution unit finishes executing a given instruction, the next instruction is usually ready for immediate execution without delays caused by instruction fetching. Figure 2-4 shows parallel fetching and executing in these CPUs.

Because the BIU is usually busy fetching instructions for the pipeline, the bus is more fully utilized. Another benefit of this parallel operation is that since the execution unit seldom needs to wait for the BIU to fetch the next instruction, there is less need for the BIU to fetch data quickly. Maximum performance and processing power is thus achieved without high speed memory devices in the system.

This parallel operation of the BIU and EU is transparent to the user, except when program execution transfers to a new, non-sequential address. When this happens, the bus interface unit is given the new address by the execution unit; it then begins fetching instructions sequentially from the new address. The execution unit must wait for the next instruction to be fetched the way most CPUs wait for every instruction to be fetched. After the first instruction is fetched from the new location, the bus interface unit continues to fill the pipeline with instructions, and fetch-time becomes transparent.

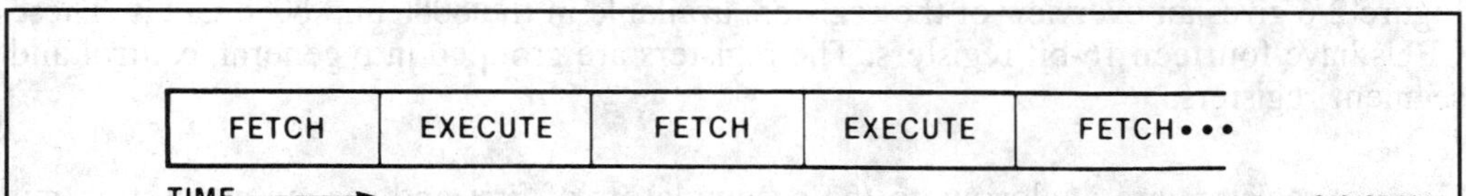

Figure 2-2. Program Execution in Standard Microprocessor

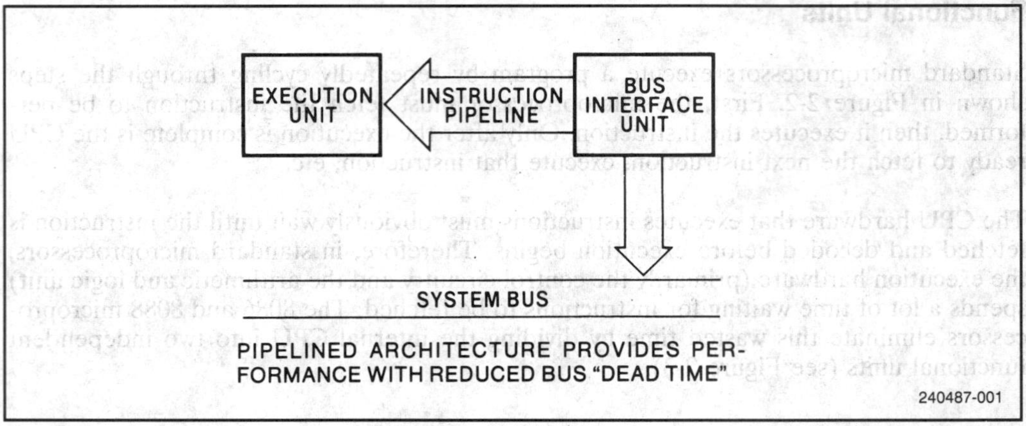

Figure 2-3. Pipelined Internal Architecture

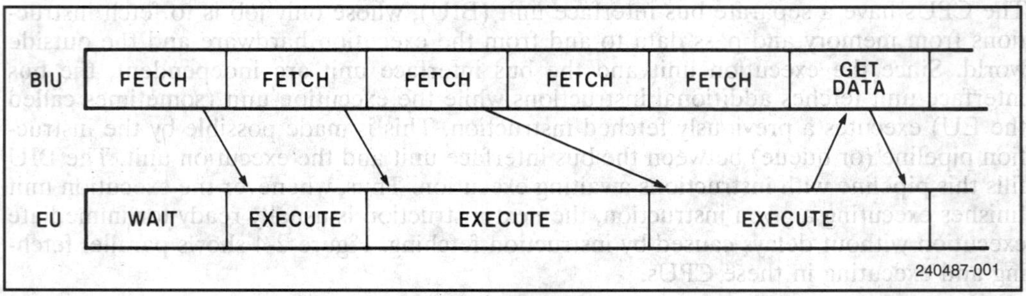

Figure 2-4. Parallel Operation in CPU

Bus Structure

A summary of the 8086/8088 bus structure is shown in Figure 2-5. There are two types of busses: system and local. Both busses may be shared by multiple processors, i.e., both are multimaster busses. Microprocessors are always connected to a local bus, and memory and I/O components usually reside on a system bus. The 8086 and 8088 bus interface components link a local bus to a system bus.

Register Resources

Figure 2-6 gives an overview of the registers available in the 8086 and 8088 CPUs. These CPUs have fourteen 16-bit registers. The registers are grouped into general, control and segment registers.

General registers are analogous to the accumulators of first and second generation microprocessors. They are, in turn, grouped into data, index and pointer registers. The function of all registers is described in more detail in the following paragraphs.

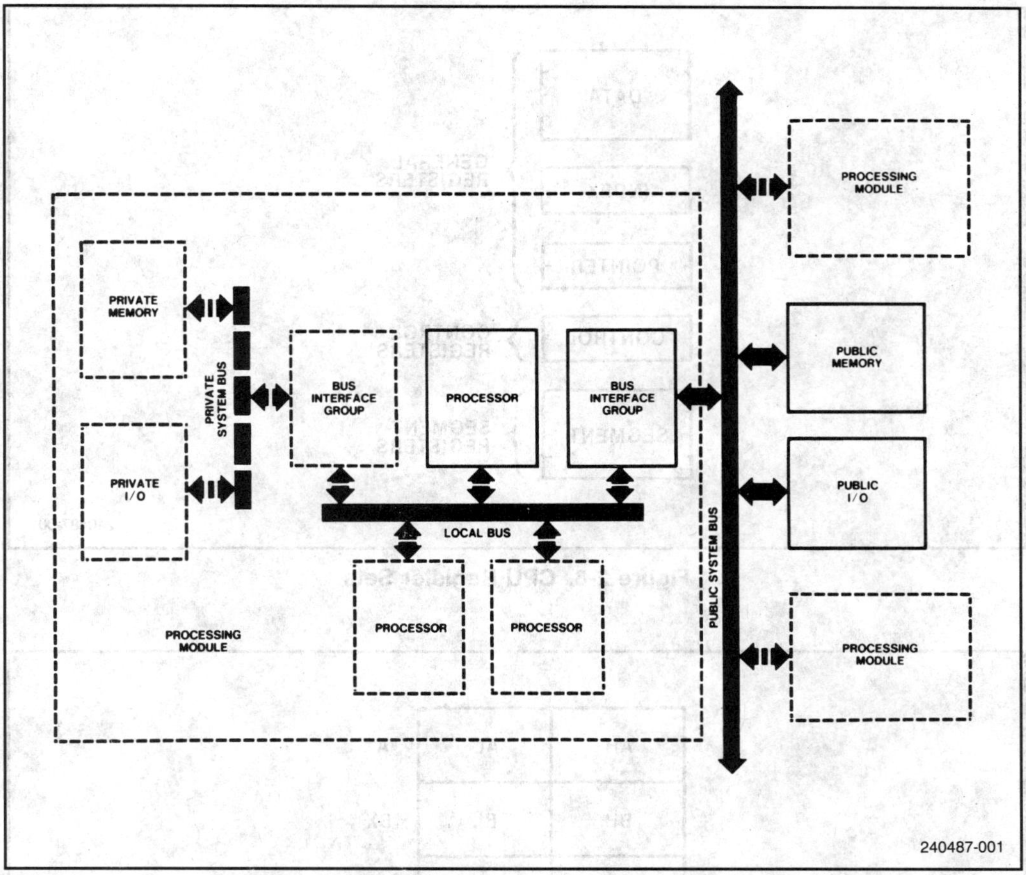

Figure 2-5. General 8086/8088 Bus Structure

Data Registers

The data registers are unique in that their upper and lower halves are separately addressable. This means that each data register can be used interchangeably as a 16-bit register, or as two 8-bit registers. In their 16-bit form, the data registers are the AX, BX, CX and DX registers (Figure 2-7). For 8-bit operations, they are divided into high byte and low byte. AH is the high byte of the AX register, AL is the low byte of the AX register, and so on. As mentioned, these registers have general usage for arithmetic and logical operations.

Some registers have additional special functions, which are performed in the execution of certain instructions. For example, the CX register is frequently used to contain a count value during repetitive instructions, and the BX register is used as a base register in some of the more powerful addressing modes. This implicit use of registers allows a very compact instruction encoding.

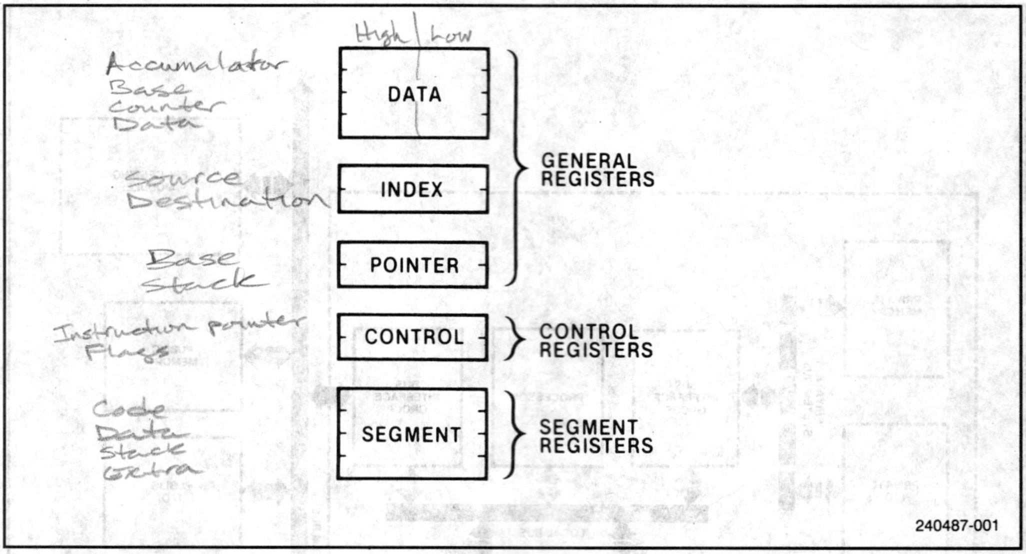

Figure 2-6. CPU Register Sets

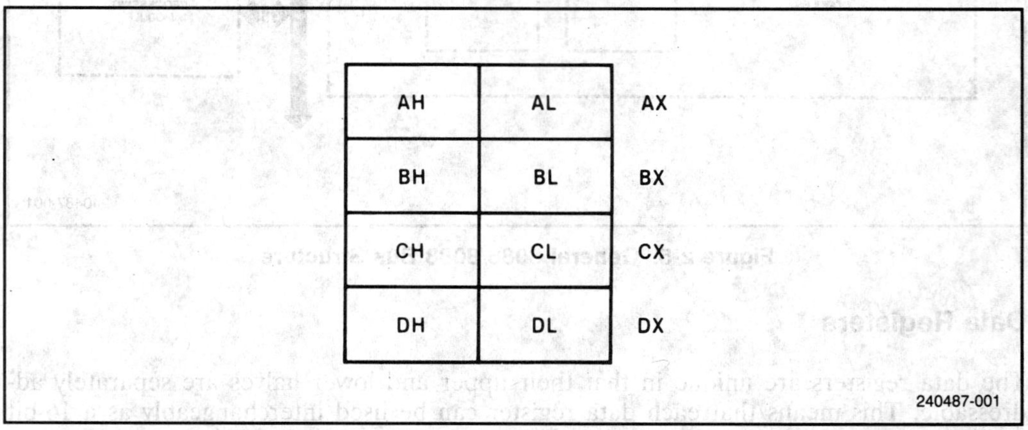

Figure 2-7. Data Group Registers

Pointer and Index Registers

Figure 2-8 shows the pointer and index registers. The BP and SP registers both point to the stack, a linear array in the memory used for subroutine parameters, subroutine return addresses, or other data temporarily saved during execution of a program.

Most microprocessors have a single stack pointer register called the SP. The 8086/8088 have an additional pointer into the stack called the BP (base pointer) register. While the SP is used similarly to the stack pointer in other machines (for pointing to subroutine and interrupt return addresses), the BP register can contain an old stack pointer value,

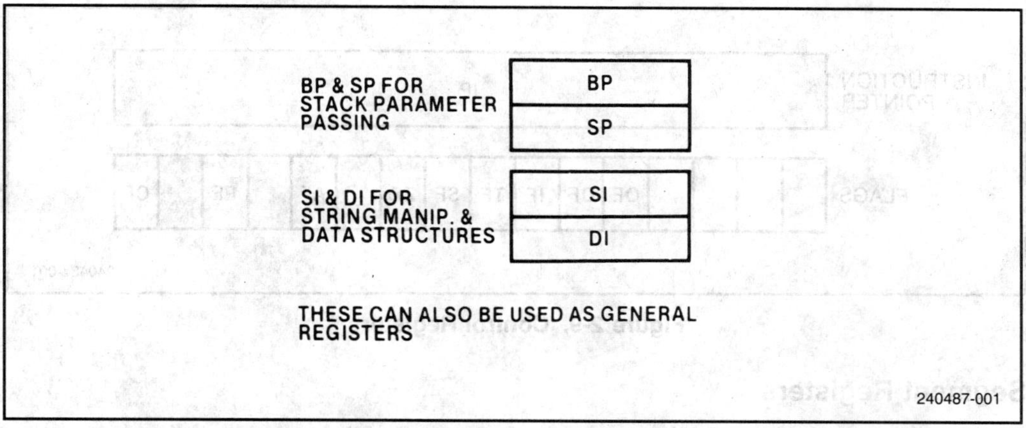

Figure 2-8. Base and Index Registers

or it can mark a place in the subroutine stack independent of the SP register. Using the BP register to mark the stack saves the juggling of a single stack pointer to reference subroutine parameters and addresses.

The two index registers are the SI (source index) register and the DI (destination index) register (Figure 2-8). These are both 16-bits wide and are used by string manipulation instructions and in building some of the more powerful 8086/8088 data structures and addressing modes. Both the SI and the DI registers have auto-incrementing and auto-decrementing capabilities.

All base and index registers have general arithmetic and logical capabilities in addition to their special functions.

Control Registers

The control registers consist of two special purpose registers, the IP or instruction pointer and the Flags register (see Figure 2-9). The IP is similar to a Program Counter used in some microprocessors, except that the IP points to the next instruction to be fetched (by the BIU), whereas the traditional program counter points to the next instruction to be executed. For 8086 instructions that manipulate the IP, however, its contents are adjusted to point to the next instruction to be executed.

The Flags register contains the flags or condition codes that reflect the results of arithmetic or logical operations as they are performed by the execution unit. The condition codes are described in detail in Chapter 3.

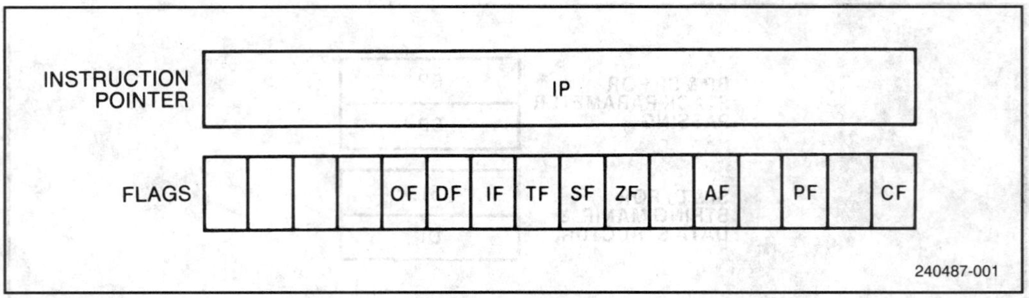

Figure 2-9. Control Registers

Segment Registers

Four 16-bit special purpose registers, called segment registers, are provided in a segment register file. They are the code segment (CS), stack segment (SS), data segment (DS) and extra segment (ES). Segment registers are used by the 8086/8088 in the formulation of memory addresses. Their usage is described in the following section on memory addressing.

MEMORY ADDRESSING

Memory is organized in sets of segments. Each segment consists of a linear sequence of up to 64K bytes. These bytes are stored sequentially from byte 00000 to byte FFFFF hex. The memory is addressed using a two-component address (a pointer) that consists of a 16-bit segment base (specifying the beginning address of the segment in memory) and a 16-bit offset (specifying the address relative to the beginning of the segment). The base values are contained in one of the four internal segment registers (CS, DS, SS, ES). A 20-bit physical memory address is calculated by shifting the base value in the appropriate segment register left by four bits and adding the 16-bit offset value to it (Figure 2-10). This form of addressing allows access to one million bytes of memory.

Every 20-bit memory address points either to program code, data, or stack area in memory (Figure 2-11). Each of the four different memory spaces is pointed to by one of the segment base registers (Figure 2-12). The code segment register points to the base of the program currently executing, the stack segment register points to the base of the stack, the data segment register points to the base of one data area, and the extra segment register points to the base of another area where data may be stored.

Generating Addresses

Each time the CPU needs to generate a memory address, one of the segment registers is automatically chosen and its contents added to a logical address.

For an instruction fetch, the code segment register is automatically added to the logical address (in this case, the contents of the instruction pointer) to compute the value of the instruction address.

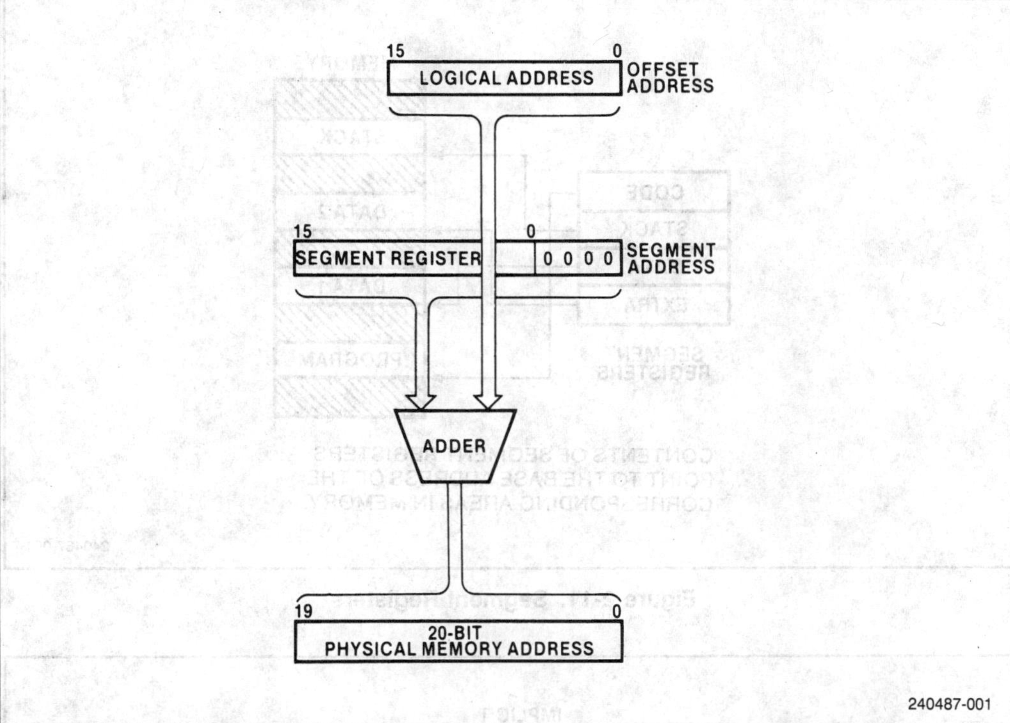

Figure 2-10. Memory Addressing

For an instruction referencing the stack, the stack segment register is automatically added to the logical address (the SP or BP register contents) to compute the value of the stack address.

For a data reference operation, where either the data or extra segment register are chosen as the base, the logical address can be made up of many different types of values: it can be simply the immediate data value contained in the instruction, or it can be the sum of an immediate data value, plus a base register, plus an index register. Generally, the selection of the DS or ES register is made automatically, though provisions do exist to override this selection.

Since logical addresses are 16-bits wide, up to 64K (65,536) bytes in a given segment may be addressed without changing the value of the segment base register. In systems that use 64K or fewer bytes of memory for each memory area (code, stack, data and extra), the segment registers can be initialized to zero at the beginning of the program and then ignored, since zero plus a 16-bit offset yields a 16-bit address. In a system where the total amount of memory is 64K bytes or less, it is possible to set all segment registers equal and have fully overlapping segments.

Segment registers are also very useful for large programming tasks, which require isolation of program code from the data area, or isolation of module data from the stack information, etc.

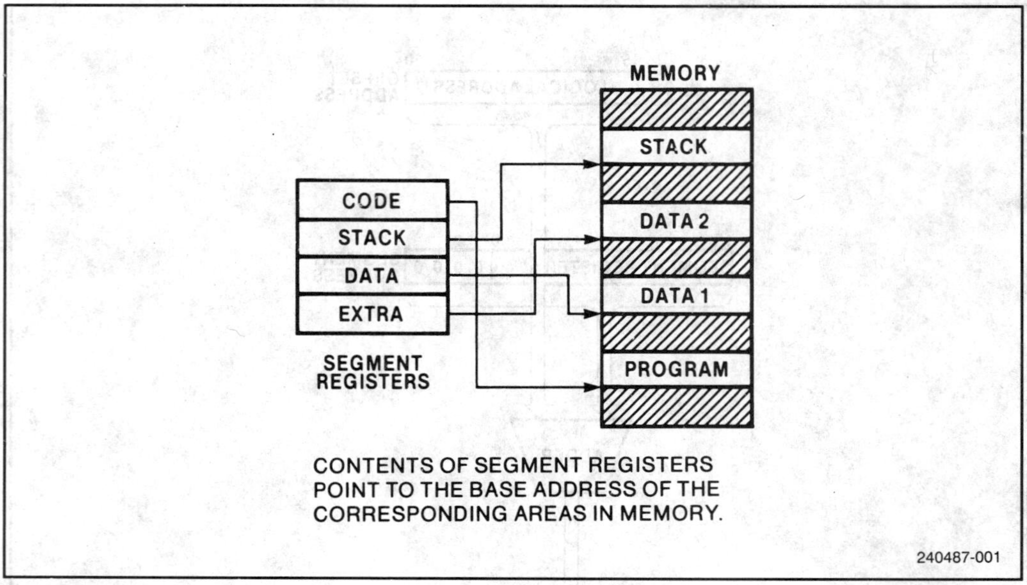

Figure 2-11. Segment Registers

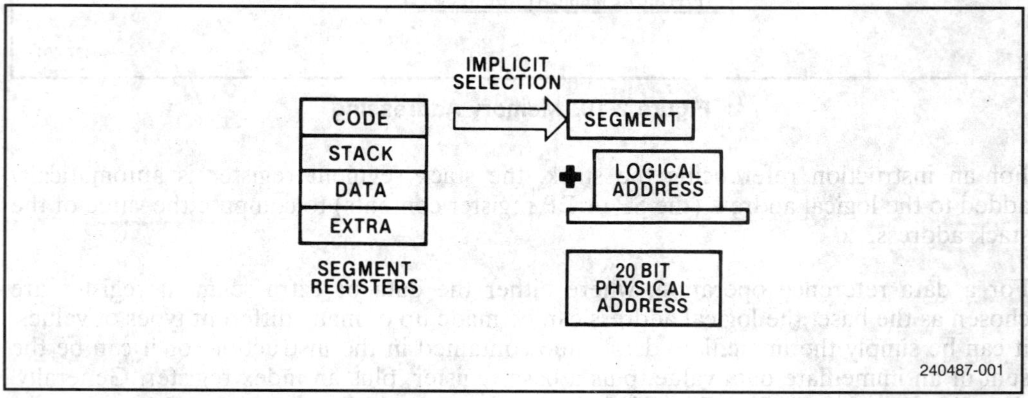

Figure 2-12. How an Address is Built

Segmentation makes it easy to build relocatable and reentrant programs. In many cases, the task of relocating a program (relocation means having the ability to run the same program in several different areas of memory without changing addresses in the program itself) simply requires moving the program code and then adjusting the code segment register to point to the base of the new code area. Since programs can be written for the 8086 or 8088 in which all branches and jumps are relative to the instruction pointer, it does not matter what value is kept in the code segment register.

Figure 2-13 shows how an entire process, consisting of code, stack and data areas, can be relocated. Likewise, in a reentrant program, a single program uses multiple data areas.

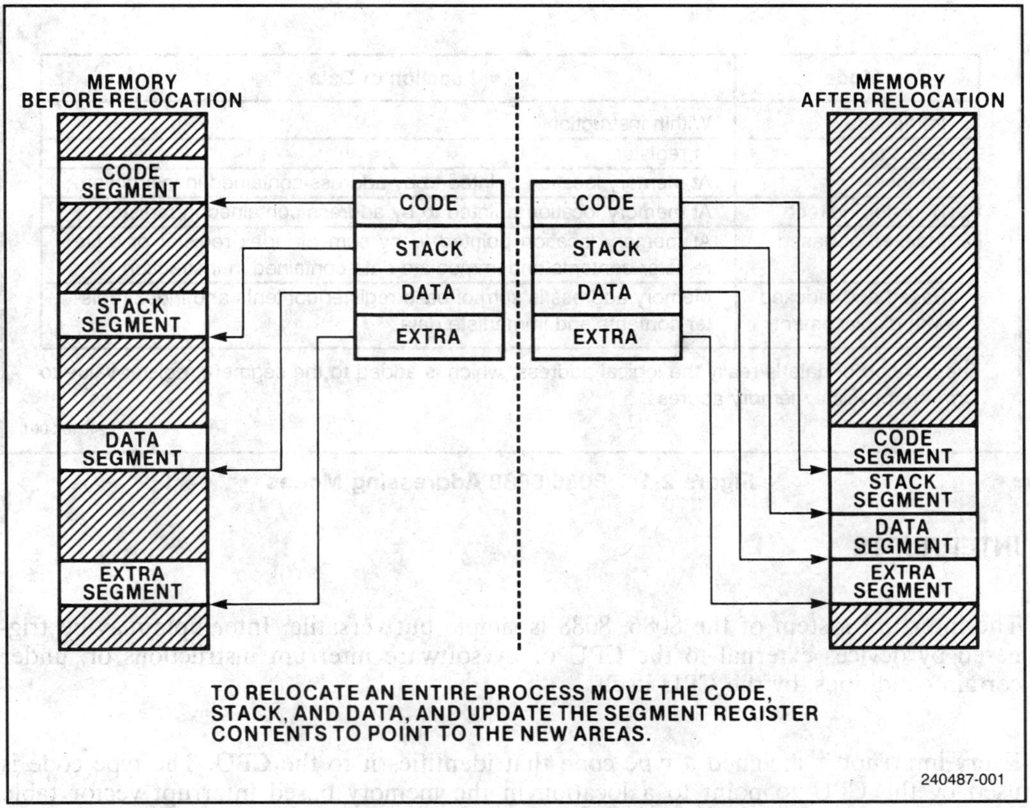

Figure 2-13. Process Relocation

Before the reentrant code is entered the second time, the data segment register value is changed so that a different data area is made available to the program.

Addressing Modes

The 8086, 8088 provide 24 different addressing modes. Various logical address combinations are shown in Figure 2-14, from the simplest immediate data mode to the register addressing mode, where a selected register contains the data being used by the instruction. In the direct addressing mode, the instruction itself contains the address of the data. In the register indirect mode, the instruction points to a register containing the memory address of the desired data. There are both indexed and based addressing modes where the contents of an index or base register is added to an immediate data value contained in the instruction to form the memory address.

Exactly how the 8086/8088 select an addressing mode for a given instruction is encoded within the bits of the instruction code. This is decribed in more detail in Chapter 3.

Mode	Location of Data
Immediate	Within instruction
Register	In register
Direct	At memory location pointed to by address contained in instruction.
Register Indirect	At memory location pointed to by address contained in register.
Indexed or based	At memory location pointed to by sum of index register or base register contents and immediate data contained in instruction.
Based and indexed with displacement	Memory address is sum of base register contents and index register contents and immediate data.

The location of data is really the logical address, which is added to the segment register value to form the physical memory address.

240487-001

Figure 2-14. 8086/8088 Addressing Modes

INTERRUPTS

The interrupt system of the 8086, 8088 is simple but versatile. Interrupts may be triggered by devices external to the CPU or by software interrupt instructions or, under certain conditions, by the CPU itself.

Every interrupt is assigned a type code that identifies it to the CPU. The type code is used by the CPU to point to a location in the memory based interrupt vector table containing the address of the interrupt routine. This interrupt vector table can contain up to 256 vectors for different interrupt types. Interrupts 0-31 are reserved by Intel.

The following sections provide a general introduction to interrupt processing for the 8086 and 8088 CPUs. For more detailed information see the section "Interrupt Structure," in Chapter 4.

External Interrupts

The 8086/8088 have two inputs that may be used by external devices to signal interrupts, the INTR (Interrupt Request) line, and the NMI (Non-Maskable Interrupt) line. The INTR line is usually driven by a PIC, such as Intel's 8259A Programmable Interrupt Controller, which in turn is connected to the devices that need interrupt service.

On the 8086/8088 CPUs, the NMI input line is generally used to signal the CPU of a "catastrophic" event, such as imminent loss of power, memory error, or bus parity error. Interrupt requests arriving on the NMI cannot be disabled. They are latched by the CPU, and have higher priority than an interrupt request on INTR or INT0-3.

Internal Interrupts

Internal interrupts are generated by two instructions (INT and INTO), by conditions resulting from the execution of two instructions (DIV, IDIV), and by most instructions when the Single Step flag in the Flags is set.

A detailed discussion of interrupts is included in Chapter 4 and Chapter 6.

MINIMUM AND MAXIMUM MODES

A unique feature of the 8086/8088 CPUs is the ability of a user to define a subset of the CPU's control signal outputs to tailor it to its intended system environment.

In the minimum mode, the CPU supports small, single-processor systems (usually single board) that consist of a few devices, and that use a local bus rather than support the MULTIBUS® architecture. In this mode, the CPU itself generates all bus control signals and the command output signal. It also provides a mechanism for requesting bus access that is compatible with bus master type controllers.

In the maximum mode (typically used for multiple board systems), an Intel 82C88 Bus Controller is added to provide a sophisticated bus control function and compatibility with the MULTIBUS architecture. In this mode, the bus controller, rather than the CPU, provides all bus control and command outputs, and allows pins previously delegated to these functions to be redefined to support multiprocessing functions. This mode is also required to support processor extensions, i.e., the 8087 Numerical Processor Extension.

THE 8087

The 8087 Numeric Processor Extension (NPX) performs arithmetic and comparison operations (using 80-bit internal registers) on a variety of numeric data types. It also executes numerous built-in transcendental functions such as log, tangent, etc. In conjunction with the maximum mode 8086/8088 CPU, the NPX effectively extends the register and instruction sets of the host CPU and adds several new data types as well. The 8087 block diagram is shown in Figure 2-15.

The 8087 uses the standard 86 family instruction set plus over fifty numeric instructions. Programs can be written in ASM-86 assembly language, or in the Intel high-level languages, PL/M-86, Fortran-86 and Pascal-86. From the stand-point of the programmer the NPX is not perceived as a separate device; instead, the computational abilities of the CPU appear greatly expanded.

The 8087 adds extensive high-speed numeric processing capabilities to the CPU. It conforms to the IEEE format for single- and double-precision floating point numbers. Even for programmers who are not expert in the problems of numerical analysis (for instance,

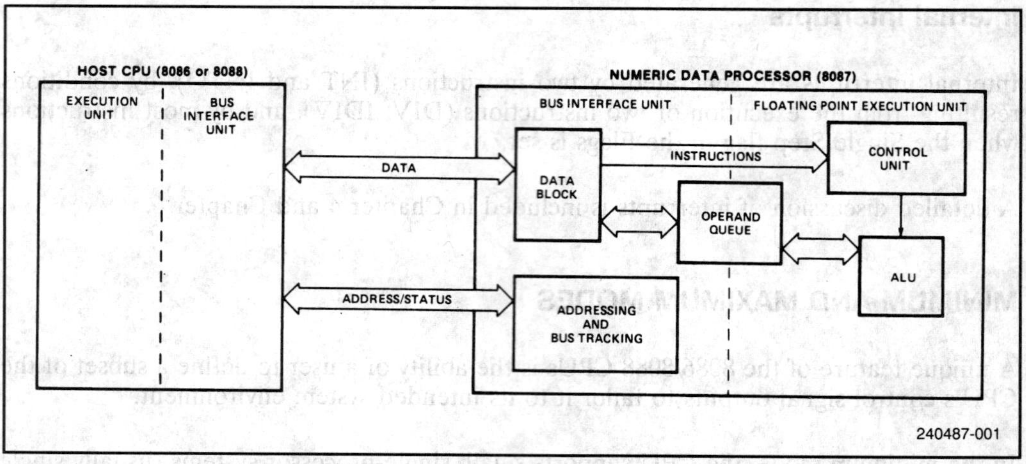

Figure 2-15. Numeric Data Processor Block Diagram

the accumulation of rounding errors which may result from a long chain of floating point calculations), the 8087 will provide correct results, and is straightforward and easy to program. Chapter 5 describes the software aspects of the 8087; Chapter 7 covers the hardware.

The 8086/8088 Architecture and Instructions 3

CHAPTER 3
THE 8086/8088 ARCHITECTURE AND INSTRUCTIONS

INTRODUCTION

This chapter describes the programmer's architecture of the 8086/8088 CPUs. It is divided into the following sections:

- CPU Architecture
- Register Structure
- Memory Structure
- I/O Port Organization
- Addressing Modes
- Instruction Set
- Programming Examples

CPU ARCHITECTURE

The two independently operating functional units of the CPU, the BIU and EU, are able, under most circumstances, to extensively overlap instruction fetch with execution. The result is that, in most cases, the time normally required to fetch instructions "disappears" because the EU executes instructions that have already been fetched by the BIU. Figure 3-1 illustrates this overlap and compares it with traditional microprocessor operation. In the example, overlapping reduces the elapsed time required to execute three instructions, and allows two additional instructions to be prefetched as well.

Execution Unit

In the execution unit, a 16-bit ALU maintains the CPU status and control flags, and manipulates the general registers and instruction operands. All registers and data paths within the EU are 16 bits wide (Figure 3-2).

The EU has no connection to the system bus, the "outside world." It obtains instructions from a queue maintained by the BIU. Likewise, when an instruction requires access to memory or to a peripheral device, the EU requests the BIU to fetch or store the data. All addresses manipulated by the EU are 16 bits wide. However, the address relocation facility provided by the BIU provides the EU with access to a full megabyte of memory space.

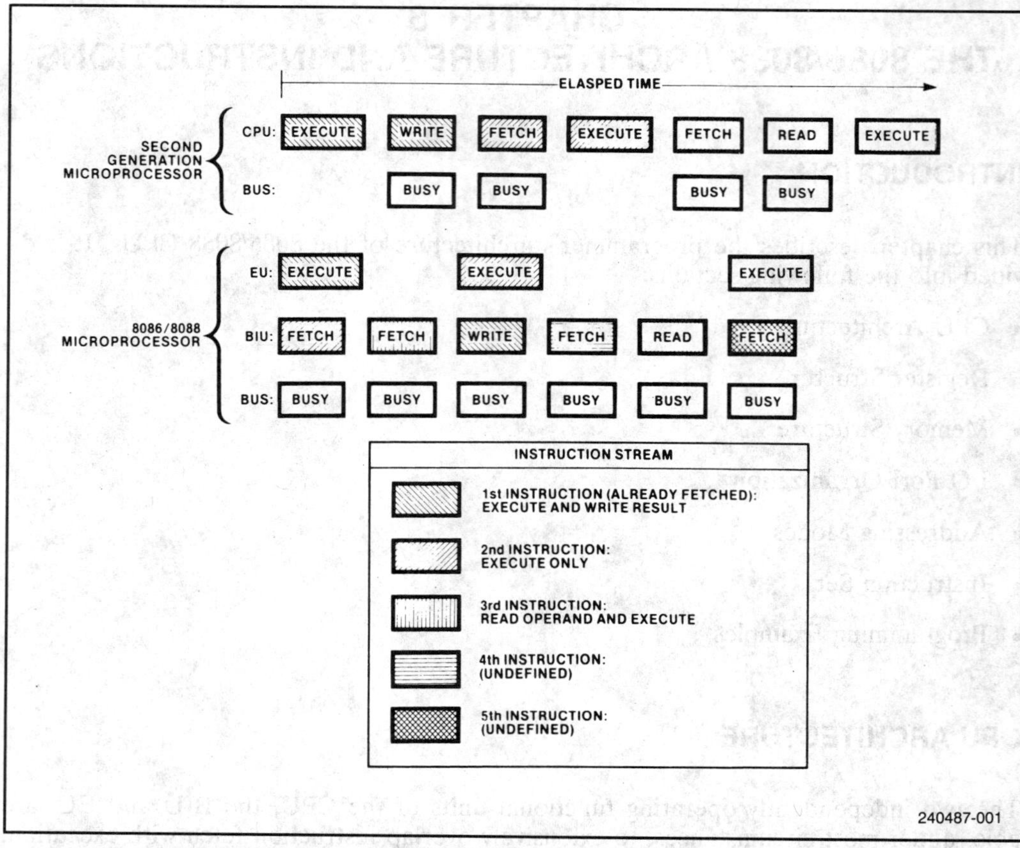

Figure 3-1. Overlapped Instruction Fetch and Execution

Bus Interface Unit

The BIUs of the 8088 and the 8086 are functionally identical, but are implemented differently to match the data path size of their busses, which are 8 bits and 16 bits respectively.

The BIU performs all bus operations for the EU. Data is transferred between the CPU and memory or I/O devices upon demand from the EU.

In addition, during periods when the EU is busy executing instructions, the BIU "looks ahead" and fetches more instructions from memory. The instructions are stored in an internal RAM array called the instruction stream queue. The 8088 instruction queue holds up to four bytes of the instruction stream, while the 8086 queue can store up to six instruction bytes. These queue sizes keep the EU supplied with prefetched instructions under most conditions without monopolizing the system bus.

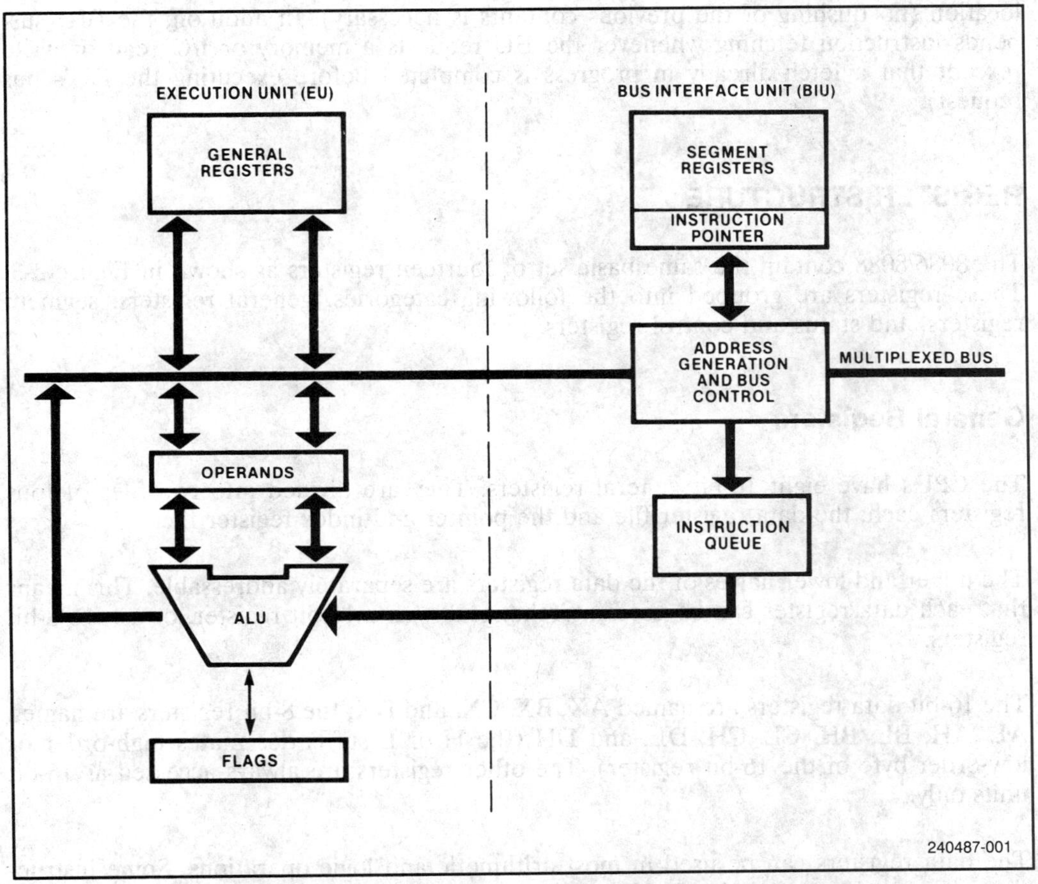

Figure 3-2. Execution and Bus Interface Units (EU and BIU)

he 8088 BIU fetches another instruction byte whenever there is one empty byte in its queue, and there is no active request for bus access from the EU. The 8086 BIU operates similarly except that it does not normally initiate a fetch until there are two empty bytes in its queue.

The 8086 BIU will generally obtain two instruction bytes per fetch; if a program transfer forces fetching from an odd address, the BIU automatically reads one byte from the odd address and then resumes fetching two-byte words from the subsequent even address.

Under most circumstances, the queue contains at least one byte of the instruction stream, and the EU does not have to wait for instructions to be fetched. The instructions in the queue are those stored in the memory locations immediately adjacent to and higher than the instruction currently being executed. That is, they are the next logical instructions so long as execution proceeds serially. If the EU executes an instruction that transfers control to another location, the BIU fetches the instruction from the new address, passes it immediately to the EU, and then begins refilling the queue from the new location (no flushing of the previous contents is necessary). In addition, the BIU suspends instruction fetching whenever the EU requests a memory or I/O read or write (except that a fetch already in progress is completed before executing the EU's bus request).

REGISTER STRUCTURE

The 8086/8088 contain the same basic set of fourteen registers as shown in Figure 3-3. These registers are grouped into the following categories: general registers, segment registers, and status and control registers.

General Registers

The CPUs have eight 16-bit general registers. They are divided into two files of four registers each: the data register file and the pointer and index register file.

The upper and lower halves of the data registers are separately addressable. This means that each data register can be used interchangeably as a 16-bit register, or as two 8-bit registers.

The 16-bit data registers are named AX, BX, CX, and DX; the 8-bit registers are named AL, AH, BL, BH, CL, CH, DL, and DH (the H or L suffix designates high-order or low-order byte of the 16-bit register). The other registers are always accessed as 16-bit units only.

The data registers can be used in most arithmetic and logic operations. Some instructions (e.g., string instructions), however, require certain general registers for specific uses (see Table 3-1). This implicit register use allows a more compact instruction encoding.

The pointer and index registers consist of the 16-bit registers SP, BP, SI, and DI as shown in Figure 3-3. They can also be used in most arithmetic and logic operations. These registers usually contain offset addresses for addressing within a segment. They reduce program size by eliminating the need for each instruction to specify frequently used addresses. These registers serve another function; they provide for dynamic logical address computation as described in the section on operand addressing. The pointer and index registers are also used implicitly in some instructions (Table 3-1).

As shown in Figure 3-3, this register file is divided into the pointer subfile (SP and BP) and the index subfile (SI and DI). The pointer registers provide convenient access to the current stack segment (as opposed to the data segment). Unless otherwise specified in the instruction, pointer registers refer to the current stack segment while index registers refer to the current data segment. In certain instances, specific uses of these four registers are indicated by the mnemonic phrases "stack pointer," "base pointer," "source index," and "destination index."

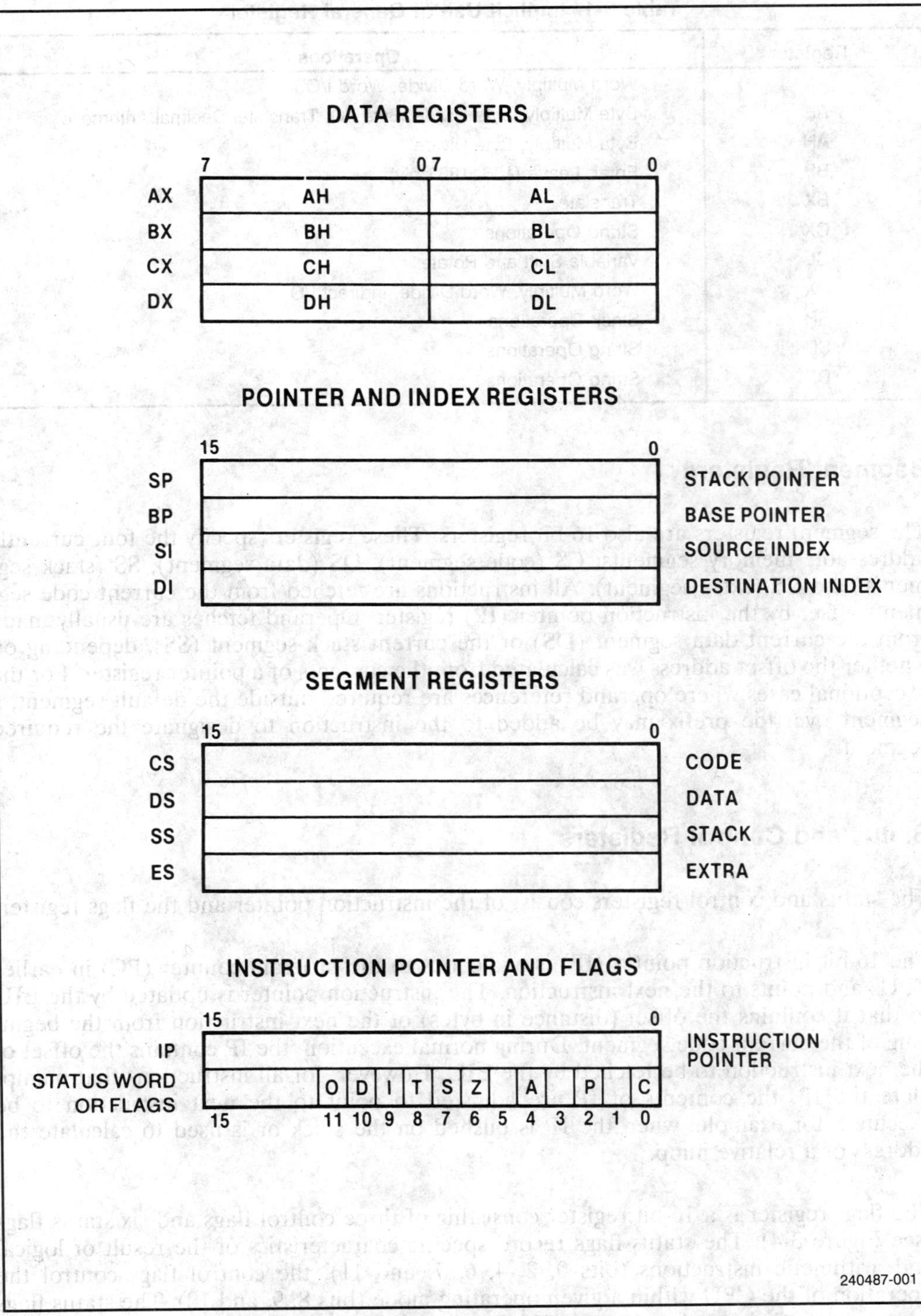

Figure 3-3. Register Structure

Table 3-1. Implicit Use of General Register

Register	Operations
AX	Word Multiply, Word Divide, Word I/O
AL	Byte Multiply, Byte Divide, Byte I/O, Translate, Decimal Arithmetic
AH	Byte Multiply, Byte Divide
BP	Enter, Leave (186, 188 only)
BX	Translate
CX	String Operations
CL	Variable Shift and Rotate
DX	Word Multiply, Word Divide, Indirect I/O
SP	Stack Operations
SI	String Operations
DI	String Operations

Segment Registers

The segment registers are also 16-bit registers. These registers specify the four currently addressable memory segments: CS (code segment), DS (data segment), SS (stack segment), and ES (extra segment). All instructions are fetched from the current code segment, offset by the instruction pointer (IP) register. Operand fetches are usually made from the current data segment (DS) or the current stack segment (SS), depending on whether the offset address was calculated from the contents of a pointer register. For the exceptional cases where operand references are required outside the default segment, a segment override prefix may be added to the instruction to designate the required segment.

Status and Control Registers

The status and control registers consist of the instruction pointer and the flags register.

The 16-bit instruction pointer (IP) is analogous to the program counter (PC) in earlier CPUs and points to the next instruction. The instruction pointer is updated by the BIU so that it contains the offset (distance in bytes) of the next instruction from the beginning of the current code segment. During normal execution, the IP contains the offset of the next instruction to be fetched by the BIU. However, for all instructions that manipulate the IP, the contents of IP are adjusted to point to the next instruction to be executed, for example, when the IP is pushed on the stack or is used to calculate the address of a relative jump.

The flags register is a 16-bit register consisting of three control flags and six status flags (see Figure 3-4). The status flags record specific characteristics of the result of logical and arithmetic instructions (bits 0, 2, 4, 6, 7, and 11); the control flags control the operation of the CPU within a given operating mode (bits 8, 9, and 10). The status flags provide status information that the EU posts to reflect certain properties of the result of an arithmetic or logic operation. A group of instructions is available that allows a program to alter its execution depending on the contents of the status flags, that is, on the result of a prior operation. Table 3-2 summarizes the flag register bit functions.

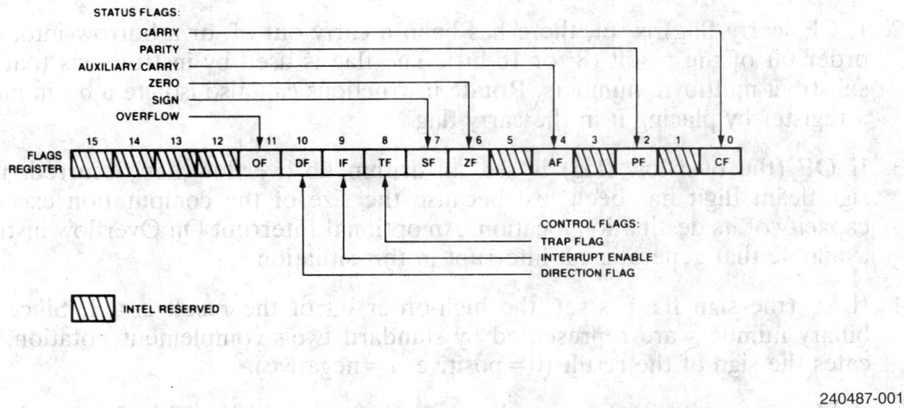

Figure 3-4. Flags Register Format

Table 3-2. Flags Register Bit Functions

Bit Position	Name	Function
0	CF	Carry Flag — Set on high-order bit carry or borrow; cleared otherwise
2	PF	Parity Flag — Set if low-order 8 bits of result contain an even number of 1-bits; cleared otherwise
4	AF	Set on carry from or borrow to the low order four bits of AL; cleared otherwise
6	ZF	Zero Flag — Set if result is zero; cleared otherwise
7	SF	Sign Flag — Set equal to high-order bit of result (0 if positive, 1 if negative)
8	TF	Single Step Flag — Once set, a single step interrupt occurs after the next instruction executes. TF is cleared by the single step interrupt
9	IF	Interrupt-enable Flag — When set, maskable interrupts will cause the CPU to transfer control to an interrupt vector specified location
10	DF	Direction Flag — Causes string instructions to auto decrement the appropriate index register when set. Clearing DF causes auto increment
11	OF	Overflow Flag — Set if the signed result cannot be expressed within the number of bits in the destination operand; cleared otherwise

Different instructions affect the status flags differently; in general, however, the flags reflect the following conditions:

1. If AF (the auxiliary flag) is set, there has been a carry out of the low nibble (the low order 4-bits of a byte) into the high nibble or a borrow from the high nibble into the low nibble of an 8-bit quantity (low-order byte of a 16-bit quantity). This flag is used by decimal arithmetic instructions.

2. If CF (carry flag) is set, there has been a carry out of, or a borrow into, the high-order bit of the result (8- or 16-bit). The flag is used by instructions that add and substract multibyte numbers. Rotate instructions can also isolate a bit in memory or a register by placing it in the carry flag.

3. If OF (the overflow flag) is set, an arithmetic overflow has occurred; that is, a significant digit has been lost because the size of the computation exceeded the capacity of its destination location. An optional Interrupt On Overflow instruction is available that generates an interrupt in this situation.

4. If SF (the sign flag) is set, the high-order bit of the result is a 1. Since negative binary numbers are represented by standard two's complement notation, SF indicates the sign of the result (0 = positive, 1 = negative).

5. If PF (the parity flag) is set, the result has even parity. This flag can be used to check for data transmission errors. (Only the low-order 8 bits are tested.) If ZF (zero flag) is set, the result of the operation is 0.

6. The three control flags are used by programs to alter processor operations in specified ways. The direction flag controls the direction of the string manipulations, the interrupt flag enables or disables external interrupts, and the trap flag puts the processor into a single-step mode for debugging.

The three control flags are used by programs to alter processor operations in specified ways. The direction flag controls the direction of the string manipulations, the interrupt flag enables or disables external interrupts, and the trap flag puts the processor into a single-step mode for debugging.

The control flags are set and cleared as follows:

1. Setting DF (the direction flag) causes string instructions to auto-decrement, that is, to process strings from high addresses to low addresses, or from right to left. Clearing DF causes string instructions to auto-increment, or to process strings from left to right.

2. Setting IF (the interrupt-enable flag) allows the CPU to recognize maskable, external interrupt requests. Clearing IF disables these interrupts. IF has no effect on either nonmaskable external or internally generated interrupts.

3. Setting TF (the trap flag) puts the processor into single-step mode for debugging. In this mode, the CPU automatically generates an internal interrupt after each instruction, allowing a program to be inspected as it executes, instruction by instruction.

MEMORY STRUCTURE

The memory and input/output space of the 8086/8088 are treated in parallel and are collectively referred to as the memory structure. Code and data reside in the memory space, while (non-memory-mapped) peripheral devices reside in the I/O space. This section describes how memory is functionally organized and used.

Memory Space

The memory in an 8086/8088 system is a sequence of up to one million (1,048,576) bytes. A *word* is any two consecutive bytes in memory (word alignment is not required). Words are stored in memory with the most significant byte at the higher memory address.

The memory can be conceived of as an arbitrary number of segments, each containing a maximum of 64K bytes. The starting address of each segment is evenly divisible by 16 (the four least significant address bits are 0). At any moment, the program can immediately access the contents of four such segments:

1. the current code segment
2. the current data segment
3. the current stack segment
4. the current extra segment

Each of these segments can be identified by placing the 16 most significant bits of the segment's starting address into one of the four 16-bit segment registers. Instructions can refer to bytes or words within a segment by using a 16-bit offset address. The processor constructs the 20-bit byte or word address automatically by adding the 16-bit offset address (also called the logical address) to the contents of a 16-bit segment register, with four low-order zeros appended (see Figure 3-5).

Storage Organization

From the storage point of view, memory spaces are organized as arrays of 8-bit bytes (Figure 3-6). Instructions, byte data and word data may be freely stored at any byte address without regard for alignment, thereby saving memory space by allowing code to be densely packed in memory (Figure 3-7).

Word data is always stored with the most-significant byte in the higher memory location (Figure 3-8). Most of the time this storage convention is transparent to the programmer, except when monitoring the system bus or reading memory dumps.

Pointers addressing data and code that are outside the currently-addressable segments are stored as doublewords. The lower-addressed word of a pointer contains an offset value; the higher-addressed word contains a segment base address. By convention, each word is stored with the higher-addressed byte holding the most-significant eight bits of the word (Figure 3-9).

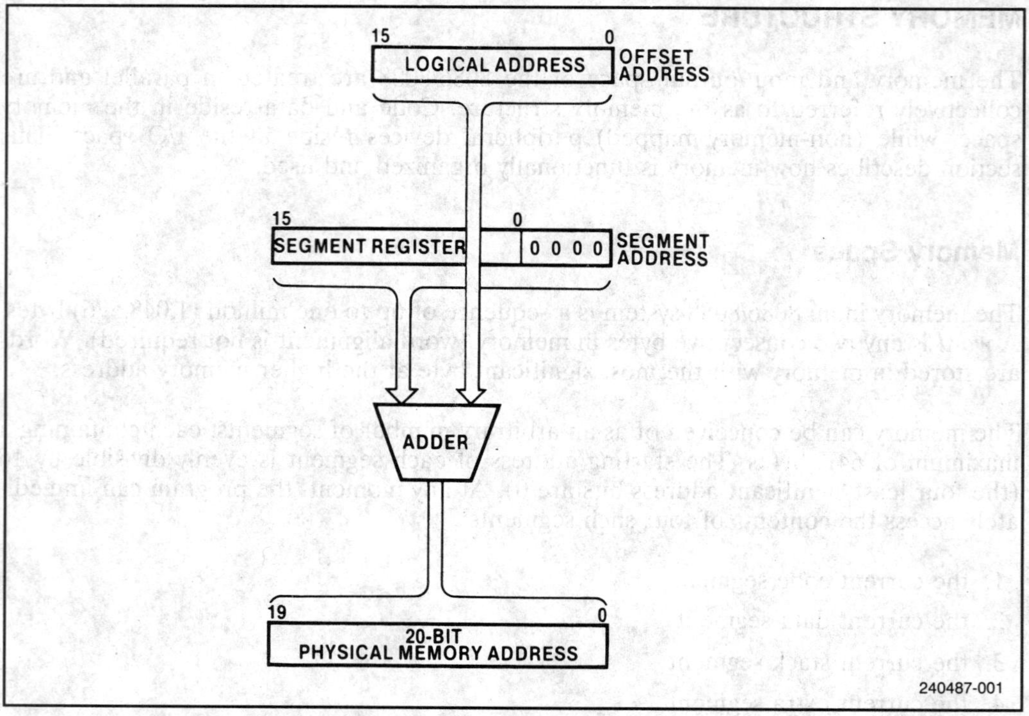

Figure 3-5. How to Address One Million Bytes

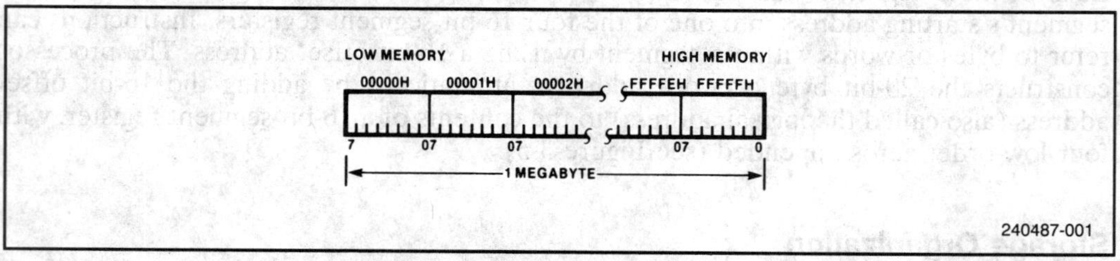

Figure 3-6. Storage Organization

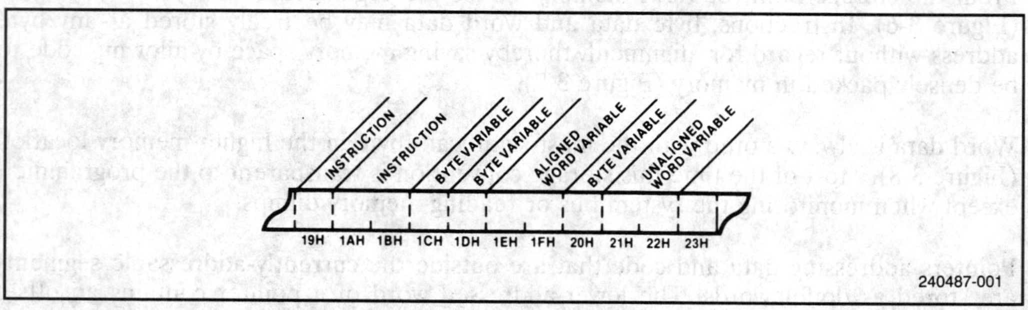

Figure 3-7. Instruction and Variable Storage

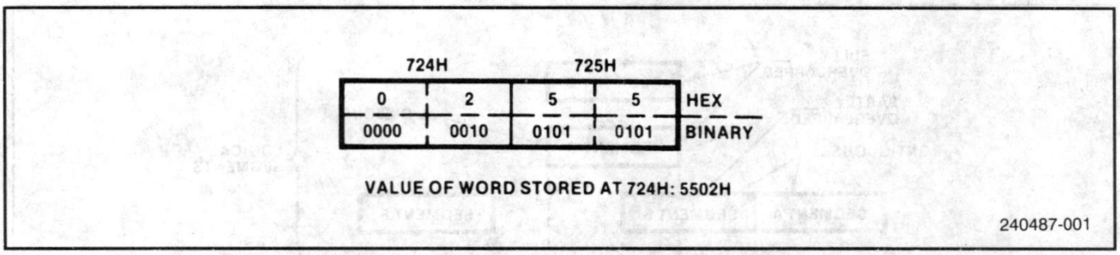

Figure 3-8. Storage of Word Variables

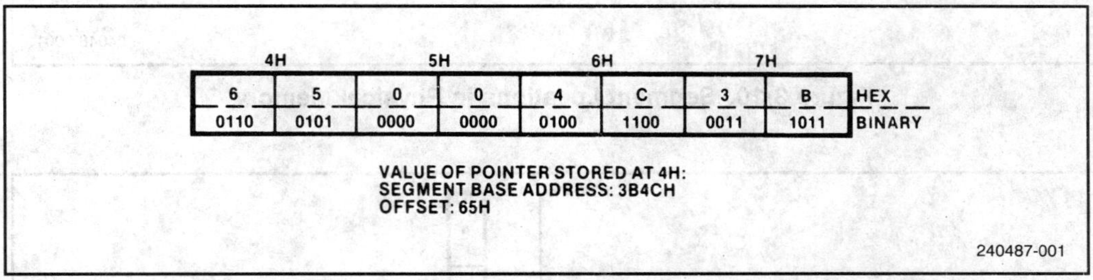

Figure 3-9. Storage of Pointer Variables

Segmentation

Programs view memory space as a group of segments defined by the application. A segment is a logical unit of memory that may be up to 64K bytes long. Each segment is made up of contiguous memory locations and is an independent, separately addressable unit. Every segment is assigned (by software) a base address, which is its starting location in the memory space. All segments start on 16-byte memory boundaries. There are no other restrictions on segment locations. Segments may be adjacent, disjoint, partially overlapped, or fully overlapped (Figure 3-10). A physical memory location may be mapped into (contained in) one or more logical segments.

The segment registers point to (contain the base address values of) the four immediately addressable segments (Figure 3-11). Programs obtain access to code and data in other segments by changing the segment registers to point to the desired segments.

Every application will define and use segments differently. The currently addressable segments provide a generous work space: 64K bytes for code, a 64K byte stack and 128K bytes of data storage. Many applications can be written to simply initialize the segment registers and then forget them. Larger applications should be designed with careful consideration given to segment definition. This segmented structure of the memory space supports modular software design by discouraging very large, monolithic programs. Segments can also be used to advantage in many programming situations. An example is the case of an editor for several on-line terminals. A 64K byte text buffer (say, an extra segment) could be assigned to each terminal. A single program could maintain all the buffers by simply changing register ES to point to the buffer of the terminal requiring service.

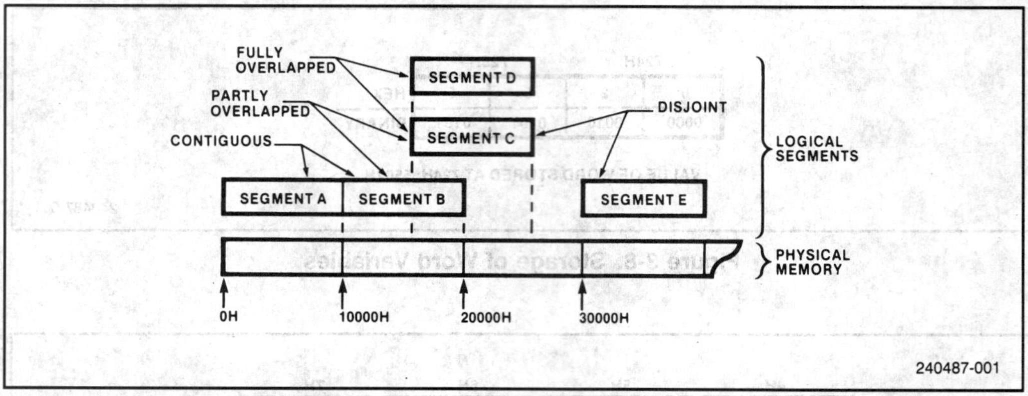

Figure 3-10. Segment Locations in Physical Memory

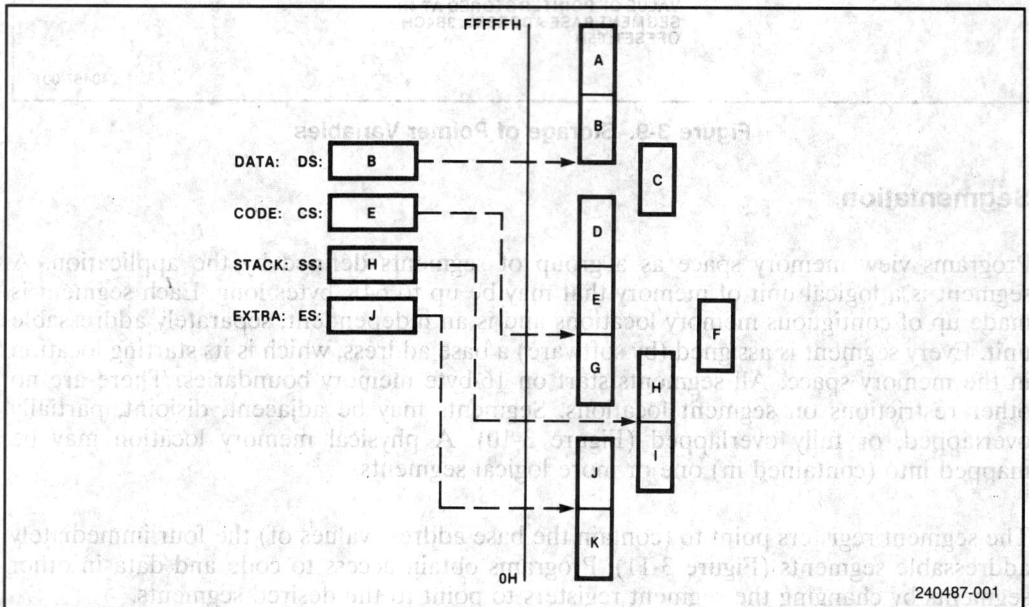

Figure 3-11. Currently Addressable Segments

Physical Address Generation

It is useful to think of every memory location as having two kinds of addresses — physical and logical. A physical address is the 20-bit value that uniquely identifies each byte location in the memory space. Physical addresses may range from 0H through FFFFFH. All exchanges between the CPU and memory components use this physical address.

Programs, however, deal with logical rather than physical addresses. The use of logical addresses allows code to be developed without prior knowledge of where the code is to be located in memory, and facilitates dynamic management of memory resources.

A logical address consists of a segment base value and an offset value. For any given memory location, the segment base value locates the first byte of the containing segment and the offset value is the distance, in bytes, of the target location from the beginning of the segment. Segment base and offset values are unsigned 16-bit quantities: the lowest-addressed byte in a segment has an offset of 0. Many different logical addresses can map to the same physical location as shown in Figure 3-12.

Whenever the BIU accesses memory – to fetch an instruction or to obtain or store a variable – it generates a physical address from a logical address. This is done by shifting the segment base value four bit positions and adding the offset as illustrated in Figure 3-13. This addition process provides for modulo 64K addresses (addresses wrap around from the end of a segment to the beginning of the same segment).

The BIU obtains the logical address of a memory location from different sources depending on the type of reference that is being made (see Table 3-3).

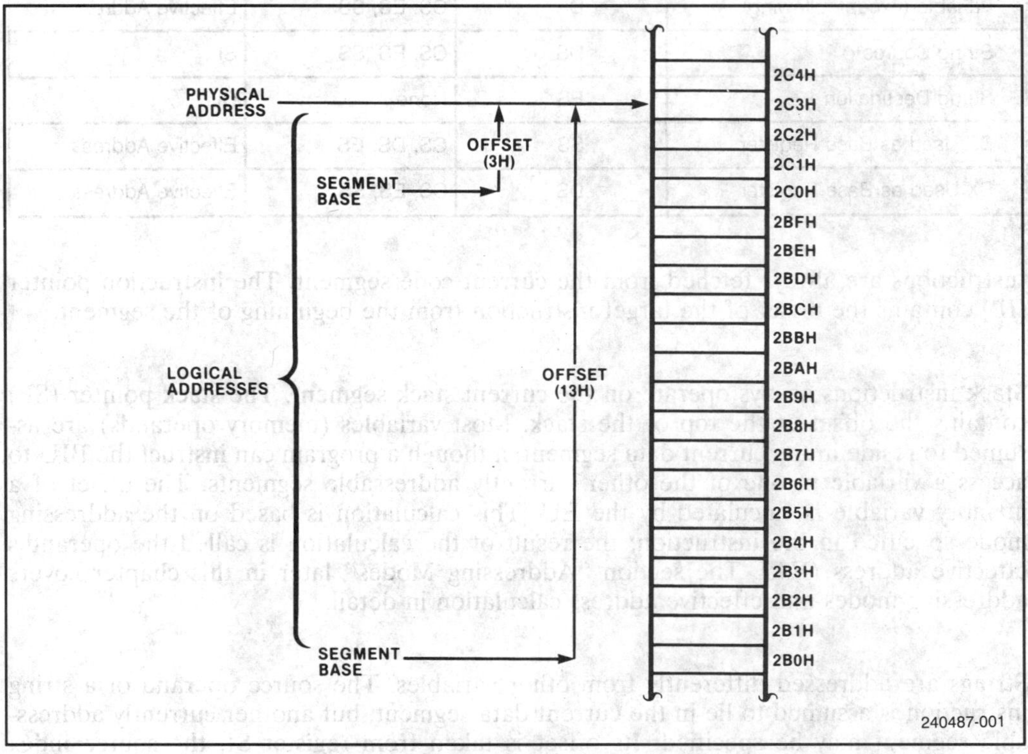

Figure 3-12. Logical and Physical Addresses

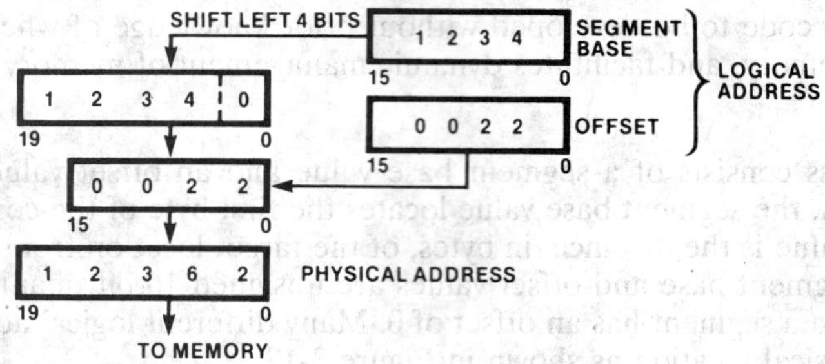

Figure 3-13. Physical Address Generation

Table 3-3. Logical Address Sources

Type of Memory Reference	Default Segment Base	Alternate Segment Base	Offset
Instruction Fetch	CS	None	IP
Stack Operation	SS	None	SP
Variable (except following)	DS	CS, ES, SS	Effective Address
String Source	DS	CS, ES, SS	SI
String Destination	ES	None	DI
BP Used as Base Register	SS	CS, DS, ES	Effective Address
BX Used as Base Register	DS	CS, ES, SS	Effective Address

Instructions are always fetched from the current code segment. The instruction pointer (IP) contains the offset of the target instruction from the beginning of the segment.

Stack instructions always operate on the current stack segment. The stack pointer (SP) contains the offset of the top of the stack. Most variables (memory operands) are assumed to reside in the current data segment, although a program can instruct the BIU to access a variable in one of the other currently addressable segments. The offset of a memory variable is calculated by the EU. This calculation is based on the addressing mode specified in the instruction; the result of the calculation is called the operand's effective address (EA). The section "Addressing Modes" later in this chapter covers addressing modes and effective address calculation in detail.

Strings are addressed differently from other variables. The source operand of a string instruction is assumed to lie in the current data segment, but another currently addressable segment may be specified. Its offset is taken from register SI, the source index register. The destination operation of a string instruction always resides in the current extra segment (ES). Its offset is taken from the DI, the destination index register. The string instructions automatically adjust SI and DI as they process the strings one byte or word at a time.

When register BP, the base pointer register is designated as a base register in an instruction, the variable is assumed to reside in the current stack segment. Register BP thus provides a convenient way to address data on the stack. BP can be used, however, to access data in any of the other currently addressable segments.

In most cases, the BIU's segment assumptions are a convenience to the programmer, since they are based on the most frequent typical usage. It is possible, however, to explicitly direct the BIU to access a variable in any of the currently addressable segments (the only exception is the destination operand of a string instruction which must be in the extra segment). This is done by preceding an instruction with a segment override prefix. This one-byte machine instruction tells the BIU which segment register to use to access a variable referenced in the following instruction.

Dynamically Relocatable Code

The segmented memory structure of the 8086/8088 makes it possible to write programs that are position-independent, or dynamically relocatable. Dynamic relocation allows a multi-programming or multitasking system to make particularly effective use of the available memory. Inactive programs can be written to disk, and the space they occupied allocated to other programs. If a disk-resident program is needed later, it can be read back into any available memory location and restarted. Similarly, if a program needs a large contiguous block of storage, and the total amount is available only in nonadjacent fragments, other program segments can be compacted to free up a continuous space. This process is shown graphically in Figure 3-14.

In order to be dynamically relocatable, a program must not load or alter its segment registers and must not transfer directly to a location outside the current code segment. In other words, all offsets in the program must be relative to fixed values contained in the segment registers. This allows the program to be moved anywhere in memory as long as the segment registers are updated to point to the new base addresses.

Stack Implementation

Stacks are located in memory and are accessed by the stack segment register (SS) and the stack pointer register (SP). A system may have an unlimited number of stacks, and a stack may be up to 64K bytes long, the maximum length of a segment. (An attempt to expand a stack beyond 64K bytes overwrites the beginning of the stack.) One stack is directly addressable at a time, the current stack, generally referred to simply as the stack. SS contains the base address of this stack and SP points to the top of the stack (TOS). In other words, SP contains the offset of the top of the stack from the stack segment's base address. The stack's base address (contained in SS), however, is not the bottom of the stack.

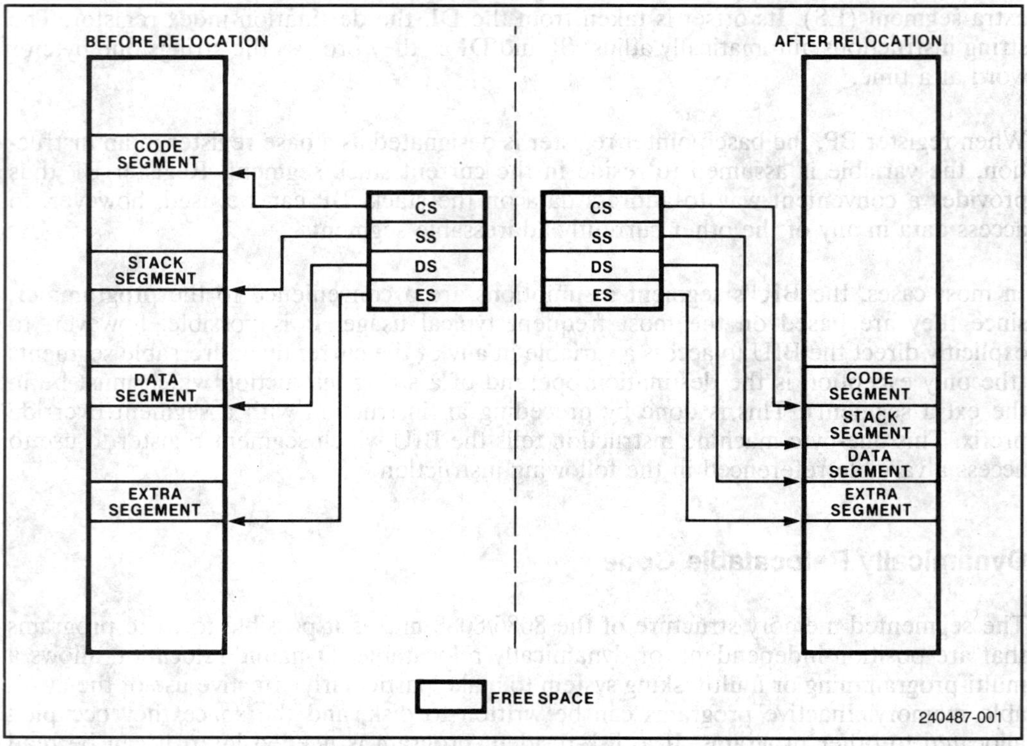

Figure 3-14. Dynamic Code Relocation

Stacks are 16-bits wide; thus, instructions that operate on stacks add and remove stack items one word at a time. A word is pushed onto the stack by *decrementing* SP by 2 and writing the item at the new TOS (see Figure 3-15). A word is popped off the stack by copying it from TOS and then *incrementing* SP by 2.

In other words, the stack grows *down* in memory towards its base address. Stack operations never move items on the stack, nor do they erase them. The top of the stack changes only as a result of updating the stack pointer.

Dedicated and Reserved Memory Locations

Two areas in extreme low and high memory are dedicated to specific processor functions or are reserved by Intel Corporation for use by Intel hardware and software products. As shown in Figure 3-16, the locations are: 0H through 7FH (128 bytes) and FFFF0H through FFFFFH (16 bytes). These areas are used for interrupt and system reset processing. Application systems should not use these areas for any other purpose. Doing so may make these systems incompatible with future Intel products.

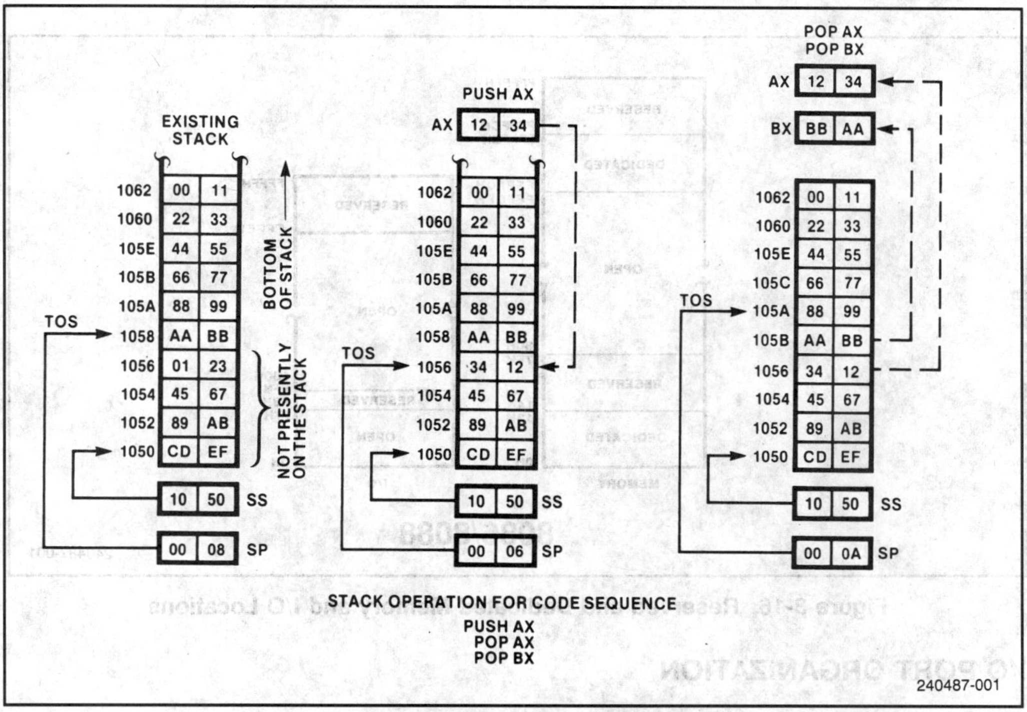

Figure 3-15. Stack Operation

8086 and 8088 Memory Access Differences

The 8086 can access either 8 or 16 bits of memory at a time. If an instruction refers to a word variable, and that variable is located at an even-numbered address, the 8086 accesses the complete word in one bus cycle. If the word is located at an odd-numbered address, it is accessed one byte at a time in two consecutive bus cycles.

Thus, to maximize throughput in 8086-based systems, 16-bit data should be stored at even addresses (i.e., it should be word aligned). This is particularly true of stacks. Unaligned stacks can slow a system's response to interrupts. Nevertheless, except for the performance penalty, word alignment is totally transparent to software, allowing maximum data packaging where memory space is constrained.

The 8086 always fetch the instruction stream in words from even addresses, except that the first fetch after a program transfer to an odd address obtains a byte. The instruction stream is disassembled inside the processor, and instruction alignment will not materially affect the performance of most systems.

The 8088 always accesses memory in bytes. Word operands are accessed in two bus cycles regardless of their alignment. Instructions are also fetched one byte at a time. Although alignment of word operands does not affect the performance of the 8088 locating 16-bit data on even addresses will insure maximum throughput if the system is ever transferred to an 8086.

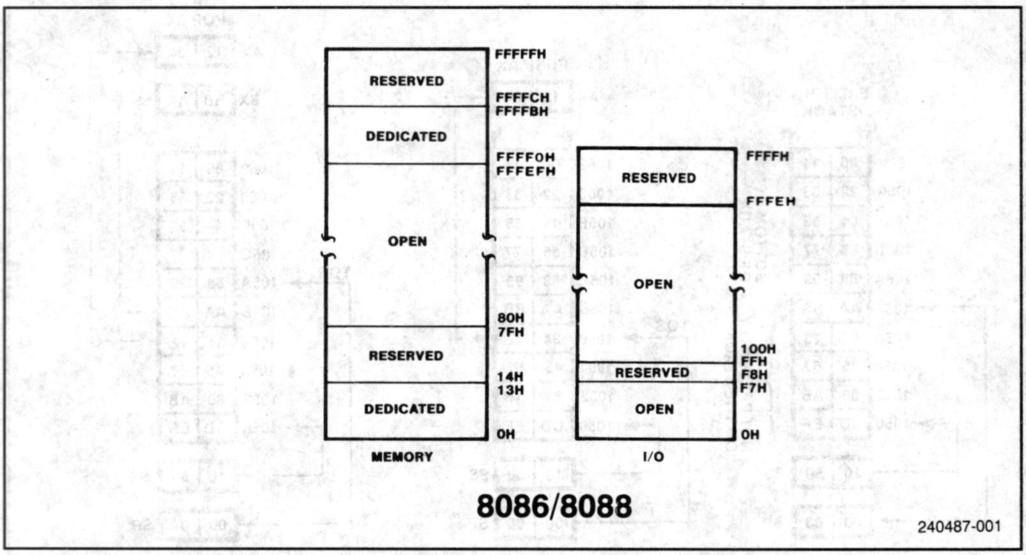

Figure 3-16. Reserved and Dedicated Memory and I/O Locations

I/O PORT ORGANIZATION

The 8086/8088 have a versatile set of input/output facilities. The processors provide a large I/O space that is separate from the memory space. I/O devices may also be placed in the memory space to bring the power of the full instruction set and addressing modes to input/output processing. For high speed transfers, the 8086/8088 may be used with traditional direct memory access controllers.

I/O Space

The I/O space can accommodate up to 64K 8-bit ports or up to 32K 16-bit ports. Ports are addressed the same way as memory except that there are no port segment registers. All ports are considered to be in one segment.

A 16-bit device should be located at an even address so that words will be transferred in a single bus cycle. An 8-bit device may be located at either an even or odd address. Thus, internal registers in a given 8-bit device will have all even or all odd addresses.

To access a port, the BIU places the port address (0-FFFFH) on the lower 16 lines of the address bus. Different forms of the I/O instructions allow the address to be specified as a fixed value in the instruction or as a variable taken from register DX. The IN and OUT (input and output) instructions transfer data between the accumulator (AL for byte transfers, AX for word transfers) and ports located in the I/O space.

The first 256 ports are directly addressable (address in the instruction) by some input/output instructions; other instructions let the programmer address the total of 64K ports indirectly (address in a register).

Restricted I/O Locations

As shown in Figure 3-16, on both the 8086/8088 processors, locations F8H through FFH (eight of the 64K locations) in the I/O space are reserved by Intel Corporation for use by future Intel hardware and software products. Using these locations for any other purpose may inhibit compatibility with future Intel products. On the 8086/8088, locations FFFE and FFFF are reserved.

Memory-Mapped I/O

I/O devices may also be placed in the memory space. This memory-mapped I/O provides additional programming flexibility. Any instruction that references memory may be used to access an I/O port located in the memory space. A group of terminals, for example, could be treated as an array in memory, with an index register selecting one of the terminals in the array.

Memory reference instructions take longer to execute, however, and are less compact than the simpler IN and OUT instructions.

ADDRESSING MODES

The 8086/8088 provides many different ways of addressing operands. Operands may be contained in registers, within the instruction itself, in memory or in I/O ports. In addition, the addresses of memory and I/O port operands can be calculated in several different ways. These addressing modes greatly extend the flexibility and convenience of the instruction set.

Register and Immediate Operands

Instructions that specify only register operands are generally the most compact and fastest executing. This is because the register addresses are encoded in instructions in just a few bits, and because these operations are performed entirely within the CPU (no bus cycles are run). Registers may serve as source operands, destination operands, or both.

Immediate operands are constant data contained in an instruction. The data may be either 8 or 16 bits long. Immediate operands can be accessed quickly because they are available directly from the instruction queue; (as in the case of register operands, no bus cycles need to be run to obtain an immediate operand). The limitations of immediate operands are that they may only serve as source operands and that they are constant values.

Memory Addressing Modes

Unlike register and immediate operands, which are directly accessible to the EU, memory operands must be transferred to and from the CPU over the bus. When the EU needs to read or write a memory operand, it must pass an offset value to the BIU. The BIU adds the offset to the (shifted) contents of a segment register, producing a 20-bit physical address, and then executes the bus cycle(s) needed to access the operand.

The Effective Address

The offset that the EU calculates for a memory operand is called the operand's effective address or EA. It is an unsigned 16-bit number that expresses the operand's distance in bytes from the beginning of the segment in which it resides. The EU can calculate the effective address in several different ways. Information encoded in the second byte of the instruction tells the EU how to calculate the effective address of each memory operand. A compiler or assembler derives this information from the statement or instruction written by the programmer. Assembly language programmers have access to all addressing modes.

As shown in Figure 3-17, the EU calculates the EA by summing a displacement, the contents of a base register, and the contents of an index register. The fact that any combination of these three components may be present in a given instruction results in the great variety of memory addressing modes provided by the 8086/8088.

The displacement element is an 8- or 16-bit number that is contained in the instruction. The displacement generally is derived from the position of the operand name (a variable or label) in the program. The programmer can also modify this value or specify the displacement explicitly.

A programmer may specify that either BX or BP is to serve as a base register whose contents are to be used in the EA computation. Similarly, either SI or DI may be specified as an index register. Whereas the displacement value is a constant, the contents of the base and index registers may change during the execution. This makes it possible for one instruction to access different memory locations as determined by the current value in the base and/or index registers.

Effective address calculations with the BP are made, by default, using the SS register, though either the DS or the ES registers may be specified instead.

Direct Addressing

Direct addressing (see Figure 3-18) is the simplest memory addressing mode. No registers are involved; the EA is taken directly from the displacement field of the instruction. Direct addressing typically is used to access simple variables (scalars).

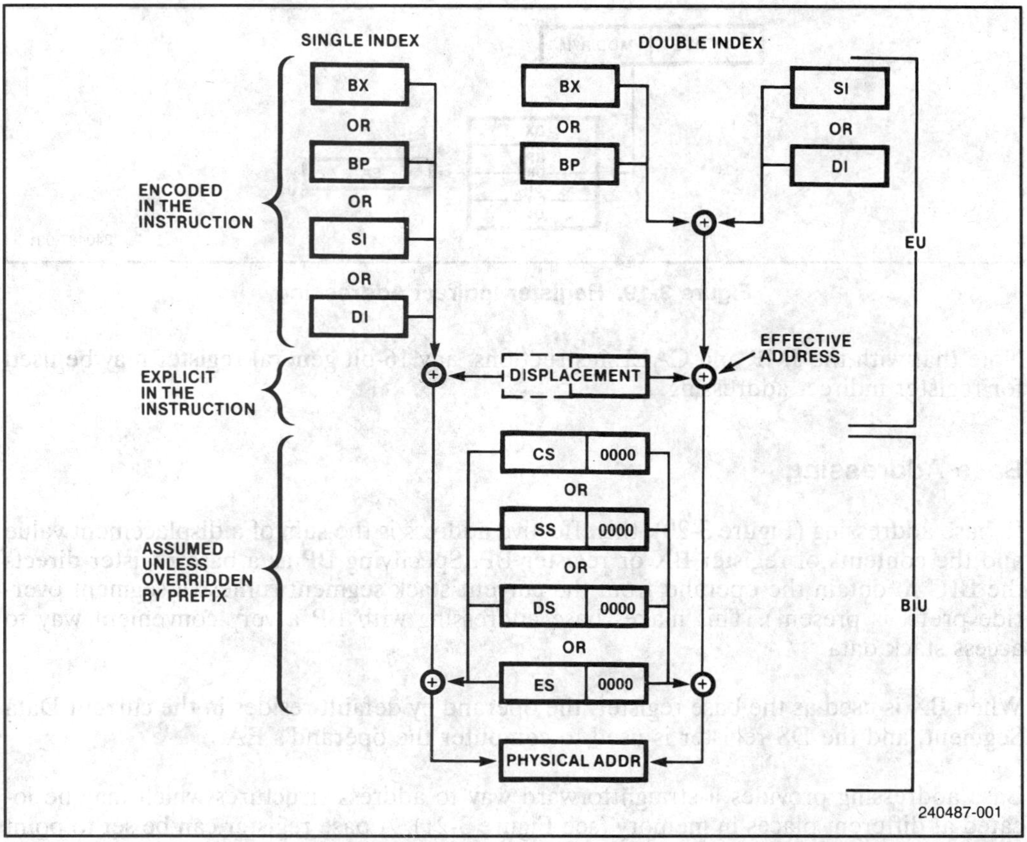

Figure 3-17. Memory Address Computation

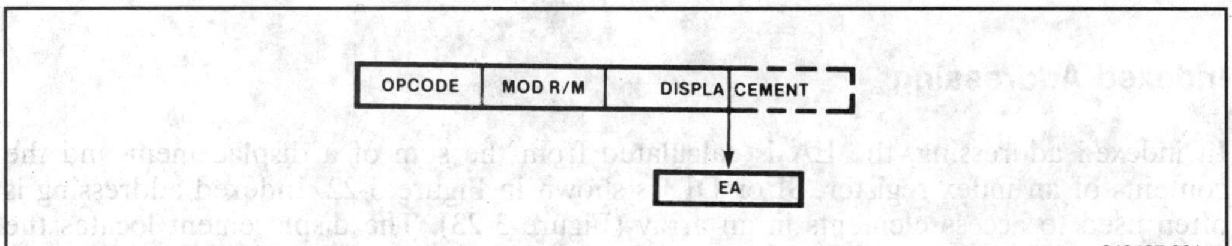

Figure 3-18. Direct Addressing

Register Indirect Addressing

The EA of a memory operand may be taken directly from the BP, BX, SI or DI register (see Figure 3-19). One instruction can operate on many different memory locations if the value in the pointer or index register is updated appropriately. The load effective address (LEA) and arithmetic instructions might be used to change the register value.

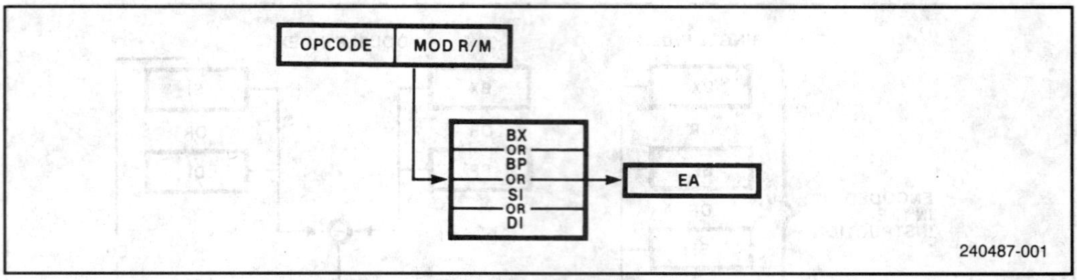

Figure 3-19. Register Indirect Addressing

Note that with the JMP and CALL instructions, any 16-bit general register may be used for register indirect addressing.

Base Addressing

In base addressing (Figure 3-20), the effective address is the sum of a displacement value and the contents of register BX or register BP. Specifying BP as a base register directs the BIU to obtain the operand from the current stack segment (unless a segment override prefix is present). This makes base addressing with BP a very convenient way to access stack data.

When BX is used as the base register, the operand by default resides in the current Data Segment, and the DS register is used to computer the operand's EA.

Base addressing provides a straightforward way to address structures which may be located at different places in memory (see Figure 3-21). A base register can be set to point to the base of the structure, and elements of the structure can then be addressed by their displacement from the base. Different copies of the same structure can be accessed by simply changing the base register.

Indexed Addressing

In indexed addressing, the EA is calculated from the sum of a displacement and the contents of an index register, SI or DI, as shown in Figure 3-22. Indexed addressing is often used to access elements in an array (Figure 3-23). The displacement locates the beginning of the array, and the value of the index register selects one element (the first element is selected if the index register contains 0). Since all array elements are the same length, simple arithmetic on the index register will select any element.

Based Indexed Addressing

Based indexed addressing generates an effective address that is the sum of a base register (BX or BP), an index register (SI or DI) and a displacement (Figure 3-24). Based indexed addressing is a very flexible mode because two address components can be varied at execution time.

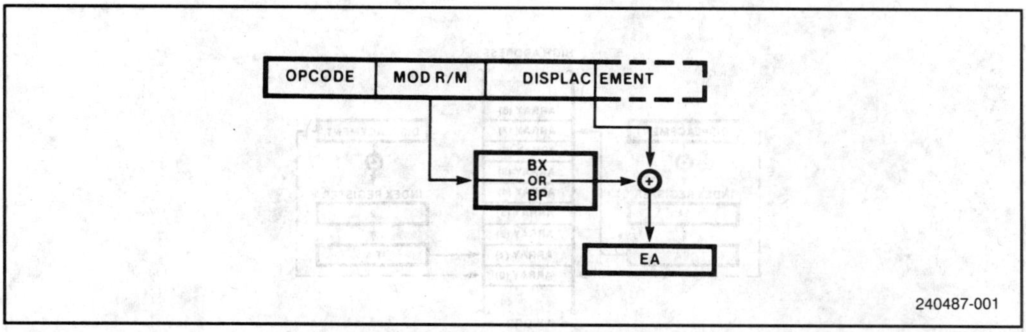

Figure 3-20. Based Addressing

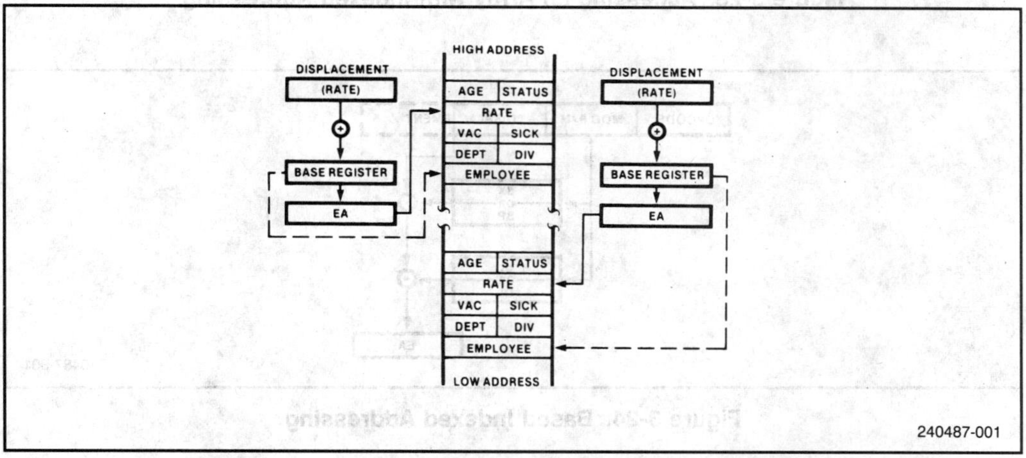

Figure 3-21. Accessing a Structure with Based Addressing

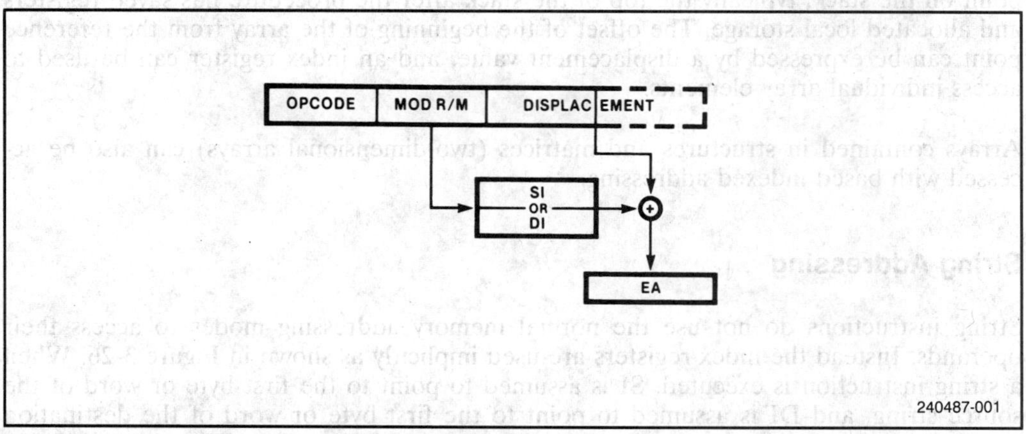

Figure 3-22. Indexed Addressing

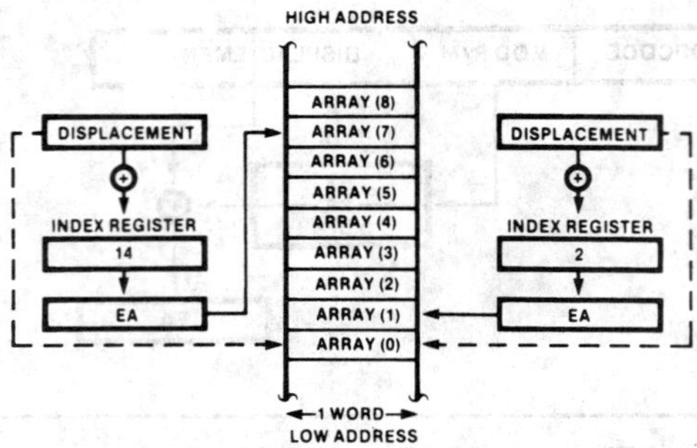

240487-001

Figure 3-23. Accessing an Array with Indexed Addressing

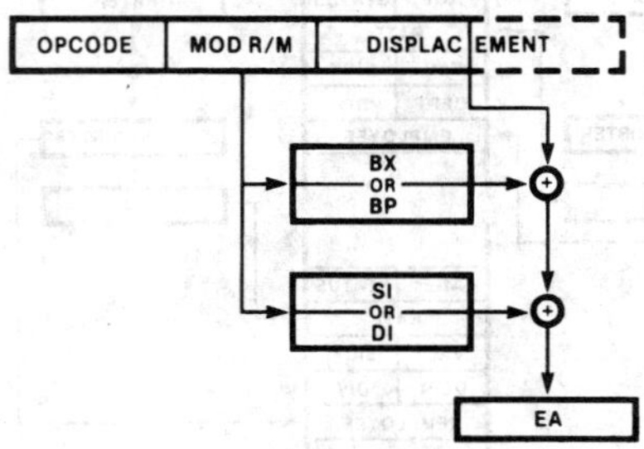

240487-001

Figure 3-24. Based Indexed Addressing

Based indexed addressing provides a convenient way for a procedure to address an array allocated on a stack (Figure 3-25). Register BP can contain the offset of a reference point on the stack, typically the top of the stack after the procedure has saved registers and allocated local storage. The offset of the beginning of the array from the reference point can be expressed by a displacement value, and an index register can be used to access individual array elements.

Arrays contained in structures and matrices (two-dimensional arrays) can also be accessed with based indexed addressing.

String Addressing

String instructions do not use the normal memory addressing modes to access their operands. Instead the index registers are used implicitly as shown in Figure 3-26. When a string instruction is executed, SI is assumed to point to the first byte or word of the source string, and DI is assumed to point to the first byte or word of the destination string. In a repeated string operation, the CPU automatically adjusts SI and DI to obtain subsequent bytes or words.

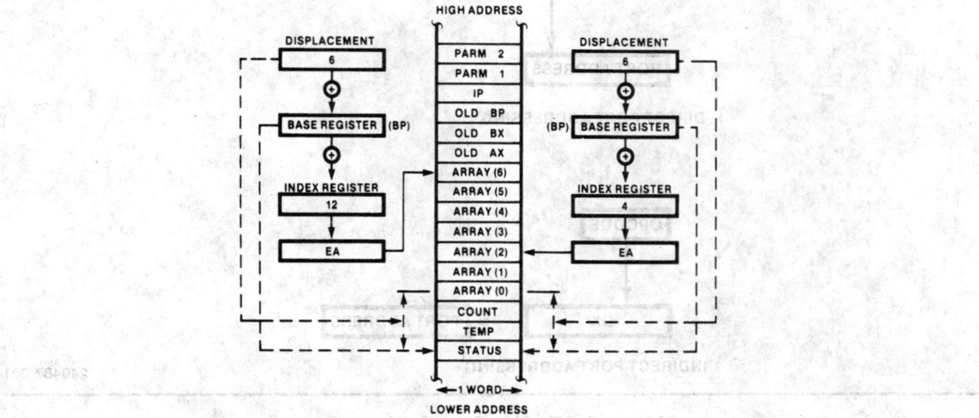

Figure 3-25. Accessing a Stack Array with Based Indexed Addressing

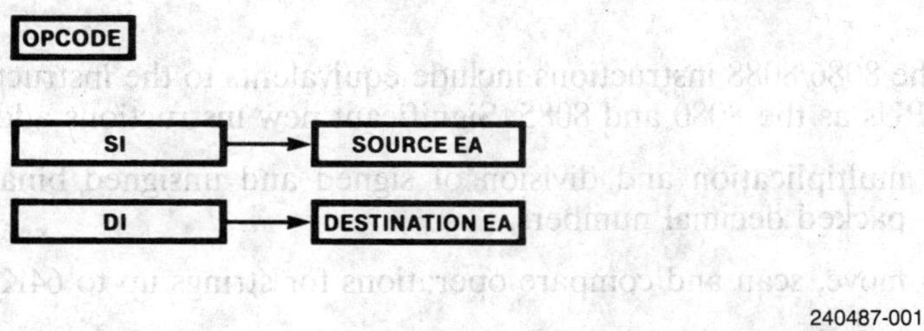

Figure 3-26. String Operand Addressing

I/O Port Addressing

If an I/O port is memory mapped, any of the memory operand addressing modes may be used to access the port (for example, a group of terminals can be accessed as an array). String instructions can also be used to transfer data to memory-mapped ports with an appropriate hardware interface.

To access ports located in the I/O space, the two different addressing modes illustrated in Figure 3-27 can be used. In direct port addressing, the port number is an 8-bit immediate operand. This allows fixed access to ports numbered 0 to 255. Indirect port addressing is similar to register indirect addressing of memory operands. The port number

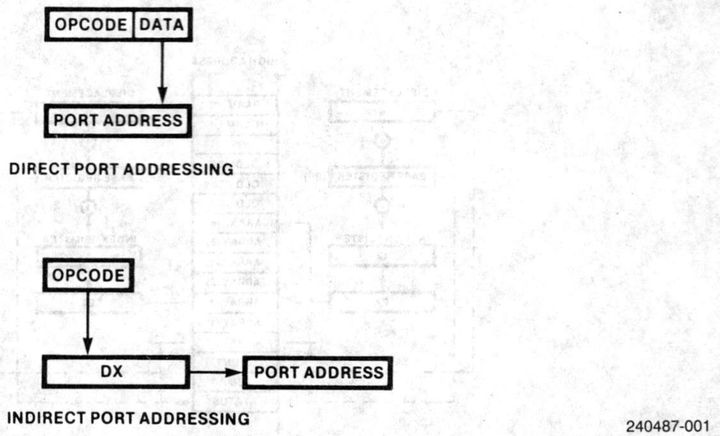

Figure 3-27. I/O Port Addressing

is taken from register DX and can range from 0 to 65,535 (providing access to any port in the I/O space). A group of adjacent ports can be accessed using a simple software loop that adjusts the value in DX.

THE INSTRUCTION SET

The 8086/8088 instructions include equivalents to the instructions typically found in such CPUs as the 8080 and 8085. Significant new instructions added by the 8086 are:

- multiplication and division of signed and unsigned binary numbers as well as unpacked decimal numbers,
- move, scan and compare operations for strings up to 64K bytes in length,
- non-destructive bit testing,
- byte translation from one code to another,
- additional software-generated interrupts, and
- a group of instructions that can help coordinate the activities of multiprocessor systems.

All instructions treat different types of operands uniformly. Nearly every instruction can operate on either byte or word data. Register, memory and immediate operands may be specified interchangeably in most instructions. The exception is that immediate values may only serve as source and not destination operands. In particular, memory variables can be added to, subtracted from, shifted, compared, and so on, in place, without moving them in and out of registers. This saves instructions, registers, and execution time in assembly language programs. In high-level languages, where most variables are memory-based, compilers, such as PL/M-86, can produce faster and shorter object programs.

The instruction set can be viewed as existing at two levels: the assembly level and the machine level. To the assembly language programmer the 8086 appears to have about 100 instructions. One MOV (move) instruction, for example, transfers a byte or a word from a register or a memory location or an immediate value to either a register or a memory location. The CPUs, however, recognize 28 different MOV machine instructions (move byte register to memory, move word immediate to register, etc.). The ASM-86 assembler translates the assembly-level instructions written by a programmer into the machine-level instructions that are actually executed by the CPU. Compilers such as the PL/M-86 translate high-level language statements directly into machine-level instructions.

The two levels of the instruction set address two different requirements: efficiency and simplicity. The numerous – about 300 in all – forms of machine-level instructions allow these instructions to make very efficient use of storage. For example, the machine instruction that increments a memory operand is three or four bytes long because the address of the operand must be encoded in the instruction. To increment a register, however, does not require as much information, so the instruction can be shorter. In fact, the 8086/8088 has eight different machine-level instructions that increment a different 16-bit register; these instructions are only one byte long.

This section presents the instruction set from two perspectives. First, the assembly-level instructions are described in functional terms. They are then presented in a reference table format that specifies all permissible operand combinations, provides execution times and machine instruction length, and shows the effect that the intruction has on the CPU flags.

The details of the syntax of the instruction set are described fully in Intel's *ASM86 Language Reference Manual*, #121703. A shorter treatment of the assembly language can be found in Intel's *An Introduction to ASM86* manual, #121689.

Instruction Set Organization

The instructions are divided into the following functional groups:

- Data transfer
- Arithmetic
- Bit manipulation
- String manipulation
- Control transfer
- Processor control

Data Transfer Instructions

The data transfer instructions (Table 3-4) move single bytes, words, and doublewords between memory and registers, as well as between register AL or AX and I/O ports. The stack manipulation instructions are included in this group, as are instructions for transferring flag contents and for loading segment registers.

Sub-groups of the data transfer instructions are the general purpose data transfer, I/O, address object, and flag transfer instructions.

GENERAL PURPOSE DATA TRANSFERS

MOV, *destination, source*

MOV transfers a byte or a word from the source operand to the destination operand.

PUSH *source*

PUSH decrements SP (the stack pointer) by two and then transfers a word from the source operand to the top of the stack now pointed to by SP. PUSH is often used to place parameters on the stack before calling a procedure; more generally, it is the basic means of storing temporary data on the stack.

Table 3-4. Data Transfer Instructions

General Purpose	
MOV	Move byte or word
PUSH	Push word onto stack
POP	Pop word off stack
XCHG	Exchange byte or word
XLAT	Translate byte
Input/Output	
In	Input byte or word
Out	Output byte or word
Address Object	
LEA	Load effective address
LDS	Load pointer using DS
LES	Load pointer using ES
Flag Transfer	
LAHF	Load AH register from flags
SAHF	Store AH register in flags
PUSHF	Push flags onto stack
POPF	Pop flags off stack

POP *destination*

POP transfers the word at the current top of stack (pointed to by SP) to the destination operand, and then increments SP by two to point to the new top of the stack. POP can be used to move temporary variables from the stack to registers or memory.

XCHG *translate-table*

XCHG (exchange) switches the contents of the source and destination (byte or word) operands. When used in conjunction with the LOCK prefix, XCHG can test and set a semaphore that controls access to a resource shared by multiple processors.

XLAT *translate-table*

XLAT (translate) replaces a byte in the AL register with a byte from a 256-byte, user-coded translation table. Register BX is assumed to point to the beginning of the table. The byte in AL is used as an index into the table and is replaced by the byte at the offset in the table corresponding to AL's binary value. The first byte in the table has an offset of 0. For example, if AL contains 5H, and the sixth element of the translation table contains 33H, then AL will contain 33H following the instruction. XLAT is useful for translating characters from one code to another, such as ASCII to EBCDIC or the reverse.

INPUT/OUTPUT

IN, *accumulator,port*

IN transfers a byte or a word from an input port to the AL register or the AX register respectively. The port number may be specified either with an immediate byte constant, allowing access to ports numbered 0 through 255, or with a number previously placed in the DX register, allowing variable access (by changing the value in DX) to ports numbered from 0 through 65,535.

OUT, *port, accumulator*

OUT transfers a byte or a word from the AL register or the AX register, respectively, to an output port. The port number may be specified either with an immediate byte constant, allowing access to ports numbered 0 through 255, or with a number previously placed in register DX, allowing variable access (by changing the value in DX) to ports numbered from 0 through 65,535.

ADDRESS OBJECT TRANSFERS

These instructions manipulate the addresses of variables rather than the contents or values of variables. They are most useful for list processing, based variables, and string operations.

LEA, *destination, source*

LEA (load effective address) transfers the offset of the source operand (rather than its value) to the destination operand. The source operand must be a memory operand, and the destination operand must be a 16-bit general register. LEA does not affect any flags. The XLAT and string instructions assume that certain registers point to operands. LEA can be used to load these registers (e.g., loading BX with the address of the translate table used by the XLAT instruction).

LDS, *destination, source*

LDS (load pointer using DS) transfers a 32-bit pointer variable from the source operand, which must be a memory operand, to the destination operand and register DS. The offset word of the pointer is transferred to the destination operand, which may be any 16-bit general register. The segment word of the pointer is transferred to register DS. Specifying SI as the destination operand is a convenient way to prepare to process a source string that is not in the current data segment (string instructions assume that the source string is located in the current data segment and that SI contains the offset of the string).

LES, *destination, source*

LES (load pointer using ES) transfers a 32-bit pointer variable from the source operand, which must be a memory operand, to the destination operand and register ES. The offset word of the pointer is transferred to the destination operand, which may be any 16-bit register. The segment word of the pointer is transferred to register ES. Specifying DI as the destination operand is a convenient way to prepare to process a destination string that is not in the current extra segment. (The destination string must be located in the extra segment, and DI must contain the offset of the string.)

FLAG TRANSFERS

LAHF

LAHF (load register AH from flags) copies SF, ZF, AF, PF and CF (the 8080/8085 flags) into bits 7, 6, 4, 2 and 0 respectively, of register AH (see Figure 3-28). The contents of bits 5, 3 and 1 is undefined; the flags themselves are not affected. LAHF is provided primarily for converting 8080/8085 assembly language programs to run on 8086 CPUs.

SAHF

SAHF (store register AH into flags) transfers bits 7, 6, 4, 2 and 0 from register AH into SF, ZF, AF, PF and CF respectively, replacing whatever values these flags previously had. OF, DF, IF and TF are not affected. This instruction is provided for 8080/8085 compatibility.

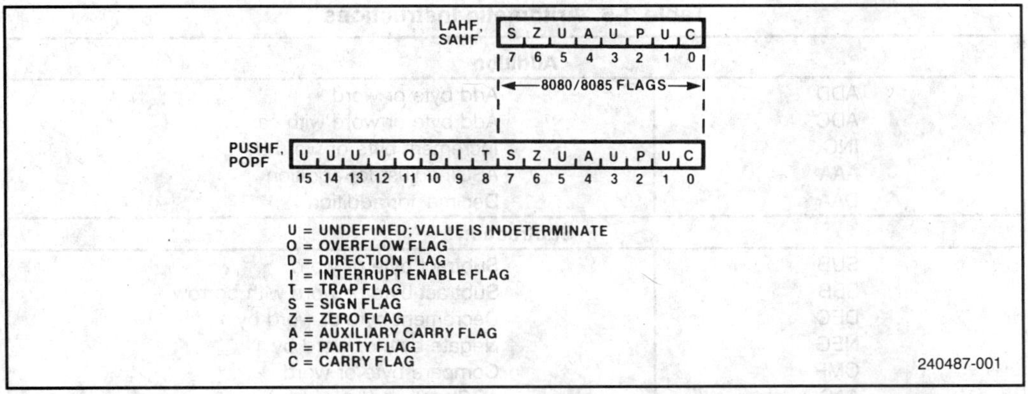

Figure 3-28. Flag Storage Formats

PUSHF

PUSHF decrements SP (the stack pointer) by two and then transfers all flags to the word at the top of stack pointed to by SP (see Figure 3-28). The flags themselves are not affected.

POPF

POPF transfers specific bits from the word at the current top of stack (pointed to by register SP) into flags, replacing whatever values the flags previously contained (see Figure 3-28). SP is then incremented by two to point to the new top of stack. PUSHF and POPF allow a procedure to save and restore a calling program's flags.

Arithmetic Instructions

Arithmetic operations (Table 3-5) may be performed on four types of numbers: unsigned binary, signed binary (integers), unsigned packed decimal and unsigned unpacked decimal (see Table 3-6). Binary numbers may be 8 or 16 bits long.

Decimal numbers are stored in bytes, two digits per byte for packed decimal and one digit per byte for unpacked decimal. The processor always assumes that the operands specified in arithmetic instructions contain data that represents valid numbers for the type of instruction being performed. Invalid data may produce unpredictable results.

Unsigned binary numbers may be either 8 or 16 bits long; all bits are considered in determining a number's magnitude. The value range of an 8-bit unsigned binary number is 0-255. Values from 0 to 65,535 can be represented by 16 bits. Addition, subtraction, multiplication and division operations are available for unsigned binary numbers.

Signed binary numbers (integers) may be 8 or 16 bits long. The high-order (leftmost) bit is interpreted as the number's sign: 0 = positive and 1 = negative. Negative numbers are represented in standard two's complement notation. Since the high-order bit is used as a sign, the range of an 8-bit integer is -128 through $+127$; 16-bit integers may range

Table 3-5. Arithmetic Instructions

Addition	
ADD	Add byte or word
ADC	Add byte or word with carry
INC	Increment byte or word by 1
AAA	ASCII adjust for addition
DAA	Decimal for addition
Subtraction	
SUB	Subtract byte or word
SBB	Subtract byte or word with borrow
DEC	Decrement byte or word by 1
NEG	Negate byte or word by 1
CMP	Compare byte or word
AAS	ASCII adjust for subtraction
DAS	Decimal adjust for subtraction
Multiplication	
MUL	Multiply byte or word unsigned
IMUL	Integer multiply byte or word
AAM	ASCII adjust for multiply
Division	
DIV	Divide byte or word unsigned
IDIV	Integer divide byte or word
AAD	ASCII adjust for division
CBW	Convert byte to word
CWD	Convert word to doubleword

Table 3-6. Arithmetic Interpretation of 8-bit Numbers

Hex	Bit Pattern	Unsigned Binary	Signed Binary	Unpacked Decimal	Packed Decimal
07	0 0 0 0 0 1 1 1	7	+7	7	7
89	1 0 0 0 1 0 0 1	137	−119	Invalid	89
C5	1 1 0 0 0 1 0 1	197	−59	Invalid	Invalid

from −32,768 through +32,767. The value of zero has a positive sign. Multiplication and division operations are provided for signed binary numbers. Addition and subtraction are performed with the unsigned binary instructions. Conditional jump instructions, as well as an "interrupt on overflow" instruction, can be used following an unsigned operation on an integer to detect overflow into the sign bit.

Packed decimal numbers are stored as unsigned byte quantities. The byte is treated as having one decimal digit in each half-byte (nibble); the digit in the high-order half-byte is the most significant. Hexadecimal values 0-9 are valid in each half-byte, and the range of a packed decimal number is 0-99. Addition and subtraction are performed in two steps. First an unsigned binary instruction is used to produce an intermediate result in register AL. Then an adjustment operation is performed which changes the intermediate value in AL to a final correct packed decimal result. Multiplication and division adjustment are not available for packed decimal numbers.

register AL. Then an adjustment operation is performed which changes the intermediate value in AL to a final correct packed decimal result. Multiplication and division adjustment are not available for packed decimal numbers.

Unpacked decimal numbers are stored as unsigned byte quantities. The magnitude of the number is determined from the low-order half-byte. Hexadecimal values 0-9 are valid and are interpreted as decimal numbers. The high-order half-byte must be zero for multiplication and division; it may contain any value for addition and subtraction. Arithmetic operations on unpacked decimal numbers are performed in two steps. The unsigned binary addition, subtraction and multiplication operations are used to produce an intermediate result in register AL. An adjustment instruction then changes the value in AL to a final correct unpacked decimal number. Division is performed similarly, except that the adjustment is carried out on the numerator operand in register AL first, and then a following unsigned binary division instruction produces a correct result.

Unpacked decimal numbers are similar to the ASCII character representations of the digits 0-9. Note, however, that the high-order half-byte of an ASCII numeral is always 3H. Unpacked decimal arithmetic may be performed on ASCII numeric characters under the following conditions:

- the high-order half-byte of an ASCII numeral must be set to 0H prior to multiplication or division.
- unpacked demical arithmetic leaves the high-order half-byte set to 0H; it must be set to 3H to produce a valid ASCII numeral.

Arithmetic Instructions and Flags

Arithmetic instructions post certain characteristics of the result of the operation to six flags. Most of these flags can be tested by following the arithmetic instruction with a conditional jump instruction, and the INTO (interrupt on overflow) instruction may also be used. The various instructions affect the flags differently, as explained in the instruction descriptions. However, they follow these general rules:

- **CF (carry flag):** If an addition results in a carry out of the high-order bit of the result, then CF is set; otherwise CF is cleared. If a subtraction results in a borrow into the high-order bit of the result, then CF is set; otherwise CF is cleared. Note that a signed carry is indicated by CF = OF (overflow flag). CF can be used to detect an unsigned overflow. Two instructions, ADC (add with carry) and SBB (subtract with borrow), incorporate the carry flag in their operations and can be used to perform multibyte (e.g., 32-bit, 64-bit) addition and subtraction.
- **AF (auxiliary carry flag):** If an addition results in a carry out of the low-order half-byte of the result, then AF is set; otherwise AF is cleared. If a subtraction results in a borrow into the low-order half-byte of the result, then AF is set; otherwise AF is cleared. The auxiliary carry flag is provided for the decimal adjust instructions and ordinarily is not used for any other purpose.
- **SF (sign flag):** Arithmetic and logical instructions set the sign flag equal to the high-order bit (bit 7 or 15) of the result. For signed binary numbers, the sign flag will be 0 for positive results and 1 for negative results (so long as overflow does not occur). A

conditional jump instruction can be used following addition or subtraction to alter the flow of the program depending on the sign of the result. Programs performing unsigned operations typically ignore SF since the high-order bit of the result is interpreted as a digit rather than a sign.

- **ZF (zero flag):** If the result of an arithmetic or logical operation is zero, then ZF is set; otherwise ZF is cleared. A conditional jump instruction can be used to alter the flow of the program if the result is or is not zero.
- **PF (parity flag):** If the low-order eight bits of an arithmetic or logical result contain an even number of 1-bits, then the parity flag is set; otherwise it is cleared. PF is provided for 8080/8085 compatibility. It can also be used to check ASCII characters for correct parity.
- **OF (overflow flag):** If the result of an operation is too large a positive number, or too small a negative number to fit in the destination operand (excluding the sign bit), then OF is set; otherwise OF is cleared. OF thus indicates signed arithmetic overflow. It can be tested with a conditional jump or the INTO (interrupt on overflow) instruction. OF may be ignored when performing unsigned arithmetic. OF is set if the operation results in a carry into the high-order bit of the result but not a carry out of the high-order bit, or vice versa; otherwise OF is cleared.

ADDITION

ADD, *destination, source*

The sum of two operands, which may be bytes or words, replaces the destination operand. Both operands may be signed or unsigned binary numbers (see AAA and DAA). ADD updates AF, CF, OF, PF, SF and ZF.

ADC, *destination, source*

ADC (add with carry) sums the operands, which may be bytes or words, adds one if CF is set and replaces the destination operand with the result. Both operands may be signed or unsigned binary numbers (see AAA and DAA). ADC updates AF, CF, OF, PF, SF and ZF. Since ADC incorporates a carry from a previous operation, it can be used to write routines to add numbers longer than 16 bits.

INC *destination*

INC (increment) adds one to the destination operand. The operand may be a byte or a word and is treated as an unsigned binary number (see AAA and DAA). INC updates AF, OF, PF, SF and ZF; it does not effect CF.

AAA

AAA (ASCII adjust for addition) changes the contents of register AL to a valid unpacked decimal number; the high-order half-byte is zeroed. AAA updates AF and CF; the contents of OF, PF, SF and ZF is undefined following execution of AAA.

DAA

DAA (decimal adjust for addition) corrects the result of previously adding two valid packed decimal operands (the destination operand must have been register AL). DAA changes the contents of AL to a pair of valid packed decimal digits. It updates AF, CF, PF, SF and ZF; the contents of OF is undefined following execution of DAA.

SUBTRACTION

SUB, *destination, source*

The source operand is subtracted from the destination operand, and the result replaces the destination operand. The operands may be signed or unsigned binary numbers (see AAS and DAS). SUB updates AF, CF, OF, PF, SF and ZF.

SBB, *destination, source*

SBB (subtract with borrow) subtracts the source from the destination, subtracts one if CF is set, and returns the result to the destination operand. Both operands may be bytes or words. Both operands may be signed or unsigned binary numbers (see AAS and DAS). SBB updates AF, CF, OF, PF, SF and ZF. Since it incorporates a borrow from a previous operation, SBB may be used to write routines that subtract numbers longer than 16 bits.

DEC *destination*

DEC (decrement) subtracts one from the destination, which may be a byte or a word. DEC updates AF, OF, PF, SF and ZF; it does not affect CF.

NEG *destination*

NEG and returns the result to the destination. This forms the two's complement of the number, effectively reversing the sign of an integer. If the operand is zero, its sign is not changed. Attempting to negate a byte containing −128 or a word containing −32,768 causes no change to the operand and sets OF. NEG updates AF, CF, OF, PF, SF and ZF. CF is always set except when the operand is zero, in which case it is cleared.

CMP , source

CMP (compare) subtracts the source from the destination, which may be bytes or words, but does not return the result. The operands are unchanged, but the flags are updated and can be tested by a subsequent conditional jump instruction. CMP updates AF, CF, OF, PF, SF and ZF. The comparison reflected in the flags is that of the destination to the source. If a CMP instruction is followed by a JG (jump is greater) instruction, for example, the jump is taken if the destination operand is greater than the source operand.

AAS

AAS (ASCII adjust for subtraction) corrects the result of a previous subtraction of two valid unpacked decimal operands (the destination operand must have been specified as register AL). AAS changes the contents of AL to a valid unpacked decimal number; the high-order half-byte is zeroed. AAS updates AF and CF; the contents of OF, PF, SF and ZF is undefined following execution of AAS.

DAS

DAS (decimal adjust for subtraction) corrects the results of a previous subtraction of two valid packed decimal operands (the destination operand must have been specified as register AL). DAS changes the contents of AL to a pair of valid packed decimal digits. DAS updates AF, CF, PF, SF and ZF; the contents of OF is undefined following execution of DAS.

MULTIPLICATION

MUL *source*

MUL (multiply) performs an unsigned multiplication of the source operand and the accumulator. If the source is a byte, then it is multiplied by register AL, and the double-length result is returned in AH and AL. If the source operand is a word, then it is multiplied by register AX, and the double-length result is returned in registers DX and AX. The operands are treated as unsigned binary numbers (see AAM). If the upper half of the results (AH for byte source, DX for word source) is nonzero, CF and OF are set; otherwise they are cleared. When CF and OF are set, they indicate that AH and DX contains significant digits of the result. The contents of AF, PF, SF and ZF is undefined following execution of MUL.

IMUL *source*

IMUL (integer multiply) performs a signed multiplication of the source operand and the accumulator. If the source is a byte, then it is multiplied by register AL, and the double-length results is returned in register AH and AL. If the source is a word, then it is multiplied by register AX, and the double-length result is returned in registers DX and AX. If the upper half of the result (AH for byte source, DX for word source) is not the sign extension of the lower half of the result, CF and OF are set; otherwise they are cleared. When CF and OF are set, they indicate that AH or DX contains significant digits of the result. The content of AF, PF, SF and ZF is undefined following execution of IMUL.

AAM

AAM (ASCII adjust for multiply) corrects the result of a previous multiplication of two valid unpacked decimal operands. A valid 2-digit unpacked decimal number is derived from the content of AH and AL and is returned to AH and AL. The high-order half-bytes of the multiplied operands must have been 0H for AAM to produce a correct result. AAM updates PF, SF and ZF; the content of AF, CF and OF is undefined following execution of AAM.

DIVISION

DIV *source*

DIV (divide) performs an unsigned division of the accumulator (and its extension) by the source operand. If the source operand is a byte, it is divided into the double-length dividend assumed to be in register AH and AL. The single-length quotient is returned in AL, and the single-length remainder in AH. If the source operand is a word, it is divided into the double-length dividend in registers DX and AX. The single-length quotient is returned in AX, and the single-length remainder is returned in DX. If the quotient exceeds the capacity of its destination register (FFH for byte source, 0FFFFH for word source), as when division by zero is attempted, a type 0 interrupt is generated, and the quotient and the remainder are undefined. Nonintegral quotients are truncated to integers. The content of AF, CF, OF, PF, SF and ZF is undefined following execution of DIV.

IDIV *source*

IDIV (integer divide) performs a signed division of the accumulator (and its extension) by the source operand. If the source operand is a byte, it is divided into the double-length dividend assumed to be in registers AH and AL. The single-length quotient is returned in AL, and the single-length remainder is returned in AH. For byte integer division, the maximum positive quotient is +127 (7FH) and the minimum negative quotient is −127 (81H). If the source operand is a word, it is divided into the double-length dividend in registers DX and AX (the high-order 16 bits are in DX and the low-order 16 bits in AX). The single-length quotient is returned in AX, and the single-length remainder is returned in DX. For word integer division, the maximum positive quotient is +32,767 (7FFFH) and the minimum negative quotient is −32,767 (8001H). If the quotient is positive and exceeds the maximum, or is negative and is less than the minimum, the quotient and the remainder are undefined, and a type 0 interrupt is generated. In particular, this occurs if division by 0 is attempted. Nonintegral quotients are truncated (toward 0) to integers, and the remainder has the same sign as the dividend. The content of AF, CF, OF, PF, SF and ZF is undefined following execution of IDIV.

AAD

AAD (ASCII adjust for division) modifies the numerator in AL before dividing two valid unpacked decimal operands so that the quotient produced by the division will be a valid unpacked decimal number. AH must be zero for the subsequent DIV to produce the correct result. The quotient is returned in AL, and the remainder is returned in AH; both high-order half-bytes are zeroed. AAD updates PF, SF and ZF; the content of AF, CF and OF is undefined following execution of AAD.

CBW

CBW (convert byte to word) extends the sign of the byte in register AL throughout register AH. CBW does not affect any flags. CBW can be used to produce a double-length (word) dividend from a byte prior to performing byte division.

CWD

CWD (convert word to doubleword) extends the sign of the word in register AX throughout register DX. CWD does not affect any flags. CWD can be used to produce a double-length (doubleword) dividend from a word prior to performing word division.

Bit Manipulation Instructions

Three groups of instructions (Table 3-7) are available for manipulating bits within both bytes and words: logical, shift and rotates.

LOGICAL

The logical instructions include the boolean operators "not," "and," "inclusive or," and "exclusive or," plus a TEST instruction that sets the flags, but does not alter either of its operands.

Table 3-7. Bit Manipulation Instructions

Logicals	
NOT	"Not" byte or word
AND	"And" byte or word
OR	"Inclusive or" byte or word
XOR	"Exclusive or" byte or word
TEST	"Test" byte or word
Shifts	
SHL/SAL	Shift logical/arithmetic left byte or word
SHR	Shift logical right byte or word
SAR	Shift arithmetic right byte or word
Rotates	
ROL	Rotate left byte or word
ROR	Rotate right byte or word
RCL	Rotate through carry left byte or word
RCR	Rotate through carry right byte or word

AND, OR, XOR and TEST affect the flags as follows:

The overflow (OF) and carry (CF) flags are always cleared by logical instructions, and the contents of the auxiliary carry (AF) flag is always undefined following execution of a logical instruction.

The sign (SF), zero (ZF) and parity (PF) flags are always posted to reflect the result of the operation and can be tested by conditional jump instructions. The interpretation of these flags is the same as for arithmetic instructions. SF is set if the result is negative (high-order bit is 1), and is cleared if the result is positive (high-order bit is 0). ZF is set if the result is zero, cleared otherwise. PF is set if the lower 8-bits of the result contains an even number of 1-bits (has even parity) and is cleared if the number of 1-bits is odd (the result has odd parity).

Note that NOT has no effect on the flags.

NOT *destination*

NOT inverts the bits (forms the one's complement) of the byte or word operand.

AND, *destination, source*

AND performs the logical "and" of the two operands (byte or word) and returns the result to the destination operand. A bit in the result is set if both corresponding bits of the original operands are set; otherwise the bit is cleared.

OR, *destination, source*

OR performs the logical "inclusive or" of the two operands (byte or word) and returns the result to the destination operand. A bit in the result is set if either or both corresponding bits in the original operands are set; otherwise the result bit is cleared.

XOR, *destination, source*

XOR (exclusive or) performs the logical "exclusive or" of the two operands and returns the result to the destination operand. A bit in the result is set if the corresponding bits of the original operands contain opposite values (one is set, the other is cleared); otherwise the result bit is cleared.

TEST, *destination, source*

TEST performs the logical "and" of the two operands (byte or word), updates the flags, but does not return the result, i.e., neither operand is changed. If a TEST instruction is followed by a JNZ (jump if not zero) instruction, the jump will be taken if there are any corresponding 1-bits in both operands.

SHIFTS

The bits in bytes and words may be shifted arithmetically or logically. On the 8086/8088 up to 255 shifts may be performed, according to the value of the count operand coded in the instruction. The count may be specified as the constant 1, or as register CL, allowing the shift count to be a variable supplied at execution time.

Arithmetic shifts may be used to multiply and divide binary numbers by powers of two (see note in description of SAR). Logical shifts can be used to isolate bits in bytes or words.

Shift instructions affect the flags as follows:

AF is always undefined following a shift operation. PF, SF and ZF are updated normally, as in the logical instructions. CF always contains the value of the last bit shifted out of the destination operand. The contents of OF is always undefined following a multibit shift. In a single-bit shift, OF is set if the value of the high-order (sign) bit was changed by the operation; if the sign bit retains its original value, OF is cleared.

SHL/SAL, *destination, count*

SHL and SAL (shift logical left and shift arithmetic left) perform the same operation and are physically the same instruction. The destination byte or word is shifted left by the number of bits specified in the count operand. Zeroes are shifted in on the right. If the sign bit retains its original value, then OF is cleared.

SHR , *destination, source*

SHR (shift logical right) shifts the bits in the destination operand (byte or word) to the right by the number of bits specified in the count operand. Zeros are shifted in on the left. If the sign bit retains its original value, then OF is cleared.

SAR, *destination, count*

SAR (shift arithmetic right) shifts the bits in the destination operand (byte or word) to the right by the number of bits specified in the count operand. Bits equal to the original high-order (sign) bit are shifted in on the left, preserving the sign of the original value. Note that SAR does not produce the same result as the dividend of an "equivalent" IDIV instruction if the destination operand is negative and 1-bits are shifted out. For example, shifting −5 right by one bit yields −3, while integer division of −5 by 2 yields −2. The difference in the instructions is that IDIV truncates all numbers toward zero, while SAR truncates positive numbers toward zero and negative numbers toward negative infinity.

ROTATES

Bits in bytes and words may also be rotated. Bit rotated out of an operand are not lost as in a shift, but are "circled" back into the other "end" of the operand. As in the shift instructions, the number of bits to be rotated is taken from the count operand, which may specify either a constant 1, or the CL register. The carry flag may act as an extension of the operand in two of the rotate instructions, allowing a bit to be isolated in CF and then tested by a JC (jump if carry) or JNC (jump if not carry) instruction.

Rotates affect only the carry and overflow flags. CF always contains the value of the last bit rotated out. On multibit rotates, the value of OF is always undefined. In single-bit rotates, OF is set if the operation changes the high-order (sign) bit of the destination operand. If the sign bit retains its original value, OF is cleared.

ROL, *destination, count*

ROL (rotate left) rotates the destination byte or word by the number of bits specified in the count operand.

ROR, *destination, count*

ROR (rotate right) operates similar to ROL except that the bits in the destination byte or word are rotated right instead of left.

RCL, *destination, count*

RCL (rotate through carry left) rotates the bits in the byte or word destination operand to the left by the number of bits specified in the count operand. The carry flag (CF) is treated as "part of" the destination operand; that is, its value is rotated into the low-order bit of the destination, and itself is replaced by the high-order bit of the destination.

RCR, *destination, count*

RCR (rotate through carry right) operates exactly like RCL except that the bits are rotated right instead of left.

String Instructions

The basic string instructions, also called primitives, operate on strings of bytes or words, one element (byte or word) at a time. Strings of up to 128K bytes may be manipulated with these instructions. Instructions are available to move, compare and scan for a value, as well as for moving string elements to and from the accumulator (see Table 3-8).

The string instructions operate similarly in many respects; the common characteristics are covered here and in Table 3-9 and in Figure 3-29, rather than in the descriptions of the individual instructions. A string instruction may have a source operand, a destination operand, or both. The hardware assumes that a source string resides in the current data segment; a segment prefix byte may be used to override this assumption. A destination string must be in the current extra segment. The assembler checks the attributes of the operands to determine if the elements of the strings are bytes or words. The assembler does not, however, use the operand names to address the strings. Rather, the contents of register SI (source index) is used as an offset to address the current element of the source string, and the contents of register DI (destination index) is taken as the offset of

Table 3-8. String Instruction

REP	Repeat
REPE/REPZ	Repeat while equal/zero
REPNE/REPNZ	Repeat while not equal/not zero
MOVS	Move byte or word string
MOVSB/MOVSW	Move byte or word string
CMPS	Compare byte or word string
SCAS	Scan byte or word string
LODS	Load byte or word string
STOS	Store byte or word string

Table 3-9. String Instruction Register and Flag Use

SI	Index (offset) for source string
DI	Index (offset) for destination string
DX	Port address
CX	Repetition counter
AL/AX	Scan value Destination for LODS Source for STOC
DF	0 = auto-increment SI, DI 1 = auto-decrement SI, DI
ZF	Scan/compare terminator

the current destination string element. These registers must be initialized to point to the source/destination strings before executing the string instruction; the LDS, LES and LEA instructions are useful in this regard.

The string instructions automatically update SI and/or DI in anticipation of processing the next string element. The setting of DF (direction flag) determines whether the index registers are auto-incremented (DF = 0) or auto-decremented (DF = 1). If byte strings are being processed, SI and/or DI is adjusted by 1. The adjustment is 2 for word strings.

If a repeat prefix has been coded, then register CX (count register) is decremented by 1 after each repetition of the string instruction. CX must be initialized to the number of repetitions desired before the string instruction is executed. If CX is 0, the string instruction is not executed, and control goes to the following instruction.

The section "8086/8088 Programming Examples," near the end of this chapter, contains examples illustrating the use of string instructions.

REP/REPE/REPZ/REPNE/REPNZ

Repeat, Repeat While Equal, Repeat While Zero, Repeat While Not Equal, and Repeat While Not Zero are five mnemonics for three forms of the prefix byte that controls repetition of a subsequent string instruction. The different mnemonics are provided to improve program clarity. The repeat prefixes do not affect the flags.

REP is used in conjunction with the MOVS (move string), the STOS (store string), the INS (in string) and OUTS (out string) instructions and is interpreted as "repeat while not end-of-string" (CX not 0). REPE and REPZ operate identically and are physically

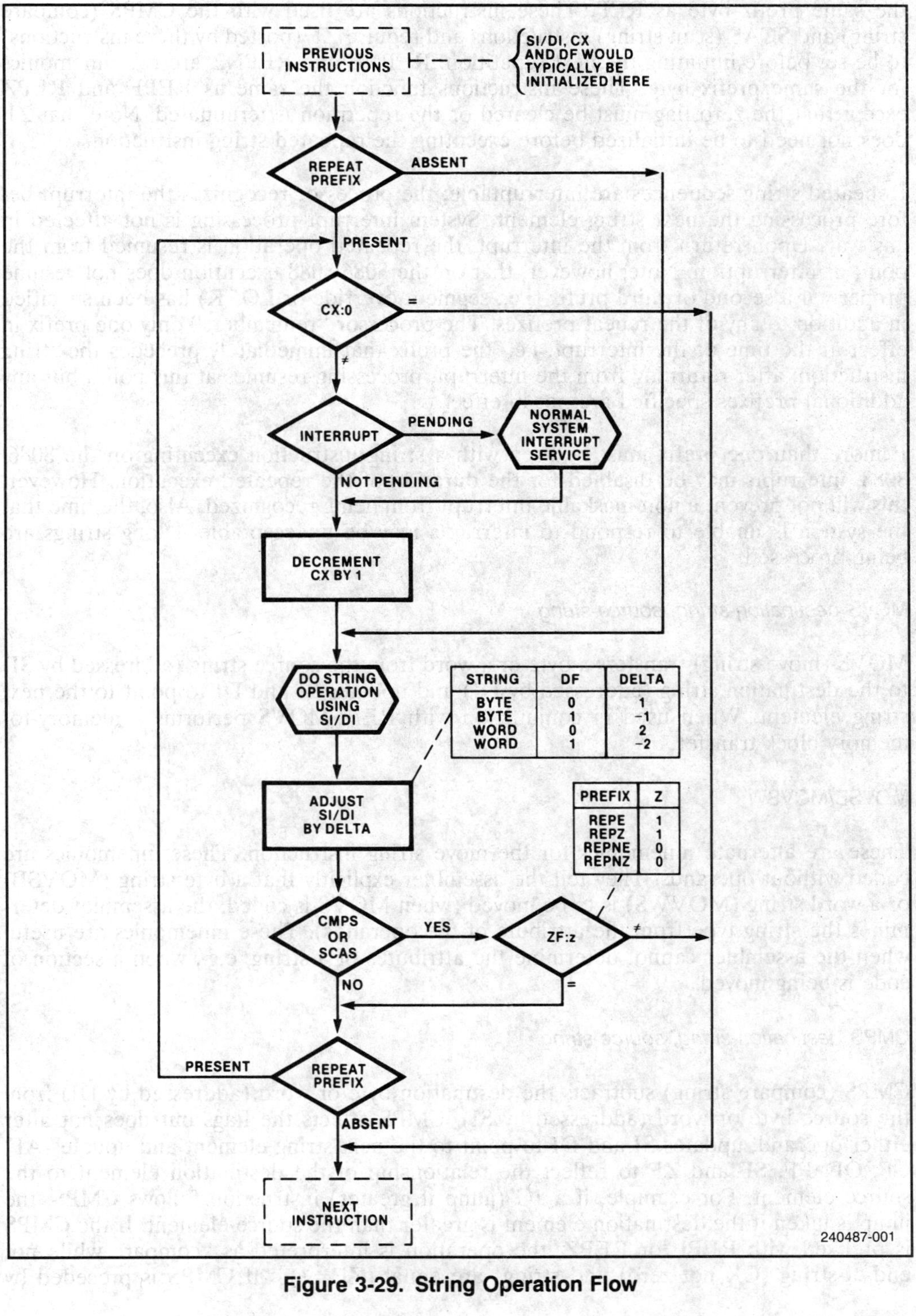

Figure 3-29. String Operation Flow

the same prefix byte as REP. These instructions are used with the CMPS (compare string) and SCAS (scan string) instructions and require ZF (posted by these instructions) to be set before initiating the next repetition. REPNE and REPNZ are two mnemonics for the same prefix byte. These instructions function the same as REPE and REPZ except that the zero flag must be cleared or the repetition is terminated. Note that ZF does not need to be initialized before executing the repeated string instruction.

Repeated string sequences are interruptable; the processor recognizes the interrupt before processing the next string element. System interrupt processing is not affected in any way. Upon return from the interrupt, the repeated operation is resumed from the point of interruption. Note, however, that on the 8086/8088 execution does not resume properly if a second or third prefix (i.e., segment override or LOCK) has been specified in addition to any of the repeat prefixes. The processor "remembers" only one prefix in effect at the time of the interrupt, i.e., the prefix that immediately precedes the string instruction; after returning from the interrupt, processing resumes at this point, but any additional prefixes specified are not in effect.

If more than one prefix must be used with a string instruction executing on the 8086/8088, interrupts may be disabled for the duration of the repeated execution. However, this will not prevent a non-maskable interrupt from being recognized. Also, the time that the system is unable to respond to interrupts may be unacceptable if long strings are being processed.

MOVS *destination-string, source-string*

MOVS (move string) transfers a byte or a word from the source string (addressed by SI) to the destination string (addressed by DI) and updates SI and DI to point to the next string element. When used in conjunction with REP, MOVS performs a memory-to-memory block transfer.

MOVSB/MOVSW

These are alternate mnemonics for the move string instruction. These mnemonics are coded without operands. They tell the assembler explicitly that a byte string (MOVSB) or a word string (MOVWS) is to be moved (when MOVS is coded, the assembler determines the string type from the attribute of the operands). These mnemonics are useful when the assembler cannot determine the attributes of a string, e.g., when a section of code is being moved.

CMPS *destination-string, source-string*

CMPS (compare string) subtracts the destination byte or word (addressed by DI) from the source byte or word (addressed by SI). CMPS affects the flags but does not alter either operand, updates SI and DI to point to the next string element and updates AF, CF, OF, PF, SF and ZF to reflect the relationship of the destination element to the source element. For example, if a JG (jump if greater) instruction follows CMPS, the jump is taken if the destination element is greater than the source element. If the CMPS is prefixed with REPE or REPZ, the operation is interpreted as "compare while not end-of-string (CX not zero) and strings are equal (ZF = 1)." If CMPS is preceded by

REPNE or REPNZ, the operation is interpreted as "compare while not end-of-string (CX not zero) and strings are not equal (ZF=0)." Thus, CMPS can be used to find matching or differing string elements.

SCAS *destination-string*

SCAS (scan string) subtracts the destination string element (byte or word) addressed by DI from the contents of AL (byte string) or AX (word string) and updates the flags, but does not alter the destination string or the accumulator. SCAS also updates DI to point to the next string element and AF, CF, OF, PF, SF and ZF to reflect the relationship of the scan value in AL/AX to the string element. If SCAS is prefixed with REPE or REPZ, the operation is interpreted as "scan while not end-of-string (CX not 0) and string-element scan-value (ZF=1)." This form may be used to scan for departure from a given value. If SCAS is prefixed with REPNE or REPNZ, the operation is interpreted as "scan while not end-of-string (CX not 0) and string-element is not equal to scan-value (ZF=0)." This may be used to locate a value in a string.

LODS *destination-string*

LODS (load string) transfers the byte or word string element addressed by SI to register AL or AX, and updates SI to point to the next element in the string. This instruction is not ordinarily repeated since the accumulator would be overwritten by each repetition, and only the last element would be retained. However, LODS is very useful in software loops as part of a more complex string function built up from string primitives and other instructions.

STOS *destination-string*

STOS (store string) transfers a byte or word from register AL or AX to the string element addressed by DI and updates DI to point to the next location in the string. As a repeated operation, STOS provides a convenient way to initialize a string to a constant value (e.g., to blank out a print line).

Control Transfer Instructions

The sequence of instructions executing in an 8086/8088 program is determined by the contents of the code segment register (CS) and the instruction pointer (IP). The CS register contains the base address of the current code segment, the 64K portion of memory from which instructions are presently being fetched. The IP is used as an offset from the beginning of the code segment; the combination of CS and IP points to the memory location from which the next instruction is to be fetched. (Under most operating conditions, the next instruction to be executed has already been fetched from memory and is waiting in the CPU instruction queue.) The program transfer instructions operate on the instruction pointer and on the CS register; changing the contents of these causes normal sequential execution to be altered. When a program transfer occurs, the queue no longer contains the correct instruction, and the queue no longer contains the correct instruction, and the BIU obtains the next instruction from memory using the new IP and CS values, passes the instruction directly to the EU, and then begins refilling the queue from the new location.

Four groups of program transfers are available (see Table 3-10): unconditional transfers, conditional transfers, iteration control instructions and interrupt-related instructions. Only the interrupt-related instructions affect any CPU flags. However, the execution of many of the program transfer instructions is affected by the states of the flags.

Table 3-10. Program Transfer Instructions

Unconditional Transfers	
CALL	Call procedure
RET	Return from procedure
JMP	Jump
Conditional Transfers	
JA/JNBE	Jump if above/not below nor equal
JAE/JNB	Jump if above or equal/nor below
JB/JNAE	Jump if below/not above not equal
JBE/JNA	Jump if below or equal/not above
JC	Jump if carry
JE/JZ	Jump if equal/zero
JG/JNLE	Jump if greater/not less nor equal
JGE/JNL	Jump if greater or equal/not less
JL/JNGE	Jump if less/not greater nor equal
JLE/JNG	Jump if less or equal/not greater
Unconditional Transfers	
JNC	Jump if not carry
JNE/JNZ	Jump if not equal/not zero
JNO	Jump if not overflow
JNP/JPO	Jump if not parity/parity odd
JNS	Jump if not sign
JO	Jump if overflow
JP/JPE	Jump if parity/parity even
JS	Jump if sign
Iteration Controls	
LOOP	Loop
LOOPE/LOOPZ	Loop if equal/zero
LOOPNE/LOOPNZ	Loop if not equal/not zero
JCXZ	Jump if register CX=0
Interrupts	
INT	Interrupt
INTO	Interrupt if overflow
IRET	Interrupt return

The unconditional transfer instructions may transfer control to a target instruction within the current code segment (intrasegment transfer) or to a different code segment (intersegment transfer). (The ASM-86 assembler terms an intrasegment target NEAR and an intersegment target FAR.) The transfer is made unconditionally any time the instruction is executed.

CALL *procedure-name*

CALL activates an out-of-line procedure, saving information on the stack to permit a RET (return) instruction in the procedure to transfer control back to the instruction following the CALL. The assembler generates a different type of CALL instruction depending on whether the programmer has defined the procedure name as NEAR or FAR. For control to return properly, the type of CALL instruction must match the type of RET instruction that exits from the procedure. (The potential for mismatch exists if the procedure and the CALL are contained in separately assembled programs.) Different forms of the CALL instruction allow the address of the target procedure to be obtained from the instruction itself (direct CALL) or from a memory location or register referenced by the instruction (indirect CALL).

In the following descriptions, bear in mind that the processor automatically adjusts IP to point to the next instruction to be executed before saving it on the stack.

For an intrasegment *direct* CALL, SP is decremented by two and IP is pushed onto the stack. The relative displacement (up to plus or minus 32K) of the target procedure from the CALL instruction is then added to the instruction pointer. This form of the CALL instruction is "self-relative" and is appropriate for position-independent (dynamically relocatable) routines in which the CALL and its target are in the same segment and are moved together.

An intrasegment *indirect* CALL may be made through memory or through a register. SP is decremented by two and IP is pushed onto the stack. The offset of the target procedure is obtained from the memory word or 16-bit general register referenced in the instruction and replaces IP.

For an intersegment *direct* CALL, SP is decremented by two, and CS is pushed onto the stack. CS is replaced by the segment word contained in the instruction. SP again is decremented by two. IP is pushed onto the stack and is replaced by the offset word contained in the instruction.

For an intersegment *indirect* CALL (which may only be made through memory), SP is decremented by two, and CS is pushed onto the stack. CS is then replaced by the contents of the second word of the doubleword memory pointer referenced by the instruction. SP again is decremented by two, and IP is pushed onto the stack and is replaced by the contents of the first word of the doubleword pointer referenced by the instruction.

RET *optional-pop-value*

RET (return) transfers control from a procedure back to the instruction following the CALL that activated the procedure. The assembler generates an intrasegment RET if the programmer has defined the procedure NEAR, or an intersegment RET if the procedure has been defined as FAR. RET pops the word at the top of the stack (pointed to by register SP) into the instruction pointer and increments SP by two. If RET is intersegment, the word at the new top of stack is popped into the CS register, and SP is again incremented by two. If an optional pop value has been specified, RET adds that value to SP. This feature may be used to discard parameters pushed onto the stack before the execution of the CALL instruction.

JMP *target*

JMP unconditionally transfers control to the target location. Unlike a CALL instruction, JMP does not save any information on the stack, and no return to the instruction following the JMP is expected. Like CALL, the address of the target operand may be obtained from the instruction itself (direct JMP) or from memory or a register referenced by the instruction (indirect JMP).

An intrasegment direct JMP changes the instruction pointer by adding the relative displacement of the target from the JMP instruction. If the assembler can determine that the target is within 127 bytes of the JMP, it automatically generates a two-byte form of this instruction called a SHORT JMP; otherwise, it generates a NEAR JMP that can address a target within plus or minus 32K. Intrasegment direct JUMPs are self-relative and are appropriate in position-independent (dynamically relocatable) routines in which the JMP and its target are in the same segment and are moved together.

An intrasegment indirect JMP may be made either through memory or through a 16-bit general register. In the first case, the contents of the word referenced by the instruction replaces the instruction pointer. In the second case, the new IP value is taken from the register named in the instruction.

An intersegment direct JMP replaces IP and CS with values contained in the instruction.

An intersegment indirect JMP may be made only through memory. The first word of the doubleword pointer referenced by the instruction replaces IP, and the second word replaces CS.

CONDITIONAL TRANSFERS

The conditional transfer instructions are jumps that may or may not transfer control depending on the state of the CPU flags at the time the instruction is executed. These instructions (see Table 3-11) each test a different combination of flags for a condition. If the condition is "true," then control is transferred to the target specified in the instruction. If the condition is "false," then control passes to the instruction that follows the conditional jump. All conditional jumps are SHORT, that is, the target must be in the current code segment and within −128 to +127 bytes of the first byte of the next

Table 3-11. Interpretation of Conditional Transfers

Mnemonic	Condition Tested	"Jump if..."
JA/JNBE	(CF OR ZF) = 0	above/not below nor equal
JAE/JNB	CF = 0	above or equal/not below
JB/JNAE	CF = 1	below/not above nor equal
JBE/JNA	(CF OR ZF) = 1	below or equal/not above
JC	CF = 1	carry
JE/JZ	ZF = 1	equal/zero
JB/JNLE	((SF XOR OF) OR ZF) = 0	greater/not less nor equal
JGE/JNL	(SF XOR OF) = 0	greater or equal/not less
JL/JNGE	(SF XOR OF) = 1	less/not greater nor equal
JLE/JNG	((SF XOR OF) OR ZF) = 1	less or equal/not greater
JNC	CF = 0	not carry
JNE/JNZ	ZF = 0	not equal/not zero
JNO	OF = 0	not overflow
JNP/JPO	PF = 0	not parity/parity odd
JNS	SF = 0	not sign
JO	OF = 1	overflow
JP/JPE	PF = 1	parity/parity equal
JS	SF = 1	sign

NOTE: "above" and "below" refer to the relationship of two unsigned values; "greater" and "less" refer to the relationship of two signed values.

instruction (JMP 00H jumps to the first byte of the next instruction). Since the jump is made by adding the relative displacement of the target to the instruction pointer, all conditional jumps are self-relative and are appropriate for position-independent routines.

ITERATION CONTROL

The iteration control instructions can be used to regulate the repetition of software loops. These instructions use the CX register as a counter. Like the conditional transfers, the iteration control instructions are self-relative and may only transfer to targets that are within −128 to +127 bytes of themselves, i.e., they are SHORT transfers.

LOOP *short-label*

LOOP decrements CX by 1 and transfers control to the target operand if CX is not 0; otherwise the instruction following LOOP is executed.

LOOP/LOOPNZ *short-label*

LOOPE and LOOPZ (loop while equal and loop while zero) are different mnemonics for the same instruction (similar to the REPE and REPZ repeat prefixes). CX is decremented by 1, and control is transferred to the target operand if CX is not 0 and if ZF is set; otherwise the instruction following LOOPE/LOOPZ is executed.

LOOPNE/LOOPNZ *short-label*

LOOPNE/LOOPNZ (loop while not equal and loop while not zero) are also synonyms for the same instruction. CX is decremented by 1, and control is transferred to the target operand if CX is not 0 and if ZF is clear; otherwise the next sequential instruction is executed.

JCXZ *short-label*

JCXZ (jump if CX zero) transfers control to the target operand if CX is 0. This instruction is useful at the beginning of a loop to bypass the loop if CX has a zero value, i.e., to execute the loop zero times.

INTERRUPT INSTRUCTIONS

The interrupt instructions allow interrupt service routines to be activated by programs as well as by external hardware devices. The effect of software interrupts is similar to hardware-initiated interrupts. However, the processor does not execute an interrupt acknowledge bus cycle if the interrupt originates in software or with an NMI (non-maskable interrupt). The effect of the interrupt instructions on the flags is covered in the description of each instruction.

INT *interrupt-type*

INT (interrupt) activates the interrupt procedure specified by the interrupt-type operand. INT decrements the stack pointer by two, pushes the flags onto the stack, and clears the trap (TF) and interrupt-enable (IF) flags to disable single-step and maskable interrupts. The flags are stored in the same format used by the PUSHF instruction. SP is decremented again by two, and the CS register is pushed onto the stack. The address of the interrupt pointer is calculated by multiplying interrupt-type by four; the second word of the interrupt pointer replaces CS. SP again is decremented by two, and IP is pushed onto the stack and is replaced by the first word of the interrupt pointer. If interrupt-type = 3, the assembler generates a short (1 byte) form of the instruction, known as the breakpoint interrupt.

Software interrupts can be used as "supervisor calls," i.e., requests for service that the operating system could supply for an application program. A different interrupt-type can be used for each type of service that the operating system could supply for an application program. Software interrupts also may be used to check out interrupt service procedures written for hardware-initiated interrupts.

INTO

INTO (interrupt on overflow) generates a software interrupt if the overflow flag (OF) is set; otherwise control proceeds to the following instruction without activating an interrupt procedure. INTO addresses the target interrupt procedure (its type is 4) through the interrupt pointer at location 10H; it clears the TF and IF flags and otherwise operates like INT. INTO may be written following an arithmetic or logical operation to activate an interrupt procedure if overflow occurs.

IRET

IRET (interrupt return) transfers control back to the point of interruption by popping IP, CS and the flags from the stack. IRET thus affects all flags by restoring them to previously saved values. IRET is used to exit any interrupt procedure, whether activated by hardware or software.

Processor Control Instructions

These instructions (see Table 3-12) allow programs to control various CPU functions. One group of instructions updates flags, and another group is used primarily for synchronizing the processor with external events. A final instruction causes the CPU to do nothing. Except for the flag operations, none of the processor instructions affect the flags.

Table 3-12. Processor Control Instructions

Flag Operations	
STC	Set carry flag
CLC	Clear carry flag
CMC	Complement carry flag
STD	Set direction flag
CLD	Clear direction flag
Flag Operations	
STI	Set interrupt enable flag
CLI	Clear interrupt enable flag
HLT	Halt until interrupt or reset
WAIT	Wait for TEST pin active
ESC	Escape to external processor
LOCK	Lock bus during next instruction
No Operation	
NOP	No operation

FLAG OPERATIONS

CLC

CLC (clear carry flag) zeroes the carry flag (CF) and affects no other flags. It (and CMC and STC) is useful in conjunction with the RCL and RCR instructions.

CMC

CMC (complement carry flag) "toggles" CF to its opposite state and affects no other flags.

STC

STC (set carry flag) sets CF to 1 and affects no other flags.

CLD

CLD (clear direction flag) zeroes DF causing the string instructions to auto-increment the SI and/or DI index registers. CLD does not affect any other flags.

STD

STD (set direction flag) sets DF to 1 causing the string instructions to auto-decrement the SI and/or DI index registers. STD does not affect any other flags.

CLI

CLI (clear interrupt-enable flag) zeroes IF. When the interrupt-enable flag is cleared, the processor does not recognize an external interrupt request that appears on the INTR line; in other words maskable interrupts are disabled. A non-maskable interrupt appearing on the NMI line, however, is honored, as is a software interrupt. CLI does not affect any other flags.

STI

STI (set interrupt-enable flag) sets IF to 1, enabling processor recognition of maskable interrupt requests appearing on the INTR line. Note, however, that a pending interrupt will not actually be recognized until the instruction following STI has executed. STI does not affect any other flags.

EXTERNAL SYNCHRONIZATION

HLT

HLT (halt) causes the processor to enter the halt state. The processor leaves the halt state upon activation of the RESET line, upon receipt of a non-maskable interrupt request on NMI, or, if interrupts are enabled, upon receipt of a maskable interrupt request on INTR. HLT does not affect any flags. It may be used as an alternative to an endless software loop in situations where a program must wait for an interrupt.

WAIT

WAIT causes the CPU to enter the wait state while its TEST line is not active. WAIT does not affect any flags.

ESC *external-opcode, source*

ESC (escape) provides a means for an external processor to obtain an opcode and possibly a memory operand from the 8086. The external opcode is a 6-bit immediate constant that the assembler encodes in the machine instruction it builds. An external processor may monitor the system bus and capture this opcode when the ESC is fetched. Then, using the second byte of the opcode, the CPU performs an operand access. If the source operand is a register, the processor does nothing. If the source operand is a memory variable, the processor obtains the operand from memory and discards it. An external processor may capture the memory operand and the memory operand's 20-bit address when the processor reads it from memory.

LOCK

LOCK is a one-byte prefix that causes the processors to assert their bus LOCK signals while the following instructions execute. LOCK does not affect any flags.

NO OPERATION

NOP

NOP (no operation) causes the CPU to do nothing. NOP does not affect any flags.

Instruction Set Reference

The instruction set summary which follows provides detailed operational information for the 8086/8088 instruction set. The information is presented from the point of view of utility to the assembly language programmer.

Instruction timings are represented as the number of clock periods required to execute a particular form (register-to-register, immediate-to-memory, etc.) of instruction. At 5 MHz clock, the clock period is 200 ns; at 8 MHz, the clock period is 125 ns. The 8086/8088 instruction timings which use memory operands, " + EA" denotes the number of additional clock periods needed to calculate the operand's effective address.

For control transfer instructions, the timings given include any additional clocks required to reinitialize the instruction queue as well as the time required to fetch the target instruction. For the 8086, four clocks should be added for each instruction reference to a word operand located at an odd memory address to reflect any additional operand bus cycles required. The required number of data references is listed in the instruction set summary for each instruction to aid in this calculation.

All of the instruction times given are of the form "n" where n is the number of clocks required for the 8086 to execute the given instruction. The number of clocks required for the 8088 will be n for 8-bit operations and n + (4 * transfers) for 16-bit operations.

For instructions which repeat a specified number of times, the value n consists of two parts in the relation "x + y/rep," where x is the initial number of clocks required to start the instruction, and y is the number of clocks corresponding to the number of iterations specified. For 16-bit repeated instructions on the 8088, when the expression "(4 * transfers)" has to be added to n, it should be added to the y part of the expression before it is multiplied by the number of repetitions.

Several additional factors can increase actual execution time over the figures shown in Table 3-13 the instruction reference. The time provided assumes that the instruction has already been prefetched and that it is waiting in the instruction queue, an assumption that is valid under most, but not all, operating conditions. A series of fast executing (fewer than two clocks per opcode byte) instructions can drain the queue and increase execution time. Execution time also is slightly impacted by interaction of the EU and BIU when memory operands must be read or written. If the EU needs access to memory, it may have to wait for up to one clock if the BIU has already started an instruction fetch bus cycle. (The EU can detect the need for a memory operand and post a bus request far enough in advance of its need for this operand to avoid waiting a full 4-clock bus cycle.) Of course the EU does not have to wait when the queue is full, because the BIU is idle. (This assumes that the BIU can obtain the bus on demand, i.e., no other processors are competing for the bus.)

With typical instruction mixes, the time actually required to execute a sequence of instructions will typically be within 5-10% of the sum of the individual timings given in the instruction set summary. Cases can be constructed, however, in which execution time may be much higher than the sum of the figures provided in the table. The execution time for a given sequence of instructions, however, is always repeatable, assuming comparable external conditions (interrupts, coprocessor activity, etc.). If the execution time for a given series of instructions must be determined exactly, the instructions should be run on an execution vehicle such as the iSBC® 88/25 or the 86/30 board.

REF — REFERENCES FOR INSTRUCTION SET

Table 3-13. Key to Following Instruction Set Reference Pages

Identifier	Used In	Explanation
destination	data transfer, bit manipulation	A register or memory location that may contain data operated on by the instruction, and which receives (is replaced by) the result of the operation.
source	data transfer, arithmetic, bit manipulation	A register, memory location or immediate value that is used in the operation, but is not altered by the instruction.
source-table	XLAT	Name of memory translation table addressed by register BX.
target	JMP, CALL	A label to which control is to be transferred directly, or a register or memory location whose *content* is the address of the location to which control is to be transferred indirectly.
short-label	cond. transfer, iteration control	A label to which control is to be conditionally transferred; must lie within −128 to +127 bytes of the first byte of the next instruction.
accumulator	IN, OUT	Register AX for word transfers, AL for bytes.
port	IN, OUT	An I/O port number; specified as an immediate value of 0-255, or register DX (which contains port number in range 0-64K).
source-string	string ops.	Name of a string in memory that is addressed by register SI; used only to identify string as byte or word and specify segment override, if any. This string is used in the operation, but is not altered.
dest-string	string ops.	Name of string in memory that is addressed by register DI; used only to identify string as byte or word. This string receives (is replaced by) the result of the operation.
count	shifts, rotates	Specifies number of bits to shift or rotate; written as immediate value 1 or register CL (which contains the count in the range 0-255).
interrupt-type	INT	Immediate value of 0-255 identifying interrupt pointer number.
optional-pop-value	RET	Number of bytes (0-64K, ordinarily an even number) to discard from stack.
external-opcode	ESC	Immediate value (0-63) that is encoded in the instruction for use by an external processor.
above-below	conditional jumps	Above and below refer to the relationship of two unsigned values.
greater-less	conditional jumps	Greater and less refer to the relationship of two signed values.

Table 3-13. Key to Operand Types

Identifier	Explanation
(no operands)	No operands are written
register	An 8- or 16-bit general register
reg 16	A 16-bit general register
seg-reg	A segment register
accumulator	Register AX or AL
immediate	A constant in the range 0-FFFFH
immed8	A constant in the range of 0-FFH
memory	An 8- or 16-bit memory location[1]
mem8	An 8-bit memory location[1]
mem16	A 16-bit memory location[1]
source-table	Name of 256-byte translate table
source-string	Name of string addressed by register SI
dest-string	Name of string, addressed by register DI
DX	Register DX
short-label	A label within −128 to +127 bytes of the end of the instruction
near-label	A label in current code segment
far-label	A label in another code segment
near-proc	A procedure in current code segment
far-proc	A procedure in another code segment
memptr16	A word containing the offset of the location in the current code segment to which control is to be transferred[1]
memptr32	A doubleword containing the offset and the segment base address of the location in another code segment to which control is to be transferred[1]
regptr16	A 16-bit general register containing the offset of the location in the current code segment to which control is to be transferred
repeat	A string instruction repeat prefix

[1] Any addressing mode − direct, register indirect, based, indexed, or based indexed − may be used (see the section "Addressing Modes").

Table 3-14. Effective Address Calculation Time

EA Components		Clocks*
Displacement Only		6
Base or Index Only	(BX,BP,SI,DI)	5
Displacement + Base or Index	(BX,BP,SI,DI)	9
Base + Index	BP + DI, BX + SI	7
	BP + SI, BX + DI	8
Displacement + Base + Index	BP + DI + DISP BX + SI + DISP	11
	BP + SI + DISP BX + DI + DISP	12

*Add 2 clocks for segment override

Notation Key
+ Addition
− Subtraction
* Multiplication
/ Division
% Modulo
: Concatenation
& And
← Assignment

"reg" Field Bit Assignments

16-Bit (w = 1)	8-Bit (w = 0)	Segment
000 AX	000 AL	00 EC
001 CX	001 CL	01 CS
010 DX	010 DL	10 SS
011 BX	011 BL	11 DS
100 SP	100 AH	
101 BP	101 CH	
110 SI	110 DH	
111 DI	111 BH	

"mod" Field Bit Assignments

mod xxx r/m

mod	Displacement
00	DISP = 0*, disp-low and disp-high are absent
01	DISP = disp-low sign-extended to 16-bits, disp-high is absent
10	DISP = disp-high: disp-low
11	r/m is treated as a "reg" field

"r/m" Field Bit Assignments

r/m	Operand Address
000	(BX) + (SI) + DISP
001	(BX) + (DI) + DISP
010	(BP) + (SI) + DISP
011	(BP) + (DI) + DISP
100	(SI) + DISP
101	(DI) + DISP
110	(BP) + DISP
111	(BX) + DISP

DISP follows 2nd byte of instruction (before data if required).
*except if mod = 00 and r/m = 110 then EA = disp-high: disp-low.

AAA — ASCII ADJUST FOR ADDITION

Operation

if ((AL) & 0FH) >9 or (AF) = 1 then
  (AL) ← (AL) + 6
  (AH) ← (AH) + 1
  (AF) ← 1
(CF) ← (AF)
(AL) ← (AL) & 0FH

Flags Affected

AF, CF
OF, PF, XF, ZF undefined

Description

AA (ASCII Adjust for Addition) changes the contents of register AL to a valid unpacked decimal number; the high-order half-byte is zeroed. AAA updates AF and CF; the content of OF, PF, SF and ZF is undefined following execution of AAA.

Encoding

0 0 1 1 0 1 1 1

AAA Operands	Clocks	Transfers	Bytes	AAA Coding Example
(no operands)	8	—	1	AAA

AAD — ASCII ADJUST FOR DIVISION

Operation

(AL) ← (AH) *0AH + (AL)
(AH) ← 0

Flags Affected

PF, SF, ZF
AF, CF, OF undefined

Description

AAD (ASCII Adjust for Division) modifies the numerator in AL *before* dividing two valid unpacked decimal operands so that the quotient produced by the division will be a valid unpacked decimal number. AH must be zero for the subsequent DIV to produce the correct result. The quotient is returned in AL, and the remainder is returned in AH; both high-order half-bytes are zeroed. AAD updates PF, SF and ZF; the content of AF, CF and OF is undefined following execution of AAD.

Encoding

1 1 0 1 0 1 0 1	0 0 0 0 1 0 1 0

AAD Operands	Clocks	Transfers	Bytes	AAD Coding Example
(no operands)	60	—	2	AAD

AAM — ASCII ADJUST FOR MULTIPLY

Operation

(AH) ← (AL)/0AH
(AL) ← (AL)%0AH

Flags Affected

PF, SF, ZF
AF, CF, OF undefined

Description

AAM (ASCII Adjust for Multiply) corrects the result of a previous multiplication of two valid unpacked decimal operands. A valid 2-digit unpacked decimal number is derived from the content of AH and AL and is returned to AH and AL. The high-order half-bytes of the multiplied operands must have been 0H for AAM to produce a correct result. AAM updates PF, SF and ZF; the content of AF, CF and OF is undefined following execution of AAM.

Encoding

1 1 0 1 0 0 0 0	0 0 0 0 1 0 1 0

AAM Operands	Clocks	Transfers	Bytes	AAM Coding Example
(no operands)	83	—	2	AAM

AAS — ASCII ADJUST FOR SUBTRACTION

Operation

if ((AL) & 0FH) >9 or (AF) = 1 then
  (AL) ← (AL) −6
  (AH) ← (AH) −1
  (AF) ← 1(CF) ← (AF)
(AL) ← (AL) & 0FH

Flags Affected AF, CFOF, PF, SF, ZF undefined

Description AAS (ASCII Adjust for Subtraction) corrects the result of a previous subtraction of two valid unpacked decimal operands (the destination operand must have been specified as register AL). AAS changes the content of AL to a valid unpacked decimal number; the high-order half-byte is zeroed. AAS updates AF and CF; the content of OF, PF, SF and ZF is undefined following execution of AAS.

Encoding

0 0 1 1 1 1 1 1

AAS Operands	Clocks	Transfers	Bytes	AAS Coding Example
(no operands)	8	—	1	AAS

ADC — ADD WITH CARRY

Operation if (CF) = 1 then (DEST) ← (LSRC) + (RSRC) + 1
else (DEST) ← (LSRC) + (RSRC)

Flags Affected AF, CF, OF, PF, SF, ZF

Description ADC *destination, source*

ADC (Add with Carry) sums the operands, which may be bytes or words, adds one if CF is set and replaces the destination operand with the result. Both operands may be signed or unsigned binary numbers (see AAA and DAA). ADC updates AF, CF, OF, PF, SF and ZF. Since ADC incorporates a carry from a previous operation, it can be used to write routines to add numbers longer than 16 bits.

Encoding

Memory or Register Operand with Register Operand

0 0 0 1 0 0 d w	mod reg r/m

if d = 1 then LSRC = REG, RSRC = EA, DEST = REG
else LSRC = EA, RSRC = REG, DEST = EA

Immediate Operand to Memory or Register Operand

1 0 0 0 0 0 s w	mod 0 1 0 r/m	data	data if s:w=01

LSRC = EA, RSRC = data, DEST = EA

Immediate Operand to Accumulator

0 0 0 1 0 1 0 w	data	data if w=1

if w = 0 then LSRC = AL, RSRC = data, DEST = AL
else LSRC = AX, RSRC = data, DEST = AX

ADC Operands	Clocks	Transfers	Bytes	ADC Coding Example
register, register	3	—	2	ADC AX, SI
register, memory	9 + EA	1	2-4	ADD DX, BETA [SI]
memory, register	16 + EA	2	2-4	ADC ALPHA [BX][SI],DI
register, immediate	4	—	3-4	ADC BX, 256
memory, immediate	17 + EA	2	3-6	ADC GAMMA, 30H
accumulator, immediate	4	—	2-3	ADC AL, 5

ADD — ADDITION

Operation (DEST) ← (LSRC) + (RSRC)

Flags Affected AF, CF, OF, PF, SF, ZF

Description **ADD** *destination, source*

The sum of the two operands, which may be bytes or words, replaces the destination operand. Both operands may be signed or unsigned binary numbers (see AAA and DAA). ADD updates AF, CF, OF, PF, SF and ZF.

Encoding

Memory or Register Operand with Register Operand

0 0 0 0 0 0 d w	mod reg r/m

if d = 1 then LSRC = REG, RSRC = EA, DEST = REG
else LSRC = EA, RSRC = REG, DEST = EA

Immediate Operand to Memory or Register Operand

1 0 0 0 0 0 s w	mod 0 0 0 r/m	data	data if s:w=01

LSRC = EA, RSRC = data, DEST = EA

Immediate Operand to Accumulator

0 0 0 0 0 1 0 w	data	data if w=1

if w = 0 then LSRC = AL, RSRC = data, DEST = AL
else LSRC = AX, RSRC = data, DEST = AX

ADD Operands	Clocks	Transfers	Bytes	ADD Coding Example
register, register	3	—	2	ADD CX, DX
register, memory	9 + EA	1	2-4	ADD DI, [BX],ALPHA
memory, register	16 + EA	2	2-4	ADD TEMP, CL
register, immediate	4	—	3-4	ADD CL, 2
memory, immediate	17 + EA	2	3-6	ADD ALPHA, 2
accumulator, immediate	4	—	2-3	ADD AX, 200

AND — AND LOGICAL

Operation

(DEST) ← (LSRC) & (RSRC)
(CF) ← 0
(OF) ← 0

Flags Affected

CF, OF, PF, SF, ZFAF undefined

Description

AND *destination, source*

AND performs the logical "and" of the two operands (byte or word) and returns the result to the destination operand. A bit in the result is set if both corresponding bits of the original operands are set; otherwise the bit is cleared.

Encoding

Memory or Register Operand with Register Operand

0 0 1 0 0 0 d w	mod reg r/m

if d = 1 then LSRC = REG, RSRC = EA, DEST = REG
else LSRC = EA, RSRC = REG, DEST = EA

Immediate Operand to Memory or Register Operand

1 0 0 0 0 0 0 w	mod 1 0 0 r/m	data	data if w=1

LSRC = EA, RSRC = data, DEST = EA

Immediate Operand to Accumulator

0 0 1 0 0 1 0 w	data	data if w=1

if w = 0 then LSRC = AL, RSRC = data, DEST = AL
else LSRC = AX, RSRC = data, DEST = AX

AND Operands	Clocks	Transfers	Bytes	AND Coding Example
register, register	3	—	2	AND AL, BL
register, memory	9 + EA	1	2-4	AND CX, FLAG_WORD
memory, register	16 + EA	2	2-4	AND ASCII [DI],AL
register, immediate	4	—	3-4	AND CX, 0F0H
memory, immediate	17 + EA	2	3-6	AND BETA, 01H
accumulator, immediate	4	—	2-3	AND AX, 01010000B

CALL — CALL PROCEDURE

Operation

if Inter-Segment then
  (SP) ← (SP) − 2
  ((SP) + 1:(SP)) ← (CS)
  (CS) ← SEG
  (SP) ← (SP) − 2
  ((SP) + 1:(SP)) ← (IP)
(IP) ← DEST

Flags Affected

None

Description

CALL *procedure-name*

CALL activates an out-of-line procedure, saving information on the stack to permit a RET (return) instruction in the procedure to transfer control back to the instruction following the CALL. The assembler generates a different type of CALL instruction depending on whether the programmer has defined the procedure name as NEAR or FAR. For control to return properly, the type of CALL instruction must match the type of RET instruction that exits from the procedure. (The potential for a mismatch exists if the procedure and the CALL are contained in separately assembled programs.) Different forms of the CALL instruction allow the address of the target procedure to be obtained from the instruction itself (direct CALL) or from a memory location or register referenced by the instruction (indirect CALL). In the following descriptions, bear in mind that the processor automatically adjusts IP to point to the next instruction to be *executed* before saving it on the stack.

For an intrasegment direct CALL, SP (the stack pointer) is decremented by two and IP is pushed onto the stack. The target procedure's relative displacement (up to ±32K) from the CALL instruction is then added to the instruction pointer. This CALL instruction form is "self-relative" and appropriate for position-independent (dynamically relocatable) routines in which the CALL and its target are moved together in the same segment.

An intrasegment indirect CALL may be made through memory or a register. SP is decremented by two; IP is pushed onto the stack. The target procedure offset is obtained from the memory word or 16-bit general register referenced in the instruction and replaces IP.

For an intersegment direct CALL, SP is decremented by two, and CS is pushed onto the stack. CS is replaced by the segment word contained in the instruction. SP again is decremented by two. IP is pushed onto the stack and replaced by the offset word in the instruction.

For an intersegment indirect CALL (which only may be made through memory), SP is decremented by two, and CS is pushed onto the stack. CS is then replaced by the content of the second word of the doubleword memory pointer referenced by the instruction. SP again is decremented by two, and IP is pushed onto the stack and replaced by the content of the first word of the doubleword pointer referenced by the instruction.

CALL — CALL PROCEDURE

Encoding

Intra-Segment Direct

1 1 1 0 1 0 0 0	disp-low	disp-high

DEST = (EA)

Intra-Segment Indirect

1 1 1 1 1 1 1 1	mod 0 1 0 r/m

DEST = (IP) + disp

Inter-Segment Direct

1 0 0 1 1 0 1 0	offset-low	offset-high
	seg-low	seg-high

DEST = offset, SEG = seg

Inter-Segment Indirect

1 1 1 1 1 1 1 1	mod 0 1 1 r/m

DEST = (EA), SEG = (EA +2)

CALL Operands	Clocks	Transfers	Bytes	CALL Coding Example
near-proc	19	1	3	CALL NEAR PROC
far-proc	28	2	5	CALL FAR PROC
memptr16	21 + EA	2	2-4	CALL PROC TABLE [SI]
regptr16	16	1	2	CALL AX
memptr32	37 + EA	4	2-4	CALL [BX].TASK [SI]

CBW — CONVERT BYTE TO WORD

Operation if (AL) < 80H then (AH) ← 0 else (AH) ← FFH

Flags Affected None

Description CBW (Convert Byte to Word) extends the sign of the byte in register AL throughout register AH. CBW does not affect any flags. CBW can be used to produce a double-length (word) dividend from a byte prior to performing byte division.

Encoding

1 0 0 1 1 0 0 0

CBW Operands	Clocks	Transfers	Bytes	CBW Coding Example
(no operands)	2	—	1	CBW

CLC — CLEAR CARRY

Operation (CF) ← 0

Flags Affected CF

Description CLC (Clear Carry flag) zeroes the carry flag (CF) and affects no other flags. It (and CMC and STC) is useful in conjunction with the RCL and RCR instructions.

Encoding

1 1 1 1 1 0 0 0

CLC Operands	Clocks	Transfers	Bytes	CLC Coding Example
(no operands)	2	—	1	CLC

CLD — CLEAR DIRECTION FLAG

Operation (DF) ← 0

Flags Affected DF

Description CLD (Clear Direction flag) zeroes DF causing the string instructions to auto-increment the SI and/or DI index registers. CLD does not affect any other flags.

Encoding

1 1 1 1 1 1 0 0

CLD Operands	Clocks	Transfers	Bytes	CLD Coding Example
(no operands)	2	—	1	CLD

CLI — CLEAR INTERRUPT-ENABLE FLAG

Operation (IF) ← 0

Flags Affected IF

Description CLI (Clear Interrupt-enable flag) zeroes IF. When the interrupt-enable flag is cleared, the 8086 and 8088 do not recognize an external interrupt request that appears on the INTR line; in other words maskable interrupts are disabled. A non-maskable interrupt appearing on NMI line, however, is honored, as is a software interrupt. CLI does not affect any other flags.

Encoding

1 1 1 1 1 0 1 0

CLI Operands	Clocks	Transfers	Bytes	CLI Coding Example
(no operands)	2	—	1	CLI

CMC — COMPLEMENT CARRY FLAG

Operation if (CF) = 0 then (CF) ← 1 else (CF) ← 0

Flags Affected CF

Description CMC (Complement Carry flag) "toggles" CF to its opposite state and affects no other flags.

Encoding

1 1 1 1 0 1 0 1

CMC Operands	Clocks	Transfers	Bytes	CMC Coding Example
(no operands)	2	—	1	CMC

CMP — COMPARE

Operation (LSRC) − (RSRC)

Flags Affected AF, CF, OF, PF, SF, ZF

Description **CMP** *destination,source*

CMP (Compare) subtracts the source from the destination, which may be bytes or words, but does not return the result. The operands are unchanged, but the flags are updated and can be tested by a subsequent conditional jump instruction. CMP updates AF, CF, OF, PF, SF and ZF. The comparison reflected in the flags is that of the destination to the source. If a CMP instruction is followed by a JG (jump if greater) instruction, for example, the jump is taken if the destination operand is greater than the source operand.

Encoding

Memory or Register Operand with Register Operand

0 0 1 1 1 0 d w	mod reg r/m

if d = 1 then LSRC = REG, RSRC = EA
else LSRC = EA, RSRC = REG

Immediate Operand with Memory or Register Operand

1 0 0 0 0 0 s w	mod 1 1 1 r/m	data	data if s:w=01

LSRC = EA, RSRC = data

Immediate Operand with Accumulator

0 0 1 1 1 1 0 w	data	data if w=1

if w = 0 then LSRC = AL, RSRC = data
else LSRC = AX, RSRC = data

CMP Operands	Clocks	Transfers	Bytes	CMP Coding Example
register, register	3	—	2	CMP BX, CX
register, memory	9 + EA	1	2-4	CMP DH, ALPHA
memory, register	9 + EA	1	2-4	CMP [BP+2],SI
register, immediate	4	—	3-4	CMP BL, 02H
memory, immediate	10 + EA	1	3-6	CMP [BX].RADAR [DI],3420H
accumulator, immediate	4	—	2-3	CMP AL, 00010000B

CMPS — COMPARE STRING (BYTE OR WORD)

Operation

(LSRC) − (RSRC)
if (DF) = 0 then
  (SI) ← (SI) + DELTA
  (DI) ← (DI) + DELTA
else
  (SI) ← (SI) − DELTA
  (DI) ← (DI) − DELTA

Flags Affected AF, CF, OF, PF, SF, ZF

Description **CMPS** *destination-string,source-string*

CMPS (Compare String) subtracts the destination byte or word (addressed by DI) from the source byte or word (addressed by SI). CMPS affects the flags but does not alter either operand, updates SI and DI to point to the next string element and updates, AF, CF, OF, PF, SF and ZF to reflect the relationship of the destination element to the source element. For example, if a JG (Jump if Greater) instruction follows CMPS, the jump is taken if the destination element is greater than the source element. If CMPS is prefixed with REPE or REPZ, the operation is interrupted as "compare while not end-of-string (CX not zero) and strings are equal (ZF = 1)." If CMPS is preceded by REPNE or REPNZ, the operation is interrupted as "compare while not end-of-string (CX not zero) and strings are not equal (ZF =0)." Thus, CMPS can be used to find matching or differing string elements.

Encoding

1 0 1 0 0 1 1 w

w = 0 then LSRC = (SI), RSRC = (DI), DELTA = 1
else LSRC = (SI) + 1:(SI), RSRC = (DI) + 1:(DI), DELTA = 2

CMPS Operands	Clocks	Transfers	Bytes	CMPS Coding Example
dest-string, source-string	22	2	1	CMPS BUFF1, BUFF2
(repeat) dest-string, string-source	9 + 22	2/rep	1	REP COMPS ID, KEY

CWD — CONVERT WORD TO DOUBLEWORD

Operation if (AX) < 8000H then (DX) ← 0
else (DX) ← FFFFH

Flags Affected None

Description CWD (Convert Word to Doubleword) extends the sign of the word in register AX throughout register DX. CWD does not affect any flags. CWD can be used to produce a double-length (doubleword) dividend from a word prior to performing word division.

Encoding

1 0 0 1 1 0 0 1

CWD Operands	Clocks	Transfers	Bytes	CWD Coding Example
(no operands)	5	—	1	CWD

DAA — DECIMAL ADJUST FOR ADDITION

Operation

if ((AL) & 0FH) >9 or (AF) = 1 then
  (AL) ← (AL) + 6
  (AF) ← 1
if (AL) > 9FH or (CF) = 1 then
  (AL) ← (AL) + 60H
  (CF) ← 1

Flags Affected

AF, CF, PF, SF, ZF
OF undefined

Description

DAA (Decimal Adjust for Addition) corrects the result of previously adding two valid packed decimal operands (the destination operand must have been register AL). DAA changes the content of AL to a pair of valid packed decimal digits. It updates AF, CF, PF, SF and ZF; the content of OF is undefined following execution of DAA.

Encoding

0 0 1 0 0 1 1 1

DAA Operands	Clocks	Transfers	Bytes	DAA Coding Example
(no operands)	4	—	1	DAA

DAS — DECIMAL ADJUST FOR SUBTRACTION

Operation

if ((AL) & 0FH) > 9 or (AF) = 1 then
  (AL) ← (AL) − 6
  (AF) ← 1
if (AL) > 9FH or (CF) = 1 then
  (AL) ← (AL) − 60H
  (CF) ← 1

Flags Affected

AF, CF, PF, SF, ZF
OF undefined

Description

DAS (Decimal Adjust for Subtraction) corrects the result of a previous subtraction of two valid packed decimal operands (the destination operand must have been specified as register AL). DAS changes the content of AL to a pair of valid packed decimal digits. DAS updates AF, CF, PF, SF and ZF; the content of OF is undefined following execution of DAS.

Encoding

0 0 1 0 1 1 1 1

DAS Operands	Clocks	Transfers	Bytes	DAS Coding Example
(no operands)	4	—	1	DAS

DEC — DECREMENT

Operation (DEST) ← (DEST) – 1

Flags Affected AF, OF, PF, SF, ZF

Description DEC (Decrement) subtracts one from the destination operand. The operand may be a byte or a word and is treated as an unsigned binary number (see AAA and DAA). DEC updates AF, OF, PF, SF and ZF; it does not affect CF.

Encoding

1 1 1 1 1 1 1 w	mod 0 0 1 r/m

DEST = EA

16-Bit Register Operand

0 1 0 0 1 reg

DEST = REG

DEC Operands	Clocks	Transfers	Bytes	DEC Coding Example
reg16	3	–	1	DEC AX
reg8	3	–	2	DEC AL
memory	15+EA	2	2-4	DEC ARRAY [SI]

DIV — DIVIDE

Operation

(temp) ← (NUMR)
if (temp)/(DIVR) > MAX then the
  following, in sequence
  (QUO),(REM) undefined
  (SP) ← (SP) − 2
  ((SP) + 1:(SP)) ← FLAGS
  (IF) ← 0
  (TF) ← 0
  (SP) ← (SP) − 2
  ((SP) + 1:(SP)) ← (CS)
  (CS) ← (2) i.e., the contents of
    memory locations 2 and 3
  (SP) ← (SP) − 2
  ((SP) + 1:(SP)) ← (IP)
  (IP) ← (0) i.e., the contents of
    locations 0 and 1
else
  (QUO) ← (temp)/(DIVR),where
    / is unsigned division
  (REM) ← (temp) %
(DIVR) where

% is unsigned modulo

Flags Affected

AF, CF, OF, PF, SF, ZF undefined

Description

DIV *source*

DIV (divide) performs an unsigned division of the accumulator (and its extension) by the source operand. If the source operand is a byte, it is divided into the two-byte dividend assumed to be in registers AL and AH. The byte quotient is returned in AL, and the byte remainder is returned in AH. If the source operand is a word, it is divided into the two-word dividend in registers AX and DX. The word quotient is returned in AX, and the word remainder is returned in DX. If the quotient exceeds the capacity of its destination register (FFH for byte source, FFFFH for word source), as when division by zero is attempted, a type 0 interrupt is generated, and the quotient and remainder are undefined. Nonintegral quotients are truncated to integers. The content of AF, CF, OF, PF, SF and ZF is undefined following execution of DIV.

Encoding

1 1 1 1 0 1 1 w	mod 1 1 0 r/m

if w = 0 then NUMR = AX, DIVR = EA, QUO = AL, REM = AH, MAX = FFH
else NUMR = DX:AX, DIVR = EA, QUO = AX, REM = DX, MAX = FFFFH

DIV Operands	Clocks	Transfers	Bytes	DIV Coding Example
reg8	80-90	—	2	DIV CL
reg16	144-162	—	2	DIV BX
mem8	86-96 + EA	1	2-4	DIV ALPHA
mem16	154-172 + EA	1	2-4	DIV TABLE [SI]

ESC — ESCAPE

Operation if mod ≠ 11 then data bus ← (EA)

Flags Affected None

Description The ESC (Escape) instruction provides a mechanism by which other processors (coprocessors) may receive their instructions from the 8086 or 8088 instruction stream and make use of the 8086 or 8088 addressing modes. The CPU (8086 or 8088) does a no operation (NOP) for the ESC instruction other than to access a memory operand and place it on the bus.

Encoding

1 1 0 1 1 x	mod x r/m

ESC Operands	Clocks	Transfers	Bytes	ESC Coding Example
immediate, memory	8+EA	1	2-4	ESC 6, ARRAY [SI]
immediate, register	2	—	2	ESC 20, AL

HLT — HALT

Operation None

Flags Affected None

Description HLT (Halt) causes the CPU to enter the halt state. The processor leaves the halt state upon activation of the RESET line, upon receipt of a non-maskable interrupt request on NMI, or, if interrupts are enabled, upon receipt of a maskable interrupt request on INTR. HLT does not affect any flags. It may be used as an alternative to an endless software loop in situations where a program must wait for an interrupt.

Encoding

1 1 1 1 0 1 0 0

HLT Operands	Clocks	Transfers	Bytes	HLT Coding Example
(no operands)	2	—	1	HLT

IDIV – INTEGER DIVIDE

Operation

```
(temp) ← (NUMR)
if (temp)/(DIVR) > 0 and (temp)
   /(DIVR) > MAX
or (temp)/(DIVR) < 0 and (temp)
   /(DIVR) < 0 – MAX – 1 then
   (QUO), (REM) undefined
   (SP) ← (SP) – 2
   ((SP) + 1:(SP)) ← FLAGS
   (IF) ← 0
   (TF) ← 0
   (SP) ← (SP) – 2
   ((SP) + 1:(SP)) ← (CS)
   (CS) ← (2)
   (SP) ← (SP) – 2
   ((SP) + 1:(SP)) ← (IP)
   (IP) ← (0)
else
   (QUO) ← (temp)/(DIVR), where
      / is signed division
   (REM) ← (temp) % (DIVR) where
      % is signed modulo
```

Flags Affected AF, CF, OF, PF, SF, ZF undefined

Description **IDIV** *source*

IDIV (Integer Divide) performs a signed division of the accumulator (and its extension) by the source operand. If the source operand is a byte, it is divided into the double-length dividend assumed to be in registers AL and AH; the single-length quotient is returned in AL, and the single-length remainder is returned in AH. For byte integer division, the maximum positive quotient is +127 (7FH) and the minimum negative quotient is –127 (81H). If the source operand is a word, it is divided into the double-length dividend in registers AX and DX; the single-length quotient is returned in AX, and the single-length remainder is returned in DX. For word integer division, the maximum positive quotient is +32,767 (7FFFH) and the minimum negative quotient is –32,767 (8001H). If the quotient is positive and exceeds the maximum, or is negative and is less than the minimum, the quotient and remainder are undefined, and a type 0 interrupt is generated. In particular, this occurs if division by 0 is attempted. Nonintegral quotients are truncated (toward 0) to integers, and the remainder has the same sign as the dividend. The content of AF, CF, OF, PF, SF and ZF is undefined following IDIV.

Encoding

1 1 1 1 0 1 1 w	mod 1 1 1 r/m

if w = 0 then NUMR = AX, DIVR = EA, QUO = AL, REM = AH, MZX = 7FH
else NUMR = DX:AX, DIVR = EA, QUO = AX, REM = DX, MAX = 7FFFH

IDIV Operands	Clocks	Transfers	Bytes	IDIV Coding Example
reg8	101-112	—	2	IDIV BL
reg16	165-184	—	2	IDIV CX
mem8	107-118 + EA	1	2-4	IDIV DIVISOR_BYTE[SI]
mem16	171-190 + EA	1	2-4	IDIV [BX].DIVISOR_WORD

IMUL — INTEGER MULTIPLY

Operation

(DEST) ← (LSRC) * (RSRC) where
  * is signed multiply
if (ext) = sign-extension of (LOW)
  then (CF) ← 0
else (CF) ← 1;
(OF) ← (CF)

Flags Affected

CF, OF
AF, PF, SF, ZF undefined

Description

IMUL *source*

IMUL (Integer Multiply) performs a signed multiplication of the source operand and the accumulator. If the source is a byte, then it is multiplied by register AL, and the double-length result is returned in AH and AL. If the source is a word, then it is multiplied by register AX, and the double-length result is returned in registers DX and AX. If the upper half of the result (AH for byte source, DX for word source) is not the sign extension of the lower half of the result, CF and OF are set; otherwise they are cleared. When CF and OF are set, they indicate that AH or DX contains significant digits of the result. The content of AF, PF, SF and ZF is undefined following execution of IMUL.

Encoding

1 1 1 1 0 1 1 w	mod 1 0 1 r/m

if w = 0 then LSRC = AL, RSRC = EA, DEST = AH, EXT = AH, LOW = AL
else LSRC = AX, RSRC = EA, DEST = DX:AX, EXT = DX, LOW = AX

IMUL Operands	Clocks	Transfers	Bytes	IMUL Coding Example
reg8	80-98	—	2	IMUL CL
reg16	128-154	—	2	IMUL BX
mem8	86-104+EA	1	2-4	IMUL RATE_BYTE
mem16	134-160+EA	1	2-4	IMUL RATE_WORD[BP][DI]

IN — INPUT BYTE OR WORD

Operation (DEST) ← (SRC)

Flags Affected None

Description **IN** *accumulator,port*

IN transfers a byte or a word from an input port to the AL register or the AX register, respectively. The port number may be specified either with an immediate byte constant, allowing access to ports numbered 0 through 255, or with a number previously placed in the DX register, allowing variable access (by changing the value in DX) to ports numbered from 0 through 65,535.

Encoding

Fixed Port

1 1 1 0 0 1 0 w	port

if w = 0 then SRC = port, DEST = AL
else SRC = port + 1:port, DEST = AX

Variable Port

1 1 1 0 1 1 0 w

if w = 0 then SRC = (DX), DEST = AL
else SRC = (DX) + 1:(DX), DEST = AX

IN Operands	Clocks	Transfers	Bytes	IN Coding Example
accumulator, immed8	10	1	2	IN AL, OEAH
accumulator,DX	8	1	1	IN AX, DX

INC — INCREMENT

Operation (DEST) ← (DEST) +1

Flags Affected AF, OF, PF, SF, ZF

Description **INC** *destination*

INC (Increment) adds one to the destination operand. The operand may be byte or a word and is treated as an unsigned binary number (see AAA and DAA). INC updates AF, OF, PF, SF and ZF; it does not affect CF.

Encoding

Memory or Register Operand

1 1 1 1 1 1 1 w	mod 0 0 0 r/m

DEST = EA

16-Bit Register Operand

0 1 0 0 0 reg

DEST = REG

INC Operands	Clocks	Transfers	Bytes	INC Coding Example
reg16	3	–	1	INC CX
reg8	3	–	2	INC BL
memory	15+EA	2	2-4	INC ALPHA [DI][BX]

INT — INTERRUPT

Operation

(SP) ← (SP) − 2
((SP) + 1:(SP))←FLAGS
(IF)←0
(TF)←0
(SP)←(SP) − 2
((SP) + 1:(SP))←(CS)
(CS)←(TYPE * 4 + 2)
(SP)←(SP) − 2
((SP) + 1:(SP))←(IP)
(IP)←(TYPE * 4)

Flags Affected

IF, TF

Description

INT *interrupt-type*

INT (Interrupt) activates the interrupt procedure specified by the interrupt-type operand. INT decrements the stack pointer by two, pushes the flags onto the stack, and clears the trap (TF) and interrupt-enable (IF) flags to disable single-step and maskable interrupts. The flags are stored in the format used by the PUSHF instruction. SP is decremented again by two, and the CS register is pushed onto the stack. The address of the interrupt pointer is calculated by multiplying interrupt-type by four; the second word of the interrupt pointer replaces CS. SP again is decremented by two, and IP is pushed onto the stack and is replaced by the first word of the interrupt pointer. If interrupt-type = 3, the assembler generates a short (1 byte) form of the instruction, known as the breakpoint interrupt.

Software interrupts can be used as "supervisor calls," i.e., requests for service from an operating system. A different interrupt-type can be used for each type of service that the operating system could supply for an application program. Software interrupts also may be used to check out interrupt service procedures written for hardware-initiated interrupts.

Encoding

1 1 0 0 1 1 0 v	type if v=1

if v = 0 then TYPE = 3
else TYPE = type

INT Operands	Clocks	Transfers	Bytes	INT Coding Example
immed8(type =3)	52	5	1	INT 3
immed8(type ≠ 3)	51	5	2	INT 67

INTO — INTERRUPT ON OVERFLOW

Operation

```
if (OF) = 1 then
   (SP)←(SP) − 2
   ((SP) + 1:(SP))←FLAGS
   (IF)←0
   (TF)←0
   (SP)←(SP) − 2
   ((SP) + 1:(SP))←(CS)
   (CS)←(12H)
   (SP)←(SP) − 2
   ((SP) + 1:(SP))←(IP)
   (IP)←(10H)
```

Flags Affected None

Description

INTO (Interrupt on Overflow) generates a software interrupt if the overflow flag (OF) is set; otherwise control proceeds to the following instruction without activating an interrupt procedure. INTO addresses the target interrupt procedure (its type is 4) through the interrupt pointer at location 10H; it clears the TF and IF flags and otherwise operates like INT. INTO may be written following an arithmetic or logical operation to activate an interrupt procedure if overflow occurs.

Encoding

1 1 0 0 1 1 1 0

INTO Operands	Clocks	Transfers	Bytes	INTO Coding Example
(no operands)	53 or 4	5	1	INTO

IRET — INTERRUPT RETURN

Operation

(IP)←((SP)+1:(SP))
(SP)←(SP)+2
(CS)←((SP)+1:(SP))
(SP)←(SP)+2
FLAGS←((SP)+1:(SP))
(SP)←(SP)+2

Flags Affected All

Description

IRET (Interrupt Return) transfers control back to the point of interruption by popping IP, CS and the flags from the stack. IRET thus affects all flags by restoring them to previously saved values. IRET is used to exit any interrupt procedure, whether activated by hardware or software.

Encoding

1 1 0 0 1 1 1 1

IRET Operands	Clocks	Transfers	Bytes	IRET Coding Example
(no operands)	32	3	1	IRET

JA — JUMP ON ABOVE
JNBE — JUMP ON NOT BELOW OR EQUAL

Operation if (CF) & (ZF) = 0 then
(IP) ← (IP) + disp (sign-extended to 16-bits)

Flags Affected None

Description Jump on Above (JA)/Jump on Not Below or Equal (JNBE) transfers control to the target operand (IP + displacement) if CF and ZF = 0.

Encoding

0 1 1 1 0 1 1 1	disp

JA/JNBE Operands	Clocks	Transfers	Bytes	JA Coding Example
short-label	16 or 4	—	2	JA ABOVE
				JNBE Coding Example
				JNBE ABOVE

JAE — JUMP ON ABOVE OR EQUAL
JNB — JUMP ON NOT BELOW

Operation if (CF) = 0 then
(IP)←(IP) + disp (sign-extended to 16-bits)

Flags Affected None

Description JAE (Jump on Above or Equal)/JNB (Jump on Not Below) transfers control to the target operand (IP + displacement) if CF = 0.

Encoding

0 1 1 1 0 0 1 1	disp

JAE/JNB Operands	Clocks	Transfers	Bytes	JAE Coding Example
short-label	16 or 4	—	2	JAE ABOVE_EQUAL

JB — JUMP ON BELOW
JNAE — JUMP ON NOT ABOVE OR EQUAL

Operation if (CF) = 1 then
(IP)←(IP) + disp (sign-extended to 16-bits)

Flags Affected None

Description JB (Jump on Below)/JNAE (Jump on Not Above or Equal) transfers control to the target operand (IP + displacement) if CF = 1.

Encoding

0 1 1 1 0 0 1 0	disp

JB/JNAE Operands	Clocks	Transfers	Bytes	JB Coding Example
short-label	16 or 4	—	2	JB BELOW

JBE — JUMP ON BELOW OR EQUAL
JNA — JUMP ON NOT ABOVE

Operation if (CF) or (ZF) = 1 then
(IP) ← (IP) + disp (sign-extended to 16-bits)

Flags Affected None

Description JBE (Jump on Below or Equal)/JNA (Jump on Not Above) transfers control to the target operand (IP + displacement) if CF or ZF = 1.

Encoding

0 1 1 1 0 1 1 0	disp

JBE/JNA Operands	Clocks	Transfers	Bytes	JNA Coding Example
short-label	16 or 4	—	2	JNA NOT_ABOVE

JC — JUMP ON CARRY

Operation if (CF) = 1 then
(IP)←(IP) + disp (sign-extended to 16-bits)

Flags Affected None

Description JC (Jump on Carry) transfers control to the target operand (IP + displacement) on the condition CF = 1.

Encoding

0 1 1 1 0 0 1 0	disp

JC Operands	Clocks	Transfers	Bytes	JC Coding Example
short-label	16 or 4	–	2	JC CARRY_SET

JCXZ — JUMP IF CX REGISTER ZERO

Operation

if (CX) = 0 then
(IP)←(IP) + disp (sign-extended to 16-bits)

Flags Affected

None

Description

JCXZ *short-label*

JCXZ (Jump if CX Zero) transfers control to the target operand if CX is 0. This instruction is useful at the beginning of a loop to bypass the loop if CX has a zero value, i.e., to execute the loop zero times.

Encoding

1 1 1 0 0 0 1 1	disp

JCXZ Operands	Clocks	Transfers	Bytes	JCXZ Coding Example
short-label	18 or 6	—	2	JCXZ COUNT_DONE

JE — JUMP ON EQUAL
JZ — JUMP ON ZERO

Operation if (ZF) = 1 then
(IP)←(IP) + disp (sign-extended to 16-bits)

Flags Affected None

Description JE (Jump on Equal)/JZ (Jump on Zero) transfers control to the target operand (IP + displacement) if ZF = 1.

Encoding

0 1 1 1 0 1 0 0	disp

JE/JZ Operands	Clocks	Transfers	Bytes	JZ Coding Example
short-label	16 or 4	—	2	JZ ZERO

JG — JUMP ON GREATER
JNLE — JUMP ON NOT LESS OR EQUAL

Operation if ((SF) = (OF)) or (ZF) = 0 then
(IP)←(IP) + disp (sign-extended to 16-bits)

Flags Affected None

Description JG (Jump on Greater Than)/JNLE (Jump on Not Less Than or Equal) transfers control to the target operand (IP + displacement) if the conditions ((SF XOR OF) or ZF = 0) are greater than/not less than or equal to the tested value.

Encoding

0 1 1 1 1 1 1 1	disp

JG/JNLE Operands	Clocks	Transfers	Bytes	JG Coding Example
short-label	16 or 4	—	2	JG GREATER

JGE — JUMP ON GREATER OR EQUAL
JNL — JUMP ON NOT LESS

Operation if (SF) = (OF) then
(IP)←(IP) + disp (sign-extended to 16-bits)

Flags Affected None

Description JGE (Jump on Greater Than or Equal)/JNL (Jump on Not Less Than) transfers control to the target operand (IP + displacement) if the condition (SF XOR OF = 0) is greater than or equal/not less than the tested value.

Encoding

0 1 1 1 1 1 0 1	disp

JGE/JNL Operands	Clocks	Transfers	Bytes	JGE Coding Example
short-label	16 or 4	—	2	JGE GREATER_EQUAL

JL — JUMP ON LESS
JNGE — JUMP ON NOT GREATER OR EQUAL

Operation if (SF) ≠ (OF) then
(IP)←(IP) + disp (sign-extended to 16-bits)

Flags Affected None

Description JL (Jump on Less Than)/JNGE (Jump on Not Greater Than or Equal), transfers control to the target operand if the condition (SF XOR OF=1) is less than/not greater than or equal to the tested value.

Encoding

0 1 1 1 1 1 0 0	disp

JL/JNGE Operands	Clocks	Transfers	Bytes	JL Coding Example
short-label	16 or 4	—	2	JL LESS

JLE — JUMP ON LESS OR EQUAL
JNG — JUMP ON NOT GREATER

Operation if ((SF) ≠ (OF)) or ((ZF) = 1) then
(IP)←(IP) + disp (sign-extended to 16-bits)

Flags Affected None

Description JLE (Jump on Less Than or Equal to)/JNG (Jump on Not Greater Than) transfers control to the target operand (IP + displacement) if the conditions tested ((SF XOR OF) or ZF = 1) are less than or equal to/not greater than the tested value.

Encoding

0 1 1 1 1 1 1 0	disp

JLE/JNG Operands	Clocks	Transfers	Bytes	JNG Coding Example
short-label	16 or 4	—	2	JNG NOT_GREATER

JMP — JUMP UNCONDITIONALLY

Operation if Inter-Segment then (CS)←SEG
(IP)←DEST

Flags Affected None

Description **JMP** *target*

JMP unconditionally transfers control to the target location. Unlike a CALL instruction, JMP does not save any information on the stack; no return to the instruction following the JMP is expected. Like CALL, the address of the target operand may be obtained from the instruction itself (direct JMP), or from memory or a register referenced by the instruction (indirect JMP).

An intrasegment direct JMP changes the instruction pointer by adding the relative displacement of the target from the JMP instruction. If the assembler can determine that the target is within 127 bytes of the JMP, it automatically generates a two-byte instruction form called a SHORT JMP; otherwise, it generates a NEAR JMP that can address a target within ±32K. Intrasegment direct JMPS are self-relative and appropriate in position-independent (dynamically relocatable) routines in which the JMP and its target are moved together in the same segment.

An intrasegment indirect JMP may be made either through memory or a 16-bit general register. In the first case, the word content referenced by the instruction replaces the instruction pointer. In the second case, the new IP value is taken from the register named in the instruction.

An intersegment direct JMP replaces IP and CS with values contained in the instruction.

An intersegment indirect JMP may be made only through memory. The first word of the doubleword pointer referenced by the instruction replaces IP and the second word replaces CS.

Encoding

Intra-Segment Direct

1 1 1 0 1 0 0 1	disp-low	disp-high

DEST = (IP) + disp

Intra-Segment Direct Short

1 1 1 0 1 0 1 1	disp

DEST = (IP) + disp sign extended to 16-bits

Intra-Segment Indirect

1 1 1 1 1 1 1 1	mod 1 0 0 r/m

DEST = (EA)

Inter-Segment Direct

1 1 1 0 1 0 1 0	offset-low	offset-high
	seg-low	seg-high

DEST = offset, SEG = seg

Inter-Segment Indirect

1 1 1 1 1 1 1 1	mod 1 0 1 r/m

DEST = (EA), SEG = (EA + 2)

JMP Operands	Clocks	Transfers	Bytes	JMP Coding Example
short-label	15	—	2	JMP SHORT
near-label	15	—	3	JMP WITHIN_SEGMENT
far-label	15	—	5	JMP FAR_LABEL
memptr16	18+EA	—	2-4	JMP[BX].TARGET
regptr16	11	—	2	JMP CX
memptr32	24+EA	—	2-4	JMP OTHER.SEG[SI]

JNC — JUMP ON NOT CARRY

Operation

if (CF) = 0 then
(IP)←(IP) + disp (sign-extended to 16-bits)

Flags Affected

None

Description

JNC (Jump on Not Carry) transfers control to the target operand (IP + displacement) on the condition CF = 0.

Encoding

0 1 1 1 0 0 1 1	disp

JNC Operands	Clocks	Transfers	Bytes	JNC Coding Example
short-label	16 or 4	—	2	JNC NO_CARRY

JNE — JUMP ON NOT EQUAL
JNZ — JUMP ON NOT ZERO

Operation if (ZF) = 0 then
(IP)←(IP) + disp (sign-extended to 16-bits)

Flags Affected None

Description JNE (Jump on Not Equal to)/JNZ (Jump on Not Zero) transfers control to the target operand (IP + displacement) if the condition tested (ZF = 0) is true.

Encoding

0 1 1 1 0 1 0 1	disp

JNE/JNZ Operands	Clocks	Transfers	Bytes	JNE Coding Example
short-label	16 or 4	—	2	JNE NOT_EQUAL

JNO — JUMP ON NOT OVERFLOW

Operation

if (OF) = 0 then
(IP)←(IP) + disp (sign-extended to 16-bits)

Flags Affected

None

Description

JNO (Jump on Not Overflow) transfers control to the target operand (IP + displacement) if the condition tested (OF = 0) is true.

Encoding

0 1 1 1 0 0 0 1	disp

JNO Operands	Clocks	Transfers	Bytes	JNO Coding Example
short-label	16 or 4	—	2	JNO NO_OVERFLOW

JNS — JUMP ON NOT SIGN

Operation if (SF) = 0 then
(IP)←(IP) + disp (sign-extended to 16-bits)

Flags Affected None

Description JNS (Jump on Not Sign) transfers control to the target operand (IP + displacement) when the tested condition (SF = 0) is true.

Encoding

0 1 1 1 1 0 0 1	disp

JNS Operands	Clocks	Transfers	Bytes	JNS Coding Example
short-label	16 or 4	—	2	JNS POSITIVE

JNP — JUMP ON NOT PARITY
JPO — JUMP ON PARITY ODD

Operation if (PF) = 0 then
(IP)←(IP) + disp (sign-extended to 16-bits)

Flags Affected None

Description JNP (Jump on Not Parity)/JPO (Jump on Parity Odd) transfers control to the target operand if the condition tested (PF = 0) is true.

Encoding

0 1 1 1 1 0 1 1	disp

JNP/JPO Operands	Clocks	Transfers	Bytes	JPO Coding Example
short-label	16 or 4	—	2	JPO ODD_PARITY

JO — JUMP ON OVERFLOW

Operation if (OF) = 1 then
(IP)←(IP) + disp (sign-extended to 16-bits)

Flags Affected None

Description JO (Jump on Overflow) transfers control to the target operand (IP + displacement) if the tested condition (OF = 1) is true.

Encoding

0 1 1 1 0 0 0 0	disp

JO Operands	Clocks	Transfers	Bytes	JO Coding Example
short-label	16 or 4	—	2	JO SIGNED_OVERFLOW

JP — JUMP ON PARITY
JPE — JUMP ON PARITY EQUAL

Operation if (PF) = 1 then
(IP)←(IP) + disp (sign-extended to 16-bits)

Flags Affected None

Description JP (Jump on Parity)/JPE (Jump on Parity Equal) transfers control to the target operand (IP + displacement) if the condition tested (PF = 1) is true.

Encoding

0 1 1 1 1 0 1 0	disp

JP/JPE Operands	Clocks	Transfers	Bytes	JPE Coding Example
short-label	16 or 4	–	2	JPE EVEN_PARITY

JS — JUMP ON SIGN

Operation if (SF) = 1 then
(IP)←(IP) + disp (sign-extended to 16-bits)

Flags Affected None

Description JS (Jump on Sign) transfers control to the target operand (IP + displacement) if the tested condition (SF = 1) is true.

Encoding

0 1 1 1 1 0 0 0	disp

JS Operands	Clocks	Transfers	Bytes	JS Coding Example
short-label	16 or 4	—	2	JS NEGATIVE

LAHF — LOAD REGISTER AH FROM FLAGS

Operation (AH)←(SF):(ZF):X:(AF):X:(PF):X:(CF)

Flags Affected None

Description LAHF (load register AH from flags) copies SF, ZF, AF, PF and CF (the 8080/8085 flags) into bits 7, 6, 4, 2 and 0, respectively, of register AH. The content of bits 5, 3 and 1 is undefined; the flags themselves are not affected. LAHF is provided primarily for converting 8080/8085 assembly language programs to run on an 8086 or 8088.

Encoding

1 0 0 1 1 1 1 1

LAHF Operands	Clocks	Transfers	Bytes	LAHF Coding Example
(no operands)	4	—	1	LAHF

LDS — LOAD POINTER USING DS

Operation

(REG)←(EA)
(DS)←(EA +2)

Flags Affected

None

Description

LDS *destination,source*

LDS (load pointer using DS) transfers a 32-bit pointer variable from the source operand, which must be a memory operand, to the destination operand and register DS. The offset word of the pointer is transferred to the destination operand, which may be any 16-bit general register. The segment word of the pointer is transferred to register DS. Specifying SI as the destination operand is a convenient way to prepare to process a source string that is not in the current data segment (string instructions assume that the source string is located in the current data segment and that SI contains the offset of the string).

Encoding

1 1 0 0 0 1 0 1	mod reg r/m

if mod = 11 then undefined operation

LDS Operands	Clocks	Transfers	Bytes	LDS Coding Example
reg16,mem32	16+EA	2	2-4	LDS SI, DATA.SEG[DI]

LEA — LOAD EFFECTIVE ADDRESS

Operation (REG)←EA

Flags Affected None

Description **LEA** *destination,source*

LEA (load effective address) transfers the offset of the source operand (rather than its value) to the destination operand. The source operand must be a memory operand, and the destination operand must be a 16-bit general register. LEA does not affect any flags. The XLAT and string instructions assume that certain registers point to operands; LEA can be used to load these registers (e.g., loading BX with the address of the translate table used by the XLAT instruction).

Encoding

1 0 0 0 1 1 0 1	mod reg r/m

if mod = 11 then undefined operation

LEA Operands	Clocks	Transfers	Bytes	LEA Coding Example
reg16,mem16	2+EA	—	2-4	LEA BX,[BP][DI]

LES — LOAD POINTER USING ES

Operation (REG)←(EA)
(ES)←(EA + 2)

Flags Affected None

Description **LES** *destination,source*

LES (load pointer using ES) transfers a 32-bit pointer variable from the source operand, which must be a memory operand, to the destination operand and register ES. The offset word of the pointer is transferred to the destination operand, which may be any 16-bit general register. The segment word of the pointer is transferred to register ES. Specifying DI as the destination operand is a convenient way to prepare to process a destination string that is not in the current extra segment. (The destination string must be located in the extra segment, and DI must contain the offset of the string.)

Encoding

1 1 0 0 0 1 0 0	mod reg r/m

if mod = 11 then undefined operation

LES Operands	Clocks	Transfers	Bytes	LES Coding Example
reg16,mem32	16+EA	2	2-4	LES DI,[BX].TEXT_BUFF

LOCK — LOCK THE BUS

Operation None

Flags Affected None

Description

LOCK is a one-byte prefix that causes the 8088 (configured in maximum mode) to assert its bus LOCK signal while the following instruction executes. LOCK does not affect any flags.

The instruction most useful in this context is an exchange register with memory. A simple software lock may be implemented with the following code sequence:

```
Check       MOV     AL,1        ;set AL to 1 (implies locked)
  LOCK      XCHG    Sema,AL     ;test and set lock
            TEST    AL,AL       ;set flags based on AL
            JNZ     Check       ;retry if lock already set
            •
            •
            MOV     Sema,0      ;clear the lock when done
```

The LOCK prefix may be combined with the segment override and/or REP prefixes.

Encoding

1 1 1 1 0 0 0 0

LOCK Operands	Clocks	Transfers	Bytes	LOCK Coding Example
(no operands)	2	—	1	LOCK XCHG FLAG, AL

LODS — LOAD STRING (BYTE OR WORD)

Operation

(DEST)←(SRC)
if (DF) = 0 then (SI)←(SI) + DELTA
else (SI)←(SI) − DELTA

Flags Affected None

Description **LODS** *source-string*

LODS (Load String) transfers the byte or word string element addressed by SI to register AL or AX, and updates SI to point to the next element in the string. This instruction is not ordinarily repeated since the accumulator would be overwritten by each repetition, and only the last element would be retained. However, LODS is very useful in software loops as part of a more complex string function built up from string primitives and other instructions.

Encoding

1 0 1 0 1 1 0 w

if w = 0 then SRC = (SI), DEST = AL, DELTA = 1
else SRC = (SI) + 1:(SI), DEST = AX, DELTA = 2

LODS Operands	Clocks	Transfers	Bytes	LODS Coding Example
source-string	12	1	1	LODS CUSTOMER_NAME
(repeat) source-string	9 + 13	1/rep	1	REP LODS NAME

LOOP — LOOP

Operation

(CX)←(CX) − 1
if (CX)≠0 then
  (IP)←(IP) + disp (sign-extended to 16-bits)

Flags Affected None

Description **LOOP** *short-label*

LOOP decrements CX by 1 and transfers control to the target operand if CX is not 0; otherwise the instruction following LOOP is executed.

Encoding

1 1 1 0 0 0 1 0	disp

LOOP Operands	Clocks	Transfers	Bytes	LOOP Coding Example
short-label	17 or 5	—	2	LOOP AGAIN

LOOPE — LOOP WHILE EQUAL
LOOPZ — LOOP WHILE ZERO

Operation

(CX)←(CX) −1
if (ZF) = 1 and (CX) ≠ 0 then
(IP)←(IP) + disp (sign-extended to 16-bits)

Flags Affected None

Description **LOOPE/LOOPZ** *short-label*

LOOPE and LOOPZ (Loop While Equal and Loop While Zero) are different mnemonics for the same instruction (similar to the REPE and REPZ repeat prefixes). CX is decremented by 1, and control is transferred to the target operand if CX is not 0 and if ZF is set; otherwise the instruction following LOOPE/LOOPZ is executed.

Encoding

1 1 1 0 0 0 0 1	disp

LOOPE/LOOPZ Operands	Clocks	Transfers	Bytes	LOOPE Coding Example
short-label	18 or 6	—	2	LOOPE AGAIN

LOOPNZ — LOOP WHILE NOT ZERO
LOOPNE — LOOP WHILE NOT EQUAL

Operation

(CX)←(CX) −1
if (ZF) = 0 and (CX) ≠ 0 then
(IP)←(IP) + disp (sign-extended to 16-bits)

Flags Affected

None

Description

LOOPNE/LOOPNZ *short-label*

LOOPNE and LOOPNZ (Loop While Not Equal and Loop While Not Zero) are also synonyms for the same instruction. CX is decremented by 1, and control is transferred to the target operand if CX is not 0 and if ZF is clear; otherwise the next sequential instruction is executed.

Encoding

1 1 1 0 0 0 0 0	disp

LOOPNE/LOOPNZ Operands	Clocks	Transfers	Bytes	LOOPNE Coding Example
short-label	19 or 5	—	2	LOOPNE AGAIN

MOV — MOVE (BYTE OR WORD)

Operation (DEST)←(SRC)

Flags Affected None

Description **MOV** *destination,source*

MOVE transfers a byte or a word from the source operand to the destination operand.

Encoding

Memory or Register Operand to/from Register Operand

1 0 0 0 1 0 d w	mod reg r/m

if d = 1 then SRC = EA, DEST = REG
else SRC = REG, DEST = EA

Immediate Operand to Memory or Register Operand

1 1 0 0 0 1 1 w	mod 0 0 0 r/m	data	data if w=1

SRC = data, DEST = EA

Immediate Operand to Register

1 0 1 1 w reg	data	data if w=1

SRC = data, DEST = REG

Memory Operand to Accumulator

1 0 1 0 0 0 0 w	addr-low	addr-high

if w = 0 then SRC = addr, DEST = AL
else SRC = addr + 1:addr, DEST = AX

Accumulator to Memory Operand

1 0 1 0 0 0 1 w	addr-low	addr-high

if w = 0 then SRC = AL, DEST = addr
else SRC = AX, DEST = addr + 1:addr

Memory or Register Operand to Segment Register

1 0 0 0 1 1 1 0	mod 0 reg r/m

if reg ≠ 01 then SRC = EA, DEST = REG
else undefined operation

Segment Register to Memory or Register Operand

1 0 0 0 1 1 0 0	mod 0 reg r/m

SRC = REG,DEST = EA

MOV Operands	Clocks	Transfers	Bytes	MOV Coding Example
memory,accumulator	10	1	3	MOV ARRAY AL
accumulator,memory	10	1	3	MOV AX, TEMP_RESULT
register,register	2	—	2	MOV AX, CX
register,memory	8+EA	1	2-4	MOV BP, STACK_TOP
memory,register	9+EA	1	2-4	MOV COUNT [DI],CX
register, immediate	4	—	2-3	MOV CL, 2
memory,immediate	10+EA	1	3-6	MOV MASK[BX][SI],2CH
seg-reg,reg16	2	—	2	MOV ES, CX
seg-reg,mem16	8+EA	1	2-4	MOV DS, SEGMENT_BASE
reg16,seg-reg	2	—	2	MOV BP, SS
memory,seg-reg	9+EA	1	2-4	MOV[BX]SEG_SAVE,CX

MOVS — MOVE STRING

Operation (DEST)←(SRC)

Flags Affected None

Description **MOVS** *destination-string,source-string*

MOVS (Move String) transfers a byte or a word from the source string (addressed by SI) to the destination string (addressed by DI) and updates SI and DI to point to the next string element. When used in conjunction with REP, MOVS performs a memory-to-memory block transfer.

Encoding

1 0 1 0 0 1 0 w

if w = 0 then SRC = (SI), DEST = AL, DELTA = 1
else SRC = (SI) + 1:(SI), DEST = AX, DELTA = 2

MOVS Operands	Clocks	Transfers	Bytes	MOVS Coding Example
dest-string, source-string	18	2	1	MOVS LINE_EDIT_DATA
(repeat) dest-string, source-string	9+17/rep	2/rep	1	REP MOVS SCREEN, BUFFER

MUL — MULTIPLY

Operation

(DES)←(LSRC) * (RSRC), where * is unsigned multiply
if (EXT) = 0 then (CF)←0
else (CF)←1;
(OF)←(CF)

Flags Affected

CF, OF
AF, PF, SF, ZF undefined

Description

MUL *source*

MUL (Multiply) performs an unsigned multiplication of the source operand and the accumulator. If the source is a byte, then it is multiplied by register AL, and the double-length result is returned in AH and AL. If the source operand is a word, then it is multiplied by register AX, and the double-length result is returned in registers DX and AX. The operands are treated as unsigned binary numbers (see AAM). If the upper half of the result (AH for byte source, DX for word source) is non-zero, CF and OF are set; otherwise they are cleared. When CF and OF are set, they indicate that AH or DX contains significant digits of the result. The content of AF, PF, SF and ZF is undefined following execution of MUL.

Encoding

1 1 1 1 0 1 1 w	mod 1 0 0 r/m

if w = 0 then LSRC = AL, RSRC = EA, DEST = AX, EXT = AH
else LSRC = AX, RSRC = EA, DEST = DX:AX, EXT = DX

MUL Operands	Clocks	Transfers	Bytes	MUL Coding Example
reg8	70-77	—	2	MUL BL
reg16	118-113	—	2	MUL CX
mem8	76-83 + EA	1	2-4	MUL MONTH[SI]
mem16	124-139 + EA	1	2-4	MUL BAUD_RATE

NEG — NEGATE

Operation (EA)←SRC − (EA)
(EA)←(EA) + 1 (affecting flags)

Flags Affected AF, CF, OF, PF, SF, ZF

Description **NEG** *destination*

NEG (Negate) subtracts the destination operand, which may be a byte or a word, from 0 and returns the result to the destination. This forms the two's complement of the number, effectively reversing the sign of an integer. If the operand is zero, its sign is not changed. Attempting to negate a byte containing −128 or a word containing −32,768 causes no change to the operand and sets OF. NEG updates AF, CF, OF, PF, SF and ZF. CF is always set except when the operand is zero, in which case it is cleared.

Encoding

1 1 1 1 0 1 1 w	mov 0 1 1 r/m

if w = 0 then SRC = FFH
else SRC = FFFFH

NEG Operands	Clocks	Transfers	Bytes	NEG Coding Example
register	3	—	2	NEG AL
memory	16+EA	2	2-4	NEG MULTIPLIER

NOP — NO OPERATION

Operation None

Flags Affected None

Description **NOP**

NOP (No Operation) causes the CPU to do nothing. NOP does not affect any flags.

Encoding

1 0 0 1 0 0 0 0

NOP Operands	Clocks	Transfers	Bytes	NOP Coding Example
(no operands)	3	—	1	NOP

NOT — LOGICAL NOT

Operation (EA)←SRC − (EA)

Flags Affected None

Description **NOT** *destination*

NOT inverts the bits (forms the one's complement) of the byte or word operand.

Encoding

1 1 1 1 0 1 1 w	mod 0 1 0 r/m

if w = 0 then SRC = FFH
else SRC = FFFFH

NOT Operands	Clocks	Transfers	Bytes	NOT Coding Example
register	3	—	—	NOT AX
memory	16 + EA	2	—	NOT CHARACTER

OR — LOGICAL OR

Operation

(DEST)←(LSRC) or (RSRC)
(CF)←0
(OF)←0

Flags Affected

CF, OF, PF, SF, ZF
AF undefined

Description

OR *destination,source*

OR performs the logical "inclusive or" of the two operands (byte or word) and returns the result to the destination operand. A bit in the result is set if either or both corresponding bits in the original operands are set; otherwise the result bit is cleared.

Encoding

Memory or Register Operand with Register Operand

0 0 0 0 1 0 d w	mod reg r/m

if d = 1 then LSRC = REG, RSRC = EA, DEST = REG
else LSRC = EA, RSRC = REG, DEST = EA

Immediate Operand to Memory or Register Operand

1 0 0 0 0 0 0 w	mod 0 0 1 r/m	data	data if w=

LSRC = EA, RSRC = data, DEST = EA

Immediate Operand to Accumulator

0 0 0 0 1 1 0 w	data	data if w=1

if w = 0 then LSRC = AL, RSRC = data, DEST = AL
else LSRC = AX, RSRC = data, DEST = AX

OR Operands	Clocks	Transfers	Bytes	OR Coding Example
register,register	3	—	2	OR AL,BL
register,memory	9+EA	1	2-4	OR DX,PORT_ID[DI]
memory,register	16+EA	2	2-4	OR FLAG_BYTE, CL
accumulator,immediate	4	—	2-3	OR AL, 01101100B
register,immediate	4	—	3-4	OR CX, 01H
register,immediate memory,immediate	17+EA	2	3-6	OR[BX].CMD_WORD,0CFH

OUT — OUTPUT

Operation (DEST)←(SRC)

Flags Affected None

Description **OUT** *port,accumulator*

OUT transfers a byte or a word from the AL register or the AX register, respectively, to an output port. The port number may be specified either with an immediate byte constant, allowing access to ports numbered 0 through 255, or with a number previously placed in register DX, allowing variable access (by changing the value in DX) to ports numbered from 0 through 65,535.

Encoding

Fixed Port

1 1 1 0 0 1 1 w	port

if w = 0 then SRC = AL, DEST = port
else SRC = AX, DEST = port+1:port

Variable Port

1 1 1 0 1 1 1 w

if w = 0 then SRC = AL, DEST = (DX)
else SRC = AX, DEST = (DX)+1:(DX)

OUT Operands	Clocks	Transfers	Bytes	OUT Coding Example
immed8,accumulator	10	1	2	OUT 44,AX
DX,accumulator	8	1	1	OUT DX,AL

POP — POP

Operation (DEST)←((SP) + 1:(SP))
(SP)←(SP) + 2

Flags Affected None

Description **POP** *destination*

POP transfers the word at the current top of stack (pointed to by SP) to the destination operand, and then increments SP by two to point to the new top of stack. POP can be used to move temporary variables from the stack to registers or memory.

Encoding

Memory or Register Operand

1 0 0 0 1 1 1 1	mod 0 0 0 r/m

DEST = EA

Register Operand

0 1 0 1 1 reg

DEST = REG

Segment Register

0 0 0 reg 1 1 1

if reg ≠ 01 then DEST = REG
else undefined operation

POP Operands	Clocks	Transfers	Bytes	POP Coding Example
register	8	1	1	POP DX
seg-reg(CS illegal)	8	1	1	POP DS
memory	17+EA	2	2-4	POP PARAMETER

POPF — POP FLAGS

Operation Flags←((SP)+1:(SP))
(SP)←(SP)+2

Flags Affected All

Description **POPF**

POPF transfers specific bits from the word at the current top of stack (pointed to by register SP) into the 8086/8088 flags, replacing whatever values the flags previously contained (see Figure 2-32). SP is then incremented by two to point to the new top of stack. PUSHF and POPF allow a procedure to save and restore a calling program's flags. They also allow a program to change the setting of TF (there is no instruction for updating this flag directly). The change is accomplished by pushing the flags, altering bit 8 of the memory-image and then popping the flags.

Encoding

1 0 0 1 1 1 0 1

POPF Operands	Clocks	Transfers	Bytes	POPF Coding Example
(no operands)	8	1	1	POPF

PUSH — PUSH

Operation (SP)←(SP) −2
((SP)+1:(SP))←(SRC)

Flags Affected None

Description **PUSH** *source*

PUSH decrements SP (the stack pointer) by two and then transfers a word from the source operand to the top of stack now pointed to by SP. PUSH often is used to place parameters on the stack before calling a procedure; more generally, it is the basic means of storing temporary data on the stack.

Encoding

Memory or Register Operand

1 1 1 1 1 1 1 1	mod 1 1 0 r/m

SRC = EA

Register Operand

0 1 0 1 0 reg

SRC = REG

Segment Register

0 0 0 reg 1 1 0

SRC = REG

PUSH Operands	Clocks	Transfers	Bytes	PUSH Coding Example
register	11	1	1	PUSH SI
seg-reg (CS legal)	10	1	1	PUSH ES
memory	16+EA	2	2-4	PUSH RETURN_CODE[SI]

PUSHF — PUSH FLAGS

Operation

(SP)←(SP) −2
((SP)+1:(SP))← Flags

Flags Affected

None

Description

PUSHF

PUSHF decrements SP (the stack pointer) by two and then transfers all flags to the word at the top of stack pointed to by SP. The flags themselves are not affected.

Encoding

1 0 0 1 1 1 0 0

PUSHF Operands	Clocks	Transfers	Bytes	PUSHF Coding Example
(no operands)	10	1	1	PUSHF

RCL — ROTATE THROUGH CARRY LEFT

Operation

```
(temp)←COUNT
do while (temp) ≠ 0
   (tmpcf)←(CF)
   (CF)←high-order bit of (EA)
   (EA)←(EA) * 2 + (tmpcf)
   (temp)←(temp) – 1
if COUNT = 1 then
   if high-order bit of (EA) ≠ (CF) then (OF)←1
   else (OF)←0
else (OF) undefined
```

Flags Affected CF, OF

Description **RCL** *destination,count*

RCL (Rotate through Carry Left) rotates the bits in the byte or word destination operand to the left by the number of bits specified in the count operand. The carry flag (CF) is treated as "part of" the destination operand; that is, its value is rotated into the low-order bit of the destination, and itself is replaced by the high-order bit of the destination.

Encoding

Rotate by 1 or CL:

1 1 0 1 0 0 v w	mod 0 1 0 r/m

if v = 0 then COUNT = 1
else COUNT = (CL)

RCL Operands	Clocks	Transfers	Bytes	RCL Coding Example
register, 1	2	—	2	RCL CX, 1
register, CL	8+4/bit	—	2	RCL AL, CL
memory, 1	15+EA	2	2-4	RCL ALPHA, 1
memory, CL	20+4/bit+EA	2	2-4	RCL[BP].PARAM, CL

RCR — ROTATE THROUGH CARRY RIGHT

Operation

```
(temp)←COUNT
do while (temp)≠0
   (tmpcf)←(CF)
   (CF)←low-order bit of (EA)
   (EA)←(EA)/2
   high-order bit of (EA)←(tmpcf)
   (temp)←(temp) − 1
if COUNT = 1 then
   if high-order bit of (EA)≠next-to-high-order bit of (EA)
   then (OF)←1
   else(OF)←0
else (OF) undefined
```

Flags Affected CF, OF

Description **RCR** *destination,count*

RCR (Rotate through Carry Right) operates exactly like RCL except that the bits are rotated right instead of left.

Encoding

Rotate by 1 or CL:

1 1 0 1 0 0 v w	mod 0 1 1 r/m

if v = 0 then COUNT = 1
else COUNT = (CL)

RCR Operands	Clocks	Transfers	Bytes	RCR Coding Example
register, 1	2	—	2	RCR BX, 1
register, CL	8+4/bit	—	2	RCR BL, CL
memory, 1	15+EA	2	2-4	RCR [BX].STATUS, 1
memory, CL	20+4/bit+EA	2	2-4	RCR ARRAY[DI], CL

REP — REPEAT
REPE/REPZ — REPEAT WHILE EQUAL/REPEAT WHILE ZERO
REPNE/REPNZ — REPEAT WHILE NOT EQUAL/REPEAT WHILE NOT ZERO

Operation

do while (CX) ≠ 0
  service pending interrupts (if any) execute primitive string operation in
    succeeding byte
  (CX)←(CX) − 1
  if primitive operation is CMPB, CMPW, SCAB, or SCAW and (ZF)≠z
    then exit from while loop

Flags Affected

None

Description

REP/REPE/REPZ/REPNE/REPNZ

Repeat, Repeat While Equal, Repeat While Zero, Repeat While Not Equal and Repeat While Not Zero are mnemonics for two forms of the prefix byte that controls subsequent string instruction repetition. The different mnemonics are provided to improve program clarity. The repeat prefixes do not affect the flags.

REP is used in conjunction with the MOVS (Move String) and STOS (Store String) instructions and is interpreted as "repeat while not end-of-string" (CX not 0). REPE and REPZ operate identically and are physically the same prefix byte as REP. These instructions are used with the CMPS (Compare String) and SCAS (Scan String) instructions and require ZF (posted by these instructions) to be set before initiating the next repetition. REPNE and REPNZ are mnemonics for the same prefix byte. These instructions function the same as REPE and REPZ except that the zero flag must be cleared or the repetition is terminated. ZF does not need to be initialized before executing the repeated string instruction.

Repeated string sequences are interruptable; the processor will recognize the interrupt before processing the next string element. System interrupt processing is not affected in any way. Upon return from the interrupt, the repeated operation is resumed from the point of interruption. However, execution does *not* resume properly if a second or third prefix (i.e., segment override or LOCK) has been specified in addition to any of the repeat prefixes. At interrupt time, the processor "remembers" only the prefix that immediately precedes the string instruction. After returning from the interrupt, processing resumes, but any additional prefixes specified are not in effect. If more than one prefix must be used with a string instruction, interrupts may be disabled for the duration of the repeated execution. However, this will not prevent a non-maskable interrupt from being recognized. Also, the time that the system is unable to respond to interrupts may be unacceptable if long strings are being processed.

Encoding

1 1 1 1 0 0 1 z

REP Operands	Clocks	Transfers	Bytes	REP Coding Example
(no operands)	2	–	1	REP MOVS DEST, SRCE
REPE/REPZ Operands	**Clocks**	**Transfers**	**Bytes**	**REPE Coding Example**
(no operands)	2	–	1	REPE CMPS DATA, KEY
REPNE/REPNZ Operands	**Clocks**	**Transfers**	**Bytes**	**REPNE Coding Example**
(no operands)	2	–	1	REPNE SCAS INPUT_LINE

RET — RETURN

Operation

(IP)←((SP) = 1:(SP))
(SP)←(SP) +2
if Inter-Segment then
  (CS)←((SP) + 1:(SP))
  (SP)←(SP) + 2
if Add Immediate to Stack Pointer
  then (SP)←(SP) + data

Flags Affected None

Description RET *optional-pop-value*

RET (Return transfers control from a procedure back to the instruction following the CALL that activated the procedure. The assembler generates an intrasegment RET if the programmer has defined the procedure NEAR, or an intersegment RET if the procedure has been defined as FAR. RET pops the word at the top of the stack (pointed to by register SP) into the instruction pointer and increments SP by two. If RET is intersegment, the word at the new top of stack is popped into the CS register, and SP is again incremented by two. If an optional pop value has been specified, RET adds that value to SP. This feature may be used to discard parameters pushed onto the stack before the execution of the CALL instruction.

Encoding

Intra-Segment

1 1 0 0 0 0 1 1

Intra-Segment and Add Immediate to Stack Pointer

1 1 0 0 0 0 1 0	data-low	data-high

Inter-Segment

1 1 0 0 1 0 1 1

Inter-Segment and Add Immediate to Stack Pointer

1 1 0 0 1 0 1 0	data-low	data-high

RET Operands	Clocks	Transfers	Bytes	RET Coding Example
(intra-segment, no pop)	16	1	1	RET
(intra-segment, pop)	20	1	3	RET 4
(inter-segment, no pop)	26	2	1	RET
(inter-segment, pop)	25	2	3	RET 2

ROL — ROTATE LEFT

Operation

```
(temp)←COUNT
do while (temp)≠0
   (CF)←high-order bit of (EA)
   (EA)←(EA) * 2 + (CF)
   (temp)←(temp) −1
if COUNT = 1 then
   if high-order bit of (EA) ≠ (CF) then (OF)←1
   else (OF)←0
else (OF) undefined
```

Flags Affected CF, OF

Description **ROL** *destination,count*

ROL (Rotate Left) rotates the destination byte or word left by the number of bits specified in the count operand.

Encoding

Rotate by 1 or CL:

1 1 0 1 0 0 v w	mov 0 0 0 r/m

if v = 0 then COUNT = 1
else COUNT = (CL)

ROL Operands	Clocks	Transfers	Bytes	ROL Coding Example
register, 1	2	—	2	ROL BX, 1
register, CL	8+4/bit	—	2	ROL DI, CL
memory, 1	15+EA	2	2-4	ROL FLAG_BYTE[DI],1
memory, CL	20+4/bit+EA	2	2-4	ROL ALPHA, CL

ROR — ROTATE RIGHT

Operation

```
(temp)←COUNT
do while (temp)≠0
   (CF)←low-order bit of (EA)
   (EA)←(EA)/2
   high-order bit of (EA)←(CF)
   (temp)←(temp) −1
if COUNT = 1 then
   if high-order bit of (EA)≠next-to-high-order bit of (EA)
then (OF)←1
   else (OF)←0
else (OF) undefined
```

Flags Affected CF, OF

Description **ROR** *destination,count*

ROR (Rotate Right) operates similar to ROL except that the bits in the destination byte or word are rotated right instead of left.

Encoding

Rotate by 1 or CL:

1 1 0 1 0 0 v w	mod 0 0 1 r/m

if v = 0 then COUNT = 1
else COUNT = (CL)

ROR Operands	Clocks	Transfers	Bytes	ROR Coding Example
register, 1	2	—	2	ROR AL, 1
register, CL	8+4/bit	—	2	ROR BX, CL
memory, 1	15+EA	2	2-4	ROR PORT_STATUS, 1
memory, CL	20+4/bit+EA	2	2-4	ROR CMD_WORD, CL

SAHF — STORE REGISTER AH INTO FLAGS

Operation (SF):(ZF):X:(AF):X:(PF):X:(CF)←(AH)

Flags Affected AF, CF, PF, SF, ZF

Description **SAHF**

SAHF (store register AH into flags) transfers bits 7, 6, 4, 2 and 0 from register AH into SF, ZF, AF, PF and CF, respectively, replacing whatever values these flags previously had. OF, DF, IF and TF are not affected. This instruction is provided for 8080/8085 compatibility.

Encoding

1 0 0 1 1 1 1 0

SAHF Operands	Clocks	Transfers	Bytes	SAHF Coding Example
(no operands)	4	—	1	SAHF

SAL — SHIFT ARITHMETIC LEFT
SHL—SHIFT LOGICAL LEFT

Operation

```
(temp)←COUNT
do while (temp)≠0
   (CF)←high-order bit of (EA)
   (EA)←(EA) * 2
   (temp)←(temp) − 1
if COUNT = 1 then
   if high-order bit of (EA)≠(CE)
      then (OF)←1
   else (OF)←0
else (OF) undefined
```

Flags Affected CF, OF, PF, SF, ZF
AF undefined

Description **SHL/SAL** *destination,count*

SHL and SAL (Shift Logical Left and Shift Arithmetic Left) perform the same operation and are physically the same instruction. The destination byte or word is shifted left by the number of bits specified in the count operand. Zeros are shifted in on the right. If the sign bit retains its original value, then OF is cleared.

Encoding

Shift by 1 or CL:

1 1 0 1 0 0 v w	mod 1 0 0 r/m

if v = 0 then COUNT = 1
else COUNT = (CL)

SAL/SHL Operands	Clocks	Transfers	Bytes	SAL/SHL Coding Example
register, 1	2	—	2	SAL AH, 1
register, CL	8+4/bit	—	2	SHL DI, CL
memory, 1	15+EA	2	2-4	SHL[BX].OVERDRAW, 1
memory, CL	20+4/bit+EA	2	2-4	SAL STORE_COUNT, CL

SAR — SHIFT ARITHMETIC RIGHT

Operation

(temp)←COUNT
do while (temp)≠0
  (CF)←low-order bit of (EA)
  (EA)←(EA)/2, where / is equivalent to signed division, rounding down
  (temp)←(temp) −1
if COUNT = 1 then
  if high-order bit of (EA)≠next-to-high-order bit of (EA)
    then (OF)←1
  else (OF)←0
else (OF)←0

Flags Affected

CF, OF, PF, SF, ZF
AF undefined

Description

SAR *destination,count*

SAR (Shift Arithmetic Right) shifts the bits in the destination operand (byte or word) to the right by the number of bits specified in the count operand. Bits equal to the original high-order (sign) bit are shifted in on the left, preserving the sign of the original value. Note that SAR does not produce the same result as the dividend of an "equivalent" IDIV instruction if the destination operand is negative and 1-bits are shifted out. For example, shifting −5 right by one bit yields −3, while integer division −5 by 2 yields −2. The difference in the instructions is that IDIV truncates all numbers toward zero, while SAR truncates positive numbers toward zero and negative numbers toward negative infinity.

Encoding

Shift by 1 or CL:

1 1 0 1 0 0 v w	mod 1 1 1 r/m

if v = 0 then COUNT = 1
else COUNT = (CL)

SAR Operands	Clocks	Transfers	Bytes	SAR Coding Example
register, 1	2	—	2	SAR DX, 1
register, CL	8+4/bit	—	2	SAR DI, CL
memory, 1	15+EA	2	2-4	SAR N_BLOCKS, 1
memory, CL	20+4/bit+EA	2	2-4	SAR N_BLOCKS, CL

SBB — SUBTRACT WITH BORROW

Operation if (CF) = 1 then (DEST) = (LSRC) − (RSRC) − 1
else (DEST)←(LSRC) − (RSRC)

Flags Affected AF, CF, OF, PF, SF, ZF

Description **SBB** *destination,source*

SBB (Subtract with Borrow) subtracts the source from the destination, subtracts one if CF is set, and returns the result to the destination operand. Both operands may be bytes or words. Both operands may be signed or unsigned binary numbers (see AAS and DAS). SBB updates AF, CF, OF, PF, SF, and ZF. Since it incorporates a borrow from a previous operation, SBB may be used to write routines that subtract numbers longer than 16 bits.

Encoding

Memory or Register Operand and Register Operand

0 0 0 1 1 0 d w	mod reg r/m

if d = 1 then LSRC = REG, RSRC = EA, DEST = REG
else LSRC = EA, RSRC = REG, DEST = EA

Immediate Operand from Memory or Register Operand

1 0 0 0 0 0 s w	mod 0 1 1 r/m	data	data if s:w=01

LSRC = EA, RSRC = data, DEST = EA

Immediate Operand from Accumulator

0 0 0 1 1 1 0 w	data	data if w=1

if w = 0 then LSRC = AL, RSRC = data, DEST = AL
else LSRC = AX, RSRC = data, DEST = AX

SBB Operands	Clocks	Transfers	Bytes	SBB Coding Example
register, register	3	—	2	SBB BX, CX
register, memory	9+EA	1	2-4	SBB DI,[BX].PAYMENT
memory, register	16+EA	2	2-4	SBB BALANCE, AX
accumulator, immediate	4	—	2-3	SBB AX, 2
register, immediate	4	—	3-4	SBB CL, 2
memory, immediate	17+EA	2	3-6	SBB COUNT [SI], 10

SCAS — SCAN (BYTE OR WORD) STRING

Operation

(LSRC) − (RSRC)
if (DF) = 0 then (DI)←(DI) + DELTA
else (DI)←(DI) − DELTA

Flags Affected

AF, CF, OF, PF, SF, ZF

Description

SCAS *destination-string*

SCAS (Scan String) subtracts the destination string element (byte or word) addressed by DI from the content of AL (byte string) or AX (word string) and updates the flags, but does not alter the destination string or the accumulator. SCAS also updates DI to point to the next string element and AF, CF, OF, PF, SF and ZF to reflect the relationship of the scan value in AL/AX to the string element. If SCAS is prefixed with REPE or REPZ, the operation is interpreted as "scan while not end-of-string (CX not 0) and string-element = scan-value (ZF = 1)." This form may be used to scan for departure from a given value. If SCAS is prefixed with REPNE or REPNZ, the operation is interpreted as "scan while not end-of-string (CX not 0) and string-element is not equal to scan-value (ZF = 0)." This form may be used to locate a value in a string.

Encoding

1 0 1 0 1 1 1 w

if w = 0 then LSRC = AL, RSRC = (DI), DELTA = 1
else LSRC = AX, RSRC = (DI) +1:(DI), DELTA = 2

SCAS Operands	Clocks	Transfers	Bytes	SCAS Coding Example
dest-string	15	1	1	SCAS INPUT_LINE
dest-string	9+15	1/rep	1	REPNE SCAS BUFFER

SHR — SHIFT LOGICAL RIGHT

Operation

```
(temp)←COUNT
do while (temp)≠0
   CF)←low-order bit of (EA
   (EA)←(EA)/2, where / is equivalent to unsigned division
   (temp)←(temp) − 1
if COUNT = 1 then
   if high-order bit of (EA)≠next-to-high-order bit of (EA)
      then (OF)←1
   else (OF)←0
else (OF) undefined
```

Flags Affected CF, OF, PF, SF, ZF
AF undefined

Description **SHR** *destination,source*

SHR (Shift Logical Right) shifts the bits in the destination operand (byte or word) to the right by the number of bits specified in the count operand. Zeros are shifted in on the left. If the sign bit retains its original value, then OF is cleared.

Encoding

Shift by 1 or CL:

1 1 0 1 0 0 v w	mod 1 0 1 r/m

if v = 0 then COUNT = 1
else COUNT = (CL)

SHR Operands	Clocks	Transfers	Bytes	SHR Coding Example
register, 1	2	—	2	SHR SI, 1
register, CL	8+4/bit	—	2	SHR SI, CL
memory, 1	15+EA	2	2-4	SHR ID_BYTE[SI][BX], 1
memory, CL	20+4/bit+EA	2	2-4	SHR INPUT_WORD, CL

STC — SET CARRY

Operation (CF)←1

Flags Affected CF

Description **STC**

STC (Set Carry flag) sets CF to 1 and affects no other flags.

Encoding

1 1 1 1 1 0 0 1

STC Operands	Clocks	Transfers	Bytes	STC Coding Example
(no operands)	2	—	1	STC

STD — SET DIRECTION FLAG

Operation (DF)←1

Flags Affected DF

Description **STD**

STD (Set Direction flag) sets DF to 1 causing the string instructions to auto-decrement the SI and/or DI index registers. STD does not affect any other flags.

Encoding

1 1 1 1 1 1 0 1

STD Operands	Clocks	Transfers	Bytes	STD Coding Example
(no operands)	2	—	1	STD

STI — SET INTERRUPT ENABLE FLAG

Operation (IF)←1

Flags Affected IF

Description **STC**

STI (Set Interrupt-enable flag) sets IF to 1, enabling processor recognition of maskable interrupt requests appearing on the INTR line. Note however, that a pending interrupt will not actually be recognized until the instruction following STI has executed. STI does not affect any other flags.

Encoding

1 1 1 1 1 0 1 1

STI Operands	Clocks	Transfers	Bytes	STI Coding Example
(no operands)	2	—	1	STI

STOS — STORE (BYTE/OR/WORD) STRING

Operation

(DEST)←(SRC)
if(DF) = 0 then (DI)←(DI) + DELTA
else (DI)←(DI) − DELTA

Flags Affected

None

Description

STOS *destination-string*

STOS (Store String) transfers a byte or word from register AL or AX to the string element addressed by DI and updates DI to point to the next location in the string. As a repeated operation. STOS provides a convenient way to initialize a string to a constant value (e.g., to blank out a print line).

Encoding

1 0 1 0 1 0 1 w

if w = 0 then SRC = AL, DEST = (DI), DELTA = 1
else SRC = AX, DEST = (DI) + 1:(DI), DELTA = 2

STOS Operands	Clocks	Transfers	Bytes	STOS Coding Example
dest-string	11	1	1	STOP PRINT_LINE
(repeat) dest-string	9+10/rep	1/rep	1	REP STOS DISPLAY

SUB — SUBTRACT

Operation (DEST)←(LSRC) – (RSRC)

Flags Affected AF, CF, OF, PF, SF, ZF

Description **SUB** *destination,source*

The source operand is subtracted from the destination operand, and the result replaces the destination operand. The operands may be bytes or words. Both operands may be signed or unsigned binary numbers (see AAS and DAS). SUB updates AF, CF, OF, PF, SF and ZF.

Encoding

Memory or Register Operand and Register Operand

0 0 1 0 1 0 d w	mod reg r/m

if d = 1 then LSRC = REG, RSRC = EA, DEST = REG
else LSRC = EA, RSRC = REG, DEST = EA

Immediate Operand from Memory or Register Operand

1 0 0 0 0 0 s w	mod 1 0 1 r/m	data	data if s:w=01

LSRC = EA, RSRC = data, DEST = EA

Immediate Operand from Accumulator

0 0 1 0 1 1 0 w	data	data if w=1

if w = 0 then LSRC = AL, RSRC = data, DEST = AL
else LSRC = AX, RSRC = data, DEST = AX

SUB Operands	Clocks	Transfers	Bytes	SUB Coding Example
register, register	3	—	2	SUB CX, BX
register, memory	9+EA	1	2-4	SUB DX,MATH_TOTAL[SI]
memory, register	16+EA	2	2-4	SUB[BP+2], CL
accumulator, immediate	4	—	2-3	SUB AL, 10
register, immediate	4	—	3-4	SUB SI, 5280
memory, immediate	17+EA	2	3-6	SUB[BP].BALANCE, 1000

TEST — TEST

Operation (LSRC) & (RSRC)
(CF)←0
(OF)←0

Flags Affected CF, OF, PF, SF, ZF
AF undefined

Description **TEST** *destination,source*

TEST performs the logical "and" of the two operands (byte or word), updates the flags, but does not return the result, i.e., neither operand is changed. If a TEST instruction is followed by a JNZ (jump if not zero) instruction, the jump will be taken if there are any corresponding 1-bits in both operands.

Encoding

Memory or Register Operand with Register Operand

1 0 0 0 0 1 0 w	mod reg r/m

LSRC = REG, RSRC = EA

Immediate Operand with Memory or Register Operand

1 1 1 1 0 1 1 w	mod 0 0 0 r/m	data	data if w=1

LSRC = EA, RSRC = data

Immediate Operand with Accumulator

1 0 1 0 1 0 0 w	data	data if w=0

if w = 0 then SRC = AL, RSRC = data
else LSRC = AX, RSRC = data

TEST Operands	Clocks	Transfers	Bytes	TEST Coding Example
register, register	3	—	2	TEST SI, DI
register, memory	9+EA	1	2-4	TEST SI, END_
accumulator, immediate	4	—	2-3	TEST AL, 00100000B
register, immediate	5	—	3-4	TEST BX, 0CC4H
memory, immediate	11+EA	—	3-6	TEST RETURN_CODE,01H

WAIT — WAIT

Operation None

Flags Affected None

Description WAIT causes the CPU to enter the wait state while its TEST line is not active. WAIT does not affect any flags.

Encoding

1 0 0 1 1 0 1 1

WAIT Operands	Clocks	Transfers	Bytes	WAIT Coding Example
(no operands)	4+5n	—	1	WAIT

XCHG — EXCHANGE

Operation

(temp)←(DEST)
(DEST)←(SRC)
(SRC)←(temp)

Flags Affected

None

Description

XCHG *destination,source*

XCHG (exchange) switches the contents of the source and destination (byte or word) operands. When used in conjunction with the LOCK prefix, XCHG can test and set a semaphore that controls access to a resource shared by multiple processors (see the section "Minimum and Maximum Modes" in Chapter 2).

Encoding

Memory or Register Operand with Register Operand

1 0 0 0 0 1 1 w	mod reg r/m

SRC = EA, DEST = REG

Register Operand with Accumulator

1 0 0 1 0 reg

SRC = REG, DEST = AX

XCHG Operands	Clocks	Transfers	Bytes	XCHG Coding Example
accumulator, reg16	3	—	1	XCHG AX, BX
memory, register	17+EA	2	2-4	XCHG SEMAPHORE, AX
register, register	4	—	2	XCHG AL, BL

XLAT — TRANSLATE

Operation AL←((BX) + (AL))

Flags Affected None

Description **XLAT** *translate-table*

XLAT (translate) replaces a byte in the AL register with a byte from a 256-byte, user-coded translation table. Register BX is assumed to point to the beginning of the table. The byte in AL is used as an index into the table and is replaced by the byte at the offset in the table corresponding to AL's binary value. The first byte in the table has an offset of 0. For example, if AL contains 5H, and the sixth element of the translation table contains 33H, then AL will contain 33H following the instruction. XLAT is useful for translating characters from one code to another, the classic example being ASCII to EBCDIC or the reverse.

Encoding

1 1 0 1 0 1 1 1

XLAT Operands	Clocks	Transfers	Bytes	XLAT Coding Example
source-table	11	1	1	XLAT ASCII_TAB

XOR — EXCLUSIVE OR

Operation (DEST)←(LSRC) XOR (RSRC)
(CF)←0
(OF)←0

Flags Affected CF, OF, PF, SF, ZF
AF undefined

Description **XOR** *destination,source*

XOR (Exclusive Or) performs the logical "exclusive or" of the two operands and returns the result to the destination operand. A bit in the result is set if the corresponding bits of the original operands contain opposite values (one is set, the other is cleared); otherwise the result bit is cleared.

Encoding

Memory or Register Operand with Register Operand

0 0 1 1 0 0 d w	mod reg r/m

if d = 1 then LSRC = REG, RSRC = EA, DEST = REG
else LSRC = EA, RSRC = REG, DEST = EA

Immediate Operand to Memory or Register Operand

1 0 0 0 0 0 0 w	mod 1 1 0 r/m	data	data if w=1

LSRC = EA, RSRC = data, DEST = EA

Immediate Operand to Accumulator

0 0 1 1 0 1 0 w	data	data if w=1

if w = 0 then LSRC = AL, RSRC = data, DEST = AL
else LSRC = AX, RSRC = data, DEST = AX

XOR Operands	Clocks	Transfers	Bytes	XOR Coding Example
register,register	3	—	2	XOR CX, BX
register,memory	9+EA	1	2-4	XOR CL, MASK_BYTE
memory,register	16+EA	2	2-4	XOR ALPHA[SI],DX
accumulator,immediate	4	—	2-3	XOR AL, 01000010B
register,immediate	4	—	3-4	XOR SI, 00C2H
memory,immediate	17+EA	2	3-6	XOR RETURN_CODE,0D2H

8086/8088 PROGRAMMING EXAMPLES

In this section and the section following, specific programming examples are provided which illustrate how the instruction set and addressing modes may be used in various commonly encountered programming situations.

The programs are primarily written in ASM-86. ASM-86 is the 8086 assembly language. It provides the programmer who is familiar with the CPU architecture, access to all processor features. For critical code segments within programs that make sophisticated use of the hardware, have extremely demanding performance or memory constraints. ASM-86 is the best choice. For detailed information about Intel's 8086 assembly language see: *ASM86 Language Reference Manual*, 121703.

Programs can also be written in high-level languages such as PL/M-86. PL/M-86 is a high-level language suitable for most microprocessor applications. It is easy to use, even by programmers who have little experience with microprocessors. Because it reduces software development time, PL/M-86 is ideal for most of the programming in any application, especially applications that must get to market quickly.

The languages are completely compatible, and a judicious combination of the two often makes good sense. Prototype software can be developed rapidly with a high-level language. When the system is operating correctly, it can then be analyzed to see which sections can best profit from being written in ASM-86. Since the logic of these sections has already been debugged, selective rewriting can be done quickly and with low risk.

The programming examples in this section address the following topics:

- Procedures
- JMP and CALL (jump, call)
- Bit manipulation
- Dynamic code relocation
- Memory mapped I/O
- Breakpoints
- Interrupt handling
- String operations

The examples are intended to show one way to use the instruction set and addressing modes. They do not demonstrate the "best" way to solve a particular problem. The flexibility of the 8086 application differences plus variations in programming style usually add up to a number of ways to implement a programming solution.

Procedures (parameters, reentrancy)

The code in Figure 3-30 illustrates several techniques that are typically used in writing ASM-86 procedures. In this example a calling program invokes a procedure (called EXAMPLE) twice, passing it a different byte array each time. Two parameters are passed on the stack; the first contains the number of elements in the array, and the second contains the address (offset in DATA2SEG) of the first array element. This same technique can be used to pass a variable-length parameter list to a procedure (the "array" could be any series of parameters or parameter addresses). Thus, although the procedure always receives two parameters, these can be used to indirectly access any number of variables in memory.

Any results returned by a procedure should be placed in registers or in memory, but not on the stack. AX or AL is often used to hold a single word or byte result. Alternatively, the calling program can pass the address (or addresses) of a result area to the procedure

```
STACK_SEG       SEGMENT
                DW          20 DUP (?)       ; ALLOCATE 20-WORD STACK
STACK_TOP       LABEL       WORD             ; LABEL INITIAL TOS
STACK_SEG       ENDS

DATA_SEG        SEGMENT
ARRAY_1         DB          10 DUP (?)       ; 10-ELEMENT BYTE ARRAY
ARRAY_2         DB          5 DUP (?)        ; 5-ELEMENT BYTE ARRAY
DATA_SEG        ENDS

PROC_SEG        SEGMENT
ASSUME  CS:PROC_SEG,DS:DATA_SEG,SS:STACK_SEG,ES:NOTHING

EXAMPLE         PROC        FAR              ; MUST BE ACTIVATED BY
                                             ;     INTERSEGMENT CALL

; PROCEDURE PROLOG
                PUSH        BP               ; SAVE BP
                MOV         BP, SP           ; ESTABLISH BASE POINTER
                PUSH        CX               ; SAVE CALLER'S
                PUSH        BX               ;     REGISTERS
                PUSHF                        ;     AND FLAGS
                SUB         SP, 6            ; ALLOCATE 3 WORDS LOCAL STORAGE
                ; END OF PROLOG
; PROCEDURE BODY
                MOV         CX, [BP+8]       ; GET ELEMENT COUNT
                MOV         BX, [BP+6]       ; GET OFFSET OF 1ST ELEMENT
                ; PROCEDURE CODE GOES HERE
                ; FIRST PARAMETER CAN BE ADDRESSED:
                ;   [BX]
                ; LOCAL STORAGE CAN BE ADDRESSED:
                ;       [BP-8], [BP-10], [BP-12]
                ; END OF PROCEDURE BODY
```

Figure 3-30. Procedure Example 1

```
; PROCEDURE EPILOG
                ADD     SP, 6           ; DE-ALLOCATE LOCAL STORAGE
                POPF                    ; RESTORE CALLER'S
                POP     BX              ;  REGISTERS
                POP     CX              ;  AND
                POP     BP              ;  FLAGS
                ; END OF EPILOG
; PROCEDURE RETURN
                RET     4               ; DISCARD 2 PARAMETERS

EXAMPLE         ENDP                    ; END OF PROCEDURE "EXAMPLE"

PROC_SEG        ENDS
CALLER_SEG      SEGMENT
; GIVE ASSEMBLER SEGMENT/REGISTER CORRESPONDENCE
ASSUME          CS:CALLER_SEG,
&               DS:DATA_SEG,
&               SS:STACK_SEG,
&               ES:NOTHING              ; NO EXTRA SEGMENT IN THIS PROGRAM

; INITIALIZE SEGMENT REGISTERS
START:          MOV     AX,DATA_SEG
                MOV     DS,AX
                MOV     AX,STACK_SEG
                MOV     SS,AX
                MOV     SP,OFFSET STACK_TOP   ; POINT SP TO TOS

; ASSUME ARRAY_1 IS INITIALIZED
;
; CALL "EXAMPLE", PASSING ARRAY_1, THAT IS, THE NUMBER OF ELEMENTS
;   IN THE ARRAY, AND THE LOCATION OF THE FIRST ELEMENT.
                MOV     AX,SIZE ARRAY_1
                PUSH    AX
                MOV     AX,OFFSET ARRAY_1
                PUSH    AX
                CALL    EXAMPLE

; ASSUME ARRAY_2 IS INITIALIZED
;
; CALL "EXAMPLE" AGAIN WITH DIFFERENT SIZE ARRAY.
                MOV     AX,SIZE ARRAY_2
                PUSH    AX
                MOV     AX,OFFSET ARRAY_2
                PUSH    AX
                CALL    EXAMPLE
CALLER_SEG              ENDS

                END     START
```

Figure 3-30. Procedure Example 1 (Cont'd.)

as a parameter. It is good practice for ASM-86 programs to follow the calling conventions used by PL/M-86.

EXAMPLE is defined as a FAR procedure, meaning it is in a different segment than the calling program. The calling program must use an intersegment CALL to activate the procedure. Note that this type of CALL saves CS and IP on the stack. If EXAMPLE were defined as NEAR (in the same segment as the caller) then an intrasegment CALL would be used, and only IP would be saved on the stack. It is the responsibility of the calling program to know how the procedure is defined and to issue the correct type of CALL.

Figure 3-31 shows the stack before the caller pushes the parameters onto it. Figure 3-32 shows the stack as the procedure receives it after the CALL has been executed.

EXAMPLE is divided into four sections. The "prolog" sets up register BP so it can be used to address data on the stack (specifying BP as a base register in an instruction automatically refers to the stack segment unless a segment override prefix is coded). The next step in the prolog is to save the "state of the machine" as it existed when the procedure was activated. This is done by pushing any registers used by the procedure (only CX and BP in this case) onto the stack. If the procedure changes the flags, and the caller expects the flags to be unchanged following execution of the procedure, they also may be saved on the stack. The last instruction in the prolog allocates three words on the

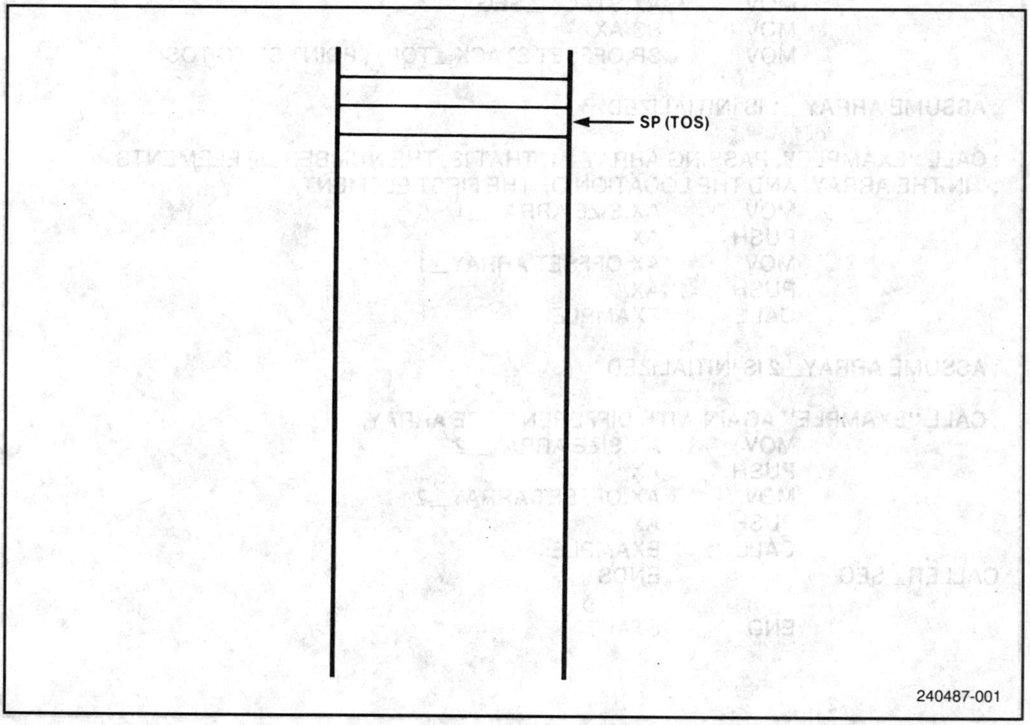

Figure 3-31. Stack Before Pushing Parameters

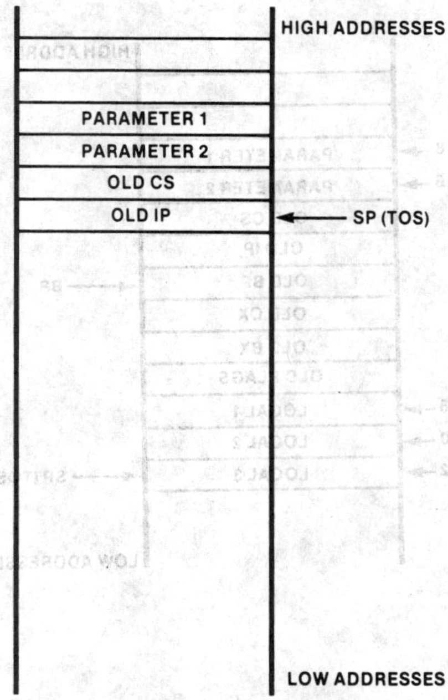

Figure 3-32. Stack at Procedure Entry

stack for the procedure to use as local temporary storage. Figure 3-33 shows the stack at the end of the prolog. Note that PL/M procedures assume that all registers except SP and BP can be used without saving and restoring.

The procedure "body" does the actual processing (none in the example). The parameters on the stack are addressed relative to BP. Note that if EXAMPLE were a NEAR procedure, CS would not be on the stack and the parameters would be two bytes "closer" to BP. BP also is used to address the local variables on the stack. Local constants are best stored in a data or extra segment.

The procedure "epilog" reverses the activities of the prolog, leaving the stack as it was when the procedure was entered (see Figure 3-34).

The procedure "return" restores CS and IP from the stack and discards the parameters. As Figure 3-35 shows, when the calling program is resumed, the stack is in the same state as it was before any parameters were pushed onto it.

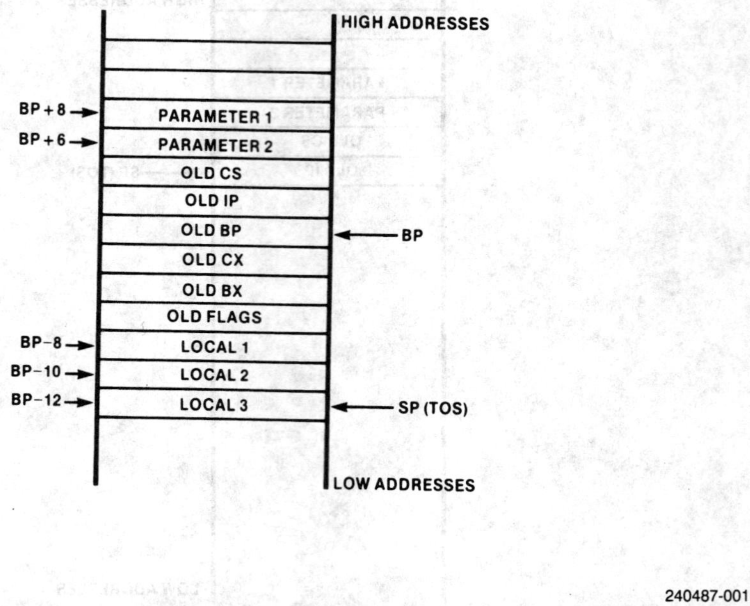

Figure 3-33. Stack Following Procedure Prolog

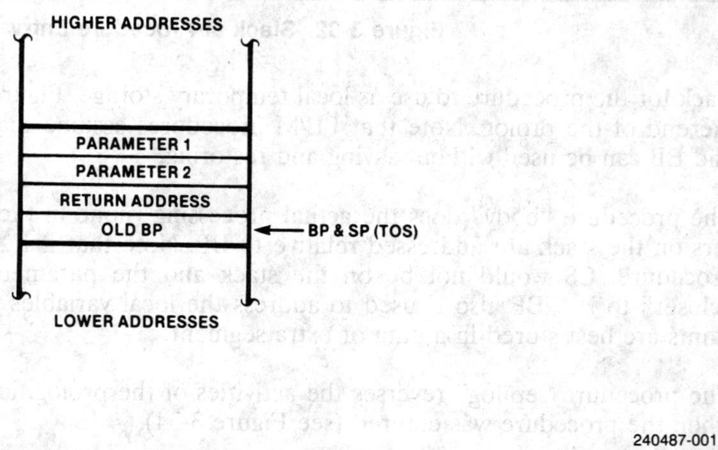

Figure 3-34. Stack Following Procedure Epilog

Figure 3-35. Stack Following Procedure Return

Figure 3-36 shows a simple procedure that uses an ASM-86 structure to address the stack. Register BP points to the base of the structure, which is the top of the stack since the stack grows toward lower addresses (see Figure 3-37). Any structure element can then be addressed by specifying BP as a base register:

```
[BP].structure_element
```

Figure 3-38 shows a different approach to using an ASM-86 structure to define the stack layout. As shown in Figure 3-39 register BP is pointed at the middle of the structure (at OLD_BP) rather than at the base of the structure. Parameters and the return address are thus located at positive displacements (high addresses) from BP, while local variables are at negative displacements (lower addresses) from BP. This means that the local variables will be "closer" to the beginning of the stack segment and increase the likelihood that the assembler will be able to produce shorter instructions to access these variables, i.e., their offset from SS may be 255 bytes or less and can be expressed as a 1-byte value rather than 1 2-byte value. Exit from the subroutine also is slightly faster because a MOV instruction can be used to deallocate the local storage instead of an ADD (compare Figure 3-30).

```
CODE            SEGMENT
                ASSUME CS:CODE
MAX             PROC
; THIS PROCEDURE IS CALLED BY THE FOLLOWING
;       SEQUENCE:
;               PUSH PARM1
;               PUSH PARM2
;               CALL MAX
; IT RETURNS THE MAXIMUM OF THE TWO WORD
;     PARAMETERS IN AX.

; DEFINE THE STACK LAYOUT AS A STRUCTURE.
STACK_LAYOUT STRUC
OLD_BP          DW ?        ; SAVED BP VALUE—BASE OF STRUCTURE
RETURN_ADDR     DW ?        ; RETURN ADDRESS
PARM_2          DW ?        ; SECOND PARAMETER
PARM_1          DW ?        ; FIRST PARAMETER
STACK_LAYOUT ENDS

; PROLOG
                PUSH        BP                  ; SAVE IN OLD_BP
                MOV         BP, SP              ; POINT TO OLD_BP
; BODY
                MOV         AX, [BP].PARM_1     ; IF FIRST
                CMP         AX, [BP].PARM_2     ; > SECOND
                JG          FIRST_IS_MAX        ; THEN RETURN FIRST
                MOV         AX, [BP].PARM_2     ; ELSE RETURN SECOND
; EPILOG
FIRST_IS_MAX:   POP         BP                  ; RESTORE BP (& SP)
; RETURN
                RET         4                   ; DISCARD PARAMETERS
MAX             ENDP

CODE            ENDS
                END
```

Figure 3-36. Procedure Example 2 – The Stack as a Structure

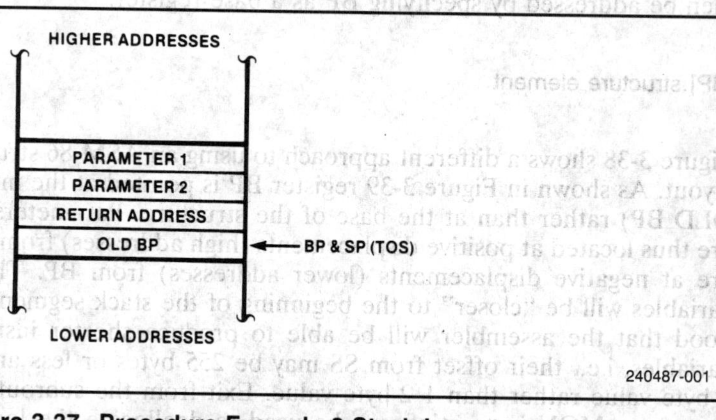

Figure 3-37. Procedure Example 2 Stack Layout

```
EXTRA           SEGMENT
; CONTAINS STRUCTURE TEMPLATE THAT "NEARPROC"
;    USES TO ADDRESS AN ARRAY PASSED BY ADDRESS.
DUMMY           STRUC
PARM_ARRAY      DB          256 DUP ?
DUMMY           ENDS
EXTRA           ENDS

CODE            SEGMENT
                ASSUME CS:CODE,ES:EXTRA
NEARPROC        PROC
; LAY OUT THE STACK (THE DYNAMIC STORAGE AREA OR DSA).
DSASTRUC        STRUC
I               DW          ?                   ; LOCAL VARIABLES FIRST
LOC_ARRAY       DW          10 DUP (?)
OLD_BP          DW          ?                   ; ORIGINAL BP VALUE
RETADDR         DW          ?                   ; RETURN ADDRESS
POINTER         DD          ?                   ; 2ND PARM—POINTER TO "PARM_ARRAY".
COUNT           DB          ?                   ; 1ST PARM—A BYTE OCCUPIES
                DB          ?                   ;      A WORD ON THE STACK
DSASTRUC        ENDS

; USE AN EQU TO DEFINE THE BASE ADDRESS OF THE
;    DSA. CANNOT SIMPLY USE BP BECAUSE IT WILL
;    BE POINTING TO "OLD_BP" IN THE MIDDLE OF
;    THE DSA.
DSA             EQU         [BP - OFFSET OLD_BP]

; PROCEDURE ENTRY
                PUSH        BP                  ; SAVE BP
                MOV         BP, SP              ; POINT BP AT OLD_BP
                SUB         SP, OFFSET OLD_BP ; ALLOCATE LOC_ARRAY & I

; PROCEDURE BODY
                ; ACCESS LOCAL VARIABLE I
                MOV         AX,DSA.I

                ; ACCESS LOCAL ARRAY (3) I.E., 4TH ELEMENT
                MOV         SI,6                ; WORD ARRAY-INDEX IS 3*2
                MOV         AX,DSA.LOC_ARRAY [SI]

                ; LOAD POINTER TO ARRAY PASSED BY ADDRESS
                LES         BX,DSA.POINTER

                ; ES:BX NOW POINTS TO PARM_ARRAY (0)
                ; ACCESS SI'TH ELEMENT OF PARM_ARRAY
                MOV         AL,ES:[BX].PARM_ARRAY [SI]

                ; ACCESS THE BYTE PARAMETER
                MOV         AL,DSA.COUNT
```

Figure 3-38. Procedure Example 3

```
; PROCEDURE EXIT
                MOV     SP,BP           ; DE-ALLOCATE LOCALS
                POP     BP              ; RESTORE BP
                ; STACK NOW AS RECEIVED FROM CALLER
                RET     6               ; DISCARD PARAMETERS

NEARPROC        ENDP
CODE            ENDS
                END
```

Figure 3-38. Procedure Example 3 (Cont'd.)

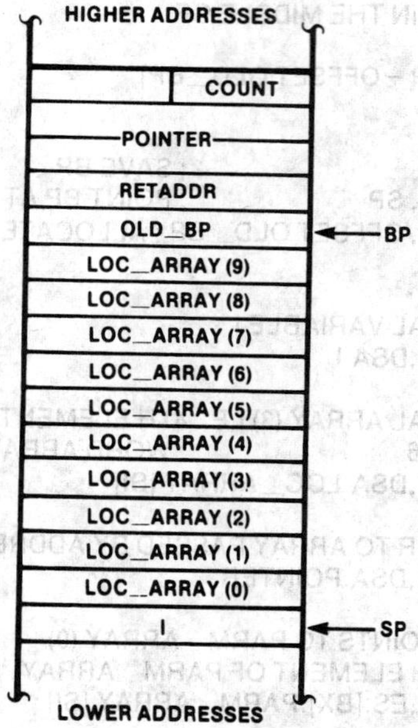

Figure 3-39. Procedure Example 3 Stack Layout

It is possible for a procedure to be activated a second time before it has returned from its first activation. For example, procedure A may call procedure B, and an interrupt may occur while procedure B is executing. If the interrupt service procedure calls B, then procedure B is reentered and must be written to handle this situation correctly, i.e., the procedure must be made reentrant.

In PL/M-86 this can be done by simply writing:

```
B:PROCEDURE(PARM1,PARM2)REENTRANT;
```

An ASM-86 procedure will be reentrant if it uses the stack for storing all local variables. When the procedure is reentered, a new "generation" of variables will be located on the stack. The stack will grow, but the sets of variables (and the parameters and return addresses as well) will automatically be kept straight. The stack must be large enough to accommodate the maximum "depth" of procedure activation that can occur under actual running conditions. In addition, any procedure called by a reentrant procedure must itself be reentrant.

A related situation that also requires reentrant procedures is recursion:

- A calls A (direct recursion),
- A calls B, B calls A (indirect recursion),
- A calls B, B calls C, C calls A (indirect recursion).

Jumps and Calls

The instruction set contains many different types of JMP and CALL instructions (e.g., direct, indirect, through register, indirect through memory, etc.). These varying types of transfer provide efficient use of space and execution time in different programming situations. Figure 3-40 illustrates typical use of the different forms of these instructions. Note that the ASM-86 assembler uses the terms "NEAR" and "FAR" to denote intra-segment and intersegment transfers, respectively.

The procedure in Figure 3-40 illustrates how a PL/M-86 DO CASE construction may be implemented in ASM-86. It also shows:

- an indirect CALL through memory to a procedure located in another segment,
- a direct JMP to a label in another segment,
- an indirect JMP through memory to a label in the same segment,
- an indirect JMP through a register to a label in the same segment,
- a direct CALL to a procedure in another segment,
- a direct CALL to a procedure in the same segment,
- direct JMPs to labels in the same segment, within −128 to +127 bytes ("SHORT") and farther than −128 to +127 bytes ("NEAR").

```
DATA            SEGMENT
; DEFINE THE CASE TABLE (JUMP TABLE) USED BY PROCEDURE
;     "DO_CASE." THE OFFSET OF EACH LABEL WILL
;     BE PLACED IN THE TABLE BY THE ASSEMBLER.
CASE_TABLE      DW          ACTION0, ACTION1, ACTION2,
&                           ACTION3, ACTION4, ACTION5
DATA            ENDS

; DEFINE TWO EXTERNAL (NOT PRESENT IN THIS
;     ASSEMBLY BUT SUPPLIED BY R & L FACILITY)
;     PROCEDURES. ONE IS IN THIS CODE SEGMENT
;     (NEAR) AND ONE IS IN ANOTHER SEGMENT (FAR).
                EXTRN       NEAR_PROC: NEAR, FAR_PROC: FAR

; DEFINE AN EXTERNAL LABEL (JUMP TARGET) THAT
;     IS IN ANOTHER SEGMENT.
                EXTRN       ERR_EXIT: FAR

CODE            SEGMENT
                ASSUME      CS: CODE, DS: DATA
; ASSUME DS HAS BEEN SET UP
;     BY CALLER TO POINT TO "DATA" SEGMENT.

DO_CASE         PROC        NEAR
; THIS EXAMPLE PROCEDURE RECEIVES TWO
;     PARAMETERS ON THE STACK. THE FIRST
;     PARAMETER IS THE "CASE NUMBER" OF
;     A ROUTINE TO BE EXECUTED (0-5). THE SECOND
;     PARAMETER IS A POINTER TO AN ERROR
;     PROCEDURE THAT IS EXECUTED IF AN INVALID
;     CASE NUMBER (>5) IS RECEIVED.

; LAY OUT THE STACK.
STACK_LAYOUT STRUC
OLD_BP          DW     ?
RETADDR         DW     ?
ERR_PROC_ADDR   DD     ?
CASE_NO         DB     ?
                DB     ?
STACK_LAYOUT ENDS

; SET UP PARAMETER ADDRESSING
                PUSH        BP
                MOV         BP, SP

; CODE TO SAVE CALLER'S REGISTERS COULD GO HERE.

; CHECK THE CASE NUMBER
                MOV         BH, 0
                MOV         BL, [BP].CASE_NO
                CMP         BX, LENGTH CASE_TABLE
                JLE         OK            ; ALL CONDITIONAL JUMPS
                                          ; ARE SHORT DIRECT
```

Figure 3-40. JMP and CALL Examples

```
; CALL THE ERROR ROUTINE WITH A FAR
;    INDIRECT CALL. A FAR INDIRECT CALL
;    IS INDICATED SINCE THE OPERAND HAS
;    TYPE "DOUBLEWORD."
                    CALL        [BP].ERR_PROC_ADDR

; JUMP DIRECTLY TO A LABEL IN ANOTHER SEGMENT.
;    A FAR DIRECT JUMP IS INDICATED SINCE
;    THE OPERAND HAS TYPE "FAR."
                    JMP         ERR_EXIT

OK:
; MULTIPLY CASE NUMBER BY 2 TO GET OFFSET
;    INTO CASE_TABLE (EACH ENTRY IS 2 BYTES).
                    SHL         BX, 1
; NEAR INDIRECT JUMP THROUGH SELECTED
;    ELEMENT OF CASE_TABLE. A NEAR
;    INDIRECT JUMP IS INDICATED SINCE THE
;    OPERAND HAS TYPE "WORD."
                    JMP         CASE_TABLE [BX]

ACTION0:            ; EXECUTED IF CASE_NO = 0
    ; CODE TO PROCESS THE ZERO CASE GOES HERE.
    ; FOR ILLUSTRATION PURPOSES, USE A
    ;    NEAR INDIRECT JUMP THROUGH A
    ;    REGISTER TO BRANCH TO THE POINT
    ;    WHERE ALL CASES CONVERGE.
    ;    A DIRECT JUMP (JMP ENDCASE) IS
    ;    ACTUALLY MORE APPROPRIATE HERE.
                    MOV         AX, OFFSET ENDCASE
                    JMP         AX

ACTION1:            ; EXECUTED IF CASE_NO = 1
    ; CALL A FAR EXTERNAL PROCEDURE. A FAR
    ;    DIRECT CALL IS INDICATED SINCE OPERAND
    ;    HAS TYPE "FAR."
                    CALL        FAR_PROC
    ; CALL A NEAR EXTERNAL PROCEDURE.
                    CALL        NEAR_PROC
    ; BRANCH TO CONVERGENCE POINT USING NEAR
    ;    DIRECT JUMP. NOTE THAT "ENDCASE"
    ;    IS MORE THAN 127 BYTES AWAY
    ;    SO A NEAR DIRECT JUMP WILL BE USED.
                    JMP         ENDCASE

ACTION2:            ; EXECUTED IF CASE_NO = 2
    ; CODE GOES HERE
                    JMP         ENDCASE        ; NEAR DIRECT JUMP
```

Figure 3-40. JMP and CALL Examples (Cont'd.)

```
ACTION3:            ; EXECUTED IF CASE_NO = 3
     ; CODE GOES HERE
                    JMP        ENDCASE      ; NEAR DIRECT JMP

; ARTIFICIALLY FORCE ''ENDCASE'' FURTHER AWAY
;     SO THAT ABOVE JUMPS CANNOT BE ''SHORT.''
                    ORG        500

ACTION4:            ; EXECUTED IF CASE_NO = 4
     ; CODE GOES HERE
                    JMP        ENDCASE      ; NEAR DIRECT JUMP

ACTION5:            ; EXECUTED IF CASE_NO = 5
     ; CODE GOES HERE.
     ; BRANCH TO CONVERGENCE POINT USING
     ;     SHORT DIRECT JUMP SINCE TARGET IS
     ;     WITHIN 127 BYTES. MACHINE INSTRUCTION
     ;     HAS 1-BYTE DISPLACEMENT RATHER THAN
     ;     2-BYTE DISPLACEMENT REQUIRED FOR
     ;     NEAR DIRECT JUMPS. ''SHORT'' IS
     ;     WRITTEN BECAUSE ''ENDCASE'' IS A FORWARD
     ;     REFERENCE, WHICH ASSEMBLER ASSUMES IS
     ;     ''NEAR.'' IF ''ENDCASE'' APPEARED PRIOR
     ;     TO THE JUMP, THE ASSEMBLER WOULD
     ;     AUTOMATICALLY DETERMINE IF IT WERE REACHABLE
     ;     WITH A SHORT JUMP.
                    JMP        SHORT ENDCASE

ENDCASE:            ; ALL CASES CONVERGE HERE.

     ; POP CALLER'S REGISTERS HERE.
     ; RESTORE BP & SP, DISCARD PARAMETERS
     ;     AND RETURN TO CALLER.
                    MOV        SP, BP
                    POP        BP
                    RET        6

DO_CASE             ENDP
CODE                ENDS
                    END        ; OF ASSEMBLY
```

Figure 3-40. JMP and CALL Examples (Cont'd.)

Bit Manipulation w/RECORD

Figure 3-41 shows the ASM-86 RECORD facility may be used to manipulate bit data. The example shows how to:

- right-justify a bit field,
- test for a value,
- assign a constant known at assembly time,
- assign a variable,
- set or clear a bit field.

Position-Independent Code

The following considerations apply to position-independent code sequences:

- A label that is referenced by a direct FAR (intersegment) transfer is not moveable.
- A label that is referenced by an indirect transfer (either NEAR or FAR) is moveable so long as the register or memory pointer to the label contains the label's current address.
- A label that is referenced by a SHORT (e.g., conditional jump) or a direct NEAR (intrasegment) transfer is moveable so long as the referencing instruction is moved with the label as a unit. These transfers are self-relative; that is, they require only that the label maintain the same distance from the referencing instruction, and actual addresses are immaterial.
- Data is segment-independent, but not offset-independent. That is, a data item may be moved to a different segment, but it must maintain the same offset from the beginning of the segment. Placing constants in a unit of code also effectively makes the code offset-dependent, and therefore is not recommended.
- A procedure should not be moved while it is active or while any procedure it has called is active.
- A section of code that has been interrupted should not be moved.

The segment that is receiving a section of code must have "room" for the code. If the MOVS (or MOVSB or MOVSW) instruction attempts to auto-increment DI past 64K, it wraps around to 0 and causes the beginning of the segment to be overwritten. If a segment override is needed for the source operand, code similar to the following can be used to properly resume the instruction if it is interrupted:

```
RESUME:REP MOVS                    DESTINATION,ES:SOURCE
; IF CX NOT=0 THEN INTERRUPT HAS OCCURRED
    AND CX,CX                    ; CX=0?
    JNZ RESUME                   ; NO,FINISH EXECUTION
    ; CONTROL COMES HERE WHEN STRING HAS BEEN MOVED.
```

```
DATA            SEGMENT
; DEFINE A WORD ARRAY
XREF            DW 3000 DUP (?)
; EACH ELEMENT OF XREF CONSISTS OF 3 FIELDS:
;       A 2-BIT TYPE CODE,
;       A 1-BIT FLAG,
;       A 13-BIT NUMBER.
; DEFINE A RECORD TO LAY OUT THIS ORGANIZATION.
LINE_REC        RECORD      LINE_TYPE: 2,
&                           VISIBLE: 1,
&                           LINE_NUM: 13
DATA            ENDS

CODE            SEGMENT
                ASSUME CS: CODE,    DS: DATA
; ASSUME SEGMENT REGISTERS ARE SET UP PROPERLY
;     AND THAT SI INDEXES AN ELEMENT OF XREF.

; A RECORD FIELD-NAME USED BY ITSELF RETURNS
;   THE SHIFT COUNT REQUIRED TO RIGHT-JUSTIFY
;   THE FIELD. ISOLATE ''LINE_TYPE'' IN THIS
;   MANNER.
                MOV         AL, XREF [SI]
                MOV         CL, LINE_TYPE
                SHR         AX, CL

; THE ''MASK'' OPERATOR APPLIED TO A RECORD
;   FIELD-NAME RETURNS THE BIT MASK
;   REQUIRED TO ISOLATE THE FIELD WITHIN
;   THE RECORD. CLEAR ALL BITS EXCEPT
;   ''LINE_NUM.''
                MOV         DX, XREF[SI]
                AND         DX, MASK LINE_NUM
; DETERMINE THE VALUE OF THE ''VISIBLE'' FIELD
                TEST        XREF[SI], MASK VISIBLE
                JZ          NOT_VISIBLE
; NO JUMP IF VISIBLE = 1
NOT_VISIBLE:    ; JUMP HERE IF VISIBLE = 0

; ASSIGN A CONSTANT KNOWN AT ASSEMBLY-TIME
;     TO A FIELD, BY FIRST CLEARING THE BITS
;     AND THEN OR'ING IN THE VALUE. IN
;     THIS CASE ''LINE_TYPE'' IS SET TO 2 (10B).
                AND         XREF[SI], NOT MASK LINE_TYPE
                OR          XREF[SI],2 SHL LINE_TYPE
; THE ASSEMBLER DOES THE MASKING AND SHIFTING.
; THE RESULT IS THE SAME AS:
                AND         XREF[SI], 3FFFH
                OR          XREF[SI], 8000H
;   BUT IS MORE READABLE AND LESS SUBJECT
;   TO CLERICAL ERROR.
```

Figure 3-41. RECORD Example

```
; ASSIGN A VARIABLE (THE CONTENT OF AX)
;       TO LINE_TYPE.
                    MOV       CL, LINE_TYPE   ; SHIFT COUNT
                    SHL       AX, CL   ; SHIFT TO ''LINE UP'' BITS
                    AND       XREF[SI], NOT MASK LINE_TYPE   ; CLEAR BITS
                    OR        XREF[SI], AX   ; OR IN NEW VALUE

; NO SHIFT IS REQUIRED TO ASSIGN TO THE
;     RIGHT-MOST FIELD. ASSUMING AX CONTAINS
;     A VALID NUMBER (HIGH 3 BITS ARE 0),
;     ASSIGN AX TO ''LINE_NUM.''
                    AND       XREF[SI], NOT MASK LINE_NUM
                    OR        XREF[SI], AX

; A FIELD MAY BE SET OR CLEARED WITH
;   ONE INSTRUCTION. CLEAR THE ''VISIBLE''
;   FLAG AND THEN SET IT.
                    AND       XREF[SI], NOT MASK VISIBLE
                    OR        XREF[SI], MASK VISIBLE

CODE                ENDS
                    END       ; OF ASSEMBLY
```

Figure 3-41. RECORD Example (Cont'd.)

On the 8086/8088, if the MOVS is interrupted, the CPU "remembers" the segment override but "forgets" the presence of the REP prefix when execution resumes. Testing CX indicates whether the instruction is completed or not. Jumping back to the instruction resumes it where it left off. Note that a segment override cannot be specified with MOVSB or MOVSW.

Dynamic Code Relocation

Figure 3-42 illustrates one approach to moving programs in memory at execution time. A "supervisor" program (which is not moved) keeps a pointer variable that contains the current location (offset and segment base) of a position-independent procedure. The supervisor always calls the procedure through this pointer. The supervisor also has access to the procedure's length in bytes. The procedure is moved with the MOVSB instruction. After the procedure is moved, its pointer is updated with the new location. The ASM-86 WORD PTR operator is written to inform the assembler that one word of the double-word pointer is being updated at a time.

```
MAIN_DATA       SEGMENT
; SET UP POINTERS TO POSITION-INDEPENDENT PROCEDURE
;     AND FREE SPACE.
PIP_PTR         DD          EXAMPLE
FREE_PTR        DD          TARGET_SEG
; SET UP SIZE OF PROCEDURE IN BYTES
PIP_SIZE        DW          EXAMPLE_LEN
MAIN_DATA       ENDS

STACK           SEGMENT
                DW          20 DUP (?)          ; 20 WORDS FOR STACK

STACK_TOP       LABEL       WORD                ; TOS BEGINS HERE
STACK           ENDS

SOURCE_SEG      SEGMENT
; THE POSITION-INDEPENDENT PROCEDURE IS INITIALLY IN THIS SEGMENT.
; OTHER CODE MAY PRECEDE IT, I.E., ITS OFFSET NEED NOT BE ZERO.
ASSUME          CS:SOURCE_SEG
EXAMPLE         PROC        FAR
    ; THIS PROCEDURE READS AN 8-BIT PORT UNTIL
    ; BIT 3 OF THE VALUE READ IS FOUND SET. IT
    ; THEN READS ANOTHER PORT. IF THE VALUE READ
    ; IS GREATER THAN 10H IT WRITES THE VALUE TO
    ; A THIRD PORT AND RETURNS; OTHERWISE IT STARTS
    ; OVER.
STATUS_PORT     EQU         0D0H
PORT_READY      EQU         008H
INPUT_PORT      EQU         0D2H
THRESHOLD       EQU         010H
OUTPUT_PORT     EQU         0D4H
```

Figure 3-42. Dynamic Code Relocation Example

```
CHECK_AGAIN:  IN     AL,STATUS_PORT     ; GET STATUS
              TEST   AL,PORT_READY      ; DATA READY?
              JNE    CHECK_AGAIN        ; NO, TRY AGAIN
              IN     AL,INPUT_PORT      ; YES, GET DATA
              CMP    AL,THRESHOLD       ; > 10H?
              JLE    CHECK_AGAIN        ; NO, TRY AGAIN
              OUT    OUTPUT_PORT,AL     ; YES, WRITE IT

              RET    ; RETURN TO CALLER
; GET PROCEDURE LENGTH
EXAMPLE_LEN   EQU    (OFFSET THIS BYTE)—(OFFSET CHECK_AGAIN)
              ENDP   EXAMPLE  ENDP
SOURCE_SEG    ENDS

TARGET_SEG    SEGMENT
; THE POSITION-INDEPENDENT PROCEDURE
;     IS MOVED TO THIS SEGMENT, WHICH IS
;     INITIALLY "EMPTY."
; IN TYPICAL SYSTEMS, A "FREE SPACE MANAGER" WOULD
;     MAINTAIN A POOL OF AVAILABLE MEMORY SPACE
; FOR ILLUSTRATION PURPOSES, ALLOCATE ENOUGH
;     SPACE TO HOLD IT
              DB     EXAMPLE_LEN DUP (?)
TARGET_SEG    ENDS

MAIN_CODE     SEGMENT
; THIS ROUTINE CALLS THE EXAMPLE PROCEDURE
; AT ITS INITIAL LOCATION, MOVES IT, AND
; CALLS IT AGAIN AT THE NEW LOCATION.

ASSUME        CS:MAIN_CODE,SS:STACK,
&             DS:MAIN_DATA,ES:NOTHING

; INITIALIZE SEGMENT REGISTERS & STACK POINTER.
START:        MOV    AX,MAIN_DATA
              MOV    DS,AX
              MOV    AX,STACK
              MOV    SS,AX
              MOV    SP,OFFSET STACK_TOP

; CALL EXAMPLE AT INITIAL LOCATION.
              CALL   PIP_PTR

; SET UP CX WITH COUNT OF BYTES TO MOV
              MOV    CX,PIP_SIZE
```

Figure 3-42. Dynamic Code Relocation Example (Cont'd.)

```
; SAVE DS, SET UP DS/SI AND ES/DI TO
;     POINT TO THE SOURCE AND DESTINATION
;     ADDRESSES.
                    PUSH        DS
                    LES         DI,FREE__PTR
                    LDS         SI,PIP__PTR
; MOVE THE PROCEDURE.
                    CLD                           ; AUTO INCREMENT
                    REP MOVSB

; RESTORE OLD ADDRESSABILITY.
                    MOV         AX,DS             ; HOLD TEMPORARILY
                    POP         DS
; UPDATE POINTER TO POSITION-INDEPENDENT PROCEDURE
                    MOV         WORD PTR PIP__PTR+2,ES
                    SUB         DI,PIP__SIZE      ; PRODUCES OFFSET
                    MOV         WORD PTR PIP__PTR,DI
; UPDATE POINTER TO FREE SPACE
                    MOV         WORD PTR FREE__PTR+2,AX
                    SUB         SI,PIP__SIZE      ; PRODUCES OFFSET
                    MOV         WORD PTR FREE__PTR,SI

; CALL POSITION-INDEPENDENT PROCEDURE AT
;     NEW LOCATION AND STOP
                    CALL        PIP__PTR
MAIN__CODE          ENDS
                    END         START
```

Figure 3-42. Dynamic Code Relocation Example (Cont'd.)

Memory Mapped I/O

Figure 3-43 shows how memory-mapped I/O can be used to address a group of communication lines as an "array." In the example, indexed addressing is used to poll the array of status ports, one port at a time. Any of the other memory addressing modes may be used in conjunction with memory-mapped I/O devices as well.

In Figure 3-44 a MOVS instruction is used to perform a high-speed transfer to a memory-mapped line printer. Using this technique requires the hardware to be set up as follows. Since the MOVS instruction transfers characters to successive memoryaddresses, the decoding logic must select the line printer if any of these locations is written. One way of accomplishing this is to have the chip select logic decode only the upper 12 lines of the address bus (A19-A8), ignoring the contents of the lower eight lines (A7-A0). When data is written to any address in this 256-byte block, the upper 12 lines will not change, so the printer will be selected.

```
COM_LINES       SEGMENT   AT 800H
; THE FOLLOWING IS A MEMORY MAPPED ''ARRAY''
;       OF EIGHT 8-BIT COMMUNICATIONS CONTROLLERS
;       (E.G., 8251 USARTS). PORTS HAVE ALL-ODD
;       OR ALL-EVEN ADDRESSES (EVERY OTHER BYTE
;       IS SKIPPED) FOR 8086-COMPATIBILITY.

COM_DATA        DB      ?
                DB      ?                       ; SKIP THIS ADDRESS
COM_STATUS      DB      ?
                DB      ?                       ; SKIP THIS ADDRESS
                DB      28      DUP (?)         ; REST OF ''ARRAY''
COM_LINES       ENDS

CODE            SEGMENT
; ASSUME STACK IS SET UP, AS ARE SEGMENT
;       REGISTERS (DS POINTING TO COM_LINES).
;       FOLLOWING CODE POLLS THE LINES.

CHAR_RDY        EQU     00000010B       ; CHARACTER PRESENT
START_POLL:     MOV     CX, 8           ; POLL 8 LINES ZERO
                SUB     SI, SI          ; ARRAY INDEX

POLL_NEXT:      TEST    COM_STATUS [SI], CHAR_RDY
                JE      READ_CHAR ; READ IF PRESENT
                ADD     SI, 4           ; ELSE BUMP TO NEXT LINE
                LOOP    POLL_NEXT ; CONTINUE POLLING UNTIL
                                  ;     ALL 8 HAVE BEEN CHECKED
                JMP     START_POLL; START OVER

READ_CHAR:      MOV     AL,COM_DATA [SI]    ;GET THE DATA
; ETC.
CODE            ENDS
```

Figure 3-43. Memory-Mapped I/O "Array"

```
PRINTER         SEGMENT
; THIS SEGMENT CONTAINS A "STRING" THAT
;     IS ACTUALLY A MEMORY-MAPPED LINE PRINTER.
;     THE SEGMENT (PRINTER) MUST BE ASSIGNED (LOCATED)
;     TO A BLOCK OF THE ADDRESS SPACE SUCH
;     THAT WRITING TO ANY ADDRESS IN THE
;     BLOCK SELECTS THE PRINTER.

PRINT_SELECT    DB 133      DUP (?)             ; "STRING" REPRESENTING PRINTER
                DB 123      DUP (?)             ; REST OF 256-BYTE BLOCK
PRINTER         ENDS

DATA            SEGMENT
PRINT_BUF       DB 133      DUP (?)             ; LINE TO BE PRINTED
PRINT_COUNT     DB 1        ?                   ; LINE LENGTH
; OTHER PROGRAM DATA
DATA            ENDS

CODE            SEGMENT
; ASSUME STACK AND SEGMENT REGISTERS HAVE
;       BEEN SET UP (DS POINTS TO DATA SEGMENT).
;       FOLLOWING CODE TRANSFERS A LINE TO
;       THE PRINTER.

                ASSUME      ES: PRINTER
                MOV         AX, PRINTER         ; PREVENT SEGMENT OVERRIDE
                MOV         ES, AX
                SUB         DI, DI              ; CLEAR SOURCE AND
                SUB         SI, SI              ;    DESTINATION POINTERS
                MOV         CX, PRINT_COUNT
                CLD         ; AUTO-INCREMENT
        REP     MOVS        PRINT_SELECT, PRINT_BUF
                ; ETC.
CODE            ENDS
                END
```

Figure 3-44. Memory-Mapped Block Transfer Example

Breakpoints

Figure 3-45 illustrates how a program may set a breakpoint. In the example, the breakpoint routine puts the processor into single-step mode, but the same general approach could be used for other purposes as well. A program passes the address where the break is to occur to a procedure that saves the byte located at that address and replaces it with an INT 3 (breakpoint) instruction. When the CPU encounters the breakpoint instruction, it calls the type 3 interrupt procedure. In the example, this procedure places the processor into single-step mode starting with the instruction where the breakpoint was placed.

Interrupt Handling

Figure 3-46 is a block diagram of a hypothetical 8086/8088 system that is used to illustrate three different examples of interrupt handling: an external (maskable) interrupt, an external non-maskable interrupt and a software interrupt.

In this hypothetical system, an 8253 Programmable Interval Timer is used to generate a time base. One of the three timers on the 8253 is programmed to repeatedly generate interrupt requests at 50 millisecond intervals. The output from this timer is tied to one of the eight interrupt request lines of an 8259A Programmable Interrupt Controller. The 8259A, in turn, is connected to the INTR line of an 8086.

A power-down circuit is used in the system to illustrate one application of the NMI (non-maskable interrupt) line. If the ac line voltage drops below a certain threshold, the power supply activates ACLO. The power-down circuit then sends a power-fail interrupt (PFI) pulse to the CPU's NMI input. After 5 milliseconds, the power-down circuit activates MPRO (memory protect) to disable reading from and writing to the system's battery-powered RAM. This protects the RAM from fluctuations that may occur when power is actually lost 7.5 milliseconds after the power failure is detected. The system software must save all vital information in the battery-powered RAM segment within 5 milliseconds of the activation of NMI.

When power returns, the power-down circuit activates the system RESET line. Pressing the "cold start" switch also produces a system RESET. The PFS (power fail status) line, which is connected to the low-order bit of port E0, identifies the source of the RESET. If the bit is set, the software executes a "warm start" to restore the information saved by the power-fail routine. If the PFS bit is cleared, the software executes a "cold start" from the beginning of the program. In either case, the software writes a "one" to the low-order bit of port E2. This line is connected to the power-down circuit's PFSR (power failure status reset) signal and is used to enable the battery-powered RAM segment.

A software interrupt is used to update a simple real-time clock. This procedure is written in PL/M-86, while the rest of the system is written in ASM-86 to demonstrate the interrupt handling capability of both languages. The system's main program simply initializes the system following receipt of a RESET and then waits for an interrupt. An example of this interrupt procedure is given in Figure 3-47.

```
INT__PTR__TAB   SEGMENT
; INTERRUPT POINTER TABLE-LOCATE AT 0H
TYPE__0         DD      ?                   ; NOT DEFINED IN EXAMPLE
TYPE__1         DD      SINGLE__STEP
TYPE__2         DD      ?                   ; NOT DEFINED IN EXAMPLE
TYPE__3         DD      BREAKPOINT
INT__PTR__TAB   ENDS

SAVE__SEG       SEGMENT
SAVE__INSTR     DB 1    DUP (?)             ; INSTRUCTION REPLACED
                                            ; BY BREAKPOINT
SAVE__SEG       ENDS

MAIN__CODE      SEGMENT
; ASSUME STACK AND SEGMENT REGISTERS ARE SET UP.

; ENABLE SINGLE-STEPPING WITH INSTRUCTION AT
;    LABEL "NEXT" BY PASSING SEGMENT AND
;    OFFSET OF "NEXT" TO "SET__BREAK" PROCEDURE
                PUSH    CS
                LEA     AX, CS: NEXT
                PUSH    AX
                CALL    FAR SET__BREAK
; ETC.

NEXT:           IN      AL, 0FFFH           ; BREAKPOINT SET HERE
                ; ETC.

MAIN__CODE      ENDS

BREAK           SEGMENT
SET__BREAK      PROC    FAR
; THIS PROCEDURE SAVES AN INSTRUCTION BYTE (WHOSE
;     ADDRESS IS PASSED BY THE CALLER) AND WRITES
;     AN INT 3 (BREAKPOINT) MACHINE INSTRUCTION
:     AT THE TARGET ADDRESS.

TARGET          EQU     DWORD PTR [BP + 6]

; SET UP BP FOR PARM ADDRESSING & SAVE REGISTERS
                PUSH    BP
                MOV     BP, SP
                PUSH    DS
                PUSH    ES
                PUSH    AX
                PUSH    BX
; POINT DS/BX TO THE TARGET INSTRUCTION
                LDS     BX, TARGET
```

Figure 3-45. Breakpoint Example

```
; POINT ES TO THE SAVE AREA
                    MOV         AX, SAVE_SEG
                    MOV         ES, AX
; SWAP THE TARGET INSTRUCTION FOR INT 3 (0CCH)
                    MOV         AL, 0CCH
                    XCHG        AL, DS: [BX]
; SAVE THE TARGET INSTRUCTION
                    MOV         ES: SAVE_INSTR, AL
; RESTORE AND RETURN
                    POP         BX
                    POP         AX
                    POP         ES
                    POP         DS
                    POP         BP
                    RET         4
SET_BREAK           ENDP

BREAKPOINT          PROC        FAR
; THE CPU WILL ACTIVATE THIS PROCEDURE WHEN IT
;    EXECUTES THE INT 3 INSTRUCTION SET BY THE
;    SET_BREAK PROCEDURE. THIS PROCEDURE
;    RESTORES THE SAVED INSTRUCTION BYTE TO ITS
;    ORIGINAL LOCATION AND BACKS UP THE
;    INSTRUCTION POINTER IMAGE ON THE STACK
;    SO THAT EXECUTION WILL RESUME WITH
;    THE RESTORED INSTRUCTION. IT THEN SETS
;    TF (THE TRAP FLAG) IN THE FLAG-IMAGE
;    ON THE STACK. THIS PUTS THE PROCESSOR
;    IN SINGLE-STEP MODE WHEN EXECUTION
;    RESUMES.
    FLAG_IMAGE          EQU         WORD PTR [BP + 6]
    IP_IMAGE            EQU         WORD PTR [BP + 2]
NEXT_INSTR          EQU         DWORD PTR [BP + 2]
; SET UP BP TO ADDRESS STACK AND SAVE REGISTERS
                    PUSH        BP
                    MOV         BP, SP
                    PUSH        DS
                    PUSH        ES
                    PUSH        AX
                    PUSH        BX
; POINT ES AT THE SAVE AREA
                    MOV         AX, SAVE_SEG
                    MOV         ES, AX
; GET THE SAVED BYTE
                    MOV         AL, ES: SAVE_INSTR

; GET THE ADDRESS OF THE TARGET + 1
;    (INSTRUCTION FOLLOWING THE BREAKPOINT)
                    LDS         BX, NEXT_INSTR
```

Figure 3-45. Breakpoint Example (Cont'd.)

```
; BACK UP IP-IMAGE (IN BX) AND REPLACE ON STACK
                  DEC          BX
                  MOV          IP_IMAGE, BX

; RESTORE THE SAVED INSTRUCTION
                  MOV          DS: [BX], AL
; SET TF ON STACK
                  AND          FLAG_IMAGE, 0100H
; RESTORE EVERYTHING AND EXIT
                  POP          BX
                  POP          AX
                  POP          ES
                  POP          DS
                  POP          BP
                  IRET
BREAKPOINT        ENDP

SINGLE   STEP     PROC         FAR
; ONCE SINGLE-STEP MODE HAS BEEN ENTERED,
;     THE CPU "TRAPS" TO THIS PROCEDURE
;     AFTER EVERY INSTRUCTION THAT IS NOT IN
;     AN INTERRUPT PROCEDURE. IN THE CASE
;     OF THIS EXAMPLE, THIS PROCEDURE WILL
;     BE EXECUTED IMMEDIATELY FOLLOWING THE
;     "IN AL, 0FFFH" INSTRUCTION (WHERE THE
;     BREAKPOINT WAS SET) AND AFTER EVERY
;     SUBSEQUENT INSTRUCTION. THE PROCEDURE
;     COULD "TURN ITSELF OFF" BY CLEARING
;     TF ON THE STACK.
; SINGLE-STEP CODE GOES HERE.
; SINGLE_STEP    ENDP

BREAK             ENDS

                  END          ;
```

Figure 3-45. Breakpoint Example (Cont'd.)

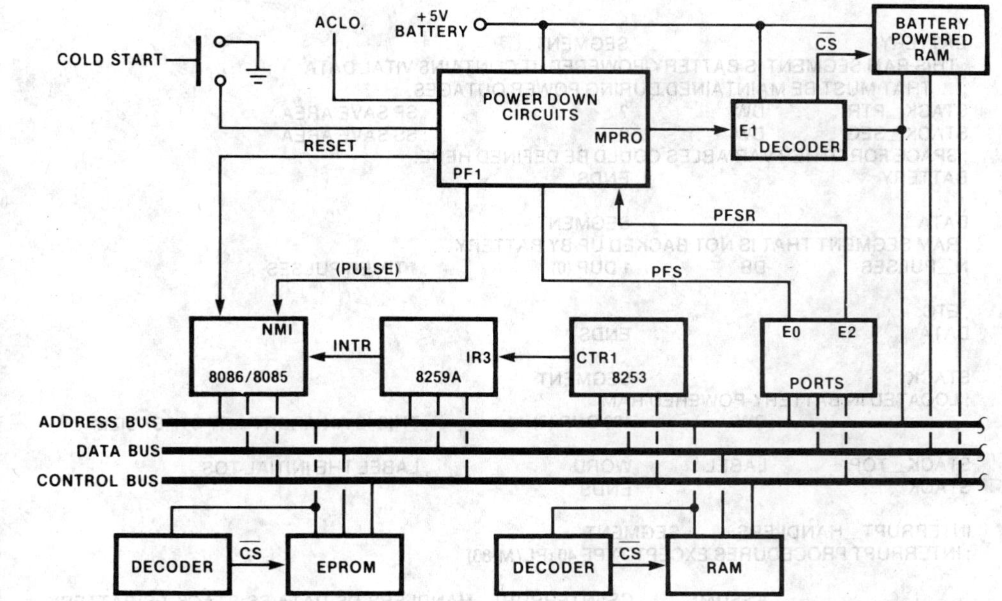

240487-001

Figure 3-46. Interrupt Example Block Diagram

```
INT_POINTERS                     SEGMENT
; INTERRUPT POINTER TABLE, LOCATE AT 0H, ROM-BASED
TYPE_0          DD               ?                ; DIVIDE-ERROR NOT SUPPLIED IN EXAMPLE.
TYPE_1          DD               ?                ; SINGLE-STEP NOT SUPPLIED IN EXAMPLE.
TYPE_2          DD               POWER_FAIL       ; NON-MASKABLE INTERRUPT
TYPE_3          DD               ?                ; BREAKPOINT NOT SUPPLIED IN EXAMPLE.
TYPE_4          DD               ?                ; OVERFLOW NOT SUPPLIED IN EXAMPLE.
; SKIP RESERVED PART OF EXAMPLE
                ORG              32*4
TYPE_32         DD               ?                ; 8259A IR0 - AVAILABLE
TYPE_33         DD               ?                ; 8259A IR1 - AVAILABLE
TYPE_34         DD               ?                ; 8259A IR2 - AVAILABLE
TYPE_35         DD               TIMER_PULSE      ; 8259A IR3
TYPE_36         DD               ?                ; 8259A IR4 - AVAILABLE
TYPE_37         DD               ?                ; 8259A IR5 - AVAILABLE
TYPE_38         DD               ?                ; 8259A IR6 - AVAILABLE
TYPE_39         DD               ?                ; 8259A IR7 - AVAILABLE
;
; POINTER FOR TYPE 40 SUPPLIED BY PL/M-86 COMPILER
;
INT_POINTERS                     ENDS
```

240487-001

Figure 3-47. 8086/8088 Interrupt Procedures Example

```
BATTERY                               SEGMENT
; THIS RAM SEGMENT IS BATTERY-POWERED. IT CONTAINS VITAL DATA
;     THAT MUST BE MAINTAINED DURING POWER OUTAGES.
STACK_PTR           DW                ?                    ; SP SAVE AREA
STACK_SEG           DW                ?                    ; SS SAVE AREA
; SPACE FOR OTHER VARIABLES COULD BE DEFINED HERE.
BATTERY                               ENDS

DATA                                  SEGMENT
; RAM SEGMENT THAT IS NOT BACKED UP BY BATTERY
N_PULSES            DB                1 DUP (0)            ; # TIMER PULSES

; ETC.
DATA                                  ENDS

STACK                                 SEGMENT
; LOCATED IN BATTERY-POWERED RAM
                    DW                100 DUP (?)          ; THIS IS AN ARBITRARY STACKSIZE

STACK_TOP           LABEL             WORD                 ; LABEL THE INITIAL TOS
STACK                                 ENDS

INTERRUPT_HANDLERS            SEGMENT
; INTERRUPT PROCEDURES EXCEPT TYPE 40 (PL/M-86)

                    ASSUME:     CS:INTERRUPT_HANDLERS,DS:DATA,SS:STACK,ES:BATTERY

POWER_FAIL                            PROC                 ; TYPE 2 INTERRUPT
; POWER FAIL DETECT CIRCUIT ACTIVATES NMI LINE ON CPU IF POWER IS
;     ABOUT TO BE LOST. THIS PROCEDURE SAVES THE PROCESSOR STATE IN
;     RAM (ASSUMED TO BE POWERED BY AN AUXILIARY SOURCE) SO THAT IT
;     CAN BE RESTORED BY A WARM START ROUTINE IF POWER RETURNS

; IP, CS, AND FLAGS ARE ALREADY ON THE STACK.
;    SAVE THE OTHER REGISTERS.
                    PUSH              AX
                    PUSH              BX
                    PUSH              CX
                    PUSH              DX
                    PUSH              SI
                    PUSH              DI
                    PUSH              BP
                    PUSH              DS
                    PUSH              ES

; CRITICAL MEMORY VARIABLES COULD ALSO BE SAVED ON THE STACK AT THIS
;     POINT. ALTERNATIVELY, THEY COULD BE DEFINED IN THE "BATTERY"
;     SEGMENT, WHERE THEY WILL AUTOMATICALLY BE PROTECTED IF MAIN POWER
;     IS LOST.

; SAVE SP AND SS IN FIXED LOCATIONS THAT ARE KNOWN BY WARM START ROUTINE.
                    MOV               AX,BATTERY
                    MOV               ES,AX
                    MOV               ES:STACK_PTR,SP
                    MOV               ES:STACK_SEG,SS

; STOP GRACEFULLY
                    HLT
POWER_FAIL                            ENDP
```

Figure 3-47. 8086/8088 Interrupt Procedures Example (Cont'd.)

```
TIMER_PULSE             PROC            ; TYPE 35 INTERRUPT
; THIS PROCEDURE HANDLES THE 50MS INTERRUPTS GENERATED BY THE 8253.
;     IT COUNTS THE INTERRUPTS AND ACTIVATES THE TYPE 40 INTERRUPT
;     PROCEDURE ONCE PER SECOND.
;
; DS IS ASSUMED TO BE POINTING TO THE DATA SEGMENT
;
; THE 8253 IS RUNNING FREE, AND AUTOMATICALLY LOWERS ITS INTERRUPT
;     REQUEST. IF A DEVICE REQUIRED ACKNOWLEDGEMENT, THE CODE MIGHT GO HERE.
;
; NOW PERFORM PROCESSING THAT MUST NOT BE INTERRUPTED (EXCEPT FOR NMI).
                        INC     N_PULSES
; ENABLE HIGHER-PRIORITY INTERRUPTS AND DO LESS CRITICAL PROCESSING
                        STI
                        CMP     N_PULSES,200    ; 1 SECOND PASSED?
                        JBE     DONE            ; NO, GO ON.
                        MOV     N_PULSES,0      ; YES, RESET COUNT.
                        INT     40              ; UPDATE CLOCK
; SEND NON-SPECIFIC END-OF-INTERRUPT COMMAND TO 8259A, ENABLING EQUAL
;     OR LOWER PRIORITY INTERRUPTS.
DONE:                   MOV     AL,020H         ; EOI COMMAND
                        OUT     0C0H,AL         ; 8259A PORT
                        IRET
TIMER_PULSE                     ENDP

INTERRUPT_HANDLERS              ENDS

CODE                    SEGMENT
; THIS SEGMENT WOULD NORMALLY RESIDE IN ROM.

                        ASSUME  CS:CODE,DS:DATA,SS:STACK,ES:NOTHING
INIT                    PROC    NEAR
; THIS PROCEDURE IS CALLED FOR BOTH WARM AND COLD STARTS TO INITIALIZE
;     THE 8253 AND THE 8259A. THIS ROUTINE DOES NOT USE STACK, DATA, OR
;     EXTRA SEGMENTS, AS THEY ARE NOT SET PREDICTABLY DURING A WARM START.
;     INTERRUPTS ARE DISABLED BY VIRTUE OF THE SYSTEM RESET.

; INITIALIZE 8253 COUNTER 1 - OTHER COUNTERS NOT USED.
; CLK INPUT TO COUNTER IS ASSUMED TO BE 1.23 MHZ.

LO50MS                  EQU     000H            ; COUNT VALUE IS
HI50MS                  EQU     0F0H            ;     61440 DECIMAL.
CONTROL                 EQU     0D6H            ; CONTROL PORT ADDRESS
COUNT_1                 EQU     0D2H            ; COUNTER 1 ADDRESS
MODE2                   EQU     01110100B       ; MODE 2, BINARY

                        MOV     DX,CONTROL      ; LOAD CONTROL BYTE
                        MOV     AL,MODE2
                        OUT     DX,AL
                        MOV     DX,COUNT_1      ; LOAD 50MS DOWNCOUNT
                        MOV     AL,LO50MS
                        OUT     DX,AL
                        MOV     AL,HI50MS
                        OUT     DX,AL
                        ; COUNTER NOW RUNNING, INTERRUPTS STILL DISABLED.
```

Figure 3-47. 8086/8088 Interrupt Procedures Example (Cont'd.)

```
; INITIALIZE 8259A TO: SINGLE INTERRUPT CONTROLLER, EDGE-TRIGGERED,
;    INTERRUPT TYPES 32-40 (DECIMAL) TO BE SENT TO CPU FOR INTERRUPT
;    REQUESTS 0-7 RESPECTIVELY, 8086 MODE, NON-AUTOMATIC END-OF-INTERRUPT.
;    MASK OFF UNUSED INTERRUPT REQUEST LINES.

ICW1            EQU      00010011B         ; EDGE-TRIGGERED, SINGLE 8259A, ICW4 REQUIRED.
ICW2            EQU      00100000B         ; TYPE 20H, 32 - 40D
ICW4            EQU      00000001B         ; 8086 MODE, NORMAL EOI
OCW1            EQU      11110111B         ; MASK ALL BUT IR3
PORT_A          EQU      0C0H              ; ICW1 WRITTEN HERE
PORT_B          EQU      0C2H              ; OTHER ICW'S WRITTEN HERE

                MOV      DX,PORT_A         ; WRITE 1ST ICW
                MOV      AL,ICW1
                OUT      DX,AL
                MOV      DX,PORT_B         ; WRITE 2ND ICW
                MOV      AL,ICW2
                OUT      DX,AL
                MOV      AL,ICW4           ; WRITE 4TH ICW
                OUT      DX,AL
                MOV      AL,0CW1           ; MASK UNUSED IR'S
                OUT      DX,AL
; INITIALIZATION COMPLETE, INTERRUPTS STILL DISABLED
                RET
INIT            ENDP

USER_PGM:
; "REAL" CODE WOULD GO HERE. THE EXAMPLE EXECUTES AN ENDLESS LOOP
;    UNTIL AN INTERRUPT OCCURS.
                JMP      USER_PGM

; EXECUTION STARTS HERE WHEN CPU IS RESET.
POWER_FAIL_STATUS        EQU    0E0H       ; PORT ADDRESS
ENABLE_RAM               EQU    0E2H       ; PORT ADDRESS

; ENABLE BATTERY-POWERED RAM SEGMENT
START:          MOV      AL,001H
                OUT      ENABLE_RAM,AL

; DETERMINE WARM OR COLD START
                IN       AL,POWER_FAIL_STATUS
                RCR      AL,1              ; ISOLATE LOW BIT
                JC       WARM_START

COLD_START:
; INITIALIZE SEGMENT REGISTERS AND STACK POINTER.
                ASSUME   CS:CODE,DS:DATA,SS:STACK,ES:NOTHING
                ; RESET TAKES CARE OF CS AND IP.
                MOV      AX,DATA
                MOV      DS,AX
                MOV      AX,STACK
                MOV      SS,AX
                MOV      SP,OFFSET STACK_TOP

; INITIALIZE 8253 AND 8259A.
                CALL     INIT

; ENABLE INTERRUPTS
                STI
```

Figure 3-47. 8086/8088 Interrupt Procedures Example (Cont'd.)

```
; START MAIN PROCESSING
                    JMP         USER_PGM
WARM_START:
; INITIALIZE 8253 AND 8259A.
                    CALL        INIT
; RESTORE SYSTEM TO STATE AT THE TIME POWER FAILED
                    ; MAKE BATTERY SEGMENT ADDRESSABLE
                          MOV     AX,BATTERY
                          MOV     DX,AX
                    ; VARIABLES SAVED IN THE ''BATTERY'' SEGMENT WOULD BE MOVED
                    ;   BACK TO UNPROTECTED RAM NOW. SEGMENT REGISTERS AND
                    ;   ''ASSUME'' DIRECTIVES WOULD HAVE TO BE WRITTEN TO GAIN
                    ;   ADDRESSABILITY.

                    ; RESTORE THE OLD STACK
                          MOV     SS,DS:STACK_SEG
                          MOV     SP,DS:STACK_PTR
                    ; RESTORE THE OTHER REGISTERS
                          POP     ES
                          POP     DS
                          POP     BP
                          POP     DI
                          POP     SI
                          POP     DX
                          POP     CX
                          POP     BX
                          POP     AX
                    ; RESUME THE ROUTINE THAT WAS EXECUTING WHEN NMI WAS ACTIVATED.
                    ;   I.E., POP CS, IP, & FLAGS, EFFECTIVELY ''RETURNING'' FROM THE
                    ;   NMI PROCEDURE.
                          IRET
CODE                ENDS

                    ; TERMINATE ASSEMBLY AND MARK BEGINNING OF THE PROGRAM.
                                       END        START

  TYPE$40:   DO;
    DECLARE (HOUR, MIN, SEC) BYTE PUBLIC;
    UPDATE$TOD: PROCEDURE INTERRUPT 40;
      /*THE PROCESSOR ACTIVATES THIS PROCEDURE
       *TO HANDLE THE SOFTWARE INTERRUPT
       *GENERATED EVERY SECOND BY THE TYPE 35
       *EXTERNAL INTERRUPT PROCEDURE. THIS
       *PROCEDURE UPDATES A REAL-TIME CLOCK.
       *IT DOES NOT PRETEND TO BE ''REALISTIC''
       *AS THERE IS NO WAY TO SET THE CLOCK.*/

    SEC = SEC + 1;
    IF SEC = 60 THEN DO;
      SEC = 0;
      MIN = MIN + 1;
      IF MIN = 60 THEN DO;
        MIN = 0;
        HOUR = HOUR + 1;
        IF HOUR = 24 THEN DO;
          HOUR = 0;
          END;
        END;
      END;
    END UPDATE$TOD;
  END;
```

Figure 3-47. 8086/8088 Interrupt Procedures Example (Cont'd.)

String Operations

Figure 3-48 illustrates typical use of string instructions and repeat prefixes. The XLAT instruction also is demonstrated. The first example simply moves 80 words of a string, as might be done in a sort. Next a string is scanned from right to left (the index register is auto-decremented) to find the last period (".") in the string. Finally a byte string of EBCDIC characters is translated to ASCII. The translation is stopped at the end of the string or when a carraige return character is encountered, whichever occurs first. This is an example of using the string primitives in combination with other instructions to build up more complex string processing operations.

```
ALPHA           SEGMENT
; THIS IS THE DATA THE STRING INSTRUCTIONS WILL USE
OUTPUT          DW 100      DUP (?)
INPUT           DW 100      DUP (?)
NAME_1          DB 'JONES, JONA'
NAME_2          DB 'JONES, JOHN'
SENTENCE        DB 80       DUP (?)
EBCDIC_CHARS    DB 80       DUP (?)
ASCII_CHARS     DB 80       DUP (?)
CONV_TAB        DB 64       DUP(0H)                   ; EBCDIC TO ASCII
   ; ASCII NULLS ARE SUBSTITUTED FOR "UNPRINTABLE" CHARS
                DB 1        20H
                DB 9        DUP (0H)
                DB 7        '¢', '.', '<', '(', '+', 0H, '&'
                DB 9        DUP (0H)
                DB 8        '!', '$', '*', ')', ';', ' ', '-', '/'
                DB 8        DUP (0H)
                DB 6        ',', ',', '%', '_', '>', '?'
                DB 9        DUP (0H)
                DB 17       ' ', ':', '#', '@', ''', '=', '"',
                            0H, 'a', 'b', 'c', 'd', 'e', 'f', 'g', 'h', 'i'
                DB 7        DUP (0H)
                DB 9        'j', 'k', 'l', 'm', 'n', 'o', 'p', 'q', 'r'
                DB 7        DUP (0H)
                DB 9        '≃', 's', 't', 'u', 'v', 'w', 'x', 'y', 'z'
                DB 22       DUP (0H)
                DB 10       ' ', 'A', 'B', 'C', 'D', 'E', 'F', 'G', 'H', 'I'
                DB 6        DUP (0H)
                DB 10       ' ', 'J', 'K', 'L', 'M', 'N', 'O', 'P', 'Q', 'R'
                DB 6        DUP (0H)
                DB 10       ' ', 0H, 'S', 'T', 'U', 'V', 'W', 'X', 'Y', 'Z'
                DB 6        DUP (0H)
                DB 10       '0', '1', '2', '3', '4', '5', '6', '7', '8', '9'
                DB 6        DUP (0H)

ALPHA           ENDS
```

Figure 3-48. String Examples

```
STACK           SEGMENT
                DW 100      DUP (?)         ; THIS IS AN ARBITRARY STACK SIZE
                                            ; FOR ILLUSTRATION ONLY.
STACK_BASE      LABEL       WORD            ; INITIAL TOS
STACK           ENDS

CODE            SEGMENT
BEGIN:          ; SET UP SEGMENT REGISTERS. NOTICE THAT
                ; ES & DS POINT TO THE SAME SEGMENT, MEANING
                ; THAT THE CURRENT EXTRA & DATA
                ; SEGMENTS FULLY OVERLAP. THIS ALLOWS
                ; ANY STRING IN "ALPHA" TO BE USED
                ; AS A SOURCE OR A DESTINATION.
                ASSUME CS: CODE, SS: STACK,
&                           DS: ALPHA, ES: ALPHA
                MOV         AX, STACK
                MOV         SS, AX
                MOV         SP, OFFSET STACK_BASE ; INITIAL TOS
                MOV         AX, ALPHA
                MOV         DS, AX
                MOV         ES, AX
; MOVE THE FIRST 80 WORDS OF "INPUT" TO
;     THE LAST 80 WORDS OF "OUTPUT".
                LEA         SI, INPUT           ; INITIALIZE
                LEA         DI, OUTPUT + 20     ; INDEX REGISTERS
                MOV         CX, 80              ; REPETITION COUNT
                CLD                             ; AUTO-INCREMENT
        REP     MOVS        OUTPUT, INPUT
; FIND THE ALPHABETICALLY LOWER OF 2 NAMES.
                MOV         SI, OFFSET NAME_1   ; ALTERNATIVE
                MOV         DI, OFFSET NAME_2   ; TO LEA
                MOV         CX, SIZE NAME_2     ; CHAR. COUNT
                CLD                             ; AUTO-INCREMENT
        REPE    CMPS        NAME_2, NAME_1      ; "WHILE EQUAL"
                JB          NAME_2_LOW
NAME_1_LOW:                 ; NOT IN THIS EXAMPLE
NAME_2_LOW:                 ; CONTROL COMES HERE IN THIS EXAMPLE.
                            ; DI POINTS TO BYTE ('H') THAT
                            ; COMPARED UNEQUAL.
```

Figure 3-48. String Examples (Cont'd.)

```
ALPHA              SEGMENT
; THIS IS THE DATA THE STRING INSTRUCTIONS WILL USE
OUTPUT             DW 100       DUP (?)
INPUT              DW 100       DUP (?)
NAME_1             DB 'JONES, JONA'
NAME_2             DB 'JONES, JOHN'
SENTENCE           DB 80        DUP (?)
EBCDIC_CHARS       DB 80        DUP (?)
ASCII_CHARS        DB 80        DUP (?)
CONV_TAB           DB 64        DUP(0H)                  ; EBCDIC TO ASCII

     ; ASCII NULLS ARE SUBSTITUTED FOR ''UNPRINTABLE'' CHARS
                   DB 1         20H
                   DB 9         DUP (0H)
                   DB 7         '¢', '.', '<', '(', '+', 0H, '&'
                   DB 9         DUP (0H)
                   DB 8         '!', '$', '*', ')', ';', ' ', '–', '/'
                   DB 8         DUP (0H)
                   DB 6         ' ', ',', '%', '_', '>', '?'
                   DB 9         DUP (0H)
                   DB 17        ' ', ':', '#', '@', ''', '=', '"',
                                0H, 'a', 'b', 'c', 'd', 'e', 'f', 'g', 'h', 'i'
                   DB 7         DUP (0H)
                   DB 9         'j', 'k', 'l', 'm', 'n', 'o', 'p', 'q', 'r'
                   DB 7         DUP (0H)
                   DB 9         '≃', 's', 't', 'u', 'v', 'w', 'x', 'y', 'z'
                   DB 22        DUP (0H)
                   DB 10        ' ', 'A', 'B', 'C', 'D', 'E', 'F', 'G', 'H', 'I'
                   DB 6         DUP (0H)
                   DB 10        ' ', 'J', 'K', 'L', 'M', 'N', 'O', 'P', 'Q', 'R'
                   DB 6         DUP (0H)
                   DB 10        ' ', 0H, 'S', 'T', 'U', 'V', 'W', 'X', 'Y', 'Z'
                   DB 6         DUP (0H)
                   DB 10        '0', '1', '2', '3', '4', '5', '6', '7', '8', '9'
                   DB 6         DUP (0H)

ALPHA              ENDS
```

Figure 3-48. String Examples (Cont'd.)

8086/8088 Hardware Design Overview 4

CHAPTER 4
8086/8088 HARDWARE DESIGN OVERVIEW

INTRODUCTION

This chapter discusses the hardware design of the 8086/8088 on the functional level. Electrical characteristics and other hardware references are discussed in Chapter 6.

This chapter includes the following topics:

- Multiprocessing Features
- Bus Organization
- Processor Control
- Interfacing with Processor Extensions

MULTIPROCESSING FEATURES

The 8086 architecture supports multiprocessor systems based on the concept of a shared system bus (see Figure 4-1). All CPU's in the system communicate with each other and share resources using the system bus. The bus may be either the Intel® MULTIBUS®

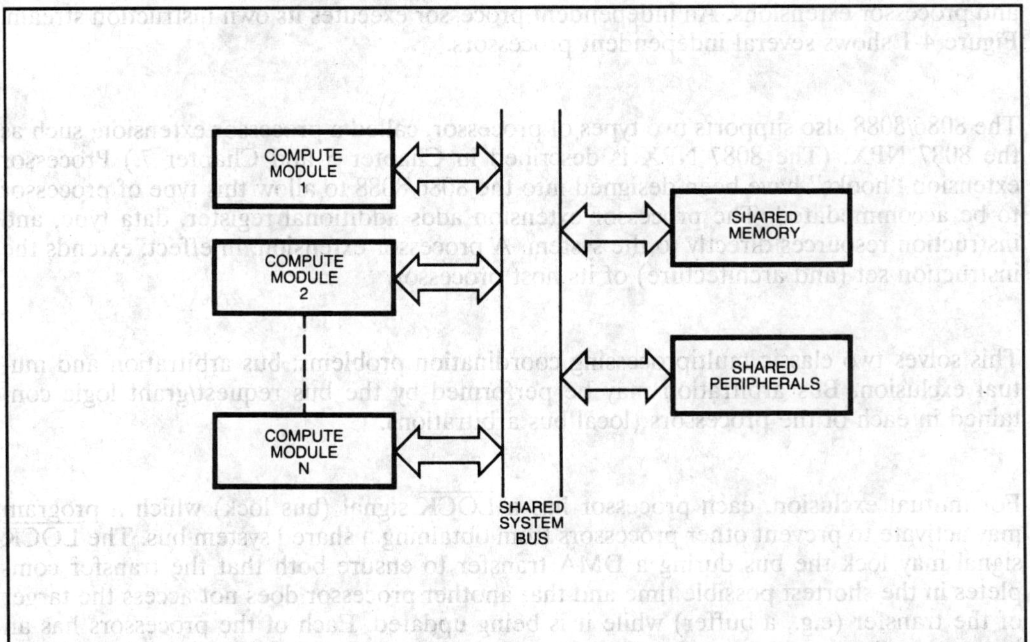

Figure 4-1. Multiprocessing System

system bus or an extension of the system bus. Arbitration logic consists of the major addition required to the demultiplexed system bus to control access to the system bus. As each CPU asynchronously requests access to the shared bus, the arbitration logic resolves priorities and grants bus access to the highest priority CPU. Having gained access to the bus, the CPU completes its transfer and will either relinquish the bus or wait to be forced to relinquish the bus. For discussion on MULTIBUS arbitration techniques, refer to Application Note AP-28A, "Intel MULTIBUS Interfacing."

In general, using multiple processors offers several significant advantages over the centralized approach that relies on a single CPU and extremely fast memory:

1. System tasks may be allocated to special-purpose processors whose designs are optimized to perform specific (or classes of) tasks simply and efficiently;

2. Very high levels of performance can be attained when processors can execute simultaneously (parallel/distributed processing);

3. Partitioning of the system promotes parallel development of subsystems, breaks the application into smaller, more manageable tasks, and helps isolate the effects of system modifications.

The 8086/8088 architecture supports two types of processors: independent processors and processor extensions. An independent processor executes its own instruction stream. Figure 4-1 shows several independent processors.

The 8086/8088 also supports two types of processor, called a processor extension, such as the 8087 NPX. (The 8087 NPX is described in Chapter 5 and Chapter 7.) Processor extension "hooks" have been designed into the 8086/8088 to allow this type of processor to be accommodated. The processor extension adds additional register, data type, and instruction resources directly to the system. A processor extension, in effect, extends the instruction set (and architecture) of its host processor.

This solves two classic multiprocessing coordination problems: bus arbitration and mutual exclusion. Bus arbitration may be performed by the bus request/grant logic contained in each of the processors (local bus arbitration).

For mutual exclusion, each processor has a $\overline{\text{LOCK}}$ signal (bus lock) which a program may activate to prevent other processors from obtaining a shared system bus. The $\overline{\text{LOCK}}$ signal may lock the bus during a DMA transfer to ensure both that the transfer completes in the shortest possible time and that another processor does not access the target of the transfer (e.g., a buffer) while it is being updated. Each of the processors has an instruction that examines and updates a memory byte with the bus locked. This instruction can be used to implement a semaphore mechanism for controlling the access of multiple processors to shared resources.

Bus Organization

The 8086/8088 bus structure can be divided into a local or Resident Bus, and a system bus. The major distinction between the two is that the local or Resident Bus has one master, while the system bus can have several masters (multi-master system bus).

LOCAL OR RESIDENT BUS

The local bus is optimized for use by the 8086/8088 CPUs. Since standard memory and I/O components are not attached to the local bus, information can be multiplexed and encoded to make efficient use of processor pins. This allows several pins to be dedicated to coordinating the activity of multiple processors sharing the local bus. Both independent processors and processor extensions may share a local bus; on-chip arbitration logic determines which processor drives the bus. Because the processors on the local bus share the same bus interface components, the local configuration of multiple processors provides a compact and inexpensive multiprocessing system.

SYSTEM BUS

A system bus carries several signals designed to meet the needs of memory and I/O devices:

- Address bus
- Data bus
- Control lines
- Interrupt lines

A group of bus interface components transforms the signals of a local bus into a system bus. The number of bus interface components required to generate a system bus depends on the size and complexity of the system. Three main variables determine the configuration of a bus interface group: address space size, data bus width and arbitration needs.

The 8086/8088 system bus can easily be made compatible with the MULTIBUS system. MULTIBUS is a general-purpose multiprocessing bus designed by Intel. The MULTIBUS has been proposed for adoption by IEEE as the IEEE 796 standard bus. It is the standard design used in Intel's iSBC® single-board microcomputer products. This compatibility gives system designers access to a wide variety of computer, memory, communication and other modules that may be incorporated into products. Many other manufacturers offer products that are compatible with the MULTIBUS architecture as well. The MULTIBUS is described in more detail later in this chapter.

Bus Lock

When configured in maximum mode, the 8086 and 8088 provide the $\overline{\text{LOCK}}$ (bus lock) signal. The BIU activates $\overline{\text{LOCK}}$ when the EU executes the one-byte LOCK prefix instruction. The $\overline{\text{LOCK}}$ signal remains active throughout execution of the instruction that follows the LOCK prefix. Interrupts are *not* affected by the LOCK prefix. If another processor requests use of the bus (via the request/grant lines, which are discussed later in this chapter), the CPU records the request, but does not honor it until execution of the locked instruction has been completed.

Note that the $\overline{\text{LOCK}}$ signal remains active for the duration of a *single* instruction. If two consecutive instructions are each preceded by a LOCK prefix, there will still be an unlocked period between these instructions. In the case of a locked repeated string instruction, $\overline{\text{LOCK}}$ does remain active for the duration of the block operation.

When the 8086 or 8088 is configured in minimum mode, the $\overline{\text{LOCK}}$ signal is not available. The LOCK prefix can be used, however, to delay the generation of a HOLDA response to a HOLD request until execution of the locked instruction is completed.

$\overline{\text{LOCK}}$ may be used in multiprocessing systems to coordinate access to a common resource, such as a buffer or a pointer. If access to the resources is not controlled, one processor can read an erroneous value from the resource when another processor is updating it (see Figure 4-2).

Access can be controlled (see Figure 4-3) by using the LOCK prefix in conjunction with the XCHG (exchange register with memory) instruction. The basis for controlling access to a given resource is a semaphore, a software-settable flag or switch that indicates whether the resource is "available" (semaphore = 0) or "busy" (semaphore = 1). Processors that share the bus agree by convention not to use the resource unless the semaphore indicates that it is available. They likewise agree to set the semaphore when they are using the resource and to clear it when they are finished.

The XCHG instruction can obtain the current value of the semaphore and set it to "busy" in a single instruction. The instruction, however, requires two bus cycles to swap 8-bit values. It is possible for another processor to obtain the bus between these two cycles and to gain access to the partially-updated semaphore. This can be prevented by preceding the XCHG instruction with a LOCK prefix, as illustrated in Figure 4-4. The bus lock establishes control over access to the semaphore and thus to the shared resource.

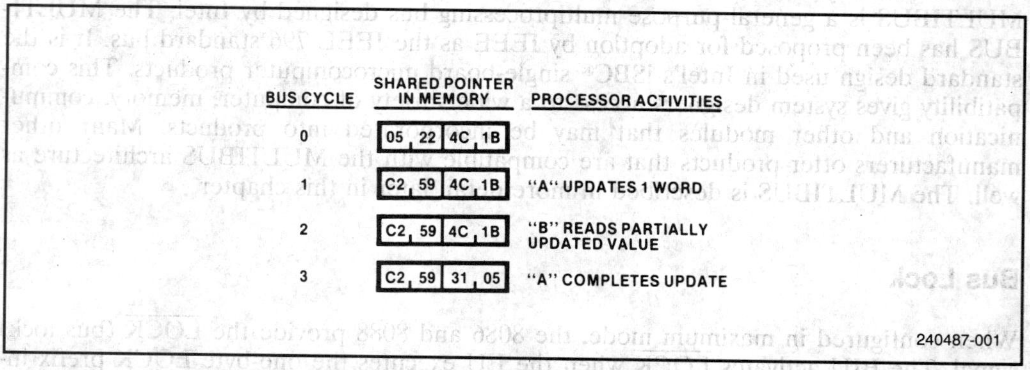

Figure 4-2. Uncontrolled Access to Shared Resource

BUS CYCLE	SEMAPHORE	SHARED POINTER IN MEMORY	PROCESSOR ACTIVITIES
0	0	05, 22 | 4C, 1B	
1	1	05, 22 | 4C, 1B	"A" OBTAINS EXCLUSIVE USE
2	1	C2, 59 | 4C, 1B	"A" UPDATES 1 WORD
3	1	C2, 59 | 4C, 1B	"B" TESTS SEMAPHORE AND WAITS
4	1	C2, 59 | 31, 05	"A" COMPLETES UPDATE
5	1	C2, 59 | 31, 05	"B" TESTS SEMAPHORE AND WAITS
6	0	C2, 59 | 31, 05	"A" RELEASES RESOURCE
7	1	C2, 59 | 31, 05	"B" OBTAINS EXCLUSIVE USE
8	1	C2, 59 | 31, 05	"B" READS UPDATED VALUE
9	0	C2, 59 | 31, 05	"B" RELEASES RESOURCE

240487-001

Figure 4-3. Controlled Access to Shared Resource

WAIT and $\overline{\text{TEST}}$

The 8086 and 8088 (in either maximum or minimum mode) can be synchronized to an external event with the WAIT (wait for TEST) instruction and the TEST input signal. When the EU executes a WAIT instruction, the result depends on the state of the $\overline{\text{TEST}}$ input line. If $\overline{\text{TEST}}$ is inactive, the processor enters an idle state and repeatedly retests the $\overline{\text{TEST}}$ line at five-clock intervals. If $\overline{\text{TEST}}$ is active, execution continues with the instruction following the WAIT.

Escape

The ESC (escape) instruction provides a way for another processor to obtain an instruction and/or a memory operand from an 8086/8088 program. When used in conjunction with WAIT and TEST, ESC can initiate a "subroutine" that executes concurrently in another processor (see Figure 4-5). An example of the use of the WAIT, TEST and ESC instructions is the application of an 8087 NPX processor extension.

Six bits in the ESC instruction may be specified by the programmer when the instruction is written. By monitoring the bus and control lines, another processor (e.g., an 8087 NPX) can capture the ESC instruction when it is fetched by the BIU. The six bits may then direct the external processor to perform some predefined activity.

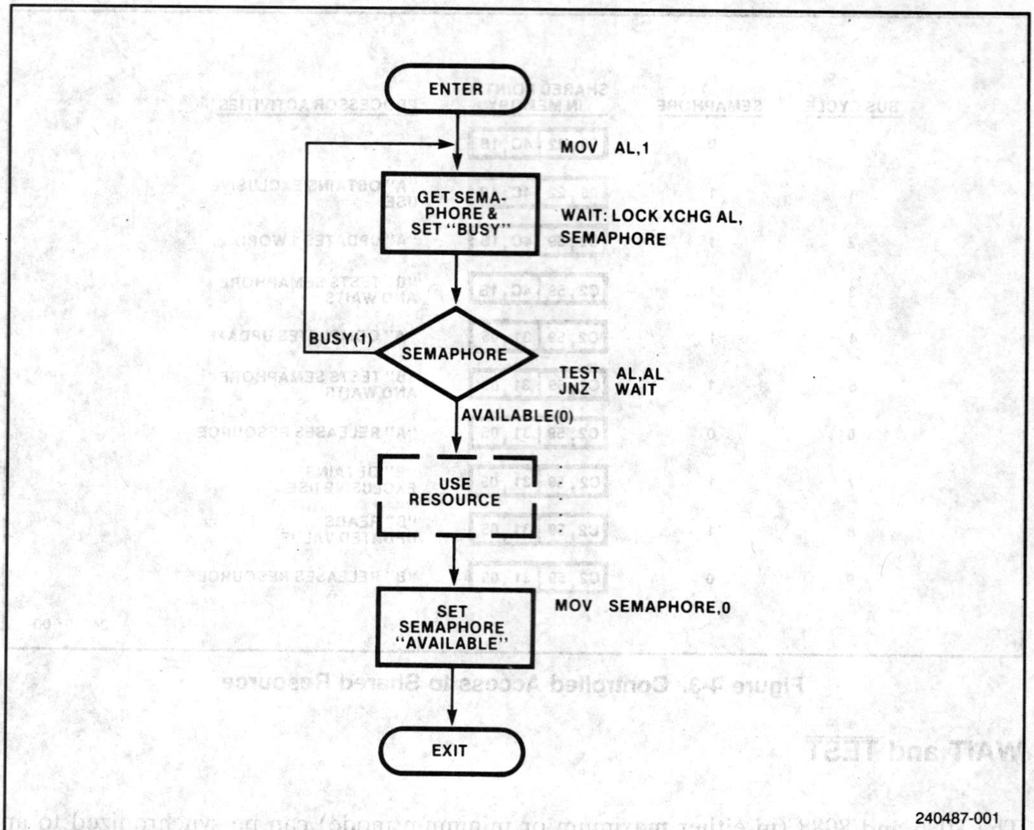

Figure 4-4. Using XCHG and LOCK

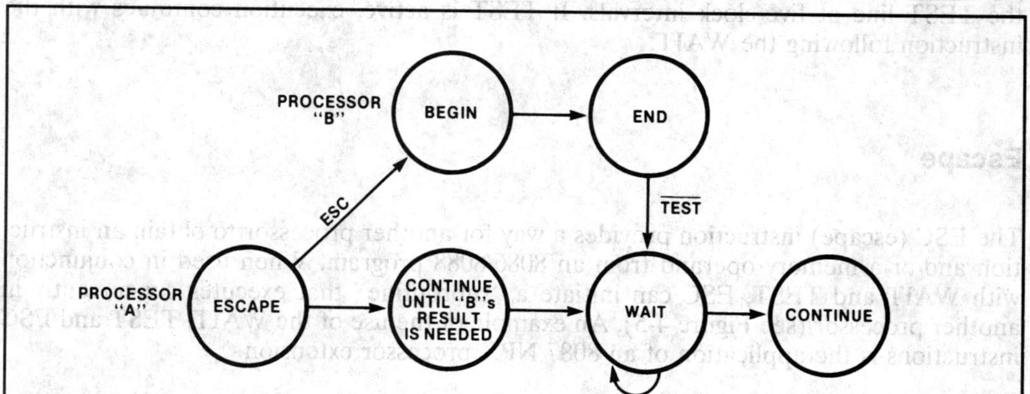

Figure 4-5. Using ESC with WAIT and TEST

If an 8086 or 8088 is configured in maximum mode, the external processor, having determined that an ESC has been fetched, can monitor QS0 and QS1 (the queue status lines) and determine when the ESC instruction is executed. If the instruction references memory the external processor can then monitor the bus and capture the operand's physical address and/or operand itself.

Note that fetching an ESC instruction is not tantamount to executing it. The ESC may be preceded by a jump that causes the queue to be reinitialized. This event also can be determined from the queue status lines.

Request/Grant Lines

When the 8086 or 8088 is configured in maximum mode, the HOLD and HLDA lines evolve into two more sophisticated signals called RQ(/)GT0 and RQ(/)GT1. These are bidirectional lines that can be used to share a local bus between an 8086 or 8088 and two other processors via a handshake sequence.

The request/grant sequence is a three-phase cycle: request, grant and release. First, the processor desiring the bus pulses a request/grant line. The CPU returns a pulse on the same line indicating that it is entering the "hold acknowledge" state and is relinquishing the bus. The BIU is logically disconnected from the bus during this period. The EU, however, will continue to execute instructions until an instruction requires bus access or the queue is emptied, whichever occurs first. When the other processor has finished with the bus, it sends a final pulse to the 8086/8088 indicating that the request has ended and that the CPU may reclaim the bus.

RQ(/)GT0 has higher priority than RQ(/)GT1. If requests arrive simultaneously on both lines, the grant goes to the processor on RQ(/)GT0 and RQ(/)GT12 is acknowledged after the bus has been returned to the CPU. If however, a request arrives on RQ(/)GT0 while the CPU is processing a prior request on RQ(/)GT1, the second request is not honored until the processor on RQ(/)GT1 releases the bus.

MULTIBUS® Architecture

When the 8086 or 8088 is configured in maximum modes, the 82C88 Bus Controller outputs signals that are electrically compatible with the MULTIBUS protocol. Designers of multiprocessing systems may want to consider using the MULTIBUS architecture in the design of their products to reduce development cost and time, and to obtain compatibility with the wide variety of boards available in the iSBC product line.

MULTIBUS architecture provides a versatile communications channel that can be used to coordinate a wide variety of computing modules (see Figure 4-6). Modules in a MULTIBUS system are designated as masters or slaves. Masters may obtain use of the bus and initiate data transfers on it. Slaves are the objects of data transfers only.

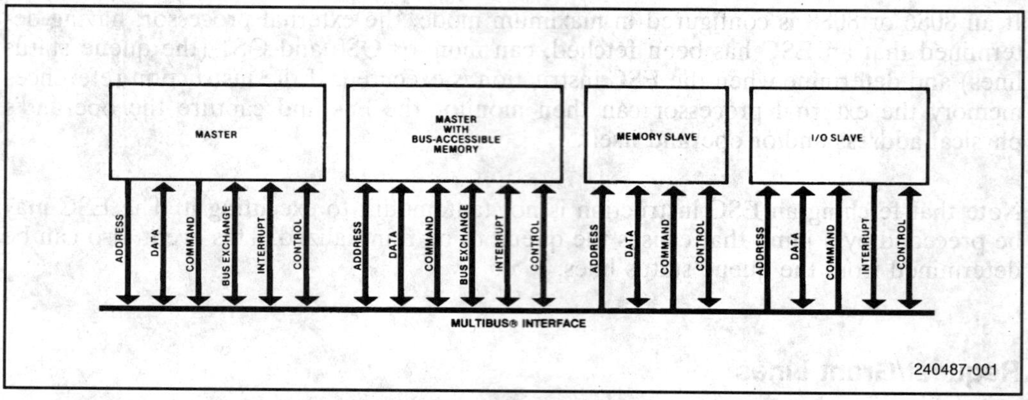

Figure 4-6. MULTIBUS®-Based System

Both 8- and 16-bit masters can be intermixed in such a system. In addition to 16 data lines, the bus design has 20 address lines, eight multilevel interrupt lines, and control and arbitration lines. An auxiliary power bus also is provided to route standby power to memories if the normal supply fails.

The MULTIBUS architecture maintains its own clock, independent of the clocks of the modules it links together. This allows different speed masters to share the bus and allows masters to operate asynchronously with respect to each other. The arbitration logic of the bus permits slow-speed masters to compete equitably for use of the bus. Once a module has obtained the bus, however, transfer speeds are dependent only on the capabilities of the transmitting and receiving modules. Finally, the MULTIBUS standard defines the form factors and physical requirements of modules that communicate on this bus.

INTERRUPT STRUCTURE

Interrupts play an important role in the control of the CPU. In 8086/8088 based systems, each interrupt is assigned a type code that identifies it. Interrupts may be initiated by devices external to the CPU; in addition, they also may be triggered by software interrupt instructions and, under certain conditions, by the CPU itself (see Figure 4-7). Figure 4-8 illustrates the basic response of the 8086/8088 to an interrupt. The next sections elaborate on the information presented in this drawing. Interrupts 0-31 are reserved by Intel.

External Interrupts

The 8086/8088 CPUs have two lines that external devices may use to signal interrupts (INTR and NMI). The INTR (Interrupt Request) line is usually driven by an Intel 8259A Programmable Interrupt Controller (PIC), which in turn is connected to the devices that need interrupt services. The 8259A is a very flexible circuit that is controlled by software commands from the 8086/8088 (the PIC appears as a set of I/O ports to the

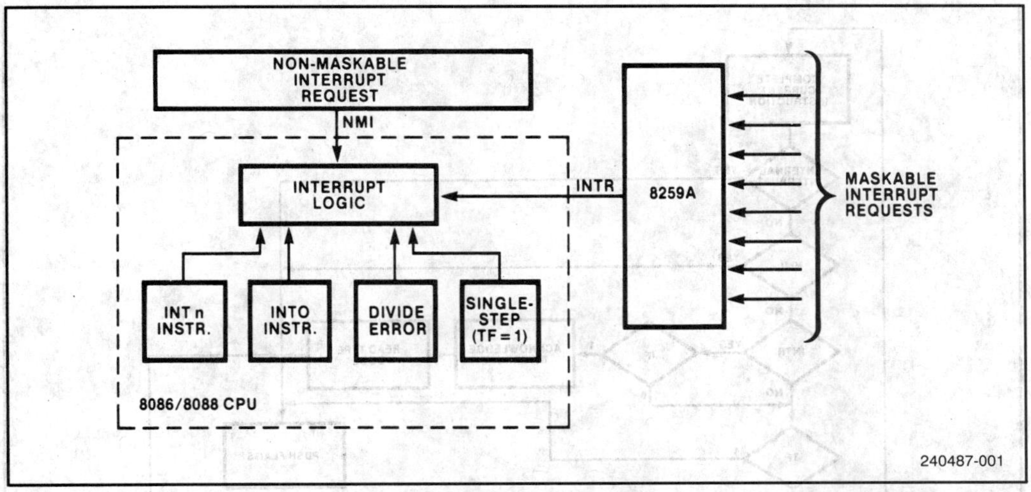

Figure 4-7. Interrupt Sources

software). Its main job is to accept interrupt requests from the devices attached to it, determine which requesting device has the highest priority, and then activate the 8086,8088 INTR line if the selected device has higher priority than the device currently being serviced (if there is one).

When INTR is active, the CPU takes different action depending on the state of the interrupt-enable flag (IF). No action takes place, however, until the currently-executing instruction has been completed. Then, if IF is clear (meaning that interrupts signaled on INTR are masked or disabled), the CPU ignores the interrupt request and processes the next instruction. The INTR signal is not latched by the CPU, so it must be held active until response is received or the request is withdrawn. If interrupts on INTR are enabled (if IF is set), then the CPU recognizes the interrupt request and processes it. Interrupt request arriving on INTR can be enabled by executing an STI (set interrupt-enable flag) instruction. They also may be selectively masked (some types enabled, some disabled) by writing commands to the 8259A. It should be noted that in order to reduce the likelihood of excessive stack buildup, the STI and IRET instructions will reenable interrupts only after the end of the following instruction. (The IRET instruction reenables interrupts only if they were enabled prior to the execution of the interrupt procedure.)

There are a few cases in which an interrupt request is not recognized until after the following instruction. Repeat, LOCK and segment override prefixes are considered "part of" the instructions they prefix; no interrupt is recognized between execution of a prefix and an instruction. A MOV (move) to segment register instruction and a POP segment register instruction are treated similarly: no interrupt is recognized until after the following instruction. This mechanism protects a program that is changing to a new stack (by updating SS and SP). If an interrupt were recognized after SS had been changed, but before SP had been altered, the processor would push the flags, CS and IP into the wrong area of memory. It follows from this that whenever a segment register and another value must be updated together, the segment register should be changed first, followed immediately by the instruction that changes the other value.

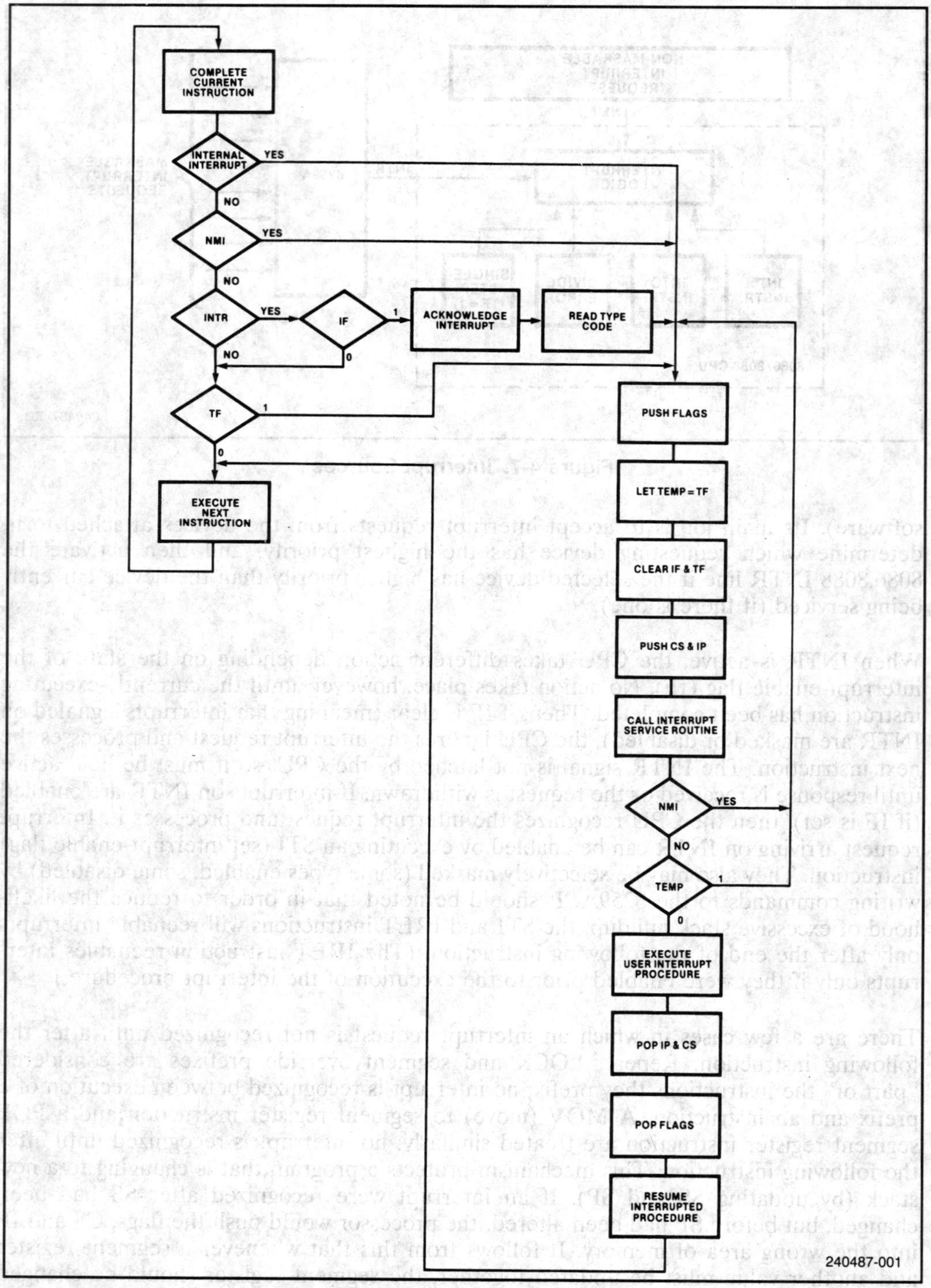

Figure 4-8. Interrupt Processing Sequence

In two cases, WAIT and repeated string instructions, an interrupt request is recognized in the middle of an instruction. In these cases, interrupts are accepted after any completed primitive operation or wait test cycle.

The CPU acknowledges the interrupt request by executing two consecutive interrupt acknowledge (INTA) bus cycles. If a bus hold request arrives (via the HOLD or request/grant lines) during the INTA cycles, it is not honored until the cycles have been completed. In addition, if the CPU is configured in maximum mode, it activates the $\overline{\text{LOCK}}$ signal during these cycles to indicate to other processors that they should not attempt to obtain the bus. The first cycle signals the 8259A that the request has been honored. During the second INTA cycle, the 8259A responds by placing a byte on the data bus that contains the interrupt type (0-255) associated with the device requesting service. (The type assignment is made when the 8259A is initialized by software in the 8086/8088.) The CPU reads this type code and uses it to call the corresponding interrupt procedure.

An external interrupt request also may arrive on another CPU line, NMI (non-maskable interrupt). This line is edge-triggered (INTR is level triggered) and is generally used to signal the CPU of a "catastrophic" event, such as the imminent loss of power, memory error detection or bus parity error. Interrupt requests arriving on NMI cannot be disabled; they are latched by the CPU and have higher priority than an interrupt request on INTR. If an interrupt request arrives on both lines during the execution of an instruction, NMI will be recognized first. Non-maskable interrupts are predefined as type 2; the processor does not need to be supplied with a type code to call the NMI procedure, and it does not run the INTA bus cycles in response to a request on NMI.

The time required for the CPU to recognize an external interrupt request (interrupt latency) depends on how many clock periods remain in the exception of the current instruction. On the average, the longest latency occurs when a multiplication, division or variable-bit shift or rotate instruction is executing when the interrupt request arrives. (See the section "The Instruction Set," in Chapter 3 for detailed instruction timing data.) As mentioned previously, in a few cases, worst-case latency will span two instructions rather than one.

Software-Generated Interrupts

An INT (interrupt) instruction generates an interrupt immediately upon completion of its execution. The Interrupt type coded into the instruction supplies the CPU with the type code needed to call the procedure to process the interrupt. Since any type code may be specified, software interrupts may be used to test interrupt procedures written to service external devices.

The CPU generates a type 0 interrupt immediately following execution of a DIV or IDIV (divide, integer divide) instruction if the calculated quotient is larger than the specified destination.

If the trap flag (TF) is set, the CPU generates a type 1 interrupt following most instructions. This is called single-step execution and is a powerful debugging tool that is discussed in more detail later in this chapter.

If the overflow flag (OF) is set, an INTO (interrupt on overflow) instruction generates a type 4 interrupt upon completion of its execution.

All internal interrupts (INT, INTO, divide error, and single step) share these characteristics:

1. The interrupt type code is either contained in the instruction or is predefined.
2. No INTA bus cycles are run.
3. Internal interrupts cannot be disabled, except for single-step.
4. Any internal interrupt (except single-step) has higher priority than any external interrupt (see Table 4-1). If interrupt requests arrive on NMI and/or INTR during execution of an instruction that causes an internal interrupt (e.g., divide error), the internal interrupt is processed first.

Interrupt Pointer Table

The interrupt pointer (or interrupt vector) table (Figure 4-9) is the link between an interrupt type code and the procedure that has been designated to service interrupts associated with that code. The interrupt pointer table occupies up to the first 1K bytes of low memory. There may be up to 256 entries in the table, one for each interrupt type that can occur in the system. Each entry in the table is a doubleword pointer containing the address of the procedure that is to service interrupts of that type. The higher-addressed word of the pointer contains the base address of the segment containing the procedure. The lower-addressed word contains the procedure's offset from the beginning of the segment. Since each entry is four bytes long, the CPU can calculate the location of the correct entry for a given interrupt type by simply multiplying (type*4).

Space at the high end of the table that would be occupied by entries for interrupt types that cannot occur in a given application may be used for other purposes. The dedicated and reserved portions of the interrupt pointer table (locations 0H through 7FH), however, should not be used for any other purpose to insure proper system operation and to preserve compatibility with future Intel hardware and software products.

Table 4-1. Interrupt Priorities

Interrupt	Priority
Divide error, INT n, INTO	highest
NMI	
INTR	
Single-step	lowest

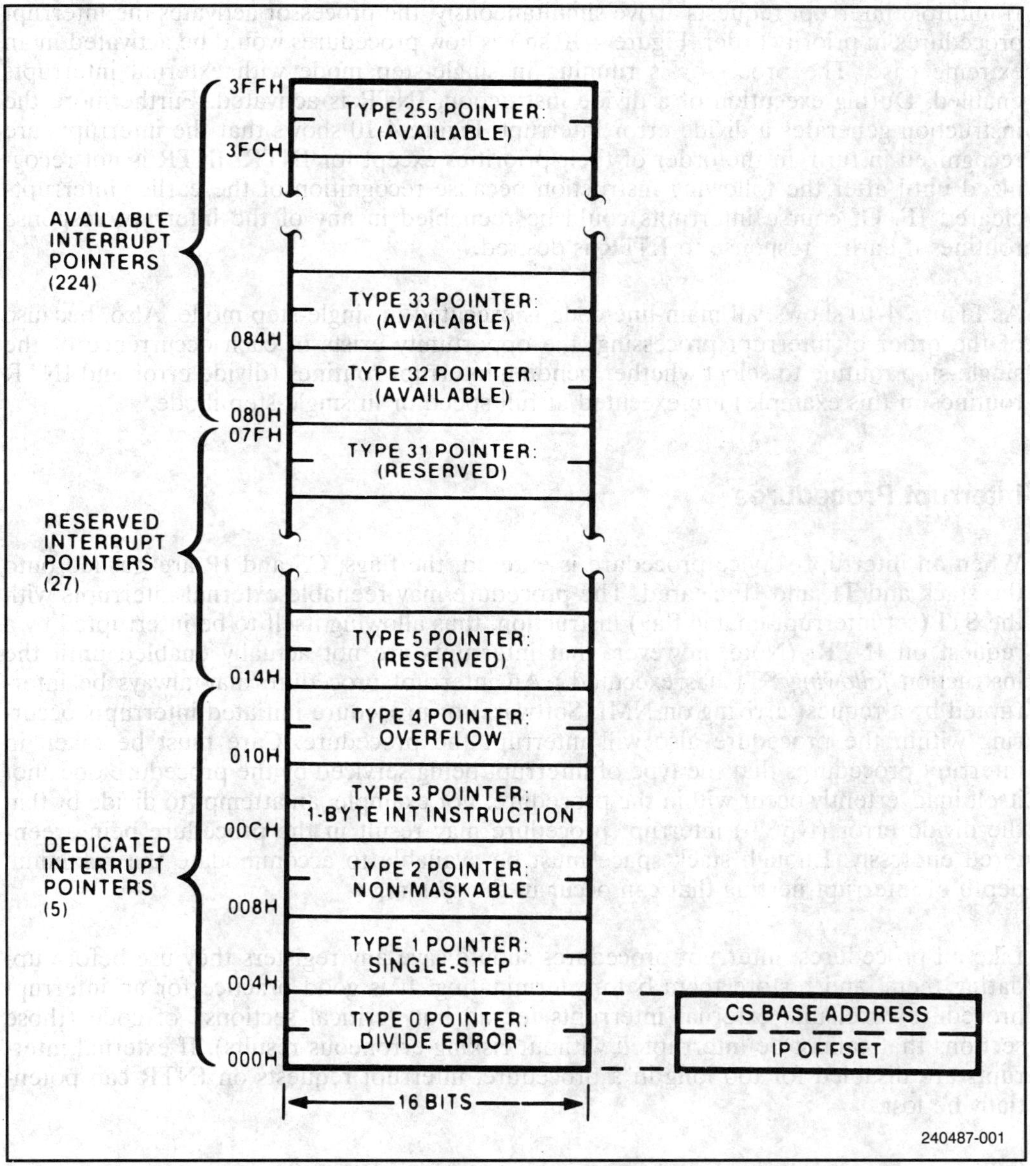

Figure 4-9. Interrupt Pointer Table

After pushing the flags onto the stack, the 8086/8088 CPUs activate an interrupt procedure by executing the equivalent of an intersegment indirect CALL instruction. The target of the "CALL" is the address contained in the interrupt pointer table element located at (type*4). The CPU saves the address of the next instruction by pushing CS and IP onto the stack. These are then replaced by the second and first words of the table element, thus transferring control to the procedure.

If multiple interrupt requests arrive simultaneously, the processor activates the interrupt procedures in priority order. Figure 4-10 shows how procedures would be activated in an extreme case. The processor is running in single-step mode with external interrupts enabled. During execution of a divide instruction, INTR is activated. Furthermore the instruction generates a divide error interrupt. Figure 4-10 shows that the interrupts are recognized in turn, in the order of their priorities except for INTR. INTR is not recognized until after the following instruction because recognition of the earlier interrupts cleared IF. Of course interrupts could be reenabled in any of the interrupt response routines if earlier response to INTR is desired.

As Figure 4-10 shows, all main-line code is executed in single-step mode. Also, because of the order of interrupt processing, the opportunity exists in each occurrence of the single-step routine to select whether pending interrupt routines (divide error and INTR routines in this example) are executed at full speed or in single-step mode.

Interrupt Procedures

When an interrupt service procedure is entered, the flags, CS and IP are pushed onto the stack and TF and IF cleared. The procedure may reenable external interrupts with the STI (set interrupt-enable flag) instruction, thus allowing itself to be interrupted by a request on INTR. (Note, however, that interrupts are not actually enabled until the instruction *following* STI has executed.) An interrupt procedure may always be interrupted by a request arriving on NMI. Software- or procedure-initiated interrupts occurring within the procedure also will interrupt the procedure. Care must be taken in interrupt procedures that the type of interrupt being serviced by the procedure does not itself inadvertently occur within the procedure. For example, an attempt to divide by 0 in the divide error (type 0) interrupt procedure may result in the procedure being reentered endlessly. Enough stack space must be available to accommodate the maximum depth of interrupt nesting that can occur in the system.

Like all procedures, interrupt procedures should save any registers they use before updating them, and restore them before terminating. It is good practice for an interrupt procedure to enable external interrupts for all but "critical sections" of code (those sections that cannot be interrupted without risking erroneous results). If external interrupts are disabled for too long in a procedure, interrupt requests on INTR can potentially be lost.

All interrupt procedures should be terminated with an IRET (interrupt return) instruction. The IRET instruction assumes that the stack is in the same condition as it was when the procedure was entered. It pops the top three stack words into IP, CS and the flags, thus returning to the instruction that was about to be executed when the interrupt procedure was activated. The actual processing done by the procedure is dependent upon the application. If the procedure is servicing an external device, it should output a command to the device instructing it to remove its interrupt request. It might then read status information from the device, determine the cause of the interrupt and then take action accordingly. See the section "8086/8088 Programming Examples," near the end of Chapter 3 for examples of interrupt procedures.

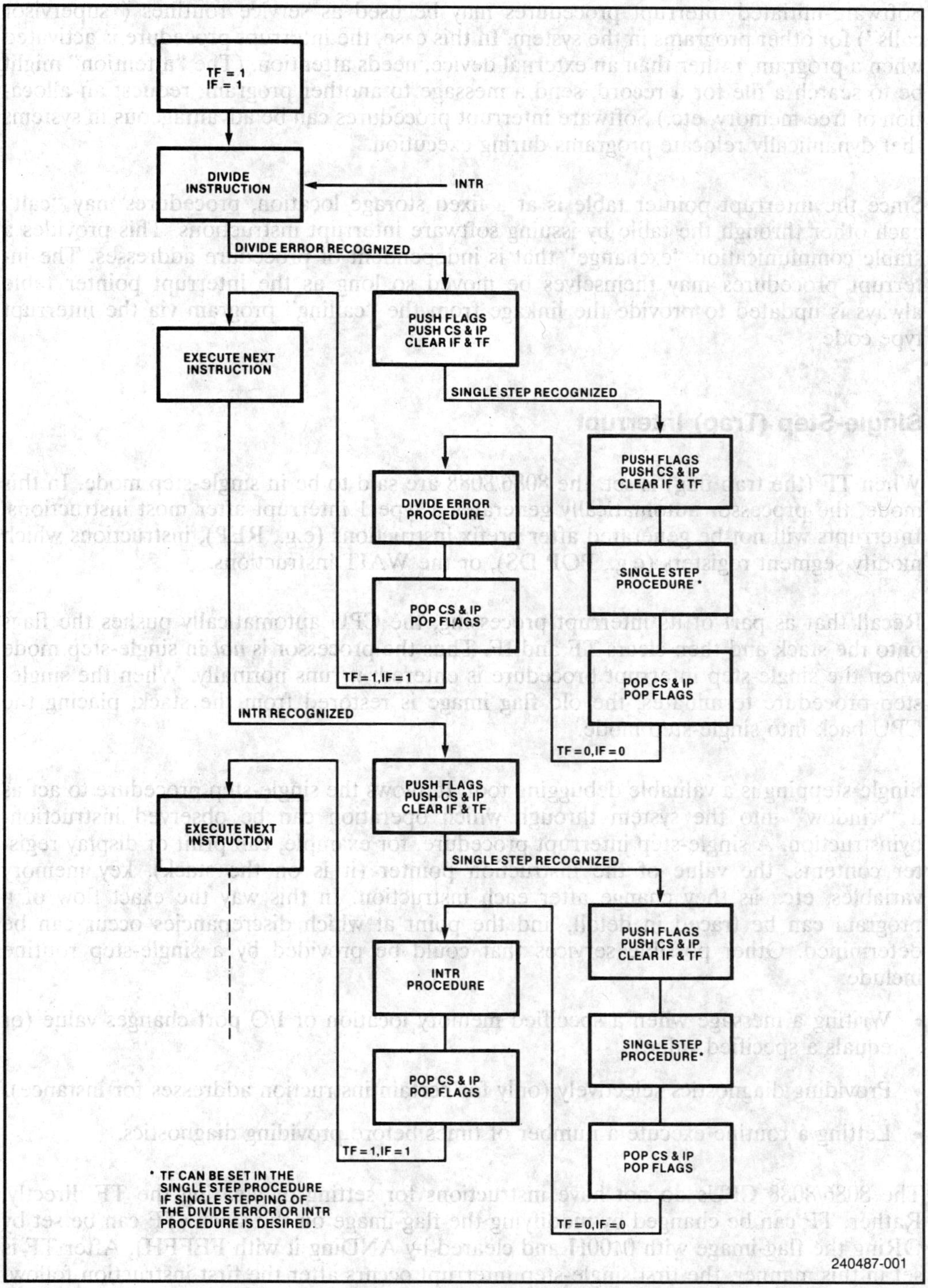

Figure 4-10. Processing Simultaneous Interrupts

Software-initiated interrupt procedures may be used as service routines ("supervisor calls") for other programs in the system. In this case, the interrupt procedure is activated when a program, rather than an external device, needs attention. (The "attention" might be to search a file for a record, send a message to another program, request an allocation of free memory, etc.) Software interrupt procedures can be advantageous in systems that dynamically relocate programs during execution.

Since the interrupt pointer table is at a fixed storage location, procedures may "call" each other through the table by issuing software interrupt instructions. This provides a stable communication "exchange" that is independent of procedure addresses. The interrupt procedures may themselves be moved so long as the interrupt pointer table always is updated to provide the linkage from the "calling" program via the interrupt type code.

Single-Step (Trap) Interrupt

When TF (the trap flag) is set, the 8086/8088 are said to be in single-step mode. In this mode, the processor automatically generates a type 1 interrupt after most instructions. Interrupts will not be generated after prefix instructions (e.g., REP), instructions which modify segment registers (e.g., POP DS), or the WAIT instructions.

Recall that as part of its interrupt processing, the CPU automatically pushes the flags onto the stack and then clears TF and IF. Thus the processor is *not* in single-step mode when the single-step interrupt procedure is entered; it runs normally. When the single-step procedure terminates, the old flag image is restored from the stack, placing the CPU back into single-step mode.

Single-stepping is a valuable debugging tool. It allows the single-step procedure to act as a "window" into the system through which operation can be observed instruction-byinstruction. A single-step interrupt procedure, for example, can print or display register contents, the value of the instruction pointer (it is on the stack), key memory variables, etc., as they change after each instruction. In this way the exact flow of a program can be traced in detail, and the point at which discrepancies occur can be determined. Other possible services that could be provided by a single-step routine include:

- Writing a message when a specified memory location or I/O port changes value (or equals a specified value).
- Providing diagnostics selectively (only for certain instruction addresses for instance).
- Letting a routine execute a number of times before providing diagnostics.

The 8086/8088 CPUs do not have instructions for setting or clearing the TF directly. Rather, TF can be changed by modifying the flag-image on the stack (TF can be set by ORing the flag-image with 0100H and cleared by ANDing it with FEFFH). After TF is set in this manner, the first single-step interrupt occurs after the first instruction following the IRET from the single-step procedure.

If the processor is single-stepping, it processes an interrupt (either internal or external) as follows. Control is passed normally (flags, CS and IP are pushed) to the procedure designated to handle the type of interrupt that has occurred. However, before the first instruction of that procedure is executed, the single-step interrupt is "recognized" and control is passed normally (flags, CS and IP are pushed) to the type 1 interrupt procedure. When single-step procedure terminates, control returns to the previous interrupt procedure. Figure 4-10 illustrates this process in a case where two interrupts occur when the processor is in single-step mode.

Breakpoint Interrupt

A type 3 interrupt is dedicated to the breakpoint interrupt. A breakpoint is generally any place in a program where normal execution is arrested so that some sort of special processing may be performed. Breakpoints typically are inserted into programs during debugging as a way of displaying registers, memory locations, etc., at crucial points in the program.

The INT 3 (breakpoint) instruction is one byte long. This makes it easy to "plant" a breakpoint anywhere in a program. The section "8086/8088 Programming Examples" in Chapter 3 contains an example that shows how a breakpoint may be set, and how a breakpoint procedure may be used to place the processor into single-step mode.

The breakpoint instruction also may be used to "patch" a program (insert new instructions) without recompiling or reassembling it. This may be done by saving an instruction byte, and replacing it with an INT 3 (CCH) machine instruction. The breakpoint procedure would contain the new machine instructions, plus code to restore the saved instruction byte and decrement IP on the stack before returning, so that the displaced instruction would be executed after the patch instructions. The breakpoint example in the section "8086/8088 Programming Examples" in Chapter 3 illustrate these principles.

Note that patching a program requires machine-instruction programming and should be undertaken with considerable caution; it is easy to add new bugs to a program in an attempt to correct existing ones. Note also that a patch is only a temporary measure to be used in exceptional conditions. The affected code should be updated and retranslated as soon as possible.

System Reset

The 8086/8088 RESET lines provide an orderly way to start or restart an executing system. When the processor detects the positive-going edge of a pulse on RESET, it terminates all activities until the signal goes low, at which time it initializes the system as shown in Table 4-2.

Table 4-2. CPU State Following RESET

CPU Component	Content
Flags	Clear
Instruction Pointer	0000H
CS Register	FFFFH
DS Register	0000H
SS Register	0000H
ES Register	0000H
Queue	Empty

Since the code segment register contains FFFFH and the instruction pointer contains 0H, the processor executes its first instruction following system reset from absolute memory location FFFF0H. This location normally contains an intersegment direct JMP instruction from information in the program that identifies its first instruction. As external (maskable) interrupts are disabled by system reset, the system software should reenable interrupts as soon as the system is initialized to the point where they can be processed.

Instruction Queue Status

When configured in maximum mode, the 8086/8088 provide information about instruction queue operations on QS0 and QS1. Table 4-3 interprets the four states that these lines can represent.

The queue status lines are provided for external processors that receive instructions and/or operands via the ESC (escape) instruction (see the section "Multiprocessing Features," earlier in this chapter). Such a processor may monitor the bus to see when an ESC instruction is fetched and then track the instruction through the queue to determine when (and if) the instruction is executed.

Processor Halt

When the HALT (halt) instruction is executed, the processor enters the halt state. This condition may be interpreted as "stop all operations until an external interrupt occurs or the system is reset." No signals are floated during the halt state, and the content of the address and data buses is undefined. A bus hold request arriving on the HOLD line (minimum mode) or either request/grant line (maximum mode) is acknowledge normally while the processor is halted.

The halt state can be used when an event prevents the system from functioning correctly. An example might be a power-fail interrupt. After recognizing that loss of power is imminent, the CPU could use the remaining time to move registers, flags and vital variables to (for example) a battery-powered CMOS RAM area – or EEPROM area and then halt until the return of power was signaled by an interrupt or system reset.

Status Lines

When configured in maximum mode, the 8086/8088 CPUs emit eight status signals that can be used by external devices. Lines $\overline{S0}$, $\overline{S1}$ and $\overline{S2}$ identify the type of bus cycle that the CPU is starting to execute (Table 4-4). These lines are typically decoded by the 8288 Bus Controller. S3 and S4 indicate which segment register was used to construct the physical addressed used in this bus cycle (see Table 4-5). Line S5 reflects the state of the interrupt-enable flag. S6 is always 0. S7 is a spare line whose content is undefined.

Table 4-3. Queue Status Signals (Maximum Mode Only)

QS_0	QS_1	Queue Operation in Last CLK Cycle
0	0	No operation; default value
0	1	First byte of an instruction was taken from the queue
1	0	Queue was reinitialized
1	1	Subsequent byte of an instruction was taken from the queue

Table 4-4. Bus Cycle Status Signals

$\overline{S}_2$	$\overline{S}_1$	$\overline{S}_0$	Types of Bus Cycle
0	0	0	Interrupt Acknowledge
0	0	1	Read I/O
0	1	0	Write I/O
0	1	1	HALT
1	0	0	Instruction Fetch
1	0	1	Read Memory
1	1	0	Write Memory
1	1	1	Passive; no bus cycle

Table 4-5. Segment Register Status Lines

S_4	S_3	Segment Register
0	0	ES
0	1	SS
1	0	CS or none (I/O or Interrupt Vector)
1	1	DS

8087 NPX Programming Design

5

CHAPTER 5
8087 NUMERIC PROCESSOR EXTENSION PROGRAMMING DESIGN

INTRODUCTION

This chapter describes the 8087 Numeric Processor Extension (NPX). It is divided into the following sections:

- Processor Overview
- Processor Architecture
- Computation Fundamentals
- Instruction Set
- Programming Facilities
- Special Features
- Programming Examples

The processor overview section covers both hardware and software topics at a general level. Special Features describes those features of the NPX that will be of interest to specialized groups of users; it is not necessary to understand this section to successfully use the 8087 in most applications. Hardware coverage in this chapter is limited to discussing processor facilities in functional terms. Timing, electrical characteristics, and other physical interface data may be found in Chapter 7.

Note that throughout this chapter the term "CPU" refers to an 8086/8088 configured in maximum mode. To make best use of the material in this chapter readers should have a good understanding of the operation of the 8086/8088.

PROCESSOR OVERVIEW

The 8087 Numeric Processor Extension (NPX) peforms arithmetic and comparison operations on a variety of numeric data types; it also executes numerous built-in transcendental functions (e.g., tangent and log functions). As a processor extension to a maximum mode 8086/8088, the NPX effectively extends the register and instruction sets of the host CPU and adds several new data types as well. The programmer generally does not perceive the 8087 as a separate device; instead, the computational capabilities of the CPU appear greatly expanded.

The 8087 adds extensive high-speed numeric processing capabilities to an 8086/8088-based system. It is specifically designed to deliver stable, correct results when used in a straightforward fashion by programmers who are not expert in numerical analysis. Its applicability to accounting and financial environments, in addition to scientific and engineering settings, further distinguishes the 8087 from the "floating point accelerators" employed in many computer systems, including minicomputers and mainframes. The NPX is housed in a standard 40-pin dual in-line package (Figure 5-1) and requires a single +5V power source.

The description of the 8087 in this section deliberately omits some operating details in order to provide a coherent overall view of the processor's capabilities. Subsequent sections of the chapter will describe these capabilities, and others, in more detail.

Evolution

The performance of first- and second-generation microprocessor-based systems was limited in three principal areas: storage capacity, input/output speed, and numeric computation. The 8086/8088 CPU broke the 64K memory barrier, allowing larger and more time-critical applications to be undertaken. The 8087 Numeric Processor Extension clears the third roadblock by enabling applications with significant computational requirements to be implemented with microprocessor technology.

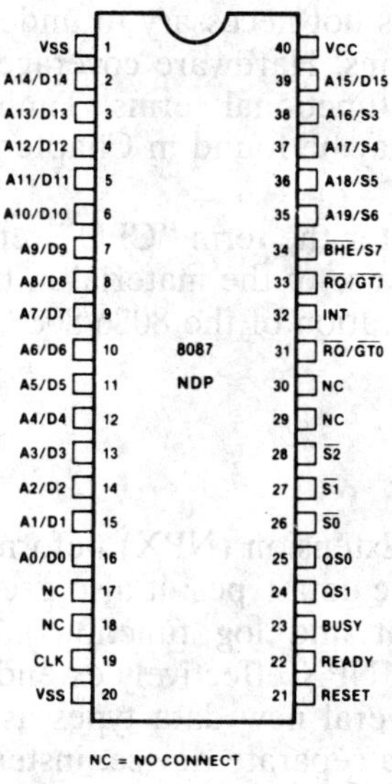

Figure 5-1. 8087 Numeric Data Processor Pin Diagram

Figure 5-2 illustrates the progression of Intel® numeric products and events that have led to the development of the 8087. In the mid-1970's, Intel made the commitment to expand the computational capabilities of microprocessors from addition and subtraction of integers to an array of widely useful operations on real numbers. (Real numbers encompass integers, fractions, and irrational numbers such as π and $\sqrt{2}$.) In 1977, the corporation adopted a standard for representing real numbers in a "floating point" format. Intel's Floating Point Arithmetic Library (FPAL) was the first product to utilize this standard format. FPAL is a set of subroutines for the 8080/8085 microprocessors. These routines perform arithmetic and limited standard functions on single precision (32-bit) real numbers; an FPAL multiply executes in about 1.5 ms (1.6 MHz 8080A CPU). The next product, the iSBC® 310 High Speed Math Unit, essentially implements FPAL in a single iSBC card, reducing a single-precision multiply to about 100 μs. The Intel 8232 is a single-chip arithmetic processor for the 8080/8085 family. The 8232 accepts double precision (64-bit) operands as well as single precision numbers. It performs a single precision multiply in about 100 μs and multiplies double precision numbers in about 875 μs (2 MHz version).

In 1979, a working committee of the Institute for Electrical and Electronic Engineers (IEEE) proposed an industry standard for minicomputer and microcomputer floating point arithmetic (J. Coonen, W. Kahan, J. Palmer, T. Pittman, D. Stevenson, "A Proposed Standard for Binary Floating Point Arithmetic," *ACM SIGNUM Newsletter*, October 1979). The intent of the standard is to promote portability of numeric programs between computers and to provide a uniform programming environment that encourages the development of accurate, reliable software. The proposed standard specifies requirements and options for number formats as well as the results of computations on these numbers. The floating point number formats are identical to those previously adopted by Intel and used in the products described in this section.

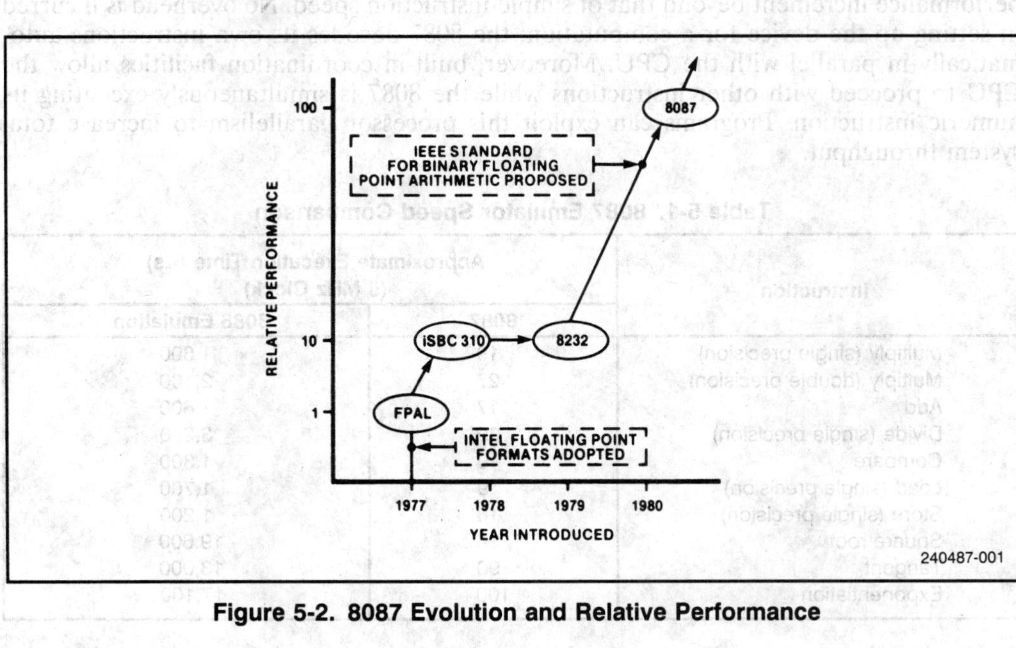

Figure 5-2. 8087 Evolution and Relative Performance

The 8087 Numeric Processor Extension is the most advanced development in Intel's continuing effort to provide improved tools for numerically-oriented microprocessor applications. It is a single-chip hardware implementation of the proposed IEEE standard, including all its options for single and double precision numbers. As such, it is compatible with previous Intel numerics products; programs written for the 8087 will be transportable to future products that conform to the proposed IEEE standard. The NPX also provides many additional functions that are extensions to the proposed standard.

Performance

As Figure 5-2 indicates, the 8087 provides about 10 times the instruction speed of the 8232 and a 100-fold improvement over FPAL. The 8087 multiplies 32-bit and 64-bit real numbers in about 19 μs and 27 μs respectively. Of course, the actual performance of the NPX in a given system depends on numerous application-specific factors.

Table 5-1 compares the execution times of several 8087 instructions with the equivalent operations executed in software on a 5 MHz 8086. The software equivalents are highly optimized assembly language procedures from the 8087 emulator, an NPX development tool discussed later in this section.

The performance figures quoted in this section are for operations on real (floating point) numbers. The 8087 also has instructions that enable it to utilize fixed point binary and decimal integers of up to 64 bits and 18 digits, respectively. Using an 8087, rather than multiple precision software algorithms for integer operations, can provide speed improvements of 10-100 times.

The 8087's unique processor extension interface to the CPU can yield an additional performance increment beyond that of simple instruction speed. No overhead is incurred in setting up the device for a computation; the 8087 decodes its own instructions automatically in parallel with the CPU. Moreover, built-in coordination facilities allow the CPU to proceed with other instructions while the 8087 is simultaneously executing its numeric instruction. Programs can exploit this processor parallelism to increase total system throughput.

Table 5-1. 8087 Emulator Speed Comparison

Instruction	Approximate Execution Time (μs) (5 MHz Clock)	
	8087	8086 Emulation
Multiply (single precision)	19	1,600
Multiply (double precision)	27	2,100
Add	17	1,600
Divide (single precision)	39	3,200
Compare	9	1,300
Load (single precision)	9	1,700
Store (single precision)	18	1,200
Square root	36	19,600
Tangent	90	13,000
Exponentiation	100	17,100

Usability

Viewed strictly from the standpoint of raw speed, the 8087 enables serious computation-intensive tasks to be performed by microprocessors for the first time. The 8087 offers more than just high performance, however. By synthesizing advances made by numerical analysts in the past several years, the NPX provides a level of usability that surpasses existing minicomputer and mainframe arithmetic units. In fact, the charter of the 8087 design team was first to achieve exceptional functionality and then to obtain high performance.

The 8087 is explicitly designed to deliver stable, accurate results when programmed using straightforward "pencil and paper" algorithms. While this statement may seem trivial, experienced users of "floating point processors" will recognize its fundamental importance. For example, most computers can overflow when two single precision floating point numbers are multiplied together and then divided by a third, even if the final result is a perfectly valid 32-bit number. The 8087 delivers the correctly rounded result. Other typical examples of undesirable machine behavior in straightforward calculations occur when solving for roots of a quadratic equations:

$$\frac{-b \pm \sqrt{b^2 - 4ac}}{2a}$$

for computing financial rate of return, which involves the expression: $(1 + i)^n$. Straightforward algorithms will not deliver consistently correct results (and will not indicate when they are incorrect) on most machines. To obtain correct results on traditional machines under all conditions usually requires sophisticated numerical techniques that are foreign to most programmers. General application programmers using straightforward algorithms will produce much more reliable programs on the 8087. This simple fact greatly reduces the software investment required to develop safe, accurate computation-based products.

Beyond traditional numerics support for "scientific" applications, the 8087 has built-in facilities for "commercial" computing. It can process decimal numbers of up to 18 digits without rounding off errors, and it performs *exact arithmetic* on integers as large as 2^{64}. Exact arithmetic is vital in accounting applications where rounding errors may introduce money losses that cannot be reconciled.

The NPX contains a number of facilities that can optionally be invoked by sophisticated users. Examples of these advanced features include two models of infinity, directed rounding, gradual underflow, and traps to user-written exception handling software.

Applications

The NPX's versatility and performance make it appropriate for a broad array of numerically-oriented applications. In general, applications that exhibit any of the following characteristics can benefit by implementing numeric processing on the 8087:

- Numeric data vary over a wide range of values, or include non-integral values.
- Algorithms produce very large or very small intermediate results.

- Computations must be very precise, i.e., a large number of significant digits must be maintained.
- Performance requirements exceed the capacity of traditional microprocessors.
- Consistently safe, reliable results must be delivered using a programming staff that is not expert in numerical techniques.

Note also that the 8087 can reduce software development costs and improve the performance of systems that do not utilize real numbers but operate on multi-precision binary or decimal integer values.

A few examples, which show how the 8087 might be utilized in specific numerics applications, are described below. In many cases, these types of systems have been implemented in the past with minicomputers. The advent of the 8087 brings the size and cost savings of microprocessor technology to these applications for the first time.

- Business data processing — The NPX's ability to accept decimal operands and produce exact decimal results of up to 18 digits greatly simplifies accounting programming. Financial calculations which use power functions can take advantage of the 8087's exponentiation and logarithmic instructions.
- Process control — The 8087 solves dynamic range problems automatically, and its extended precision allows control functions to be fine-tuned for more accurate and efficient performance. Control algorithms implemented with the NPX also contribute to improved reliability and safety, while the 8087's speed can be exploited in real-time operations.
- Numerical control — The 8087 can move and position machine tool heads with extreme accuracy. Axis positioning also benefits from the hardware trigonometric support provided by the 8087.
- Robotics — Coupling small size and modest power requirements with powerful computational abilities, the NPX is ideal for on-board six-axis positioning.
- Navigation — Very small, light weight, and accurate inertial guidance systems can be implemented with the 8087. Its built-in trigonometric functions can speed and simplify the calculation of position from bearing data.
- Graphics terminals — The 8087 can be used in graphics terminals to locally perform many functions which normally demand the attention of a main computer; these include rotation, scaling, and interpolation. Very powerful and highly self-sufficient terminals can be built from a relatively small number of 8086/8088 family parts.
- Data acquisition — The 8087 can be used to scan, scale, and reduce large quantities of data as it is collected, thereby lowering storage requirements as well as the time required to process the data for analysis.

The preceding examples are oriented toward "traditional" numerics applications. There are, in addition, many other types of systems that do not appear to the end user as "computational," but can employ the 8087 to advantage. Indeed, the 8087 presents the imaginative system designer with an opportunity similar to that created by the introduction of the microprocessor itself. Many applications can be viewed as numerically-based if sufficient computational power is available to support this view. This is analogous to the thousands of successful products that have been built around "buried" microprocessors, even though the products themselves bear little resemblance to computers.

Programming Interface

The combination of an 8086/8088 CPU and an 8087 generally appears to the programmer as a single machine. The 8087, in effect, adds new data types, registers, and instructions to the CPU. The programming languages and the coprocessor architecture take care of most interprocessor coordination automatically.

Table 5-2 lists the seven 8087 data types. Internally, the 8087 holds all numbers in the temporary real format; the extended range and precision of this format are key contributors to the NPX's ability to consistently deliver stable, expected results. The 8087's load and store instructions convert operands between the other formats and temporary real. The fact that these conversions are made, and that calculations may be performed on converted numbers, is transparent to the programmer. Integer operands, whether binary or decimal, yield correct integer results, just as real operands yield correct real results. Moreover, a rounding error does not occur when a number in an external format is converted to temporary real.

Computations in the 8087 center on the processor's register stack. These eight 80-bit registers provide the equivalent capacity of 40 of the 16-bit registers found in typical CPUs. This generous register space allows more constants and intermediate results to be held in registers during calculations, reducing memory access and consequently improving execution speed as well as bus availability. The 8087 register set is unique in that it can be accessed both as a stack, with instructions operating implicitly on the top one or two stack elements, and as a fixed register set, with instructions operating on explicitly designated registers.

Table 5-2. Data Types

Data Type	Bits	Significant Digits (Decimal)	Approximate Range (Decimal)
Word integer	16	4	$-32,768 \le X \le +32,767$
Short integer	32	9	$-2 \times 10^9 \le X \le 2 \times 10$
Long integer	64	18	$-9 \times 10^{18} \le X \le 9 \times 10^{18}$
Packed decimal	80	18	$-99...99 \le X \le +99...99$(18 digits)
Short real*	32	6-7	$8.43 \times 10^{-37} \le \lvert X \rvert \le 3.37 \times 10^{38}$
Long real*	64	15-16	$4.19 \times 10^{-307} \le \lvert X \rvert \le 1.67 \times 10^{308}$
Temporary real	80	19	$3.4 \times 10^{-4932} \le \lvert X \rvert \le 1.2 \times 10^{4932}$

*The short and long real data types correspond to the single and double precision data types defined in other Intel numerics products.

Table 5-3 lists the 8087's major instructions by class. Assembly language programs are written in ASM-86, the 8086/8088/8087 common assembly language. ASM-86 provides directives for defining all 8087 data types and mnemonics for all instructions. The fact that some instructions in a program are executed by the 8087 and others by the CPU is usually of no concern to the programmer. All 8086/8088 addressing modes may be used to access memory-based 8087 operands, enabling convenient processing of numeric arrays, structures, based variables, etc.

NPX routines may also be written in PL/M-86, Intel's high-level language for the 8086/8088 CPUs. PL/M-86 provides the programmer with access to many 8087 facilities while reducing the programmer's need to understand the architecture of the chip.

Two features of the 8087 hardware further simplify numeric application programming. First, the 8087 is invoked directly by the programmer's instructions. There is no need to write instructions that "address" the NPX as an "I/O device," or to incur the overhead of setting up a DMA operation to perform data transfers. Second, the NPX automatically detects exception conditions that can potentially damage a calculation at run-time. On-chip exception handlers are automatically invoked by default to field these exceptions, so that a reasonable result is produced and execution may proceed without program intervention. Alternatively, the 8087 can interrupt the CPU and thus trap to a user procedure when an exception is detected.

Besides the assembler and compiler, Intel provides a software emulator for the 8087. The 8087 emulator (E8087) is a software package that provides the functional equivalent of an 8087; it executes entirely on an 8086/8088 CPU. The emulator allows 8087 routines to be developed and checked out on an 8086/8088 execution vehicle before prototype 8087 hardware is operational.

At the source code level, there is no difference between a routine that will ultimately run on an 8087 or on a CPU emulation of an 8087. At link time, the decision is made whether to use the NPX or the software emulator; no recompilation or re-assembly is necessary. Source programs are independent of the numeric execution vehicle: except for timing, the operation of the emulated NPX is the same as for "real hardware." The emulator also makes it simple for a product to offer the NPX as a "plug-in" performance option without the necessity of maintaining two sets of source code.

Table 5-3. Principal Instructions

Class	Instructions
Data Transfer	Load (all data types), Store (all data types), Exchange
Arithmetic	Add, Subtract, Multiply, Divide, Subtract Reversed, Divide Reversed, Square Root, Scale, Remainder, Integer Part, Change Sign, Absolute Value, Extract
Comparison	Compare, Examine, Test
Transcendental	Tangent, Arctangent, $2^X - 1$, $YLog_2(X+1)$, $YLog_2(X)$
Constants	0, 1, π, $Log_{10}2$, Log_e2, Log_210, Log_2e
Processor Control	Load Control Word, Store Control Word, Store Status Word, Load Environment, Store Environment, Save, Restore, Enable Interrupts, Disable Interrupts, Clear Exceptions, Initialize

Hardware Interface

As a processor extension to an 8086/8088, the 8087 is wired directly to the CPU as shown in Figure 5-3. The CPU's queue status lines (QS0 and QS1) enable the NPX to obtain and decode instructions in synchronization with the CPU. The NPX's BUSY signal informs the CPU that the NPX is executing; the CPU WAIT instruction tests this signal to ensure that the NPX is ready to execute a subsequent instruction. The NPX can interrupt the CPU when it detects an exception. The NPX's interrupt request line is typically routed to the CPU through an 8259A Programmable Interrupt Controller. The NPX uses one of its host CPU's request/grant lines to obtain control of the local bus for data transfer (loads and stores). The other CPU request/grant line is available for general system use.

The 8086, 8088 and 8087 all utilize the same clock generator and system bus interface components (bus controller, latches, transceivers, and bus arbiter). Thus, no additional hardware beyond the 8087 is required to add powerful computational capabilities to 8086/8088-based systems.

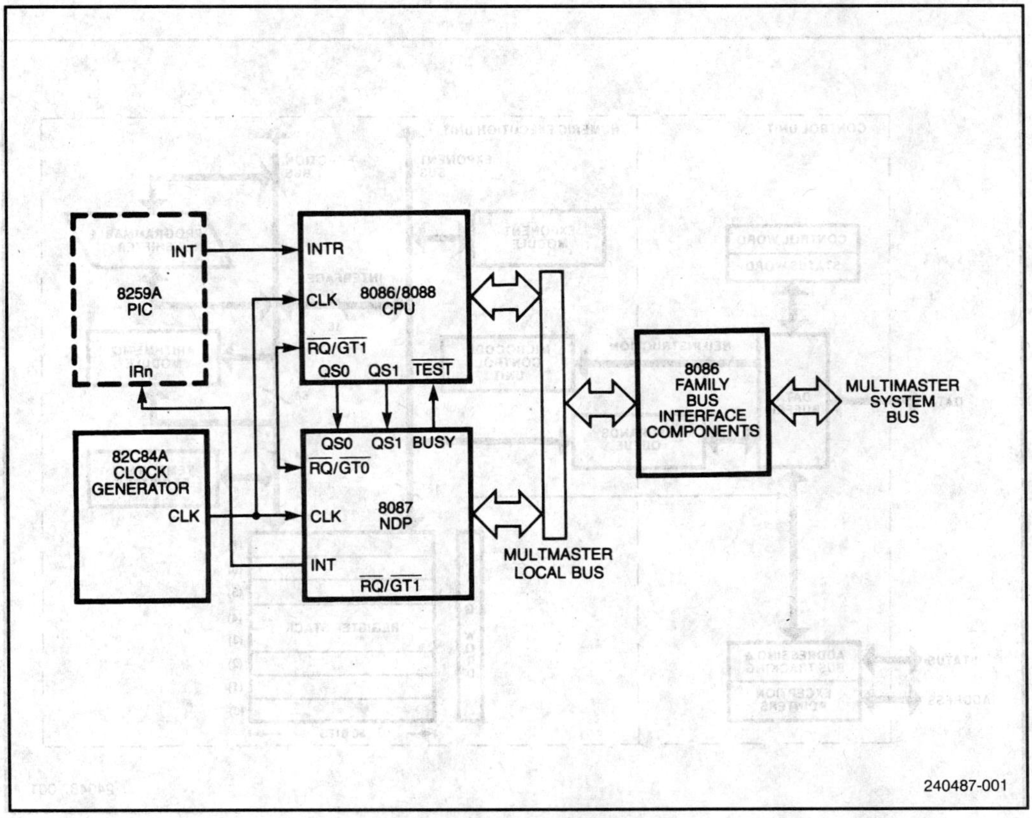

Figure 5-3. NDP Interconnect

PROCESSOR ARCHITECTURE

As shown in Figure 5-4, the NPX is internally divided into two processing elements, the control unit (CU) and the numeric execution unit (NEU). In essence, the NEU executes all numeric instructions, while the CU fetches instructions, reads and writes memory operands, and executes the processor control class of instructions. The two elements are able to operate independently of one another, allowing the CU to maintain synchronization with the CPU while the NEU executes numeric instructions.

Control Unit

The CU keeps the 8087 operating in synchronization with its host CPU. 8087 instructions are intermixed with CPU instructions in a single instruction stream fetched by the CPU. By monitoring the status signals emitted by the CPU, the NPX control unit can determine when an instruction is being fetched. When the instruction byte or word becomes available on the local bus, the CU taps the bus in parallel with the CPU and obtains that portion of the instruction.

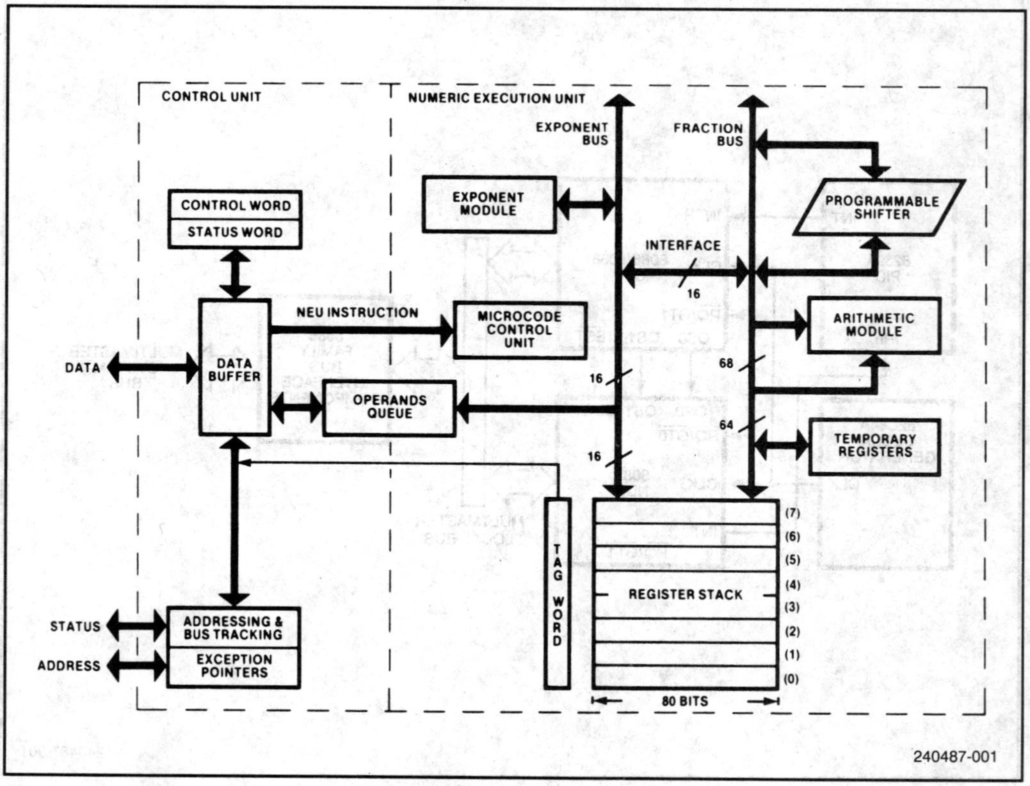

Figure 5-4. 8087 Block Diagram

The CU maintains an instruction queue that is identical to the queue in the host CPU. By monitoring the CPU's queue status lines, the CU is able to obtain and decode instructions from the queue in synchronization with the CPU. In effect, both processors fetch and decode the instruction stream in parallel.

The two processors execute the instruction stream differently, however. The first five bits of all 8087 machine instructions are identical; these bits designate the coprocessor escape (ESC) class of instructions. The control unit ignores all instructions that do not match these bits, since these instructions are directed to the CPU only. When the CU decodes an instruction containing the escape code, it either executes the instruction itself, or passes it to the NEU, depending on the type of instruction.

The CPU distinguishes between ESC instructions that reference memory and those that do not. If the instruction refers to a memory operand, the CPU calculates the operand's address and then performs a "dummy read" of the word at that location. This is a normal read cycle, except that the CPU ignores the data it receives. If the ESC instruction does not contain a memory reference, the CPU simply proceeds to the next instruction.

A given 8087 instruction (an ESC to the CPU) will either require loading an operand from memory into the 8087, or will require storing an operand from the 8087 into memory, or will not reference memory at all. In the first two cases, the CU makes use of the "dummy read" cycle initiated by the CPU. The CU captures and saves the operand address that the CPU places on the bus early in the "dummy read." If the instruction is an 8087 load, the CU additionally captures the first (and possibly only) word of the operand when it becomes available on the bus. If the operand to be loaded is longer than one word, the CU immediately obtains the bus from the CPU and reads the rest of the operand in consecutive bus cycles. In a store operation, the CU captures and saves the operand address as in a load, and ignores the data word that follows in the "dummy read" cycle. When the 8087 is ready to perform the store, the CU obtains the bus from the CPU and writes the operand at the saved address using as many consecutive bus cycles as are necessary to store the operand.

Numeric Execution Unit

The NEU executes all instructions that involve the register stack; these include arithmetic, comparison, transcendental, constant, and data transfer instructions. The data path in the NEU is 68 bits wide and allows internal operand transfers to be performed at very high speeds.

Register Stack

Each of the eight registers in the 8087's register stack is 80 bits wide, and each is divided into the "fields" shown in Figure 5-5. This format corresponds to the NPX's temporary real data type that is used for all calculations. The section "Programming Facilities," later in this chapter describes in detail how numbers are represented in the temporary real format.

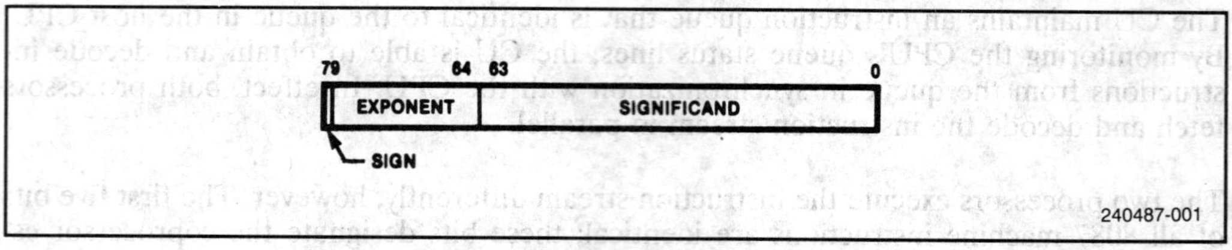

Figure 5-5. Register Structure

At a given point in time, the ST field in the status word (described shortly) identifies the current top-of-stack register. A load ("push") operation decrements ST by 1 and loads a value into the new top register. A store-and-pop operation stores the value from the current top register and then increments ST by 1. Thus, like 8086 stacks in memory, the 8087 register stack grows "down" toward lower-addressed registers.

Instructions may address registers either implicitly or explicitly. Many instructions operate on the register at the top of the stack. These instructions implicitly address the register pointed to by ST. For example, the ASM-86 instruction FSQRT replaces the number at the top of the stack with its square root; this instruction takes no operands because the top-of-stack register is implied as the operand. Other instructions allow the programmer to explicitly specify the register that is to be used. Explicit register addressing is "top-relative" where the ASM-86 expression ST denotes the current stack top and ST (*i*) refers to the *i*th register from ST in the stack (0 *i* 7). For example, if ST contains 011B (register 3 is the top of the stack), the following instruction would add registers 3 and 5:

```
FADD ST,ST(2)
```

In typical use, the programmer may conceptually "divide" the registers into a fixed group and an adjustable group. The fixed registers are used like the conventional registers in a CPU, to hold constants, accumulations, etc. The adjustable group is used like a stack, with operands pushed on and results popped off. After loading, the registers in the fixed group are addressed explicitly, while those in the adjustable group are addressed implicitly. Of course, all registers may be addressed using either mode, and the "definition" of the fixed versus the adjustable areas may be altered at any time. The section "Programming Facilities," later in this chapter, contains a programming example that illustrates typical register stack use.

The stack organization and top-relative addressing of the register simplify subroutine programming. Passing subroutine parameters on the register stack eliminates the need for the subroutine to "know" which registers actually contain the parameters and allows different routines to call the same subroutine without having to observe a convention for passing parameters in dedicated registers. So long as the stack is not full, each routine simply loads the parameters on the stack and calls the subroutine. The subroutine addresses the parameters as ST, ST (1), etc., even though ST may, for example, refer to register 3 in one invocation and register 5 in another.

Status Word

The status word reflects the overall condition of the 8087; it may be examined by storing it into memory with an NPX instruction and then inspecting it with CPU code. The status word is divided into the fields shown in Figure 5-6. The busy field (bit 15) indicates whether the NPX is executing an instruction (B=1) or is idle (B=0).

Several 8087 instructions (for example, the comparison instructions) post their results to the condition code (bits 14 and 10-8 of the status word). The principal use of the condition code is for conditional branching. This may be accomplished by executing an instruction that sets the condition code, storing the status word in memory and then examining the condition code with CPU instructions.

Bits 13-11 of the status word point to the 8087 register that is the current stack top (ST). Note that if ST=000B, a "push" operation, which decrements ST, produces ST=111B; similarly, popping the stack with ST=111B yields ST=000B.

Bit 7 is the interrupt request field. The NPX sets this field to record a pending interrupt to the CPU.

Bits 5-0 are set to indicate that the NEU has detected an exception while executing an instruction. The next major section "Computation Fundamentals," explains these exceptions.

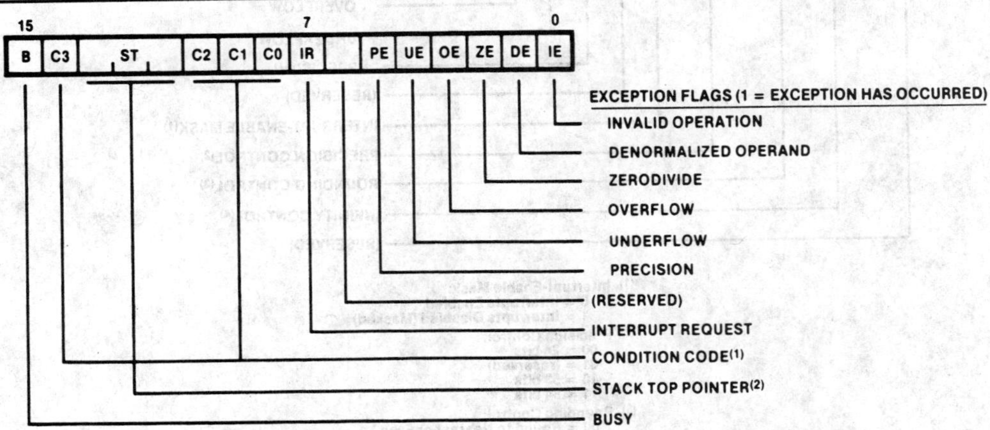

(1) See descriptions of compare, test, examine and remainder instructions in section S.7 for condition code interpretation.
(2) ST values:
000 = register 0 is stack top
001 = register 1 is stack top
•
•
•
111 = register 7 is stack top

240487-001

Figure 5-6. Status Word Format

Control Word

To satisfy a broad range of application requirements, the NPX provides several processing options which are selected by loading a word from memory into the control word. Figure 5-7 shows the format and encoding of the fields in the control word; it is provided here for reference. The next major section, "Computation Fundamentals," explains the use of each of these 8087 facilities except the interrupt-enable control field, which is covered in Chapter 7.

Tag Word

The tag word marks the content of each register as shown in Figure 5-8. The principal function of the tag word is to optimize the NPX's performance under certain circumstances, and programmers ordinarily need not be concerned with it.

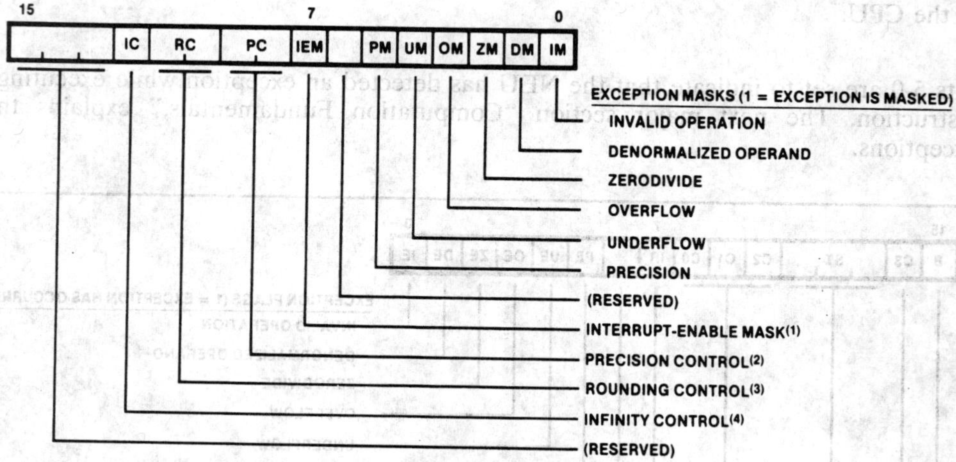

(1) Interrupt-Enable Mask:
0 = Interrupts Enabled
1 = Interrupts Disabled (Masked)

(2) Precision Control:
00 = 24 bits
01 = (reserved)
10 = 53 bits
11 = 64 bits

(3) Rounding Control:
00 = Round to Nearest or Even
01 = Round Down (toward −∞)
10 = Round Up (toward +∞)
11 = Chop (Truncate Toward Zero)

(4) Infinity Control:
0 = Projective
1 = Affine

240487-001

Figure 5-7. Control Word Format

Exception Pointers

The exception pointers (see Figure 5-9) are provided for user-written exception handlers. Whenever the 8087 executes an instruction, the CU saves the instruction address and the instruction opcode in the exception pointers. In addition, if the instruction references a memory operand, the address of the operand is retained also. An exception handler can store these pointers in memory and thus obtain information concerning the instruction that caused the exception.

COMPUTATION FUNDAMENTALS

This section covers 8087 programming concepts that are common to all applications. It describes the 8087's internal number system and the various types of numbers that can be employed in NPX programs. The most commonly used options for rounding, precision and infinity (selected by fields in the control word) are described, with exhaustive coverage of less frequently used facilities deferred to the section "Special Topics," near the end of this chapter. Exception conditions which may arise during execution of NPX instructions are also described, along with the options that are available for responding to these exceptions.

Number System

The system of real numbers that people use for pencil and paper calculations is conceptually infinite and continuous. There is no upper or lower limit to the magnitude of the numbers one can employ in a calculation, or to the precision (number of significant digits) that the numbers can represent. When considering any real number, there are always an infinity of numbers both larger and smaller. There is also an infinity of numbers between (i.e., with more significant digits than) any two real numbers. For example, between 2.5 and 2.6 are 2.51, 2.5897, 2.500001, etc.

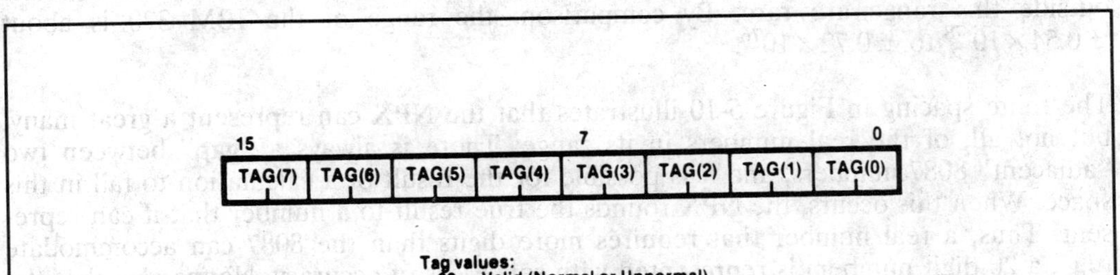

Figure 5-8. Tag Word Format

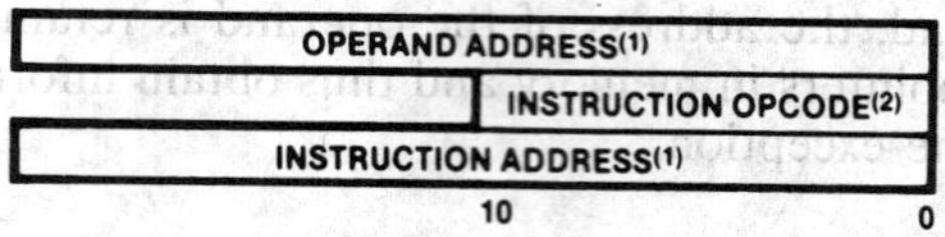

(1) 20-bit physical address
(2) 11 least significant bits of opcode; 5 most significant bits are always 8087 hook (11011B)

240487-001

Figure 5-9. Exception Pointers Format

Ideally, it would be desirable for a computer to be able to operate on the entire real number system. In practice this is not possible. Computers, no matter how large, ultimately have fixed size registers and memories that limit the system of numbers that can be accommodated. These limitations proscribe both the range and the precision of numbers. The result is a set of numbers that is finite and discrete, rather than infinite and continuous. This sequence is a subset of the real numbers, which is designed to form a useful *approximation* of the real number system.

Figure 5-10 superimposes the basic 8087 real number system on a real number line (decimal numbers are shown for clarity, although the 8087 actually represents numbers in binary). The dots indicate the subset of real numbers the 8087 can represent as the data and final results of calculations. The 8087's range is approximately $\pm 4.19 \times 10^{-307}$ to $\pm 1.67 \times 10^{308}$. Applications that are required to deal with data and final results outside this range are rare. By comparison, the range of the IBM 370 is about $\pm 0.54 \times 10^{-78}$ to $\pm 0.72 \times 10^{76}$.

The finite spacing in Figure 5-10 illustrates that the NPX can represent a great many, but not all, of the real numbers in its range. There is always a "gap" between two "adjacent" 8087 numbers, and it is possible for the result of a calculation to fall in this space. When this occurs, the NPX rounds the true result to a number that it can represent. Thus, a real number that requires more digits than the 8087 can accommodate (e.g., a 20 digit number) is represented with some loss of accuracy. Notice also that the 8087's representable numbers are not distributed evenly along the real number line. There are, in fact, an equal number of representable numbers between successive powers of 2 (i.e., there are as many representable numbers between 2 and 4 as between 65,536 and 131,072). Therefore, the "gaps" between representable numbers are "larger" as the numbers increase in magnitude. All integers in the range $\pm 2^{64}$, however, are exactly representable.

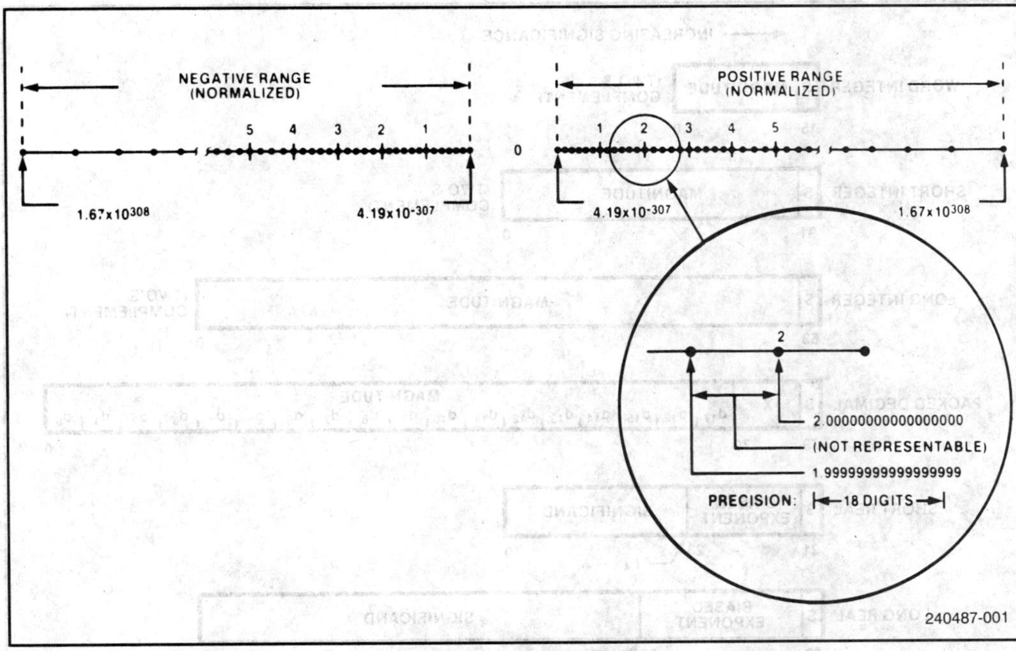

Figure 5-10. 8087 Number System

In its internal operations, the 8087 actually employs a number system that is a substantial superset of that shown in Figure 5-10. The internal format (called temporary real) extends the 8087's range to about $\pm 3.4 \times 10^{-4932}$ to $\pm 1.2 \times 10^{4932}$, and its precision to about 19 (equivalent decimal) digits. This format is designed to provide extra range and precision for constants and intermediate results, and is not normally intended for data or final results.

From a practical standpoint, the 8087's set of real numbers is sufficiently "large" and "dense" so as not to limit the vast majority of microprocessor applications. Compared to most computers, including mainframes, the NPX provides a very good approximation of the real number system. It is important to remember, however, that it is not an exact representation, and that arithmetic on real numbers is inherently approximate.

Conversely, and equally important, the 8087 does perform exact arithmetic on its integer subset of the reals. That is, an operation on two integers returns an exact integral result, provided that the true result is an integer and is in range. For example, $4 \div 2$ yields an exact integer, $1 \div 3$ does not, and $2^{40} \times 2^{30} + 1$ does not, because the result requires greater than 64 bits of precision.

Data Types and Formats

The 8087 recognizes seven numeric data types, divided into three classes: binary integers, packed decimal integers, and binary reals. Figure 5-11 summarizes the format of

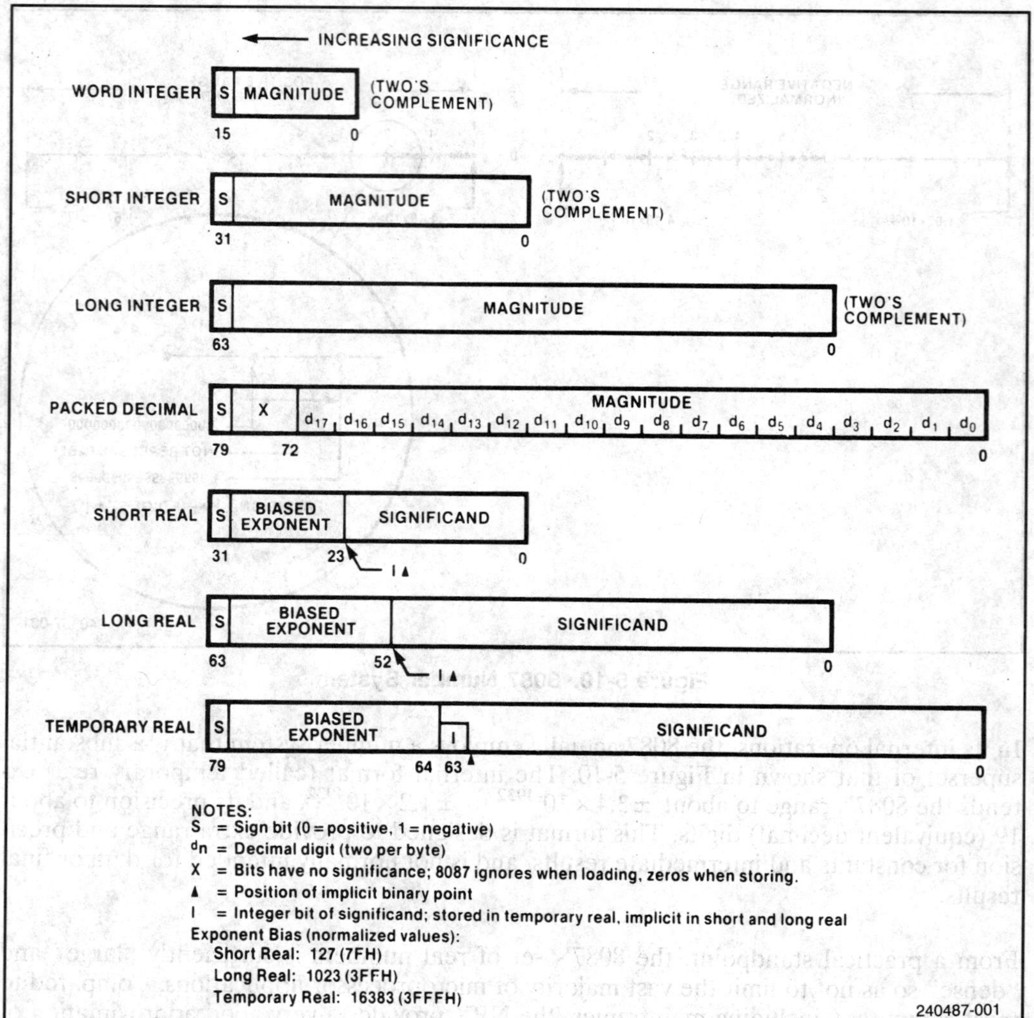

Figure 5-11. Data Formats

each data type. In the figure, the most significant digits of all numbers (and fields within numbers) are the leftmost digits. Table 5-2 provides the range and number of significant (decimal) digits that each format can accommodate.

BINARY INTEGERS

The three binary integer formats are identical except for length, which governs the range that can be accommodated in each format. The leftmost bit is interpreted as the number's sign: 0 = positive and 1 = negative. Negative numbers are represented in standard two's complement notation (the binary integers are the only 8087 format to use two's complement). The quantity zero is represented with a positive sign (all bits are 0). The 8087 word integer format is identical to the 16-bit signed integer data type of the 8086/8088.

DECIMAL INTEGERS

Decimal integers are stored in packed decimal notation, with two decimal digits "packed" into each byte, except the leftmost byte, which carries the sign bit (0 = positive, 1 = negative). Negative numbers are not stored in two's complement form and are distinguished from positive numbers only by the sign bit. The most significant digit of the number is the leftmost digit. All digits must be in the range 0H-9H.

REAL NUMBERS

The 8087 stores real numbers in a three-field binary format that resembles scientific, or exponential, notation. The number's significant digits are held in the *significand* field, the *exponent* field locates the binary point within the significant digits (and therefore determines the number's magnitude), and the *sign* field indicates whether the number is positive or negative. (The exponent and significand are analogous to the terms "characteristic" and "mantissa" used to describe floating point numbers on some computers.) Negative numbers differ from positive numbers only in their sign bits.

Table 5-4 shows how the real number 178.125 (decimal) is stored in the 8087 short real format. The table lists a progression of equivalent notations that express the same value to show how a number can be converted from one form to another. The ASM-86 and PL/M-86 language translators perform a similar process when they encounter programmer-defined real number constants. Note that not every decimal fraction has an exact binary equivalent. The decimal number 1/10, for example, cannot be expressed exactly in binary (just as the number 1/3 cannot be expressed in decimal). When a translator encounters such a value, it produces a rounded binary approximation of the decimal value.

Table 5-4. Real Number Notation

Notation	Value		
Ordinary Decimal	178.125		
Scientific Decimal	1Δ78125E2		
Scientific Binary	1Δ0110010001E111		
Scientific Binary (Biased Exponent)	1Δ011001001E100000110		
8087 Short Real (Normalized)	**Sign**	**Biased Exponent**	**Significand**
	0	10000110	01100100010000000000000 1Δ (implicit)

The NPX usually carries the digits of the significand in normalized form. This means that, except for the value zero, the significand is an *integer* and a *fraction* as follows:

1 Δ fff...ff

where Δ indicates an assumed binary point. The number of fraction bits varies according to the real format: 23 for short, 52 for long and 63 for temporary real. By normalizing real numbers so that their integer bit is always a 1, the 8087 eliminates leading zeros in small values ($| \times | < 1$). This technique maximizes the number of significant digits that can be accommodated in a significand of a given width.

Note that in the short and long real formats the integer bit is *implicit* and is not actually stored; the integer bit is physically present in the temporary real format only.

If one were to examine only the significand with its assumed binary point, all normalized, real numbers would have values between 1 and 2. The exponent field locates the *actual* binary point in the significant digits. Just as in decimal scientific notation, a positive exponent has the effect of moving the binary point to the right, and a negative exponent effectively moves the binary point to the left, inserting leading zeros as necessary. An unbiased exponent of zero indicates that the position of the assumed binary point is also the position of the actual binary point. The exponent field, then, determines a real number's magnitude.

In order to simplify comparing real numbers (e.g., for sorting), the 8087 stores exponents in a biased form. This means that a constant is added to the *true exponent* described above. The value of this bias is different for each real format (see Figure 5-11). It has been chosen so as to force the *biased exponent* to be a positive value. This allows two real numbers (of the same format and sign) to be compared as if they are unsigned binary integers. That is, when comparing them bitwise from left to right (beginning with the left-most exponent bit), the first bit position that differs orders the numbers; there is no need to proceed further with the comparison. A number's true exponent can be determined simply by subtracting the bias value of its format.

The short and long real formats exist in memory only. If a number in one of these formats is loaded into a register, it is automatically converted to temporary real, the format used for all internal operations. Likewise, data in registers can be converted to short or long real for storage in memory. The temporary real format may be used in memory also, typically to store intermediate results that cannot be held in registers.

Most applications should use the long real form to store real number data and results; it provides sufficient range and precision to return correct results with a minimum of programmer attention. The short real format is appropriate for applications that are constrained by memory, but it should be recognized that this format provides a smaller margin of safety. It is also useful for debugging algorithms because roundoff problems will manifest themselves more quickly in this format. The temporary real format should normally be reserved for holding intermediate results, loop accumulations, and constants. Its extra length is designed to shield final results from the effects of rounding and overflow/underflow in intermediate calculations. When the temporary real format is used to hold data or to deliver final results, the safety features built into the 8087 are compromised. Furthermore, the range and precision of the long real form are adequate for most microcomputer applications.

SPECIAL VALUES

Besides being able to represent positive and negative numbers, the 8087 data formats may be used to describe other entities. These special values provide extra flexibility but most users do not need to understand them in detail to use the 8087 successfully. Accordingly, they are discussed here only briefly; expanded coverage, including the bit encoding of each value, is provided in the section "Special Topics."

The value zero may be signed positive or negative in the real and decimal integer formats; the sign of a binary integer zero is always positive. The fact that zero may be signed, however, is transparent to the programmer.

The real number formats allow for the representation of the special values $+\infty$ and $-\infty$. The 8087 may generate these values as its built-in response to exceptions such as division by zero, or the attempt to store a result that exceeds the upper range limit of the destination format. Infinities may participate in arithmetic and comparison operations, and in fact the processor provides two different conceptual models for handling these special values.

If a programmer attempts an operation for which the 8087 cannot deliver a reasonable result, it will, at the programmer's discretion, either request an interrupt, or return the special value *indefinite*. Taking the square root of a negative number is an example of this type of invalid operation. The recommended action in this situation is to stop the computation by trapping to a user-written exception handler. If, however, the programmer elects to continue the computation, the specially coded *indefinite* value will propagate through the calculation and thus flag the erroneous computation when it is eventually delivered as the result. Each format has an encoding that represents the special value *indefinite*.

In the real formats, a whole range of special values, both positive and negative, is designated to represent a class of values called NAN (Not-A-Number). The special value *indefinite* is a reserved NAN encoding, but all other encodings are made available to be defined in any way by application software. Using a NAN as an operand raises the invalid operation exception, and can trap to a user-written routine to process the NAN. Alternatively, the 8087's built-in exception handler will simply return the NAN itself as the result of the operation; in this way NANs, including *indefinite*, may be propagated through a calculation and delivered as a final, special-valued, result. One use for NANs is to detect uninitialized variables.

As mentioned earlier, the 8087 stores non-zero real numbers in "normalized floating point" form. It also provides for storing and operating on reals that are not normalized, i.e., whose significands contain one or more leading zeros. Nonnormals arise when the result of a calculation yields a value that is too small to be represented in normal form. The leading zeros of nonnormals permit smaller numbers to be represented, at the cost of some lost precision (the number of significant digits is reduced by the leading zeros).

In typical algorithms, extremely small values are most likely to be generated as intermediate, rather than final results. By using the NPX's temporary real format for holding intermediates, values as small as $\pm 3.4 \times 10^{-4932}$ can be represented; this makes the occurrence of nonnormal numbers a rare phenomenon in 8087 applications. Nevertheless, the NPX can load, store and operate on nonnormalized real numbers.

Rounding Control

Internally, the 8087 employs three extra bits (guard, round and sticky bits) which enable it to represent the infinitely precise true result of a computation; these bits are not accessible to programmers. Whenever the destination can represent the infinitely precise true result, the 8087 delivers it. Rounding occurs in arithmetic and store operations when the format of the destination cannot exactly represent the infinitely precise true result. For example, a real number may be rounded if it is stored in a shorter real format, or in an integer format. Or, the infinitely precise true result may be rounded when it is returned to a register.

The NPX has four rounding modes, selectable by the RC field in the control word (see Figure 5-7). Given a true result *b* that cannot be represented by the target data type, the 8087 determines the two representable numbers *a* and *c* that most closely bracket *b* in value ($a < b < c$). The processor then rounds (changes *b* to *a* or to *c* according to the mode selected by the RC field as shown in Table 5-5. Rounding introduces an error in a result that is less than one unit in the last place to which the result is rounded.

"Round to nearest or even" is the default mode and is suitable for most applications; it provides the most accurate and statistically unbiased estimate of the true result. The "chop" mode is provided for integer arithmetic applications.

"Round up" and "round down" are termed directed rounding and can be used to implement interval arithmetic. Interval arithmetic generates a certifiable result independent of the occurrence of rounding and other errors. The upper and lower bounds of an interval may be computed by executing an algorithm twice, rounding up in one pass and down in the other.

Table 5-5. Rounding Modes

RC Field	Rounding Mode	Rounding Action
00	Round to nearest	Closer to *b* of *a* or *c*; if equally close, select even number (the one whose least significant bit is zero).
01	Round down (toward $-\infty$)	*a*
10	Round up (toward $+\infty$)	*c*
11	Chop (toward 0)	Smaller in magnitude of *a* or *c*

Precision Control

The 8087 allows results to be calculated with 64, 53, or 24 bits of precision as selected by the PC field of the control word. The default setting, and the one that is best-suited for most applications, is the full 64 bits. The other settings are required by the proposed IEEE standard, and are provided to obtain compatibility with the specifications of certain existing programming languages. Specifying less precision nullifies the advantages of the temporary real format's extended fraction length, and does not improve execution speed. When reduced precision is specified, the rounding of the fraction zeros the unused bits on the right.

Infinity Control

The 8087's system of real numbers may be closed by either of two models of infinity. These two means of closing the number system, projective and affine closure, are illustrated schematically in Figure 5-12. The setting of the IC field in the control word selects one model or the other. The default means of closure is projective, and this is recommended for most computations. When projective closure is selected, the NPX treats the special values $+\infty$ and $-\infty$ as a single unsigned infinity (similar to its treatment of signed zeros). In the affine mode the NPX respects the signs of $+\infty$ and $-\infty$.

While affine mode may provide more information than projective, there are occasions when the sign may in fact represent misinformation. For example, consider an algorithm that yields an intermediate result x of $+0$ and -0 the (the same numeric value) in different executions. If 1/x were then computed in affine mode, two entirely different values ($+\infty$ and $-\infty$) would result from numerically identical values of x. Projective mode on the other hand, provides less information but never returns misinformation. In general, then, projective mode should be used globally, with affine mode reserved for local computations where the programmer can take advantage of the sign and knows for certain that the nature of the computation will not produce misleading results.

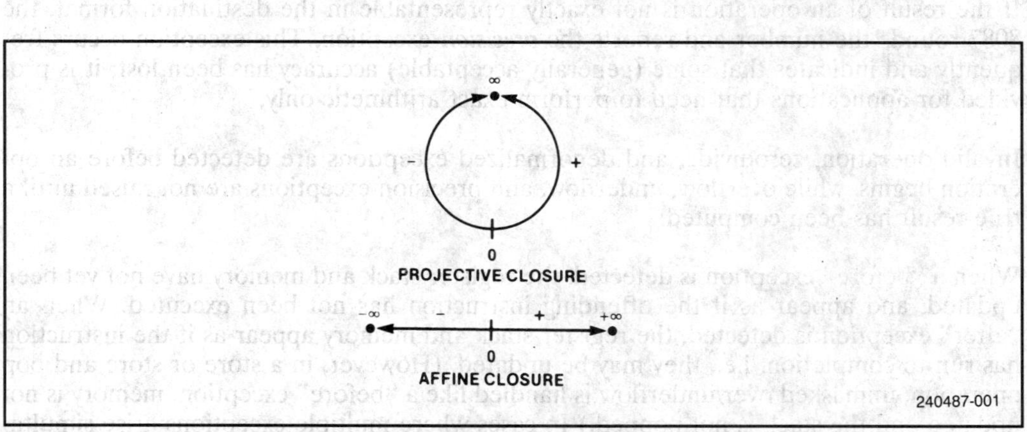

Figure 5-12. Projective versus Affine Closure

Exceptions

During the execution of most instructions, the 8087 checks for six classes of exception conditions.

The 8087 reports *invalid operation* if any of the following occurs:

- An attempt to load a register that is not empty, (e.g., Stack overflow).
- An attempt to pop an operand from an empty register (e.g., stack underflow).
- An operand is a NAN.
- The operands cause the operation to be indeterminate (0/0, square root of a negative number, etc.).

An invalid operation generally indicates a program error.

If the exponent of the true result is too large for the destination real format, the 8087 signals *overflow*. Conversely, a true exponent that is too small to be represented results in the *underflow* exception. If either of these occur, the result of the operation is outside the range of the destination real format.

Typical algorithms are most likely to produce extremely large and small numbers in the calculation of intermediate, rather than final, results. Because of the great range of the temporary real format (recommended as the destination format for intermediates), overflow and underflow are relatively rare events in most 8087 applications.

If division of a finite non-zero operand by zero is attempted, the 8087 reports the *zero-divide* exception.

If an instruction attempts to operate on a denormal, the NPX reports the *denormalized* exception. This exception is provided for users who wish to implement, in software, an option of the proposed IEEE standard which specifies that operands must be prenormalized before they are used.

If the result of an operation is not exactly representable in the destination format, the 8087 rounds the number and reports the *precision* exception. This exception occurs frequently and indicates that some (generally acceptable) accuracy has been lost; it is provided for applications that need to perform exact arithmetic only.

Invalid operation, zerodivide, and denormalized exceptions are detected before an operation begins, while overflow, underflow, and precision exceptions are not raised until a true result has been computed.

When a "before" exception is detected, the register stack and memory have not yet been updated, and appear as if the offending instruction has not been executed. When an "after" exception is detected, the register stack and memory appear as if the instruction has run to completion, i.e., they may be updated. (However, in a store or store and pop operation, unmasked over/underflow is handled like a "before" exception; memory is not updated and the stack is not popped.) In cases where multiple exceptions arise simultaneously, one exception is signaled according to the following precedence sequence:

- Denormalized (if unmasked)
- Invalid operation
- Zerodivide
- Denormalized (if masked)
- Over/underflow
- Precision

(The terms "masked" and "unmasked" are explained shortly.) This means, for example, that zero divided by zero will result in an invalid operation and not a zerodivide exception.

The 8087 reports an exception by setting the corresponding flag in the status word to 1. It then checks the corresponding exception mask in the control word to determine if it should "field" the exception (mask=1), or if it should issue an interrupt request to invoke a user-written exception handler (mask=0). In the first case, the exception is said to be *masked* (from user software) and the NPX executes its on-chip *masked response* for that exception. In the second case, the exception is *unmasked*, and the processor performs its *unmasked response*. The masked response always produces a standard result and then proceeds with the instruction. The unmasked response always traps to user software by interrupting the CPU (assuming the interrupt path is clear). These responses are summarized in Table 5-6. The section "Special Topics," later in this chapter, contains a complete description of all exception conditions and the NPX's masked responses. Note that when exceptions are masked, the NPX may detect multiple

Table 5-6. Exception and Response Summary

Exception	Masked Response	Unmasked Response
Invalid Operation	If one operand is NAN, return it; if both are NANs, return NAN with larger absolute value; if neither is NAN, return *indefinite*.	Request interrupt.
Zerodivide	Return ∞ signed with "exclusive or" of operand signs.	Request interrupt.
Denormalized	Memory operand: proceed as usual. Register operand: convert to valid unnormal, then re-evaluate for exceptions.	Request interrupt.
Overflow	Return properly signed ∞.	Register destination: adjust exponent*, store result, request interrupt. Memory destination: request interrupt.
Underflow	Denormalize result.	Register destination: adjust exponent*, store result, request interrupt. Memory destination: request interrupt.
Precision	Return rounded result.	Return rounded result, request interrupt.

exceptions in a single instruction, since it continues executing the instruction after performing its masked response. For example, the 8087 could detect a denormalized operand, perform its masked response to this exception, and then detect an underflow.

By writing different values into the exception masks of the control word, the user can accept responsibility for handling exceptions, or delegate this to the NPX. Exception handling software is often difficult to write, and the 8087's masked responses have been tailored to deliver the most "reasonable" result for each condition. The majority of applications will find that masking all exceptions other than invalid operation will yield satisfactory results with the least programming investment. An invalid operation exception normally indicates a fatal error in a program that must be corrected; this exception should not normally be masked.

The exception flags are "sticky" and can be cleared only by executing the FCLEX (clear exceptions) instruction, by reinitializing the processor, or by overwriting the flags with an FRSTOR or FLDENV instruction. This means that the flags can provide a cumulative record of the exceptions encountered in a long calculation. A program can therefore mask all exceptions (except, typically, invalid operation), run the calculation and then inspect the status word to see if any exceptions were detected at any point in the calculation.

Note that the 8087 has another set of internal exception flags that it clears before each instruction. It is these flags and not those in the status word that actually trigger the 8087's exception response. The flags in the status word provide a cumulative record of exceptions for the programmer only.

If the NPX executes an unmasked response to an exception, it is assumed that a user exception handler will be invoked via an interrupt from the 8087. The 8087 sets the IR (interrupt request) bit in the status word, but this, in itself, does not guarantee an immediate CPU interrupt. The interrupt request may be blocked by the IEM (interrupt-enable mask) in the 8087 control word, by the 8259A Programmable Interrupt Controller, or by the CPU itself. *If any exception flag is unmasked, it is imperative that the interrupt path to the CPU is eventually cleared so that the user's software can field the exception and the offending task can resume execution.* Note that the 8087 remains "busy" pending CPU intervention. Interrupts are covered in detail in Chapter 7.

A user-written exception handler takes the form of an 8086/8088 interrupt procedure. Although exception handlers will vary widely from one application to the next, most will include these basic steps:

- Store the 8087 environment (control, status and tag words, operand and instruction pointers) as it existed at the time of the exception;
- Clear the exception bits in the status word;
- Enable interrupts on the CPU;
- Identify the exception by examining the status and control words in the saved environment;
- Take application-dependent action;
- Return to the point of interruption, resuming normal execution.

Possible "application-dependent actions" include:

- Incrementing an exception counter for later display or printing;
- Printing or displaying diagnostic information (e.g., the 8087 environment and registers);
- Aborting further execution of the calculation causing the exception;
- Aborting all further execution;
- Using the exception pointers to build an instruction that will run without exception and executing it;
- Storing a diagnostic value (a NAN) in the result and continuing with the computation.

Notice that an exception may or may not constitute an error, depending on the application. For example, an invalid operation caused by a stack overflow could signal an ambitious exception handler to extend the register stack to memory and continue running.

INSTRUCTION SET

This section describes the operation of each of the 8087's 69 instructions. The first part of the section describes the function of each instruction in detail. For this discussion, the instructions are divided into six functional groups: data transfer, arithmetic, comparisons, transcendental, constant, and processor control. The second part provides instruction attributes such as execution speed, bus transfers, and exceptions, as well as coding example for each combination of operands accepted by the instruction. This information is concentrated in a table, organized alphabetically by instruction mnemonic, for easy reference.

Throughout this section, the instruction set is described as it appears to the ASM-86 programmer who is coding a program. Table 6-23, in Section Two, "Hardware," covers the actual machine instruction encodings, which are principally of use to those reading unformatted memory dumps, monitoring instruction fetches on the bus, or writing exception handlers.

The instruction descriptions in this section concentrate on describing the normal function of each operation. Table 5-17 lists the exceptions that can occur for each instruction. Table 5-29 details the causes of exceptions as well as the 8087's masked responses.

The typical NPX instruction accepts one or two operands as "inputs," operates on these, and produces a result as an "output." Operands are most often (the contents of) register of memory locations. The operands of some instructions are predefined; for example, FSQRT always takes the square root of the number in the top stack element. Others allow, or require, the programmer to explicitly code the operand(s) along with the instruction mnemonic. Still others accept one explicit operand and one implicit operand, which is usually the top stack element.

Whether supplied by the programmer or utilized automatically, there are two basic types of operands, *sources* and *destinations*. A source operand simply supplies one of the "inputs" to an instruction; it is not altered by the instruction. Even when an instruction converts the source operand from one format to another (e.g., real to integer), the conversion is actually performed in an internal work area to avoid altering the source operand. A destination operand may also provide an "input" to an instruction. It is distinguished from a source operand, however, because its contents may be altered when it receives the result produced by the operation; that is, the destination is replaced by the result.

Many instructions allow their operands to be coded in more than one way. For example, FADD (add real) may be written without operands, with only a source or with a destination and a source. The instruction descriptions in this section employ the simple convention of separating alternative operand forms with slashes; the slashes, however, are not coded. Consecutive slashes indicate an option of no explicit operands. The operands for FADD are thus described as:

//source/destination,source

This means that FADD may be written in any of three ways.

FADD
FADD *source*
FADD *destination,source*

When reading this section, it is important to bear in mind that memory operands may be coded with any of the CPU's memory addressing modes. Table 5-19 in this chapter also provides several addressing mode examples.

Data Transfer Instructions

These instructions (summarized in Table 5-7) move operands among elements of the register stack, and between the stack top and memory. Any of the seven data types can be converted to temporary real and loaded (pushed) onto the stack in a single operation; they can be stored to memory in the same manner. The data transfer instructions automatically update the 8087 tag word to reflect the register contents following the instruction.

FLD *source*

FLD (load real) loads (pushes) the source operand onto the top of the register stack. This is done by decrementing the stack pointer by one and then copying the contents of the source to the new stack top. The source may be a register on the stack (ST(i)) or any of the real data types in memory. Short and long real source operands are converted to temporary real automatically. Coding FLD ST(0) duplicates the stack top.

Table 5-7. Data Transfer Instructions

Real Transfers	
FLD	Load real
FST	Store real
FSTP	Store real and pop
FXCH	Exchange registers
Integer Transfers	
FILD	Integer load
FIST	Integer store
FISTP	Integer store and pop
Packed Decimal Transfers	
FBLD	Packed decimal (BCD) load
FBSTP	Packed decimal (BCD) store and pop

FST *destination*

FST (store real) transfers the stack top to the destination, which may be another register on the stack, or a short or long real memory operand. If the destination is short or long real, the significand is rounded to the width of the destination according to the RC field of the control word, and the exponent is converted to the width and bias of the destination format.

If, however, the stack top is tagged special (it contains, a NAN, or a denormal) then the stack top's significand is not rounded but is chopped (on the right) to fit the destination. Neither is the exponent converted, but it also is chopped on the right and transferred, "as is." This preserves the value's identification as or a NAN (exponent all ones) or a denormal (exponent all zeros) so that it can be properly loaded and tagged later in the program if desired.

FSTP *destination*

FSTP (store real and pop) operates identically to FST except that the stack is popped following the transfer. This is done by tagging the top stack element empty and then incrementing ST. FSTP permits storing to a temporary real memory variable while FST does not. Coding FSTP ST(0) is equivalent to popping the stack with no data transfer.

FXCH//*destination*

FXCH (exchange registers) swaps the contents of the destination and the stack top registers. If the destination is not coded explicitly, ST(1) is used. Many 8087 instructions operate only on the stack top; FXCH provides a simple means of effectively using these instructions on lower stack elements. For example, the following sequence takes the square root of the third register from the top:

```
FXCH ST(3)
FSQRT
FXCH ST(3)
```

FILD *source*

FILD (integer load) coverts the source memory operand from its binary integer format (word, short, or long) to temporary real and loads (pushes) the result onto the stack. The (new) stack top is tagged zero if all bits in the source were zero, and is tagged valid otherwise.

FIST *destination*

FIST (integer store) rounds the contents of the stack top to an integer according to the RC field of the control word and transfers the result to the destination. The destination may define a word or short integer variable. Negative zero is stored in the same encoding as positive zero: 0000...00.

FISTP *destination*

FISTP (integer store and pop) operates like FIST and also pops the stack following the transfer. The destination may be any of the binary integer data types.

FBLD *source*

FBLD (packed decimal (BCD) load) converts the contents of the source operand from packed decimal to temporary real and loads (pushes) the result onto the stack. The sign of the source is preserved, including the case where the value is negative zero. FBLD is an exact operation; the source is loaded with no rounding error.

The packed decimal digits of the source are assumed to be in the range 0-9H. The instuction does not check for invalid digits (A-FH) and the result of attempting to load an invalid encoding is undefined.

FBSTP *destination*

FBSTP (packed decimal (BCD) store and pop) converts the contents of the stack top to a packed decimal integer, stores the result at the destination in memory, and pops the stack. FBSTP produces a rounded integer from a non-integral value by adding a value close to 0.5 to the value and chopping. Users who are concerned about rounding may precede FBSTP with FRNDINT.

Arithmetic Instructions

The 8087's arithmetic instruction set (Table 5-8) provides a wealth of variations on the basic add, subtract, multiply, and divide operations, and a number of other useful functions. These range from a simple absolute value to a square root instruction that executes faster than ordinary division; 8087 programmers no longer need to spend valuable time eliminating square roots from algorithms because they run too slowly. Other arithmetic instructions perform exact modulo division, round real numbers to integers, and scale values by powers of two.

Table 5-8. Arithmetic Instructions

Addition	
FADD	Add real
FADDP	Add real and pop
FIADD	Integer add
Subtraction	
FSUB	Subtract real
FUSBP	Subtract real and pop
FISUB	Integer subtract
FSUBR	Subtract real reversed
FSUBRP	Subtract real reversed and pop
FISUBR	Integer subtract reversed
Multiplication	
FMUL	Multiply real
FMULP	Multiply real and pop
FIMUL	Integer multiply
Division	
FDIV	Divide real
FDIVP	Divide real and pop
FIDIV	Integer divide
FDIVR	Divide real reversed
FDIVRP	Divide real reversed and pop
FIDIVR	Integer divide reversed
Other Operations	
FSQRT	Square root
FSCALE	Scale
FPREM	Partial remainder
FRNDINT	Round to integer
FXTRACT	Extract exponent and significand
FABS	Absolute value
FCHS	Change sign

The 8087's basic arithmetic instructions (addition, subtraction, multiplication, and division) are designed to encourage the development of very efficient algorithms. In particular, they allow the programmer to minimize memory references and to make optimum use of the NPX register stack.

Table 5-9 summarizes the available operation/operand forms that are provided for basic arithmetic. In addition to the four normal operations, two "reversed" instructions make subtraction and division "symmetrical" like addition and multiplication. The variety of instruction and operand forms give the programmer unusual flexibility:

- operands may be located in registers or memory;
- results may be deposited in a choice of registers;
- operands may be a variety of NPX data types: temporary real, long real, short real, short integer or word integer, with automatic conversion to temporary real performed by the 8087.

Table 5-9. Arithmetic Instructions and Operands

Instruction Form	Mnemonic Form	Operand Forms destination,source	ASM-86 Example	
Classical stack	F*op*	{ST(1),ST}	FADD	
Register	F*op*	ST(i),ST or ST,ST(i)	FSUB	ST,ST(3)
Register pop	F*op*P	ST(i),ST	FMULP	ST(2),ST
Real memory	F*op*	{ST,} short-real/long-real	FDIV	AZIMUTH
Integer memory	FI*op*	{ST,} word-integer/short-integer	FIDIV	N_PULSES

NOTES:

Braces { } surround *implicit operands; these are not coded, and are shown here for information only.*

op =	ADD	destination ←destination + source
	SUB	destination←source
	SUBR	destination←source − destination
	MUL	destination←destination • source
	DIV	destination←destination ÷ source
	DIVR	destination←source ÷ destination

Five basic instruction forms may be used across all six operations, as shown in Table 5-9. The classical stack form may be used to make the 8087 operate like a classical stack machine. No operands are coded in this form, only the instruction mnemonic. The NDP picks the source operand from the stack top and the destination from the next stack element. It then pops the stack, performs the operation, and returns the result to the new stack top, effectively replacing the operands by the result. (Note that FADD, FSUB, FMUL and FDIV also pop if no operands are specified, in spite of the fact that the mnemonics do not have P as a last character.)

Addition

```
FADD    //source/destination,source
FADDP   destination,source
FIADD   source
```

The addition instructions (add real, add real and pop, integer add) add the source and destination operands and return the sum to the destination. The operand at the stack top may be doubled by coding:

```
FADD    ST,ST(0)
```

Normal Subtraction

```
FSUB    //source/destination,source
FSUBP   destination,source
FISUB   source
```

The normal subtraction instructions (subtract real, subtract real and pop, integer subtract) subtract the source operand from the destination and return the difference to the destination.

Reversed Subtraction

FSUBR *//source/destination,source*
FSUBRP *//destination,source*
FISUBR *source*

The reversed subtraction instruction (subtract real reversed, subtract real reversed and pop, integer subtract reversed) subtract the destination from the source and return the difference to the destination.

Multiplication

FMUL *//source/destination,source*
FMULP *destination,source*
FIMUL *source*

The multiplication instructions (muliply real, multiply real and pop, integer multiply) multiply the source and destination operands and return the product to the destination. Coding FMUL ST,ST(0) squares the contents of the stack top.

Normal Division

FDIV *//source/destination,source*
FDIVP *destination,source*
FIDIV *source*

The normal division instructions (divide real, divide real and pop, integer divide) divide the destination by the source and return the quotient to the destination.

Reversed Division

FDIVR *//source/destination,source*
FDIVRP *destination,source*
FIDIVR *source*

The reversed division instructions (divide real reversed, divide real reversed and pop, integer divide reversed) divide the source operand by the destination and return the quotient to the destination.

FSQRT

FSQRT (square root) replaces the contents of the top stack element with its square root. (Note: the square root of −0 is defined to be −0.)

FSCALE

FSCALE (scale) interprets the value contained in ST(1) as an integer, and adds this value to the exponent of the number in ST.

This is equivalent to:

$ST < -ST2^{ST(1)}$

thus, FSCALE provides rapid multiplication or division by integral powers of 2. It is particularly useful for scaling the elements of a vector.

Note that FSCALE assumes the scale factor if ST(1) is an integral value in the range $-2^{15} \leq \times 2^{15}$. If the value is not integral, but is in-range and is greater in magnitude than 1, FSCALE uses the nearest integer smaller in magnitude, i.e., it chops the value toward 0. If the value is out of range, or $0<|X|<1$, the instruction will produce an undefined result and will not signal an exception. The recommended practice is to load the scale factor from a word integer to ensure correct operation.

FPREM

FPREM (partial remainder) performs modulo division of the top stack element by the next stack element, i.e., ST(1) is the modulus.

FPREM produces an *exact* result; the precision exception does not occur. The sign of the remainder is the same as the sign of the original dividend.

FPREM operates by performing successive scaled subtractions; obtaining the exact remainder when the operands differ greatly in magnitude can consume large amounts of execution time. Since the 8087 can only be preempted between instructions, the remainder function could seriously increase interrupt latency in these cases. Accordingly, the instruction is designed to be executed iteratively in a software-controlled loop.

FPREM can reduce a magnitude difference of up to 2^{64} in one execution. If FPREM produces a remainder that is less than the modulus, the function is complete and bit C2 of the status word condition code is cleared. If the function is incomplete, C2 is set to 1; the result in ST is then called the partial remainder. Software can inspect C2 by storing the status word following execution of FPREM and reexecute the instruction (using the partial remainder in ST as the dividend), until "C" is cleared. Alternatively, a program can determine when the function is complete by comparing ST to ST(1). If ST > ST(1) then FPREM must be executed again; if ST = ST(1) then the remainder is 0; if ST < ST(1) then the remainder is ST. A higher priority interrupting routine which needs the 8087 can force a context switch between the instructions in the remainder loop.

An important use for FPREM is to reduce arguments (operands) of periodic transcendental functions to the range permitted by these instructions. For example, the FPTAN (tangent) instruction requires its argument to be less than $\pi/4$. Using $\pi/4$ as a modulus,

FPREM will reduce an argument so that it is in range of FPT. Because FPREM produces an exact result, the argument reduction does *not* introduce roundoff error into the calculation, even if several iterations are required to bring the argument into range. (The rounding of pi does not create the effect of a rounded argument, but of a rounded period.)

FPREM also provides the least-significant three bits of the quotient generated by FPREM (in C_0, C_3, C_1). This is also important for transcendental argument reduction since it locates the original angle in the correct one of eight $\pi 4$ segments of the unit circle.

The FPREM instruction also functions as a "universal normalizer." If the top stack element is unnormal and the modulus is greater than the top stack element, the top stack element will be normalized. In addition, if the number is normalized and the precision mode of the 8087 is set to less than 64 bits, the extra precision bits of the normalized element will be cleared.

FRNDINT

FRNDINT (round to integer) rounds the top stack element to an integer. For example, assume that ST contains the 8087 real number encoding of the decimal value 155.625. FRNDINT will change the value to 155 if the RC field of the control word is set to down or chop, or to 156 if it is set up or nearest.

FXTRACT

FXTRACT (extract exponent and significand) "decomposes" the number in the stack top into two numbers that represent the actual value of the operand's exponent and significand fields. The "exponent" replaces the original operand on the stack and the significand is pushed onto the stack. Following execution of FXTRACT, ST (the new stack top) contains the value of the original significand expressed as a real number: its sign is the same as the operand's, its exponent is 0 true (16,383 or 3FFFH biased), and its significand is identical to the original operand's. ST(1) contains the value of the original operand's true (unbiased) exponent expressed as a real number. If the original operand is zero, FXTRACT produces zeros in ST and ST(1) and *both* are signed as the original operand.

To clarify the operation of FXTRACT, assume ST contains a number whose true exponent is +4 (i.e., its exponent field contains 4003H). After executing FXTRACT, ST(1) will contain the real number +4.0; its sign will be positive, its exponent field will contain 4001H (+2 true) and its significand field will contain 1 Δ 00...00B. In other words, the value in ST(1) will be $1.0 \times 2^2 = 4$. If ST contains an operand whose true exponent is −7 (i.e., its exponent field contains 3FF8H), then FXTRACT will return an "exponent" of −7.0; after the instruction executes, ST(1)'s sign and exponent fields will contain C001H (negative sign, true exponent of 2) and its significand will be 1 Δ 1100...00B. In other words, the value in ST(1) will be $-1.11\ 2^2 = -7.0$. In both cases, following FXTRACT, ST's sign and significand fields will be the same as the original operand's, and its exponent field will contain 3FFFH, (0 true).

FXTRACT is useful in conjunction with FBSTP for converting numbers in 8087 temporary real format to decimal representations (e.g., for printing or displaying). It can also be useful for debugging, since it allows the exponent and significand parts of a real number to be examined separately.

FABS

FABS (absolute value) changes the top stack element to its absolute value by making its sign positive.

FCHS

FCHS (change sign) complements (reverses) the sign of the top stack element.

Comparison Instructions

Each of these instructions (Table 5-10) analyzes the top stack element, often in relationship to another operand, and reports the result in the status word condition code. The basic operations are compare, test (compare with zero), and examine (report tag, sign, and normalization). Special forms of the compare operation are provided to optimize algorithms by allowing direct comparisons with binary integers and real numbers in memory, as well as popping the stack after a comparison.

The FSTSW (store status word) instruction may be used following a comparison to transfer the condition code to memory for inspection.

Note that instructions other than those in the comparison group may update the condition code. To insure that the status word is not altered inadvertently, store it immediately following a comparison operation.

Table 5-10. Comparison Instructions

FCOM	Compare real
FCOMP	Compare real and pop
FCOMPP	Compare real and pop twice
FICOM	Integer compare
FICOMP	Integer compare and pop
FTST	Test
TXAM	Examine

FCOM//*source*

FCOM (compare real) compares the stack top to the source operand. The source operand may be a register on the stack, or a short or long real memory operand. If an operand is not coded, ST is compared to ST(1). Positive and negative forms of zero compare identically as if they were unsigned. Following the instruction, the condition codes reflect the order of the operands as follows:

C3	C2	C0	Order
0	0	0	ST > source
0	0	1	ST < source
1	0	0	ST = source
1	1	1	ST?source

NANs and ∞ (projective) cannot be compared and return C3 = C0 = 1 as shown above.

FCOMP//*source*

FCOMP (compare real and pop) operates like FCOM, and in addition pops the stack.

FCOMPP

FCOMPP (compare real and pop twice) operates like FCOM and additionally pops the stack twice, discarding both operands. The comparison is of the stack top to ST(1); no operands may be explicitly coded.

FICOM*source*

FICOM (integer compare) converts the source operand, which may reference a word or short binary integer variable, to temporary real and compares the stack top to it.

FICOMP*source*

FICOMP (integer compare and pop) operates identically to FICOM and additionally discards the value in ST by popping the stack.

FTST

FTST (test) tests the top stack element by comparing it to zero. The result is posted to the condition codes as follows:

C3	C2	C0	Result
0	0	0	ST is positive and nonzero
0	0	1	ST is negative and nonzero
1	0	0	ST is zero (+ or −)
1	1	1	ST is not comparable (i.e., it is a NAN or projective ∞)

FXAM

FXAM (examine) reports the contents of the top stack element as positive/negative and NAN/unnormal/denormal/normal/zero, or empty. Table 5-11 lists and interprets all the condition code values that FXAM generates. Although four different encodings may be returned for an empty register, bits C3 and C0 of the condition code are both 1 in all encodings. Bits C2 and C1 should be ignored.

Transcendental Instructions

The instructions in this group (Table 5-12) perform the time-consuming *core calculations* for all common trigonometric, hyperbolic, inverse hyperbolic, logarithmic and exponential functions. Prologue and epilogue software may be used to reduce arguments to the range accepted by the instructions and to adjust the result to correspond to the original arguments if necessary. The transcendentals operate on the top one or two stack elements and they return their results to the stack also.

Table 5-11. FXAM Condition Code Settings

Condition Code				Interpretation
C3	C2	C1	C0	
0	0	0	0	+ Unnormal
0	0	0	1	+ NAN
0	0	1	0	− Unnormal
0	0	1	1	− NAN
0	1	0	0	+ Normal
0	1	0	1	+ ∞
0	1	1	0	− Normal
0	1	1	1	− ∞
1	0	0	0	+ 0
1	0	0	1	Empty
1	0	1	0	− 0
1	0	1	1	Empty
1	1	0	0	+ Denormal
1	1	0	1	Empty
1	1	1	0	− Denormal
1	1	1	1	Empty

Table 5-12. Transcendental Instructions

FPTAN	Partial tangent
FPATAN	Partial arctangent
F2XM1	$2^X - 1$
FYL2X	$Y \log_2 X$
FYL2XP1	$Y \log_2(X+1)$

The transcendental instructions assume that their operands are *valid and in-range*. The instruction descriptions in this section provide the range of each operation. To be considered valid, an operand to a transcendental must be normalized; denormals, unnormals, infinities and NANs are considered invalid. (Zero operands are accepted by some functions and are considered out-of-range by others.) If a transcendental operand is invalid or out of range, the instruction will produce an undefined result without signalling an exception. It is the programmer's responsibility to ensure that operands are valid and in-range before executing a transcendental. For periodic functions, FPREM may be used to bring a valid operand into range.

FPTAN

FPTAN (partial tangent) computes the function Y/X = TAN (Θ). Θ is taken from the top of the stack element; it must lie in the range Θ = or < Θ = or < π4. The result of the operation is a ratio; Y replaces Θ in the stack and X is pushed, becoming the new stack top.

The ratio result of FPTAN and the ratio argument of FPATAN are designed to optimize the calculation of the other trigonometric functions, including SIN, COS, ARCSIN and ARCCOS. These can be derived from TAN and ARCTAN via standard trigonometric identities.

FPATAN

FPATAN (partial arctangent) computes the function Θ = ARCTAN (Y/X). X is taken from the top stack element and Y from ST(1). Y and X must observe the inequality $0 < Y < X < \infty$. The instruction pops the stack and returns Θ to the (new) stack top, overwriting the Y operand; both original operands are destroyed.

F2XM1

F2XM1 (2 to the X minus 1) calculates the function $Y = 2^X - 1$. X is taken from the stack top and must be in the range $0 \leq X \leq 0.5$. The result Y replaces X at the stack top.

This instruction is designed to produce a very accurate result even when X is close to zero. To obtain $Y = 2^X$, add 1 to the result delivered by F2XM1.

The following formulas show how values other than 2 may be raised to a power of X:

$10^X = 2^{X \cdot LOG\ 10}$

$e^X = 2^{X \cdot LOG\ e}$

$Y^X = 2^{X \cdot LOG\ y}$

As shown in the next section, the 8087 has built-in instructions for loading the constants $LOG_2 10$ and $LOG_2 e$, and the FYL2X instruction may be used to calculate $X \cdot LOG_2 Y$.

FYL2X

FYL2X (Y log base 2 of X) calculates the function $Z = Y \cdot LOG_2X$. X is taken from the stack top and y from ST(1). The operands must be in the ranges $0<x<\infty$ and $-\infty<Y<+\infty$. The instruction pops the stack and returns Z at the (new) stack top, replacing the Y operand; both original operands are destroyed.

This function optimizes the calculation of log to any base other than two since a multiplication is always required:

$$LOG_nX = LOG_n2 \cdot LOG_2X$$

FYL2XP1

FYL2XP1 (Y log base 2 of (X + 1) calculates the function $Z = Y \cdot LOG_2 (X=1)$. X is taken from the stack top and must be in the range $0<|X|<(1-(\sqrt{2}/2))$. Y is taken from ST(1) and must be in the range $-\infty < Y < \infty$. FYL2XP1 pops the stack and returns Z at the (new) stack top, replacing Y.

This instruction provides improved accuracy over FYL2X when computing the log of a number very close to 1, for example $1 + \epsilon$ where $\epsilon < <1$. Providing ϵ rather than $1 + \epsilon$ as the input to the function allows more significant digits to be retained.

For example, this instruction is useful for any calculation (i.e., compounded interest rates) requiring a logarithm of $1.0+N$ where $0</N<0.29$. If only the FYL2X instruction were available, the value 1.0 would have to be added to N, potentially losing many significant bits in the result. By avoiding the addition of 1.0 to N, the result of the FYL2XPI will be as accurate (to within 3 units of temporary real precision) as N.

Constant Instructions

Each of these instructions (Table 5-13) loads (pushes) a commonly-used constant onto the stack. The values have full temporary real precision (80 bits) and are accurate to approximately 19 decimal digits. Since a temporary real constant occupies 10 memory bytes, the constant instructions, which are only two bytes long, save storage and improve execution speed, in addition to simplifying programming.

Table 5-13. Constant Instructions

Instruction	Operation
FLDZ	Load +0.0
FLD1	Load +1.0
FLDPI	Load π
FLDL2T	Load $\log_2 10$
FLDL2E	Load $\log_2 e$
FLDLG2	Load $\log_{10} 2$
FLDLN2	Load $\log_e$

FLDZ

FLDZ (load zero) loads (pushes) +0.0 onto the stack.

FLD1

FLD1 (load one) loads (pushes) +1.0 onto the stack.

FLDPI

FLDPI (load pi) loads (pushes) pi onto the stack.

FLDL2T

FLDL2T (load log base 2 of 10) loads (pushes) value $LOG_2 10$ onto the stack.

FLDL2E

FLDL2E (load log base 2 of e) loads (pushes) the value $LOG_2 e$ onto the stack.

FLDLG2

FLDLG2 (load log base 10 of 2) loads (pushes) the value $LOG_{10} 2$ onto the stack.

FLDLN2

FLDLN2 (load log base e of 2) loads (pushes) the value $LOG_e 2$ onto the stack.

Processor Control Instructions

Most of these instructions (Table 5-14) are not used in computations; they are provided principally for system-level activities. These include initialization, exception handling and task switching.

As shown in Table 5-14, an alternate mnemonic is available for many of the processor control instructions. This mnemonic, distinguished by a second character of "N," instructs the assembler *not* to prefix the instruction with a CPU WAIT instruction (instead, a CPU NOP precedes the instruction). This "no-wait" form is intended for use in critical code regions where a WAIT instruction is not desired. When CPU interrupts are enabled, as will normally be the case when an application task is running, the "wait" forms of these instructions should be used.

Except for FNSTENV and FNSAVE, all instructions which provide a no-wait mnemonic are self-synchronizing and can be executed back-to-back in any combination without intervening FWAITs. These instructions can be executed by the 8087 CU while the NEU is busy with a previously decoded instruction. To insure that the processor control instruction executes after completion of any operation in progress in the NEU, the "wait" form of that instruction should be used.

Table 5-14. Processor Control Instructions

FINIT/FNINIT	Initialize processor
FDISI/FNDISI	Disable interrupts
FENI/FNENI	Enable interrupts
FLDCW	Load control word
FSTCW/FNSTCW	Store control word
FSTSW/FNSTSW	Store status word
FCLEX/FNCLEX	Clear exceptions
FSTENV/FNSTENV	Store environment
FLDENV	Load environment
FSAVE/FNSAVE	Save state
FRSTOR	Restore state
FINCSTP	Increment stack pointer
FDECSTP	Decrement stack pointer
FFREE	Free register
FNOP	No operation
FWAIT	CPU wait

The register form is a generalization of the classical stack form; the programmer specifies the stack top as one operand and any register on the stack as the other operand. Coding the stack top as the destinationprovides a convenient way to access a constant, held elsewhere in the stack, from the stack top. The converse coding (ST is the source operand) allows, for example, adding the top into a register used as an accumulator.

Often the operand in the stack top is needed for one operation but then is of no further use in the compuation. The register pop form can be used to pick up the stack top as the source operand, and then discard it by popping the stack. Coding operand of ST(1),ST with a register pop mnemonic is equivalent to a classical stack operation; the top is popped and the result is left at the new top.

The two memory forms increase the flexibility of the 8087's arithmetic instructions. They permit a real number or a binary integer in memory to be used directly as a source operand. This is a very useful facility in situations where operands are not used frequently enough to justify holding them in registers. Note that any memory addressing mode may be used to define these operands, so they may be elements in arrays, structures or other data organizations, as well as simple scalars.

The six basic operations are discussed further in the next paragraphs, and descriptions of the remaining seven arithmetic operations follow.

FINIT/FNINIT

FINIT/FNINIT (initialize processor) performs the functional equivalent of a hardware RESET except that it does not affect the instruction fetch synchronization of the 8087 and its CPU.

For compatibility with the 8087 emulator, a system should call the INIT87 procedure in lieu of executing FINIT/FNINIT when the processor is first initialized (see the section "Programming Facilities," later in this chapter, for details). Note that if FNINIT is executed while a previous 8087 memory referencing instruction is running, 8087 bus cycles in progress will be aborted.

FDISI/FNDISI

FDISI/FNDISI (disable interrupts) sets the interrupt enable mask in the control word and prevents the NPX from issuing an interrupt request.

FENI/FNENI

FENI/FNENI (enable interrupts) clears the interrupt enable mask in the control word, allowing the 8087 to generate interrupt requests.

FLDCW *source*

FLDCW (load control word) replaces the current processor control word with the word defined by the source operand. This instruction is typically used to establish, or change, the 8087's mode of operation.

Note that if an exception bit in the status word is set, loading a new control word that unmasks that exception and clears the interrupt enable mask will generate an immediate interrupt request before the next instruction is executed. When changing modes, the recommended procedure is to first clear any exceptions and then load the new control word.

FSTCW/FNSTCW *destination*

FSTCW/FNSTCW (store control word) writes the current processor control word to the memory location defined by the destination.

FSTSW/FNSTSW *destination*

FSTSW/FNSTSW destination (store status word) writes the current value of the 8087 status word to the destination operand in memory. The instruction has many uses:

- to implement conditional branching following a comparison of FPREM instruction (FSTSW);
- to poll the 8087 to determine if it is busy (FNSTSW);
- to invoke exception handlers in environments that do not use interrupts (FSTSW).

If busy is set, the status bits are not valid.

FCLEX/FNCLEX

FCLEX/FNCLEX (clear exceptions) clears all exception flags, the interrupt request flag and the busy flag in the status word. As a consequence, the 8087's INT and BUSY lines go inactive. An exception handler must issue this instruction before returning to the interrupted computation, or another interrupt request will be generated immediately, and an endless loop may result.

FSAVE/FNSAVE *destination*

FSAVE/FNSAVE (save state) writes the full 8087 state – environment plus register stack – to the memory location defined by the destination operand. Figure 5-13 shows the layout of the 94-byte save area; typically the instruction will be coded to save this image on the CPU stack. If an instruction is executing in the 8087 NEU when FNSAVE is decoded, the CPU queues the FNSAVE and delays its execution until the running instruction completes normally encounters an unmasked exception. Thus, the save image reflects the state of the NPX FOLLOWING THE COMPLETION OF ANY running instruction. After writing the state image to memory, FSAVE/FNSAVE initializes the 8087 as if FINIT/FNINIT has been executed.

FSAVE/FNSAVE is useful whenever a program wants to save the current state of the NPX and initialize it for a new routine. Three examples are:

- an operating system needs to perform a context switch (suspend the task that had been running and give control to a new task);
- an interrupt handler needs to use the 8087;
- an application task wants to pass a "clean" 8087 to a subroutine.

FNSAVE must be "protected" by executing it in a critical region, i.e., with CPU interrupts disabled. This prevents an interrupt handler from executing a second FNSAVE (or other "no-wait" processor control instruction that reference memory) which could destroy the first FNSAVE if it is queued in the 8087. An FWAIT should be executed before CPU interrupts are enabled or any subsequent 8087 instruction is executed.

FRSTOR *source*

FRSTOR (restore state) reloads the 8087 from the 94-byte memory area defined by the source operand. This information should have been written by a previous FSAVE/FNSAVE instruction and not altered by any other instruction. CPU instructions (that do not reference the save image) may immediately follow FRSTOR, but no NPX instruction should be without an intervening FWAIT or an assembler-generated WAIT.

Note that the 8087 "reacts" to its new state at the conclusion of the FRSTOR; it will for example generate an immediate interrupt request if the exception and mask bits in the memory image so indicate.

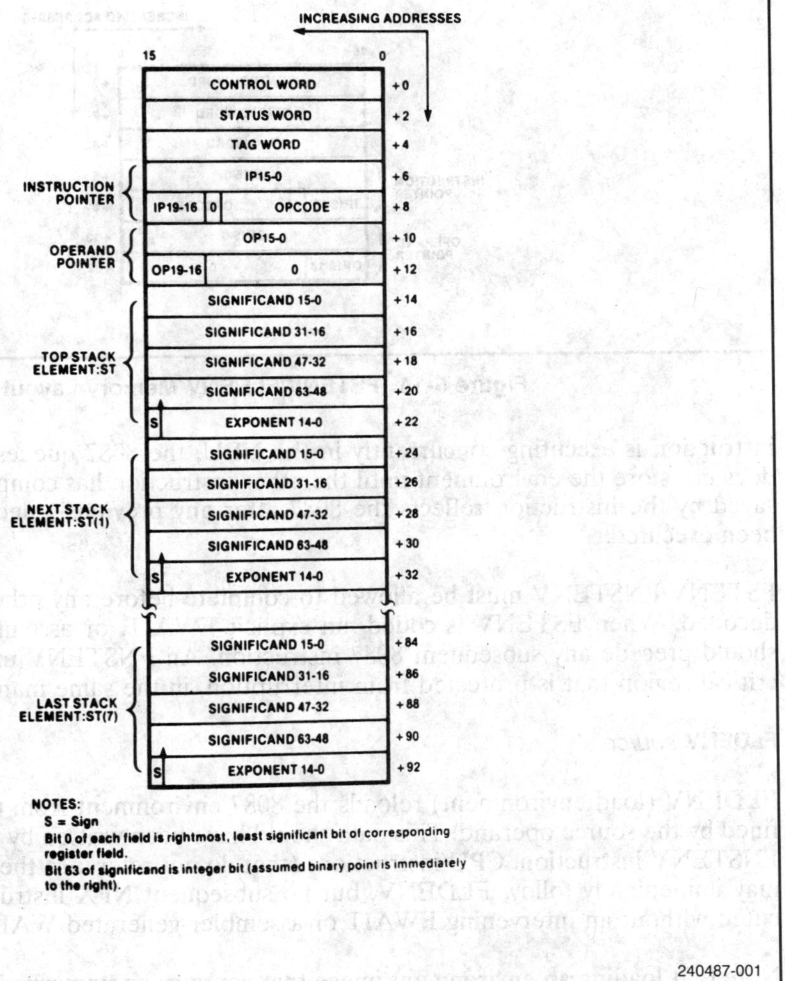

Figure 5-13. FSAVE/FRSTOR Memory Layout

FSTENV/FNSTENV *destination*

FSTENV/FNSTENV (store environment) writes the 8087's basic status – control, status and tag words, and exception pointers – to the memory location defined by the destination operand. Typically the environment is saved on the CPU stack. FSTENV/FNSTENV is often used by exception handlers because it provides access to the exception pointers which identify the offending instruction and operand. After saving the environment, FSTENV/FNSTENV sets all exception masks (masking all exceptions) in the processor; it does not affect the interrupt-enable mask. Figure 5-14 shows the format of the environment data in memory. If FNSTENV is decoded while another

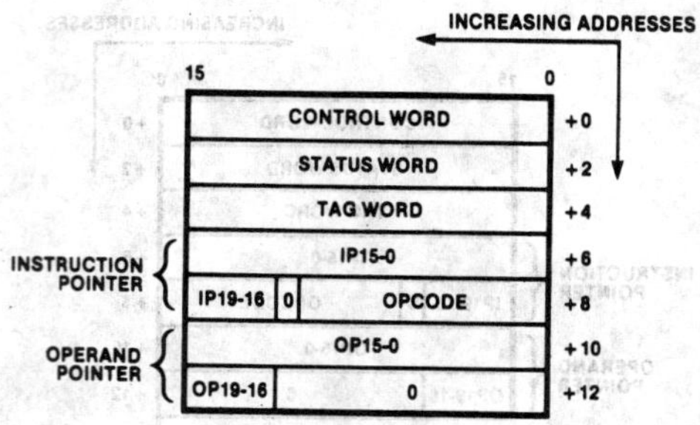

Figure 5-14. FSTENV/FLDENV Memory Layout

instruction is executing concurrently in the NEU, the 8087 queues the FNSTENV and does not store the environment until the other instruction has completed. Thus, the data saved by the instruction reflects the 8087 after any previously decoded instruction has been executed.

FSTENV/FNSTENV must be allowed to complete before any other 8087 instruction is decoded. When FSTENV is coded, an explicit FWAIT, or assembler-generate WAIT, should precede any subsequent 8087 instruction. An FNSTENV must be executed in a critical region that is protected from interruption, in the same manner as FNSAVE.

FLDENV *source*

FLDENV (load environment) reloads the 8087 environment from the memory area defined by the source operand. This data should have been written by a previous FSTENV/FNSTENV instruction. CPU instructions (that do not reference the environment image) may immediately follow FLDENV, but no subsequent NPX instruction should be executed without an intervening FWAIT or assembler-generated WAIT.

Note that loading an environment image that contains an unmasked exception will cause an immediate interrupt request from the 8087 (assuming IEM-0 in the environment image).

FINCSTP

FINCSTP (increment stack pointer) adds 1 to the stack top pointer (ST) in the status word. It does not alter tags or register contents, nor does it transfer data. It is not equivalent to popping the transfer data since it does not set the tag of the previous stack top to empty. Incrementing the stack pointer when ST = 7 produces ST = 0.

FDECSTP

FDECSTP (decrement stack pointer) subtracts 1 from ST, the stack top pointer in the status word. No tags or registers are altered, nor is any data transferred. Executing FDECSTP when ST=0 produces ST=7.

FFREE *destination*

FFREE (free register) changes the destination register's tag to empty; the contents of the register is unaffected.

FNOP

FNOP (no operation) stores the stack top to the stack top (FST ST,ST(0)) and thus effectively performs no operation.

FWAIT (CPU instruction)

FWAIT is not actually an 8087 instruction, but an alternate mnemonic for the CPU WAIT instruction described in the section "Addressing Modes," in Chapter 3. The FWAIT mnemonic should be coded whenever the programmer wants to synchronize the CPU to the NPX, that is, to suspend further instruction decoding until the NPX has completed the current instruction. *A CPU instruction should not attempt to access a memory operand that has been read or written by a previous 8087 instruction until the 8087 instruction has completed.* The following coding shows how FWAIT can be used to force the CPU instruction to wait for the 8087:

```
FNSAVE     STATUS
   FWAIT   Wait for FNSAVE
MOV        AX,SAVE AREA STATUS
```

Programmers should not code WAIT to synchronize the CPU and the NPX. The routines that alter an object program for 8087 emulation eliminate FWAITs (and assemblergenerated WAITs) but do not change any explicitly coded WAITs. The program will wait forever if a WAIT is encountered in emulated execution, since there is no 8087 to drive the CPU's TEST pin active.

Instruction Set Reference Information

Table 5-17 lists the operating characteristics of all the 8087 instructions. There is one table entry for each instruction mnemonic; the entries are in alphabetical order for quick lookup. Each entry provides the general operand forms accepted by the instruction as well as a list of all exceptions that may be detected during the operation.

There is one entry for each combination of operand types that can be coded with the mnemonic. Table 5-15 explains the operand identifiers allowed in Table 5-17. Following this entry are columns that provide execution time in clocks, the number of bus transfers run during the operation, the length of the instruction in bytes, and an ASM-86 coding sample.

Table 5-15. Key to Operand Types

Identifier	Explanation
ST	Stack top; the register currently at the top of the stack.
ST(1)	A register in the stack i (0≤i≤7) stack elements from the top. ST(1) is the next-on-stack register, ST(2) is below ST(1), etc.
Short-real	A short real (32-bits) number in memory.
Long-real	A long real (64 bits) number in memory.
Temp-real	A temporary real (80 bits) number in memory.
Packed-decimal	A packed decimal integer (18 digits, 10 bytes) in memory.
Word-integer	A word binary integer (16 bits) in memory.
Short-integer	A short binary integer (32 bits) in memory.
Long-integer	A long-binary integer (64 bits) in memory.
nn-bytes	A memory area nn bytes long.

EXECUTION TIME

The execution of an 8087 instruction involves three principal activities, each of which may contribute to the total duration (execution time) of the operation:

- Instruction fetch
- Instruction execution
- Operand transfer

The CPU and NPX simultaneously prefetch and queue their common instruction stream from memory. This activity is performed during spare bus cycles and proceeds in parallel with the execution of instructions from the queue. Because of their complexity, 8087 instructions typically take much longer to execute than to fetch. This means that in a typical sequence of 8087 instructions the processors have a relatively large amount of time available to maintain full instruction queues. Instruction fetching is therefore fully overlapped with execution and does not contribute to the overall duration of a series of instructions.

Fetch time does become apparent when a CPU jump or call instruction alters the normal sequential execution. This empties the queues and delays execution of the target instruction until it is fetched from memory. The time required to fetch the instruction depends on its length, the type of CPU (8086 or 8088), and, if the CPU is an 8086, whether the instruction is located at an even or odd address. (Slow memories, which force the insertion of wait states in bus cycles, and the bus activities of other processors in the system, may also lengthen fetch time.)

Table 5-17 quotes a typical execution time and a range for each instruction. Dividing the figures in the table by 5 (assuming a 5 MHz clock) produces execution time in microseconds. The typical case is an estimate for operand values that normally characterize most applications. The range encompasses best- and worst-case operand values that may be found in extreme circumstances. Where applicable, the figures *include* all overhead incurred by the CPU's execution of the ESC instruction, local bus arbitration (request/grant time), and the average overhead imposed by a preceding WAIT instruction (half of the 5-clock cycle that it uses to examine the TEST(pin)).

The execution times assume that no exceptions are detected. Invalid operation, denormalized (unmasked), and zerodivide exceptions usually decrease execution time from the typical figure, but it will still fall within the quoted range. The precision exception has no effect on execution time. Unmasked overflow and underflow, and masked denormalized exceptions, impose the penalties shown in Table 5-16. Absolute worst-case execution time is therefore the high range figure plus the largest penalty that may be encountered.

For instructions that transfer operands to or from memory, the execution times in Table 5-17 show that the time required for the CPU to calculate the operand's effective address (EA) should be added. Effective address calculation time varies according to addressing mode and to the CPU processor (8086/8088) used; Table 3-14 supplies the figures.

BUS TRANSFERS

Instructions that reference memory execute bus cycles to transfer operands. Each transfer requires one bus cycle. The number of transfers depends on the length of the operand, the type of CPU, and the alignment of the operand if the CPU is an 8086. The figures in Table 5-17 *include* the "dummy read" transfer(s) performed by the CPU in its execution of the escape instruction. The first 8086 figure is for even-addressed operands, and the second is for odd-addressed operands.

A bus cycle (transfer) consumes four clocks if the bus is immediately available and if the memory is running at processor speed, without wait states. Additional time is required if slow memories are employed, because these insert wait states into the bus cycle. In multiprocessor environments, the bus may not be available immediately if a higher priority processor is using it; this also can increase effective transfer time.

Table 5-16. Execution Penalties

Exception	Additional Clocks
Overflow (unmasked)	14
Underflow (unmasked)	16
Denormalized (masked)	33

INSTRUCTION LENGTH

Instructions that do not reference memory are two bytes long. Memory reference instructions vary between two and four bytes. The third and fourth bytes are used for 8- or 16-bit displacement values; the assembler generates the short displacement whenever possible. No displacements are required in memory references that use only CPU register contents to calculate an operand's effective address. Note that the lengths quoted in Table 5-17 do not include the one byte CPU WAIT instruction that the assembler automatically inserts in front of all NPX instructions (except those coded with a "no-wait" mnemonic).

Table 5-17. Instruction Set Reference Data

FABS — FABS (no operands) Absolute value — Exceptions: I

Operands	Execution Clocks		Transfers		Bytes	Coding Example
	Typical	Range	8086	8088		
(no operands)	14	10-17	0	0	2	FABS

FADD — FADD //source/destination,source Add real — Exceptions: I, D, O, U, P

Operands	Execution Clocks		Transfers		Bytes	Coding Example
	Typical	Range	8086	8088		
//ST,ST(i)/ST(i),ST	85	70-100	0	0	2	FADD ST,ST(4)
short-real	105+EA	90-120+EA	2/4	4	2-4	FADD AIR_TEMP [SI]
long-real	110+EA	95-125+EA	4/6	8	2-4	FADD [BX].MEAN

FADDP — FADDP destination,source Add real and pop — Exceptions: I, D, O, U, P

Operands	Execution Clocks		Transfers		Bytes	Coding Example
	Typical	Range	8086	8088		
ST(i),ST	90	75-105	0	0	2	FADDP ST(2),ST

Table 5-17. Instruction Set Reference Data (Cont'd.)

FBLD

FBLD source
Packed decimal (BCD) load

Exceptions: I

Operands	Execution Clocks		Transfers		Bytes	Coding Example
	Typical	Range	8086	8088		
packed-decimal	300+EA	290-310+EA	5/7	10	2-4	FBLD YTD_SALES

FBSTP

FBSTP destination
Packed decimal (BCD) store and pop

Exceptions: I

Operands	Execution Clocks		Transfers		Bytes	Coding Example
	Typical	Range	8086	8088		
packed-decimal	530+EA	520-540+EA	6/8	12	2-4	FBSTP [BX].FORECAST

FCHS

FCHS (no operands)
Change sign

Exceptions: I

Operands	Execution Clocks		Transfers		Bytes	Coding Example
	Typical	Range	8086	8088		
(no operands)	15	10-17	0	0	2	FCHS

FCLEX/FNCLEX

FCLEX (no operands)
Clear exceptions

Exceptions: None

Operands	Execution Clocks		Transfers		Bytes	Coding Example
	Typical	Range	8086	8088		
(no operands)	5	2-8	0	0	2	FNCLEX

FCOM

FCOM //source
Compare real

Exceptions: I, D

Operands	Execution Clocks		Transfers		Bytes	Coding Example
	Typical	Range	8086	8088		
//ST(i)	45	40-50	0	0	2	FCOM ST(1)
short-real	65+EA	60-70+EA	2/4	4	2-4	FCOM [BP].UPPER_LIMIT
long-real	70+EA	65-75+EA	4/6	8	2-4	FCOM WAVELENGTH

Table 5-17. Instruction Set Reference Data (Cont'd.)

FCOMP

FCOMP //source
Compare real and pop

Exceptions: I, D

Operands	Execution Clocks		Transfers		Bytes	Coding Example
	Typical	Range	8086	8088		
//ST(i)	47	42-52	0	0	2	FCOMP ST(2)
short-real	68+EA	63-73+EA	2/4	4	2-4	FCOMP [BP+2].N_READINGS
long-real	72+EA	67-77+EA	4/6	8	2-4	FCOMP DENSITY

FCOMPP

FCOMPP (no operands)
Compare real and pop twice

Exceptions: I, D

Operands	Execution Clocks		Transfers		Bytes	Coding Example
	Typical	Range	8086	8088		
(no operands)	50	45-55	0	0	2	FCOMPP

FDECSTP

FDECSTP (no operands)
Decrement stack pointer

Exceptions: None

Operands	Execution Clocks		Transfers		Bytes	Coding Example
	Typical	Range	8086	8088		
(no operands)	9	6-12	0	0	2	FDECSTP

FDISI/FNDISI

FDISI (no operands)
Disable interrupts

Exceptions: None

Operands	Execution Clocks		Transfers		Bytes	Coding Example
	Typical	Range	8086	8088		
(no operands)	5	2-8	0	0	2	FDISI

FDIV

FDIV //source/destination,source
Divide real

Exceptions: I, D, Z, O, U, P

Operands	Execution Clocks		Transfers		Bytes	Coding Example
	Typical	Range	8086	8088		
//ST(i),ST	198	193-203	0	0	2	FDIV
short-real	220+EA	215-225+EA	2/4	4	2-4	FDIV DISTANCE
long-real	225+EA	220-230+EA	4/6	8	2-4	FDIV ARC [DI]

Table 5-17. Instruction Set Reference Data (Cont'd.)

FDIVP

FDIVP destination,source
Divide real and pop

Exceptions: I, D, Z, O, U, P

Operands	Execution Clocks		Transfers		Bytes	Coding Example
	Typical	Range	8086	8088		
ST(i),ST	202	197-207	0	0	2	FDIVP ST(4),ST

FDIVR

FDIVR //source/destination,source
Divide real reversed

Exceptions: I, D, Z, O, U, P

Operands	Execution Clocks		Transfers		Bytes	Coding Example
	Typical	Range	8086	8088		
//ST,ST(i)/ST(i),ST	199	194-204	0	0	2	FDIVR ST(2),ST
short-real	221+EA	216-226+EA	2/4	6	2-4	FDIVR [BX].PULSE_RATE
long-real	226+EA	221-231+EA	4/6	8	2-4	FDIVR RECORDER.FREQUENCY

FDIVRP

FDIVRP destination,source
Divide real reversed and pop

Exceptions: I, D, Z, O, U, P

Operands	Execution Clocks		Transfers		Bytes	Coding Example
	Typical	Range	8086	8088		
ST(i),ST	203	198-208	0	0	2	FDIVRP ST(1),ST

FENI/FNENI

FENI (no operands)
Enable interrupts

Exceptions: None

Operands	Execution Clocks		Transfers		Bytes	Coding Example
	Typical	Range	8086	8088		
(no operands)	5	2-8	0	0	2	FNENI

FFREE

FFREE destination
Free register

Exceptions: None

Operands	Execution Clocks		Transfers		Bytes	Coding Example
	Typical	Range	8086	8088		
ST(i)	11	9-16	0	0	2	FFREE ST(1)

Table 5-17. Instruction Set Reference Data (Cont'd.)

FIADD

FIADD source
Integer add

Exceptions: I, D, O, P

Operands	Execution Clocks		Transfers		Bytes	Coding Example
	Typical	Range	8086	8088		
word-integer	120+EA	102-137+EA	1/2	2	2-4	FIADD DISTANCE_TRAVELLED
short-integer	125+EA	108-143+EA	2/4	4	2-4	FIADD PULSE_COUNT [SI]

FICOM

FICOM source
Integer compare

Exceptions: I, D

Operands	Execution Clocks		Transfers		Bytes	Coding Example
	Typical	Range	8086	8088		
word-integer	80+EA	72-86+EA	1/2	2	2-4	FICOM TOOL.N_PASSES
short-integer	85+EA	78-91+EA	2/4	4	2-4	FICOM [BP+4].PARM_COUNT

FICOMP

FICOMP source
Integer compare and pop

Exceptions: I, D

Operands	Execution Clocks		Transfers		Bytes	Coding Example
	Typical	Range	8086	8088		
word-integer	82+EA	74-88+EA	1/2	2	2-4	FICOMP [BP].LIMIT [SI]
short-integer	87+EA	80-93+EA	2/4	4	2-4	FICOMP N_SAMPLES

FIDIV

FIDIV source
Integer divide

Exceptions: I, D, Z, O, U, P

Operands	Execution Clocks		Transfers		Bytes	Coding Example
	Typical	Range	8086	8088		
word-integer	230+EA	224-238+EA	1/2	2	2-4	FIDIV SURVEY.OBSERVATIONS
short-integer	236+EA	230-243+EA	2/4	4	2-4	FIDIV RELATIVE_ANGLE [DI]

FIDIVR

FIDIVR source
Integer divide reversed

Exceptions: I, D, Z, O, U, P

Operands	Execution Clocks		Transfers		Bytes	Coding Example
	Typical	Range	8086	8088		
word-integer	230+EA	225-239+EA	1/2	2	2-4	FIDIVR [BP].X_COORD
short-integer	237+EA	231-245+EA	2/4	4	2-4	FIDIVR FREQUENCY

Table 5-17. Instruction Set Reference Data (Cont'd.)

FILD

FILD source
Integer load

Exception: I

Operands	Execution Clocks		Transfers		Bytes	Coding Example
	Typical	Range	8086	8088		
word-integer	50+EA	46-54+EA	1/2	2	2-4	FILD [BX].SEQUENCE
short-integer	56+EA	52-60+EA	2/4	4	2-4	FILD STANDOFF [DI]
long-integer	64+EA	60-68+EA	4/6	8	2-4	FILD RESPONSE.COUNT

FIMUL

FIMUL source
Integer multiply

Exceptions: I, D, O, P

Operands	Execution Clocks		Transfers		Bytes	Coding Example
	Typical	Range	8086	8088		
word-integer	130+EA	124-138+EA	1/2	2	2-4	FIMUL BEARING
short-integer	136+EA	130-144+EA	2/4	4	2-4	FIMUL POSITION.Z_AXIS

FINCSTP

FINCSTP (no operands)
Increment stack pointer

Exceptions: None

Operands	Execution Clocks		Transfers		Bytes	Coding Example
	Typical	Range	8086	8088		
(no operands)	9	6-12	0	0	2	FINCSTP

FINIT/FNINIT

FINIT (no operands)
Initialize processor

Exceptions: None

Operands	Execution Clocks		Transfers		Bytes	Coding Example
	Typical	Range	8086	8088		
(no operands)	5	2-8	0	0	2	FINIT

FIST

FIST destination
Integer store

Exceptions: I, P

Operands	Execution Clocks		Transfers		Bytes	Coding Example
	Typical	Range	8086	8088		
word-integer	86+EA	80-90+EA	2/4	4	2-4	FIST OBS.COUNT [SI]
short-integer	88+EA	82-92+EA	3/5	6	2-4	FIST [BP].FACTORED_PULSES

Table 5-17. Instruction Set Reference Data (Cont'd.)

FISTP

FISTP destination
Integer store and pop

Exceptions: I, P

Operands	Execution Clocks		Transfers		Bytes	Coding Example
	Typical	Range	8086	8088		
word-integer	88+EA	82-92+EA	2/4	4	2-4	FISTP BX ALPHA COUNT SI
short-integer	90+EA	84-94+EA	3/5	6	2-4	FISTP CORRECTED TIME
long-integer	100+EA	94-105+EA	5/7	10	2-4	FISTP PANEL N READINGS

FISUB

FISUB source
Integer subtract

Exceptions: I, D, O, P

Operands	Execution Clocks		Transfers		Bytes	Coding Example
	Typical	Range	8086	8088		
word-integer	120+EA	102-137+EA	1/2	2	2-4	FISUB BASE FREQUENCY
short-integer	125+EA	108-143+EA	2/4	4	2-4	FISUB TRAIN SIZE [DI]

FISUBR

FISUBR source
Integer subtract reversed

Exceptions: I, D, O, P

Operands	Execution Clocks		Transfers		Bytes	Coding Example
	Typical	Range	8086	8088		
word-integer	120+EA	103-139+EA	1/2	2	2-4	FISUBR FLOOR [BX] [SI]
short-integer	125+EA	109-144+EA	2/4	4	2-4	FISUBR BALANCE

FLD

FLD source
Load real

Exceptions: I, D

Operands	Execution Clocks		Transfers		Bytes	Coding Example
	Typical	Range	8086	8088		
ST(i)	20	17-22	0	0	2	FLD ST(0)
short-real	43+EA	38-56+EA	2/4	4	2-4	FLD READING [SI].PRESSURE
long-real	46+EA	40-60+EA	4/6	8	2-4	FLD [BP].TEMPERATURE
temp-real	57+EA	53-65+EA	5/7	10	2-4	FLD SAVEREADING

FLDCW

FLDCW source
Load control word

Exceptions: None

Operands	Execution Clocks		Transfers		Bytes	Coding Example
	Typical	Range	8086	8088		
2-bytes	10+EA	7-14+EA	1/2	2	2-4	FLDCW CONTROL_WORD

Table 5-17. Instruction Set Reference Data (Cont'd.)

FLDENV

FLDENV source
Load environment

Exceptions: None

Operands	Execution Clocks		Transfers		Bytes	Coding Example
	Typical	Range	8086	8088		
14-bytes	40+EA	35-45+EA	7/9	14	2-4	FLDENV [BP+6]

FLDLG2

FLDLG2 (no operands)
Load $\log_{10} 2$

Exceptions: I

Operands	Execution Clocks		Transfers		Bytes	Coding Example
	Typical	Range	8086	8088		
(no operands)	21	18-24	0	0	2	FLDLG2

FLDLN2

FLDLN2 (no operands)
Load $\log_e 2$

Exceptions: I

Operands	Execution Clocks		Transfers		Bytes	Coding Example
	Typical	Range	8086	8088		
(no operands)	20	17-23	0	0	2	FLDLN2

FLDL2E

FLDL2E (no operands)
Load $\log_2 e$

Exceptions: I

Operands	Execution Clocks		Transfers		Bytes	Coding Example
	Typical	Range	8086	8088		
(no operands)	18	15-21	0	0	2	FLDL2E

FLDL2T

FLDL2T (no operands)
Load $\log_2 10$

Exceptions: I

Operands	Execution Clocks		Transfers		Bytes	Coding Example
	Typical	Range	8086	8088		
(no operands)	19	16-22	0	0	2	FLDL2T

Table 5-17. Instruction Set Reference Data (Cont'd.)

FLDPI

FLDPI (no operands)
Load π

Exceptions: I

Operands	Execution Clocks		Transfers		Bytes	Coding Example
	Typical	Range	8086	8088		
(no operands)	19	16-22	0	0	2	FLDPI

FLDZ

FLDZ (no operands)
Load +0.0

Exceptions: I

Operands	Execution Clocks		Transfers		Bytes	Coding Example
	Typical	Range	8086	8088		
(no operands)	14	11-17	0	0	2	FLDZ

FLD1

FLD1 (no operands)
Load +1.0

Exceptions: I

Operands	Execution Clocks		Transfers		Bytes	Coding Example
	Typical	Range	8086	8088		
(no operands)	18	15-21	0	0	2	FLD1

FMUL

FMUL //source/destination,source
Multiply real

Exceptions: I, D, O, U, P

Operands	Execution Clocks		Transfers		Bytes	Coding Example
	Typical	Range	8086	8088		
//ST(i),ST/ST,ST(i)[1]	97	90-105	0	0	2	FMUL ST,ST(3)
//ST(i),ST/ST,ST(i)	138	130-145	0	0	2	FMUL ST,ST(3)
short-real	118+EA	110-125+EA	2/4	4	2-4	FMUL SPEED_FACTOR
long-real[1]	120+EA	112-126+EA	4/6	8	2-4	FMUL [BP].HEIGHT
long-real	161+EA	154-168+EA	4/6	8	2-4	FMUL [BP].HEIGHT

[1] occurs when one or both operands is "short"—it has 40 trailing zeros in its fraction (e.g., it was loaded from a short-real memory operand).

FMULP

FMULP destination,source
Multiply real and pop

Exceptions: I, D, O, U, P

Operands	Execution Clocks		Transfers		Bytes	Coding Example
	Typical	Range	8086	8088		
ST(i),ST[1]	100	94-108	0	0	2	FMULP ST(1),ST
ST(i),ST	142	134-148	0	0	2	FMULP ST(1),ST

[1] occurs when one or both operands is "short"—it has 40 trailing zeros in its fraction (e.g., it was loaded from a short-real memory operand).

Table 5-17. Instruction Set Reference Data (Cont'd.)

FNOP

FNOP (no operands)
No operation

Exceptions: None

Operands	Execution Clocks		Transfers		Bytes	Coding Example
	Typical	Range	8086	8088		
(no operands)	13	10-16	0	0	2	FNOP

FPATAN

FPATAN (no operands)
Partial arctangent

Exceptions: U, P (operands not checked)

Operands	Execution Clocks		Transfers		Bytes	Coding Example
	Typical	Range	8086	8088		
(no operands)	650	250-800	0	0	2	FPATAN

FPREM

FPREM (no operands)
Partial remainder

Exceptions: I, D, U

Operands	Execution Clocks		Transfers		Bytes	Coding Example
	Typical	Range	8086	8088		
(no operands)	125	15-190	0	0	2	FPREM

FPTAN

FPTAN (no operands)
Partial tangent

Exceptions: I, P (operands not checked)

Operands	Execution Clocks		Transfers		Bytes	Coding Example
	Typical	Range	8086	8088		
(no operands)	450	30-540	0	0	2	FPTAN

FRNDINT

FRNDINT (no operands)
Round to integer

Exceptions: I, P

Operands	Execution Clocks		Transfers		Bytes	Coding Example
	Typical	Range	8086	8088		
(no operands)	45	16-50	0	0	2	FRNDINT

Table 5-17. Instruction Set Reference Data (Cont'd.)

FRSTOR

FRSTOR source
Restore saved state

Exceptions: None

Operands	Execution Clocks		Transfers		Bytes	Coding Example
	Typical	Range	8086	8088		
94-bytes	208+EA	197-207+EA	47/49	96	2-4	FRSTOR [BP]

FSAVE/FNSAVE

FSAVE destination
Save state

Exceptions: None

Operands	Execution Clocks		Transfers		Bytes	Coding Example
	Typical	Range	8086	8088		
94-bytes	208+EA	197-207+EA	48/50	94	2-4	FSAVE [BP]

FSCALE

FSCALE (no operands)
Scale

Exceptions: I, O, U

Operands	Execution Clocks		Transfers		Bytes	Coding Example
	Typical	Range	8086	8088		
(no operands)	35	32-38	0	0	2	FSCALE

FSQRT

FSQRT (no operands)
Square root

Exceptions: I, D, P

Operands	Execution Clocks		Transfers		Bytes	Coding Example
	Typical	Range	8086	8088		
(no operands)	183	180-186	0	0	2	FSQRT

FST

FST destination
Store real

Exceptions: I, O, U, P

Operands	Execution Clocks		Transfers		Bytes	Coding Example
	Typical	Range	8086	8088		
ST(i)	18	15-22	0	0	2	FST ST(3)
short-real	87+EA	84-90+EA	3/5	6	2-4	FST CORRELATION [DI]
long-real	100+EA	96-104+EA	5/7	10	2-4	FST MEAN_READING

Table 5-17. Instruction Set Reference Data (Cont'd.)

FSTCW/FNSTCW

FSTCW destination
Store control word

Exceptions: None

Operands	Execution Clocks		Transfers		Bytes	Coding Example
	Typical	Range	8086	8088		
2-bytes	15+EA	12-18+EA	2/4	4	2-4	FSTCW SAVE_CONTROL

FSTENV/FNSTENV

FSTENV destination
Store environment

Exceptions: None

Operands	Execution Clocks		Transfers		Bytes	Coding Example
	Typical	Range	8086	8088		
14-bytes	45+EA	40-50+EA	8/10	16	2-4	FSTENV [BP]

FSTP

FSTP destination
Store real and pop

Exceptions: I, O, U, P

Operands	Execution Clocks		Transfers		Bytes	Coding Example
	Typical	Range	8086	8088		
ST(i)	20	17-24	0	0	2	FSTP ST(2)
short-real	89+EA	86-92+EA	3/5	6	2-4	FSTP [BX].ADJUSTED RPM
long-real	102+EA	98-106+EA	5/7	10	2-4	FSTP TOTAL DOSAGE
temp-real	55+EA	52-58+EA	6/8	12	2-4	FSTP REG SAVE [SI]

FSTSW/FNSTSW

FSTSW destination
Store status word

Exceptions: None

Operands	Execution Clocks		Transfers		Bytes	Coding Example
	Typical	Range	8086	8088		
2-bytes	15+EA	12-18+EA	2/4	4	2-4	FSTSW SAVE STATUS

FSUB

FSUB //source/destination,source
Subtract real

Exceptions: I,D,O,U,P

Operands	Execution Clocks		Transfers		Bytes	Coding Example
	Typical	Range	8086	8088		
//ST,ST(i)/ST(i),ST	85	70-100	0	0	2	FSUB ST ST(2)
short-real	105+EA	90-120+EA	2/4	4	2-4	FSUB BASE VALUE
long-real	110+EA	95-125+EA	4/6	8	2-4	FSUB COORDINATE X

Table 5-17. Instruction Set Reference Data (Cont'd.)

FSUBP

FSUBP destination,source
Subtract real and pop

Exceptions: I,D,O,U,P

Operands	Execution Clocks		Transfers		Bytes	Coding Example
	Typical	Range	8086	8088		
ST(i),ST	90	75-105	0	0	2	FSUBP ST(2),ST

FSUBR

FSUBR //source/destination,source
Subtract real reversed

Exceptions: I,D,O,U,P

Operands	Execution Clocks		Transfers		Bytes	Coding Example
	Typical	Range	8086	8088		
//ST,ST(i)/ST(i),ST	87	70-100	0	0	2	FSUBR ST,ST(1)
short-real	105+EA	90-120+EA	2/4	4	2-4	FSUBR VECTOR[SI]
long-real	110+EA	95-125+EA	4/6	8	2-4	FSUBR [BX].INDEX

FSUBRP

FSUBRP destination,source
Subtract real reversed and pop

Exceptions: I,D,O,U,P

Operands	Executon Clocks		Transfers		Bytes	Coding Example
	Typical	Range	8086	8088		
ST(i),ST	90	75-105	0	0	2	FSUBRP ST(1),ST

FTST

FTST (no operands)
Test stack top against +0.0

Exceptions: I, D

Operands	Execution Clocks		Transfers		Bytes	Coding Example
	Typical	Range	8086	8088		
(no operands)	42	38-48	0	0	2	FTST

FWAIT

FWAIT (no operands)
(CPU) Wait while 8087 is busy

Exceptions: None (CPU instruction)

Operands	Execution Clocks		Transfers		Bytes	Coding Example
	Typical	Range	8086	8088		
(no operands)	3+5n*	3+5n*	0	0	1	FWAIT

*n = number of times CPU examines $\overline{\text{TEST}}$ line before 8087 lowers BUSY.

Table 5-17. Instruction Set Reference Data (Cont'd.)

FXAM

FXAM (no operands)
Examine stack top

Exceptions: None

Operands	Execution Clocks		Transfers		Bytes	Coding Example
	Typical	Range	8086	8088		
(no operands)	17	12-23	0	0	2	FXAM

FXCH

FXCH //destination
Exchange registers

Exceptions: I

Operands	Execution Clocks		Transfers		Bytes	Coding Example
	Typical	Range	8086	8088		
//ST(i)	12	10-15	0	0	2	FXCH ST(2)

FXTRACT

FXTRACT (no operands)
Extract exponent and significand

Exceptions: I

Operands	Execution Clocks		Transfers		Bytes	Coding Example
	Typical	Range	8086	8088		
(no operands)	50	27-55	0	0	2	FXTRACT

FYL2X

FYL2X (no operands)
$Y \cdot \log_2 X$

Exceptions: P (operands not checked)

Operands	Execution Clocks		Transfers		Bytes	Coding Example
	Typical	Range	8086	8088		
(no operands)	950	900-1100	0	0	2	FYL2X

FYL2XP1

FYL2XP1 (no operands)
$Y \cdot \log_2(X+1)$

Exceptions: P (operands not checked)

Operands	Execution Clocks		Transfers		Bytes	Coding Example
	Typical	Range	8086	8088		
(no operands)	850	700-1000	0	0	2	FYL2XP1

Table 5-17. Instruction Set Reference Data (Cont'd.)

F2XM1 — F2XM1 (no operands) 2^X-1 — Exceptions: U, P (operands not checked)

Operands	Execution Clocks		Transfers		Bytes	Coding Example
	Typical	Range	8086	8088		
(no operands)	500	310-630	0	0	2	F2XM1

PROGRAMMING FACILITIES

Writing programs for the 8087 is a natural extension, just as the NPX itself is an extension to the CPU. This section describes how PL/M-86 and ASM-86 programmers work with the 8087 in these languages. It also covers the 8087 software emulators provided for both translators.

The level of detail in this section is intended to give programmers a basic understanding of the software tools that can be used with the 8087, but this information is not sufficient to document the full capabilities of these facilities. The definitive description of ASM-86 and the full 8087 emulator is provided in *MCS®-86 Assembly Language Reference Manual*, Order No. 9800640, and *MCS®-86 Assembler Operating Instructions for ISIS-II users*, Order No. 9800641. PL/M-86 and the partial emulator are documented in *PL/M-86 Programming Manual*, Order No. 9800466 and *ISIS-II PL/M-86 Compiler Operators Manual*, Order No. 9800478. These publications may be ordered from Intel's Literature Department.

PL/M-86

High level language programmers can access a useful subset of the 8087's (real or emulated) capabilities. The PL/M-86 REAL data type corresponds to the NPX's short real (32-bit) format. This data type provides a range of about $8.43*10^{-37} \leq |X| \leq 3.38*10^{38}$, with about seven significant decimal digits. This representation is adequate for the data manipulated by many microcomputer applications.

The utility of the REAL data type is extended by the PL/M-86 compiler's practice of holding intermediate results in the 8087's temporary real format. This means that the full range and precision of the processor may be utilized for intermediate results. Underflow, overflow, and rounding errors are most likely to occur during intermediate computations rather than during calculation of an expression's final result. Holding intermediate results in temporary real format greatly reduces the likelihood of overflow and underflow and eliminates roundoff as a serious source of error until the final assignment of the result is performed.

The compiler generates 8087 code to evaluate expressions that contain REAL data types, whether variables or constants or both. This means that addition, subtraction, multiplication, division, comparison, and assignment of REALs will be performed by the NPX. INTEGER expressions, on the other hand, are evaluated on the CPU.

Five built-in procedures (Table 5-18) give the PL/M-86 programmer access to 8087 functions manipulated by the processor control instructions. Prior to any arithmetic operations, a typical PL/M-86 program will setup the NPX after power up using the INIT$REAL$MATH$UNIT procedure and then issue SET$REAL$MODE to configure the NPX. SET$REAL$MODE loads the 8087 control word, and its 16-bit parameter has the format shown in Figure 5-7. The recommended value of this parameter is 033EH (projective closure, round to nearest, 64-bit precision, interrupts enabled, all exceptions masked except invalid operation). Other settings may be used at the programmer's discretion.

If any exceptions are unmasked, an exception handler must be provided in the form of an interrupt procedure that is designated to be invoked by CPU interrupt pointer (vector) number 16. The exception handler can use the GET$REAL$ERROR procedure to obtain the low-order byte of the 8087 status word and to then clear the exception flags. The byte returned by GET$REAL$ERROR contains the exception flags; these can be examined to determine the source of the exception.

The SAVE$REAL$STATUS and RESTORE$REAL$STATUS procedures are provided for multitasking environments where a running task that uses the 8087 may be preempted by another task that also uses the 8087. It is the responsibility of the preempting task to issue SAVE$REAL$STATUS before it executes any statements that affect the 8087; these include the INIT$REAL$MATH$UNIT and SET$REAL$MODE procedures as well as arithmetic expressions. SAVE$REAL$STATUS saves the 8087 state (registers, status, and control words, etc.) on the CPU's stack. RESTORE$REAL$STATUS reloads the state information; the preempting task must invoke this procedure before terminating in order to restore the 8087 to its state at the time the running task was preempted. This enables the preempted task to resume execution from the point of its preemption.

Note that the PL/M-86 compiler prefixes every 8087 instruction with a CPU WAIT. Therefore, programmers should not code PL/M-86 statements that generate 8087 instructions if the NPX can request an interrupt and that interrupt is blocked. This may result in the endless wait condition.

Table 5-18. PL/M-86 Built-In Procedures

Procedure	8087 Instruction	Description
INIT$REAL$MATH$UNIT(1)	FINIT	Initialize processor.
SET$REAL$MODE	FLDCW	Set exception masks, rounding precision, and infinity controls.
GET$REAL$ERROR(2)	FNSTSW & FNCLEX	Store, then clear, exception flags.
SAVE$REAL$STATUS	FNSAVE	Save processor state.
RESTORE$REAL$STATUS	FRSTOR	Restore processor state.

ASM-86

The ASM-86 assembly language provides a single uniform set of facilities for all combinations of the 8086/8088/8087 processors. Assembly language programs can be written to be completely independent of the processor set on which they are destined to execute.

This means that a program written originally for an 8088 alone will execute on an 8086/8087 or 8088/8087 combination without re-assembling. The programmer's view of the hardware is a single machine with these resources:

- 160 instructions
- 12 data types
- 8 general registers
- 4 segment registers
- 8 floating-point registers, organized as a stack

The combination of the assembly language and the 8087 emulator decouples the source code from the execution vehicle. For example, the assembler automatically inserts CPU WAIT instructions in front of those 8087 instructions that require them. If the program actually runs with the emulator rather than the 8087, the WAITs are automatically removed at link time (since there is no NPX for which to wait).

DEFINING DATA

The ASM-86 directives shown in Table 5-19 allocate storage for 8087 variables and constants. As with other storage allocation directives, the assembler associates a type with any variable defined with these directives. The type value is equal to the length of the storage unit in bytes (10 for DT, 8 for DQ, etc.). The assembler checks the type of any variable coded in an instruction to be certain that it is compatible with the instruction. For example, the coding FIADD ALPHA will be flagged as an error if ALPHA's type is not 2 or 4, because integer addition is only available for word and short integer data types. The operand's type also tells the assembler which machine instruction to produce; although to the programmer there is only an FIADD instruction, a different machine instruction is required for each operand type.

Table 5-19. 8087 Storage Allocation Directives

Directive	Interpretation	8087 Data Types
DW	Define Word	Word integer
DD	Define Doubleword	Short integer, short real
DQ	Define Quadword	Long integer, long real
DT	Define Tenbyte	Packed decimal, temporary real

On occasion it is desirable to use an instruction with an operand that has no declared type. For example, if register BX points to a short integer variable, a programmer may want to code FIADD [BX]. This can be done by informing the assembler of the operand's type in the instruction, coding FIADD DWORD PTR [BX]. The corresponding overrides for the other storage allocations are WORD PTR, QWORD PTR, and TBYTE PTR.

The assembler does not, however, check the types of operands used in processor control instructions. Coding FRSTOR [BP] implies that the programmer has set up register BP to point to the stack location where the processor's 94-byte state record has been previously saved.

The initial values for 8087 constants may be coded in several different ways. Binary integer constants may be specified as bit strings, decimal integers, octal integers, or hexadecimal strings. Packed decimal values are normally written as decimal integers, although the assembler will accept and convert other representations of integers, Real values may be written as ordinary decimal real numbers (decimal point required), as decimal numbers in scientific notation, or as hexadecimal strings. Using hexadecimal strings is primarily intended for defining special values such as infinities, NANs, and nonnormalized numbers. Most programmers will find that ordinary decimal and scientific decimal provide the simplest way to initialize 8087 constants. Figure 5-15 compares several ways of setting the various 8087 data types to the same initial value.

Note that preceding 8087 variables and constants with the ASM-86 EVEN directive ensures that the operands will be word-aligned in memory. This will produce the best performance in 8086-based systems, and is good practice even for 8088/80188 software, in the event that the programs are transferred to an 8086. All 8087 data types occupy integral numbers of words so that no storage is "wasted" if blocks of variables are defined together and preceded by a single EVEN declarative.

```
; THE FOLLOWING ALL ALLOCATE THE CONSTANT: -126
; NOTE TWO'S COMPLEMENT STORAGE OF NEGATIVE BINARY INTEGERS.
;
; EVEN                                ; FORCE WORD ALIGNMENT
WORD_INTEGER   DW  1111111110000010B ; BIT STRING
SHORT_INTEGER  DD  0FFFFFF82H         ; HEX STRING MUST START WITH DIGIT
LONG_INTEGER   DQ  -126               ; ORDINARY DECIMAL
SHORT_REAL     DD  -126.0             ; NOTE PRESENCE OF '.'
LONG_REAL      DD  -1.26E2            ;''SCIENTIFIC''
PACKED_DECIMAL DT  -126               ; ORDINARY DECIMAL INTEGER
; IN THE FOLLOWING, SIGN AND EXPONENT IS 'C005',
;     SIGNIFICAND IS '7E00...00', 'R' INFORMS ASSEMBLER THAT
;     THE STRING REPRESENTS A REAL DATA TYPE.
;
TEMP_REAL      DT  0C0057E00000000000000R  ; HEX STRING
```

Figure 5-15. Sample 8087 Constants

RECORDS AND STRUCTURES

The ASM-86 RECORD and STRUC (structure declaratives can be very useful in NPX programming. The record facility can be used to define the bit fields of the control, status, and tag words.

Figure 5-16 shows one definition of the status words and how it might be used in a routine that polls the 8087 until it has completed an instruction.

Because structures allow different but related data types to be grouped together, they often provide a natural way to represent "real world" data organizations. The fact that the structure template may be "moved" about in memory adds to its flexibility. Figure 5-17 shows a simple structure that might be used to represent data consisting of a series of test score samples. A structure could also be used to define the organization of the information stored and loaded by the FSTENV and FLDENV instructions.

ADDRESSING MODES

8087 memory data can be accessed with any of the CPU's twenty-two memory addressing modes. This means that 8087 data types can be incorporated in data aggregates ranging from simple to complex according to the needs of the application. The addressing modes, and the ASM-86 notation used to specify them in instructions, make the accessing of structures, arrays, arrays of structures, and other organizations direct and straightforward.

Table 5-20 gives several examples of 8087 instructions coded with operands that illustrate different addressing modes.

8087 EMULATORS

Intel offers two software products that provide the functional equivalent of an 8087, implemented in 8086/8088 software. The full emulator (E8087) emulates all 8087 instructions. The partial emulator (PE8087) is a smaller version that implements only the instructions needed to support PL/M-86 programs. The full emulator adds about 16K bytes to a program, while the partial emulator executes in about 8K. Any emulated program will deliver the same results (except for timing) if it is executed on 8087 hardware. (The partial emulator does not support transcendental functions.)

The emulators may be viewed as consisting of emulated hardware and emulated instructions. The emulators establish in CPU memory the equivalent of the 8087 register stack, control, and status words and all other programmer-accessible elements of the NPX architecture. The emulator instructions utilize the same algorithms as their hardware counterparts. Emulator instructions are actually implemented as CPU interrupt procedures. During relocation and linkage, the 8087 machine instructions generated by the ASM-86 and PL/M-86 translators are changed to software interrupt (INT) instructions which invoke these procedures as the CPU processes its instruction stream.

```
; RESERVE SPACE FOR STATUS WORD
STATUS_WORD                 DW ?
; LAY OUT STATUS WORD FIELDS
STATUS RECORD
&    BUSY:                1,
&    COND_CODE3:          1,
&    STACK_TOP:           3,
&    COND_CODE2:          1,
&    COND_CODE1:          1,
&    COND_CODE0:          1,
&    INT_REQ:             1,
&    RESERVED:            1,
&    P_FLAG:              1,
&    U_FLAG:              1,
&    O_FLAG:              1,
&    Z_FLAG:              1,
&    D_FLAG:              1,
&    I_FLAG:              1
; POLL STATUS WORD UNTIL 8087 IS NOT BUSY
POLL:     FNSTSW   STATUS_WORD
          TEST     STATUS_WORD, MASK BUSY
          JNZ      POLL
```

Figure 5-16. Status Word RECORD Definition

```
SAMPLE      STRUC

   N_OBS          DD    ?    ;SHORT INTEGER
   MEAN           DQ    ?    ;LONG REAL
   MODE           DW    ?    ;WORD INTEGER
   STD_DEV        DQ    ?    ;LONG REAL
   ;ARRAY OF OBSERVATIONS -- WORD INTEGER
   TEST_SCORES    DW    1000 DUP (?)
SAMPLE ENDS
```

Figure 5-17. Structure Definition

Table 5-20. Addressing Mode Examples

	Coding	Interpretation
FIADD	ALPHA	ALPHA is a simple scalar (mode is direct)
FDIVR	ALPHA.BETA	BETA is a field in a structure that is "overlaid" on ALPHA (mode is direct).
FMUL	QWORD PTR [BX]	BX contains the address of a long real variable (mode is register indirect).
FSUB	ALPHA [SI]	ALPHA is an array and SI contains the offset of an array element from the start of the array (mode is indexed).
FILD	[BP].BETA	BP contains the address of a structure on the CPU stack and BETA is a field in the structure (mode is based).
FBLD	TBYTE PTR [BX] [DI]	BX contains the address of a packed decimal array and DI contains the offset of an array element (mode is based indexed).

Since the decision to produce real or emulated 8087 instructions is made at link time, a program may be switched from one mode to the other without retranslating the source code. When the PL/M-86 compiler or ASM-86 assembler places an 8087 machine instruction into an object module, it also inserts a special external reference. This reference is satisfied by linking the object module to one of two Intel-supplied libraries: the real library, or the emulator library. If the real library is specified, LINK-86 simply deletes the external references, leaving the original 8087 machine instructions.

To run on an emulated 8087, the object program is linked to the emulator library and to a file containing the code of either the full or the partial emulator. LINK-86 then adds the emulator code to the program and changes the 8087 machine instructions (and their preceding WAITs) to CPU software interrupt instructions. Any FWAIT instructions are also changed to CPU NOPs.

Note that an explicitly-coded CPU WAIT instruction will *not* be changed; if it is executed under emulation, the CPU will wait forever. This is why the FWAIT mnemonic should always be used when the external processor that the CPU is to wait for is an 8087.

In order to be compatible with E8087, ASM-86 programs should observe the following conventions:

- Their stack segment and class should be named STACK.
- Interrupt pointer (vector) 16 should be designated for the user's exception handler interrupt procedure. Interrupt pointer 16 only needs designating if any exceptions are unmasked.
- The external procedure INIT87 should be called in the program's initialization (power-up) sequence. If the emulator is being used, this procedure will initialize CPU interrupt pointers 20-31 to the addresses of emulator procedures and will execute an (emulated) FINIT instruction. If the program is not being emulated, INIT87 simply executes the FINIT instruction.

PL/M-86 automatically observes corresponding conventions.

Programming Example

Figure 5-18 and 5-19 show the PL/M-86 and ASM-86 code for a simple 8087 program, called ARRSUM. The program references an array (X$ARRAY), which contains 0-100 short real values; the integer variable NOFX indicates the number of array elements the program is to consider. ARRSUM steps through X$ARRAY accumulating three sums:

- SUM$X, the sum of the array values;
- SUM$INDEXES, the sum of each array value times its index, where the index of the first element is 1, the second is 2, etc:
- SUM$SQUARES, the sum of each array element squared.

```
ISIS-II PL/M-86 DEBUG V2.1 COMPILATION OF MODULE ARRAYSUM
OBJECT MODULE PLACED IN :F4:ARRSUM.OBJ
COMPILER INVOKED BY:  :F0:PLM86 :F4:ARRSUM.P86 XREF


             /**************************************
              *                                    *
              *    A R R A Y S U M . M O D         *
              *                                    *
              **************************************/

   1         ARRAY$SUM:  DO;

   2   1     DECLARE (SUM$X,SUM$INDEXES,SUM$SQUARES) REAL;
   3   1     DECLARE X$ARRAY (100)   REAL;
   4   1     DECLARE (N$OF$X,I)  INTEGER;
   5   1     DECLARE CONTROL$87  LITERALLY  '033EH';

             /* ASSUME X$ARRAY AND N$OF$X ARE INITIALIZED  */

             /* PREPARE THE 8087, OR ITS EMULATOR */
   6   1     CALL INIT$REAL$MATH$UNIT;
   7   1     CALL SET$REAL$MODE(CONTROL$87);

             /* CLEAR SUMS  */
   8   1     SUM$X, SUM$INDEXES, SUM$SQUARES = 0.0;

             /* LOOP THROUGH X$ARRAY, ACCUMULATING SUMS */
   9   1     DO I = 0 TO N$OF$X - 1;
  10   2       SUM$X = SUM$X + X$ARRAY(I);
  11   2       SUM$INDEXES = SUM$INDEXES +
                        (X$ARRAY(I) * FLOAT(I + 1));
  12   2       SUM$SQUARES = SUM$SQUARES + (X$ARRAY(I) * X$ARRAY(I));
  13   2     END;

             /* ETC...*/

  14   1     END ARRAY$SUM;


CROSS-REFERENCE LISTING
-----------------------

   DEFN  ADDR   SIZE  NAME, ATTRIBUTES, AND REFERENCES
  ----- ------ -----  -------------------------------


      1  0002H   151  ARRAYSUM . . . . .   PROCEDURE STACK=0002H
      5                CONTROL87. . . . .   LITERALLY       7
                       FLOAT. . . . . . .   BUILTIN         11
      4  019EH     2   I. . . . . . . . .   INTEGER          9   10   11   12
                       INITREALMATHUNIT .   BUILTIN          6
      4  019CH     2   NOFX . . . . . . .   INTEGER          9
                       SETREALMODE. . . .   BUILTIN          7
      2  0004H     4   SUMINDEXES . . . .   REAL          8 11
      2  0008H     4   SUMSQUARES . . . .   REAL          8 12
      2  0000H     4   SUMX . . . . . . .   REAL          8 10
      3  000CH   400   XARRAY . . . . . .   REAL ARRAY(100)     10   11   12


MODULE INFORMATION:

     CODE AREA SIZE     = 0099H    153D
     CONSTANT AREA SIZE = 0004H      4D
     VARIABLE AREA SIZE = 01A0H    416D
     MAXIMUM STACK SIZE = 0002H      2D
     33 LINES READ
     0 PROGRAM ERROR(S)

END OF PL/M-86 COMPILATION
```

Figure 5-18. Sample PL/M-86 Program

```
ISIS-II 8086/8087/8088 MACRO ASSEMBLER V3.0 ASSEMBLY OF MODULE ARRSUM
OBJECT MODULE PLACED IN :F1:ARRSUM.OBJ
ASSEMBLER INVOKED BY:  :F0:ASM86 :F1:ARRSUM.A86 XREF

LOC  OBJ                 SOURCE

                         ;DEFINE INITIALIZATION ROUTINE
                                 EXTRN   INIT87:FAR

                         ;ALLOCATE SPACE FOR DATA
----                             DATA            SEGMENT PUBLIC 'DATA'
0000 3E03                        CONTROL_87      DW      033EH
0002 ????                        N_OF_X          DW      ?
0004 (100                        X_ARRAY         DD      100 DUP (?)
     ????????
     )
0194 ????????                    SUM_X           DD      ?
0198 ????????                    SUM_INDEXES     DD      ?
019C ????????                    SUM_SQUARES     DD      ?
----                             DATA            ENDS

                         ;ALLOCATE CPU STACK SPACE
----                             STACK           SEGMENT STACK 'STACK'
0000 (200                                        DW      200 DUP (?)
     ????
     )

                         ;LABEL INITIAL TOP OF STACK
0190                             STACK_TOP       LABEL   WORD
----                             STACK           ENDS

----                             CODE    SEGMENT PUBLIC 'CODE'
                                 ASSUME  CS:CODE,DS:DATA,SS:STACK,ES:NOTHING

0000                     START:
0000 B8----          R           MOV     AX,DATA
0003 8ED8                        MOV     DS,AX
0005 B8----          R           MOV     AX,STACK
0008 8ED0                        MOV     SS,AX
000A BC9001          R           MOV     SP,OFFSET STACK_TOP

                         ;ASSUME X_ARRAY & N_OF_X ARE INITIALIZED.
                         ;       NOTE: PROGRAM ZEROS N_OF_X
                         ;PREPARE THE 8087 OR ITS EMULATOR.

000D 9A0000----      E           CALL    INIT87
0012 9BD92E0000      R           FLDCW   CONTROL_87

                         ;CLEAR 3 REGISTERS TO HOLD RUNNING SUMS.

0017 9BD9EE                      FLDZ
001A 9BD9EE                      FLDZ
001D 9BD9EE                      FLDZ

                         ;SETUP CX AS LOOP COUNTER & SI AS INDEX TO X_ARRAY.

0020 8B0E0200        R           MOV     CX,N_OF_X
0024 E329                        JCXZ    POP_RESULTS     ;EXIT EARLY IF X_ARRAY EMPTY
0026 B80400                      MOV     AX,TYPE X_ARRAY
0029 F7E9                        IMUL    CX
002B 8BF0                        MOV     SI,AX
```

Figure 5-19. Sample ASM-86 Program

```
LOC  OBJ                LINE     SOURCE

                          53     ;SI NOW CONTAINS INDEX OF LAST ELEMENT + 1.
                          54     ;LOOP THRU X_ARRAY ACCUMULATING SUMS.
002D                      55     SUM_NEXT:
002D 83EE04               56             SUB    SI,TYPE X_ARRAY   ;BACKUP ONE ELEMENT
0030 9BD9840400     R     57             FLD    X_ARRAY[SI]       ;PUSH IT ONTO STACK
0035 9BDCC3               58             FADD   ST(3),ST          ;ADD INTO SUM OF X
0038 9BD9C0               59             FLD    ST                ;DUPLICATE X ON TOP
003B 9BDCC8               60             FMUL   ST,ST             ;SQUARE IT
003E 9BDEC2               61             FADDP  ST(2),ST          ;ADD INTO SUM OF SQUARES
                          62                                      ;  AND DISCARD
0041 9BDE0E0200     R     63             FIMUL  N_OF_X            ;GET X TIMES ITS INDEX
0046 9BDEC2               64             FADDP  ST(2),ST          ;ADD INTO SUM OF (INDEX * X)
                          65                                      ;  AND DISCARD
0049 FF0E0200       R     66             DEC    N_OF_X            ;REDUCE INDEX FOR NEXT ITERATION
004D E2DE                 67             LOOP   SUM_NEXT          ;CONTINUE
                          68
                          69     ;POP RUNNING SUMS INTO MEMORY
004F                      70     POP_RESULTS:
004F 9BD91E9C01     R     71             FSTP   SUM_SQUARES
0054 9BD91E9801     R     72             FSTP   SUM_INDEXES
0059 9BD91E9401     R     73             FSTP   SUM_X
                          74
                          75     ;
                          76     ;ETC...
                          77     ;
----                      78     CODE    ENDS
                          79
 0000                     80             END     START

8086/8087/8088 MACRO ASSEMBLER    ARRSUM

XREF SYMBOL TABLE LISTING
---- ------ ----- -------

NAME           TYPE     VALUE  ATTRIBUTES, XREFS

??SEG . . .    SEGMENT         SIZE=0000H PARA PUBLIC
CODE. . . .    SEGMENT         SIZE=005EH PARA PUBLIC 'CODE'  22# 23 78
CONTROL_87.    V WORD   0000H  DATA  6# 37
DATA. . . .    SEGMENT         SIZE=01A0H PARA PUBLIC 'DATA'  5# 12 23 26
INIT87. . .    L FAR    0000H  EXTRN  2# 36
N_OF_X. . .    V WORD   0002H  DATA  7# 47 63 66
POP_RESULTS    L NEAR   004FH  CODE  48 70#
STACK . . .    SEGMENT         SIZE=0190H PARA STACK 'STACK'
STACK_TOP .    V WORD   0190H  STACK  19# 30
START . . .    L NEAR   0000H  CODE  25# 80
SUM_INDEXES    V DWORD  0198H  DATA  10# 72
SUM_NEXT. .    L NEAR   002DH  CODE  55# 67
SUM_SQUARES    V DWORD  019CH  DATA  11# 71
SUM_X . . .    V DWORD  0194H  DATA  9# 73
X_ARRAY . .    V DWORD  0004H  DATA  8# 49 56 57

ASSEMBLY COMPLETE, NO ERRORS FOUND
```

Figure 5-19. Sample ASM-86 Program (Cont'd.)

(A true program, of course, would go beyond these steps to store and use the results of these calculations.) The control word is set with the recommended values: projective closure, round to nearest, 64-bit precision, interrupts enabled, and all exceptions masked except invalid operation. It is assumed that an exception handler has been written to field the invalid operation, if it occurs, and that it is invoked by interrupt pointer 16. Either version of the program will run on an actual or an emulated 8087 without altering the code shown.

The PL/M-86 version of ARRSUM (Figure 5-18) is very straightforward and illustrates how easily the 8087 can be used in this language. After declaring variables, the program calls built-in procedures to initialize the processor (or its emulator) and to load the control word. The program clears the sum variables and then steps through X$ARRAY with a DO-loop. The loop control takes into account PL/M-86's practice of considering the index of the first element of an array to be 0. In the computation of SUM$INDEXES, the built-in procedure FLOAT coverts I+1 from integer to real because the language does not support "mixed mode" arithmetic. One of the strengths of the NPX, of course, is that it *does* support arithmetic on mixed data types, and assembly language programmers can take advantage of this facility.

The ASM-86 version (Figure 5-19) defines the external procedure INIT87, which makes the different initialization requirements of the processor and its emulator transparent to the source code. After defining the data, and setting up the segment registers and stack pointer, the program calls INIT87 and loads the control word. The computation begins with the next three instructions, which clear three registers by loading (pushing) zeros onto the stack. As shown in Figure 5-20, these registers remain at the bottom of the stack throughout the computation while temporary values are pushed on and popped off the stack above them.

The program uses the CPU LOOP instruction to control its iteration through X_ARRAY; register CX, which LOOP automatically decrements, is loaded with N_OF_X, the number of array elements to be summed. Register S1 is used to select (index) the array elements. The program steps through X_ARRAY from "back to front," so SI is initialized to point at the element just beyond the first element to be processed. The ASM-86 TYPE operator is used to determine the number of bytes in each array element. This permits changing X_ARRAY to a long real array by simply changing its definition (DD to DQ) and re-assembling.

Figure 5-20 shows the effect of the instructions in the program loop on the NPX register stack. The figure assumes that the program is in its first iteration, that N_OF_X is 20, and that X_ARRAY(19) (the 20th element) contains the value 2.5 When the loop terminates, the three sums are left as the top stack elements so that the program ends by simply popping them into memory variables.

SPECIAL TOPICS

This section describes features of the 8087 which will be of interest to groups of users who have special requirements. Most users will not need to understand this material in detail in order to utilize the NPX successfully. Most readers, then, can either browse this section, or skip it altogether in favor of the programming examples in the section "Programming Examples," later in this chapter.

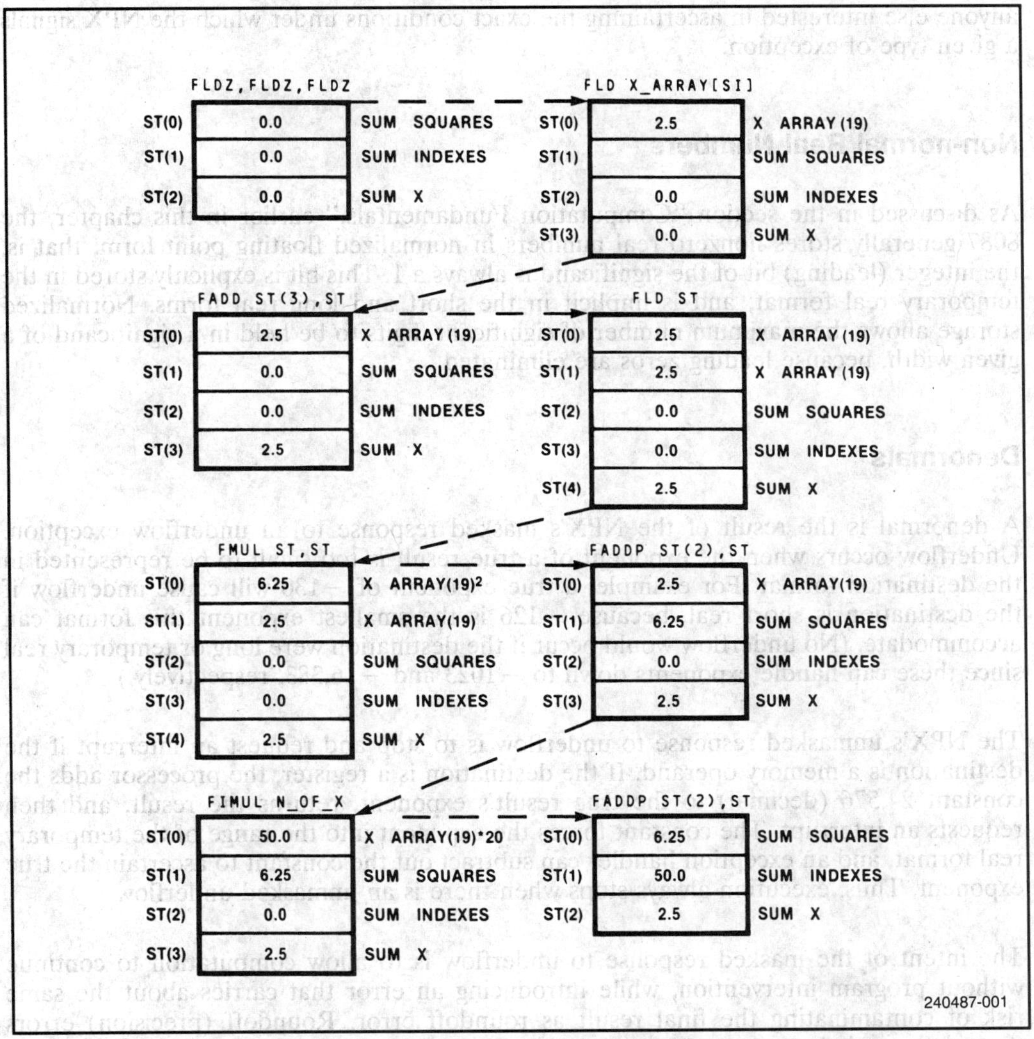

Figure 5-20. Instructions and Register Stack

The first four topics in this section cover the 8087's generation and handling of nonnormalized real values, zeros, infinities, and NANs. In the great majority of applications, these special values will either not appear at all, or in the case of zeros, will function according to the normal rules of arithmetic. Next the bit encodings of each data type are summarized in table form, including special values. This information may be of use to programmers who are sorting these data types or are decoding unformatted memory dumps or data monitored from the bus. At the end of the section is a table that lists all 8087 exception conditions by class, and the processor's masked response to each exception. This information will principally be of use to writers of exception handlers and to anyone else interested in ascertaining the exact conditions under which the NPX signals a given type of exception.

Non-normal Real Numbers

As discussed in the section "Computation Fundamentals," earlier in this chapter, the 8087 generally stores nonzero real numbers in normalized floating point form; that is, the integer (leading) bit of the significand is always a 1. This bit is explicitly stored in the temporary real format, and is implicit in the short and long real forms. Normalized storage allows the maximum number of significant digits to be held in a significand of a given width, because leading zeros are eliminated.

Denormals

A denormal is the result of the NPX's masked response to an underflow exception. Underflow occurs when the exponent of a true result is too small to be represented in the destination format. For example, a true exponent of −130 will cause underflow if the destination is short real, because −126 is the smallest exponent this format can accommodate. (No underflow would occur if the destination were long or temporary real since these can handle exponents down to −1023 and −16,383, respectively.)

The NPX's unmasked response to underflow is to stop and request an interrupt if the destination is a memory operand. If the destination is a register, the processor adds the constant 24,576 (decimal) to the true result's exponent, returns the result, and then requests an interrupt. The constant forces the exponent into the range of the temporary real format, and an exception handler can subtract out the constant to ascertain the true exponent. Thus, execution always stops when there is an unmasked underflow.

The intent of the masked response to underflow is to allow computation to continue without program intervention, while introducing an error that carries about the same risk of contaminating the final result as roundoff error. Roundoff (precision) errors occur frequently in real number calculations; sometimes they spoil the result of computation, but often they do not. Recognizing that roundoff errors are often non-fatal, computation usually proceeds and the programmer inspects the final result to see if these errors have had a significant effect. The 8087's masked underflow response allows programmers to treat underflows in a similar manner; the computation continues and the programmer can examine the final result to determine if an underflow has had important consequences. (If the underflow has had a significant effect, an invalid operation will probably be signaled later in the computation.)

Most computers underflow "abruptly"; they simply return a zero result, which is likely to produce an unacceptable final result if computation continues. The 8087, on the other hand, underflows "gradually" when the underflow exception is masked. Gradual underflow is accomplished by denormalizing the result until it is just within the exponent range of the destination. Denormalizing means incrementing the true result's exponent and inserting a corresponding leading zero in the significand, shifting the rest of the significand one place to the right. Table 5-21 illustrates how a result might be denormalized to fit a short real destination.

Denormalization produces a denormal or a zero. Denormals are readily identified by their exponents, which are always the minimum for their formats; in biased form, this is always the bit string: 00...00. This same exponent value is also assigned to the zeros, but a denormal has a nonzero significand. A denormal in a register is tagged special.

The denormalization process may cause the loss of the low-order significand bits as they are shifted off the right. In a severe case, *all* the significand bits of the true result are shifted out and replaced by the leading zeros. In this case, the result of denormalization is a true zero, and if the value is in a register, it is tagged as such. However, this is a comparatively rare occurrence, and, in any case, is no worse than "abrupt" underflow.

Denormals are rarely encountered in most applications. Typical debugged algorithms generate extremely small results during the evaluation of intermediate subexpressions; the final result is usually of an appropriate magnitude for its short or long real destination. If intermediate results are held in temporary real, as is recommended, the great range of this format makes underflow very unlikely. Denormals are likely to arise only when an application generates a great many intermediates, so many that they cannot be held on the register stack or in temporary real memory variables. If storage limitations force the use of short or long reals for intermediates, and small values are produced, underflow may occur, and if masked, may generate denormals.

Accessing a denormal may produce an exception as shown in Table 5-22. (The denormalized exception signals that a denormal has been fetched.) Denormals may have reduced significance due to lost low-order bits, and an option of the proposed IEEE standard precludes operations on non-normalized operands. This option may be implemented in the form of an exception handler that responds to unmasked denormalized exceptions. Most users will mask this exception so that computation may proceed; any loss of accuracy will be analyzed by the user when the final result is delivered.

Table 5-21. Denormalization Process

Operation	Sign	Exponent[1]	Significand
True Result	0	−129	1Δ01011100...00
Denormalize	0	−128	0Δ101011100...00
Denormalize	0	−127	0Δ0101011100...00
Denormalize	0	−126	0Δ00101011100...00
Denormal Result[2]	0	−126	0Δ00101011100...00

NOTES:

(1) Expressed as unbiased, decimal number

(2) Before storing, significand is rounded to 24 bits, integer bit is dropped, and exponent is biased by adding 126.

Table 5-22. Exceptions Due to Denormal Operands

Operation	Exception	Masked Response
FLD (short/long real)	D	Load as equivalent unnormal
Arithmetic (except following)	D	Convert (in a work area) denormal to equivalent unnormal and proceed
Compare and test	D	Convert (in a work area) denormal to equivalent unnormal and proceed
Division or FPREM with denormal divisor	I	Return real *indefinite*

As Table 5-22 shows, the division and remainder operations do not accept denormal divisors and raise the invalid operation exception. Recall, also, that the transcendental instructions require normalized operands and do *not* check for exceptions. In all other cases, the NPX converts denormals to unnormals, and the unnormal arithmetic rules then apply.

Unnormals

As unnormal is the "descendent" of a denormal and therefore of a masked underflow response. An unnormal may exist only in the temporary real format; it may have any exponent that a normal may have, but it is distinguished from a normal by the integer bit of its significand, which is always 0. An unnormal in a register is tagged valid.

Unnormals allow arithmetic to continue following an underflow while still retaining their identity as numbers which may have reduced significance. That is, unnormal operands generate unnormal results, so long as their unnormality has a significant effect on the result. Unnormals are thus prevented from "masquerading" as normals, numbers which have full significance. On the other hand, if an unnormal has an insignificant effect on a calculation with a normal, the result will be normal. For example, adding a small unnormal to a large normal yields a normal result. The converse situation yields an unnormal.

Table 5-23 shows how the instruction set deals with unnormal operands. Note that the unnormal may be the original operand or a temporary created by the 8087 from a denormal. Unnormals can be converted to normals using the FPREM instruction (refer to this instruction in the section "Instruction Set," earlier in this chapter.

Zeros and Pseudo-Zeros

As discussed in the section "Computation Fundamentals," earlier in this chapter, the real and packed decimal data types support signed zeros, while the binary integers represent a single zero, signed positive. The signed zeros behave, however, as though they are a single unsigned quantity. If necessary, the FXAM instruction may be used to determine a zero's sign.

Table 5-23. Unnormal Operands and Results

Operation	Result
Addition/subtraction	Normalization of operand with larger absolute value determines normalization of result.
Multiplication	If either operand is unnormal, result is unnormal.
Division (unnormal dividend only)	Result is unnormal.
FPREM (unnormal dividend only)	Result is normalized.
Division/FPREM (unnormal divisor)	Signal invalid operation.
Compare/FTST	Normalize as much as possible before making comparison.
FRNDINT	Normalize as much as possible before rounding.
FSQRT	Signal invalid operation.
FST, FSTP (short/long real destination)	If value is above destination's underflow boundary, then signal invalid operation; else signal underflow.
FSTP (temporary real destination)	Store as usual.
FIST, FISTP, FBSTP	Signal invalid operation.
FLD	Load as usual.
FXCH	Exchange as usual.
Transcendental instructions	Undefined; operands must be normal and are not checked.

The zeros discussed are called true zeros; if one of them is loaded or generated in a register, the register is tagged zero. Table 5-24 lists the result of instructions executed with zero operands and also shows how a true zero may be created from nonzero operands. (Nonzero operands are denoted "X" or "Y" in the table.)

Only the temporary real format may contain a special class of values called pseudo zeros. A pseudo zero is an unnormal whose significand is all zeros, but whose (biased) exponent is nonzero (true zeros have a zero exponent). Neither is a pseudo zero's exponent all ones, since this encoding is reserved for infinities and NANs. A pseudo zero result will be produced if two unnormals, containing a total of more than 64 leading zero bits in their significands, are multiplied together. This is a remote possibility in most applications, but it can happen.

Pseudo zero operands behave like unnormals, except in the following cases where they produce the same results as true zeros:

- compare and test instructions
- FRNDINT (round to integer 9)
- division, where the dividend is either a true zero or a pseudo zero (the divisor is a pseudo zero).

In addition and subtraction of a pseudo zero and a true zero or another pseudo zero, the pseudo zero(s) behave like unnormals, except for the determination of the result's sign. The sign is determined as shown in Table 5-24 for two true zero operands.

Table 5-24. Zero Operands and Results

Operation/Operands	Result	Operation/Operands	Result
FLD, FBLD[1]		Division	
+0	+0	±0 ÷ ±0	Invalid operation
−0	−0	±X ÷ ±0	Zerodivide
FILD[2]		+0 ÷ +X, −0 ÷ −X	+0
+0	+0	+0 ÷ −X, −0 ÷ +X	−0
FST, FSTP		−X ÷ −Y, +X ÷ +Y	+0, underflow[8]
+0	+0	−X ÷ +Y, +X ÷ −Y	−0, underflow[8]
−0	−0		
+X[3]	+0	FPREM	
−X[3]	−0	±0 rem ±0	Invalid operation
FBSTP		±X rem ±0	Invalid operation
+0	+0	+0 rem +X, +0 rem −X	+0
−0	−0	−0 rem +X, −0 rem −X	−0
FIST, FISTP		+X rem +Y, +X rem −Y	+0[9]
+0	+0	−X rem −Y, −X rem +Y	−0[9]
−0	+0		
+X[4]	+0	FSQRT	
−X[4]	+0	−0	−0
		+0	+0
Addition			
+0 plus +0	+0	Compare	
−0 plus −0	−0	±0 : +X	A<B
+0 plus −0, −0 plus +0	*0[5]	±0 : ±0	A=B
−X plus +X, +X plus −X	*0[5]	±0 : −X	A>B
±0 plus ±X, ±X plus ±0	†X[6]		
		FTST	
Subtraction		±0	Zero
+0 minus −0	+0	FCHS	
−0 minus +0	−0	+0	−0
+0 minus +0, −0 minus −0	*0[5]	−0	+0
+X minus +X, −X minus −X	*0[5]	FABS	
±0 minus ±X, ±X minus ±0	†X[6]	±0	+0
		F2XM1	
Multiplication		+0	+0
+0 · +0, −0 · −0	+0	−0	−0
+0 · −0, −0 · +0	−0	FRNDINT	
+0 · +X, +X · +0	+0	+0	+0
+0 · −X, −X · +0	−0	−0	−0
−0 · +X, +X · −0	−0	FXTRACT	
−0 · −X, −X · −0	+0	+0	Both +0
+X · +Y, −X · −Y	+0, underflow[7]	−0	Both −0
+X · −Y, −X · +Y	−0, underflow[7]		

NOTES:

(1) Arithmetic and compare operations with real memory operands interpret the memory operand signs in the same way.
(2) Arithmetic and compare operations with binary integers interpret the integer sign in the same manner.
(3) Severe underflows in storing to short or long real may generate zeros.
(4) Small values ($|X|<1$) stored into integers may round to zero.
(5) Sign is determined by rounding mode:
* = + for nearest, up or chop
* = − for down
(6) † = sign of X.
(7) Very small values of X and Y may yield zeros, after rounding of true result. NPX signals underflow to warn that zero has been yielded by nonzero operands.
(8) Very small X and very large Y may yield zero, after rounding of true result. NPX signals underflow to warn that zero has been yielded from nonzero operands.
(9) When Y divides into X exactly.

Infinities

The real formats support signed representations of infinities. These values are encoded with a biased exponent of all ones and a significand of 1 Δ 00...00; if the infinity is in a register, it is tagged special. The significand distinguishes infinities from NANs, including real indefinite.

A programmer may code an infinity, or it may be created by the NPX as its masked response to an overflow or a zerodivide exception. Note that when rounding is up or down, the masked response may create the largest valid value representable in the destination rather than infinity. See Table 5-31 for details. As operands, infinities behave somewhat differently depending on how the infinity control field in the control word is set (see Table 5-25). When the projective model of infinity is selected, the infinities behave as a single unsigned representation; because of this, infinity cannot be compared with any value except infinity. In affine mode, the signs of the infinities are observed, and comparisons are possible.

NANs

A NAN (Not-A-Number) is a member of a class of special values that exist in the real formats only. A NAN has an exponent of 11...11B, may have either sign, and may have any significand except 1 Δ 00...00B, which is assigned to the infinities. A NAN in a register is tagged special.

The 8087 will generate the special NAN, real *indefinite*, as its masked response to an invalid operation exception. This NAN is signed negative; its significand is encoded 1 Δ 100...00. All other NANs represent programmer-created values.

Whenever the NPX uses an operand that is a NAN, it signals invalid operation. Its masked response to this exception is to return the NAN as the operation's result. If both operands of an instruction are NANs, the result is the NAN with the larger absolute value. In this way, a NAN that enters a computation propagates through the computation and will eventually be delivered as the final result. Note, however, that the transcendental instructions do not check their operands, and a NAN will produce an undefined result.

By unmasking the invalid operation exception, the programmer can use NANs to trap to the exception handler. The generality of this approach and the large number of NAN values that are available, provide the sophisticated programmer with a tool that can be applied to a variety of special situations.

For example, a compiler could use NANs to reference uninitialized (real) array elements. the compiler could pre-initialize each array element with a NAN whose significand contained the index (relative position) of the element. If an application program attempted to access an element that it had not initialized, it would use the NAN placed there by the compiler. If the invalid operation exception where unmasked, an interrupt would occur, and the exception handler would be invoked. The exception handler could

Table 5-25. Infinity Operands and Results

Operation	Projective Result	Affine Result
Division		
± ∞ ÷ ± ∞	Invalid operation	Invalid operation
± ∞ ÷ ±X	⊕ ∞	⊕ ∞
±X ÷ ± ∞	⊕ 0	⊕ 0
FSQRT		
− ∞	Invalid operation	Invalid operation
+ ∞	Invalid operation	+ ∞
FPREM		
± ∞ rem ± ∞	Invalid operation	Invalid operation
± ∞ rem ±X	Invalid operation	Invalid operation
±Y rem ± ∞	*Y	*Y
±0 rem ± ∞	*0	*0
FRNDINT		
± ∞	* ∞	* ∞
FSCALE		
± ∞ scaled by ± ∞	Invalid operation	Invalid operation
± ∞ scaled by ±X	* ∞	* ∞
±0 scaled by ± ∞	*0	*0
±Y scaled by ± ∞	Invalid operation	Invalid operation
FXTRACT		
± ∞	Invalid operation	Invalid operation
Compare		
± ∞ : ± ∞	A=B	− ∞ < + ∞
± ∞ : ±Y	A?B (and) invalid operation	− ∞ < Y < + ∞
± ∞ : ±0	A?B (and) invalid operation	− ∞ < 0 < + ∞
FTST		
± ∞	A?B (and) invalid operation	* ∞
Addition		
+ ∞ plus + ∞	Invalid operation	+ ∞
− ∞ plus − ∞	Invalid operation	− ∞
+ ∞ plus − ∞	Invalid operation	Invalid operation
− ∞ plus + ∞	Invalid operation	Invalid operation
± ∞ plus ±X	* ∞	* ∞
±X plus ± ∞	* ∞	* ∞
Subtraction		
+ ∞ minus − ∞	Invalid operation	+ ∞
− ∞ minus + ∞	Invalid operation	− ∞
+ ∞ minus + ∞	Invalid operation	Invalid operation
− ∞ minus − ∞	Invalid operation	Invalid operation
± ∞ minus ±X	* ∞	* ∞
±X minus ± ∞	† ∞	† ∞
Multiplication		
± ∞ ± ∞	⊕ ∞	⊕ ∞
± ∞ ±Y	⊕ ∞	⊕ ∞
±0 ± ∞, ± ∞ * ±0	Invalid operation	Invalid operation

NOTES:

X = zero or nonzero operand
Y = nonzero operand
* = sign of original operand
† = sign is complement of original operand's sign
⊕ = sign is "exclusive or" original operand signs (+ if operands had same sign, − if operands had different signs)

determine which element had been accessed, since the operand address field of the exception pointers would point to the NAN, and the NAN would contain the index number of the array element.

NAN's could also be used to speed up debugging. In its early testing phase, a program often contains multiple errors. An exception handler could be written to save diagnostic information in memory whenever it was invoked. After storing the diagnostic data, it could supply a NAN as the result of the erroneous instruction, and that NAN could point to its associated diagnostic area in memory. The program would then continue, creating a different NAN for each error. When the program ended, the NAN results could be used to access the diagnostic data saved at the time the errors occurred. Many errors could thus be diagnosed and corrected in one test run.

Data Type Encoding

Tables 5-26 through 5-29 summarize how various types of values are encoded in the seven NPX data types. In all tables, the less significant bits are to the right and are stored in the lowest memory addresses. The sign bit is always the left-most bit of the highestaddressed byte.

Notice that in every format, one encoding is interpreted as representing the special value *indefinite*. The 8087 produces this encoding as its response to a masked invalid operation exception. In the case of the reals, *indefinite* can be loaded and stored like any NAN and it always retains its special identity; programmers are advised not to use this encoding for any other purpose. Packed decimal *indefinite* may be stored by the NPX in a FBSTP instruction; attempting to use this encoding in a FBLD instruction, however, will have an undefined result. In the binary integers, the same encoding may represent either *indefinite* or the largest negative number supported by the format (-2^{15}, -2^{31} or -2^{63}). The 8087 will store this encoding as its masked response to an invalid operation, or when the value in a source register represents, or rounds to, the largest negative integer representable by the destination. In situations where its origin may be ambiguous, the invalid operation exception flag can be examined to see if the value was produced by an exception response. When this encoding is loaded, or used by an integer arithmetic or compare operation, it is always interpreted as a negative number; thus *indefinite* cannot be loaded from a packed decimal or binary integer.

Exception Handling Details

Table 5-30 lists every exception condition that the NPX detects and describes the processor's response when the relevant exception mask is set. The unmasked responses are described in Table 5-6. Note that if an unmasked overflow or underflow occurs in an FST or FSTP instruction, no result is stored, and the stack and memory are left as they existed *before* the instruction was executed. This gives an exception handler the opportunity to examine the offending operand on the stack top.

Table 5-26. Binary Integer Encodings

Class		Sign	Magnitude
Positives	(Largest)	0	11...11
		.	.
	(Smallest)	0	00...01
Zero		0	00...00
Negatives	(Smallest)	1	11...11
		.	.
	(Largest/*Indefinite**)	1	00...00
		Word:	←15 bits→
		Short:	←31 bits→
		Long:	←63 bits→

Table 5-27. Packed Decimal Encodings

Class		Sign		Magnitude					
				digit	digit	digit	digit	...	digit
Positives	(Largest)	0	0000000	1 0 0 1	1 0 0 1	1 0 0 1	1 0 0 1	...	1 0 0 1
		.	.				.		
	(Smallest)	0	0000000	0 0 0 0	0 0 0 0	0 0 0 0	0 0 0 0	...	0 0 0 1
	Zero	0	0000000	0 0 0 0	0 0 0 0	0 0 0 0	0 0 0 0	...	0 0 0 0
Negatives	Zero	1	0000000	0 0 0 0	0 0 0 0	0 0 0 0	0 0 0 0	...	0 0 0 0
	(Smallest)	1	0000000	0 0 0 0	0 0 0 0	0 0 0 0	0 0 0 0	...	0 0 0 1
		.	.			.			
	(Largest)	1	0000000	1 0 0 1	1 0 0 1	1 0 0 1	1 0 0 1	...	1 0 0 1
*Indefinite**		1	1111111	1 1 1 1	1 1 1 1	U U U U**	U U U U	...	U U U U
		← 1 byte →		← 9 bytes →					

* The *packed decimal indefinite* encoding is stored by FBSTP in response to a masked invalid operation exception. Attempting to load this value via FBLD produces an undefined result.
** UUUU means bit values are undefined and may contain any value.

When rounding is directed (the RC field of the control word is set to "up" or "down"), the 8087 handles a masked overflow differently than it does for the "nearest" or "chop" rounding modes. Table 5-31 shows the NPX's masked response when the true result is too large to be represented in it's destination real format. For a normalized result, the essence of this response is to deliver ∞ or the largest valid number representable in the destination format, as dictated by the rounding mode and the sign of the true result. Thus, when RC = down, a positive overflow is rounded down to the largest positive number. Conversely, when RC = up, a negative overflow is rounded up to the largest negative number. A properly signed ∞ is returned for a positive overflow with RC = up, or a negative overflow with RC = down. For an unnormalized result, the action is similar except that the unnormal character of the result is preserved if the sign and rounding mode do not indicate that ∞ should be delivered.In all masked overflow responses for directed rounding, the overflow flag is *not* set, but the precision exception *is* raised to signal that the exact true result has not been returned.

Table 5-28. Real and Long Real Encodings

Class			Sign	Biased Exponent	Significand* Δff...ff
Positive		NANs	0 ⋮ 0	11...11 ⋮ 11...11	11...11 ⋮ 00...01
	∞		0	11...11	00...00
	Reals	Normals	0 ⋮ 0	11...10 ⋮ 00...01	11...11 ⋮ 00...00
		Denormals	0 ⋮ 0	00...00 ⋮ 00...00	11...11 ⋮ 00...01
		Zero	0	00...00	00...00
Negatives	Reals	Zero	1	00...00	00...00
		Denormals	1 ⋮ 1	00...00 ⋮ 00...00	00...01 ⋮ 11...11
		Normals	1 ⋮ 1	00...01 ⋮ 11...10	00...00 ⋮ 11...11
	∞		1	11...11	00...00
		NANs	1 ⋮	11...11 ⋮	00...01 ⋮
		Indefinite	1	11...11	10.000
		NANs	⋮ 1	⋮ 11...11	⋮ 11...11
			Short:	← 8 bits →	← 23 bits →
			Long:	← 11 bits →	← 52 bits →

*Integer bit is implied and not stored.

Table 5-29. Temporary Real Encodings

	Class	Sign	Biased Exponent	Significand Δff..ff
Positives	NANs	0 ⋮ 0	11...11 ⋮ 11...11	111...11 ⋮ 100...01
	∞	0	11...11	100...00
Positives	Reals	0 ⋮ ⋮ 0	11...10 ⋮ ⋮ 00...01	Normals 111...11 ⋮ 100...00 Unnormals 011..11 ⋮ 000...00
		0 ⋮ 0	00...00 ⋮ 00...00	Denormals 011...11 ⋮ 000...01
	Zero	0	00...00	000...00
Negatives	Zero	1	00...00	000...00
		1 ⋮ 1	00...00 ⋮ 00...00	Denormals 000...01 ⋮ 011...11
Negatives	Reals	1 ⋮ ⋮ 1	00...01 ⋮ ⋮ 11...10	Unnormals 000...00 ⋮ 011...11 Normals 100...00 ⋮ 111...11
	∞	1	11...11	100...00
Negatives		1 ⋮	11...11 ⋮	100...01 ⋮
	Indefinite	1	11...11	110...00
	NANs	⋮ 1	⋮ 11...11	⋮ 111...11
			← 15 bits →	← 64 bits →

Table 5-30. Exception Conditions and Masked Responses

Condition	Masked Response
Invalid Operation	
Source register is tagged empty (usually due to stack underflow).	Return real *indefinite.*
Destination register is not tagged empty (usually due to stack overflow).	Return real *indefinite* (overwrite destination value).
One or both operands is a NAN.	Return NAN with larger absolute value (ignore signs).
(Compare and test operations only): one or both operands is a NAN.	Set condition codes "not comparable."
(Addition operations only): closure is affine and operands are opposite-signed infinities; or closure is projective and both operands are ∞ (signs immaterial).	Return real *indefinite.*
(Subtraction operations only): closure is affine and operands are like-signed infinities; or closure is projective and both operands are ∞ (signs immaterial).	Return real *indefinite.*
(Multiplication operations only): ∞ * 0; or 0 * ∞.	Return real *indefinite.*
(Division operations only): ∞ ÷ ∞, or 0 ÷ 0; or 0 ÷ pseudo-zero; or divisor is denormal or unnormal.	Return real *indefinite.*
(FPREM instruction only): modulus (divisor) is unnormal or denormal; or dividend is ∞.	Return real *indefinite*, set condition code = "complete remainder."
(FSQRT instruction only): operand is nonzero and negative; or operand is denormal or unnormal; or closure is affine and operand is − ∞; or closure is projective and operand is ∞.	Return real *indefinite.*
(Compare operations only): closure is projective and ∞ is being compared with 0 or a normal, or ∞.	Set condition code = "not comparable."
(FTST instruction only): closure is projective and operand is ∞.	Set condition code = "not comparable."
(FIST, FISTP instructions only): source register is empty, or a NAN, or denormal, or unnormal, or ∞, or exceeds representable range of destination.	Store integer *indefinite.*
(FBSTP instruction only): source register is empty, or a NAN, or denormal, or unnormal, or ∞, or exceeds 18 decimal digits.	Store packed decimal *indefinite.*
(FST, FSTP instructions only): destination is short or long real and source register is an unnormal with exponent in range.	Store real *indefinite.*

Table 5-30. Exception Conditions and Masked Responses

Condition	Masked Response
(FXCH instruction only): one or both registers is tagged empty.	Change empty register(s) to real *indefinite* and then perform exchange.
Denormalized Operand	
(FLD instruction only): source operand is denormal.	No special action; load as usual.
(Arithmetic operations only): one or both operands is denormal.	Convert (in a work area) the operand to the equivalent unnormal and proceed.
(Compare and test operations only): one or both operands is denormal *or unnormal* (other than pseudo-zero).	Convert (in a work area) any denormal to the equivalent unnormal normalize as much as possible, and proceed with operation.
Zerodivide	
(Division operations only): divisor = 0.	Return ∞ signed with "exclusive or" of operand signs.
Overflow	
(Arithmetic operations only): rounding is nearest or chop, and exponent of true result > 16,383.	Return properly signed ∞ and signal precision exception.
(FST, FSTP instructions only): rounding is nearest or chop, and exponent of true result > +127 (short real destination) or > +1023 (long real destination).	Return properly signed ∞ and signal precision exception.
Underflow	
(Arithmetic operations only): exponent of true result < −16,382 (true).	Denormalize until exponent rises to −16,382 (true), round significand to 64 bits. If denormalized rounded significand = 0, then return true 0; else, return denormal (tag = special, biased exponent = 0).
(FST, FSTP instructions only): destination is short real and exponent of true result < −126 (true).	Denormalize until exponent rises to −126 (true), round significand to 24 bits, store true 0 if denormalized rounded significand = 0; else, store denormal (biased exponent = 0).
(FST, FSTP instructions only): destination is long real and exponent of true result < −1022 (true).	Denormalize until exponent rises to −1022 (true), round significand to 53 bits, store true 0 if rounded denormalized significand = 0; else, store denormal (biased exponent = 0).
Precision	
True rounding error occurs.	No special action.
Masked response to overflow exception earlier in instruction.	No special action.

Table 5-31. Masked Overflow Response for Directed Rounding

True Result		Rounding Mode	Result Delivered
Normalization	Sign		
Normal	+	Up	$+\infty$
Normal	+	Down	Largest finite positive number(1)
Normal	−	Up	Largest finite negative number(1)
Normal	−	Down	$-\infty$
Unnormal	+	Up	$+\infty$
Unnormal	−	Down	Largest exponent, result's significand(2)
Unnormal	+	Up	Largest exponent, result's significand(2)
Unnormal	−	Down	$-\infty$

NOTES:

(1) The largest valid representable reals are encoded:
exponent: 11...10B
significand: (1)Δ11...10B

(2) The significand retains its identity as an unnormal; the true result is rounded as usual (effectively chopped toward 0 in this case). The exponent is encoded 11...10B.

PROGRAMMING EXAMPLES

Conditional Branching

As discussed in the section "Instruction Set," earlier in this chapter, the comparison instructions post their results to the condition code bits of the 8087 status word. Although there are many ways to implement conditional branching following a comparison, the basic approach is as follows:

- execute the comparison,
- store the status word,
- inspect the condition code bits,
- jump on the result.

Figure 5-21 is a code fragment that illustrates how two memory-resident long real numbers might be compared (similar code could be used with the FTST instruction). The numbers are called A and B, and the comparison is A to B. The comparison itself simply requires loading A onto the top of the 8087 register stack and then comparing it to B and popping the stack in the same instruction. The status word is written to memory and the code waits for completion of the store before attempting to use the result.

There are four possible orderings of A and B, and bits C3 and C0 of the condition code indicate which ordering holds. These bits are positioned in the upper byte of the status word so as to correspond to the CPU's zero and carry flags (ZF and CF), if the byte is

```
        .
        .
A       DQ      ?
B       DQ      ?
STAT_87 DW      ?
        .
        .
        .
        FLD     A           ;LOAD A ONTO TOP OF 87 STACK
        FCOMP B             ;COMPARE A:B, POP A
        FSTSW STAT_87       ;STORE RESULT
        FWAIT               ;WAIT FOR STORE
        ;
        ;LOAD CPU REGISTER AH WITH BYTE OF
        ;       STATUS WORD CONTAINING CONDITION CODE
        MOV     AH, BYTE PTR STAT_87+1
        ;
        ;LOAD CONDITION CODES INTO CPU FLAGS
        SAHF
        ;
        ;USE CONDITIONAL JUMPS TO DETERMINE
        ;       ORDERING OF A AND B
        JB      A_LESS_OR_UNORDERED
        ;CF (CO) = 0
        JNE     A_GREATER
    A_EQUAL:
        ;CF (CO) = 0, ZF (C3) = 1
        .
        .
    A_GREATER:
        ;CF (CO) = 0, ZF (C3) = 0
        .
        .
        .
    A_LESS_OR_UNORDERED:
        ;CF (CO) = 1, TEST ZF (C3)
        JNE     A_LESS
    A_B_UNORDERED:
        ;CF (CO) = 1, ZF (C3) = 1
        .
        .
    A_LESS:
        ;CF (CO) = 1, ZF (C3) = 0
        .
        .
        .
```

Figure 5-21. Conditional Branching for Compares

written into the flags (see Figures 3-28 and 5-6.) The code fragment, then sets ZF and CF to the values of C3 and C0 and then uses the CPU conditional jumps to test the flags. Table 3-12 shows how each conditional jump instruction tests the CPU flags.

The FXAM instruction updates all four condition code bits. Figure 5-22 shows how a jump table can be used to determine the characteristics of the value examined. The jump table (FXAM_TBL) is initialized to contain the 16-bit displacement of 16 labels, one for each possible condition code setting. Note that four of the table entries contain the same value, since there are four condition code settings that correspond to "empty."

The program fragment performs the FXAM and stores the status word. It then manipulates the condition code bits to finally produce a number in register BX that equals the condition code times 2. This involves zeroing the unused bits in the byte that contains the code, shifting C3 to the right so that it is adjacent to C2, and then shifting the code to multiply it by 2. The resulting value is used as an index which selects one of the displacements from FXAM_TBL (the multiplication of the condition code is required because of the 2-byte length of each value in FXAM_TBL). The unconditional JMP instruction effectively vectors through the jump table to the labeled routine that contains code (not shown in the example) to process each possible result of the FXAM instruction.

Exception Handlers

There are many approaches to writing exception handlers. One useful technique is to consider the exception handler interrupt procedure as consisting of "prologue," "body" and "epilogue" sections of code. (For compatibility with the 8087 emulators, this procedure should be invoked by interrupt pointer (vector) number 16.)

At the beginning of the prologue, CPU interrupts have been disabled by the CPU's normal interrupt response mechanism. The prologue performs all functions that must be protected from possible interruption by higher-priority sources. Typically this will involve saving CPU registers and transferring diagnostic information from the 8087 to memory. When the critical processing has been completed, the prologue may enable CPU interrupts to allow higher-priority interrupt handlers to preempt the exception handler.

The exception handler body examines the diagnostic information and makes a response that is necessarily application-dependent. This response may range from halting execution, to displaying a message, to attempting to repair the problem and proceed with normal execution.

The epilogue essentially reverses the actions of the prologue, restoring the CPU and the NPX so that normal execution can be resumed. The epilogue must *not* load an unmasked exception flag into the 8087 or another interrupt will be requested immediately (assuming 8087 interrupts are also loaded as unmasked).

Figure 5-23 through 5-25 show the ASM-86 coding of three skeleton exception handlers.

```
;EXAMINE ST, STORE RESULT, WAIT FOR COMPLETION
    FXAM
    FSTSW       STAT_87
    FWAIT
;CLEAR UPPER HALF OF BX, LOAD CONDITION CODE
;   IN LOWER HALF
    MOV         BH,0
    MOV         BL, BYTE PTR STAT_87+1
;COPY ORIGINAL IMAGE
    MOV         AL,BL
;CLEAR ALL BITS EXCEPT C2-C0
    AND         BL,00000111B
;CLEAR ALL BITS EXCEPT C3
    AND         AL,01000000B
;SHIFT C3 TWO PLACES RIGHT
    SHR         AL,1
    SHR         AL,1
;SHIFT C2-C0 ONE PLACE LEFT (MULTIPLY BY 2)
    SAL         BX,1
;DROP C3 BACK IN ADJACENT TO C2 (000XXXX0)
    OR          BL,AL
;JUMP TO THE ROUTINE ''ADDRESSED'' BY CONDITION CODE
    JMP         FXAM_TBL[BX]
;
;HERE ARE THE JUMP TARGETS, ONE TO HANDLE
;   EACH POSSIBLE RESULT OF FXAM
POS_UNNORM:
    .
    .
POS_NAN:
    .
    .
NEG_UNNORM:
    .
    .
NEG_NAN:
    .
    .
POS_NORM:
    .
    .
POS_INFINITY:
    .
    .
NEG_NORM:
    .
    .
NEG_INFINITY:
    .
    .
POS_ZERO:
    .
    .
```

Figure 5-22. Conditional Branching for FXAM

```
EMPTY:
        .
        .
NEG_ZERO:
        .
        .
POS_DENORM:
        .
        .
NEG_DENORM:
        .
        .
        .
```

Figure 5-22. Conditional Branching for FXAM (Cont'd.)

They show how prologues and epilogues can be written for various situations, but only provide comments indicating where the application-dependent exception handling body should be placed.

Figure 5-23 and 5-24 are very similar; their only substantial difference is their choice of instructions to save and restore the 8087. The tradeoff here is between the increased diagnostic information provided by FNSAVE and the faster execution of FNSTENV. For applications that are sensitive to interrupt latency, or do not need to examine register contents, FNSTENV reduces the duration of the "critical region," during which the CPU will not recognize another interrupt request (unless it is a non-maskable interrupt).

After the exception handler body, the epilogues prepare the CPU and the NPX to resume execution from the point of interruption (i.e., the instruction following the one that generated the unmasked exception). Notice that the exception flags in the memory image that is loaded into the 8087 are cleared to zero prior to reloading (in fact, in these examples, the entire status word image is cleared). The prologue also provides for indicating to the interrupt controller hardware (e.g., an 8259A) that the interrupt has been processed. The actual processing done here is application-dependent, but might typically involve writing an "end of interrupt" command to the interrupt controller.

The examples in Figures 5-23 and 5-24 assume that the exception handler itself will not cause an unmasked exception. Where this is a possibility, the general approach shown in Figure 5-25 can be employed. The basic technique is to save the full 8087 state and then to load a new control word in the prologue. Note that considerable care should be taken when designing an exception handler of this type to prevent the handler from being reentered endlessly.

```
SAVE_ALL            PROC
;
; SAVE CPU REGISTERS, ALLOCATE STACK SPACER
; FOR 8087 STATE IMAGE
; NOTE! INTERRUPTS MUST BE DISABLED.
     PUSH       BP
         .
         .
         .
     MOV        BP,SP
     SUB        SP,94
;SAVE FULL 8087 STATE, WAIT FOR COMPLETION,
;ENABLE CPU INTERRUPTS
     FNSAVE     [BP-94]
     FWAIT
     STI
;
;APPLICATION-DEPENDENT EXCEPTION HANDLING
;CODE GOES HERE
;
;CLEAR EXCEPTION FLAGS IN STATUS WORD
;RESTORE MODIFIED STATE
;IMAGE
     MOV        BYTE PTR [BP-92], 0H
     FRSTOR     [BP-94]
;WAIT FOR RESTORE TO FINISH BEFORE RELEASING MEMORY
     FWAIT
;DE-ALLOCATE STACK SPACE, RESTORE CPU REGISTERS
     MOV        SP,BP
         .
         .
         .
     POP        BP
;
;CODE TO SEND ''END OF INTERRUPT'' COMMAND TO
;8259A GOES HERE
;
;RETURN TO INTERRUPTED CALCULATION
     IRET
SAVE_ALL            ENDP
```

Figure 5-23. Full State Exception Handler

```
SAVE_ENVIRONMENT PROC
;
; SAVE CPU REGISTERS, ALLOCATE STACK SPACE
; FOR 8087 ENVIRONMENT
; NOTE! INTERRUPTS MUST BE DISABLED.
        PUSH    BP
            .
            .
            .
        MOV     BP,SP
        SUB     SP,14
;SAVE ENVIRONMENT, WAIT FOR COMPLETION,
;ENABLE CPU INTERRUPTS
        FNSTENV [BP-14]
        FWAIT
        STI
;
;APPLICATION EXCEPTION-HANDLING CODE GOES HERE
;
;CLEAR EXCEPTION FLAGS IN STATUS WORD
;RESTORE MODIFIED
;ENVIRONMENT IMAGE
        MOV     BYTE PTR [BP-12], 0H
        FLDENV  [BP-14]
;WAIT FOR LOAD TO FINISH BEFORE RELEASING MEMORY
        FWAIT
;DE-ALLOCATE STACK SPACE, RESTORE CPU REGISTERS
        MOV     SP,BP
            .
            .
            .
        POP     BP
;
;CODE TO SEND ''END OF INTERRUPT'' COMMAND TO
;8259A GOES HERE
;
;RETURN TO INTERRUPTED CALCULATION
        IRET
SAVE_ENVIRONMENT ENDP
```

Figure 5-24. Reduced Latency Exception Handler

```
                .
                .
                .
          LOCAL_CONTROL  DW  ?  ;ASSUME INITIALIZED
                .
                .
                .
REENTRANT                  PROC
;
;SAVE CPU REGISTERS, ALLOCATE STACK SPACE FOR
;8087 STATE IMAGE
      PUSH      BP
          .
          .
          .
      MOV       BP,SP
      SUB       SP,94
;SAVE STATE, LOAD NEW CONTROL WORD, WAIT
;FOR COMPLETION, ENABLE CPU INTERRUPTS
      FNSAVE    [BP-94]
      FLDCW     LOCAL_CONTROL
      FWAIT
      STI
;CODE TO SEND ''END OF INTERRUPT'' COMMAND TO
;8259A GOES HERE
          .
          .
          .
;APPLICATION EXCEPTION HANDLING CODE GOES HERE.
;AN UNMASKED EXCEPTION GENERATED HERE WILL
;CAUSE THE EXCEPTION HANDLER TO BE REENTERED.
;IF LOCAL STORAGE IS NEEDED, IT MUST BE
;ALLOCATED ON THE CPU STACK.
          .
          .
          .
;CLEAR EXCEPTION FLAGS IN STATUS WORD
;RESTORE MODIFIED STATE IMAGE
      MOV       BYTE PTR [BP-92], 0H
      FRSTOR    [BP-94]
;WAIT FOR RESTORE TO FINISH BEFORE RELEASING MEMORY
      FWAIT
;DE-ALLOCATE STACK SPACE, RESTORE CPU REGISTERS
      MOV       SP,BP
          .
          .
          .
      POP       BP
;RETURN TO POINT OF INTERRUPTION
      IRET
REENTRANT                  ENDP
```

Figure 5-25. Reentrant Exception Handler

The 8086/8088 CPU 6

CHAPTER 6
THE 8086/8088 CPU

INTRODUCTION

This chapter contains specific hardware design information on the operation and functions of Intel®'s 8086/8088 Central Processing Units (CPUs). This information consists of a component overview of the 8086/88 microprocessors presenting architectural and software considerations, individual device pin functional and electrical signal definitions, a detailed description of the minimum and maximum operating modes, detailed descriptions of the operation of the address and data buses, an explanation of the protocols supported for local bus transfers to other devices, and a detailed description of interrupt operation. In addition, descriptions of the various 8086/88 family support circuits and their circuit functions appear at the end of the chapter. For more specific information of any of the 8086 family support circuits, refer to the *Microprocessor Handbook* (Order Number: 230843).

COMPONENT OVERVIEW

The 8086 and 8088 are closely related third-generation microprocessors. Both CPU's contain a 20-bit address bus (1 mega-byte of address space) and utilize an identical instruction/function format. Differences between the two devices consist essentially of their respective data bus widths. The 8088 is designed with an 8-bit external data path to memory and I/O, while the 8086 can transfer 16 bits at a time. In almost every other respect the processors are identical; software written for one CPU will execute on the other without alteration. Both chips are contained in standard 40-pin dual in-line packages and operate from a single +5V power source. Except where expressly noted, the descriptions contained in this chapter are applicable to both microprocessors.

The 8086 and 8088 Microprocessors can be used for a wide spectrum of microcomputer applications. This flexibility is one of their most outstanding characteristics. Systems can range from small uniprocessor minimal-memory designs implemented with a few chips (see Figure 6-1), to multiprocessor systems with up to a megabyte of memory.

Both the 8086 and 8088 microprocessors use a combined, or "time-multiplexed," address and data bus that permits several of the device pins to serve dual functions. Some microprocessor control pins also serve dual functions. These pins are defined according to the strapping of a single input pin (the MN/MX* pin). This feature provides configuration of the CPU's in either "minimum mode" or "maximum mode" circuits.

In the "minimum mode," the CPU is configured for small, single-processor systems. In this configuration all control signals are provided by the CPU and the dual function pins transfer signals directly to memory and input/output devices.

In the "maximum mode" these same pins take on different functions that are helpful in medium to large systems, especially systems with multiple processors. An Intel 82C88 Bus Controller is used to provide the control signal outputs. This allows several of the

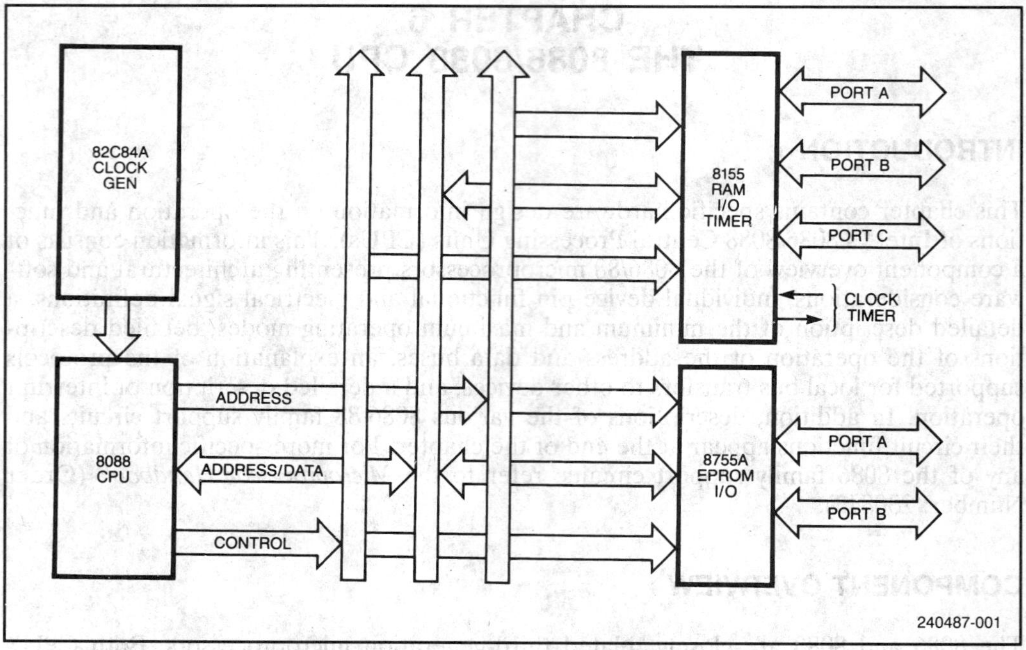

Figure 6-1. Small 8088-Based System

device pins previously delegated to these control functions to be redefined in order to support multiprocessing applications. A detailed description of this feature is presented later in the chapter.

Both the 8086 and 8088 are substantially more powerful than any microprocessor previously offered by Intel. Actual performance, of course, varies from application to application, but comparisons to the industry standard 2-MHz 8080A are instructive. The 8088 is from four to six times more powerful than the 8080A; the 8086 provides seven to ten times the 8080A's performance.

The 8086's advantage over the 8088 is the result of the 8086's 16-bit external data bus. In applications that manipulate 8-bit quantities extensively, or that are execution-bound, the 8088 can approach to within 10% of the 8086's processing throughput.

The improved performance of the 8086 and 8088 is accomplished by combining a 16-bit internal data path with a pipelined architecture that allows instructions to be prefetched during spare bus cycles. In addition, a compact instruction format that enables more instructions to be fetched in a given amount of time contributes to this high performance.

Software for 8086 and 8088 systems does not need to be written in assembly language. The CPUs are designed to provide direct hardware support for programs written in high-level languages such as Intel's PL/M-86. Most high-level languages store variables in memory; the 8086/8088 symmetrical instruction set supports direct operation on memory operands, including operands on the stack. The hardware addressing modes provide efficient, straightforward implementations of based variables, arrays, arrays of structures and other high-level language data constructs. A powerful set of memory-to-memory string operations is available for efficient character data manipulation. Finally, routines with critical performance requirements that cannot be met with PL/M-86 may be written in ASM-86 (the 8086/8088 assembly language) and linked with PL/M-86 code.

Although the 8086 and 8088 Microprocessors are totally new designs, they make the most of user's existing investments in systems designed around the 8080/8085 microprocessors. Many of the standard Intel memory, peripheral control and communication chips are compatible with the 8086 and the 8088. Software is developed in the familiar Intellec Microcomputer Development System environment, and most existing programs, whether written in ASM-80 or PL/M-80, can be directly converted to run on the 8086 and 8088.

Architectural Overview

Both the 8086 and 8088 microprocessors incorporate two separate processing units (see Figures 6-2 and 6-3). These are the Execution Unit (EU) and the Bus Interface Unit

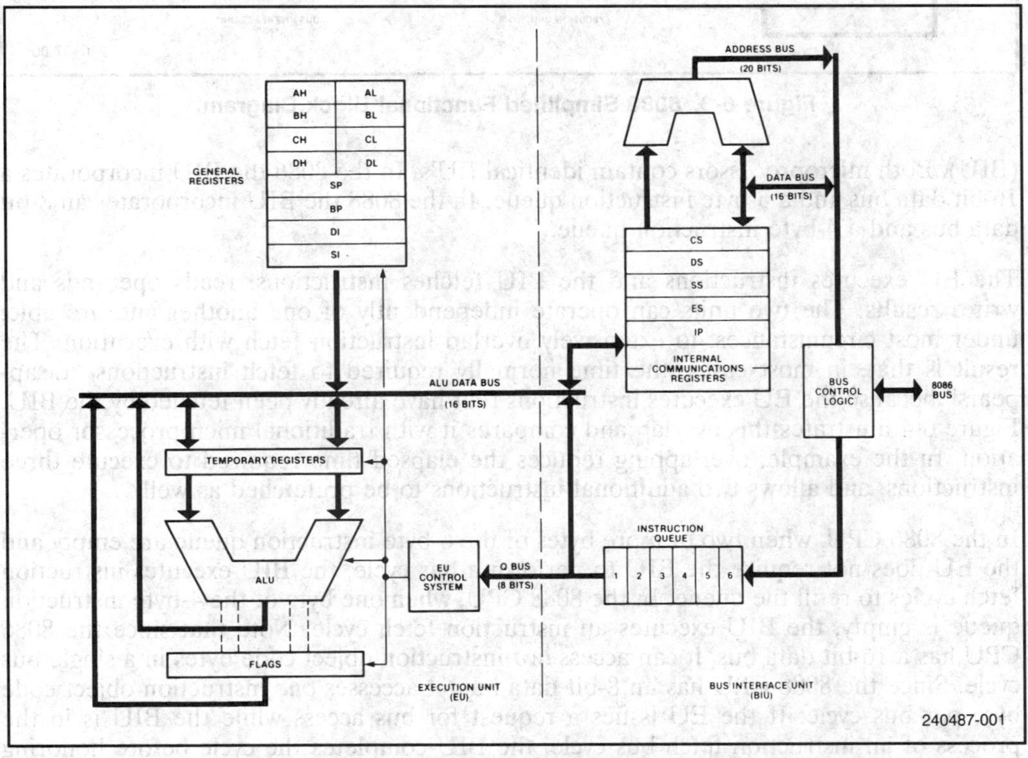

Figure 6-2. 8086 Simplified Functional Block Diagram

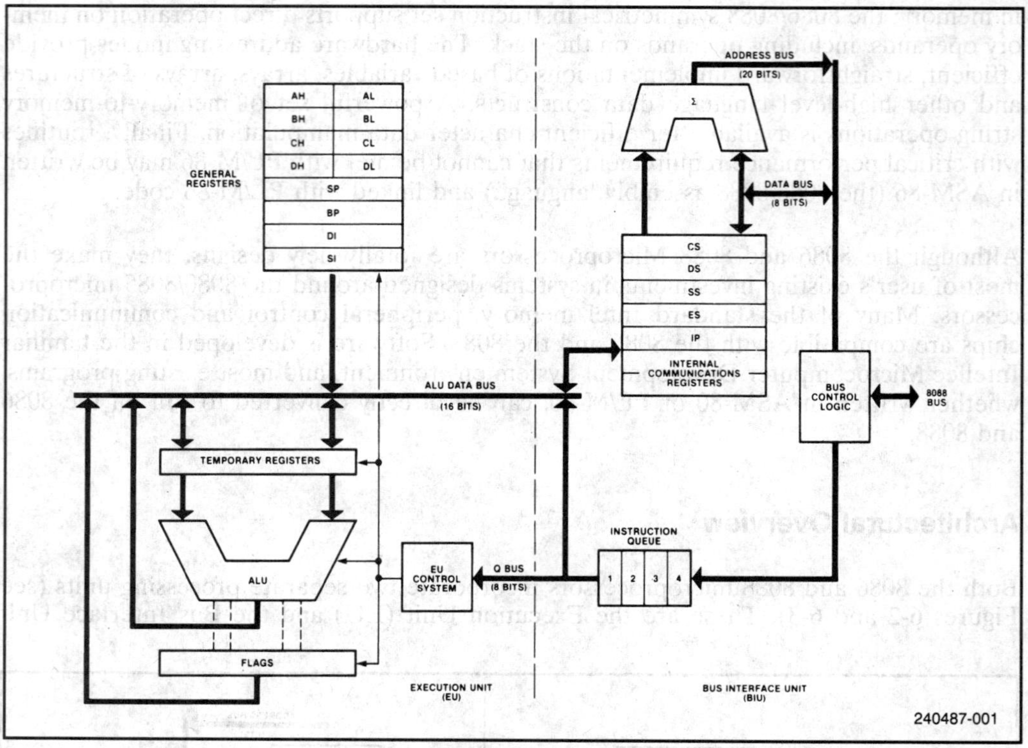

Figure 6-3. 8088 Simplified Functional Block Diagram

(BIU). Both microprocessors contain identical EU's. In the 8086 the BIU incorporates a 16-bit data bus and a 6-byte instruction queue. In the 8088 the BIU incorporates an 8-bit data bus and a 4-byte instruction queue.

The EU executes instructions and the BIU fetches instructions, reads operands and writes results. The two units can operate independently of one another and are able, under most circumstances, to extensively overlap instruction fetch with execution. The result is that, in most cases, the time normally required to fetch instructions "disappears" because the EU executes instructions that have already been fetched by the BIU. Figure 6-4 illustrates this overlap and compares it with traditional microprocessor operation. In the example, overlapping reduces the elapsed time required to execute three instructions, and allows two additional instructions to be prefetched as well.

In the 8086 CPU, when two or more bytes of the 6-byte instruction queue are empty and the EU does not require the BIU to perform a bus cycle, the BIU executes instruction fetch cycles to refill the queue. In the 8088 CPU, when one byte of the 4-byte instruction queue is empty, the BIU executes an instruction fetch cycle. Note that since the 8086 CPU has a 16-bit data bus, it can access *two* instruction object code bytes in a single bus cycle. Since the 8088 CPU has an 8-bit data bus, it accesses *one* instruction object code byte per bus cycle. If the EU issues a request for bus access while the BIU is in the process of an instruction fetch bus cycle, the BIU completes the cycle before honoring the EU's request.

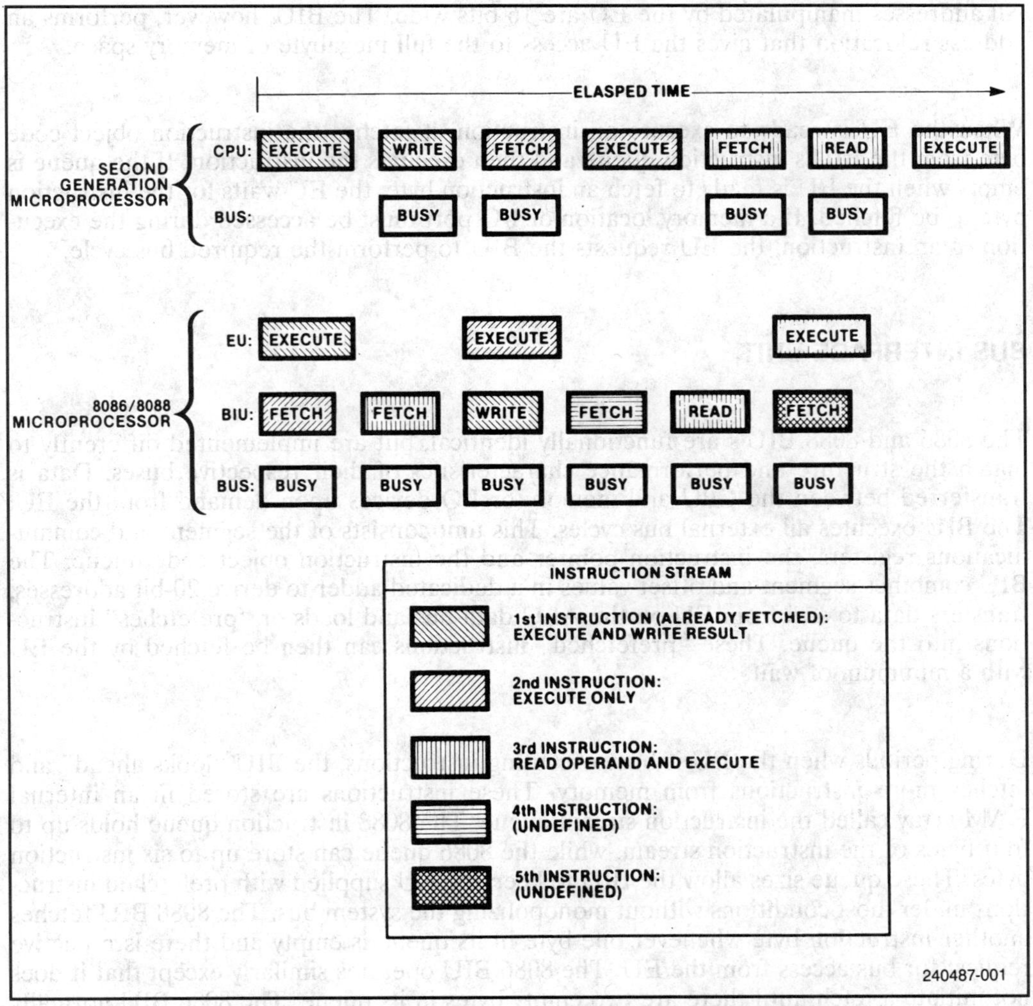

Figure 6-4. Overlapped Instruction Fetch and Execution

EXECUTION UNIT

The execution units (EU's) of the 8086 and 8088 are identical (see Figures 6-2 and 6-3). The EU is responsible for the execution of all instructions, for providing data and addresses to the BIU, and for manipulating the general registers and the flag register. A 16-bit arithmetic/logic unit (ALU) in the EU maintains the CPU status and control flags, and manipulates the general registers and instruction operands. All registers and data paths in the EU are 16 bits wide for fast internal transfers.

The EU has no connection to the system bus, the "outside world." It obtains instructions from a queue maintained by the BIU. Likewise, when an instruction requires access to memory or to a peripheral device, the EU requests the BIU to obtain and store the data.

All addresses manipulated by the EU are 16 bits wide. The BIU, however, performs an address relocation that gives the EU access to the full megabyte of memory space.

When the EU is ready to execute an instruction, it fetches the instruction object code byte from the BIU's instruction queue and then executes the instruction. If the queue is empty when the EU is ready to fetch an instruction byte, the EU waits for the instruction byte to be fetched. If a memory location or I/O port must be accessed during the execution of an instruction, the EU requests the BIU to perform the required bus cycle.

BUS INTERFACE UNIT

The 8086 and 8088 BIU's are functionally identical, but are implemented differently to match the structure and performance characteristics of their respective buses. Data is transferred between the CPU and memory or I/O devices upon demand from the EU. The BIU executes all external bus cycles. This unit consists of the segment and communications registers, the instruction pointer and the instruction object code queue. The BIU combines segment and offset values in a dedicated adder to derive 20-bit addresses, transfers data to and from EU on the ALU data bus and loads or "prefetches" instructions into the queue. These "prefetched" instructions can then be fetched by the EU with a minimum of wait.

During periods when the EU is busy executing instructions, the BIU "looks ahead" and fetches more instructions from memory. These instructions are stored in an internal RAM array called the instruction stream queue. The 8088 instruction queue holds up to four bytes of the instruction stream, while the 8086 queue can store up to six instruction bytes. These queue sizes allow the BIU to keep the EU supplied with prefetched instructions under most conditions without monopolizing the system bus. The 8088 BIU fetches another instruction byte whenever one byte in its queue is empty and there is no active request for bus access from the EU. The 8086 BIU operates similarly except that it does not initiate a fetch until there are two empty bytes in its queue. The 8086 BIU normally obtains two instruction bytes per fetch. If a program transfer forces fetching from an odd address, the 8086 automatically reads one byte from the odd address and then resumes fetching two-byte words from the subsequent even addresses.

In most circumstances the queues contain at least one byte of the instruction stream and the EU does not have to wait for instructions to be fetched. The instructions in the queue are those stored in memory locations immediately adjacent to and higher than the instruction currently being executed. That is, they are the next logical instructions so long as execution proceeds serially. If the EU executes an instruction that transfers control to another location, the BIU resets the queue, fetches the instruction from the new address, passes it immediately to the EU, and then begins refilling the queue from the new location. In addition, the BIU suspends instruction fetching whenever the EU requests a memory or I/O read or write (except that a fetch already in progress is completed before executing the EU's bus request).

GENERAL REGISTERS

Both CPU's have the same complement of eight 16-bit general registers (see Figure 6-5). The general registers are subdivided into two sets of four registers each. These are the data registers (sometimes called the H & L group for "high" and "low"), and the pointer and index registers (sometimes called the P & I group).

The data registers are unique in that their upper (high) and lower halves are separately addressable. This means that each data register can be used interchangeably as a 16-bit register, or as two 8-bit registers. The other CPU registers are always accessed as 16-bit only. The data registers can be used without constraint in most arithmetic and logic operations. In addition, some instructions use certain registers implicitly (see Table 6-1), therefore allowing compact yet powerful encoding.

The pointer and index registers can also be used in most arithmetic and logic operations. All eight general registers fit the definition of an "accumulator" as defined in first and second generation microprocessors. The P & I registers (except for BP) are also used implicitly in some instructions (see Table 6-1).

SEGMENT REGISTERS

The 8086 and 8088 memory space (up to one megabyte) is divided into logical segments of up to 64K bytes each. The CPU has direct access to four segments at a time. The base addresses (starting locations) of these memory segments are contained in the segment registers (see Figure 6-6). The CS register points to the current code segment. Instructions are fetched from the CS segment. The SS register points to the current stack

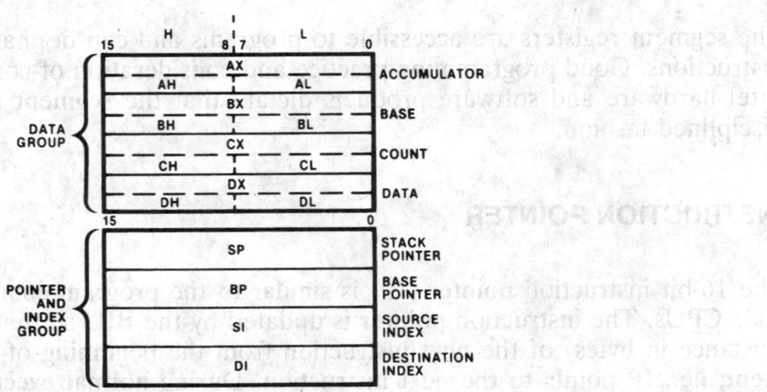

Figure 6-5. General Registers

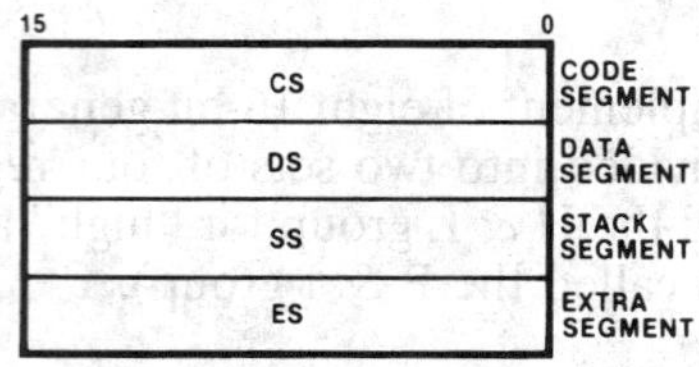

Figure 6-6. Segment Registers

Table 6-1. Implicit Use of General Registers

Register	Operations
AX	Word Multiply, Word Divide, Word I/O
AL	Byte Multiply, Byte Divide, Byte I/O, Translate, Decimal Arithmetic
AH	Byte Multiply, Byte Divide
BX	Translate
CX	String Operations, Loops
CL	Variable Shift and Rotate
DX	Word Multiply, Word Divide, Indirect I/O
SP	Stack Operations
SI	String Operations
DI	String Operations

segment. Stack operations are performed on locations in the SS segment. The DS register points to the current data segment. The DS register generally contains program variables. The ES register points to the current extra segment, which also is typically used for data storage.

The segment registers are accessible to programs and can be manipulated with several instructions. Good programming practice and consideration of compatibility with future Intel hardware and software products dictate that the segment registers be used in a disciplined fashion.

INSTRUCTION POINTER

The 16-bit instruction pointer (IP) is similar to the program counter (PC) in the 8080/8085 CPUs. The instruction pointer is updated by the BIU so that it contains the offset (distance in bytes) of the next instruction from the beginning of the current code segment; i.e., IP points to the next instruction. During normal execution, IP contains the offset of the next instruction to be *fetched* by the BIU. Whenever IP is saved on the stack, however, it is first automatically adjusted to point to the next instruction to be *executed*. Programs do not have direct access to the instruction pointer, but instructions cause it to change and to be saved on and restored from the stack.

FLAGS

The 8086 and 8088 have six 1-bit status flags (see Figure 6-7) that the EU posts to reflect certain properties of the result of an arithmetic or logic operation. A group of instructions is available that allows a program to alter its execution depending on the state of these flags, i.e., on the result of a prior operation. Different instructions affect the status flags differently; in general, however, the flags reflect the following conditions:

1. If AF (the auxiliary flag) is set, there has been a carry out of the low nibble into the high nibble or a borrow from the high nibble into the low nibble of an 8-bit quantity (low-order byte of a 16-bit quantity). This flag is used by decimal arithmetic instructions.

2. If CF (the carry flag) is set, there has been a carry out of, or a borrow into, the high-order bit of the result (8- or 16-bit). The flag is used by instructions that add and subtract multibyte numbers. Rotate instructions can also isolate a bit in memory or a register by placing it in the carry flag.

3. If OF (the overflow flag) is set, an arithmetic overflow has occurred; that is, a significant digit has been lost because the size of the result exceeded the capacity of its destination location. An Interrupt On Overflow instruction is available that will generate an interrupt in this situation.

4. If SF (the sign flag) is set, the high-order bit of the result is a 1. Since negative binary numbers are represented in the 8086 and 8088 in standard two's complement notation, SF indicates the sign of the result (0 = positive, 1 = negative).

5. If the PF (the parity flag) is set, the result has even parity, an even number of 1-bits. This flag can be used to check for data transmission errors.

6. If ZF (the zero flag) is set, the result of the operation is 0.

Three additional control flags (see Figure 6-7) can be set and cleared by programs to alter processor operations:

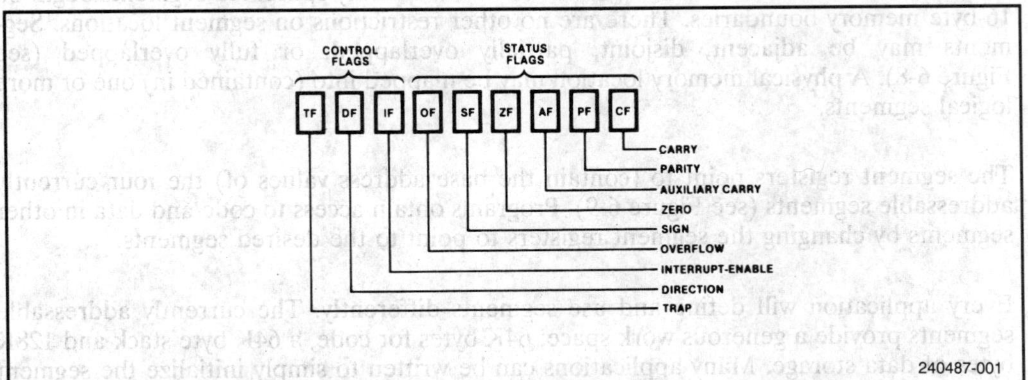

Figure 6-7. Status Flags

1. Setting DF (the direction flag) causes string instructions to auto-decrement; that is, to process strings from the high address to the low address, or from "right to left." Clearing DF causes string instructions to auto-increment, or process strings from "left to right."

2. Setting IF (the interrupt-enable flag) allows the CPU to recognize external (maskable) interrupt requests. Clearing IF disables these interrupts. IF has no affect on either non-maskable external or internally generated interrupts.

3. Setting TF (the trap flag) puts the processor into single-step mode for debugging. In this mode, the CPU automatically generates an internal interrrupt after each instruction, allowing a program to be inspected as it executes instruction by instruction.

MODE SELECTION

Each of the processors has a strap pin (MN/MX*) that defines the function of eight CPU pins in the 8086 and nine pins in the 8088. Connecting MN/MX* to +5V places the CPU in minimum mode. This configuration is designed for small systems (roughly one or two boards) and the CPU provides bus control signals needed by memory and peripherals. When MN/MX* is strapped to ground, the CPU is configured in maximum mode. In this configuration the CPU encodes control signals on three lines. An 82C88 Bus Controller is added to decode the signals for the rest of the system. The CPU uses the remaining free lines for a new set of signals designed to help coordinate the activities of other processors in the system.

SEGMENTATION

Programs for the 8086 and 8088 "view" the memory space (one megabyte) as a group of segments that are defined by application. A segment is a logical unit of memory that may be up to 64K bytes long. Each segment is made up of contiguous memory locations and is an independent, separately-addressable unit. Every segment is assigned (by software) a base address, which is its starting location in the memory space. All segments begin on 16-byte memory boundaries. There are no other restrictions on segment locations. Segments may be adjacent, disjoint, partially overlapped, or fully overlapped (see Figure 6-8). A physical memory location may be mapped into (contained in) one or more logical segments.

The segment registers point to (contain the base address values of) the four currently addressable segments (see Figure 6-9). Programs obtain access to code and data in other segments by changing the segment registers to point to the desired segments.

Every application will define and use segments differently. The currently addressable segments provide a generous work space; 64K bytes for code, a 64K byte stack and 128K bytes of data storage. Many applications can be written to simply initialize the segment registers and then forget them. Larger applications should be designed with careful consideration given to segment definition.

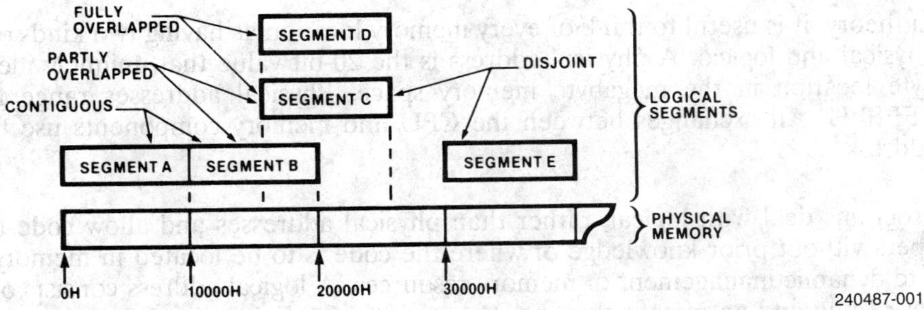

Figure 6-8. Segment Locations in Physical Memory

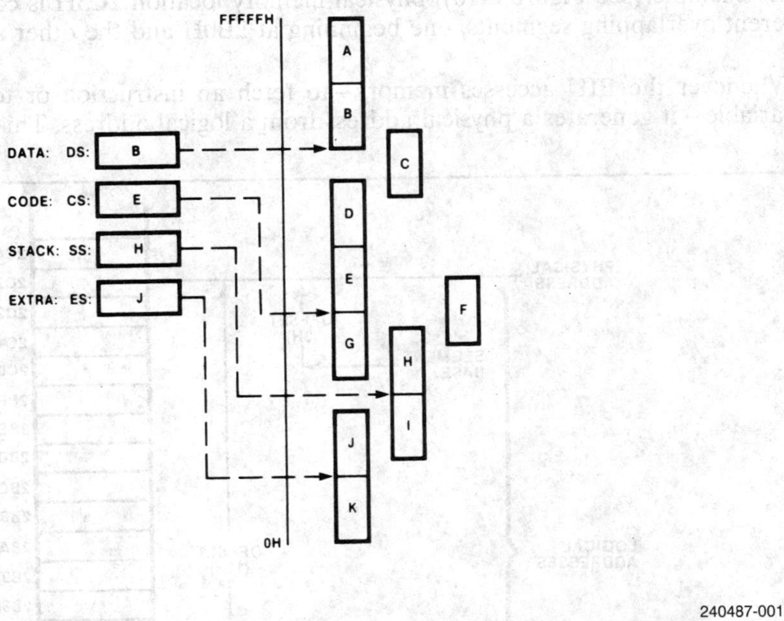

Figure 6-9. Currently Addressable Segments

The segment structure of the 8086/8088 memory space supports modular software design by discouraging huge, monolithic programs. The segments also can be used to advantage in many programming situations. Take, for example, the case of an editor for several on-line terminals. A 64K test buffer (probably an extra segment) could be assigned to each terminal. A single program could maintain all the buffers by simply changing register ES to point to the buffer of the terminal requiring service.

PHYSICAL ADDRESS GENERATION

In theory, it is useful to think of every memory location as having two kinds of addresses, physical and logical. A physical address is the 20-bit value that uniquely identifies each byte location in the megabyte memory space. Physical addresses range from 0H to FFFFFH. All exchanges between the CPU and memory components use this physical address.

Programs deal with logical, rather than physical addresses and allow code to be developed without prior knowledge of where the code is to be located in memory and facilitate dynamic management of memory resources. A logical address consists of a segment base value and an offset value. For any given memory location, the segment base value locates the first byte of the containing segment and the offset value is the distance, in bytes, of the target location from the beginning of the segment. Segment base and offset values are unsigned 16-bit quantities. The lowest-addressed byte in a segment has an offset of 0. Many different logical addresses can map to the same physical location. In the example (see Figure 6-10), physical memory location 2C3H is contained in two different overlapping segments, one beginning at 2B0H and the other at 2C0H.

Whenever the BIU accesses memory—to fetch an instruction or to obtain or store a variable—it generates a physical address from a logical address. This is done by shifting

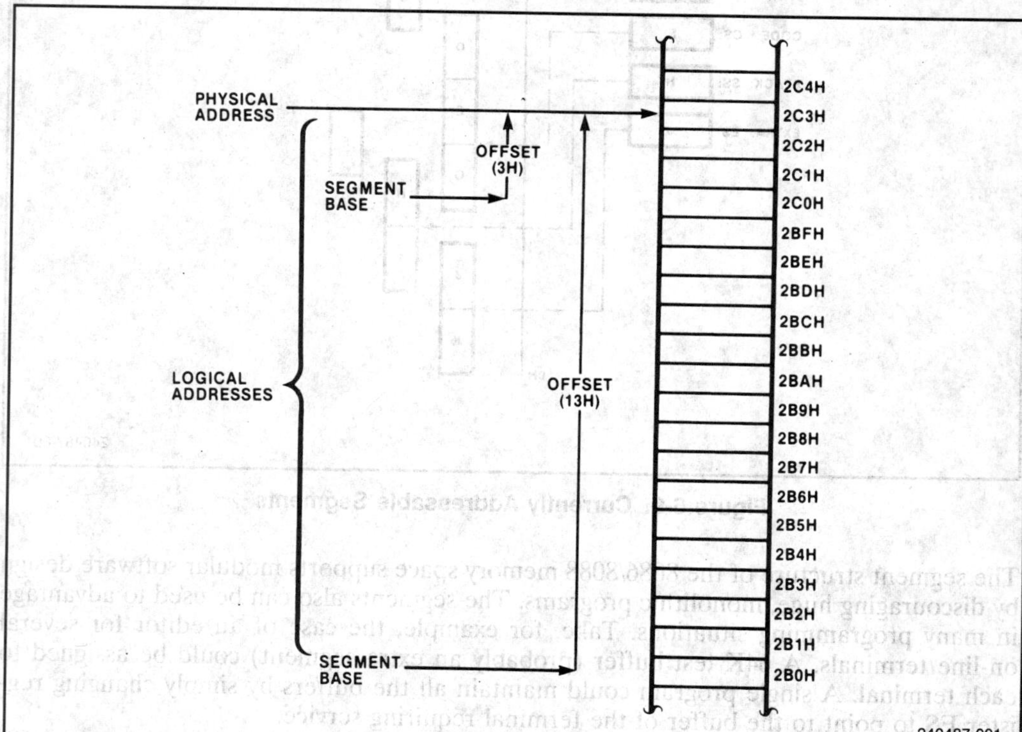

Figure 6-10. Logical and Physical Addresses

the segment base value four bit positions and adding the offset as illustrated in Figure 6-11. Note that this addition process provides for modulo 64K addressing (addresses wrap around from the end of a segment to the beginning of the same segment).

The BIU obtains the logical address of a memory location from different sources, depending on the type of reference that is being made (see Table 6-2). Instructions are always fetched from the current code segment; IP contains the offset of the target instruction from the beginning of the segment. Stack instructions always operate on the current stack segment; SP contains the offset of the top of the stack. Most variables (memory operands) are assumed to reside in the current data segment, although a program can instruct the BIU to access a variable in one of the other currently addressable segments. The offset of a memory variable is calculated by the EU. This calculation is based on the addressing mode specified in the instruction; the result is called the operand's effective address (EA).

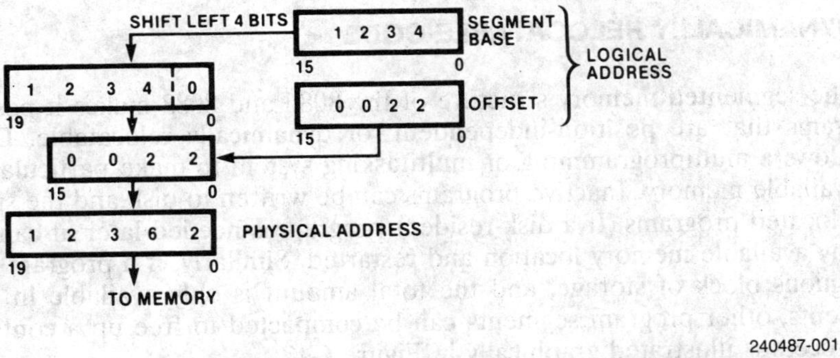

Figure 6-11. Physical Address Generation

Table 6-2. Logical Addresses Sources

Type of Memory Reference	Default Segment Base	Alternate Segment Base	Offset
Instruction Fetch	CS	None	IP
Stack Operation	SS	None	SP
Variable (except following)	DS	CS, ES, SS	Effective Address
String Source	DS	CS, ES, SS	SI
String Destination	ES	None	DI
BP Used as Base Register	SS	CS, DS, ES	Effective Address

Strings are addressed differently than other variables. The source operand of a string instruction is assumed to lie in the current data segment, but another currently addressable segment may be specified. Its offset is taken from register SI, the source index register. The destination operand of a string instruction always resides in the current extra segment; its offset is taken from DI, the destination index register. The string instruction automatically adjust SI and DI as they process the strings one byte or word at a time.When register BP, the base pointer register, is designated as a base register in an instruction, the variable is assumed to reside in the current stack segment. Therefore, register BP provides a convenient way to address data on the stack. However, BP can also be used to access data in any of the other currently addressable segments.

The BIU's segment assumptions are a convenience to programmers in most cases. However, it is possible for a programmer to explicitly direct the BIU to access a variable in any of the currently addressable segments. (The only exception is the destination operand of a string instruction which must be an extra segment.) This is done by preceding an instruction with a segment override prefix. This one-byte machine instruction tells the BIU which segment register to use to access a variable referenced in the following instruction.

DYNAMICALLY RELOCATABLE CODE

The segmented memory structure of the 8086 and 8088 makes it possible to write programs that are position-independent, or dynamically relocatable. Dynamic relocation allows a multiprogramming or multitasking system to make particularly effective use of available memory. Inactive programs can be written to disk and the space they occupied allocated programs. If a disk-resident program is needed later, it can be read back into any available memory location and restarted. Similarly, if a program needs a large contiguous block of storage, and the total amount is only available in non-adjacent fragments, other program segments can be compacted to free up a continuous space. This process is illustrated graphically in Figure 6-12.

To be dynamically relocatable, a program must not load or alter its segment registers and must not transfer directly to a location outside the current code segment. In other words, all offsets in the program must be relative to fixed values contained in the segment registers. This allows the program to be moved anywhere in memory as long as the segment registers are updated to point to the new base addresses.

STACK IMPLEMENTATION

Stacks in the 8086 and 8088 are implemented in memory and are located by the stack segment register (SS) and the stack pointer (SP). A system may have an unlimited number of stacks, and a stack may be up to 64K bytes long, the maximum length of a segment. (An attempt to expand a stack beyond 64K bytes overwrites the beginning of the segment.) One stack is directly addressable at a time; this is the current stack, often referred to simply as "the" stack. SS contains the base address of the current stack and SP points to the top of stack (TOS). In other words, SP contains the offset of the top of the stack from the stack segment's base address. However, the stack's base address (contained in SS) is not the "bottom" of the stack.

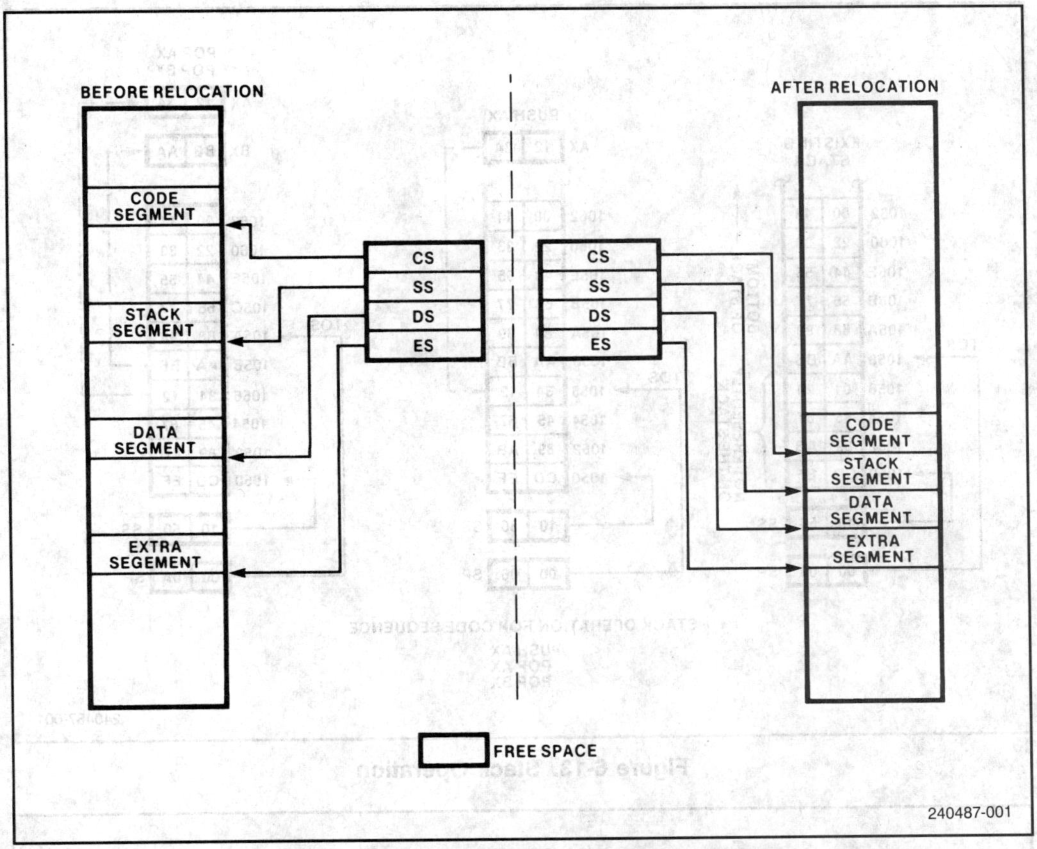

Figure 6-12. Dynamic Code Relocation

Stacks in the 8086 and 8088 are 16 bits wide; instructions that operate on a stack and remove stack items one word a time. An item is pushed onto the stack (see Figure 6-13) by *decrementing* SP by 2 and writing the item at a new TOS. An item is popped off the stack by copying it from TOS and the *incrementing* SP by 2. In other words, the stack goes *down* in memory toward its base address. Stack operations never move items on the stack, nor do they erase them. The top of the stack changes only as a result of updating the stack pointer.

RESERVED MEMORY

Two areas in extreme low and high memory (see Figure 6-14) are dedicated to specific processor functions or are reserved by Intel Corporation for use by Intel hardware and software products. The locations are 0H through 7FH (128 bytes) and FFFF0H through FFFFFH (16 bytes). These areas are used for interrupt and system reset processing. 8086 and 8088 application systems do not use these areas for any other purpose. Doing so may make these systems incompatible with future Intel products.

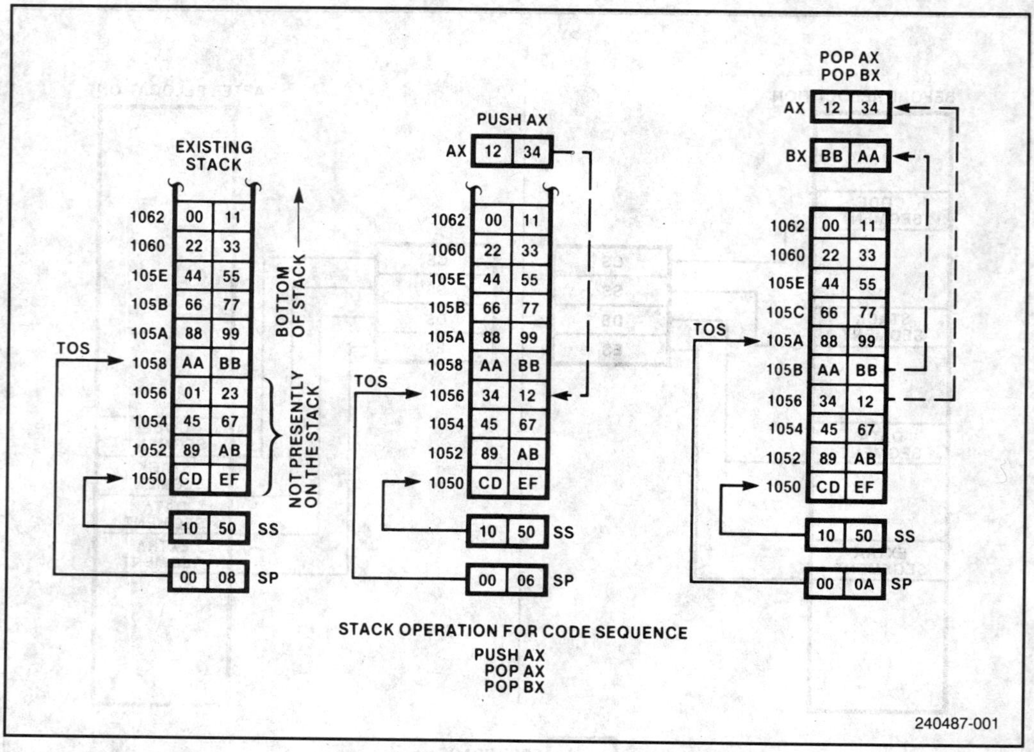

Figure 6-13. Stack Operation

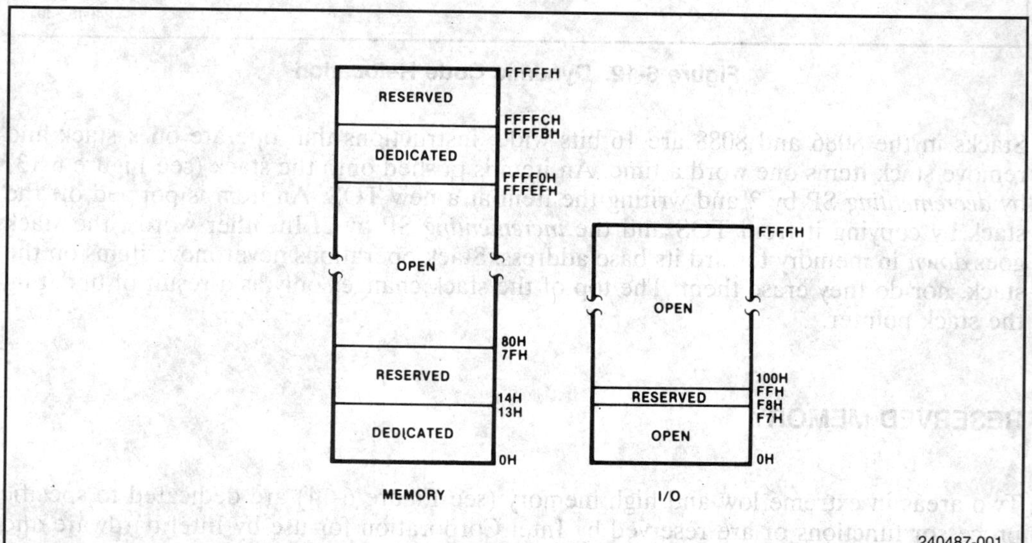

Figure 6-14. Reserved Memory and I/O Locations

8086/8088 MEMORY ACCESS DIFFERENCES

The 8086 can access either 8 or 16 bits of memory at a time. If an instruction refers to a word variable and that variable is located at an even-numbered address, the 8086 accesses the complete word in one bus cycle. If the word is located at an odd-numbered address, the 8086 accesses the word one byte at a time in two consecutive bus cycles.

To maximize throughput in 8086-based systems, 16-bit data should be stored at even addresses (should be word-aligned). This is particularly true of stacks. Unaligned stacks can slow a system's response to interrupts. Nevertheless, except for the performance penalty, word alignment is totally transparent to software. This allows maximum data packing where memory space is constrained.

The 8086 always fetches the instruction stream in words from even addresses except that the first fetch after a program transfer to an odd address obtains a byte. The instruction stream is disassembled inside the processor and instruction alignment will not materially affect the performance of most systems.

The 8088 always accesses memory in bytes. Word operands are accessed in two bus cycles regardless of their alignment. Instructions are also fetched one byte at a time. Although alignment of word operands does not affect the performance of 8088, locating 16-bit data on even addresses will insure maximum throughput if the system is ever transferred to an 8086.

Software Overview

The 8086 and 8088 execute exactly the same instructions. This instruction set includes equivalents to the instructions typically found in previous microprocessors such as the 8080/8085. Significant new operations include:

- multiplication and division of signed and unsigned binary numbers as well as unpacked decimal numbers,
- move, scan and compare operations for strings up to 64K bytes in length,
- non-destructive bit testing,
- byte translation from one code to another,
- software generated interrupts,
- a group of instructions that can help coordinate the activities of multiprocessing systems.

The following paragraphs provide a description of the instructions by category and a detailed discussion of the various operand addressing modes. In addition, a complete instruction set summary is provided in tabular form which recaps each device instruction by category, and provides timing cycles for each instruction. Information is also described on how to encode and decode machine instructions for any given assembly code instruction.

8086/8088 INSTRUCTION SET

The 8086/8088 instructions treat different types of operands uniformly. Nearly every instruction can operate on either byte or word data. Register, memory and immediate operands may be specified interchangeably in most instructions. The exception to this is that immediate values serve as "source" and not "destination" operands. In particular, memory variables may be added to, subtracted from, shifted, compared, and so on, in place, without moving them in and out of register. This saves instructions, registers, and execution time in assembly language programs. In high-level languages, where most variables are memory based, compilers can produce faster and shorter object programs.

The 8086/8088 instruction set can be viewed as existing on two levels. One is the assembly level and the other is the machine level. To the assembly language programmer, the 8086/8088 appear to have a repertoire of about 100 instructions. One MOV (move) instruction, for example, transfers a byte or a word from a register or a memory location or an immediate value to either a register or a memory location. The 8086/8088 CPU's, however, recognize 28 different MOV machine instructions ("move byte register to memory," "move word immediate to register," etc.).

The two levels of instruction set address two different requirements: efficiency and simplicity. The approximately 300 forms of machine-level instructions make very efficient use of storage. For example, the machine instructions that increments a memory operand is three or four bytes long because the address of the operand must be encoded in the instruction. To increment a register, however, does not require as much information, so the instruction can be shorter. The 8086/88 have eight different machine-level instructions that increment a different 16-bit register. Each of these instructions are only one byte long.

The assembly level instructions simplify the programmers view of the instruction set. The programmer writes one form of an INC (increment) instruction and the ASM-86 assembler examines the operand to determine which machine level instruction to generate. The following paragraphs provide a functional description of the assembly-level instructions.

Data Transfer Instructions

The 8086/8088 instruction set contains 14 data transfer instructions. These instructions move single bytes and words between memory and registers, and also move single bytes and words between the AL or AX registers and I/O ports. Table 6-3 lists the four types of data transfer instructions and their functions.

Data transfer instructions are categorized into four types: 1) general purpose; 2) input/output; 3) address object; and 4) flag transfer. The stack manipulation instructions, which are used for transferring flag contents, and the instructions for loading segment registers are also included in this group. Figure 6-15 shows the flag storage formats. These formats are used primarily by the LAHF instruction when converting 8080/8085 assembly language programs to run on the 8086 or 8088. The address object instructions manipulate the addresses of variables instead of the contents of values of the variables. This is useful for list processing, based variable and string operations.

Table 6-3. Data Transfer Instructions

General Purpose	
MOV	Move byte or word
PUSH	Push word onto stack
POP	Pop word off stack
XCHG	Exchange byte or word
XLAT	Translate byte
Input/Output	
IN	Input byte or word
OUT	Output byte or word
Address Object	
LEA	Load effective address
LDS	Load pointer using DS
LES	Load pointer using ES
Flag Transfer	
LAHF	Load AH register from flags
SAHF	Store AH register in flags
PUSHF	Push flags onto stack
POPF	Pop flags off stack

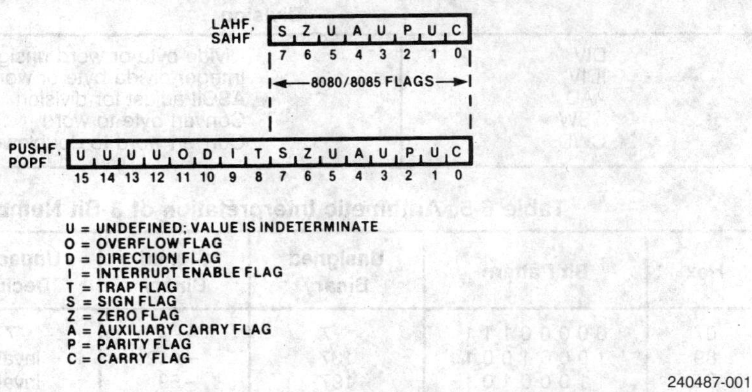

Figure 6-15. Flag Storage Formats

Arithmetic Instructions

The arithmetic instructions (see Table 6-4) perform operations on four types of numbers: 1) unsigned binary; 2) signed binary (integers); 3) unsigned packed decimal; and 4) unsigned unpacked decimal. See Table 6-5. Binary numbers may be 8 or 16 bits long. Decimal numbers are stored in bytes, two digits per byte for packed decimal and one digit per byte for unpacked decimal. The processor always assumes that the operands specified in arithmetic instructions contain data that represents valid numbers for the type of instruction being performed. Invalid data may produce unpredictable results.

Arithmetic instructions post certain characteristics of the result of an operation to six flags. Refer to Chapter 3 for a detailed description of the arithmetic instructions and flags.

Table 6-4. Arithmetic Instructions

Addition	
ADD	Add byte or word
ADC	Add byte or word with carry
INC	Increment byte or word by 1
AAA	ASCII adjust for addition
DAA	Decimal adjust for addition
Subtraction	
SUB	Subtract byte or word
SBB	Subtract byte or word with borrow
DEC	Decrement byte or word by 1
NEG	Negate byte or word
CMP	Compare byte or word
AAS	ASCII adjust for subtraction
DAS	Decimal adjust for subtraction
Multiplication	
MUL	Multiply byte or word unsigned
IMUL	Integer multiply byte or word
AAM	ASCII adjust for multiply
Division	
DIV	Divide byte or word unsigned
IDIV	Integer divide byte or word
AAD	ASCII adjust for division
CBW	Convert byte to word
CWD	Convert word to doubleword

Table 6-5. Arithmetic Interpretation of 8-Bit Numbers

Hex	Bit Pattern	Unsigned Binary	Signed Binary	Unpacked Decimal	Packed Decimal
07	0 0 0 0 0 1 1 1	7	+7	7	7
89	1 0 0 0 1 0 0 1	137	−119	invalid	89
C5	1 1 0 0 0 1 0 1	197	−59	invalid	invalid

Bit Manipulation Instructions

The 8086 and 8088 CPU's provide three groups of instructions for manipulating bits within both bytes and word. These three groups are logicals, shifts and rotates. Table 6-6 lists these three groups of bit manipulation instructions with their functions.

a. Logical

   The logical instructions include the boolean operators "not," "and," "inclusive or," and "exclusive or." A TEST instruction that sets the flags as a result of a boolean "and" operation, but does not alter either of its operands, is also included.

b. Shifts

   The bits in bytes and words may be shifted arithmetically or logically. Up to 255 shifts may be performed, according to the value of the count operand coded in the instruction. The count may be specified as a constant 1, or register CL, allowing the shift count to be a variable supplied at execution time. Arithmetic shifts may be used to multiply and divide binary numbers by powers of two. Logical shifts can be used to isolate bits in bytes or words.

c. Rotates

   Bits in bytes and words can also be rotated. Bits rotated out of an operand are not lost as in a shift, but are "circled" back into the other "end" of the operand. As in the shift instructions, the number of bits to be rotated is taken from the count operand, which may specify either a constant of 1, or the CL reigster. The carry flag may act as an extension of the operand in two of the rotate instructions, allowing a bit to be isolated in CF and then tested by a JC (jump if carry) or JNC (jump if not carry) instruction.

Table 6-6. Bit Manipulation Instructions

Logicals	
NOT	"Not" byte or word
AND	"And" byte or word
OR	"Inclusive or" byte or word
XOR	"Exclusive or" byte or word
TEST	"Test" byte or word
Shifts	
SHL/SAL	Shift logical/arithmetic left byte or word
SHR	Shift logical right byte or word
SAR	Shift arithmetic right byte or word
Rotates	
ROL	Rotate left byte or word
ROR	Rotate right byte or word
RCL	Rotate through carry left byte or word
RCR	Rotate through carry right byte or word

String Instructions

Five basic string operations, called primitives, allow strings of bytes or words to be operated on, one element (byte or word) at a time. Strings of up to 64K bytes many be manipulated with these instructions. Instructions are available to move, compare and scan for a value, as well as moving string elements to and from the accumulator. Table 6-7 lists the string instructions. These basic operations may be preceded by a special one-byte prefix that causes the instruction to be repeated by the hardware, allowing long strings to be processed much faster than would be possible with a software loop. The repetitions can be terminated by a variety of conditions, and a repeated operation may be interrupted and resumed.

The string instructions operate similarly in many respects (refer to Table 6-8). A string instruction may have a source operand, a destination operand, or both. The hardware assumes that a source string resides in the current data segment. A segment prefix may be used to override this assumption. A destination string must be in the current extra segment. The assembler checks the attributes of the operands to determine if the elements of the strings are bytes or words. However, the assembler does not use the operand names to address strings. Instead, the contents of register SI (source index) is used as an offset to address the current element of the source string. Also, the contents of register DI (destination index) is taken as the offset of the current destination string element. These registers must be initialized to point to the source/destination strings before executing the string instructions. The LDS, LES and LEA instructions are useful in performing this function.

Table 6-7. String Instructions

REP	Repeat
REPE/REPZ	Repeat while equal/zero
REPNE/REPNZ	Repeat while not equal/not zero
MOVS	Move byte or word string
MOVSB/MOVSW	Move byte or word string
CMPS	Compare byte or word string
SCAS	Scan byte or word string
LODS	Load byte or word string
STOS	Store byte or word string

Table 6-8. String Instruction Register and Flag Use

SI	Index (offset) for source string
DI	Index (offset) for destination string
CX	Repetition counter
AL/AX	Scan Value Destination for LODS Source for STOS
DF	0 = auto-increment SI, DI 1 = auto-decrement SI, DI
ZF	Scan/compare terminator

String instructions automatically update SI and/or DI in anticipation of processing the next string element. Setting DF (direction flag) determines whether the index registers are auto-incremented (DF=0) or auto-decremented (DF=1). If byte strings are being processed, SI and/or DI is adjusted by 1. The adjustment is 2 for word strings.

If a repeat prefix has been coded, then register CX (count register) is decremented by 1 after each repetition of the string instruction. CX must be initialized to the number of repetitions desired before the string instruction is executed. If CX is 0, the string instruction is not executed, and control goes to the following instruction.

Program Transfer Instructions

The sequence in which instructions are executed in the 8086/8088 is determined by the content of the code segment register (CS) and the instruction pointer (IP). The CS register contains the base address of the current code segment, the 64K portion of memory from which instructions are currently being fetched. The IP points to the memory location from which the next instruction is to be fetched. In most operating conditions, the next instruction to be executed will have already been fetched and is waiting in the CPU instruction queue. The program transfer instructions operate on the instruction pointer and on the CS register; changing the content of these causes normal sequential operation to be altered. When a program transfer occurs, the queue no longer contains the correct instruction. When the BIU obtains the next instruction from memory using the new IP and CS values, it passes the instruction directly to the EU and then begins refilling the queue from the new location.

Four groups of program transfers are available with the 8086/8088 CPU's. See Table 6-9. These are unconditional transfers, conditional transfers, iteration control instructions, and interrupt-related instructions.

a. Unconditional Transfers

   The unconditional transfer instructions may transfer control to a target instruction within the current code segment (intrasegment transfer) or to a different code segment (intersegment transfer). The ASM-86 Assembler terms an intrasegment transfer SHORT or NEAR and an intersegment transfer FAR. The transfer is made unconditionally any time the instruction is executed.

b. Conditional Transfers

   The conditional transfer instructions are jumps that may or may not transfer control depending on the state of the CPU flags at the time the instruction is executed. These 18 instructions (see Table 6-10) each test a different combination of flags for a condition. If the condition is "true" then control is transferred to the target specified in the instruction. If the condition is "false" then control passes to the instruction that follows the conditional jump. All conditional jumps are SHORT, that is, the target must be in the current code segment and within −128 to +127 bytes of the first byte of the next instruction (JMP 00H jumps to the first byte of the next instruction). Since jumps are made by adding the relative displacement of the target to the instruction pointer, all conditional jumps are self-relative and are appropriate for position-independent routines.

c. Iteration Control

The iteration control instructions can be used to regulate the repetition of software loops. These instructions use the CX register as a counter. Like the conditional transfers, the iteration control instructions are self-relative and may only transfer to targets that are within −128 to +127 bytes of themselves, i.e., they are SHORT transfers.

d. Interrupt Instructions

The interrupt instructions allow interrupt service routines to be activated by programs as well as by external hardware devices. The effect of software interrupts is similar to hardware-initiated interrupts. However, the processor does not execute an interrupt acknowledge bus cycle if the interrupt originates in software or with an NMI.

Table 6-9. Program Transfer Instructions

Unconditional Transfers	
CALL	Call procedure
RET	Return from procedure
JMP	Jump
Conditional Transfers	
JA/JNBE	Jump if above/not below nor equal
JAE/JNB	Jump if above or equal/not below
JB/JNAE	Jump if below/not above nor equal
JBE/JNA	Jump if below or equal/not above
JC	Jump if carry
JE/JZ	Jump if equal/zero
JG/JNLE	Jump if greater/not less nor equal
JGE/JNL	Jump if greater or equal/not less
JL/JNGE	Jump if less/not greater nor equal
JLE/JNG	Jump if less or equal/not greater
JNC	Jump if not carry
JNE/JNZ	Jump if not equal/not zero
JNO	Jump if not overflow
JNP/JPO	Jump if not parity/parity odd
JNS	Jump if not sign
JO	Jump if overflow
JP/JPE	Jump if parity/parity even
JS	Jump if sign
Iteration Controls	
LOOP	Loop
LOOPE/LOOPZ	Loop if equal/zero
LOOPNE/LOOPNZ	Loop if not equal/not zero
JCXZ	Jump if register CX = 0
Interrupts	
INT	Interrupt
INTO	Interrupt if overflow
IRET	Interrupt return

Processor Control Instructions

The processor control instructions (see Table 6-11) allow programs to control various CPU functions. One group of instructions updates flags, and another group is used primarily for synchronizing the 8086 or 8088 to external events. A final instruction causes the CPU to do nothing. Except for the flag operations, none of the processor control instructions affect the flags.

Table 6-10. Interpretation of Conditional Transfers

Mnemonic	Condition Tested	"Jump If ..."
JA/JNBE	(CF OR ZF) = 0	above/not below nor equal
JAE/JNB	CF = 0	above or equal/not below
JB/JNAE	CF = 1	below/not above nor equal
JBE/JNA	(CF OR ZF) = 1	below or equal/not above
JC	CF = 1	carry
JE/JZ	ZF = 1	equal/zero
JG/JNLE	((SF XOR OF) OR ZF) = 0	greater/not less nor equal
JGE/JNL	(SF XOR OF) = 0	greater or equal/not less
JL/JNGE	(SF XOR OF) = 1	less/not greater nor equal
JLE/JNG	((SF XOR OF) OR ZF) = 1	less or equal/not greater
JNC	CF = 0	not carry
JNE/JNZ	ZF = 0	not equal/not zero
JNO	OF = 0	not overflow
JNP/JPO	PF = 0	not parity/parity odd
JNS	SF = 0	not sign
JO	OF = 1	overflow
JP/JPE	PF = 1	parity/parity equal
JS	SF = 1	sign

NOTE:
"above" and "below" refer to the relationship of two unsigned values;
"greater" and "less" refer to the relationship of two signed values.

Table 6-11. Processor Control Instructions

Flag Operations	
STC	Set carry flag
CLC	Clear carry flag
CMC	Complement carry flag
STD	Set direction flag
CLD	Clear direction flag
STI	Set interrupt enable flag
CLI	Clear interrupt enable flag
External Synchronization	
HLT	Halt until interrupt or reset
WAIT	Wait for TEST pin active
ESC	Escape to external processor
LOCK	Lock bus during next instruction
No Operation	
NOP	No operation

OPERAND ADDRESSING MODES

The 8086 and 8088 access instruction operands in many different ways. Operands may be contained in registers, within the instruction itself, in memory, or at I/O ports. Also, the addresses of memory and I/O port operands can be calculated in several different ways. These addressing modes greatly extend the flexibility and convenience of the instruction set. The following paragraphs briefly describe the register and immediate modes of operand addressing, and then provide a detailed description of the memory and I/O addressing modes.

Register and Immediate Operands

Instructions that specify only register operands are generally the most compact and fastest executing of the operand addressing forms. This is because the register operand addresses are encoded in instructions in just a few bits, and because these operands are performed entirely within the CPU (no bus cycles are run). Registers may serve as source operands, destination operands, or both.

Immediate operands are constant data contained in an instruction. The data may be either 8 or 16 bits in length. Immediate operands can be accessed quickly because they are available directly from the instruction queue. Like the register operand, no bus cycles need to be run to obtain an immediate operand. The limitations on immediate operands are that they may only serve as source operands and that they are constant value.

Memory Addressing Modes

Although the EU has direct access to register and immediate operands, memory operands must be transferred to and from the CPU over the bus. When the EU needs to read or write a memory operand, it must pass an offset value to the BIU. The BIU adds the offset to the (shifted) content of a segment register producing a 20-bit physical address and then executes the bus cycle or cycles needed to access the operand.

a. The Effective Address

The offset that the EU calculates for a memory operand is called the operand's effective address of EA. This address is an unsigned 16-bit number that expresses the operand's distance in bytes from the beginning of the segment in which it resides. The EU can calculate the effective address in several different ways. Information encoded in the second byte of the instruction tells the EU how to calculate the effective address of each memory operand. A compiler or assembler derives this information from the statement or instruction written by the programmer. Assembly language programmers have access to all addressing modes.

The EU calculates the EA by summing a displacement, the content of a base register and the content of an index register (see Figure 6-16). Any combination of these three components may be present in a given instruction. This allows a variety of memory addressing modes.

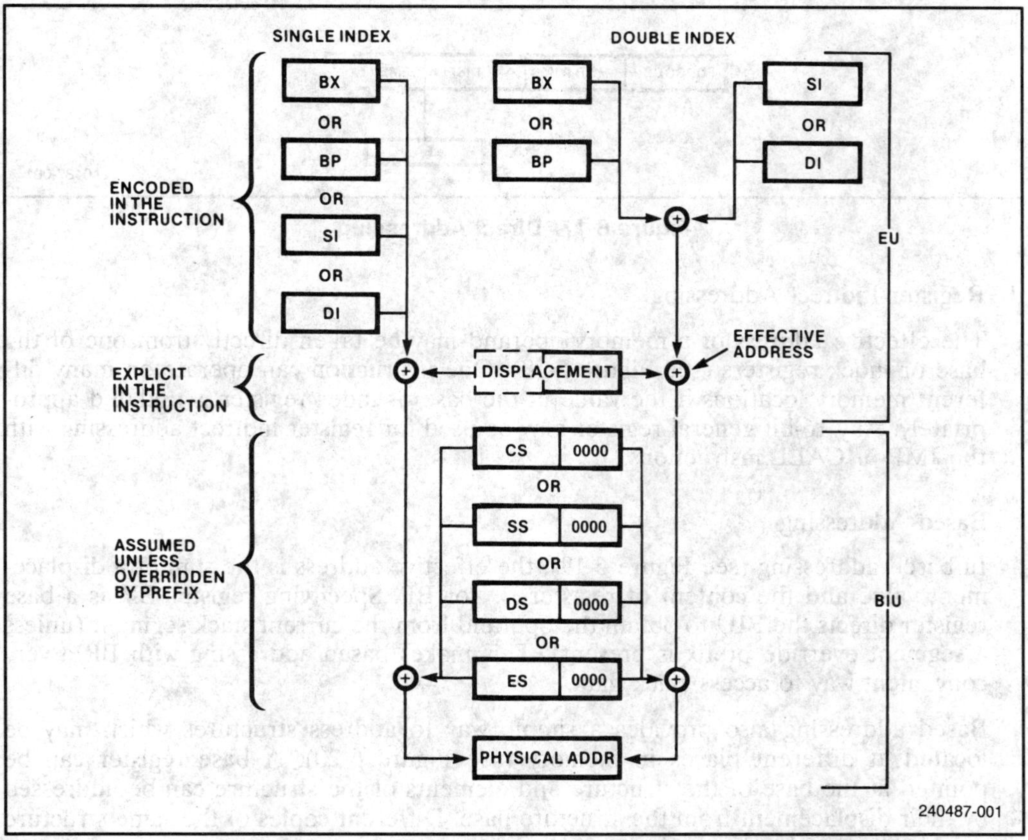

Figure 6-16. Memory Address Computation

The displacement element is an 8- or 16-bit number that is contained in the instruction. The displacement generally is derived from the position of the operand name (a variable or label) in the program. The programmer can also modify this value or explicitly specify the displacement.

A programmer may specify that either BX or BP is to serve as a base register whose content is to be used in the EA computation.

b. Similarly, either SI or DI may be specified as the index register. The displacement value is a constant. The contents of the base and index registers may change during execution. This allows one instruction to access different memory locations as determined by the current values in the base and/or index registers. Effective address calculations with the BP are made using the SS register, by default, although either the DS or the ES registers may be specified instead.

c. Direct Addressing

Direct addressing is the simplest memory addressing mode (see Figure 6-17). No registers are involved and the EA is taken directly from the displacement of the instruction. Direct addressing is typically to access simple variables (scalars).

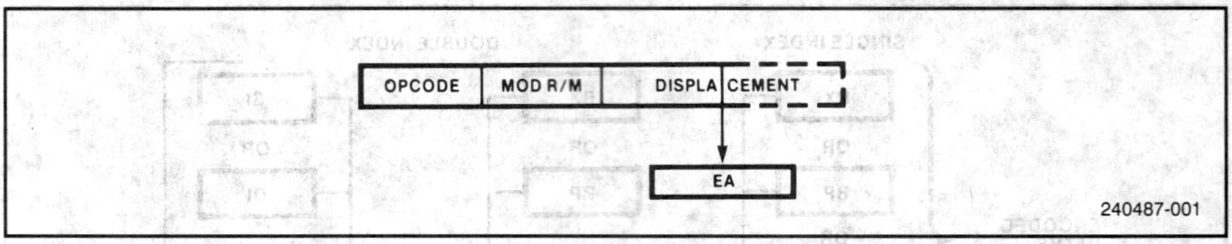

Figure 6-17. Direct Addressing

d. Register Indirect Addressing

The effective address of a memory operand may be taken directly from one of the base or index registers (see Figure 6-18). One instruction can operate on many different memory locations if the value in the base or index register is updated appropriately. Any 16-bit general register may be used for register indirect addressing with the JMP or CALL instructions.

e. Based Addressing

In based addressing (see Figure 6-19), the effective address is the sum of a displacement value and the content of register BX or BP. Specifying register BP as a base register directs the BIU to obtain the operand from the current stack segment (unless a segment override prefix is present). This makes based addressing with BP a very convenient way to access stack data.

Based addressing also provides a simple way to address structures which may be located at different places in memory (see Figure 6-20). A base register can be pointed at the base of the structure and elements of the structure can be addressed by their displacement from the structure base. Different copies of the same structure can be accessed by simply changing the base register.

f. Indexed Address

The effective address is calculated from the sum of a displacement plus the content of an index register (SI or DI) in index addressing (see Figure 6-21). Indexed address is often used to access elements in an array (see Figure 6-22). The displacement locates the beginning of the array, and the value of the index register selects one element (the first element is selected if the index register contains 0). Since all array elements are the same length, simple arithmetic on the index register may select any element.

g. Based Index Addressing

Based index addressing generates an effective address that is the sum of a base register, an index register and a displacement (see Figure 6-23). This mode of addressing is very flexible because two address components can be varied at execution time.

Based index addressing provides a convenient way for a procedure to address an array allocated on a stack (see Figure 6-24). Reigster BP can contain the offset of a reference point on the stack, typically the top of the stack after the procedure has saved registers and allocated local storage. The offset of the beginning of the array from the reference point can be expressed by a displacement value, and the index

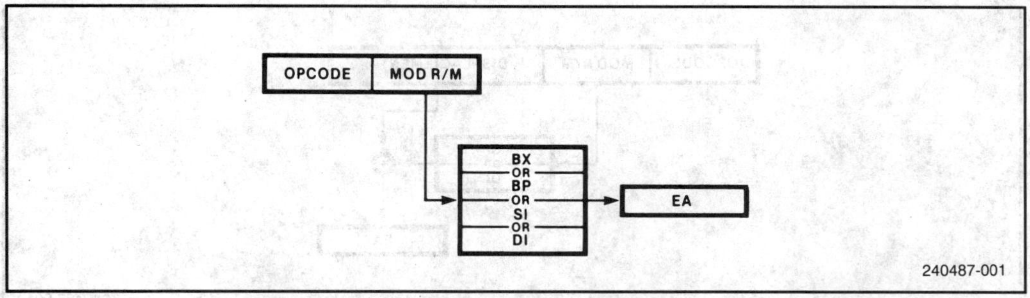

Figure 6-18. Register Indirect Addressing

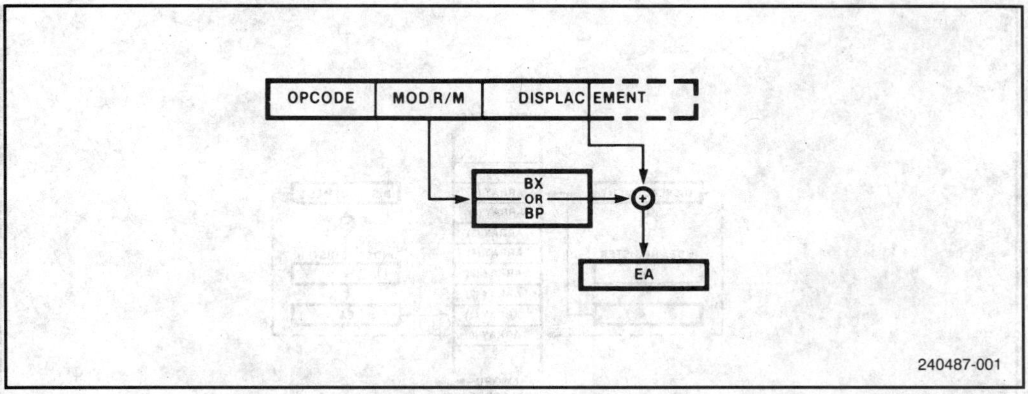

Figure 6-19. Based Addressing

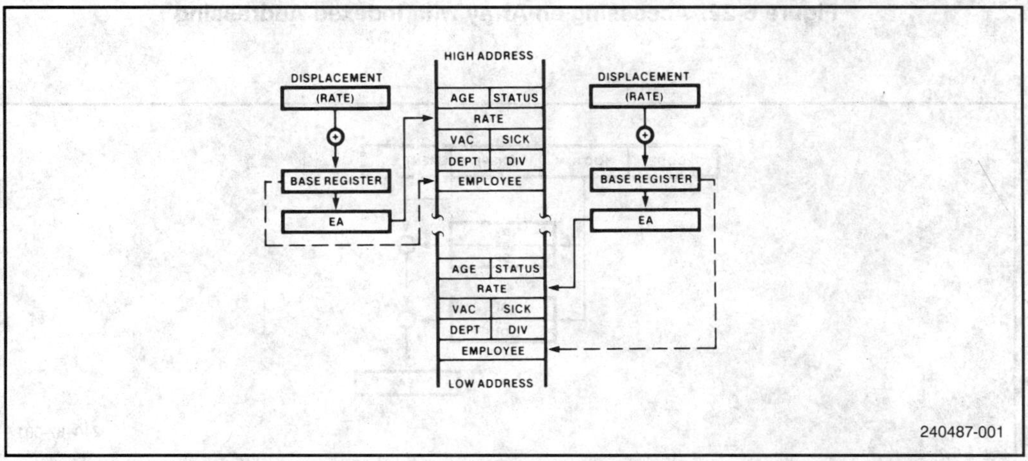

Figure 6-20. Accessing a Structure with Based Addressing

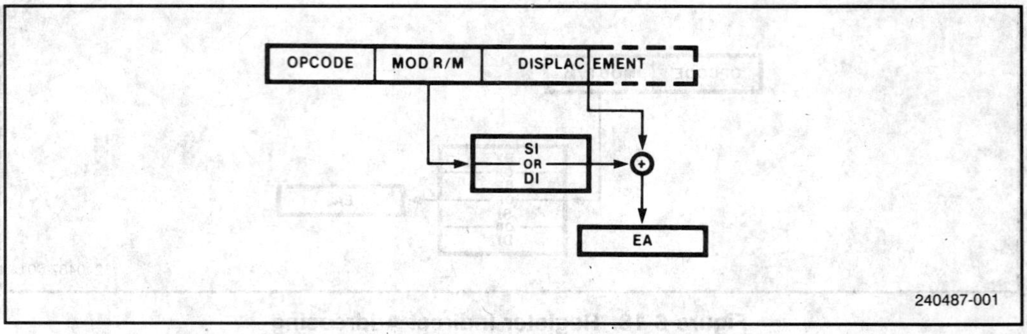

Figure 6-21. Indexed Addressing

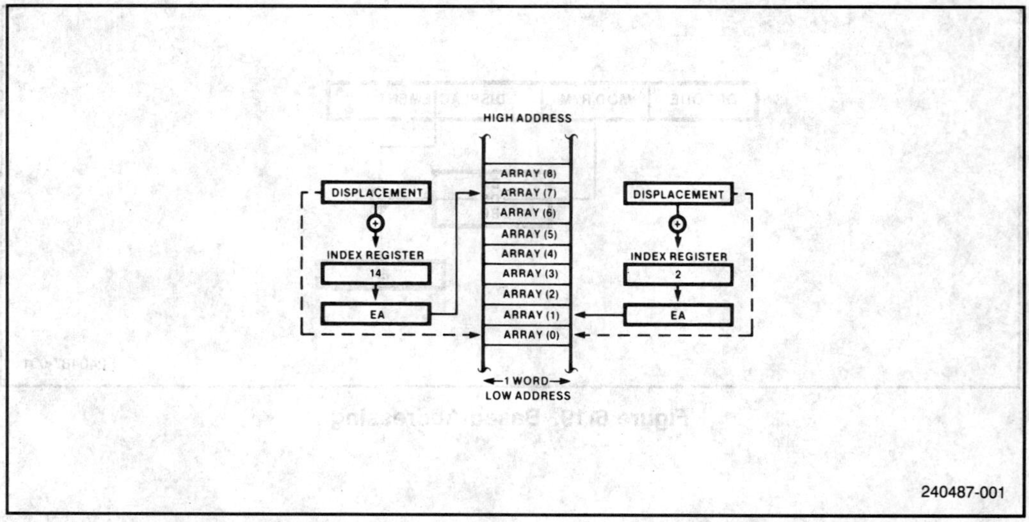

Figure 6-22. Accessing an Array with Indexed Addressing

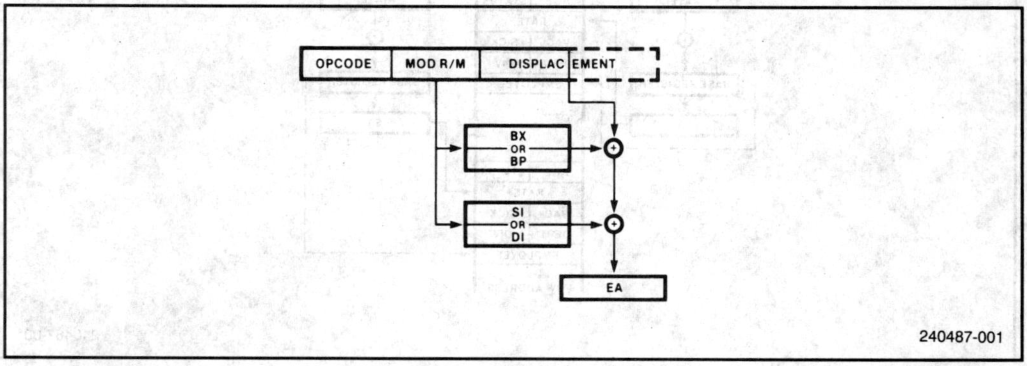

Figure 6-23. Based Index Addressing

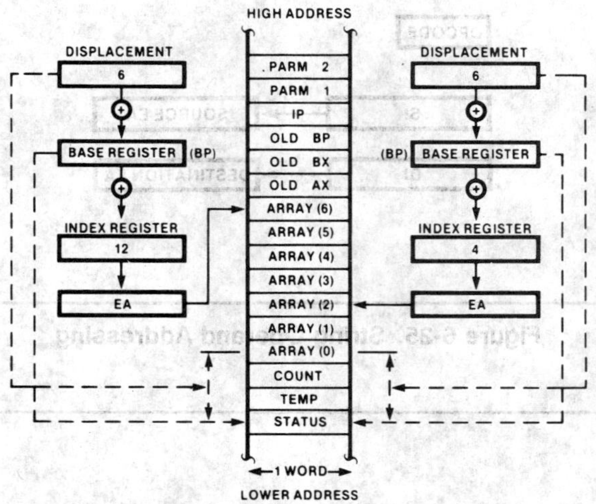

Figure 6-24. Accessing a Stacked Array with Based Index Addressing

register can be used to access individual array elements. Arrays contained in structures and matrices (two-dimensional arrays) can also be accessed with based indexed addressing.

h. String Addressing

String instructions do not use the normal memory addressing modes to access operands. Instead, the index registers are used implicitly (see Figure 6-25). When a string instruction is executed, SI is assumed to point to the first byte or word of the source string. DI is assumed to point at the first byte or word of the destination string. In a repeated string operation, the CPU's automatically adjust SI and DI to obtain subsequent bytes or words. Note that for string instructions DS is the default segment register to SI and ES is the default segment register for DI. This allows string instructions to easily operate on data located anywhere within the one megabyte address space.

I/O Port Addressing

Any of the memory operand addressing modes may be used to access an I/O port if the port is memory mapped. For example, a group of terminals can be accessed as an "array." String instructions can also be used to transfer data to memory-mapped ports with an appropriate hardware interface.

Two different addressing modes can be used to access ports located in the I/O space (see Figure 6-26). The port number is an 8-bit immediate operand for direct addressing. This

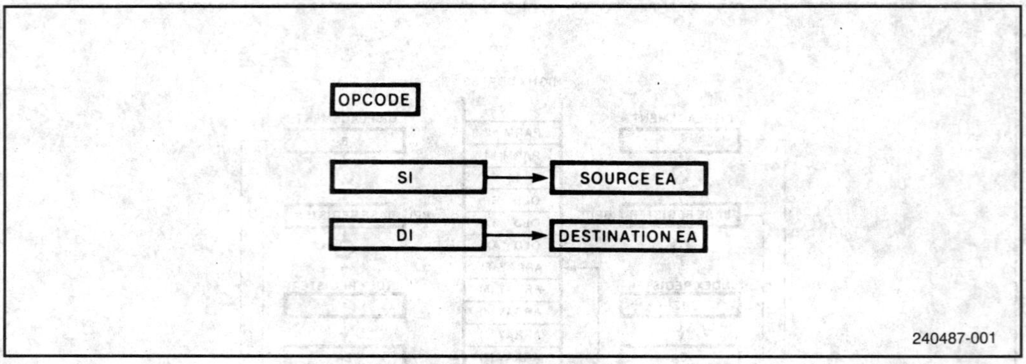

Figure 6-25. String Operand Addressing

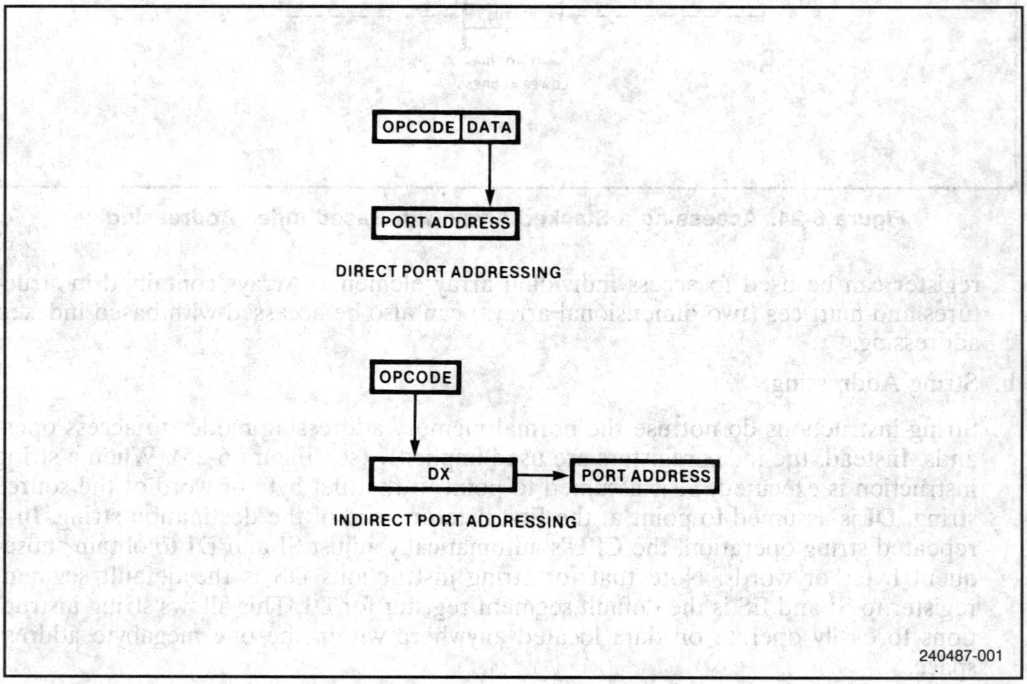

Figure 6-26. I/O Port Addressing

allows fixed access to ports numbers 0–255. Indirect I/O port addressing is similar to register indirect addressing of memory operands. The port number is taken from register DX and can range from 0 to 65,535. By previously adjusting the content of register DX, one instruction can access any port in the I/O space. A group of adjacent ports can be accessed using a simple software loop that adjusts the value of DX.

INSTRUCTION SET SUMMARY

The following paragraphs, and tables, provide detailed information for the 8086/8088 instruction set. Table 6-12, 6-13 and 6-14 explain the symbols that are used in Table 6-16, the instruction set reference data table. Machine language instruction encoding and decoding information is provided in the paragraphs immediately following the instruction set summary.

Instruction timings are presented as the number of clock periods required to execute a particular form of the instruction (register-to-register, immediate-to-memory, etc.). If the system is running with a 5 MHz maximum clock, the maximum clock period is 200 ns; at 8 MHz, the clock period is 125 ns. When memory operands are used, "+EA" indicates a variable number of additional clock periods needed to calculate the operand's effective address. Table 6-15 lists all effective address calculation times.

The timings given for control transfer instructions include any additional clocks required to reinitialize the instruction queue as well as the time required to fetch the target instructions. For instructions executing on an 8086, four clocks should be added for each instruction reference to a word operand located at an odd memory address to reflect any additional operand bus cycles required. Also, for instructions executing on an 8088, four clocks should be added to each instruction reference to a 16-bit memory operand. This includes stack operations. The required number of data references is listed for each instruction in Table 6-16 to aid in this calculation.

All of the instruction times given are of the form "n," where "n" is the number of clocks required for the 8086 to execute the given instruction. The number of clocks required for the 8088 will be n for 8-bit operations and n + (4* transfers) for 16-bit operations.

For instructions which repeat a specified number of times, the value n consists of two parts in the relation "x + y/rep," where x is the initial number of clocks required to start the instruction, and y is the number of clocks corresponding to the number of iterations specified. For 16-bit repeated instructions on the 8088 when the expression "(4 * transfers)" has to be added to n, it should be added to the y part of the expression before it is multiplied by the number of repetitions.

Several additional factors can alter the actual execution time from the figures shown in Table 6-16. The time provided assumes that the instruction has already been prefetched and that it is waiting in the instruction queue. This assumption is valid under most, but not all, operating conditions. A series of fast executing (fewer than two clocks per opcode byte) instructions can drain the queue and increase execution time. Execution time is also slightly effected by the interaction of the EU and BIU when memory operands must be read or written. If the EU needs access to memory, it may have to wait for up to one clock if the BIU has already started an instruction fetch bus cycle. (The EU can detect the need for a memory operand and post a bus request far enough in advance of its need for this operand to avoid waiting a full 4-clock bus cycle.) If the queue is full the EU does not have to wait because the BIU is idle. (This assumes the BIU can obtain the bus on demand and no other processors are competing for the bus.)

With typical instruction mixes, the time actually required to execute a sequence of instructions will be within 5-10% of the sum of the individual timings provided in Table 6-16. Cases can be constructed, however, in which execution time may be much higher than the sum of the figures provided in the table. The execution time for a given sequence of instructions is always repeatable, assuming comparable external conditions (interrupts, coprocessor activity, etc.). If the execution time for a given series of instructions must be determined exactly, the instructions should be run on an execution vehicle such as the iSBC 88/25 or 86/30 board.

Table 6-12. Key to Instruction Coding Formats

Identifier	Used In	Explanation
destination	data transfer, bit manipulation	A register or memory location that may contain data operated on by the instruction, and which receives (is replaced by) the result of the operation.
source	data transfer, arithmetic, bit manipulation	A register, memory location or immediate value that is used in the operation, but is not altered by the instruction.
source-table	XLAT	Name of memory translation table addressed by register BX.
target	JMP, CALL	A label to which control is to be transferred directly, or a register or memory location whose *content* is the address of the location to which control is to be transferred indirectly.
short-label	cond. transfer, iteration control	A label to which control is to be conditionally transferred; must lie within −128 to +127 bytes of the first byte of the next instruction.
accumulator	IN, OUT	Register AX for word transfers, AL for bytes.
port	IN, OUT	An I/O port number; specified as an immediate value of 0-255, or register DX (which contains port number in range 0-64K).
source-string	string ops.	Name of a string in memory that is addressed by register SI; used only to identify string as byte or word and specify segment override, if any. This string is used in the operation, but is not altered.
dest-string	string ops.	Name of string in memory that is addressed by register DI; used only to identify string as byte or word. This string receives (is replaced by) the result of the operation.
count	shifts, rotates	Specifies number of bits to shift or rotate; written as immediate value 1 or register CL (which contains the count in the range 0-255).
interrupt-type	INT	Immediate value of 0-255 identifying interrupt pointer number.
optional-pop-value	RET	Number of bytes (0-64K, ordinarily an even number) to discard from stack.
external-opcode	ESC	Immediate value (0-63) that is encoded in the instruction for use by an external processor.

Table 6-13. Key to Flag Effects

Identifier	Explanation
(blank)	not altered
0	cleared to 0
1	set to 1
X	set or cleared according to result
U	undefined – contains no reliable value
R	restored from previously-saved value

Table 6-14. Key to Operand Types

Identifier	Explanation
(no operands)	No operands are written
register	An 8- or 16-bit general register
reg 16	A 16-bit general register
seg-reg	A segment register
accumulator	Register AX or AL
immediate	A constant in the range 0-FFFFH
immed8	A constant in the range 0-FFH
memory	An 8- or 16-bit memory location*
mem8	An 8-bit memory location*
mem16	A 16-bit memory location*
source-table	Name of 256-byte translate table
source-string	Name of string addressed by register SI
dest-string	Name of string addressed by register DI
DX	Register DX
short-label	A label within −128 to +127 bytes of the end of the instruction
near-label	A label in current code segment
far-label	A label in another code segment
near-proc	A procedure in current code segment
far-proc	A procedure in another code segment
memptr16	A word containing the offset of the location in the current code segment to which control is to be transferred*
memptr32	A doubleword containing the offset and the segment base address of the location in another code segment to which control is to be transferred*
regptr16	A 16-bit general register containing the offset of the location in the current code segment to which control is to be transferred
repeat	A string instruction repeat prefix

*Any addressing mode – direct, register indirect, based, indexed, or based indexed – may be used.

Table 6-15. Effective Address Calculation Time

EA Components		Clocks*
Displacement Only		6
Base or Index Only (BX, BP, SI, DI)		5
Displacement + Base or Index	(BX, BP, SI, DI)	9
Base + Index	BP + DI, BX + SI	7
	BP + SI, BX + DI	8
Displacement + Base + Index	BP + DI + DISP BX + SI + DISP	11
	BP + SI + DISP BX + DI + DISP	12

*Add 2 clocks for segment override

Table 6-16. Instruction Set Reference Data

AAA	**AAA** (no operands) ASCII adjust for addition			Flags: O D I T S Z A P C U U U X U X
Operands	**Clocks**	**Transfers***	**Bytes**	**Coding Example**
(no operands)	8	—	1	AAA

AAD	**AAD** (no operands) ASCII adjust for division			Flags: O D I T S Z A P C U X X U X U
Operands	**Clocks**	**Transfers***	**Bytes**	**Coding Example**
(no operands)	60	—	2	AAD

AAM	**AAM** (no operands) ASCII adjust for multiply			Flags: O D I T S Z A P C U X X U X U
Operands	**Clocks**	**Transfers***	**Bytes**	**Coding Example**
(no operands)	83	—	2	AAM

AAS	**AAS** (no operands) ASCII adjust for subtraction			Flags: O D I T S Z A P C U U U X U X
Operands	**Clocks**	**Transfers***	**Bytes**	**Coding Example**
(no operands)	8	—	1	AAS

ADC

ADC destination, source
Add with carry

Flags O D I T S Z A P C
X X X X X X

Operands	Clocks	Transfers*	Bytes	Coding Example
register, register	3	—	2	ADC AX, SI
register, memory	9 + EA	1	2-4	ADC CX, BETA [SI]
memory, register	16 + EA	2	2-4	ADC ALPHA [BX] [SI], DI
register, immediate	4	—	3-4	ADC BX, 256
memory, immediate	17 + EA	2	3-6	ADC GAMMA, 30H
accumulator, immediate	4	—	2-3	ADC AL, 5

ADD

ADD destination, source
Addition

Flags O D I T S Z A P C
X X X X X X

Operands	Clocks	Transfers*	Bytes	Coding Example
register, register	3	—	2	ADD CX, DX
register, memory	9 + EA	1	2-4	ADD DI,[BX], ALPHA
memory, register	16 + EA	2	2-4	ADD TEMP, CL
register, immediate	4	—	3-4	ADD CL, 2
memory, immediate	17 + EA	2	3-6	ADD ALPHA, 2
accumulator, immediate	4	—	2-3	ADD AX, 200

AND

AND destination, source
Logical and

Flags O D I T S Z A P C
O X X U X O

Operands	Clocks	Transfers*	Bytes	Coding Example
register, register	3	—	2	AND AL, BL
register, memory	9 + EA	1	2-4	AND CX, FLAB WORD
memory, register	16 + EA	2	2-4	AND ASCII [DI], AL
register, immediate	4	—	3-4	AND CX, 0F0H
memory, immediate	17 + EA	2	3-6	AND BETA, 01H
accumulator, immediate	4	—	2-3	AND AX, 01010000B

CALL

CALL target
Call a procedure

Flags O D I T S Z A P C
X X X X X X

Operands	Clocks	Transfers*	Bytes	Coding Example
near-proc	19	1	3	CALL NEAR_PROC
far-proc	28	2	5	CALL FOR_PROC
memptr 16	21 + EA	2	2-4	CALL PROC_TABLE [SI]
regptr 16	16	1	2	CALL AX
memptr 32	37 + EA	4	2-4	CALL [BX].TASK [SI]

CBW

CBW (no operands)
Convert byte to word

Flags O D I T S Z A P C
U U U X U X

Operands	Clocks	Transfers*	Bytes	Coding Example
(no operands)	2	—	1	CBW

CLC

CLC (no operands)
Clear carry flag

Flags	O	D	I	T	S	Z	A	P	C
									0

Operands	Clocks	Transfers*	Bytes	Coding Example
(no operands)	2	—	1	CLC

CLD

CLD (no operands)
Clear direction flag

Flags	O	D	I	T	S	Z	A	P	C
		0							

Operands	Clocks	Transfers*	Bytes	Coding Example
(no operands)	2	—	1	CLD

CLI

CLI (no operands)
Clear interrupt flag

Flags	O	D	I	T	S	Z	A	P	C
			0						

Operands	Clocks	Transfers*	Bytes	Coding Example
(no operands)	2	—	1	CLI

CMC

CMC (no operands)
Complement carry flag

Flags	O	D	I	T	S	Z	A	P	C
									X

Operands	Clocks	Transfers*	Bytes	Coding Example
(no operands)	2	—	1	CMC

CMP

CMP destination, source
Compare destination to source

Flags	O	D	I	T	S	Z	A	P	C
	X				X	X	X	X	X

Operands	Clocks	Transfers*	Bytes	Coding Example
register, register	3	—	2	CMP BX, CX
register, memory	9 + EA	1	2-4	CMP DH, ALPHA
memory, register	9 + EA	1	2-4	CMB [BP + 2], SI
register, immediate	4 + EA	—	3-4	CMP BL, 02H
memory, immediate	10 + EA	1	3-6	CMB [BX].RADAR [DI], 3420H
accumulator, immediate	4	—	2-3	CMP AL, 00010000B

CMPS

CMPS des-string, source-string
Compare string

Flags	O	D	I	T	S	Z	A	P	C
	X				X	X	X	X	X

Operands	Clocks	Transfers*	Bytes	Coding Example
dest-string, source-string	22	2	1	CMPS BUSS1, BUFF2
(repeat) dest-string, source-string	9 + 22/rep	2/rep	1	REPE CMPS ID, KEY

CWD

CWD (no operands)
Convert word to doubleword

Flags	O	D	I	T	S	Z	A	P	C

Operands	Clocks	Transfers*	Bytes	Coding Example
(no operands)	5	—	1	CWD

DAA

DAA (no operands)
Decimal adjust for addition

Flags	O	D	I	T	S	Z	A	P	C
	X				X	X	X	X	X

Operands	Clocks	Transfers*	Bytes	Coding Example
(no operands)	4	—	1	DAA

DAS

DAS (no operands)
Decimal adjust for subtraction

Flags	O	D	I	T	S	Z	A	P	C
	U				X	X	X	X	X

Operands	Clocks	Transfers*	Bytes	Coding Example
(no operands)	4	—	1	DAS

DEC

DEC destination
Decrement by 1

Flags	O	D	I	T	S	Z	A	P	C
	X				X	X	X	X	

Operands	Clocks	Transfers*	Bytes	Coding Example
reg 16	3	—	1	DEC AX
reg 8	3	—	2	DEC AL
memory	15 + EA	2	2-4	DEC ARRAY [SI]

DIV

DIV source
Division, unsigned

Flags	O	D	I	T	S	Z	A	P	C
	U				U	U	U	U	U

Operands	Clocks	Transfers*	Bytes	Coding Example
reg 8	80-90	—	2	DIV CL
reg 16	144-162	—	2	DIV BX
mem 8	89-96 + EA	1	2-4	DIV ALPHA
mem 16	150-168 + EA	1	2-4	DIV TABLE [SI]

ENTER

ENTER
Procedure entry

Flags	O	D	I	T	S	Z	A	P	C

Operands	Clocks	Transfers*	Bytes	Coding Example
locals, level	L = 0 L = 1 L > 1 (22 + 16(n−1))	—	4	ENTER 28, 3

ESC	ESC external-opcode, source Escape			Flags O D I T S Z A P C
Operands	**Clocks**	**Transfers***	**Bytes**	**Coding Example**
immediate, memory immediate, register	8 + EA 2	1 —	2-4 2	ESC 6.ARRAY [SI] ESC 20, AL

HLT	HLT (no operands) Halt			Flags O D I T S Z A P C
Operands	**Clocks**	**Transfers***	**Bytes**	**Coding Example**
(no operands)	2	—	1	HLT

IDIV	IDIV source Integer division			Flags O D I T S Z A P C U U U U U U
Operands	**Clocks**	**Transfers***	**Bytes**	**Coding Example**
reg 8 reg 16 mem 8 mem 16	101-112 165-184 107-118 + EA 171-190 + EA	— — 1 1	2 2 2-4 2-4	IDIV BL IDIV CX IDIV DIVISOR_BYTE [SI] IDIV [BX].DIVISOR_WORD

IMUL	IMUL source Integer multiplication			Flags O D I T S Z A P C X U U U U X
Operands	**Clocks**	**Transfers***	**Bytes**	**Coding Example**
reg 8 reg 16 mem 8 mem 16	80-98 128-154 86-104 + EA 134-160 + EA	— — 1 1	2 2 2-4 2-4	IMUL CL IMUL BX IMUL RATE_BYTE IMUL RATE_WORD [BP] [DI]

IN	IN accumulator, port Input byte or word			Flags O D I T S Z A P C
Operands	**Clocks**	**Transfers***	**Bytes**	**Coding Example**
accumulator, immed 8 accumulator, DX	10 8	1 1	2 1	IN AL, 0FFEAH IN AX, DX

INC	INC destination Increment by 1			Flags O D I T S Z A P C X X X X X X
Operands	**Clocks**	**Transfers***	**Bytes**	**Coding Example**
reg 16 reg 8 memory	3 3 15 + EA	— — 2	1 2 2-4	INC CX INC BL INC ALPHA [DI] [BX]

INT

INT Interrupt-type Interrupt

Flags	O	D	I	T	S	Z	A	P	C
			0	0					

Operands	Clocks	Transfers*	Bytes	Coding Example
immed 8 (type = 3)	52	5	1	INT 3
immed 8 (type 3)	52	5	2	INT 67

INTR†

INTR (external maskable interrupt)
Interrupt if INTER and IF = 1

Flags	O	D	I	T	S	Z	A	P	C
			0	0					

Operands	Clocks	Transfers*	Bytes	Coding Example
(no operands)	61	7	N/A	N/A

INTO

INTO (no operands)
Interrupt if overflow

Flags	O	D	I	T	S	Z	A	P	C
			0	0					

Operands	Clocks	Transfers*	Bytes	Coding Example
(no operands)	53 or 4	5	1	INTO

IRET

IRET (no operands)
Interrupt Return

Flags	O	D	I	T	S	Z	A	P	C
	R	R	R	R	R	R	R	R	R

Operands	Clocks	Transfers*	Bytes	Coding Example
(no operands)	32	3	1	IRET

JA/JNBE

JA/JNBE short-label
Jump if above/Jump if not below nor equal

Flags: O D I T S Z A P C

Operands	Clocks	Transfers*	Bytes	Coding Example
short-label	16 or 4	–	2	JA ABOVE

JAE/JNB

JAE/JNB short-label
Jump if above or equal/Jump if not below

Flags: O D I T S Z A P C

Operands	Clocks	Transfers*	Bytes	Coding Example
short-label	16 or 4	–	2	JAE ABOVE_EQUAL

JB/JNAE

JB/JNAE
Jump if below/Jump if not above nor equal

Flags: O D I T S Z A P C

Operands	Clocks	Transfers*	Bytes	Coding Example
short-label	16 or 4	–	2	JB BELOW

JBE/JNA	JBE/JNA short-label Jump if below or equal/Jump if not above			Flags O D I T S Z A P C
Operands	**Clocks**	**Transfers***	**Bytes**	**Coding Example**
short-label	16 or 4	—	2	JNA NOT_ABOVE

JC	JC short-label Jump if carry			Flags O D I T S Z A P C
Operands	**Clocks**	**Transfers***	**Bytes**	**Coding Example**
short-label	16 or 4	—	2	JC CARRY_SET

JCXZ	JCXZ short-label Jump if CX is zero			Flags O D I T S Z A P C
Operands	**Clocks**	**Transfers***	**Bytes**	**Coding Example**
short-label	16 or 4	—	2	JCXZ COUNT_DONE

JE/JZ	JE/JZ short-label Jump if equal/Jump if zero			Flags O D I T S Z A P C
Operands	**Clocks**	**Transfers***	**Bytes**	**Coding Example**
short-label	16 or 4	—	2	JZ ZERO

JG/JNLE	JG/JNLE short-label Jump if greater/Jump if not less nor equal			Flags O D I T S Z A P C
Operands	**Clocks**	**Transfers***	**Bytes**	**Coding Example**
short-label	16 or 4	—	2	JG GREATER

JGE/JNL	JGE/JNL short-label Jump if greater or equal/Jump if not less			Flags O D I T S Z A P C
Operands	**Clocks**	**Transfers***	**Bytes**	**Coding Example**
short-label	16 or 4	—	2	JGE GREATER_EQUAL

JL/JNGE	JL/JNGE short-label Jump if less/Jump if not greater nor equal			Flags O D I T S Z A P C
Operands	**Clocks**	**Transfers***	**Bytes**	**Coding Example**
short-label	16 or 4	—	2	JL LESS

JLE/JNG	JLE/JNG short-label Jump if less or equal/jump if not greater			Flags O D I T S Z A P C
Operands	**Clocks**	**Transfers***	**Bytes**	**Coding Example**
short-label	16 or 4	—	2	JNG NOT_GREATER

JMP	JMP target Jump			Flags O D I T S Z A P C
Operands	**Clocks**	**Transfers***	**Bytes**	**Coding Example**
short-label	15	—	2	JMP SHORT
near-label	15	—	3	JMP WITHIN_SEGMENT
far-label	15	—	5	JMP FAR_LABEL
memptr 16	18 + EA	1	2-4	JMP [BX].TARGET
regptr 16	11	—	2	JMP CX
memptr 32	24 + EA	2	2-4	JMP OTHER.SEG [SI]

JNC	JNC short-label Jump if not carry			Flags O D I T S Z A P C
Operands	**Clocks**	**Transfers***	**Bytes**	**Coding Example**
short-label	16 or 4	—	2	JNC NOT_CARRY

JNE/JNZ	JNE/JNZ short-label Jump if not equal/Jump if not zero			Flags O D I T S Z A P C
Operands	**Clocks**	**Transfers***	**Bytes**	**Coding Example**
short-label	16 or 4	—	2	JNE NOT_EQUAL

JNO	JNO short-label Jump if not overflow			Flags O D I T S Z A P C
Operands	**Clocks**	**Transfers***	**Bytes**	**Coding Example**
short-label	16 or 4	—	2	JNO NO_OVERFLOW

JNP/JPO	JNP/JPO short-label Jump if not parity/Jump if parity odd			Flags O D I T S Z A P C
Operands	**Clocks**	**Transfers***	**Bytes**	**Coding Example**
short-label	16 or 4	—	2	JPO ODD_PARITY

JNS	JNS short-label Jump if not sign			Flags O D I T S Z A P C
Operands	**Clocks**	**Transfers***	**Bytes**	**Coding Example**
short-label	16 or 4	—	2	JNS POSITIVE

JO	JO short-label Jump if overflow			Flags O D I T S Z A P C
Operands	**Clocks**	**Transfers***	**Bytes**	**Coding Example**
short-label	16 or 4	—	2	JO SIGNED_OVERFLOW

JP/JPE	JP/JPE short-label Jump if parity/Jump if parity even			Flags O D I T S Z A P C
Operands	**Clocks**	**Transfers***	**Bytes**	**Coding Example**
short-label	16 or 4	—	2	JPE EVEN_PARITY

JS	JS short-label Jump if sign			Flags O D I T S Z A P C
Operands	**Clocks**	**Transfers***	**Bytes**	**Coding Example**
short-label	16 or 4	—	2	JS NEGATIVE

LAHF	LAHF (no operands) Load AH from flags			Flags O D I T S Z A P C
Operands	**Clocks**	**Transfers***	**Bytes**	**Coding Example**
(no operands)	4	—	1	LAHF

LDS	LDS destination, source Load pointer using DS			Flags O D I T S Z A P C
Operands	**Clocks**	**Transfers***	**Bytes**	**Coding Example**
reg 16, mem 16	16 + EA	2	2-4	LDS SI, DATA, SEG [DI]

LEA	LEA destination, source Load effective address			Flags O D I T S Z A P C
Operands	**Clocks**	**Transfers***	**Bytes**	**Coding Example**
reg 16, mem 16	2 + EA	—	2-4	LEA BX, [BP] [DI]

LES	LES destination, source Load pointer using ES			Flags O D I T S Z A P C
Operands	**Clocks**	**Transfers***	**Bytes**	**Coding Example**
reg 16, mem 32	16 + EA	2	2-4	LES DI,[BX], TXT_BUFF

LOCK	LOCK (no operands) Lock bus			Flags O D I T S Z A P C
Operands	**Clocks**	**Transfers***	**Bytes**	**Coding Example**
(no operands)	2	–	1	LOCK XCHG FLAG, AL

LODS	LODS source-string Load string			Flags O D I T S Z A P C
Operands	**Clocks**	**Transfers***	**Bytes**	**Coding Example**
source-string (repeat) source-string	12 9 + 13/rep	1 1/rep	1 1	LODS CUSTOMER_NAME REP LODS NAME

LOOP	LOOP short-label Loop			Flags O D I T S Z A P C
Operands	**Clocks**	**Transfers***	**Bytes**	**Coding Example**
short-label	17	–	2	LOOP AGAIN

LOOPE/LOOPZ	LOOPE/LOOPZ short-label Loop if equal/Loop if zero			Flags O D I T S Z A P C
Operands	**Clocks**	**Transfers***	**Bytes**	**Coding Example**
short-label	18 or 6	–	2	LOOPE AGAIN

LOOPNE/LOOPNZ	LOOPNE/LOOPNZ short-label Loop if not equal/Loop if not zero			Flags O D I T S Z A P C O O
Operands	**Clocks**	**Transfers***	**Bytes**	**Coding Example**
short-label	19 or 5	–	2	LOOPNE AGAIN

NMI†	NMI (external nonmaskable interrupt) Interrupt if NMI = 1			Flags O D I T S Z A P C
Operands	**Clocks**	**Transfers***	**Bytes**	**Coding Example**
(no operands)	50	5	N/A	N/A

MOV	**MOV** destination, source Move			**Flags** O D I T S Z A P C
Operands	**Clocks**	**Transfers***	**Bytes**	**Coding Example**
memory, accumulator	10	1	3	MOV ARRAY [SI], AL
accumulator, memory	10	1	3	MOV AZ, TEMP_RESULT
register, register	2	—	2	MOV AZ, CX
register, memory	8 + EA	1	2-4	MOV BP, STACK_TOP
memory, register	9 + EA	1	2-4	MOV COUNT [DI], CX
register, immediate	4	—	2-3	MOV CL, 2
memory, immediate	10 + EA	1	3-6	MOV MASK [BX] [SI], 2CH
seg-reg, reg 16	2	—	2	MOV ES, CX
seg-reg, mem 16	8 + EA	1	2-4	MOV DS, SEGMENT_BASE
reg 16, seg-reg	2	—	2	MOV BP, SS
memory, seg-reg	9 + EA	1	2-4	MOV [BX], SEG_SAVE, CS

MOVS	**MOVS** dest-string, source-string Mov string			**Flags** O D I T S Z A P C
Operands	**Clocks**	**Transfers***	**Bytes**	**Coding Example**
dest-string, source-string	18	2	1	MOVS LINE EDIT_DATA
(repeat) dest-string, source-string	9 + 17/rep	2/rep	1	REP MOVS SCREEN, BUFFER

MOVSB/MOVSW	**MOVSB/MOVSW** (no operands) Move string (byte/word)			**Flags** O D I T S Z A P C
Operands	**Clocks**	**Transfers***	**Bytes**	**Coding Example**
(no operands)	18	2	1	MOVSB
(repeat)(no operands)	9 + 17/rep	2/rep	1	REP MOVSW

MUL	**MUL** source Multiplication, unsigned			**Flags** O D I T S Z A P C X U U U U X
Operands	**Clocks**	**Transfers***	**Bytes**	**Coding Example**
reg 8	70-77	—	2	MUL BL
reg 16	118-133	—	2	MUL CX
mem 8	76-83 + EA	1	2-4	MUL MONTH [SI]
mem 16	124-139 + EA	1	2-4	MUL BAUD_RATE

NEG	**NEG** destination Negate			**Flags** O D I T S Z A P C
Operands	**Clocks**	**Transfers***	**Bytes**	**Coding Example**
register	3	—	2	NEG AL
memory	16 + EA	2	2-4	NEG MULTIPLIER
*0 if destination is 0				

NOP

NOP (no operands)
No operation

Flags: O D I T S Z A P C

Operands	Clocks	Transfers*	Bytes	Coding Example
(no operands)	3	–	1	NOP

NOT

NOT destination
Logical not

Flags: O D I T S Z A P C

Operands	Clocks	Transfers*	Bytes	Coding Example
register	3	–	2	NOT AX
memory	16 + EA	2	2-4	NOT CHARACTER

OR

OR destination, source
Logical inclusive or

Flags: O D I T S Z A P C
O X X U X O

Operands	Clocks	Transfers*	Bytes	Coding Example
register, register	3	–	2	OR AL, BL
register, memory	9 + EA	1	2-4	OR DX, PORT_ ID [DI]
memory, register	16 + EA	2	2-4	OR FLAG_BYTE, CL
accumulator, immediate	4	–	2-3	OR AL, 011011008
register, immediate	4	–	3-4	OR CX, 01H
memory, immediate	17 + EA	2	3-6	OR [BX], CMD_WORD, 0CFH

OUT

OUT port, accumulator
Output byte or word

Flags: O D I T S Z A P C

Operands	Clocks	Transfers*	Bytes	Coding Example
immed 8, accumulator	10	–	2	OUT 44, AX
DX, accumulator	8	1	1	OUT DX, AL

POP

POP destination
Pop word off stack

Flags: O D I T S Z A P C

Operands	Clocks	Transfers*	Bytes	Coding Example
register	8	1	1	POP DX
seg-reg (CS illegal)	8	1	1	POP DS
memory	17 + EA	2	2-4	POP PARAMETER

POPF

POPF (no operands)
Pop all registers

Flags: O D I T S Z A P C
R R R R R R R R R

Operands	Clocks	Transfers*	Bytes	Coding Example
(no operands)	8	1	1	POPF

PUSH	PUSH source Push word onto stack			Flags ODITSZAPC
Operands	**Clocks**	**Transfers***	**Bytes**	**Coding Example**
register	11	1	1	PUSH SI
seg-reg (CS legal)	10	1	1	PUSH ES
memory	16 + EA	2	2-4	PUSH RETURN_CODE [SI]

PUSHF	PUSHF (no operands) Push flags onto stack			Flags ODITSZAPC
Operands	**Clocks**	**Transfers***	**Bytes**	**Coding Example**
(no operands)	10	1	1	PUSHF

RCL	RCL destination, count Rotate left through carry			Flags ODITSZAPC X C
Operands	**Clocks**	**Transfers***	**Bytes**	**Coding Example**
register, 1	2	—	2	RCL CX, 1
register, CL	8 + 4/bit	—	2	RCL AL, CL
memory, 1	15 + EA	2	2-4	RCL ALPHA, 1
memory CL	20 + 4/bit + EA	2	2-4	RCL [BP], PARM, CL

RCR	RCR destination, count Rotate right through carry			Flags ODITSZAPC X C
Operands	**Clocks**	**Transfers***	**Bytes**	**Coding Example**
register, 1	2	—	2	RCR BX, 1
register, CL	8 + 4/bit	—	2	RCR BL, CL
memory, 1	15 + EA	2	2-4	RCR [BX], STATUS, 1
memory CL	20 + 4/bit + EA	2	2-4	RCR ARRAY, [DI], CL

REP	REP (no operands) Repeat string operation			Flags ODITSZAPC
Operands	**Clocks**	**Transfers***	**Bytes**	**Coding Example**
(no operands)	2	—	1	REP MOVS DEST, SRCE

REPE/REPZ	REPE/REPZ (no operands) Repeat string operation while equal/while zero			Flags ODITSZAPC
Operands	**Clocks**	**Transfers***	**Bytes**	**Coding Example**
(no operands)	2	—	1	REPE CMPS DATA, KEY

REPNE/REPNZ

REPNE/REPNZ (no operands)
Repeat string operation while not equal/not zero

Flags	O	D	I	T	S	Z	A	P	C
	U				U	U	X	U	X

Operands	Clocks	Transfers*	Bytes	Coding Example
(no operands)	2	—	1	REPNE SCAS INPUT_LINE

RET

RET optional-pop-value
Return from procedure

Flags	O	D	I	T	S	Z	A	P	C

Operands	Clocks	Transfers*	Bytes	Coding Example
(intra-segment, no pop)	16	1	1	RET
(intra-segment, pop)	20	1	3	RET 4
(inter-segment, no pop)	26	2	1	RET
(inter-segment, pop)	25	2	3	RET 2

ROL

ROL destination, count
Rotate left

Flags	O	D	I	T	S	Z	A	P	C
	X								X

Operands	Clocks	Transfers*	Bytes	Coding Example
register, 1	2	—	2	ROL BX, 1
register, CL	8 + 4/bit	—	2	ROL DI, CL
memory, 1	15 + EA	2	2-4	ROL FLAG_BYTE [DI], 1
memory CL	20 + 4/bit + EA	2	2-4	ROL ALPHA, CL

ROR

ROR destination, count
Rotate right

Flags	O	D	I	T	S	Z	A	P	C
	X								X

Operands	Clocks	Transfers*	Bytes	Coding Example
register, 1	2	—	2	ROR BX, 1
register, CL	8 + 4/bit	—	2	ROR BX, CL
memory, 1	15 + EA	2	2-4	ROR PORT_STATUS, 1
memory CL	20 + 4/bit + EA	2	2-4	ROR CMD_WORD, CL

SAHF

SAHF (no operands)
Store AH into flags

Flags	O	D	I	T	S	Z	A	P	C
					R	R	R	R	R

Operands	Clocks	Transfers*	Bytes	Coding Example
(no operands)	4	—	1	SAHF

SAL/SHL

SAL/SHL destination
Shift arithmetic left/Shift logical left

Flags	O	D	I	T	S	Z	A	P	C
	X								X

Operands	Clocks	Transfers*	Bytes	Coding Example
register, 1	2	—	2	SAL AL, 1
register, CL	8 + 4/bit	—	2	SAL DI, CL
memory, 1	15 + EA	2	2-4	SAL [BX], OVERDRAW, 1
memory, CL	20 + 4/bit + EA	2	2-4	SAL STORE_COUNT, CL

SAR

SAR destination, source
Shift arithmetic right

Flags	O	D	I	T	S	Z	A	P	C
	X				X	X	U	X	X

Operands	Clocks	Transfers*	Bytes	Coding Example
register, 1	2	—	2	SAR DX, 1
register, CL	8 + 4/bit	—	2	SAR DI, CL
memory, 1	15 + EA	2	2-4	SAR N_BLOCKS, 1
memory, CL	20 + 4/bit + EA	2	2-4	SAR N_BLOCKS, CL

SBB

SBB destination, source
Subtract with borrow

Flags	O	D	I	T	S	Z	A	P	C
	X				X	X	X	X	X

Operands	Clocks	Transfers*	Bytes	Coding Example
register, register	3	—	2	SBB BX, CX
register, memory	9 + EA	1	2-4	SBB DI, [BX], PAYMENT
memory, register	16 + EA	2	2-4	SBB BALANCE, AX
accumulator, immediate	4	—	2-3	SBB AX, 2
register, immediate	4	—	3-4	SBB CL, 1
memory, immediate	17 + EA	2	3-6	SBB COUNT, [SI], 10

SCAS

SCAS dest-string
Scan string

Flags	O	D	I	T	S	Z	A	P	C
	X				X	X	X	X	X

Operands	Clocks	Transfers*	Bytes	Coding Example
dest-string	15	1	1	SCAS INPUT_LINE
(repeat) dest-string	9 + 15/rep	1/rep	1	REPNE SCAS BUFFER

SEGMENT†

SEGMENT override, prefix
Override to specified segment

Flags	O	D	I	T	S	Z	A	P	C

Operands	Clocks	Transfers*	Bytes	Coding Example
(no operands)	2	—	1	MOV SS: PARAMETER AX

SHR

SHR destination, count
Shift logical right

Flags	O	D	I	T	S	Z	A	P	C
	X								X

Operands	Clocks	Transfers*	Bytes	Coding Example
register, 1	2	—	2	SHR SI, 1
register, CL	8 + 4/bit	—	2	SHR SI, CL
memory, 1	15 + EA	2	2-4	SHR ID BYTE [SI] [BX],1
memory, CL	20 + 4/bit + EA	2	2-4	SHR INPUT WORD, CL

SINGLE STEP††

SINGLE STEP (Trap flag interrupt)
Interrupt if TF = 1

Flags	O	D	I	T	S	Z	A	P	C
			0	0					

Operands	Clocks	Transfers*	Bytes	Coding Example
(no operands)	50	5	N/A	N/A

STC

STC (no operands)
Set carry flag

Flags	O	D	I	T	S	Z	A	P	C
									C

Operands	Clocks	Transfers*	Bytes	Coding Example
(no operands)	2	—	1	STC

STD

STD (no operands)
Set direction flag

Flags	O	D	I	T	S	Z	A	P	C
		1							

Operands	Clocks	Transfers*	Bytes	Coding Example
(no operands)	2	—	1	STD

STI

STI (no operands)
Set interrupt enable flag

Flags	O	D	I	T	S	Z	A	P	C
			1						

Operands	Clocks	Transfers*	Bytes	Coding Example
(no operands)	2	—	1	STI

STOS

STOS dest-string
Store byte or word string

Flags	O	D	I	T	S	Z	A	P	C

Operands	Clocks	Transfers*	Bytes	Coding Example
dest-string	11	1	1	STOS PRINT_LINE
(repeat) dest-string	9 + 10/rep	1/rep	1	REP STOS DISPLAY

SUB

SUB destination, source
Subtraction

Flags	O	D	I	T	S	Z	A	P	C
	X				X	X	X	X	X

Operands	Clocks	Transfers*	Bytes	Coding Example
register, register	3	—	2	SUB CX, BX
register, memory	9 + EA	1	2-4	SUB DX, MATH_TOTAL [SI]
memory, register	16 + EA	2	2-4	SUB [BP+2], CL
accumulator, immediate	4	—	2-3	SUB AL, 10
register, immediate	4	—	3-4	SUB SI, 5280
memory, immediate	17 + EA	2	3-6	SUB [BP], BALANCE, 1000

TEST

TEST destination, source
Test or non-destructive logical and

Flags	O	D	I	T	S	Z	A	P	C
	O				X	X	U	X	O

Operands	Clocks	Transfers*	Bytes	Coding Example
register, register	3	—	2	TEST SI, DI
register, memory	9 + EA	1	2-4	TEST SI, END_COUNT
accumulator, immediate	4	—	2-3	TEST AL, 001000008
register, immediate	5	—	3-4	TEST BX, 0CC4H
memory, immediate	11 + EA	—	3-6	TEST RETURN_COUNT, 01H

WAIT

WAIT (no operands)
Wait while TEST pin not asserted

Flags	O	D	I	T	S	Z	A	P	C

Operands	Clocks	Transfers*	Bytes	Coding Example
(no operands)	4 + 5	—	1	WAIT

XCHG

XCHG destination, source
Exchange

Flags	O	D	I	T	S	Z	A	P	C

Operands	Clocks	Transfers*	Bytes	Coding Example
accumulator, reg 16	3	—	1	XCHG AX, BX
memory, register	17 + EA	2	2-4	XCHG SEMAPHORE, AX
register, register	4	—	2	XCHG AL, BL

XLAT

XLAT source-table
Translate

Flags	O	D	I	T	S	Z	A	P	C

Operands	Clocks	Transfers*	Bytes	Coding Example
source-table	11	1	1	XLAT ASCII_TAB

XOR	XOR destination, source Logical exclusive or			Flags ODITSZAPC O XXUXO
Operands	**Clocks**	**Transfers***	**Bytes**	**Coding Example**
register, register	3	—	2	XOR CX, BX
register, memory	9 + EA	1	2-4	XOR CL, MASK_BYTE
memory, register	16 + EA	2	2-4	XOR ALPHA [SI], DX
accumulator, immediate	4	—	2-3	XOR AL, 010000108
register, immediate	4	—	2-4	XOR SI, 00C2H
memory, immediate	17 + EA	2	3-6	XOR RETURN_CODE 0D2H

*For the 8086 add four clocks for each 16-bit word transfer with an odd address. For the 8088 add four clocks for each 16-bit word transfer.

†INTR is not an instruction, it is included in Table 6-16 only for timing information.

†NMI is not an instruction, it is included in Table 6-16 only for timing information.

†ASM-86 incorporates the segment override prefix into the operand specification and not as a separate instruction. SEGMENT is included in Table 6-16 only for timing information.

††SINGLE STEP is not an instruction, it is included in Table 6-16 only for timing information.

MACHINE INSTRUCTION ENCODING AND DECODING

Machine instruction encoding and decoding is primarily the concern of the programmer. It is presented here for the hardware designer since such encoding and decoding directly affects bus activity. As an example of the encoding and decoding process, consider writing a MOV instruction in ASM-86 in the form:

```
MOV destination,source
```

This will cause the assembler to generate 1 of 28 possible forms of the MOV machine instruction. A programmer rarely needs to know the details of machine instruction formats or encoding. An exception may occur during debugging when it may be necessary to monitor instructions fetched on the bus, read unformatted memory dumps, etc. This section provides the information necessary to translate or decode an 8086 or 8088 machine instruction.

To pack instructions into memory as densely as possible, the 8086 and 8088 CPUs utilize an efficient coding technique. Machine instructions vary from one to six bytes in length. One-byte instructions, which generally operate on single registers or flags, are simple to identify; the keys to decoding longer instructions are in the first two bytes. The format of these bytes can vary, but most instructions follow the format shown in Figure 6-27.

The first six bits of a multibyte instruction generally contain an opcode that identifies the basic instruction type: ADD, XOR, etc. The following bit, called the D field, generally specifies the "direction" of the operation: 1 = the REG field in the second byte identifies the destination operand, 0 = the REG field identifies the source operand. The W field distinguishes between byte and word operations: 0 = byte, 1 = word.

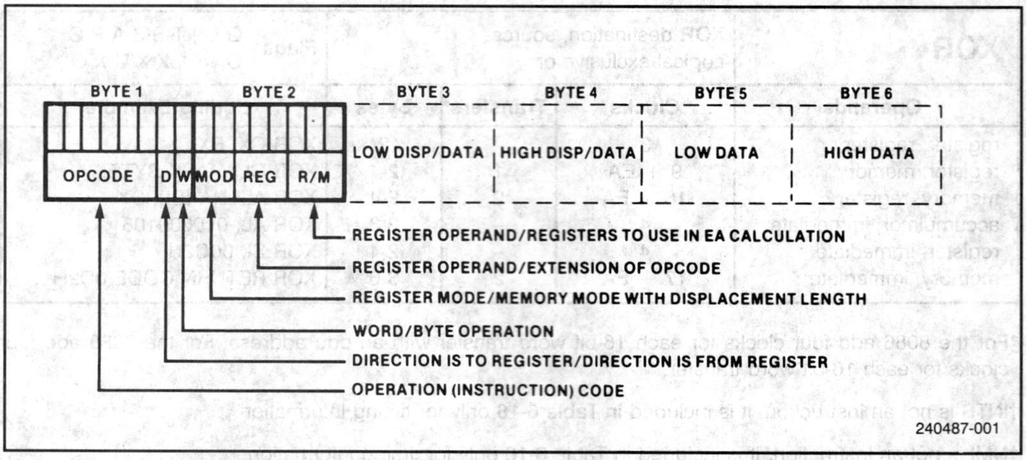

Figure 6-27. Typical 8086/8088 Machine Instruction Format

One of three additional single-bit fields, S, V or Z, appears in some instruction formats (refer to Table 6-17). S, in conjunction with W, indicates the sign extension of immediate fields in arithmetic instructions. V distinguishes between single- and variable-bit shifts and rotates. Z is a compare bit with the zero flag in conditional repeat and loop instructions.

The second byte of the instruction usually identifies the instruction's operands. The MOD (mode) field indicates whether one of the operands is in memory or whether both operands are registers (refer to Table 6-18). The REG (register) field identifies a register that is one of the instruction operands (refer to Table 6-19). In a number of instructions, particularly the immediate-to-memory variety, REG is used as an extension of the opcode to identify the type of operation. The encoding of the R/M (register/memory) field (refer to Table 6-20) depends on how the mode field is set. If MOD = 11 (register-to-register mode), then R/M identifies the second register operand. If MOD selects memory mode, then R/M indicates how the effective address of the memory operand is to be calculated.

Bytes 3 through 6 of an instruction are optional fields that usually contain the displacement value of a memory operand and/or the actual value of an immediate constant operand.

The displacement value may contain one or two bytes; the language translators generate one byte whenever possible. The MOD field indicates how many displacement bytes are present. Following Intel convention, if the displacement is two bytes, the most-significant byte is stored second in the instruction. If the displacement is only a single byte, the 8086 or 8088 automatically sign-extends this quantity to 16-bits before using the information in further address calculations. Immediate values always follow any displacement values that may be present. The second byte of a two-byte immediate value is the most significant.

Table 6-17. Single-Bit Field Encoding

Field	Value	Function
S	0	No sign extension
	1	Sign extend 8-bit immediate data to 16 bits if W=1
W	0	Instruction operates on byte data
	1	Instruction operates on word data
D	0	Instruction source is specified in REG field
	1	Instruction destination is specified in REG field
V	0	Shift/rotate count is one
	1	Shift/rotate count is specified in CL register
Z	0	Repeat/loop while zero flag is clear
	1	Repeat/loop while zero flag is set

Table 6-18. Mode (MOD) Field Encoding

Code	Explanation
00	Memory Mode, no displacement follows*
01	Memory Mode, 8-bit displacement follows
10	Memory Mode, 16-bit displacement follows
11	Register Mode (no displacement)

*Except when R/M = 110, then 16-bit displacement follows

Table 6-19. REG (Register) Field Encoding

REG	W = 0	W = 1
000	AL	AX
001	CL	CX
010	DL	DX
011	BL	BX
100	AH	SP
101	CH	BP
110	DH	SI
111	BH	DI

Table 6-20. Register/Memory Field Encoding

MOD = 11			Effective Address Calculation			
R/M	W = 0	W = 1	R/M	MOD = 00	MOD = 01	MOD = 10
000	AL	AX	000	(BX) + (SI)	(BX) + (SI) + D8	(BX) + (SI) + D16
001	CL	CX	001	(BX) + (DI)	(BX) + (DI) + D8	(BX) + (DI) + D16
010	DL	DX	010	(BP) + (SI)	(BP) + (SI) + D8	(BP) + (SI) + D16
011	BL	BX	011	(BP) + (DI)	(BP) + (DI) + D8	(BP) + (DI) + D16
100	AH	SP	100	(SI)	(SI) + D8	(SI) + D16
101	CH	BP	101	(DI)	(DI) + D8	(DI) + D16
110	DH	SI	110	DIRECT ADDRESS	(BP) + D8	(BP) + D16
111	BH	DI	111	(BX)	(BX) + D8	(BX) + D16

Table 6-22 lists the instruction encodings for all 8086/8088 instructions. This table can be used to predict the machine encoding of any ASM-86 instruction. Table 6-23 lists the 8086/8088 machine instructions in order by the binary value of their first byte. This table can be used to decode any machine instruction from its binary representation. Table 6-21 is a key to the abbreviations used in Table 6-22 and 6-23. Figure 6-28 is a more compact instruction decoding guide.

Table 6-21. Key to Machine Instruction Encoding and Decoding

Identifier	Explanation
MOD	Mode field; described in this chapter.
REG	Register field; described in this chapter.
R/M	Register/Memory field; described in this chapter.
SR	Segment register code: 00 = ES, 01 = CS, 10 = SS, 11 = DS.
W, S, D, V, Z	Single-bit instruction fields; described in this chapter.
DATA-8	8-bit immediate constant.
DATA-SX	8-bit immediate value that is automatically sign-extended to 16-bits before use.
DATA-LO	Low-order byte of 16-bit immediate constant.
DATA-HI	High-order byte of 16-bit immediate constant.
(DISP-LO)	Low-order byte of optional 8- or 16-bit unsigned displacement; MOD indicates if present.
(DISP-HI)	High-order byte of optional 16-bit unsigned displacement; MOD indicates if present.
IP-LO	Low-order byte of new IP value.
IP-HI	High-order byte of new IP value.
CS-LO	Low-order byte of new CS value.
CS-HI	High-order byte of new CS value.
IP-INC8	8-bit signed increment to instruction pointer.
IP-INC-LO	Low-order byte of signed 16-bit instruction pointer increment.
IP-INC-HI	High-order byte of signed 16-bit instruction pointer increment.
ADDR-LO	Low-order byte of direct address (offset) of memory operand; EA not calculated.
ADDR-HI	High-order byte of direct address (offset) of memory operand; EA not calculated.
— —	Bits may contain any value.
XXX	First 3 bits of ESC opcode.
YYY	Second 3 bits of ESC opcode.
REG8	8-bit general register operand.
REG16	16-bit general register operand.
MEM8	8-bit memory operand (any addressing mode).
MEM16	16-bit memory operand (any addressing mode).
IMMED8	8-bit immediate operand.
IMMED16	16-bit immediate operand.
SEGREG	Segment register operand.
DEST-STR8	Byte string addressed by DI.
SRC-STR8	Byte string addressed by SI.
DEST-STR16	Word string addressed by DI.
SRC-STR16	Word string addressed by SI.
SHORT-LABEL	Label within ±127 bytes of instruction.
NEAR-PROC	Procedure in current code segment.
FAR-PROC	Procedure in another code segment.
NEAR-LABEL	Label in current code segment but farther than −128 to +127 bytes from instruction.
FAR-LABEL	Label in another code segment.
SOURCE-TABLE	XLAT translation table addressed by BX.
OPCODE	ESC opcode operand.
SOURCE	ESC register or memory operand.

Table 6-22. 8086/8088 Instruction Encoding

DATA TRANSFER INSTRUCTIONS						
MOV = Move word variable	76543210	76543210	76543210	76543210	76543210	76543210
Memory to register	RRR00AA1	100000MM	offset if AA=01			
Register to memory	RRR00AA1	100001MM	offset if AA=01			
Memory to memory	00000AA1	100100MM	offset if AA=01	00000AA1	110011MM	offset if AA=01
MOVB = Move byte variable	76543210	76543210	76543210	76543210	76543210	76543210
Memory to register	RRR00AA0	100000MM	offset if AA=01			
Register to memory	RRR00AA0	100001MM	offset if AA=01			
Memory to memory	00000AA0	100100MM	offset if AA=01	00000AA0	110011MM	offset if AA=01
MOVBI = Move byte immediate						
Immediate to register	RRR01000	00110000	data-8			
Immediate to memory	00001AA0	010011MM	offset if AA=01	data-8		
MOVI = Move word immediate						
Immediate to register	RRR10001	00110000	data-lo	data-hi		
Immediate to memory	00010AA1	010011MM	offset if AA=01	data-lo	data-hi	
MOVP = Move pointer						
Memory to pointer register	PPP00AA1	100011MM	offset if AA=01			
Pointer register to memory	PPP00AA1	100110MM	offset if AA=01			
LPD = Load pointer with doubleword variable	PPP00AA1	100010MM	offset if AA=01			
LPDI = Load pointer with doubleword immediate	PPP10001	00001000	offset-lo	offset-hi	segment-lo	segment-hi
ARITHMETIC INSTRUCTIONS						
ADD = Add word variable						
Memory to register	RRR00AA1	101000MM	offset if AA=01			
Register to memory	RRR00AA1	110100MM	offset if AA=01			
ADDB = Add byte variable						
Memory to register	RRR00AA0	101000MM	offset if AA=01			
Register to memory	RRR00AA0	110100MM	offset if AA=01			
ADDI = Add word immediate						
Immediate to register	RRR10001	00100000	data-lo	data-hi		
Immediate to memory	00010AA1	110000MM	offset if AA=01	data-lo	data-hi	

Table 6-22. 8086/8088 Instruction Encoding (Cont'd.)

ARITHMETIC (Cont'd.)

Instruction	76543210	76543210	76543210	76543210	76543210	76543210
SUB = Subtract:						
Reg/memory and register to either	0 0 1 0 1 0 d w	mod reg r/m	(DISP-LO)	(DISP-HI)		
Immediate from register/memory	1 0 0 0 0 0 s w	mod 1 0 1 r/m	(DISP-LO)	(DISP-HI)	data	data if s: w=01
Immediate from accumulator	0 0 1 0 1 1 0 w	data	data if w=1			
SBB = Subtract with borrow:						
Reg/memory and register to either	0 0 0 1 1 0 d w	mod reg r/m	(DISP-LO)	(DISP-HI)		
Immediate from register/memory	1 0 0 0 0 0 s w	mod 0 1 1 r/m	(DISP-LO)	(DISP-HI)	data	data if s: w=01
Immediate from accumulator	0 0 0 1 1 1 0 w	data	data if w=1			
DEC Decrement:						
Register/memory	1 1 1 1 1 1 1 w	mod 0 0 1 r/m	(DISP-LO)	(DISP-HI)		
Register	0 1 0 0 1 reg					
NEG Change sign	1 1 1 1 0 1 1 w	mod 0 1 1 r/m	(DISP-LO)	(DISP-HI)		
CMP = Compare:						
Register/memory and register	0 0 1 1 1 0 d w	mod reg r/m	(DISP-LO)	(DISP-HI)		
Immediate with register/memory	1 0 0 0 0 0 s w	mod 1 1 1 r/m	(DISP-LO)	(DISP-HI)	data	data if s: w=1
Immediate with accumulator	0 0 1 1 1 1 0 w	data				
AAS ASCII adjust for subtract	0 0 1 1 1 1 1 1					
DAS Decimal adjust for subtract	0 0 1 0 1 1 1 1					
MUL Multiply (unsigned)	1 1 1 1 0 1 1 w	mod 1 0 0 r/m	(DISP-LO)	(DISP-HI)		
IMUL Integer multiply (signed)	1 1 1 1 0 1 1 w	mod 1 0 1 r/m	(DISP-LO)	(DISP-HI)		
AAM ASCII adjust for multiply	1 1 0 1 0 1 0 0	0 0 0 0 1 0 1 0	(DISP-LO)	(DISP-HI)		
DIV Divide (unsigned)	1 1 1 1 0 1 1 w	mod 1 1 0 r/m	(DISP-LO)	(DISP-HI)		
IDIV Integer divide (signed)	1 1 1 1 0 1 1 w	mod 1 1 1 r/m	(DISP-LO)	(DISP-HI)		
AAD ASCII adjust for divide	1 1 0 1 0 1 0 1	0 0 0 0 1 0 1 0	(DISP-LO)	(DISP-HI)		
CBW Convert byte to word	1 0 0 1 1 0 0 0					
CWD Convert word to double word	1 0 0 1 1 0 0 1					

LOGIC

Instruction	76543210	76543210	76543210	76543210
NOT Invert	1 1 1 1 0 1 1 w	mod 0 1 0 r/m	(DISP-LO)	(DISP-HI)
SHL/SAL Shift logical/arithmetic left	1 1 0 1 0 0 v w	mod 1 0 0 r/m	(DISP-LO)	(DISP-HI)
SHR Shift logical right	1 1 0 1 0 0 v w	mod 1 0 1 r/m	(DISP-LO)	(DISP-HI)
SAR Shift arithmetic right	1 1 0 1 0 0 v w	mod 1 1 1 r/m	(DISP-LO)	(DISP-HI)
ROL Rotate left	1 1 0 1 0 0 v w	mod 0 0 0 r/m	(DISP-LO)	(DISP-HI)

Table 6-22. 8086/8088 Instruction Encoding (Cont'd.)

LOGIC (Cont'd.)	7 6 5 4 3 2 1 0	7 6 5 4 3 2 1 0	7 6 5 4 3 2 1 0	7 6 5 4 3 2 1 0	7 6 5 4 3 2 1 0	7 6 5 4 3 2 1 0
ROR Rotate right	1 1 0 1 0 0 v w	mod 0 0 1 r/m	(DISP-LO)	(DISP-HI)		
RCL Rotate through carry flag left	1 1 0 1 0 0 v w	mod 0 1 0 r/m	(DISP-LO)	(DISP-HI)		
RCR Rotate through carry right	1 1 0 1 0 0 v w	mod 0 1 1 r/m	(DISP-LO)	(DISP-HI)		
AND = And:						
Reg/memory with register to either	0 0 1 0 0 0 d w	mod reg r/m	(DISP-LO)	(DISP-HI)		
Immediate to register/memory	1 0 0 0 0 0 0 w	mod 1 0 0 r/m	(DISP-LO)	(DISP-HI)	data	data if w=1
Immediate to accumulator	0 0 1 0 0 1 0 w	data	data if w=1			
TEST = And function to flags no result:						
Register/memory and register	0 0 0 1 0 0 d w	mod reg r/m	(DISP-LO)	(DISP-HI)		
Immediate data and register/memory	1 1 1 1 0 1 1 w	mod 0 0 0 r/m	(DISP-LO)	(DISP-HI)	data	data if w=1
Immediate data and accumulator	1 0 1 0 1 0 0 w	data				
OR = Or:						
Reg/memory and register to either	0 0 0 0 1 0 d w	mod reg r/m	(DISP-LO)	(DISP-HI)		
Immediate to register/memory	1 0 0 0 0 0 0 w	mod 0 0 1 r/m	(DISP-LO)	(DISP-HI)	data	data if w=1
Immediate to accumulator	0 0 0 0 1 1 0 w	data	data if w=1			
XOR = Exclusive or:						
Reg/memory and register to either	0 0 1 1 0 0 d w	mod reg r/m	(DISP-LO)	(DISP-HI)		
Immediate to register/memory	0 0 1 1 0 1 0 w	data	(DISP-LO)	(DISP-HI)	data	data if w=1
Immediate to accumulator	0 0 1 1 0 1 0 w	data	data if w=1			
STRING MANIPULATION						
REP = Repeat	1 1 1 1 0 0 1 z					
MOVS = Move byte/word	1 0 1 0 0 1 0 w					
CMPS = Compare byte/word	1 0 1 0 0 1 1 w					
SCAS = Scan byte/word	1 0 1 0 1 1 1 w					
LODS = Load byte/wd to AL/AX	1 0 1 0 1 1 0 w					
STDS = Stor byte/wd from AL/A	1 0 1 0 1 0 1 w					

Table 6-22. 8086/8088 Instruction Encoding (Cont'd.)

CONTROL TRANSFER

Instruction	7 6 5 4 3 2 1 0	7 6 5 4 3 2 1 0	7 6 5 4 3 2 1 0	7 6 5 4 3 2 1 0	7 6 5 4 3 2 1 0	7 6 5 4 3 2 1 0
CALL = Call:						
Direct within segment	1 1 1 0 1 0 0 0	IP-INC-LO	IP-INC-HI			
Indirect within segment	1 1 1 1 1 1 1 1	mod 0 1 0 r/m	(DISP-LO)	(DISP-HI)		
Direct intersegment	1 0 0 1 1 0 1 0	IP-lo	IP-hi			
		CS-lo	CS-hi			
Indirect intersegment	1 1 1 1 1 1 1 1	mod 0 1 1 r/m	(DISP-LO)	(DISP-HI)		
JMP = Unconditional Jump:						
Direct within segment	1 1 1 0 1 0 0 1	IP-INC-LO	IP-INC-HI			
Direct within segment-short	1 1 1 0 1 0 1 1	IP-INC8				
Indirect within segment	1 1 1 1 1 1 1 1	mod 1 0 0 r/m	(DISP-LO)	(DISP-HI)		
Direct intersegment	1 1 1 0 1 0 1 0	IP-lo	IP-hi			
		CS-lo	CS-hi			
Indirect intersegment	1 1 1 1 1 1 1 1	mod 1 0 1 r/m	(DISP-LO)	(DISP-HI)		
RET = Return from CALL:						
Within segment	1 1 0 0 0 0 1 1					
Within seg adding immed to SP	1 1 0 0 0 0 1 0	data-lo	data-hi			
Intersegment	1 1 0 0 1 0 1 1					
Intersegment adding immediate to SP	1 1 0 0 1 0 1 0	data-lo	data-hi			
JE/JZ = Jump on equal/zero	0 1 1 1 0 1 0 0	IP-INC8				
JL/JNGE = Jump on less/not greater or equal	0 1 1 1 1 1 0 0	IP-INC8				
JLE/JNG = Jump on less or equal/not greater	0 1 1 1 1 1 1 0	IP-INC8				
JB/JNAE = Jump on below/not above or equal	0 1 1 1 0 0 1 0	IP-INC8				
JBE/JNA = Jump on below or equal/not above	0 1 1 1 0 1 1 0	IP-INC8				
JP/JPE = Jump on parity/parity even	0 1 1 1 1 0 1 0	IP-INC8				
JO = Jump on overflow	0 1 1 1 0 0 0 0	IP-INC8				
JS = Jump on sign	0 1 1 1 1 0 0 0	IP-INC8				
JNE/JNZ = Jump on not equal/not zer0	0 1 1 1 0 1 0 1	IP-INC8				
JNL/JGE = Jump on not less/greater or equal	0 1 1 1 1 1 0 1	IP-INC8				
JNLE/JG = Jump on not less or equal/greater	0 1 1 1 1 1 1 1	IP-INC8				
JNB/JAE = Jump on not below/above or equal	0 1 1 1 0 0 1 1	IP-INC8				
JNBE/JA = Jump on not below or equal/above	0 1 1 1 0 1 1 1	IP-INC8				
JNP/JPO = Jump on not par/par odd	0 1 1 1 1 0 1 1	IP-INC8				
JNO = Jump on not overflow	0 1 1 1 0 0 0 1	IP-INC8				

Table 6-22. 8086/8088 Instruction Encoding (Cont'd.)

CONTROL TRANSFER (Cont'd.)

Instruction	7 6 5 4 3 2 1 0	7 6 5 4 3 2 1 0	7 6 5 4 3 2 1 0	7 6 5 4 3 2 1 0	7 6 5 4 3 2 1 0	7 6 5 4 3 2 1 0
RET = Return from CALL:						
JNS = Jump on not sign	0 1 1 1 1 0 0 1	IP-INC8				
LOOP = Loop CX times	1 1 1 0 0 0 1 0	IP-INC8				
LOOPZ/LOOPE = Loop while zero/equal	1 1 1 0 0 0 0 1	IP-INC8				
LOOPNZ/LOOPNE = Loop while not zero/equal	1 1 1 0 0 0 0 0	IP-INC8				
JCXZ = Jump on CX zero	1 1 1 0 0 0 1 1	IP-INC8				
INT = Interrupt:						
Type specified	1 1 0 0 1 1 0 1	DATA-8				
Type 3	1 1 0 0 1 1 0 0					
INTO = Interrupt on overflow	1 1 0 0 1 1 1 0					
IRET = Interrupt return	1 1 0 0 1 1 1 1					
PROCESSOR CONTROL						
CLC = Clear carry	1 1 1 1 1 0 0 0					
CMC = Complement carry	1 1 1 1 0 1 0 1					
STC = Set carry	1 1 1 1 1 0 0 1					
CLD = Clear direction	1 1 1 1 1 1 0 0					
STD = Set direction	1 1 1 1 1 1 0 1					
CLI = Clear interrupt	1 1 1 1 1 0 1 0					
STI = Set interrupt	1 1 1 1 1 0 1 1					
HLT = Halt	1 1 1 1 0 1 0 0					
WAIT = Wait	1 0 0 1 1 0 1 1					
ESC = Escape (to external device)	1 1 0 1 1 x x x	m o d y y y r / m	(DISP-LO)	(DISP-HI)		
LOCK = Bus lock prefix	1 1 1 1 0 0 0 0					
SEGMENT = Override prefix	0 0 1 reg 1 1 0					

Table 6-23. Machine Instruction Decoding Guide

1ST BYTE HEX	1ST BYTE BINARY	2ND BYTE	BYTES 3, 4, 5, 6	ASM-86 INSTRUCTION FORMAT	
00	0000 0000	MOD REG R/M	(DISP-LO),(DISP-HI)	ADD	REG8/MEM8,REG8
01	0000 0001	MOD REG R/M	(DISP-LO),(DISP-HI)	ADD	REG16/MEM16,REG16
02	0000 0010	MOD REG R/M	(DISP-LO),(DISP-HI)	ADD	REG8,REG8/MEM8
03	0000 0011	MOD REG R/M	(DISP-LO),(DISP-HI)	ADD	REG16,REG16/MEM16
04	0000 0100	DATA-8		ADD	AL,IMMED8
05	0000 0101	DATA-LO	DATA-HI	ADD	AX,IMMED16
06	0000 0110			PUSH	ES
07	0000 0111			POP	ES

Table 6-23. Machine Instruction Decoding Guide (Cont'd.)

1ST BYTE		2ND BYTE	BYTES 3,4,5,6	ASM-86 INSTRUCTION FORMAT	
HEX	BINARY				
08	0000 1000	MOD REG R/M	(DISP-LO),(DISP-HI)	OR	REG8/MEM8,REG8
09	0000 1001	MOD REG R/M	(DISP-LO),(DISP-HI)	OR	REG16/MEM16,REG16
0A	0000 1010	MOD REG R/M	(DISP-LO),(DISP-HI)	OR	REG8,REG8/MEM8
0B	0000 1011	MOD REG R/M	(DISP-LO),(DISP-HI)	OR	REG16,REG16/MEM16
0C	0000 1100	DATA-8		OR	AL,IMMED8
0D	0000 1101	DATA-LO	DATA-HI	OR	AX,IMMED16
0E	0000 1110			PUSH	CS
0F	0000 1111			(not used)	
10	0001 0000	MOD REG R/M	(DISP-LO),(DISP-HI)	ADC	REG8/MEM8,REG8
11	0001 0001	MOD REG R/M	(DISP-LO),(DISP-HI)	ADC	REG16/MEM16,REG16
12	0001 0010	MOD REG R/M	(DISP-LO),(DISP-HI)	ADC	REG8,REG8/MEM8
13	0001 0011	MOD REG R/M	(DISP-LO),(DISP-HI)	ADC	REG16,REG16/MEM16
14	0001 0100	DATA-8		ADC	AL,IMMED8
15	0001 0101	DATA-LO	DATA-HI	ADC	AX,IMMED16
16	0001 0110			PUSH	SS
17	0001 0111			POP	SS
18	0001 1000	MOD REG R/M	(DISP-LO),(DISP-HI)	SBB	REG8/MEM8,REG8
19	0001 1001	MOD REG R/M	(DISP-LO),(DISP-HI)	SBB	REG16/MEM16,REG16
1A	0001 1010	MOD REG R/M	(DISP-LO),(DISP-HI)	SBB	REG8,REG8/MEM8
1B	0001 1011	MOD REG R/M	(DISP-LO),(DISP-HI)	SBB	REG16,REG16/MEM16
1C	0001 1100	DATA-8		SBB	AL,IMMED8
1D	0001 1101	DATA-LO	DATA-HI	SBB	AX,IMMED16
1E	0001 1110			PUSH	DS
1F	0001 1111			POP	DS
20	0010 0000	MOD REG R/M	(DISP-LO),(DISP-HI)	AND	REG8/MEM8,REG8
21	0010 0001	MOD REG R/M	(DISP-LO),(DISP-HI)	AND	REG16/MEM16,REG16
22	0010 0010	MOD REG R/M	(DISP-LO),(DISP-HI)	AND	REG8,REG8/MEM8
23	0010 0011	MOD REG R/M	(DISP-LO),(DISP-HI)	AND	REG16,REG16/MEM16
24	0010 0100	DATA-8		AND	AL,IMMED8
25	0010 0101	DATA-LO	DATA-HI	AND	AX,IMMED16
26	0010 0110			ES:	(segment override prefix)
27	0010 0111			DAA	
28	0010 1000	MOD REG R/M	(DISP-LO),(DISP-HI)	SUB	REG8/MEM8,REG8
29	0010 1001	MOD REG R/M	(DISP-LO),(DISP-HI)	SUB	REG16/MEM16,REG16
2A	0010 1010	MOD REG R/M	(DISP-LO),(DISP-HI)	SUB	REG8,REG8/MEM8
2B	0010 1011	MOD REG R/M	(DISP-LO,(DISP-HI)	SUB	REG16,REG16/MEM16
2C	0010 1100	DATA-8		SUB	AL,IMMED8
2D	0010 1101	DATA-LO	DATA-HI	SUB	AX,IMMED16
2E	0010 1110			CS:	(segment override prefix)
2F	0010 1111			DAS	
30	0011 0000	MOD REG R/M	(DISP-LO),(DISP-HI)	XOR	REG8/MEM8,REG8
31	0011 0001	MOD REG R/M	(DISP-LO),(DISP-HI)	XOR	REG16/MEM16,REG16
32	0011 0010	MOD REG R/M	(DISP-LO),(DISP-HI)	XOR	REG8,REG8/MEM8
33	0011 0011	MOD REG R/M	(DISP-LO),(DISP-HI)	XOR	REG16,REG16/MEM16
34	0011 0100	DATA-8		XOR	AL,IMMED8
35	0011 0101	DATA-LO	DATA-HI	XOR	AX,IMMED16
36	0011 0110			SS:	(segment override prefix)

Table 6-23. Machine Instruction Decoding Guide (Cont'd.)

1ST BYTE		2ND BYTE	BYTES 3,4,5,6	ASM-86 INSTRUCTION FORMAT	
HEX	BINARY				
37	0011 0110			AAA	
38	0011 1000	MOD REG R/M	(DISP-LO),(DISP-HI)	CMP	REG8/MEM8,REG8
39	0011 1001	MOD REG R/M	(DISP-LO),(DISP-HI)	CMP	REG16/MEM16,REG16
3A	0011 1010	MOD REG R/M	(DISP-LO),(DISP-HI)	CMP	REG8,REG8/MEM8
3B	0011 1011	MOD REG R/M	(DISP-LO),(DISP-HI)	CMP	REG16,REG16/MEM16
3C	0011 1100	DATA-8		CMP	AL,IMMED8
3D	0011 1101	DATA-LO	DATA-HI	CMP	AX,IMMED16
3E	0011 1110			DS:	(segment override prefix)
3F	0011 1111			AAS	
40	0100 0000			INC	AX
41	0100 0001			INC	CX
42	0100 0010			INC	DX
43	0100 0011			INC	BX
44	0100 0100			INC	SP
45	0100 0101			INC	BP
46	0100 0110			INC	SI
47	0100 0111			INC	DI
48	0100 1000			DEC	AX
49	0100 1001			DEC	CX
4A	0100 1010			DEC	DX
4B	0100 1011			DEC	BX
4C	0100 1100			DEC	SP
4D	0100 1101			DEC	BP
4E	0100 1110			DEC	SI
4F	0100 1111			DEC	DI
50	0101 0000			PUSH	AX
51	0101 0001			PUSH	CX
52	0101 0010			PUSH	DX
53	0101 0011			PUSH	BX
54	0101 0100			PUSH	SP
55	0101 0101			PUSH	BP
56	0101 0110			PUSH	SI
57	0101 0111			PUSH	DI
58	0101 1000			POP	AX
59	0101 1001			POP	CX
5A	0101 1010			POP	DX
5B	0101 1011			POP	BX
5C	0101 1100			POP	SP
5D	0101 1101			POP	BP
5E	0101 1110			POP	SI
5F	0101 1111			POP	DI
60	0110 0000			(not used)	
61	0110 0001			(not used)	
62	0110 0010			(not used)	
63	0110 0011			(not used)	
64	0110 0100			(not used)	
65	0110 0101			(not used)	
66	0110 0110			(not used)	
67	0110 0111			(not used)	

Table 6-23. Machine Instruction Decoding Guide (Cont'd.)

1ST BYTE		2ND BYTE	BYTES 3,4,5,6	ASM-86 INSTRUCTION FORMAT	
HEX	BINARY				
68	0110 1000			(not used)	
69	0110 1001			(not used)	
6A	0110 1010			(not used)	
6B	0110 1011			(not used)	
6C	0110 1100			(not used)	
6D	0110 1101			(not used)	
6E	0110 1110			(not used)	
6F	0110 1111			(not used)	
70	0111 0000	IP-INC8		JO	SHORT-LABEL
71	0111 0001	IP-INC8		JNO	SHORT-LABEL
72	0111 0010	IP-INC8		JB/JNAE/ JC	SHORT-LABEL
73	0111 0011	IP-INC8		JNB/JAE/ JNC	SHORT-LABEL
74	0111 0100	IP-INC8		JE/JZ	SHORT-LABEL
75	0111 0101	IP-INC8		JNE/JNZ	SHORT-LABEL
76	0111 0110	IP-INC8		JBE/JNA	SHORT-LABEL
77	0111 0111	IP-INC8		JNBE/JA	SHORT-LABEL
78	0111 1000	IP-INC8		JS	SHORT-LABEL
79	0111 1001	IP-INC8		JNS	SHORT-LABEL
7A	0111 1010	IP-INC8		JP/JPE	SHORT-LABEL
7B	0111 1011	IP-INC8		JNP/JPO	SHORT-LABEL
7C	0111 1100	IP-INC8		JL/JNGE	SHORT-LABEL
7D	0111 1101	IP-INC8		JNL/JGE	SHORT-LABEL
7E	0111 1110	IP-INC8		JLE/JNG	SHORT-LABEL
7F	0111 1111	IP-INC8		JNLE/JG	SHORT-LABEL
80	1000 0000	MOD 000 R/M	(DISP-LO),(DISP-HI), DATA-8	ADD	REG8/MEM8,IMMED8
80	1000 0000	MOD 001 R/M	(DISP-LO),(DISP-HI), DATA-8	OR	REG8/MEM8,IMMED8
80	1000 0000	MOD 010 R/M	(DISP-LO),(DISP-HI), DATA-8	ADC	REG8/MEM8,IMMED8
80	1000 0000	MOD 011 R/M	(DISP-LO),(DISP-HI), DATA-8	SBB	REG8/MEM8,IMMED8
80	1000 0000	MOD 100 R/M	(DISP-LO),(DISP-HI), DATA-8	AND	REG8/MEM8,IMMED8
80	1000 0000	MOD 101 R/M	(DISP-LO),(DISP-HI), DATA-8	SUB	REG8/MEM8,IMMED8
80	1000 0000	MOD 110 R/M	(DISP-LO),(DISP-HI), DATA-8	XOR	REG8/MEM8,IMMED8
80	1000 0000	MOD 111 R/M	(DISP-LO),(DISP-HI), DATA-8	CMP	REG8/MEM8,IMMED8
81	1000 0001	MOD 000 R/M	(DISP-LO),(DISP-HI), DATA-LO,DATA-HI	ADD	REG16/MEM16,IMMED16
81	1000 0001	MOD 001 R/M	(DISP-LO),(DISP-HI), DATA-LO,DATA-HI	OR	REG16/MEM16,IMMED16
81	1000 0001	MOD 010 R/M	(DISP-LO),(DISP-HI), DATA-LO,DATA-HI	ADC	REG16/MEM16,IMMED16
81	1000 0001	MOD 011 R/M	(DISP-LO),(DISP-HI), DATA-LO,DATA-HI	SBB	REG16/MEM16,IMMED16

Table 6-23. Machine Instruction Decoding Guide (Cont'd.)

1ST BYTE		2ND BYTE	BYTES 3,4,5,6	ASM-86 INSTRUCTION FORMAT	
HEX	BINARY				
81	1000 0001	MOD 100 R/M	(DISP-LO),(DISP-HI), DATA-LO,DATA-HI	AND	REG16/MEM16,IMMED16
81	1000 0001	MOD 101 R/M	(DISP-LO),(DISP-HI), DATA-LO,DATA-HI	SUB	REG16/MEM16,IMMED16
81	1000 0001	MOD 110 R/M	(DISP-LO),(DISP-HI), DATA-LO,DATA-HI	XOR	REG16/MEM16,IMMED16
81	1000 0001	MOD 111 R/M	(DISP-LO),(DISP-HI), DATA-LO,DATA-HI	CMP	REG16/MEM16,IMMED16
82	1000 0010	MOD 000 R/M	(DISP-LO),(DISP-HI), DATA-8	ADD	REG8/MEM8,IMMED8
82	1000 0010	MOD 001 R/M		(not used)	
82	1000 0010	MOD 010 R/M	(DISP-LO),(DISP-HI), DATA-8	ADC	REG8/MEM8,IMMED8
82	1000 0010	MOD 011 R/M	(DISP-LO),(DISP-HI), DATA-8	SBB	REG8/MEM8,IMMED8
82	1000 0010	MOD 100 R/M		(not used)	
82	1000 0010	MOD 101 R/M	(DISP-LO),(DISP-HI), DATA-8	SUB	REG8/MEM8,IMMED8
82	1000 0010	MOD 110 R/M		(not used)	
82	1000 0010	MOD 111 R/M	(DISP-LO),(DISP-HI), DATA-8	CMP	REG8/MEM8,IMMED8
83	1000 0011	MOD 000 R/M	(DISP-LO),(DISP-HI), DATA-SX	ADD	REG16/MEM16, IMMED8
83	1000 0011	MOD 001 R/M		(not used)	
83	1000 0011	MOD 010 R/M	(DISP-LO), (DISP-HI), DATA-SX	ADC	REG16/MEM16,IMMED8
83	1000 0011	MOD 011 R/M	(DISP-LO),(DISP-HI), DATA-SX	SBB	REG16/MEM16,IMMED8
83	1000 0011	MOD 100 R/M		(not used)	
83	1000 0011	MOD 101 R/M	(DISP-LO),(DISP-HI), DATA-SX	SUB	REG16/MEM16,IMMED8
83	1000 0011	MOD 110 R/M		(not used)	
83	1000 0011	MOD 111 R/M	(DISP-LO),(DISP-HI), DATA-SX	CMP	REG16/MEM16,IMMED8
84	1000 0100	MOD REG R/M	(DISP-LO),(DISP-HI)	TEST	REG8/MEM8,REG8
85	1000 0101	MOD REG R/M	(DISP-LO),(DISP-HI)	TEST	REG16/MEM16,REG16
86	1000 0110	MOD REG R/M	(DISP-LO),(DISP-HI)	XCHG	REG8,REG8/MEM8
87	1000 0111	MOD REG R/M	(DISP-LO),(DISP-HI)	XCHG	REG16,REG16/MEM16
88	1000 1000	MOD REG R/M	(DISP-LO),(DISP-HI)	MOV	REG8/MEM8,REG8
89	1000 1001	MOD REG R/M	(DISP-LO),(DISP-HI)	MOV	REG16/MEM16/REG16
8A	1000 1010	MOD REG R/M	(DISP-LO),(DISP-HI)	MOV	REG8,REG8/MEM8
8B	1000 1011	MOD REG R/M	(DISP-LO),(DISP-HI)	MOV	REG16,REG16/MEM16
8C	1000 1100	MOD 0SR R/M	(DISP-LO),(DISP-HI)	MOV	REG16/MEM16,SEGREG
8C	1000 1100	MOD 1-- R/M		(not used)	
8D	1000 1101	MOD REG R/M	(DISP-LO),(DISP-HI)	LEA	REG16,MEM16
8E	1000 1110	MOD 0SR R/M	(DISP-LO),(DISP-HI)	MOV	SEGREG,REG16/MEM16
8E	1000 1110	MOD 1-- R/M		(not used)	
8F	1000 1111	MOD 000 R/M	(DISP-LO),(DISP-HI)	POP	REG16/MEM16
8F	1000 1111	MOD 001 R/M		(not used)	
8F	1000 1111	MOD 010 R/M		(not used)	

Table 6-23. Machine Instruction Decoding Guide (Cont'd.)

1ST BYTE HEX	BINARY	2ND BYTE	BYTES 3,4,5,6	ASM-86 INSTRUCTION FORMAT	
8F	1000 1111	MOD 011 R/M		(not used)	
8F	1000 1111	MOD 100 R/M		(not used)	
8F	1000 1111	MOD 101 R/M		(not used)	
8F	1000 1111	MOD 110 R/M		(not used)	
8F	1000 1111	MOD 111 R/M		(not used)	
90	1001 0000			NOP	(exchange AX,AX)
91	1001 0001			XCHG	AX,CX
92	1001 0010			XCHG	AX,DX
93	1001 0011			XCHG	AX,BX
94	1001 0100			XCHG	AX,SP
95	1001 0101			XCHG	AX,BP
96	1001 0110			XCHG	AX,SI
97	1001 0111			XCHG	AX,DI
98	1001 1000			CBW	
99	1001 1001			CWD	
9A	1001 1010	DISP-LO	DISP-HI,SEG-LO, SEG-HI	CALL	FAR_PROC
9B	1001 1011			WAIT	
9C	1001 1100			PUSHF	
9D	1001 1101			POPF	
9E	1001 1110			SAHF	
9F	1001 1111			LAHF	
A0	1010 0000	ADDR-LO	ADDR-HI	MOV	AL,MEM8
A1	1010 0001	ADDR-LO	ADDR-HI	MOV	AX,MEM16
A2	1010 0010	ADDR-LO	ADDR-HI	MOV	MEM8,AL
A3	1010 0011	ADDR-LO	ADDR-HI	MOV	MEM16,AL
A4	1010 0100			MOVS	DEST-STR8,SRC-STR8
A5	1010 0101			MOVS	DEST-STR16,SRC-STR16
A6	1010 0110			CMPS	DEST-STR8,SRC-STR8
A7	1010 0111			CMPS	DEST-STR16,SRC-STR16
A8	1010 1000	DATA-8		TEST	AL,IMMED8
A9	1010 1001	DATA-LO	DATA-HI	TEST	AX,IMMED16
AA	1010 1010			STOS	DEST-STR8
AB	1010 1011			STOS	DEST-STR16
AC	1010 1100			LODS	SRC-STR8
AD	1010 1101			LODS	SRC-STR16
AE	1010 1110			SCAS	DEST-STR8
AF	1010 1111			SCAS	DEST-STR16
B0	1011 0000	DATA-8		MOV	AL,IMMED8
B1	1011 0001	DATA-8		MOV	CL,IMMED8
B2	1011 0010	DATA-8		MOV	DL,IMMED8
B3	1011 1011	DATA-8		MOV	BL,IMMED8
B4	1011 0100	DATA-8		MOV	AH,IMMED8
B5	1011 0101	DATA-8		MOV	CH,IMMED8
B6	1011 0110	DATA-8		MOV	DH,IMMED8
B7	1011 0111	DATA-8		MOV	BH,IMMED8
B8	1011 1000	DATA-LO	DATA-HI	MOV	AX,IMMED16
B9	1011 1001	DATA-LO	DATA-HI	MOV	CX,IMMED16
BA	1011 1010	DATA-LO	DATA-HI	MOV	DX,IMMED16
BB	1011 1011	DATA-LO	DATA-HI	MOV	BX,IMMED16

Table 6-23. Machine Instruction Decoding Guide (Cont'd.)

1ST BYTE		2ND BYTE	BYTES 3,4,5,6	ASM-86 INSTRUCTION FORMAT	
HEX	BINARY				
BC	1011 1100	DATA-LO	DATA-HI	MOV	SP,IMMED16
BD	1011 1101	DATA-LO	DATA-HI	MOV	BP,IMMED16
BE	1011 1110	DATA-LO	DATA-HI	MOV	SI,IMMED16
BF	1011 1111	DATA-LO	DATA-HI	MOV	DI,IMMED16
C0	1100 0000			(not used)	
C1	1100 0001			(not used)	
C2	1100 0010	DATA-LO	DATA-HI	RET	IMMED16 (intraseg)
C3	1100 0011			RET	(intrasegment)
C4	1100 0100	MOD REG R/M	(DISP-LO),(DISP-HI)	LES	REG16,MEM16
C5	1100 0101	MOD REG R/M	(DISP-LO),(DISP-HI)	LDS	REG16,MEM16
C6	1100 0110	MOD 000 R/M	(DISP-LO),(DISP-HI), DATA-8	MOV	MEM8,IMMED8
C6	1100 0110	MOD 001 R/M		(not used)	
C6	1100 0110	MOD 010 R/M		(not used)	
C6	1100 0110	MOD 011 R/M		(not used)	
C6	1100 0110	MOD 100 R/M		(not used)	
C6	1100 0110	MOD 101 R/M		(not used)	
C6	1100 0110	MOD 110 R/M		(not used)	
C6	1100 0110	MOD 111 R/M		(not used)	
C7	1100 0111	MOD 000 R/M	(DISP-LO),(DISP-HI), DATA-LO,DATA-HI	MOV	MEM16,IMMED16
C7	1100 0111	MOD 001 R/M		(not used)	
C7	1100 0111	MOD 010 R/M		(not used)	
C7	1100 0111	MOD 011 R/M		(not used)	
C7	1100 0111	MOD 100 R/M		(not used)	
C7	1100 0111	MOD 101 R/M		(not used)	
C7	1100 0111	MOD 110 R/M		(not used)	
C7	1100 0111	MOD 111 R/M		(not used	
C8	1100 1000			(not used)	
C9	1100 1001			(not used)	
CA	1100 1010	DATA-LO	DATA-HI	RET	IMMED16 (intersegment)
CB	1100 1011			RET	(intersegment)
CC	1100 1100			INT	3
CD	1100 1101	DATA-8		INT	IMMED8
CE	1100 1110			INTO	
CF	1100 1111			IRET	
D0	1101 0000	MOD 000 R/M	(DISP-LO),(DISP-HI)	ROL	REG8/MEM8,1
D0	1101 0000	MOD 001 R/M	(DISP-LO),(DISP-HI)	ROR	REG8/MEM8,1
D0	1101 0000	MOD 010 R/M	(DISP-LO),(DISP-HI)	RCL	REG8/MEM8,1
D0	1101 0000	MOD 011 R/M	(DISP-LO),(DISP-HI)	RCR	REG8/MEM8,1
D0	1101 0000	MOD 100 R/M	(DISP-LO),(DISP-HI)	SAL/SHL	REG8/MEM8,1
D0	1101 0000	MOD 101 R/M	(DISP-LO),(DISP-HI)	SHR	REG8/MEM8,1
D0	1101 0000	MOD 110 R/M		(not used)	
D0	1101 0000	MOD 111 R/M	(DISP-LO),(DISP-HI)	SAR	REG8/MEM8,1
D1	1101 0001	MOD 000 R/M	(DISP-LO),(DISP-HI)	ROL	REG16/MEM16,1
D1	1101 0001	MOD 001 R/M	(DISP-LO),(DISP-HI)	ROR	REG16/MEM16,1
D1	1101 0001	MOD 010 R/M	(DISP-LO),(DISP-HI)	RCL	REG16/MEM16,1
D1	1101 0001	MOD 011 R/M	(DISP-LO),(DISP-HI)	RCR	REG16/MEM16,1
D1	1101 0001	MOD 100 R/M	(DISP-LO),(DISP-HI)	SAL/SHL	REG16/MEM16,1

Table 6-23. Machine Instruction Decoding Guide (Cont'd.)

1ST BYTE		2ND BYTE	BYTES 3,4,5,6	ASM-86 INSTRUCTION FORMAT	
HEX	BINARY				
D1	1101 0001	MOD 101 R/M	(DISP-LO),(DISP-HI)	SHR	REG16/MEM16,1
D1	1101 0001	MOD 110 R/M		(not used)	
D1	1101 0001	MOD 111 R/M	(DISP-LO),(DISP-HI)	SAR	REG16/MEM16,1
D2	1101 0010	MOD 000 R/M	(DISP-LO),(DISP-HI)	ROL	REG8/MEM8,CL
D2	1101 0010	MOD 001 R/M	(DISP-LO),(DISP-HI)	ROR	REG8/MEM8,CL
D2	1101 0010	MOD 010 R/M	(DISP-LO),(DISP-HI)	RCL	REG8/MEM8,CL
D2	1101 0010	MOD 011 R/M	(DISP-LO),(DISP-HI)	RCR	REG8/MEM8,CL
D2	1101 0010	MOD 100 R/M	(DISP-LO),(DISP-HI)	SAL/SHL	REG8/MEM8,CL
D2	1101 0010	MOD 101 R/M	(DISP-LO),(DISP-HI)	SHR	REG8/MEM8,CL
D2	1101 0010	MOD 110 R/M		(not used)	
D2	1101 0010	MOD 111 R/M	(DISP-LO),(DISP-HI)	SAR	REG8/MEM8,CL
D3	1101 0011	MOD 000 R/M	(DISP-LO),(DISP-HI)	ROL	REG16/MEM16,CL
D3	1101 0011	MOD 001 R/M	(DISP-LO),(DISP-HI)	ROR	REG16/MEM16,CL
D3	1101 0011	MOD 010 R/M	(DISP-LO),(DISP-HI)	RCL	REG16/MEM16,CL
D3	1101 0011	MOD 011 R/M	(DISP-LO),(DISP-HI)	RCR	REG16/MEM16,CL
D3	1101 0011	MOD 100 R/M	(DISP-LO),(DISP-HI)	SAL/SHL	REG16/MEM16,CL
D3	1101 0011	MOD 101 R/M	(DISP-LO),(DISP-HI)	SHR	REG16/MEM16,CL
D3	1101 0011	MOD 110 R/M		(not used)	
D3	1101 0011	MOD 111 R/M	(DISP-LO),(DISP-HI)	SAR	REG16/MEM16,CL
D4	1101 0100	00001010		AAM	
D5	1101 0101	00001010		AAD	
D6	1101 0110			(not used)	
D7	1101 0111			XLAT	SOURCE-TABLE
D8	1101 1000	MOD 000 R/M			
	1XXX	MOD YYY R/M	(DISP-LO), (DISP-HI)	ESC	OPCODE,SOURCE
DF	1101 1111	MOD 111 R/M			
E0	1110 0000	IP-INC-8		LOOPNE/ LOOPNZ	SHORT-LABEL
E1	1110 0001	IP-INC-8		LOOPE/ LOOPZ	SHORT-LABEL
E2	1110 0010	IP-INC-8		LOOP	SHORT-LABEL
E3	1110 0011	IP-INC-8		JCXZ	SHORT-LABEL
E4	1110 0100	DATA-8		IN	AL,IMMED8
E5	1110 0101	DATA-8		IN	AX,IMMED8
E6	1110 0110	DATA-8		OUT	AL,IMMED8
E7	1110 0111	DATA-8		OUT	AX,IMMED8
E8	1110 1000	IP-INC-LO	IP-INC-HI	CALL	NEAR-PROC
E9	1110 1001	IP-INC-LO	IP-INC-HI	JMP	NEAR-LABEL
EA	1110 1010	IP-LO	IP-HI,CS-LO,CS-HI	JMP	FAR-LABEL
EB	1110 1011	IP-INC8		JMP	SHORT-LABEL
EC	1110 1100			IN	AL,DX
ED	1110 1101			IN	AX,DX
EE	1110 1110			OUT	AL,DX
EF	1110 1111			OUT	AX,DX
F0	1111 0000			LOCK	(prefix)
F1	1111 0001			(not used)	
F2	1111 0010			REPNE/REPNZ	
F3	1111 0011			REP/REPE/REPZ	
F4	1111 0100			HLT	
F5	1111 0101			CMC	

Table 6-23. Machine Instruction Decoding Guide (Cont'd.)

1ST BYTE HEX	1ST BYTE BINARY	2ND BYTE	BYTES 3,4,5,6	ASM-86 INSTRUCTION FORMAT	
F6	1111 0110	MOD 000 R/M	(DISP-LO),(DISP-HI), DATA-8	TEST	REG8/MEM8,IMMED8
F6	1111 0110	MOD 001 R/M		(not used)	
F6	1111 0110	MOD 010 R/M	(DISP-LO),(DISP-HI)	NOT	REG8/MEM8
F6	1111 0110	MOD 011 R/M	(DISP-LO),(DISP-HI)	NEG	REG8/MEM8
F6	1111 0110	MOD 100 R/M	(DISP-LO),(DISP-HI)	MUL	REG8/MEM8
F6	1111 0110	MOD 101 R/M	(DISP-LO),(DISP-HI)	IMUL	REG8/MEM8
F6	1111 0110	MOD 110 R/M	(DISP-LO),(DISP-HI)	DIV	REG8/MEM8
F6	1111 0110	MOD 111 R/M	(DISP-LO),(DISP-HI)	IDIV	REG8/MEM8
F7	1111 0111	MOD 000 R/M	(DISP-LO),(DISP-HI), DATA-LO,DATA-HI	TEST	REG16/MEM16,IMMED16
F7	1111 0111	MOD 001 R/M		(not used)	
F7	1111 0111	MOD 010 R/M	(DISP-LO),(DISP-HI)	NOT	REG16/MEM16
F7	1111 0111	MOD 011 R/M	(DISP-LO),(DISP-HI)	NEG	REG16/MEM16
F7	1111 0111	MOD 100 R/M	(DISP-LO),(DISP-HI)	MUL	REG16/MEM16
F7	1111 0111	MOD 101 R/M	(DISP-LO),(DISP-HI)	IMUL	REG16/MEM16
F7	1111 0111	MOD 110 R/M	(DISP-LO),(DISP-HI)	DIV	REG16/MEM16
F7	1111 0111	MOD 111 R/M	(DISP-LO),(DISP-HI)	IDIV	REG16/MEM16
F8	1111 1000			CLC	
F9	1111 1001			STC	
FA	1111 1010			CLI	
FB	1111 1011			STI	
FC	1111 1100			CLD	
FD	1111 1101			STD	
FE	1111 1110	MOD 000 R/M	(DISP-LO),(DISP-HI)	INC	REG8/MEM8
FE	1111 1110	MOD 001 R/M	(DISP-LO),(DISP-HI)	DEC	REG8/MEM8
FE	1111 1110	MOD 010 R/M		(not used)	
FE	1111 1110	MOD 011 R/M		(not used)	
FE	1111 1110	MOD 100 R/M		(not used)	
FE	1111 1110	MOD 101 R/M		(not used)	
FE	1111 1110	MOD 110 R/M		(not used)	
FE	1111 1110	MOD 111 R/M		(not used)	
FF	1111 1111	MOD 000 R/M	(DISP-LO),(DISP-HI)	INC	MEM16
FF	1111 1111	MOD 001 R/M	(DISP-LO),(DISP-HI)	DEC	MEM16
FF	1111 1111	MOD 010 R/M	(DISP-LO),(DISP-HI)	CALL	REG16/MEM16 (intra)
FF	1111 1111	MOD 011 R/M	(DISP-LO),(DISP-HI)	CALL	MEM16 (intersegment)
FF	1111 1111	MOD 100 R/M	(DISP-LO),(DISP-HI)	JMP	REG16/MEM16 (intra)
FF	1111 1111	MOD 101 R/M	(DISP-LO),(DISP-HI)	JMP	MEM16 (intersegment)
FF	1111 1111	MOD 110 R/M	(DISP-LO),(DISP-HI)	PUSH	MEM16
FF	1111 1111	MOD 111 R/M		(not used)	

Hi \ Lo	0	1	2	3	4	5	6	7	8	9	A	B	C	D	E	F
0	ADD b.f.r/m	ADD w.f.r/m	ADD b.t.r/m	ADD w.t.r/m	ADD b.ia	ADD w.ia	PUSH ES	POP ES	OR b.f.r/m	OR w.f.r/m	OR b.t.r/m	OR w.t.r/m	OR b.i	OR w.i	PUSH CS	
1	ADC b.f.r/m	ADC w.f.r/m	ADC b.t.r/m	ADC w.t.r/m	ADC b.i	ADC w.i	PUSH SS	POP SS	SBB b.f.r/m	SBB w.f.r/m	SBB b.t.r/m	SBB w.t.r/m	SBB b.i	SBB w.i	PUSH DS	POP DS
2	AND b.f.r/m	AND w.f.r/m	AND b.t.r/m	AND w.t.r/m	AND b.i	AND w.i	SEG ES	DAA	SUB b.f.r/m	SUB w.f.r/m	SUB b.t.r/m	SUB w.t.r/m	SUB b.i	SUB w.i	SEG CS	DAS
3	XOR b.f.r/m	XOR w.f.r/m	XOR b.t.r/m	XOR w.t.r/m	XOR b.i	XOR w.i	SEG SS	AAA	CMP b.f.r/m	CMP w.f.r/m	CMP b.t.r/m	CMP w.t.r/m	CMP b.i	CMP w.i	SEG DS	AAS
4	INC AX	INC CX	INC DX	INC BX	INC SP	INC BP	INC SI	INC DI	DEC AX	DEC CX	DEC DX	DEC BX	DEC SP	DEC BP	DEC SI	DEC DI
5	PUSH AX	PUSH CX	PUSH DX	PUSH BX	PUSH SP	PUSH BP	PUSH SI	PUSH DI	POP AX	POP CX	POP DX	POP BX	POP SP	POP BP	POP SI	POP DI
6																
7	JO	JNO	JB/ JNAE	JNB/ JAE	JE/ JZ	JNE/ JNZ	JBE/ JNA	JNBE/ JA	JS	JNS	JP/ JPE	JNP/ JPO	JL/ JNGE	JNL/ JGE	JLE/ JNG	JNLE/ JG
8	Immed b.r/m	Immed w.r/m	Immed b.r/m	Immed is.r/m	TEST b.r/m	TEST w.r/m	XCHG b.r/m	XCHG w.r/m	MOV b.f.r/m	MOV w.f.r/m	MOV b.t.r/m	MOV w.t.r/m	MOV sr.f.r/m	LEA	MOV sr.t.r/m	POP r/m
9	XCHG AX	XCHG CX	XCHG DX	XCHG BX	XCHG SP	XCHG BP	XCHG SI	XCHG DI	CBW	CWD	CALL l.d	WAIT	PUSHF	POPF	SAHF	LAHF
A	MOV m → AL	MOV m → AX	MOV AL → m	MOV AX → m	MOVS	MOVS	CMPS	CMPS	TEST b.i.a	TEST w.i.a	STOS	STOS	LODS	LODS	SCAS	SCAS
B	MOV i → AL	MOV i → CL	MOV i → DL	MOV i → BL	MOV i → AH	MOV i → CH	MOV i → DH	MOV i → BH	MOV i → AX	MOV i → CX	MOV i → DX	MOV i → BX	MOV i → SP	MOV i → BP	MOV i → SI	MOV i → DI
C			RET. (i+SP)	RET	LES	LDS	MOV b.i.r/m	MOV w.i.r/m			RET. l.(i+SP)	RET l	INT Type 3	INT (Any)	INTO	IRET
D	Shift b	Shift w	Shift b.v	Shift w.v	AAM	AAD		XLAT	ESC 0	ESC 1	ESC 2	ESC 3	ESC 4	ESC 5	ESC 6	ESC 7
E	LOOPNZ/ LOOPNE	LOOPZ/ LOOPE	LOOP	JCXZ	IN b	IN w	OUT b	OUT w	CALL d	JMP d	JMP l.d	JMP si.d	IN v,b	IN v,w	OUT v,b	OUT v,w
F	LOCK		REP	REP z	HLT	CMC	Grp 1 b.r/m	Grp 1 w.r/m	CLC	STC	CLI	STI	CLD	STD	Grp 2 b.r/m	Grp 2 w.r/m

where

mod☐r/m	000	001	010	011	100	101	110	111
Immed	ADD	OR	ADC	SBB	AND	SUB	XOR	CMP
Shift	ROL	ROR	RCL	RCR	SHL/SAL	SHR	—	SAR
Grp 1	TEST	—	NOT	NEG	MUL	IMUL	DIV	IDIV
Grp 2	INC	DEC	CALL id	CALL l.id	JMP id	JMP l.id	PUSH	—

b = byte operation
d = direct
f = from CPU reg
i = immediate
ia = immed. to accum.
id = indirect
is = immed. byte, sign ext.
l = long ie. intersegment

m = memory
r/m = EA is second byte
si = short intrasegment
sr = segment register
t = to CPU reg
v = variable
w = word operation
z = zero

240487-001

Figure 6-28. Machine Instruction Encoding Matrix

DEVICE PIN DEFINITIONS

The following paragraphs present functional descriptions of all input/output signals and electrical descriptions of all of the input/output pins on the 8086 and 8088 40-pin DIP's.

Functional Description of All Signals

Figure 6-29 shows the 8086/8088 DIP pin assignments and Table 6-24 provides a complete functional description of each device pin signal and correlates the description to the pin number and associated signal symbol.

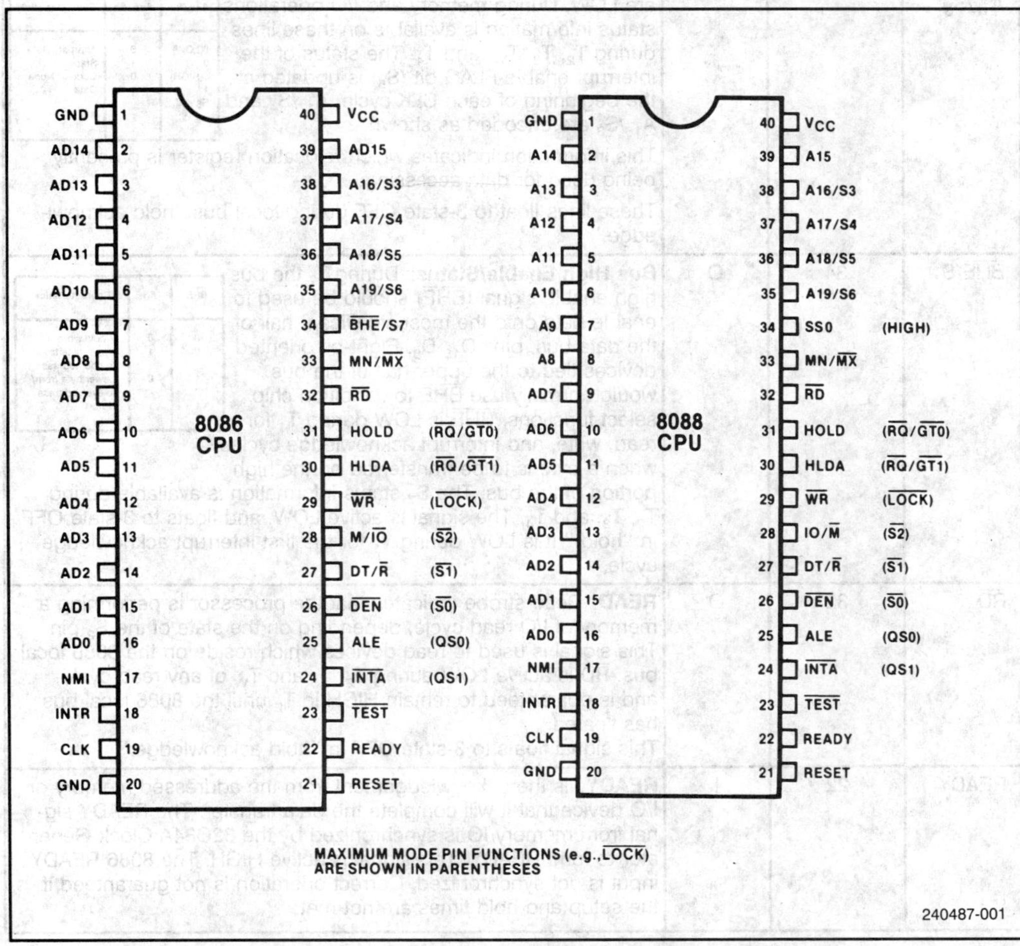

Figure 6-29. 8086/8088 DIP Pin Assignments

Table 6-24. 8086/8088 Device Pin Descriptions

The following pin function descriptions are for 8086 systems in either minimum or maximum mode. The "Local Bus" in these descriptions is the direct multiplexed bus interface connection to the 8086 (without regard to additional bus buffers).

<table>
<tr><th>Symbol</th><th>Pin No.</th><th>Type</th><th>Name and Function</th></tr>
<tr><td>AD_{15}-AD_0</td><td>2-16, 39</td><td>I/O</td><td>Address Data Bus: These lines constitute the time multiplexed memory/IO address (T_1) and data (T_2, T_3, T_W, T_4) bus. A_0 is analogous to $\overline{BHE}$ for the lower byte of the data bus, pins D_7-D_0. It is LOW during T_1 when a byte is to be transferred on the lower portion of the bus in memory or I/O operations. Eight-bit oriented devices tied to the lower half would normally use A_0 to condition chip select functions. (See $\overline{BHE}$.) These lines are active HIGH and float to 3-state OFF during interrupt acknowledge and local bus "hold acknowledge."</td></tr>
<tr><td>A_{19}/S_6,
A_{18}/S_5,
A_{17}/S_4,
A_{16}/S_3</td><td>35-38</td><td>O</td><td>Address/Status: During T_1 these are the four most significant address lines for memory operations. During I/O operations these lines are LOW. During memory and I/O operations status information is available on these lines during T_2, T_3, T_W, and T_4. The status of the interrupt enable FLAG bit (S_5) is updated at the beginning of each CLK cycle. A_{17}/S_4 and A_{16}/S_3 are encoded as shown.
<table>
<tr><th>A_{17}/S_4</th><th>A_{16}/S_3</th><th>Characteristics</th></tr>
<tr><td>0(LOW)</td><td>0</td><td>Alternate Data</td></tr>
<tr><td>0</td><td>1</td><td>Stack</td></tr>
<tr><td>1(HIGH)</td><td>0</td><td>Code or None</td></tr>
<tr><td>1</td><td>1</td><td>Data</td></tr>
<tr><td>S_6 is 0 (LOW)</td><td></td><td></td></tr>
</table>
This information indicates which relocation register is presently being used for data accessing.
These lines float to 3-state OFF during local bus "hold acknowledge."</td></tr>
<tr><td>$\overline{BHE}/S_7$</td><td>34</td><td>O</td><td>Bus High Enable/Status: During T_1 the bus high enable signal ($\overline{BHE}$) should be used to enable data onto the most significant half of the data bus, pins D_{15}-D_8. Eight-bit oriented devices tied to the upper half of the bus would normally use $\overline{BHE}$ to condition chip select functions. $\overline{BHE}$ is LOW during T_1 for read, write, and interrupt acknowledge cycles when a byte is to be transferred on the high portion of the bus. The S_7 status information is available during T_2, T_3, and T_4. The signal is active LOW, and floats to 3-state OFF in "hold." It is LOW during T_1 for the first interrupt acknowledge cycle.
<table>
<tr><th>$\overline{BHE}$</th><th>A_0</th><th>Characteristics</th></tr>
<tr><td>0</td><td>0</td><td>Whole word</td></tr>
<tr><td>0</td><td>1</td><td>Upper byte from/ to odd address</td></tr>
<tr><td>1</td><td>0</td><td>Lower byte from/ to even address</td></tr>
<tr><td>1</td><td>1</td><td>None</td></tr>
</table></td></tr>
<tr><td>$\overline{RD}$</td><td>32</td><td>O</td><td>READ: Read strobe indicates that the processor is performing a memory of I/O read cycle, depending on the state of the S_2 pin. This signal is used to read devices which reside on the 8086 local bus. $\overline{RD}$ is active LOW during T_2, T_3 and T_W of any read cycle, and is guaranteed to remain HIGH in T_2 until the 8086 local bus has floated.
This signal floats to 3-state OFF in "hold acknowledge."</td></tr>
<tr><td>READY</td><td>22</td><td>I</td><td>READY: is the acknowledgement from the addressed memory or I/O device that it will complete the data transfer. The READY signal from memory/IO is synchronized by the 82C84A Clock Generator to form READY. This signal is active HIGH. The 8086 READY input is not synchronized. Correct operation is not guaranteed if the setup and hold times are not met.</td></tr>
</table>

Table 6-24. 8086/8088 Device Pin Descriptions

The following pin function descriptions are for 8086 systems in either minimum or maximum mode. The "Local Bus" in these descriptions is the direct multiplexed bus interface connection to the 8086 (without regard to additional bus buffers).

Symbol	Pin No.	Type	Name and Function
INTR	18	I	**Interrupt Request**: is a level triggered input which is sampled during the last clock cycle of each instruction to determine if the processor should enter into an interrupt acknowledge operation. A subroutine is vectored to via an interrupt vector lookup table located in system memory. It can be internally masked by software resetting the interrupt enable bit. INTR is internally synchronized. This signal is active HIGH.
TEST	23	I	$\overline{\textbf{TEST}}$: input is examined by the "Wait" instruction. If the $\overline{\text{TEST}}$ input is LOW execution continues, otherwise the processor waits in an "Idle" state. This input is synchronized internally during each clock cycle on the leading edge of CLK.
NMI	17	I	**Non-maskable interrupt**: an edge triggered input which causes a type 2 interrupt. A subroutine is vectored to via an interrupt vector lookup table located in system memory. NMI is not maskable internally by software. A transition from a LOW to HIGH initiates the interrupt at the end of the current instruction. This input is internally synchronized.
RESET	21	I	**Reset**: causes the processor to immediately terminate its present activity. The signal must be active HIGH for at least four clock cycles. It restarts execution, as described in the Instruction Set description, when RESET returns LOW. RESET is internally synchronized.
CLK	19	I	**CLOCK**: provides the basic timing for the processor and bus controller. It is asymmetric with a 33% duty cycle to provide optimized internal timing.
V_{CC}	40		V_{CC}: +5V power supply pin.
GND	1, 20		**Ground**
MN/$\overline{\text{MX}}$	33	I	**Minimum/Maximum**: indicates what mode the processor is to operate in. The two modes are discussed in the following sections.
The following pin function descriptions are for the 8086/82C88 system in maximum mode (i.e., MN/$\overline{\text{MX}}$ = V_{SS}). Only the pin functions which are unique to maximum mode are described; all other pin functions are as described above.			
$\overline{S}_2$, $\overline{S}_1$, $\overline{S}_0$	26-28	O	**Status**: active during T_4, T_1, and T_2 and is returned to the passive state (1,1,1) during T_3 or during T_W when READY is HIGH. This status is used by the 82C88 Bus Controller to generate all memory and I/O access control signals. Any change by $\overline{S}_2$, $\overline{S}_1$, or $\overline{S}_0$ during T_4 is used to indicate the beginning of a bus cycle, and the return to the passive state in T_3 or T_W is used to indicate the end of a bus cycle. These signals float to 3-state OFF in "hold acknowledge." These status lines are encoded as shown.

$\overline{S_2}$	$\overline{S_1}$	$\overline{S_0}$	Characteristics
0(LOW)	0	0	Interrupt Acknowledge
0	0	1	Read I/O Port
0	1	0	Write I/O Port
0	1	1	Halt
1(HIGH)	0	0	Code Access
1	0	1	Read Memory
1	1	0	Write Memory
1	1	1	Passive

Table 6-24. 8086/8088 Device Pin Descriptions

The following pin function descriptions are for 8086 systems in either minimum or maximum mode. The "Local Bus" in these descriptions is the direct multiplexed bus interface connection to the 8086 (without regard to additional bus buffers).

Symbol	Pin No.	Type	Name and Function
$\overline{RQ/GT}_0$, $\overline{RQ/GT}_1$	30,31	I/O	**Request/Grant**: pins are used by other local bus masters to force the processor to release the local bus at the end of the processor's current bus cycle. Each pin is bidirectional with RQ/GT_0 having higher priority than $\overline{RQ/GT}_1$. $\overline{RQ/GT}$ has an internal pull-up resistor so may be left unconnected. The request/grant sequence is as follows (see Figure 9): 1. A pulse of 1 CLK wide from another local bus master indicates a local bus request ("hold") to the 8086 (pulse 1). 2. During a T_4 or T_1 clock cycle, a pulse 1 CLK wide from the 8086 to the requesting master (pulse 2), indicates that the 8086 has allowed the local bus to float and that it will enter the "hold acknowledge" state at the next CLK. The CPU's bus interface unit is disconnected logically from the local bus during "hold acknowledge." 3. A pulse 1 CLK wide from the requesting master indicates to the 8086 (pulse 3) that the "hold" request is about to end and that the 8086 can reclaim the local bus at the next CLK. Each master-master exchange of the local bus is a sequence of 3 pulses. There must be one dead CLK cycle after each bus exchange. Pulses are active LOW. If the request is made while the CPU is performing a memory cycle, it will release the local bus during T_4 of the cycle when all the following conditions are met: 1. Request occurs on or before T_2. 2. Current cycle is not the low byte of a word (on an odd address). 3. Current cycle is not the first acknowledge of an interrupt acknowledge sequence. 4. A locked instruction is not currently executing.
			If the local bus is idle when the request is made the two possible events will follow: 1. Local bus will be released during the next clock. 2. A memory cycle will start within 3 clocks. Now the four rules for a currently active memory cycle apply with condition number 1 already satisfied.
$\overline{LOCK}$	29	O	**$\overline{LOCK}$**: output indicates that other system bus masters are not to gain control of the system bus while $\overline{LOCK}$ is active LOW. The $\overline{LOCK}$ signal is activated by the "LOCK" prefix instruction and remains active until the completion of the next instruction. This signal is active LOW, and floats to 3-state OFF in "hold acknowledge."
QS_1,QS_0	24, 25	O	**Queue Status**: The queue status is valid during the CLK cycle after which the queue operation is performed. QS_1 and QS_0 provide status to allow external tracking of the internal 8086 instruction queue.

QS_1	QS_0	Characteristics
0(LOW)	0	No Operation
0	1	First Byte of Op Code from Queue
1(HIGH)	0	Empty the Queue
1	1	Subsequent Byte from Queue

Table 6-24. 8086/8088 Device Pin Descriptions

The following pin function descriptions are for 8086 systems in either minimum or maximum mode. The "Local Bus" in these descriptions is the direct multiplexed bus interface connection to the 8086 (without regard to additional bus buffers).

Symbol	Pin No.	Type	Name and Function
The following pin function descriptions are for the 8086 in minimum mode (i.e., $MN/\overline{MX} = V_{CC}$). Only the pin functions which are unique to minimum mode are described; all other pin functions are as described above.			
$M/\overline{IO}$	28	O	**Status line**: logically equivalent to S_2 in the maximum mode. It is used to distinguish a memory access from an I/O access. $M/\overline{IO}$ becomes valid in the T_4 preceding a bus cycle and remains valid until the final T_4 of the cycle (M = HIGH, IO = LOW). $M/\overline{IO}$ floats to 3-state OFF in local bus "hold acknowledge."
$\overline{WR}$	29	O	**Write**: indicates that the processor is performing a write memory or write I/O cycle, depending on the state of the $M/\overline{IO}$ signal. $\overline{WR}$ is active for T_2, T_3 and T_W of any write cycle. It is active LOW, and floats to 3-state OFF in local bus "hold acknowledge."
$\overline{INTA}$	24	O	**$\overline{INTA}$** is used as a read strobe for interrupt acknowledge cycles. It is active LOW during T_2, T_3 and T_W of each interrupt acknowledge cycle.
ALE	25	O	**Address Latch Enable**: provided by the processor to latch the address into the address latch. It is a HIGH pulse active during T_1 of any bus cycle. Note that ALE is never floated.
$DT/\overline{R}$	27	O	**Data Transmit/Receive**: needed in minimum system that desires to use a data bus transceiver. It is used to control the direction of data flow through the transceiver. Logically $DT/\overline{R}$ is equivalent to $\overline{S_1}$ in the maximum mode, and its timing is the same as for $M/\overline{IO}$. (T = HIGH, R = LOW.) This signal floats to 3-state OFF in local bus "hold acknowledge."
$\overline{DEN}$	26	O	**Data Enable**: provided as an output enable for the data bus transceiver in a minimum system which uses the transceiver. $\overline{DEN}$ is active LOW during each memory and I/O access and for INTA cycles. For a read or $\overline{INTA}$ cycle it is active from the middle of T_2 until the middle of T_4, while for a write cycle it is active from the beginning of T_2 until the middle of T_4. $\overline{DEN}$ floats to 3-state OFF in local bus "hold acknowledge."
HOLD, HLDA	31, 30	I/O	**HOLD**: indicates that another master is requesting a local bus "hold." To be acknowledged, HOLD must be active HIGH. The processor receiving the "hold" request will issue HLDA (HIGH) as an acknowledgement in the middle of T_1 clock cycle. Simultaneous with the issuance of HLDA the processor will float the local bus and control lines. After HOLD is detected as being LOW, the processor will LOWER the HLDA, and when the processor needs to run another cycle, it will again drive the local bus and control lines. The same rules as for $\overline{RQ}/\overline{GT}$ apply regarding when the local bus will be released. HOLD is not an asynchronous input. External synchronization should be provided if the system cannot otherwise guarantee the setup time.

Electrical Description of Pins

The absolute maximum ratings for the 8086/8088 device are as follows.

ABSOLUTE MAXIMUM RATINGS

Ambient Temperature Under Bias	0°C to 70°C
Storage Temperature	−65°C to +150°C
Voltage on Any Pin with Respect to GND	−1.0 to +7V
Power Dissipation	2.5 Watt

Stresses above those listed above may cause permanent damage to the device. These values present stress ratings only and functional operation of the device at these or any other conditions above those indicated in the operational sections of the device specifications is not implied. Exposure to absolute maximum conditions for extended period of time may affect the device reliability.

Table 6-25 presents the D.C. voltage characteristics of the 8086/8088 CPU's. Table 6-26 lists the A.C. characteristics timing requirements and timing response for minimum complexity systems, and Table 6-27 lists the A.C. characteristics timing requirements and timing responses for maximum complexity systems (using 82C88 bus controller). Figure 6-30 and Figure 6-31 present waveforms for the minimum mode and maximum mode operation related to the preceding A.C. characteristics tables.

Operating modes

One of the unique features the 8086 and 8088 CPU's allow the user is the ability to select between two functional definitions of a subset of the 8086/8088 outputs. This enables the user to tailor the intended CPU system environment. This "system tailoring" is accomplished by strapping the CPU's MN/MX* (minimum/maximum) input pin. Table 6-28 defines the 8086 and 8088 pin assignments for both the minimum and maximum modes of operation.

In the minimum mode, the CPU's support small systems by strapping the MN/MX* pin to +5V. In this mode of operation, the 8086/8088 CPU generates all bus control signals (DT/R*, DEN*, ALE and either M/IO* or IO/M*) and the command output signals (RD*, WR* or INTA*). The CPU also provides a mechanism for requesting bus access (HOLD/HLDA) that is compatible with bus master type controllers (e.g., the Intel 8237A DMA Controller).

When a bus master requires bus access in the minimum mode, it activages the HOLD input to the CPU through its request logic. In response to the "hold" request, the CPU activates HLDA as an acknowledgement to the bus master, requesting the bus, and simultaneously floats the system bus and control lines. Since a bus request is asynchronous, the CPU samples the HOLD input on the positive transition of each CLK signal and activates HLDA at the end of either the current bus cycle (if a bus cycle is in progress) or idle clock period. The CPU maintains the hold state until the bus master inactivates the HOLD input. At that time the CPU regains control of the system bus. Note that during a "hold" state, the CPU continues to execute instructions until a bus cycle is required.

Table 6-25. D.C. Characteristics

(8086: T_A = 0°C to 70°C, V_{CC} = 5V ± 10%)
(8086-1: T_A = 0°C to 70°C, V_{CC} = 5V ± 5%)
(8086-2: T_A = 0°C to 70°C, V_{CC} = 5V ± 5%)

Symbol	Parameter	Min.	Max.	Units	Test Conditions
V_{IL}	Input Low Voltage	−0.5	+0.8	V	
V_{IH}	Input High Voltage	2.0	V_{CC}+0.5	V	
V_{OL}	Output Low Voltage		0.45	V	I_{OL} = 2.5 mA
V_{OH}	Output High Voltage	2.4		V	I_{OH} = −400 μA
I_{CC}	Power Supply Current: 8086 8086-1 8086-2		340 360 350	mA	T_A = 25°C
I_{LI}	Input Leakage Current		±10	μA	0V ≤ V_{IN} ≤ V_{CC}
I_{LO}	Output Leakage Current		±10	μA	0.45V ≤ V_{OUT} ≤ V_{CC}
V_{CL}	Clock Input Low Voltage	−0.5	+0.6	V	
V_{CH}	Clock Input High Voltage	3.9	V_{CC} + 1.0	V	
C_{IN}	Capacitance of Input Buffer (All input except AD_0 – AD_{15}, $\overline{RQ}/\overline{GT}$)		15	pF	fc = 1 MHz
C_{IO}	Capacitance of I/O Buffer (AD_0 – AD_{15}, $\overline{RQ}/\overline{GT}$)		15	pF	fc = 1 MHz

Table 6-26. A.C. Timing Requirements for Minimum Complexity System

(8086: T_A = 0°C to 70°C, V_{CC} = 5V ± 10%)
(8086-1: T_A = 0°C to 70°C, V_{CC} = 5V ± 5%)
(8086-2: T_A = 0°C to 70°C, V_{CC} = 5V ± 5%)

MINIMUM COMPLEXITY SYSTEM TIMING REQUIREMENTS

Symbol	Parameter	8086		8086-1		8086-2		Units	Test Conditions
		Min.	Max.	Min.	Max.	Min.	Max.		
TCLCL	CLK Cycle Period	200	500	100	500	125	500	ns	
TCLCH	CLK Low Time	118		53		68		ns	
TCHCL	CLK High Time	69		39		44		ns	
TCH1CH2	CLK Rise Time		10		10		10	ns	From 1.0V to 3.5V
TCL2CL1	CLK Fall Time		10		10		10	ns	From 3.5V to 1.0V
TDVCL	Data in Setup Time	30		5		20		ns	
TCLDX	Data in Hold Time	10		10		10		ns	
TR1VCL	RDY Setup Time into 82C84A (see Notes 1, 2)	35		35		35		ns	
TCLR1X	RDY Hold Time into 82C84A (See Notes 1, 2)	0		0		0		ns	
TRYHCH	READY Setup Time into 8086	118		53		68		ns	
TCHRYX	READY Hold Time into 8086	30		20		20		ns	
TRYLCL	READY Inactive to CLK (See Note 3)	−8		−10		−8		ns	
THVCH	HOLD Setup Time	35		20		20		ns	
TILIH	Input Rise Time (Except CLK)		20		20		20	ns	From 0.8V to 2.0V
TIHIL	Input Fall Time (Except CLK)		12		12		12	ns	From 2.0V to 0.8V
TINVCH	INTR, NMI, TEST Setup Time (See Note 2)	30		15		15		ns	

Table 6-26. A.C. Timing Requirements for Minimum Complexity System
(8086: T_A = 0°C to 70°C, V_{CC} = 5V ±10%)
(8086-1: T_A = 0°C to 70°C, V_{CC} = 5V ± 5%)
(8086-2: T_A = 0°C to 70°C, V_{CC} = 5V ± 5%)

TIMING RESPONSES

Symbol	Parameter	8086		8086-1		8086-2		Units	Test Conditions
		Min.	Max.	Min.	Max.	Min.	Max.		
TCLAV	Address Valid Delay	10	110	10	50	10	60	ns	
TCLAX	Address Hold Time	10		10		10		ns	
TCLAZ	Address Float Delay	TCLAX	80	10	40	TCLAX	50	ns	
TLHLL	ALE Width	TCLCH-20		TCLCH-10		TCLCH-10		ns	
TCLLH	ALE Active Delay		80		40		50	ns	
TCHLL	ALE Inactive Delay		85		45		55	ns	
TLLAX	Address Hold Time to ALE Inactive	TCHCL-10		TCHCL-10		TCHCL-10		ns	
TCLDV	Data Valid Delay	10	110	10	50	10	60	ns	
TCHDX	Data Hold Time	10		10		10		ns	
TWHDX	Data Hold Time after WR	TCLCH-30		TCLCH-25		TCLCH-30		ns	
TCVCTV	Control Active Delay 1	10	110	10	50	10	70	ns	
TCHCTV	Control Active Delay 2	10	110	10	45	10	60	ns	
TCVCTX	Control Inactive Delay	10	110	10	50	10	70	ns	
TAZRL	Address Float to READ Active	0		0		0		ns	
TCLRL	$\overline{RD}$ Active Delay	10	165	10	70	10	100	ns	
TCLRH	$\overline{RD}$ Inactive Delay	10	150	10	60	10	80	ns	
TRHAV	$\overline{RD}$ Inactive to Next Address Active	TCLCL-45		TCLCL-35		TCLCL-40		ns	
TCLHAV	HLDA Valid Delay	10	160	10	60	10	100	ns	
TRLRH	$\overline{RD}$ Width	2TCLCL-75		2TCLCL-40		2TCLCL-50		ns	
TWLWH	$\overline{WR}$ Width	2TCLCL-60		2TCLCL-35		2TCLCL-40		ns	
TAVAL	Address Valid to ALE Low	TCLCH-60		TCLCH-35		TCLCH-40		ns	
TOLOH	Output Rise Time		20		20		20	ns	From 0.8V to 2.0V
TOHOL	Output Fall Time		12		12		12	ns	From 2.0V to 0.8V

NOTES:

1. Signal at 82C84A
2. Setup requirement for asynchronous signal only to guarantee recognition at next CLK.
3. Applies only to T2 state (8 ns into T3).

Table 6-27. A.C. Timing Requirements for Maximum Complexity System

MAX MODE SYSTEM (USING 82C88 BUS CONTROLLER) TIMING REQUIREMENTS

Symbol	Parameter	8086		8086-1		8086-2		Units	Test Conditions
		Min.	Max.	Min.	Max.	Min.	Max.		
TCLCL	CLK Cycle Period	200	500	100	500	125	500	ns	
TCLCH	CLK Low Time	118		53		68		ns	
TCHCL	CLK High Time	69		39		44		ns	
TCH1CH2	CLK Rise Time		10		10		10	ns	From 1.0V to 3.5V
TCL2CL1	CLK Fall Time		10		10		10	ns	From 3.5V to 1.0V
TDVCL	Data in Setup Time	30		5		20		ns	
TCLDX	Data in Hold Time	10		10		10		ns	
TR1VCL	RDY Setup Time into 82C84A (see Notes 1, 2)	35		35		35		ns	
TCLR1X	RDY Hold Time into 82C84A (See Notes 1, 2)	0		0		0		ns	
TRYHCH	READY Setup Time into 8086	118		53		68		ns	
TCHRYX	READY Hold Time into 8086	30		20		20		ns	
TRYLCL	READY Inactive to CLK (See Note 4)	−8		−10		−8		ns	
TINVCH	Setup Time for Recognition (INTR, NMI, $\overline{TEST}$) (See Note 2)	30		15		15		ns	
TGVCH	$\overline{RG}/\overline{GT}$ Setup Time	30		15		15		ns	
TCHGX	$\overline{RQ}$ Hold Time into 8086	40		20		30		ns	
TILIH	Input Rise Time (Except CLK)		20		20		20	ns	From 0.8V to 2.0V
TIHIL	Input Fall Time (Except CLK)		12		12		12	ns	From 2.0V to 0.8V

NOTES:
1. Signal at 82C84A or 82C88 shown for reference only.
2. Setup requirement for asynchronous signal only to guarantee recognition at next CLK.
3. Applies only to T3 and wait states.
4. Applies only to T2 state (8 ns into T3).
5. Change from 1985 Handbook.

Table 6-27. A.C. Timing Requirements for Maximum Complexity System (Cont'd.)

TIMING RESPONSES

Symbol	Parameter	8086		8086-1		8086-2		Units	Test Conditions
		Min.	Max.	Min.	Max.	Min.	Max.		
TCLML	Command Active Delay (See Note 1)	10	35	10	35	10	35	ns	
TCLMH	Command Inactive Delay (See Note 1)	10	35	10	35	10	35	ns	
TRYHSH	READY Active to Status Passive (See Note 3)		110		45		65	ns	
TCHSV	Status Active Delay	10	110	10	45	10	60	ns	
TCLSH	Status Inactive Delay	10	130	10	55	10	70	ns	
TCLAV	Address Valid Delay	10	110	10	50	10	60	ns	
TCLAX	Address Hold Time	10		10		10		ns	
TCLAZ	Address Float Delay	TCLAX	80	10	40	TCLAX	50	ns	
TSVLH	Status Valid to ALE High (See Note 1)		15		15		15	ns	
TSVMCH	Status Valid to MCE High (See Note 1)		15		15		15	ns	
TCLLH	CLK Low to ALE Valid (See Note 1)		15		15		15	ns	
TCLMCH	CLK Low to MCE High (See Note 1)		15		15		15	ns	
TCHLL	ALE Inactive Delay (See Note 1)		15		15		15	ns	
TCLMCL	MCE Inactive Delay (See Note 1)		15		15		15	ns	
TCLDV	Data Valid Delay	10	110	10	50	10	60	ns	
TCHDX	Data Hold Time	10		10		10		ns	
TCVNV	Control Active Delay (See Note 1)	5	45	5	45	5	45	ns	
TCVNX	Control Inactive Delay (See Note 1)	10	45	10	45	10	45	ns	
TAZRL	Address Float to Read Active	0		0		0		ns	
TCLRL	RD Active Delay	10	165	10	70	10	100	ns	
TCLRH	RD Inactive Delay	10	150	10	60	10	80	ns	
TRHAV	RD Inactive to Next Address Active	TCLCL-45		TCLCL-35		TCLCL-40		ns	
TCHDTL	Direction Control Active Delay (See Note 1)		50		50		50	ns	
TCHDTH	Direction Control Inactive Delay (See Note 1)		30		30		30	ns	
TCLGL	GT Active Delay (See Note 5)	0	85	0	38	0	50	ns	
TCLGH	GT Inactive Delay	0	85	0	45	0	50	ns	
TRLRH	RD Width	2TCLCL-75		2TCLCL-40		2TCLCL-50		ns	
TOLOH	Output Rise Time		20		20		20	ns	From 0.8V to 2.0V
TOHOL	Output Fall Time		12		12		12	ns	From 2.0V to 0.8V

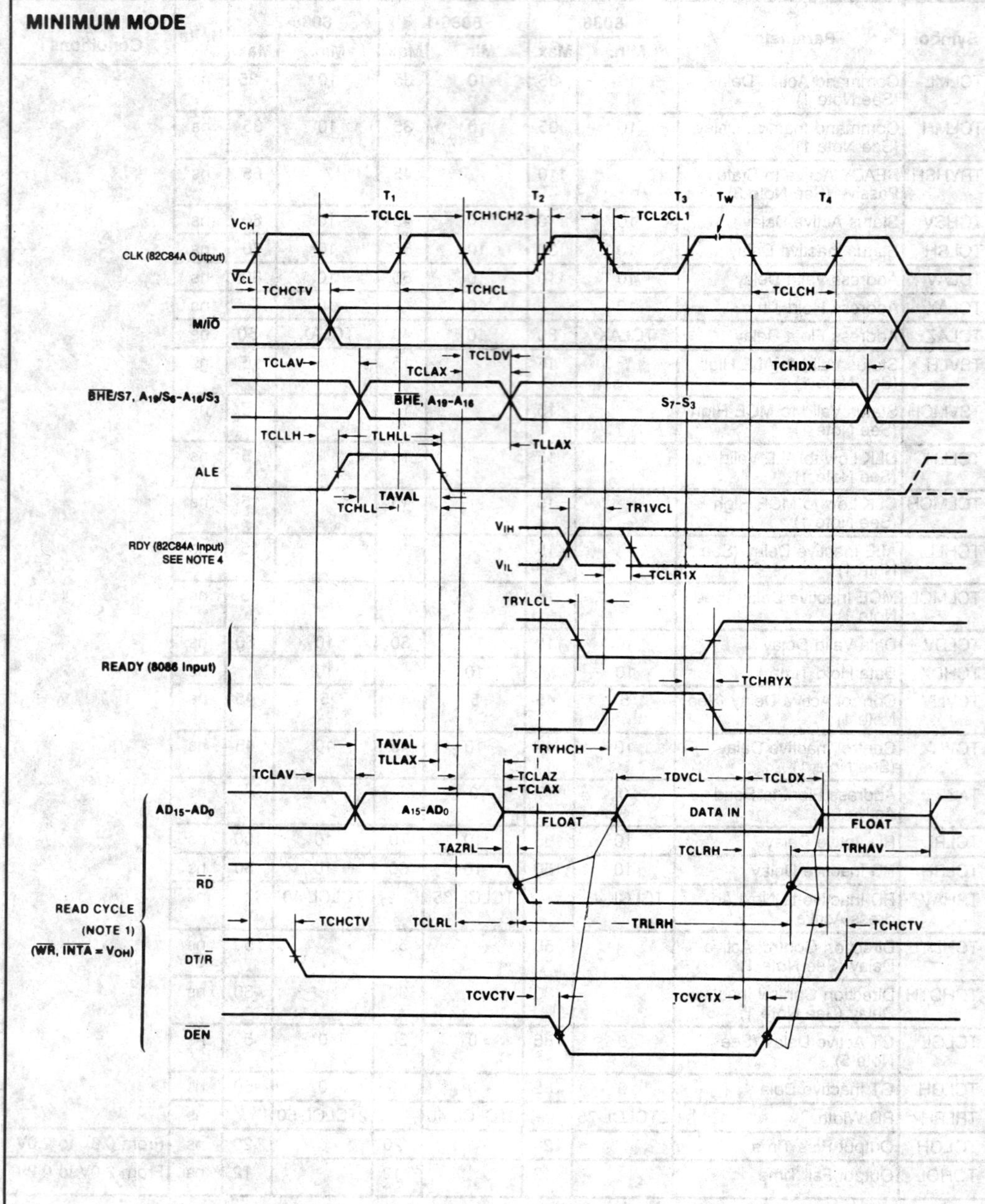

Figure 6-30. Minimum Mode Waveforms

WAVEFORMS (Continued)

MINIMUM MODE (Continued)

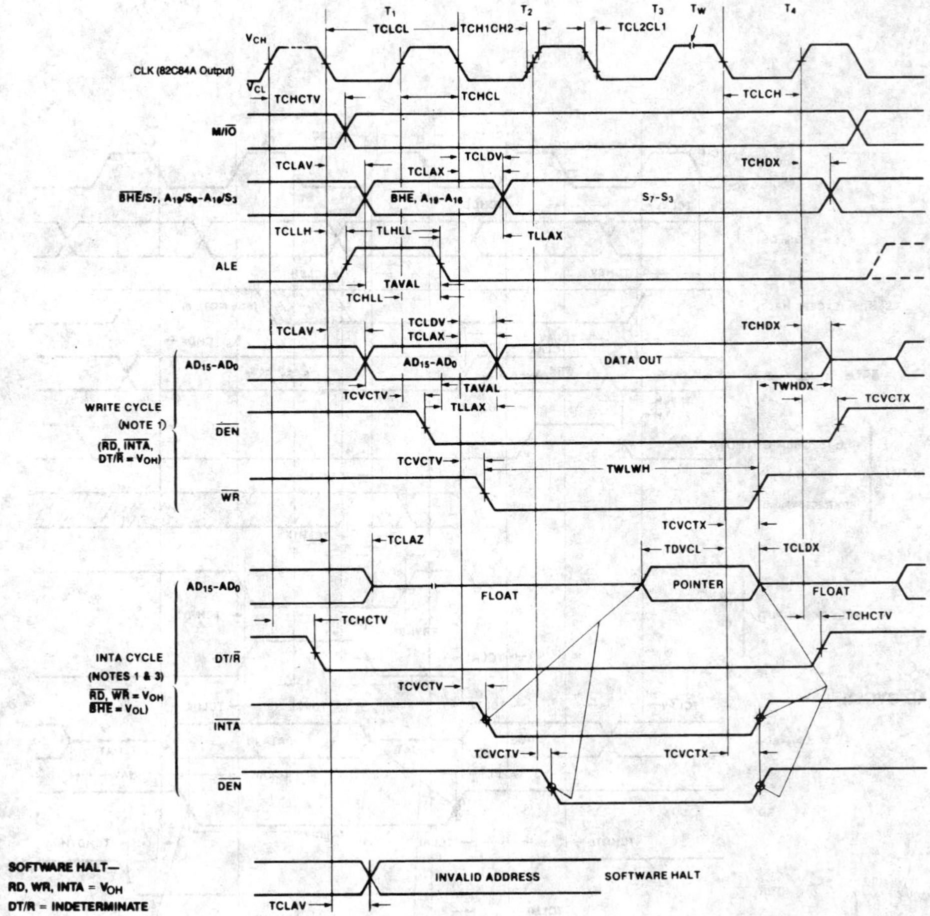

NOTES:

1. All signals switch between V_{OH} and V_{OL} unless otherwise specified.
2. RDY is sampled near the end of T_2, T_3, T_W, to determine if T_W machines states are to be inserted.
3. Two INTA cycles run back-to-back. The 8086 LOCAL ADDR/DATA BUS is floating during both INTA cycles. Control signals shown for INTA cycle.
4. Signals at 82C84A are shown for reference only.
5. All timing measurements are made at 1.5V unless otherwise noted.

240487-001

Figure 6-30. Minimum Mode Waveforms (Cont'd.)

WAVEFORMS

MAXIMUM MODE

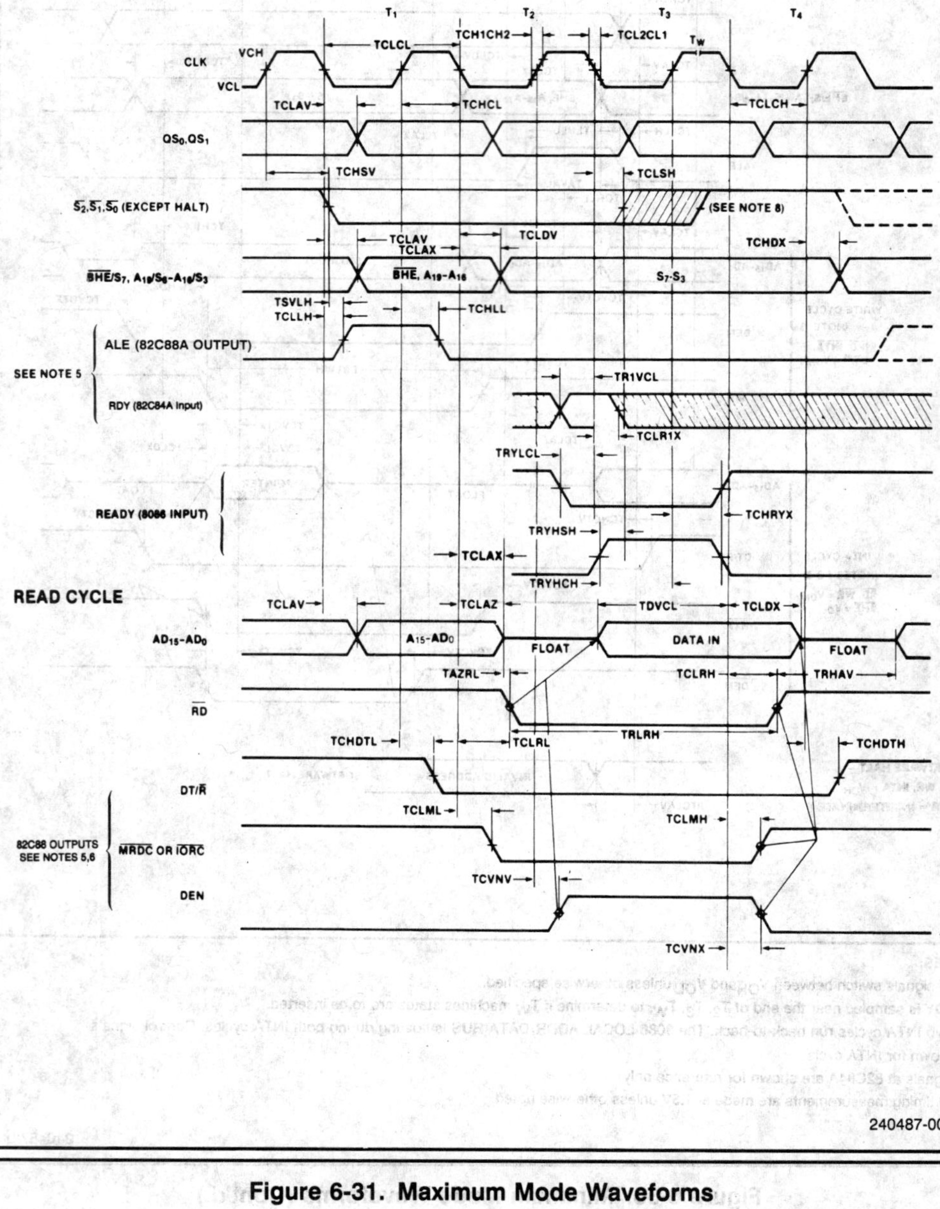

Figure 6-31. Maximum Mode Waveforms

WAVEFORMS (Continued)

MAXIMUM MODE (Continued)

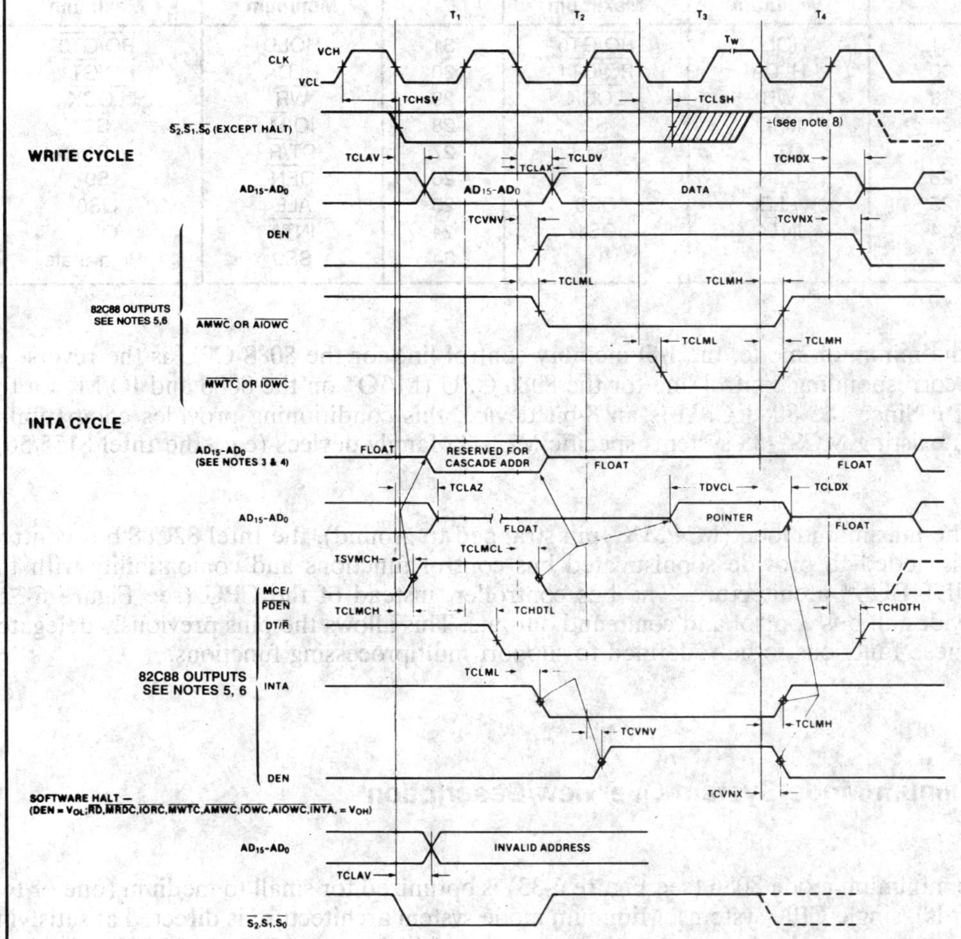

NOTES:

1. All signals switch between V_{OH} and V_{OL} unless otherwise specified.
2. RDY is sampled near the end of T_2, T_3, TW, to determine if T_W machines states are to be inserted.
3. Cascade address is valid between first and second INTA cycle.
4. Two INTA cycles run back-to-back. The 8086 LOCAL ADDR/DATA BUS is floating during both INTA cycles. Control for pointer address is shown for second INTA cycle.
5. Signals at 82C84A or 82C88 are shown for reference only.
6. The issuance of the 82C88 command and control signals ($\overline{MRDC}$, $\overline{MWTC}$, $\overline{AMWC}$, $\overline{IORC}$, $\overline{IOWC}$, $\overline{AIOWC}$, $\overline{INTA}$ and DEN) lags the active high 82C88 CEN.
7. All timing measurements are made at 1.5V unless otherwise noted.
8. Status inactive in state just prior to T_4.

240487-001

Figure 6-31. Maximum Mode Waveforms (Cont'd.)

Table 6-28. Minimum/Maximum Mode Pin Assignments

8086			8086		
Pin	Mode		Pin	Mode	
	Minimum	Maximum		Minimum	Maximum
31	HOLD	$\overline{RQ}/\overline{GT0}$	31	HOLD	$\overline{RQ}/\overline{GT0}$
30	HLDA	$\overline{RQ}/\overline{GT1}$	30	HLDA	$\overline{RQ}/\overline{GT1}$
29	$\overline{WR}$	$\overline{LOCK}$	29	$\overline{WR}$	$\overline{LOCK}$
28	M/$\overline{IO}$	$\overline{S2}$	28	IO/$\overline{M}$	$\overline{S2}$
27	DT/$\overline{R}$	$\overline{S1}$	27	DT/$\overline{R}$	$\overline{S1}$
26	$\overline{DEN}$	$\overline{S0}$	26	$\overline{DEN}$	$\overline{S0}$
25	ALE	QS0	25	ALE	QS0
24	$\overline{INTA}$	QS1	24	$\overline{INTA}$	QS1
			34	SS0	High State

In the minimum mode, the I/O-memory control line for the 8088 CPU is the reverse of the corresponding control line for the 8086 CPU (M/IO* on the 8086 and IO/M* on the 8088). Since the 8088 CPU is an 8-bit device, this conditioning provides compatibility with existing MCS®-85 systems specific MCS-85 family devices (e.g., the Intel 8155/56).

In the maximum mode (MN/MX* pin strapped to ground), the Intel 82C88 bus controller is added to provide sophisticated bus control functions and compatibility with the MULTIBUS® architecture. The bus controller, instead of the CPU (see Figure 6-32), provides all bus control and command outputs. This allows the pins previously delegated to these functions to be redefined to support multiprocessing functions.

Minimum Mode System Overview/Description

The minimum mode 8086 (see Figure 6-33) is optimized for small to medium (one or two boards), single CPU systems. Minimum mode system architecture is directed at satisfying requirements of the lower to middle segment of high performance 16-bit applications. The CPU maintains the full megabyte memory space, 64K-byte I/O space and 16-bit data path. The CPU directly provides all bus control (DT/R*, DEN*, ALE, M/IO*), commands (RD*, WR*, INTA*) and a simple CPU preemption mechanism (HOLD, HLDA) compatible with existing DMA controllers (e.g., 8259A Interrupt Controller).

In the minimum mode the 8088 CPU provides an SS0 status output. This output is equivalent to S0 in the maximum mode and can be decoded with DT/R* and –IO/M*, which are equivalent to S1* and S2* respectively, to provide the same CPU cycle status information (see Table 6-29). This type of decoding could be used in a minimum mode 8088-based system to allow dynamic RAM refresh during passive CPU cycle.

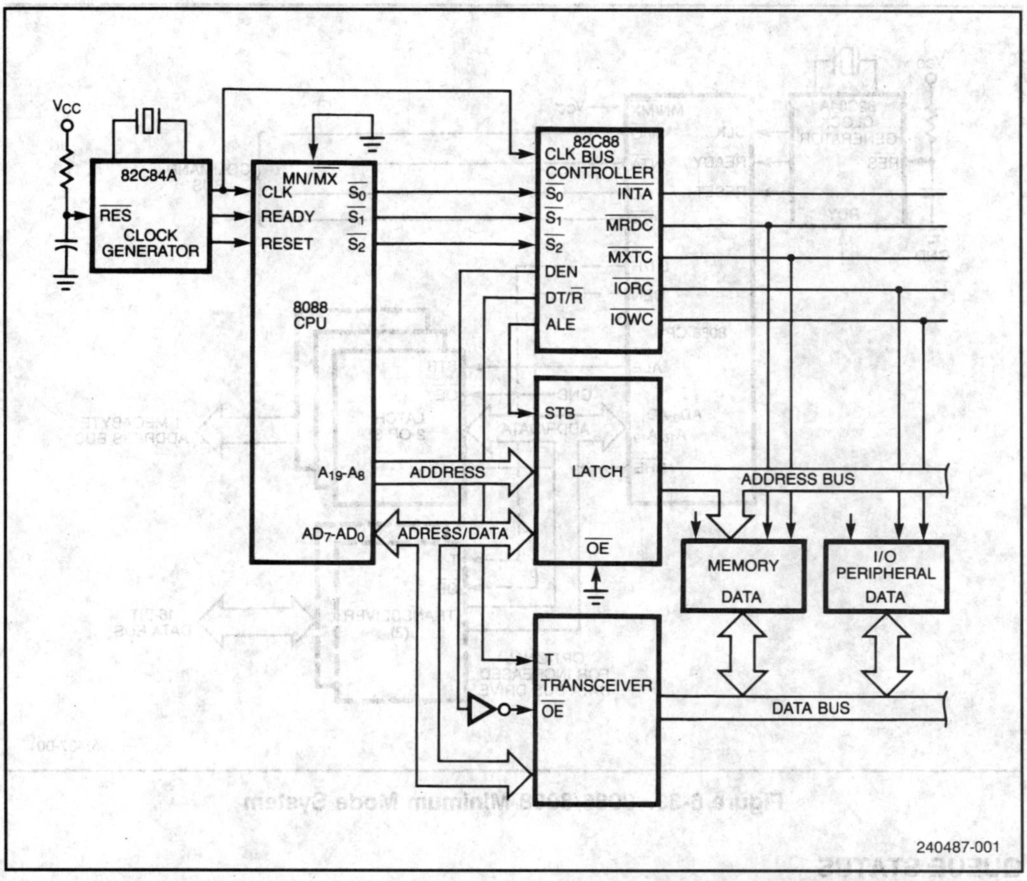

Figure 6-32. Elementary Maximum Mode System

Maximum Mode System Overview/Description

The maximum mode (see Figure 6-34) extends the system architecture to support multiprocessor configurations and local instruction set extension processors (coprocessors). By adding the 82C88 bus controller, the 8086 outputs assigned to bus control and commands in the minimum mode are redefined to allow these extensions and enhance general system performance. Specifically, (1) two prioritized levels of processor preemption (RQ*/GT0*, RQ*/GT1*) allow multiple processors to reside on the 8086's local bus and share its interface to the system bus, (2) Queue status (QS0, QS1) is available to allow external devices like ICE™-86 or special instruction set extension coprocessors (such as the 8087 Numeric Coprocessor) to track the CPU instruction execution, (3) access control to shared resources in multiprocessor systems is supported by a hardware bus lock mechanism and (4) system command and configuration options are expanded via devices like the 82C88 bus controller.

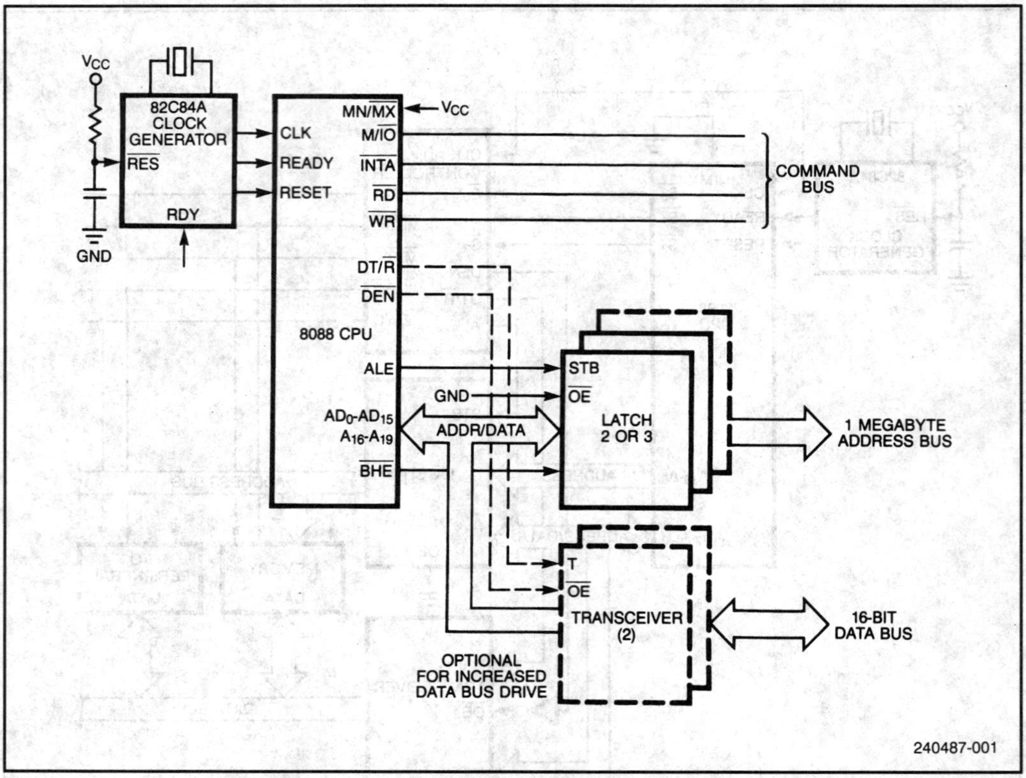

Figure 6-33. 8086/8088 Minimum Mode System

QUEUE STATUS

The queue status indicates what information is being removed from the internal queue and when the queue is being reset due to a transfer of control (Table 6-30). By monitoring the S0*, S1*, S2* status lines for instructions entering the 8086 (1, 0, 0 indicates code access while A0 and BHE* indicate word or byte) and QS0, QS1 for instructions leaving the 8086's internal queue, it is possible to track the instruction execution. Since instructions are executed from the 8086's internal queue, the queue status is presented each CPU clock cycle and is not related to the bus cycle activity. This mechanism (1) allows a coprocessor to detect execution of an ESCAPE instruction which directs the coprocessor to perform a specific task and (2) allows ICE-86 to trap execution of a specific memory location.

An example of a circuit used by ICE is given in Figure 6-35. The first up down counter tracks the depth of the queue while the second captures the queue depth on a match. The second counter decrements on further fetches from the queue until the queue is flushed or the count goes to zero indicating execution of the match address. The first counter decrements on fetch from the queue (QS0 = 1) and increments on code fetches into the queue. Note that a normal code fetch will transfer two bytes into the queue so two clock increments are given to the counter (T201 and T301) unless a single byte is loaded over the upper half of the bus (A0-P is high). Since the execution unit (EU) is not synchronized to the bus interface unit (BIU), a fetch from the queue can occur simultaneously with a transfer into the queue. The Exclusive-OR gate driving the ENP input of the first counter allows these simultaneous operations to cancel each other and not modify the queue depth.

Table 6-29. Status Bit Decoding

Status Inputs			CPU Cycle	8288 Command
$\overline{\text{S2}}$	$\overline{\text{S1}}$	$\overline{\text{S0}}$		
0	0	0	Interrupt Acknowledge	$\overline{\text{INTA}}$
0	0	1	Read I/O Port	$\overline{\text{IORC}}$
0	1	0	Write I/O Port	$\overline{\text{IOWC}}$, $\overline{\text{AIOWC}}$
0	1	1	Halt	None
1	0	0	Instruction Fetch	$\overline{\text{MRDC}}$
1	0	1	Read Memory	$\overline{\text{MRCD}}$
1	1	0	Write Memory	$\overline{\text{MWTC}}$, $\overline{\text{AMWC}}$
1	1	1	Passive	None

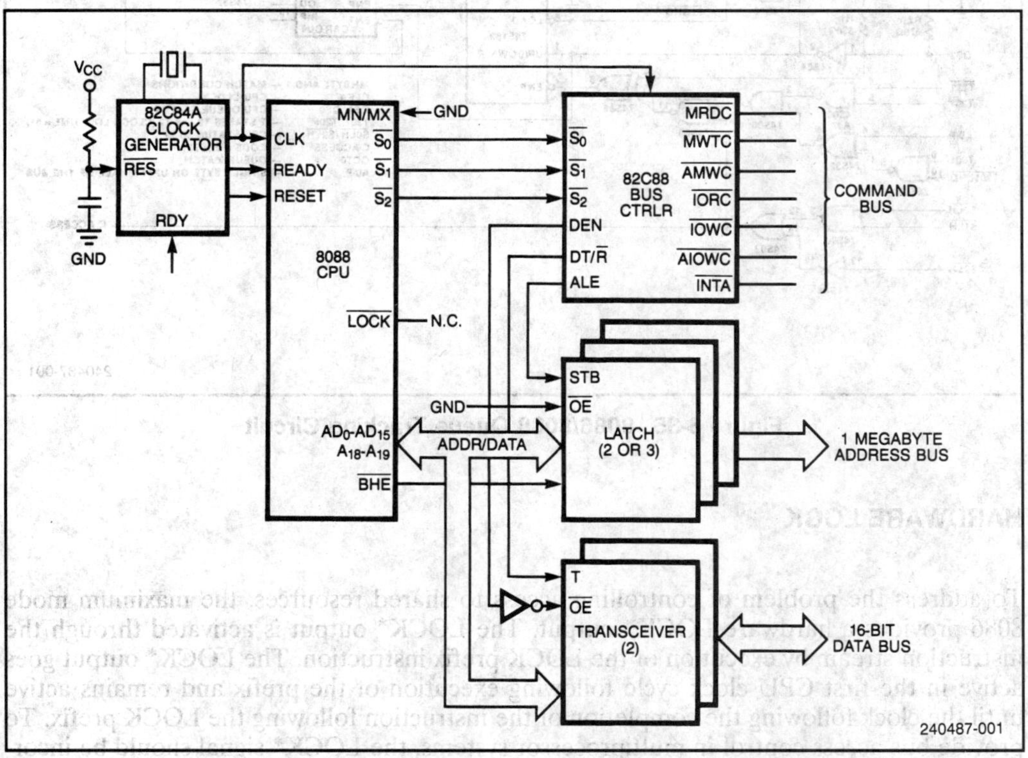

Figure 6-34. 8086/8088 Maximum Mode System

Table 6-30. Status Line Decoders

$\overline{S}_2$	$\overline{S}_1$	$\overline{S}_0$	
0 (LOW)	0	0	Interrupt Acknowledge
0	0	1	Read I/O Port
0	1	0	Write I/O Port
0	1	1	Halt
1 (HIGH)	0	0	Code Access
1	0	1	Read Memory
1	1	0	Write Memory
1	1	1	Passive

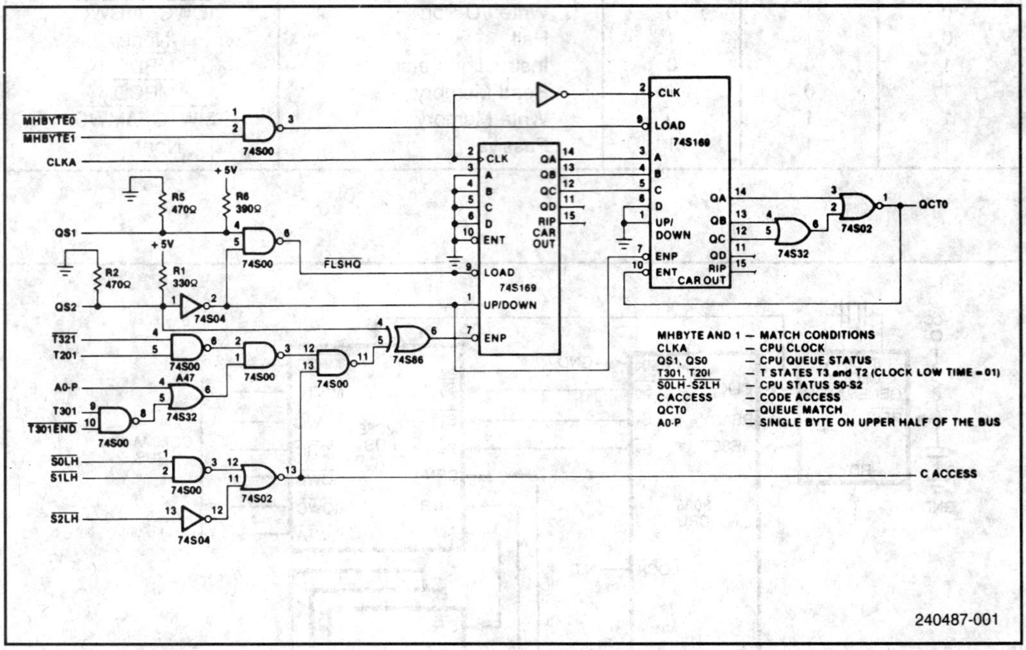

Figure 6-35. 8086/8088 Queue Tracking Circuit

HARDWARE LOCK

To address the problem of controlling access to shared resources, the maximum mode 8086 provides a hardware LOCK* output. The LOCK* output is activated through the instruction stream by execution of the LOCK prefix instruction. The LOCK* output goes active in the first CPU clock cycle following execution of the prefix and remains active until the clock following the completion of the instruction following the LOCK prefix. To provide bus access control in multiprocessor systems, the LOCK* signal should be incorporated into the system bus arbitration logic resident to the CPU.

During normal multiprocessor system operation, priority of the shared system bus is determined by the arbitration circuits on a cycle by cycle basis. As each CPU requires a transfer over the system bus, it requests access to the bus via its resident bus arbitration logic. When the CPU gains priority (determined by the system bus arbitration scheme and any associated logic), it takes control of the bus, performs its bus cycle and either maintains bus control, voluntarily releases the bus or is forced off the bus by the loss of priority. The lock mechanism prevents the CPU from losing bus control (either voluntarily or by force) and guarantees a CPU the ability to execute multiple bus cycles (during execution of the locked instruction) without intervention and possible corruption of the data by another CPU. A classic use of the mechanism is the 'TEST and SET semaphore' during which a CPU must read from a shared memory location and return data to the location without allowing another CPU to reference the same location between the TEST operation (read) and the SET operation (write). In the 8086 this is accomplished with a locked exchange instruction (see Figure 6-36).

```
LOCK XCHG reg, MEMORY ; reg is any register
                      ; MEMORY is the address of the
                      ; semaphore
```

Another application of LOCK* for multiprocessor systems consists of a locked block move which allows high speed message transfer from one CPU's message buffer to another.

During the locked instruction, a request for processor preemption (RQ*/GT*) is recorded but not acknowledged until completion of the locked instruction. The LOCK*

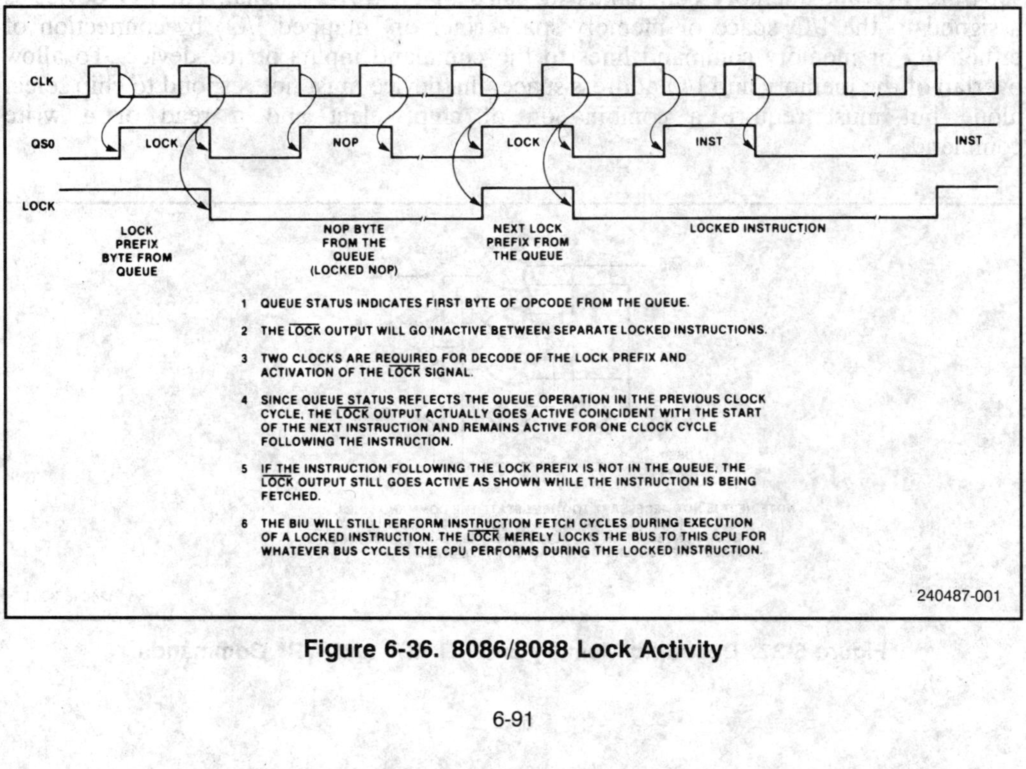

Figure 6-36. 8086/8088 Lock Activity

has no direct affect on interrupts. As an example, a locked HALT instruction will cause HOLD (or RQ*/GT*) requests to be ignored but will allow the CPU to exit the HALT state on an interrupt. In general, prefix bytes are considered extensions of the instructions they preceded. Therefore, interrupts that occur during execution of a prefix are not acknowledged (assuming interrupts are enabled) until completion of the instruction following the prefix (except for instructions which are servicing interrupts during their execution, i.e., HALT, WAIT and repeated string primitive). Note that multiple prefix bytes may precede an instruction. Another example is a 'string primitive' preceded by the repetition prefix (REP) which is interruptible after each execution of the string primitive. This holds even if the REP prefix is combined with the LOCK prefix. This prevents interrupts from being locked out during a block move or other repeated string operation. As long as the operation is not interrupted, LOCK* remains active. Further information on the operation of an interrupted string operation with multiple prefixes is presented in the section dealing with the 8086 interrupt structure.

General Design Considerations

Since the minimum mode 8086 has common read and write commands for memory and I/O, if the memory and I/O address spaces overlap, the chip selects must be qualified by M/IO* to determine which address space the devices are assigned. This restriction on chip select decoding can be removed if the I/O and memory addresses in the system do not overlap and are properly decoded, all I/O is memory mapped, or RD*, WR* and M/IO* are decoded to provide separate memory and I/O read/write commands (see Figure 6-37). The 82C88 bus controller in the maximum mode 8086 system generates separate I/O and memory commands in place of an M/IO* signal. An I/O device is assigned to the I/O space or memory space (memory mapped I/O) by connection of either I/O or memory command lines to the command inputs of the device. To allow overlap of the memory and I/O address space, the device must not respond to chip select alone but must require a combination of chip select and a read or a write command.

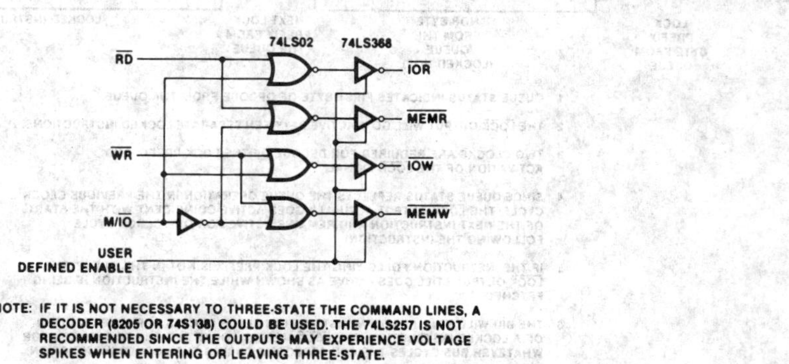

Figure 6-37. Decoding Memory and I/O RD* and WR* Commands

Linear select techniques (see Figure 6-38) for I/O devices can only be used with devices that either reside in the I/O address space or require more than one active chip select (at least one low active and one high active). Devices with a single chip select input cannot use linear select if they are memory mapped because memory address space FFFF0H-FFFFFH is assigned to reset startup and memory space 00000H-003FFH is assigned to interrupt vectors.

BUS OPERATION

In order to understand the operation of a time-multiplexed bus, the BIU's bus cycle must be understood. A bus cycle is an asynchronous event that presents the address of an I/O peripheral or memory location. The address is followed by either a read control signal to capture or read data from the addressed device, or a write control signal and the associated data to transmit or write the data to the addressed device. The selected device (memory or I/O peripheral) accepts the data on the bus during a write cycle or places the requested data on the bus during a read cycle. On termination of the specified cycle, the device latches the data written or removes the data read.

Multiplexed Address and Data Bus

The 8086/88 has a combined address and data bus commonly referred to as a time multiplexed bus. Time multiplexing makes the most efficient use of pins on the processor while permitting the use of a standard 40-pin package. This "local bus" can be buffered directly and used throughout the system with address latching provided on memory and I/O modules. In addition, the bus can also be demultiplexed at the processor with a single set of address latches if a standard non-multiplexed bus is desired for the system.

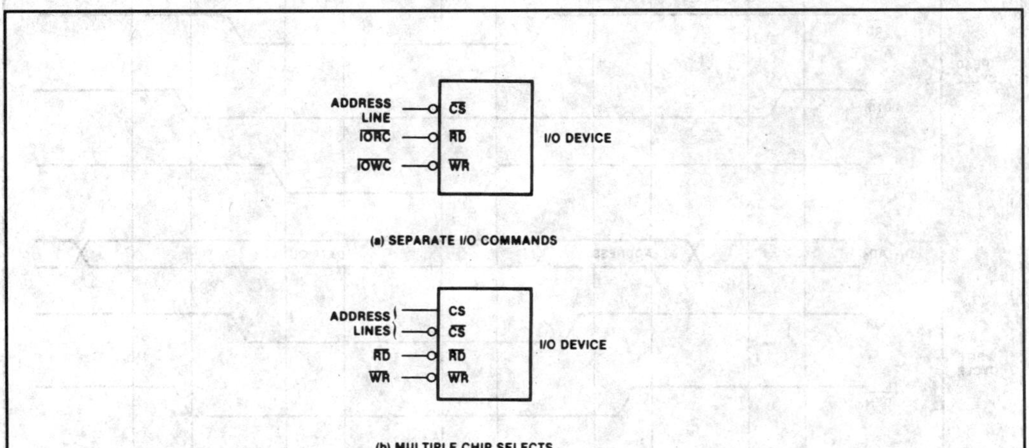

Figure 6-38. Linear Select for I/O

Bus Cycle Definition

The 8086 is a true 16-bit microprocessor with 16-bit internal and external data paths, one megabyte of memory address space (2^{20}) and a separate 64K byte (2^{16}) I/O address space. The CPU communicates with its external environment via a twenty-bit time multiplexed address, status and data bus and a command bus. To transfer data or fetch instructions, the CPU executes a bus cycle (see Figure 6-39). The minimum bus cycle consists of four CPU clock cycles ("T") states. During the first T state (T1), the CPU asserts an address on the twenty-bit multiplexed, address/data/status bus. For the second T state (T2), the CPU removes the address from the bus and either tri-states its outputs on the lower sixteen bus lines in preparation for a ready cycle or asserts write data. Data bus transceivers are enabled in either T1 or T2 depending on the 8086 system configuration and the direction of the transfer (into or out of the CPU). Read, write or interrupt acknowledge commands are always enabled in T2. The maximum mode 8086 configuration also provides a write command enabled in T3 to guarantee time for data setup prior to command activation.

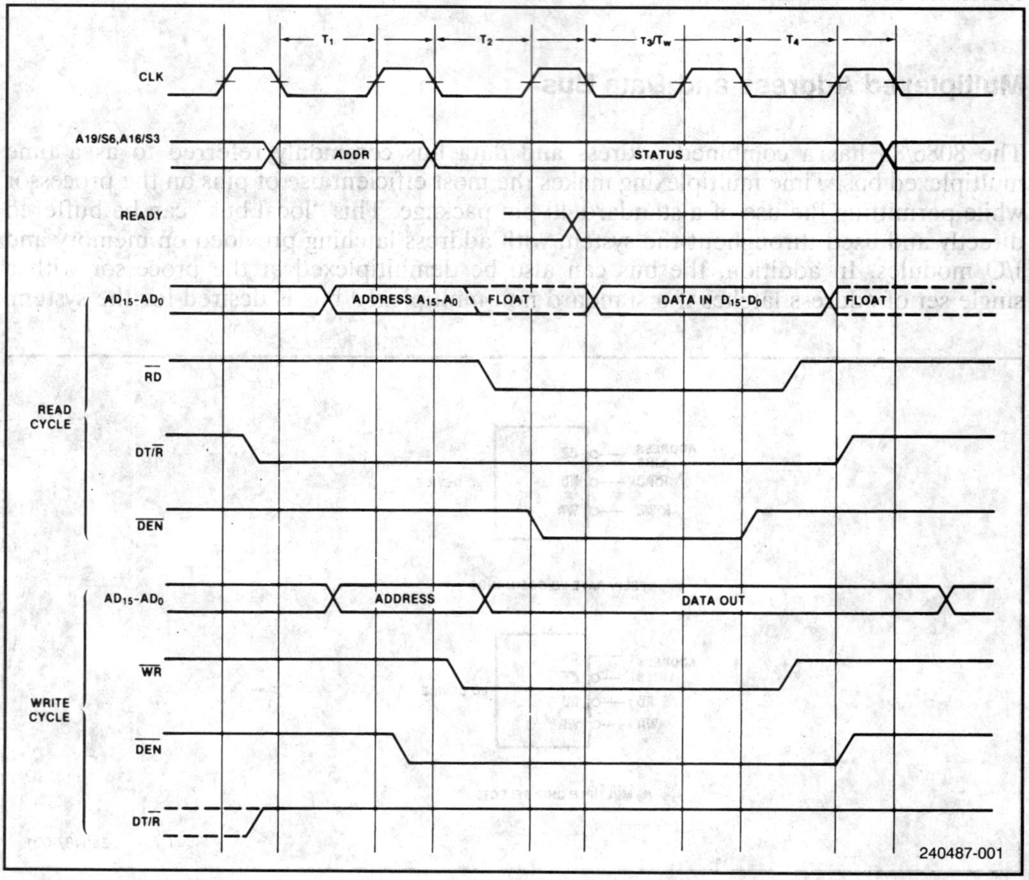

Figure 6-39. Basic 8086/8088 Bus Cycles

During T2, the upper four multiplexed bus lines switch from address (A19-A16) to bus cycle status (S6, S5, S4, S3). The status information (see Table 6-31) is available primarily for diagnostic monitoring. However, a decode of S3 and S4 could be used to select one of four banks of memory, one assigned to each segment register. This technique allows partitioning the memory by segment to expand the memory addressing beyond one megabyte. It also provides a degree of protection by preventing erroneous write operations to one segment from overlapping into, and destroying information, in another segment.

The CPU continues to provide status information on the upper four bus lines during T3 and will either continue to assert write data or sample read data on the lower sixteen bus lines. If the selected memory or I/O device is not capable of transferring data at the maximum CPU transfer rate, the device must signal the CPU "not ready" and force the CPU to insert additional clock cycles (Wait states, TW) after T3. The 'not ready' indication must be presented to the CPU by the start of T3. Bus activity during TW is the same as T3. In a "normally not ready" system, when the selected device has had sufficient time to complete the transfer, it asserts "Ready" and allows the CPU to continue from the TW states. The CPU will latch the data on the bus during the last wait state or during T3 if no wait states are requested. The bus cycle is terminated in T4 (command lines are disabled and the selected external device releases the bus). To devices in the system, the bus cycle appears as an asynchronous event consisting of an address to select the device followed by a read strobe or data and a write strobe. The selected device accepts bus data during a write cycle and drives the desired data onto the bus during a read cycle. On termination of the command, the device latches write data or disables its bus drives. The only way the device controls the bus cycle is by inserting wait cycles.

The 8086 CPU only executes a bus cycle when instructions or operands must be transferred to or from memory or I/O devices. When not executing a bus cycle, the bus interface executes idle cycles (T1). During the idle cycles, the CPU continues to drive status information from the previous bus cycle on the upper address lines. If the previous bus cycle was a write, the CPU continues to drive the write data onto the multiplexed bus until the start of the next bus cycle. If the CPU executes idle cycles following a ready cycle, the CPU will not drive the lower 16 bus lines until the next bus cycle is required.

Table 6-31. Status Information

S3	S4	
0	0	Alternative (relative to the ES segment)
1	0	Stack (relative to the SS segment)
0	1	Code/None (relative to the CS segment or a default of zero)
1	1	Data (relative to the DS segment)

S5 = IF (interrupt enable flag)
S6 = 0 (indicates the 8086 is on the bus)

Since the CPU prefetches up to six bytes of the instruction stream for storage and execution from an internal instruction queue, the relationship may be skewed in time and separated by additional instruction fetch bus cycles. In general, if the BIU fetches an instruction into the 8086's internal instruction queue, it may also fetch several additional instructions before the EU removes the instruction from the queue and executes it. If the EU executes a jump or other control transfer instruction from the queue, it ignores any instructions remaining in the queue; the CPU discards these instructions with no effect on operation. The bus activity observed during execution of a specific instruction depends on the preceding instructions; the activity, however, may always be determined within a specific sequence.

Address and Data Bus Concepts

The programmer views the 8086 memory address space as a sequence of one million bytes in which any byte may contain an eight bit data element and any two consecutive bytes may contain a 16-bit data element. There is no constraint on byte or word addresses (i.e., boundaries). The address space is physically implemented on a 16-bit data bus by dividing the address space into two banks of up to 512K bytes (see Figure 6-40). One bank connects to the lower half of the 16-bit data bus (D7-0) and contains even addressed bytes (A0=0). The other bank connects to the upper half of the data bus (D15-8) and contains odd addressed bytes (A0=1). Address lines A19-A1 select a specific byte within each bank. To perform byte transfers to even addresses (Figure 6-41), the information is transferred over the lower half of the data bus (D7-0). A0 (active low) enables the bank connected to the lower half of the data bus to participate in the transfer. Another 8086 signal, Bus High Enable (BHE*), disables the bank of the upper half of the data bus to prevent its participation in the transfer. This action prevents a write operation to the lower bank from destroying data in the upper bank. Device pin 34 (refer to the section "Device Pin Definitions," earlier in this chapter) is multiplexed between BHE* during T1 and S7 during T2 through T4. The current implementation of the 8086 equates BHE* to S7. That is, if BHE* is high during T1 then S7 will likewise be high during T2 through T4. Since BHE* is a multiplexed signal with timing identical to the A19-A16 address lines, it also should be latched during T1 with ALE to provide a stable signal during the bus cycle. To perform byte transfers to odd addresses (see Figure 6-41), the information is transferred over the upper half of the data bus (D15-D8). BHE* (active low) will enable the upper bank and A0 will disable the lower bank. Directing the data transfer to the appropriate half of the data bus and activation of S7 (BHE*) and A0 is performed by the 8086, transparent to the programmer. For example, consider loading a byte of data into the CX register (lower half of the CX register) from an odd addressed memory location (referenced over the upper half of the 16-bit data bus). The data is transferred into the 8086 over the upper 8 bits of the data bus, automatically redirected to the lower half of the 8086 internal 16-bit data path and stored in the CX register. This capability also allows byte I/O transfers with the AL register to be directed to I/O devices connected to either the upper or lower half of the 16-bit data bus.

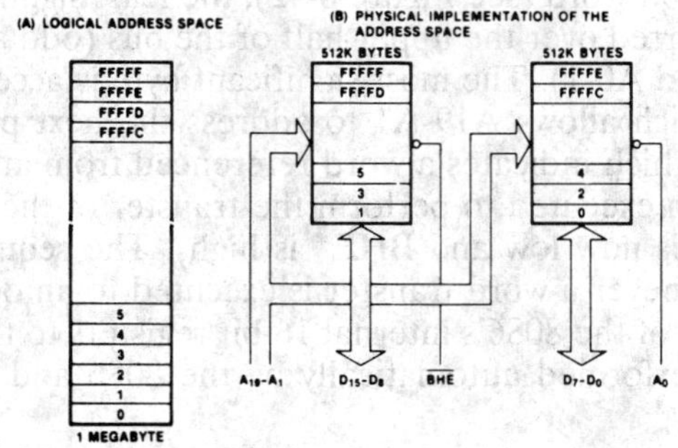

Figure 6-40. 8086 Memory

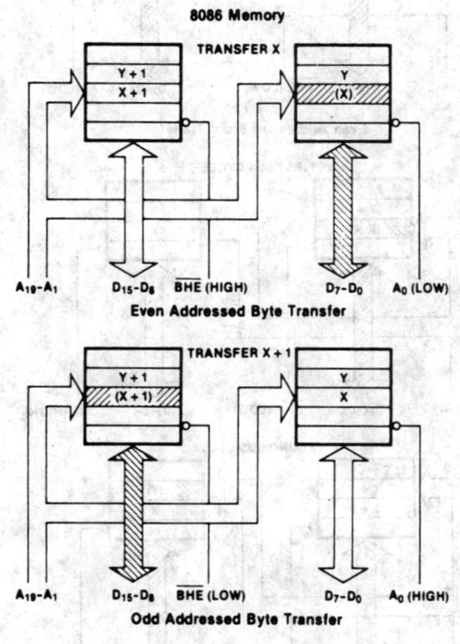

Figure 6-41. Memory Even and Odd Data Byte Transfers

To access even addressed 16-bit words (two consecutive bytes with the least significant byte at an even byte address), A19-A1 select the appropriate byte within each bank and A0 and BHE* (active low) enable both banks simultaneously (see Figure 6-42). To access an odd addressed 16-bit word (see Figure 6-42), the least significant byte (addressed by A19-A1) is first transferred over the upper half of the bus (odd addressed byte, upper bank, BHE* low active and A0-1). The most significant byte is accessed by incrementing the address (A19-A0) which allows A19-A1 to address the next physical word location (recall that A0 was high which indicates a word referenced from an odd byte boundary). A second bus cycle is then executed to perform the transfer of the most significant byte with the lower bank (A0 is now low and BHE* is high). The sequence is automatically executed by the 8086 whenever a word transfer is executed to an odd address. Directing the upper and lower bytes of the 8086's internal 16-bit registers to the appropriate halves of the data bus is also performed automatically by the 8086 and is transparent to the programmer.

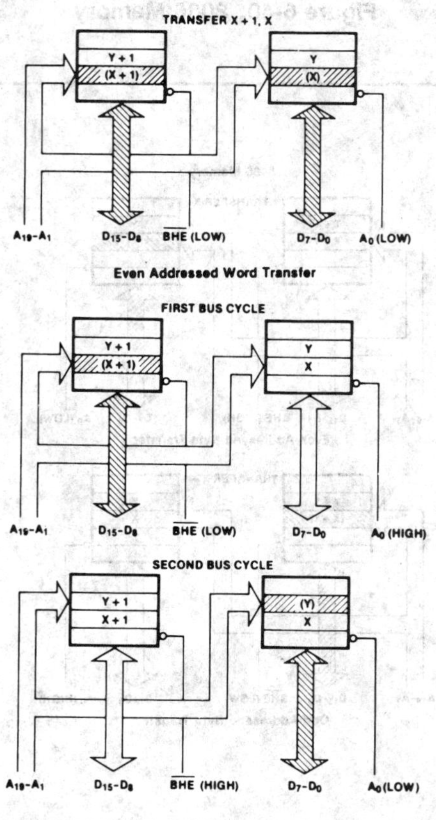

Figure 6-42. Memory Even and Odd Data Word Transfers

During a byte read, the CPU floats the entire 16-bit data bus even though data is only expected on the upper or lower half of the data bus. As will be demonstrated later, this action simplifies the chip select decoding requirements for read only devices (ROM, EPROM). During a byte write operation, the 8086 will drive the entire 16-bit data bus. The information on the half of the data bus not transferring data is indeterminate. These concepts also apply to the I/O address space. Specific examples of I/O and memory interfacing are considered in the corresponding sections.

Memory and I/O Peripherals Interface

The 8086 and 8088 CPUs have a 20-bit address bus and are capable of accessing one megabyte of memory address space. The memory is organized as a linear array of up to 1 million bytes, addressed as 00000(H) to FFFFF(H). The memory is logically divided into code, data, extra data, and stack segments of up to 64K bytes each, with each segment falling on 16-byte boundaries (see Figure 6-43).

All memory references are made relative to base addresses contained in high speed segment registers. The segment types were chosen based on the addressing needs of programs. The segment register to be selected is automatically chosen according to the rules of the following table. All information in one segment type share the same logical attributes (e.g., code or data). By structuring memory into relocatable areas of similar characteristics and by automatically selecting segment registers, programs are shorter, faster, and more structured.

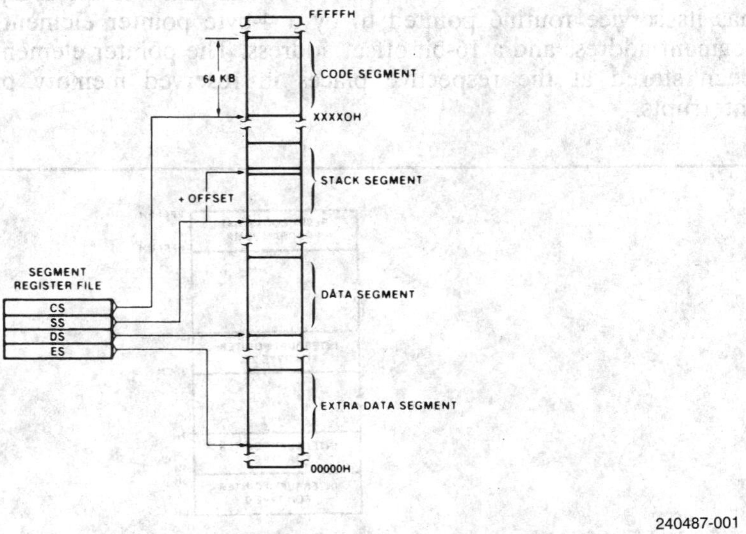

Figure 6-43. 8086/8088 Memory Organization

Word (16-bit) operands can be located on even or odd address boundaries and are thus not constrained to even boundaries as is the case in many 16-bit computers. For address and data operands, the least significant byte of the word is stored in the lower valued address location and the most significant byte in the next higher address location. The BIU automatically performs the proper number of memory accesses, one if the word operand is on an even byte boundary and two if it is on an odd byte boundary. Except for the performance penalty, this double access is transparent to the software. This performance penalty does not occur for instruction fetches, only word operands.

Physically, the memory is organized as a high bank (D15-D8) and a low bank (D7-D0) of 512K 8-bit bytes addressed in parallel by the processor's address lines A19-A1. Byte data with even addresses is transferred on the D7-D0 bus lines while odd addressed byte data (A0 HIGH) is transferred on the D15-D8 bus lines. The processor provides two enable signals, BHE* and A0, to selectively allow reading from or writing into either an odd byte location, even byte location, or both. The instruction stream is fetched from memory as words and is addressed internally by the processor to the byte level as necessary.

In referencing word data the BIU requires one or two memory cycles depending on whether or not the starting byte of the word is on an even or odd address, respectively. Consequently, in referencing word operands performance can be optimized by locating data on even address boundaries. This is an especially useful technique for using the stack, since odd address references to the stack may adversely affect the context switching time for interrupt processing or task multiplexing.

Certain locations in memory are reserved for specific CPU operations (see Figure 6-44). Locations from address FFFF0H through FFFFFH are reserved for operations including a jump to the initial program loading routine. Following RESET, the CPU will always begin execution at location FFFF0H where the jump must be. Locations 00000H through 003FFH are reserved for interrupt operations. Each of the 256 possible interrupt types has its service routine pointed to by a 4-byte pointer element consisting of a 16-bit segment address and a 16-bit offset address. The pointer elements are assumed to have been stored at the respective places in reserved memory prior to occurrence of interrupts.

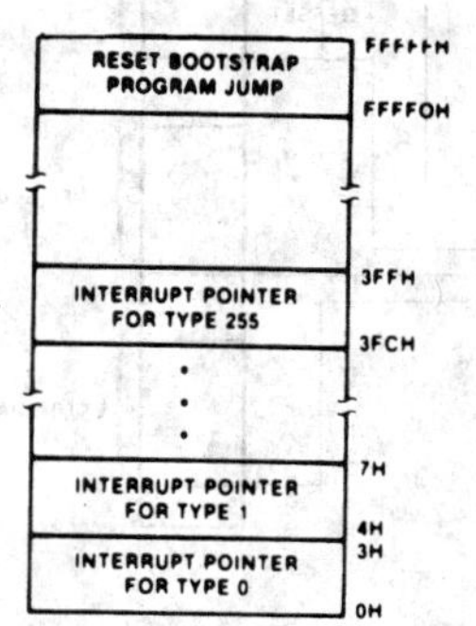

Figure 6-44. Reserved Memory Locations

MEMORY INTERFACE

The basic characteristics of 8086/8088 memory organization (see Figure 6-45) are partitioning of the 16-bit word memory into high and low 8-bit banks on the upper and lower halves of the data bus and inclusion of BHE* and A0 in selection of the banks. Specific implementations depend on the type of memory and system configuration.

ROM and EPROM

ROM's and EPROM's are the easiest devices to interface to the 8086/8088 system (see Figure 6-46). The byte format of these devices provides a simple bus interface and, since they are read only devices, A0 and BHE* do not need to be included in their chip enable/select decoding. (Chip enable is similar to chip select and also determines if the device is in active or standby power mode.) The address lines connected to the devices start with A1 and continue up to the maximum number of address lines the device can accept. The remaining address lines are used for chip enable/select decoding. To connect the devices directly to the multiplexed bus, they must have output enables. The output enable is also necessary to avoid bus contention in other configurations. No special decode techniques are required for generating chip enable/selects. Each valid decode selects one device on the upper and lower halves of bus to allow byte and word access. Byte access is achieved by reading the full word onto the bus with the 8086 only accepting the desired byte. If RD*, WR* and M/IO* are not decoded to form separate commands for memory and I/O in a minimum mode 8086, M/IO* (high active) must be a condition of chip enable/select decode. This is also true if the I/O space overlaps the memory space assigned to the EPROM/ROM. The output enable is controlled by the system memory read signal.

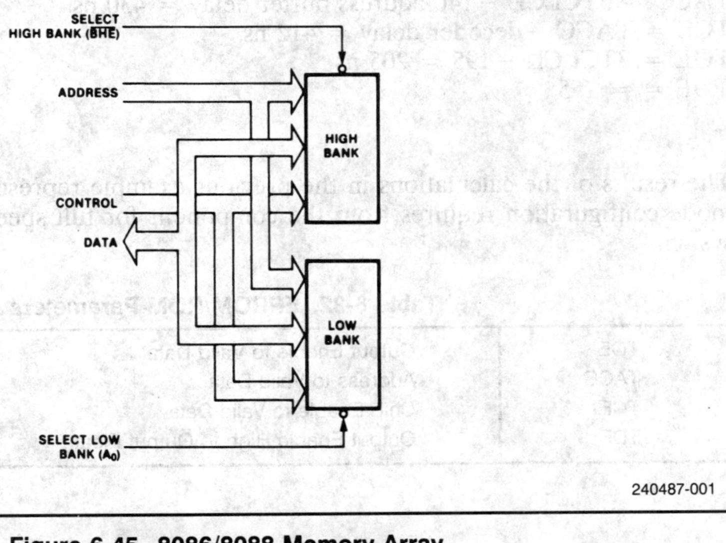

Figure 6-45. 8086/8088 Memory Array

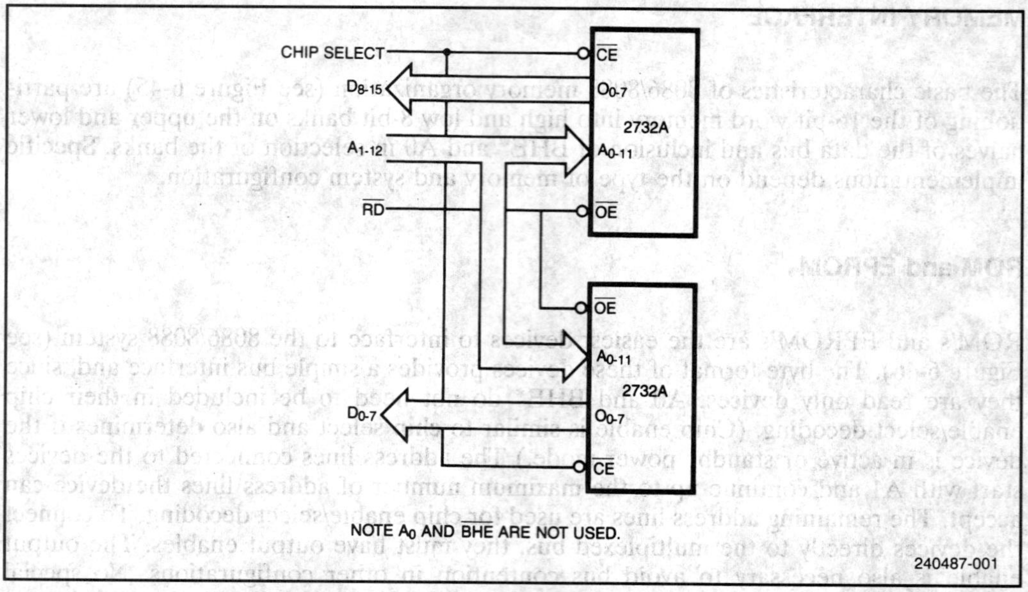

Figure 6-46. EPROM/ROM Bus Interface

Four parameters must be evaluated when determining the compatibility of static ROM's and PROM's to an 8086/8088 system. The parameters, equations and evaluation techniques given in the I/O section are also applicable to these devices. The relationship of parameters is given in Table 6-32. TACC and TCE are related to the same equation and differ only by the delay associated with the chip enable/select decoder. The following example shows a 2732A EPROM memory residing on the multiplexed bus of a minimum mode 8086 configuration:

TACC = 3TCLCL − 140 address buffer delay = 430 ns
TCE = TACC − decoder delay = 412 ns
TOE = 2TCLCL − 195 = 205 ns
TDF = = 155

The results of the calculations in the previous example represent the times a minimum mode configuration requires from the component for full speed compatibility with the system.

Table 6-32. EPROM/ROM Parameters

TOE	Output Enable to Valid Data	TRLDV
TACC	Address to Valid Data	TAVDV
TCE	Chip Enable to Valid Data	TSLDV
TDF	Output Enable High to Output Float	TRHDZ

Static RAM

Several new memory design requirements are introduced when interfacing static RAM's to the system. To begin with, A0 and BHE* must be included in the chip select/chip enable decoding of the devices and write timing must be considered in the compatibility analysis.

Data bus connections must be restricted to either the upper half or the lower half or the data bus for each device. Also, devices must not straddle the upper and lower halves of the data bus. In order to select either the upper byte, lower byte or the full 16-bit word for a write operation, BHE* must be a condition of decode for selecting the upper byte and A0 must be a condition of decode for selecting the lower byte. Several selection techniques for devices with single chip selects and no output enables are illustrated in Figure 6-47. Figure 6-48 illustrates selection techniques for devices with chip selects and output enables.

In the first examples (see Figure 6-47) A0 and BHE* must be included to decode or enable the chip selects. Since these memories do not have output enables, read and write are used as enables for chip select generation to prevent bus contention. If read and write are not used to enable the chip selects, devices with common input/output pins will be subjected to severe bus contention between chip select and write active. For devices with upper byte and A0 must be a condition of decode for selecting the buffered with the buffer enable controlled by read. This solution will only allow bus contention between memory devices in the array during chip select transition periods.

For devices with output enables (see Figure 6-48), write may be gated with BHE* and A0 to provide upper and lower bank write strobes. This simplifies chip select decoding by eliminating BHE* and A0 as a condition of decode. Although both devices are selected during a byte write operation, only one will receive a write strobe. No bus contention will exist during the write since a read command must be issued to enable the memory output drivers.

If multiple chip selects are available at the device, BHE* and A0 may directly control device selection. This allows normal chip select decoding of the address space and direct connection of the read and write commands to the devices. Alternately, the multiple chip select inputs of the device could directly decode the address space (linear select) and be combined with the separate write strobe technique to minimize the control circuits needed to generate chip selects.

As with the EPROM's and ROM's if separate commands are not provided for memory and I/O in the minimum mode 8086 and the address spaces overlap, M/IO* (high active) must be a condition of chip select decode. Also, the address lines connected to the memory devices must start with A1 rather than A0.

The write timing parameters listed in Table 6-33 may also need to be considered to analyze RAM compatibility (depending on the RAM device being considered). CPU clock relative timing is listed in Table 6-34. The equations specify the device requirements at the CPU and provide a base for determining device requirements in other

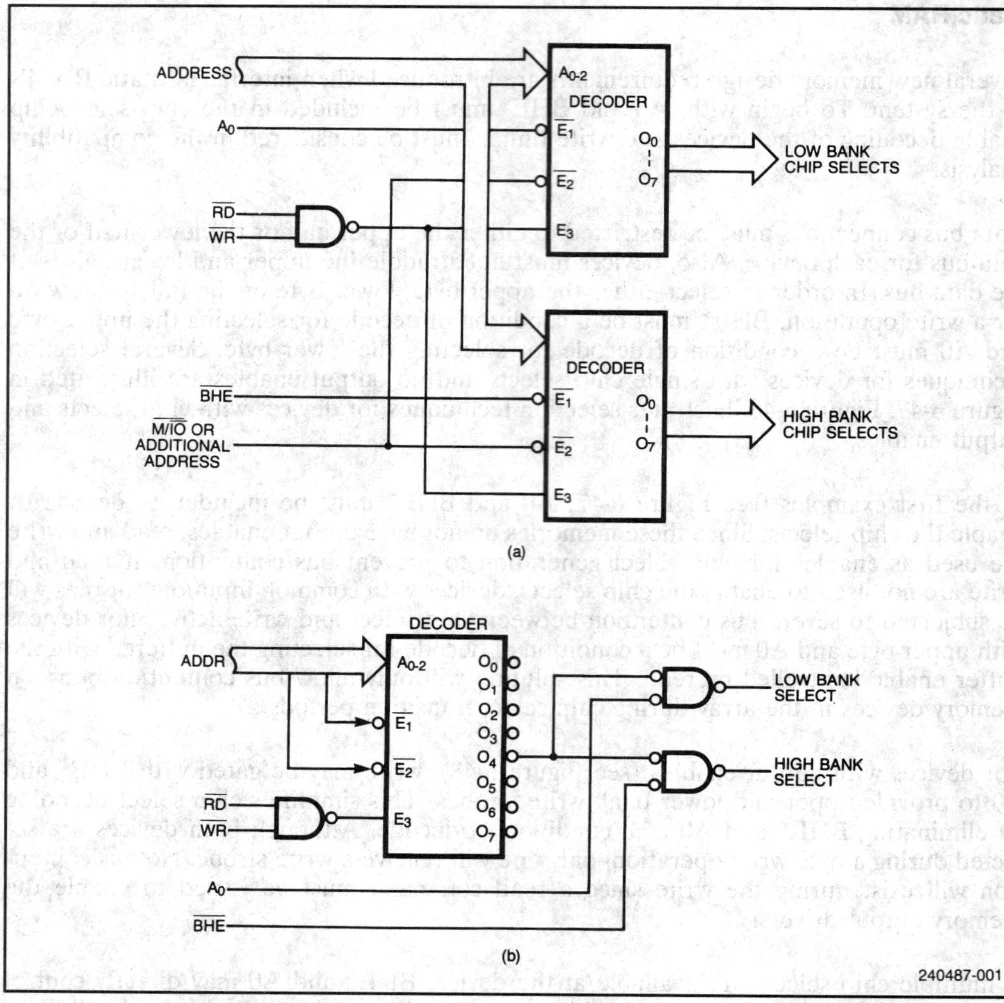

Figure 6-47. Chip Select Generation for Devices without Output Enables

configurations. For example, consider the write timing requirements of a 2148 in a maximum mode buffered 8086 system (see Figure 6-49). The write parameters of the 2148 that must be analyzed are TWP write pulse width, TWR write recovery time, TDW data valid at end of write, and TDH data hold from write time.

TWA = 2TCLCL − TCLMLmax + TCLMHmin = 375 ns

TWR = 2TCLCL − TCLMHmax + TCLLHmin + TSHOVmin = 170 ns

TDW = 2TCLCL − TCDLVmax + TCLMHmin − TIVOVmax = 265 ns

TDH = TCLCH − TCLMHmax + TCHDXmin + TIVOVmin = 95 ns

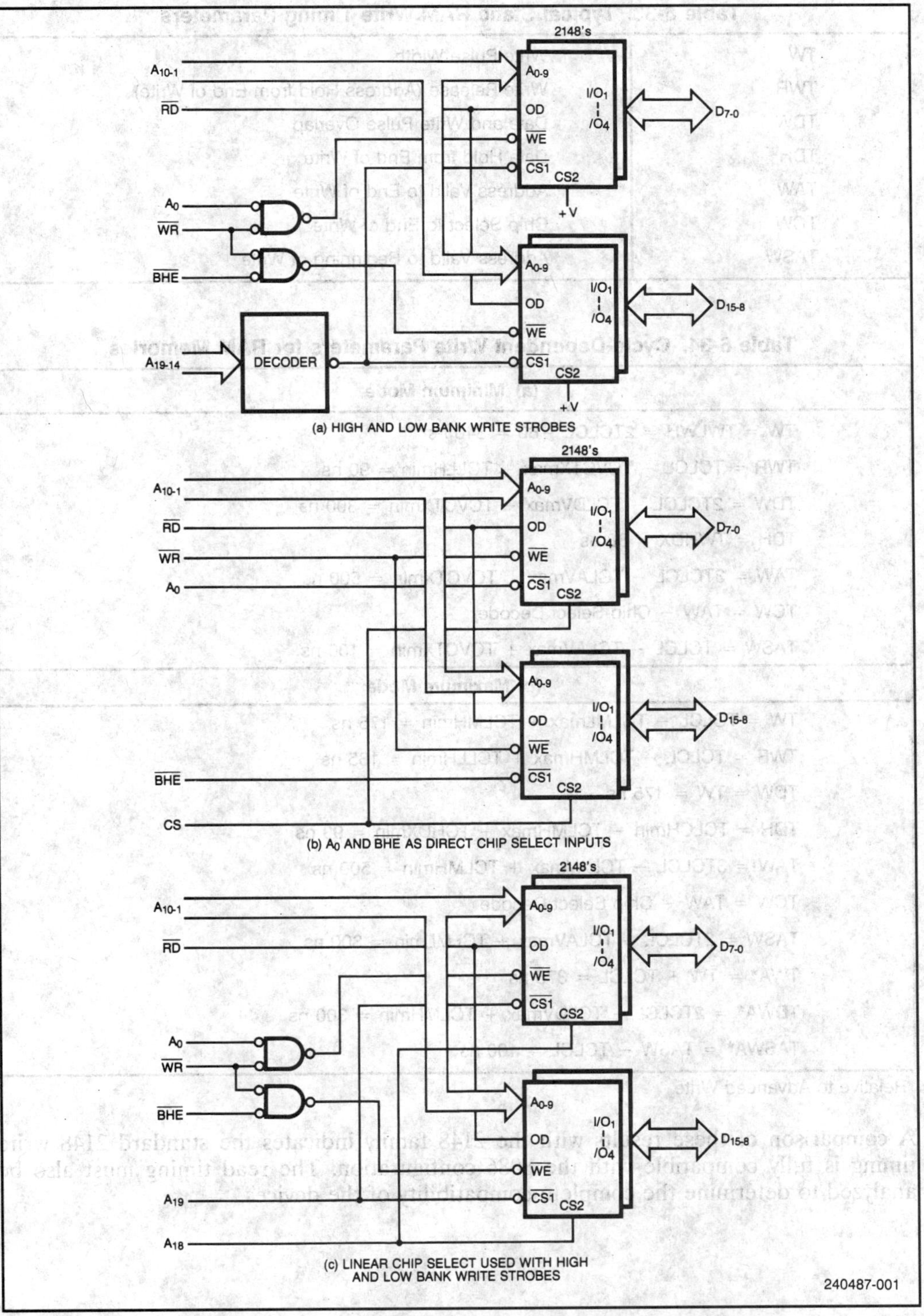

Figure 6-48. Chip Select for Devices with Output Enables

Table 6-33. Typical Static RAM Write Timing Parameters

TW	Write Pulse Width
TWR	Write Release (Address Hold from End of Write)
TDW	Data and Write Pulse Overlap
TDH	Data Hold from End of Write
TAW	Address Valid to End of Write
TCW	Chip Select to End of Write
TASW	Address Valid to Beginning of Write

Table 6-34. Cycle-Dependent Write Parameters for RAM Memories

(a) Minimum Mode
TW = TWLWH = 2TCLCL −60 = 340 ns
TWR = TCLCL − TCVCTXmax + TCLLHmin = 90 ns
TDW = 2TCLCL − TCLDVmax + TCVCTXmin = 300 ns
TDH = TWHDX = 88 ns
TAW = 3TCLCL − TCLAVmax + TCVCTXmin = 500 ns
TCW = TAW − Chip Select Decode
TASW = TCLCL − TCLAVmax + TCVCTXmin = 100 ns
(b) Maximum Mode
TW = TCLCL − TCLMLmax + TCLMHmin = 175 ns
TWR = TCLCL − TCLMHmax + TCLLHmin = 165 ns
TDW = TW = 175 ns
TDH = TCLCHmin − TCLMHmax + TCHDXmin = 93 ns
TAW = 3TCLCL − TCLAVmax + TCLMHmin = 500 ns
TCW = TAW − Chip Select Decode
TASW = 2TCLCL − TCLAVmax + TCLMLmin = 300 ns
TWA* = TW + TCLCL = 375 ns
TDWA* = 2TCLCL − TCLDVmax + TCLMHmin = 300 ns
TASWA* = TASW − TCLCL = 100 ns

*Relative to Advanced Write

A comparison of these results with the 2148 family indicates the standard 2148 write timing is fully compatible with the 8086 configuration. The read timing must also be analyzed to determine the complete compatibility of the devices.

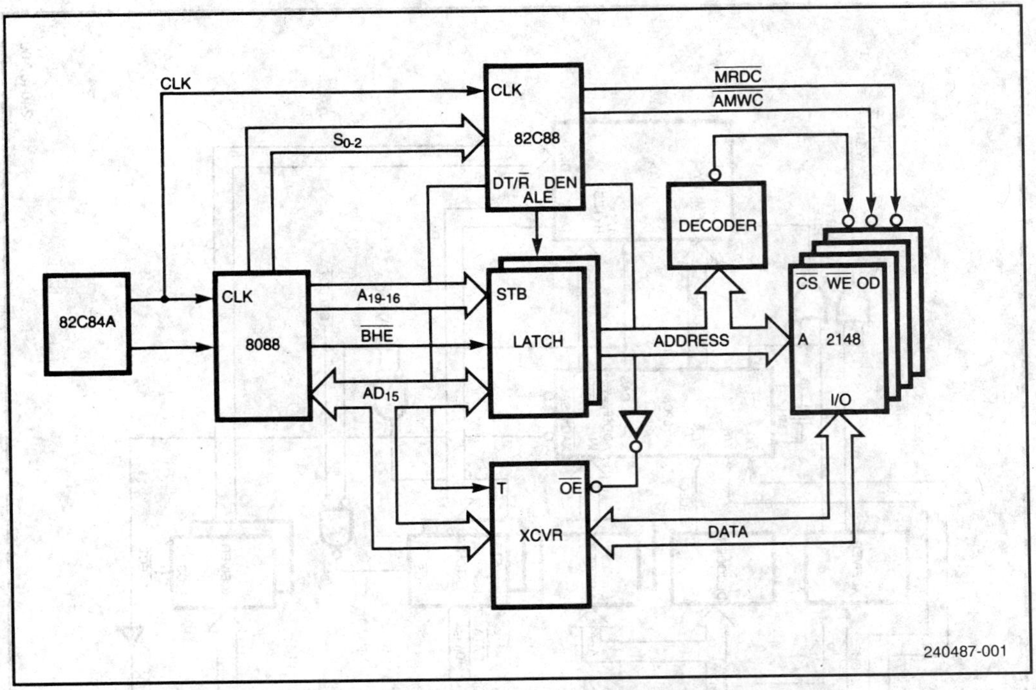

Figure 6-49. Sample Compatibility Analysis Configuration

Dynamic RAM

A dynamic RAM is one of the most complex devices to design into an 8086 system. In order to help the Design Engineer and simplify the design task somewhat, Intel provides the 8203, 8207, and 8208 dynamic RAM controllers as part of the 8086 family of peripheral devices. The following paragraphs describe the use of the 8203 with the 8086 in designing a dynamic memory system for an 8086 system.

For example, a standard interconnection for an 8203 in an 8086 system (see Figure 6-50) accommodates 64K words (128 bytes) of dynamic RAM which is addressable as words or bytes. To access the RAM, the 8086 must initiate a bus cycle with an address that selects the 8203 (via PCS*) and the appropriate transfer command (MRDC* or MWTC*). If the 8203 is not performing a refresh cycle, the access starts immediately, otherwise, the 8086 must wait for completion of the refresh. XACK* from the 8203 is connected to the 82C84A RDY input to force the CPU to wait until the RAM cycle is completed before the CPU can terminate the bus cycle. This effectively synchronizes the asynchronous events of refresh and CPU bus cycles. The normal write command (MWTC*) is used rather than the advanced command (AMWC*) to guarantee that data is valid at the dynamic RAMs before the write command is issued. Gating WE* with A0 and BHE* provides selective write strobes to the upper and lower banks of memory to allow byte and word write operations. The logic which generates the strobe for the data latches allows read data to propagate to the system as soon as the data is available and latches the data on the trailing edge of CAS*.

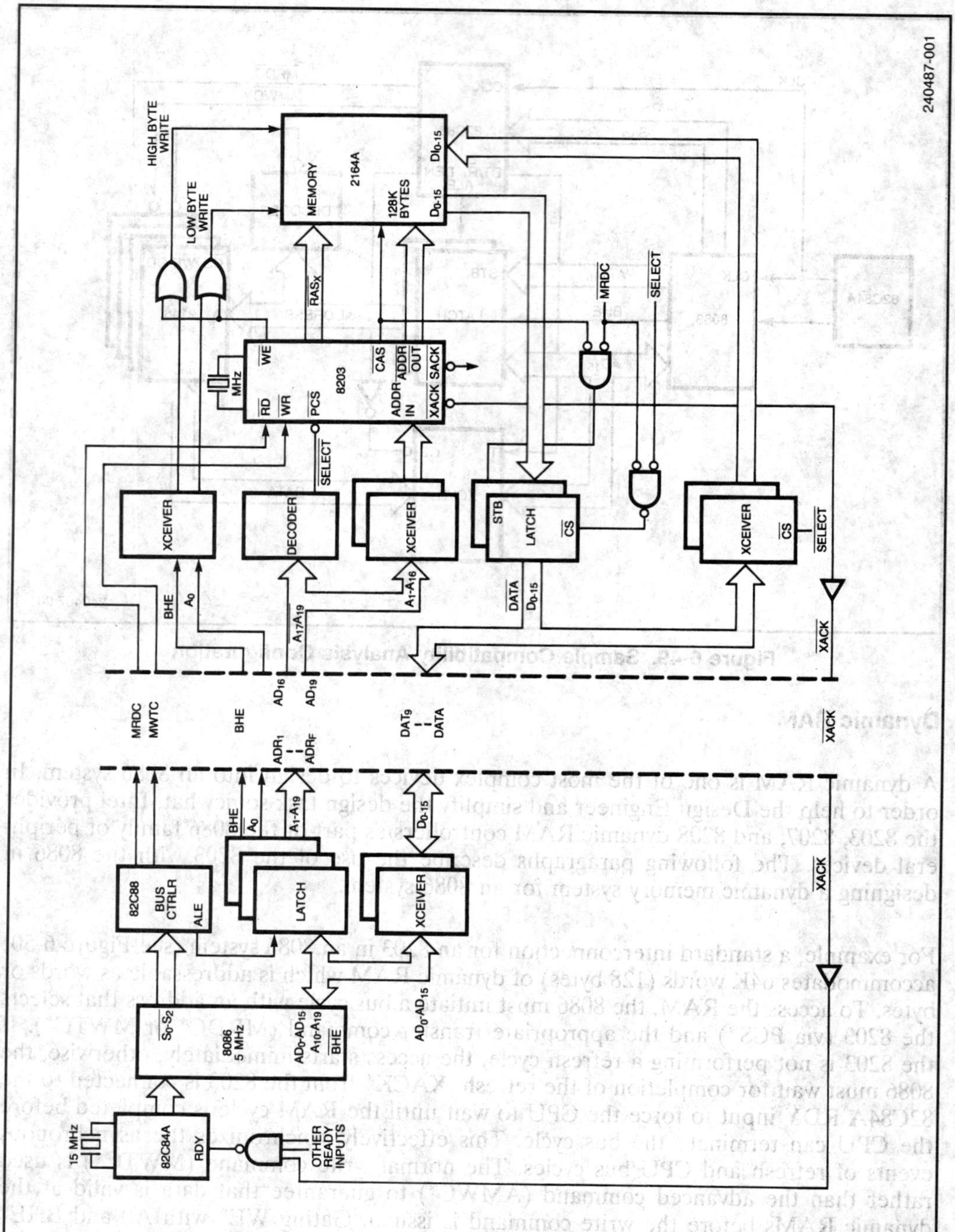

Figure 6-50. 5 MHz 8086 System using an 8203 Dynamic RAM Controller

a. Read Cycle

For no wait state operation, the 8086 requires data to be valid from MRDC* in:

2TCLCL − TCLML − TDVCL − buffer delays = 291 ns

Since the 8203 is CAS* access limited, only CAS* access time needs to be examined. The 8203/2164A guarantees data valid from 8203 RD* low to be:

(tph + 3tp + 100 ns) 8203 TCC delay + TCAC for the 2164A

A 25 MHz 8203 and 2164A provide only 297 ns, which is insufficient for no wait state operation. If only 64K bytes are accessed, the 8203 requires only (tph + 3tp = 85 ns) giving 282 ns access and no wait states required (see Figure 6-51 and 6-52). Refer to the devices respective data sheets for additional information.

b. Write Cycle

An important consideration for dynamic RAM write cycles is to guarantee data to the RAM is valid when both CAS* and WE* are active. For the 2164A, if WE* is valid prior to CAS*, the data setup is to CAS* and if CAS* is valid before WE* (as would occur during a read modify write cycle) the data setup time is to WE*.

For the 8203, the WR* to CAS* delay is analyzed to determine the data setup time to CAS* inherently provided by the 8203 command to RAS*/CAS* timing. The minimum delay from WR* to CAS* is:

TCCmin = tph + 2tp + 25 = 127 ns @ 25 MHz

Subtracting buffer delays and data setup at the 2164A, we have 83 ns to generate valid data after the write command is issued by the CPU (in this case the 82C88). Since the 8086 will not guarantee valid data until TCLAVmax − TCLMLmin = 100 ns from the advanced write signal, the normal write signal is used. The normal write MWTC* guarantees data is valid 100 ns before it is active. The worst case write pulse width is approximately 175 ns which is sufficient for all 2164A's.

c. Synchronization

To force the 8086 to wait during refresh the XACK* or SACK* lines must be returned to the 82C84A ready input. The maximum delay from RD* to SACK* (if the 8203 is not performing refresh) is TAC = tp + 40 = 80 ns. To prevent a wait state at the 8086, RDY must be valid at the 82C84A TCLCHmin − TCLMLmax − TR1VCLmax = 48 ns after the command is active. This implies that under worst case conditions, one wait state will be inserted for every read cycle. Since MWTC* does not occur until one clock later, two wait states may be inserted for writes.

The XACK* from command delay will assert RDY TCC + TCX = (tph + 3tp + 100) + (5tp + 20) = 460 ns after the command. This will typically insert one or two wait states.

Unless 2164A's are used in 64K byte or less memories, SACK* must not be used since it does not guarantee a wait state. From the previous access time analysis we saw that other configurations required a wait state.

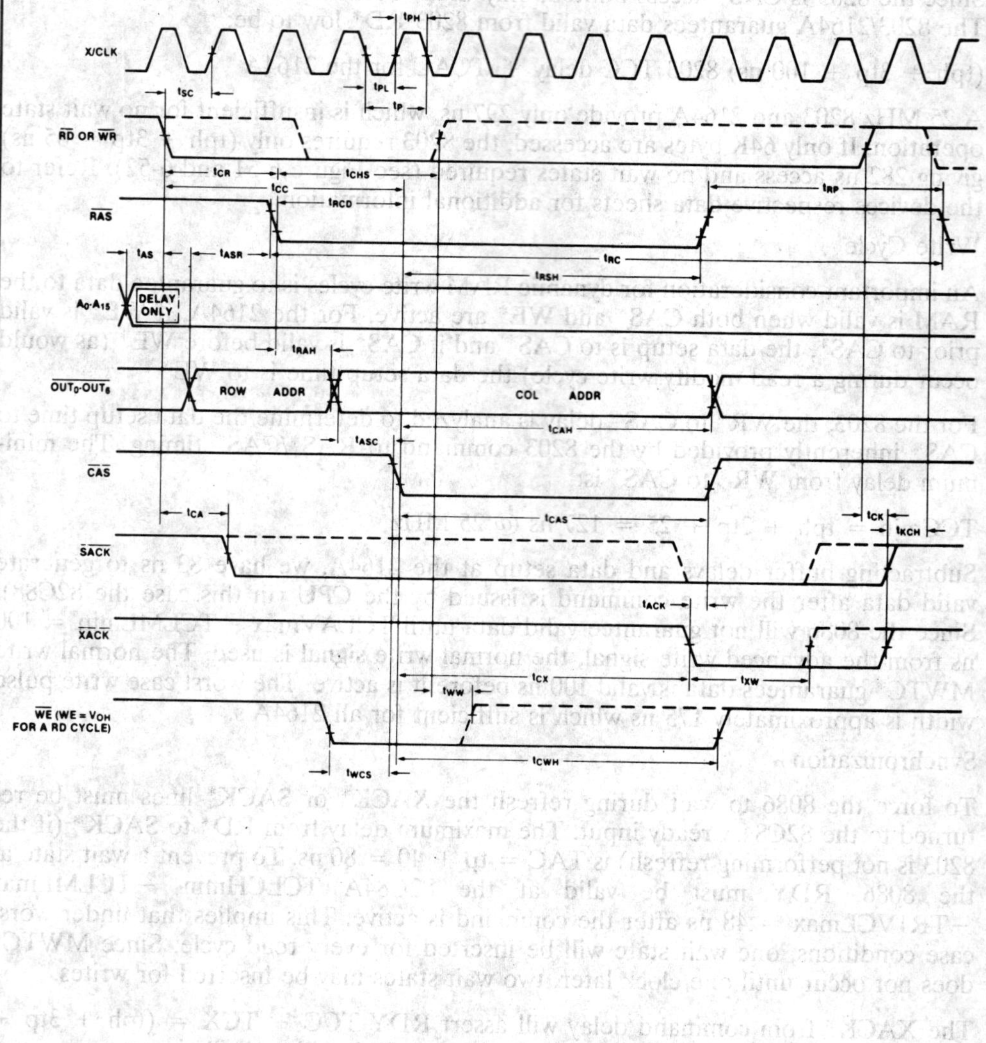

240487-001

Figure 6-51. 8203 Timing Information

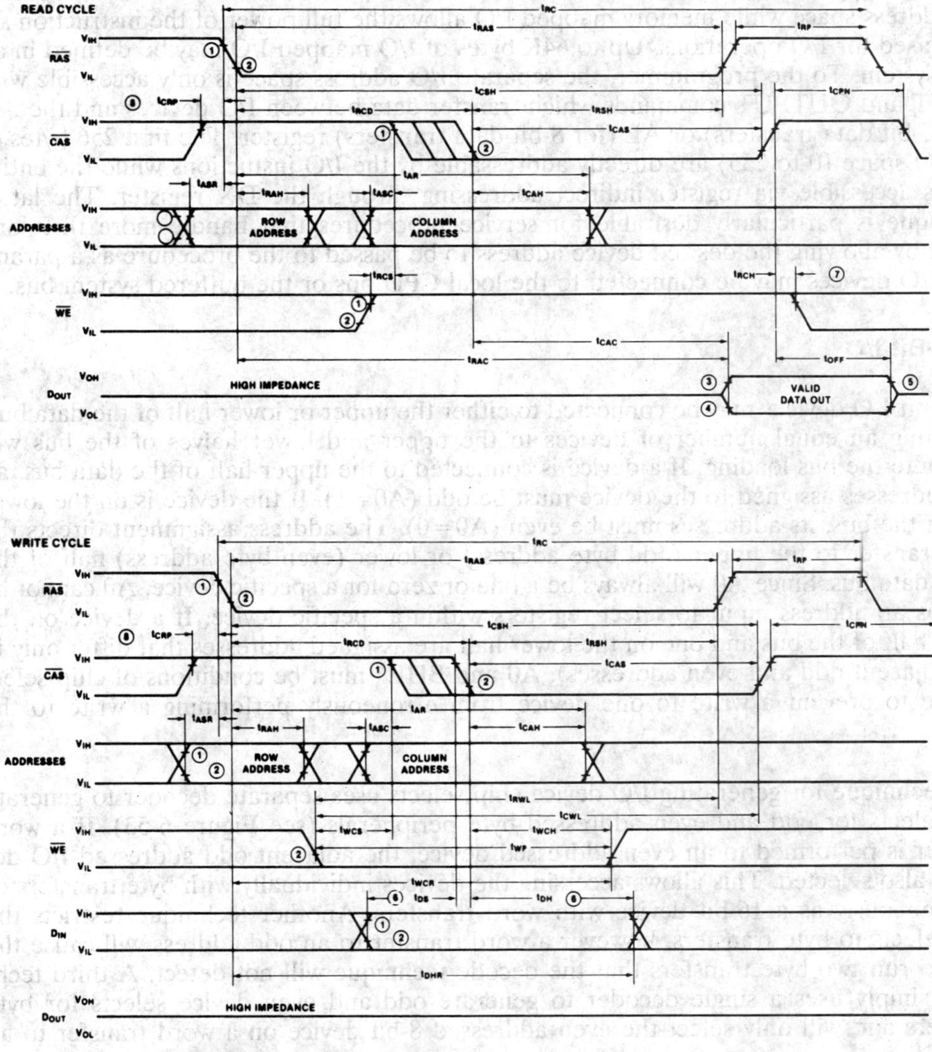

NOTES:
1,2. $V_{IH\ MIN}$ AND $V_{IL\ MAX}$ ARE REFERENCE LEVELS FOR MEASURING TIMING OF INPUT SIGNALS.
3,4. $V_{OH\ MIN}$ AND $V_{OL\ MAX}$ ARE REFERENCE LEVELS FOR MEASURING TIMING OF D_{OUT}.
5. t_{OFF} IS MEASURED TO $I_{OUT} < |I_{OL}|$.
6. t_{DS} AND t_{DH} ARE REFERENCED TO $\overline{CAS}$ OR $\overline{WE}$, WHICHEVER OCCURS LAST.
7. t_{RCH} IS REFERENCED TO THE TRAILING EDGE OF $\overline{CAS}$ OR $\overline{RAS}$, WHICHEVER OCCURS FIRST.
8. t_{CRP} REQUIREMENT IS ONLY APPLICABLE FOR $\overline{RAD}/\overline{CAS}$ CYCLES PRECEDED BY A $\overline{CAS}$-ONLY CYCLE (i.e., FOR SYSTEMS WHERE $\overline{CAS}$ HAS NOT BEEN DECODED WITH $\overline{RAS}$).

240487-001

Figure 6-52. 2164A Family Timing

I/O PERIPHERAL INTERFACE

The 8086 can interface with 8- and 16-bit I/O devices using either I/O instructions or memory mapped I/O. The I/O instructions allow the I/O devices to reside in a separate I/O address space while memory mapped I/O allows the full power of the instruction set to be used for I/O operations. Up to 64K bytes of I/O mapped I/O may be defined in an 8086 system. To the programmer, the separate I/O address space is only accessible with INPUT and OUTPUT commands which transfer data between I/O devices and the AX (for 16-bit data transfers) or AL (for 8-bit data transfers) register. The first 256 bytes of the I/O space (0 to 255) are directly addressable by the I/O instuctions while the entire 64K is accessible via register indirect addressing through the DX register. The latter technique is particularly desirable for service procedures that handle more than one device by allowing the desired device address to be passed to the procedure as a parameter. I/O devices may be connected to the local CPU bus or the buffered system bus.

Eight-Bit I/O

Eight-bit I/O devices may be connected to either the upper or lower half of the data bus. Assigning an equal number of devices to the upper and lower halves of the bus will distribute the bus loading. If a device is connected to the upper half of the data bus, all I/O addresses assigned to the device must be odd (A0=1). If the device is on the lower half of the bus, its addresses must be even (A0=0). The address assignment directs the 8-bit transfer to the upper (odd byte address) or lower (even byte address) half of the 16-bit data bus. Since A0 will always be a one or zero for a specific device, A0 cannot be used as an address input to select registers within a specific device. If a device on the upper half of the bus and one on the lower half are assigned addresses that differ only in A0 (adjacent odd and even addresses), A0 and BHE* must be conditions of chip select decode to prevent a write to one device from erroneously performing a write to the other.

One technique for generating I/O device chip selects uses separate decoder to generate chip selects for odd and even addressed byte peripherals (see Figure 6-53). If a word transfer is performed to an even addressed device, the adjacent odd addressed I/O device is also selected. This allows accessing the devices individually with byte transfers or simultaneously as a 16-bit device with word transfers. Another technique restricts the chip selects to byte transfers, however a word transfer to an odd address will cause the 8086 to run two byte transfers that the decode technique will not detect. A third technique simply uses a single decoder to generate odd and even device selects for byte transfers and will only select the even addressed 8-bit device on a word transfer to an even address.

One last technique for interfacing with 8-bit peripherals (see Figure 6-54) multiplexes the 16-bit data bus onto an 8-bit bus to accommodate byte oriented DMA or block transfers to memory mapped 8-bit I/O. Devices connected to this interface may be assigned a sequence of odd and even addresses rather than all odd or even.

If greater than 256 bytes of the I/O space or memory mapped I/O is used, additional decoding beyond these sample techniques may be necessary. This decoding can be done with additional TTL or a decoder.

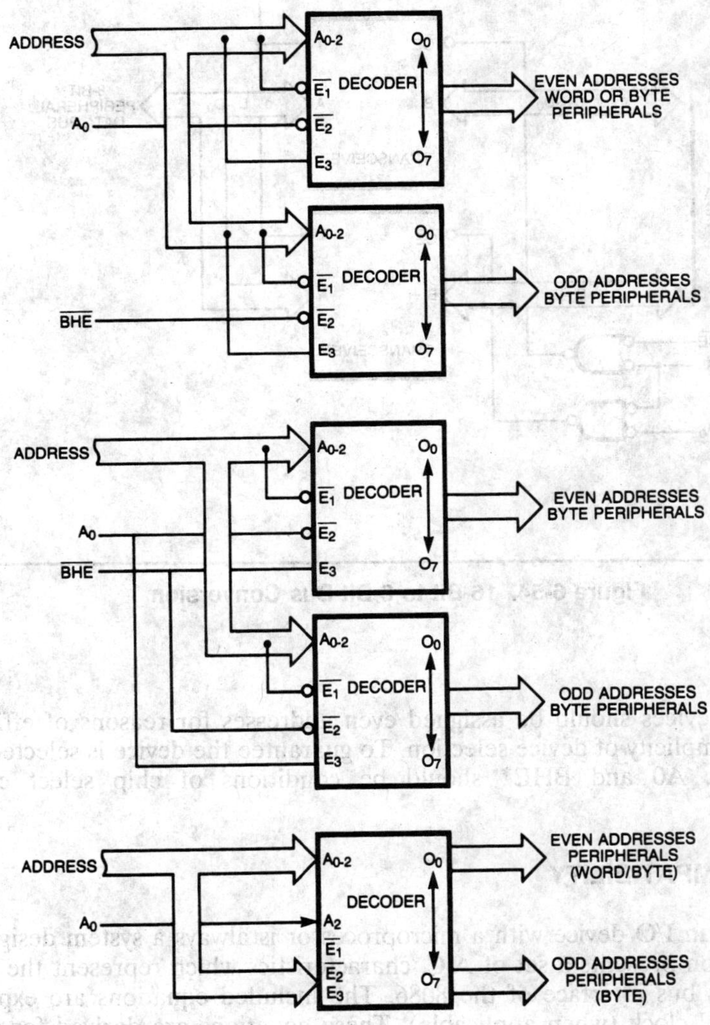

Figure 6-53. I/O Device Chip Select Techniques

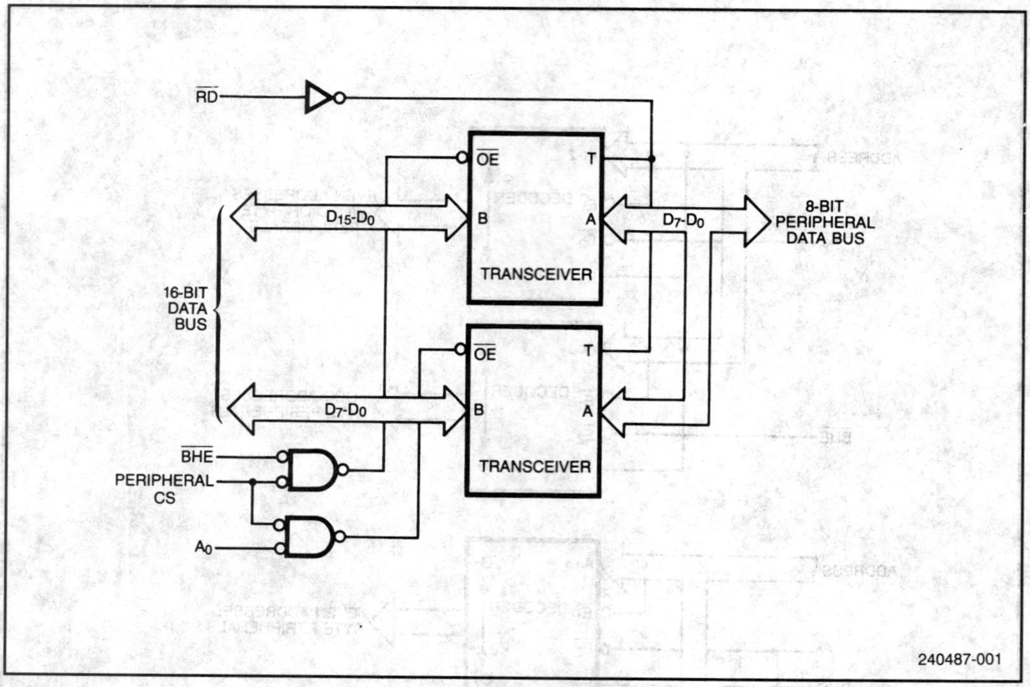

Figure 6-54. 16-Bit to 8-Bit Bus Conversion

Sixteen-Bit I/O

Sixteen-bit I/O devices should be assigned even addresses for reasons of efficient bus utilization and simplicity of device selection. To guarantee the device is selected only for word operations, A0 and BHE* should be conditions of chip select code (see Figure 6-55).

I/O DEVICE COMPATIBILITY

Compatibility of an I/O device with a microprocessor is always a system design consideration. This section presents a set of A.C. characteristics which represent the timing of the asynchronous bus interface of the 8086. The included equations are expressed in terms of the CPU clock (when applicable). These equations are derived for minimum and maximum modes of the 8086 and they represent the bus characteristics at the CPU. The results can be used to determine I/O device requirements for operation on a single CPU local bus or buffered system bus.

NOTE

These values are not applicable to a MULTIBUS system bus interface. The requirements for a MULTIBUS system bus are available in the MULTIBUS interface specification.

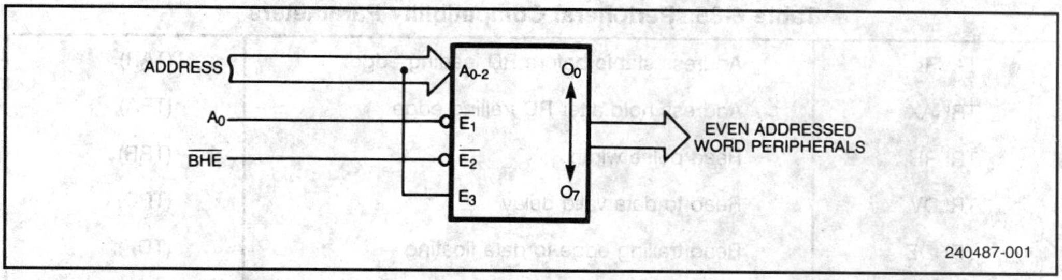

Figure 6-55. 16-Bit I/O Decode

Table 6-35 presents a list of bus parameters, their definition and how they relate to the A.C. characteristics of Intel peripherals. Table 6-36 presents Cycle dependent values of the parameters. For each equation, if more than one signal path is involved, the equation reflects the worst case path. For example:

TAVRL (address valid before read active) =
(1) Address from CPU to RD* active
(2) ALE (to enable the address through the address latches) to RD* active

The worst case delay path is (1).

For maximum mode 8086 configurations, TAVWLA, TWLWHA and TWLCLA relate to the advanced write signal while TAVWL, TWLWH and TWLCL relate to the normal write signal.

In the given list of equations, TWHDXB represents the data hold time from the trailing edge of write for the minimum mode with a buffered data bus. For this equation, TCVCTX cannot be a minimum for data hold and a maximum for write inactive. The maximum difference is 50 ns giving the result TCLCH-50. If the reader wishes to verify the equations or derive others, refer to the index under "Bus Timing" for assistance with interpreting the 8086 bus timing diagrams.

Figure 6-56 shows four representative configurations and the compatible Intel peripherals (including wait states if required) for each configuration given in Table 6-37. Configuration 1 and 2 consist of minimum mode demultiplexed bus 8086 systems without (1) and with (2) data bus transceivers. Configurations 3 and 4 consist of maximum mode systems with one (3) and two (4) levels of address and data buffering. The last configuration is characteristic of a multi-board system with bus buffers on each board. The 5 MHz parameter values for these configurations (refer to Table 6-38) demonstrate the relaxed device requirements for even a large complex configuration. The analysis assumes all components are exhibiting the specified worst case parameter values under the corresponding temperature, voltage and capacitive load conditions. If the capacitive loading on the latches or transceivers is less than the maximum, refer to the graphs of delay versus capacitive loading in the respective data sheets to determine the appropriate delay values.

Table 6-35. Peripheral Compatibility Parameters

TAVRL	Address stable before RD leading edge	(TAR)
TRHAX	Address hold after RD trailing edge	(TRA)
TRLRH	Read pulse width	(TRR)
TRLDV	Read to data valid delay	(TRD)
TRHDZ	Read trailing edge to data floating	(TDF)
TAVDV	Address to valid data delay	(TAD)
TRLRL	Read cycle time	(TRCYC)
TAVWL	Address valid before write leading edge	(TAW)
TAVWLA	Address valid before advanced write	(TAW)
TWHAX	Address hold after write trailing edge	(TWA)
TWLWH	Write pulse width	(TWW)
TWLWHA	Advanced write pulse width	(TWW)
TDVWH	Data set up to write trailing edge	(TDW)
TWHDX	Data hold from write trailing edge	(TWD)
TWLCL	Write recovery time	(TRV)
TWLCLA	Advanced write recovery time	(TRV)
TSVRL	Chip select stable before RD leading edge	(TAR)
TRHSX	Chip select hold after RD trailing edge	(TRA)
TSLDV	Chip select to data valid delay	(TRD)
TSVWL	Chip select stable before WR leading edge	(TAW)
TWHSX	Chip select hold after WR trailing edge	(TWA)
TSVWLA	Chip select stable before advanced write	(TAW)

NOTE:
Symbols in parentheses are equivalent parameters specified for Intel® peripherals

Table 6-36. Peripherals Cycle-Dependent Parameter Requirements

(a) Minimum Mode
TAVRL = TCLCL + TCLRLmin − TCLAVmax = TCLCL − 100
TRHAX = TCLCL − TCLRHmax + TCLLHmin = TCLCL − 150
TRLRH = 2TCLCL − 60 = 2TCLCL − 60
TRLDV = 2TCLCL − TCLRLmax − TDVCLmin = 2TCLCL − 195
TRHDZ = TRHAVmin = 155 ns
TAVDV = 3TCLCL − TDVCLmin − TCLAVmax = 3TCLCL − 140
TRLRL = 4TCLCL = 4TCLCL
TAVWL = TCLCL + TCVCTVmin − TCLAVmax = TCLCL − 100
TWHAX = TCLCL + TCLLHmin − TCVCTXmax = TCLCL −110
TWLWH = 2TCLCL − 40 = 2TCLCL − 40
TDVWH = 2TCLCL + TCVCTXmin − TCLDVmax = 2TCLCL − 100
TWHDX = TWHDZmin = 89
TWLCL = 4TCLCL = 4TCLCL
TWHDXB = TCLCHmin + (−TCVCTXmax + TCVCTXmin) = TCLCHmin − 50
(b) Maximum Mode
TAVRL = TCLCL + TCLMLmin − TCLAVmax = TCLCL − 100
TRHAX = TCLCL − TCLMHmax + TCLLHmin = TCLCL − 40
TRLRH = 2TCLCL − TCLMLmax + TCLMHmin = 2TCLCL − 25
TRLDV = 2TCLCL − TCLMLmax − TDVCLmin = 2TCLCL −65
TRHDZ = TRHAVmin = 155
TAVDV = 3TCLCL − TDVCLmin − TCLAVmax = 3TCLCL − 140
TRLRL = 4TCLCL = 4TCLCL
TAVWLA = TAVRL = TCLCL − 100
TAVWL = TAVRL + TCLCL = 2TCLCL −100
TWHAX = TRHAX = TCLCL − 40
TWLWHA = TRLRH = 2TCLCL − 25
TWLWH = TRLRH − TCLCL = TCLCL −25
TDVWH = 2TCLCL + TCLMHmin − TCLDVmax = 2TCLCL − 100
TWHDZ = TCLCHmin − TCLMHmax + TCHDZmin = TCLCHmin −30
TWLCL = 3TCLCL = 3TCLCL
TWLCLA = 4TCLCL = 4TCLCL

NOTE: Delays relative to chip select are a function of the chip select decode technique used and are equal to: equivalent delay from address − chip select decode delay

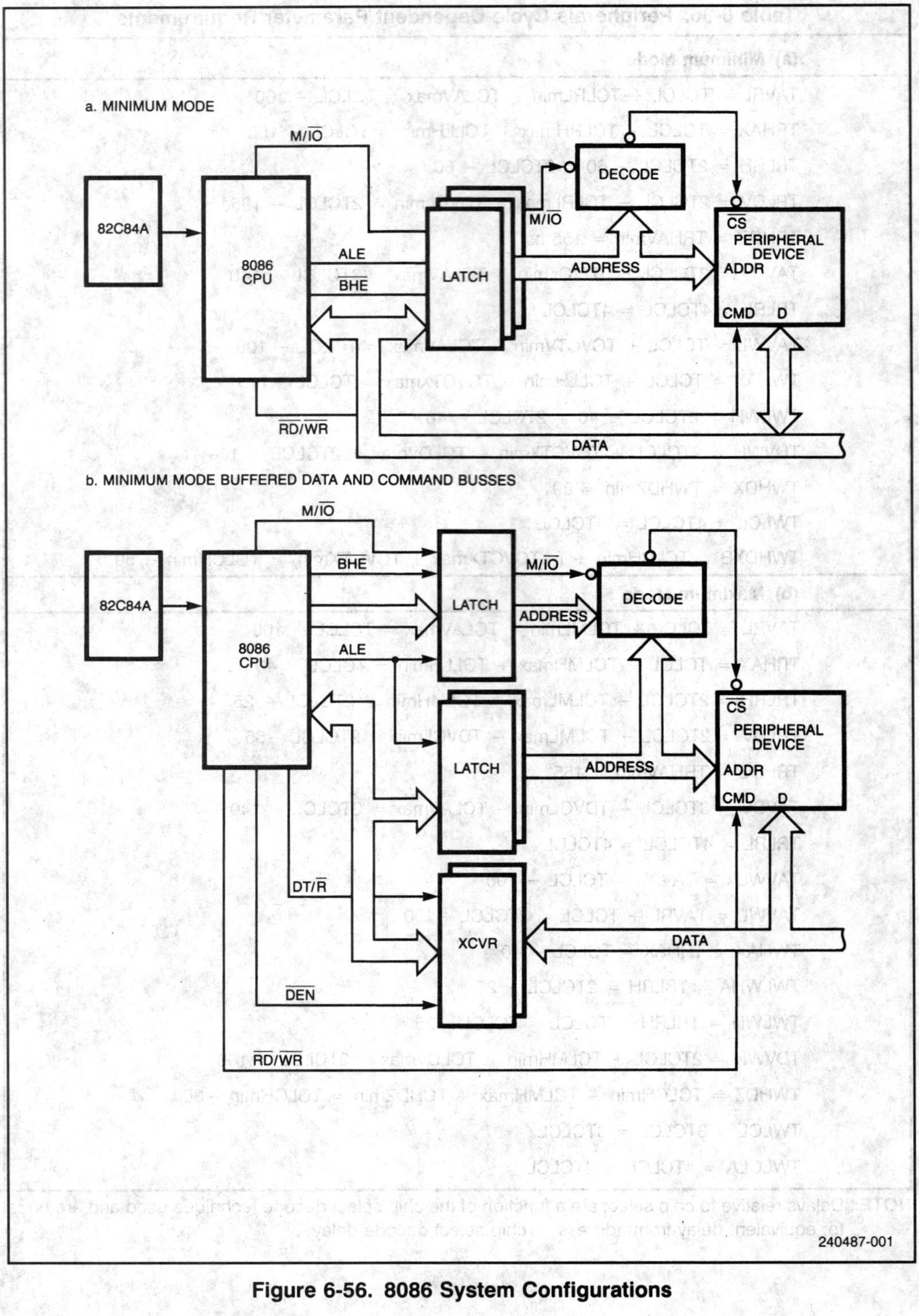

Figure 6-56. 8086 System Configurations

Table 6-37. Compatible Peripherals for a 5 MHz 8086/8088

	Configuration			
	Minimum Mode		Maximum Mode	
	Unbuffered	Buffered	Buffered	Fully Buffered
8251A	X	1W	X	X
8253-5	X	1W	X	X
8255A-5	X	1W	X	X
8257-5	X	1W	X	X
8259A	X	X	X	X
8271	X	1W	X	X
8273	X	1W	X	X
8275	X	1W	X	X
8279-5	X	1W	X	X
8041A*	X	1W	X	X
8741A	X	1W	X	X
8291	X	X	X	X

* includes other Intel® peripherals based on the 8041A (i.e., 8292, 8294, 8295).

X implies full operation with no wait states.

W implies the number of wait states required.

Table 6-38. Compatible Peripheral Requirements for Full Speed Operation with a 5 MHz 8086/8088

	Configuration			
	Maximum Mode		Maximum Mode	
	Unbuffered	Buffered	Buffered	Fully Buffered
TAVRL	70	72	70	58
TRHAX	57	27	169	141
TRLRH	340	320	375	347
TRLDV	205	150	305	261
TRHDZ	155	158	382	360
TAVDV	430	400	400	372
TRLRL	800	770	800	772
TAVWL	70	72	270	258
TAVWLA	—	—	70	58
TWHAX	97	67	169	141
TWLWH	360	340	175	147
TWLWHA	—	—	375	347
TDVWH	300	339	270	258
TWHDX	88	15	95	13
TWLCL	800	772	600	572
TWLCLA	—	—	800	772
TSVRL	52	54	52	40
TRHSX	50	50	171	143
TSLDV	412	382	382	354
TSVWL	52	54	252	240
TWHSX	90	90	171	143
TSVWLA	—	—	52	40

To determine peripheral compatibility, modify the equations given for the CPU to account for additional delays from address latches and data transceivers in the configuration. Once the system configuration is selected, determine the system requirements at the peripheral interface and use the results to evaluate compatibility of the peripheral to the system. During this process, consider: (1) can the device operate at maximum bus bandwidth and if not, how many wait states are required, and (2) are there any problems that cannot be resolved by wait states.

Examples of the first consideration include TRLRH (read pulse width) and TRLDV (read access or RD* active to output data valid). Consider address access time (valid address to valid data) for the maximum mode fully buffered configuration.

TAVDV = 3TCYC − 140 ns − address latch delay − address buffer delay − chip select decode delay − 2 transceiver delays

Assuming inverting latches, buffers and transceivers with 22 ns max delays, the result is:

TAVDV = 322 ns @ 5 MHz

This result gives the address to data valid delay required at the peripheral (in this configuration) to satisfy zero wait state CPU access time. If the maximum delay specified for the peripheral is less than the result, this parameter is compatible with zero wait state CPU operation. If not, wait states must be inserted until TAVDV + n * TCYC (n is the number of wait states) is greater than the peripherals maximum delay. If several parameters require wait states either the largest number required should always be used or different transfer cycles can insert the maximum number required for that cycle.

The second consideration includes TAVRL (address set up to read) and TWHDX (data hold after write). Incompatibilities in this area cannot be resolved by the insertion of wait states and may require either additional hardware, slowing down the CPU (if the parameter is related to the clock) or not using the device. As an example, consider address valid prior to advanced write lower (TAVWLA) for the maximum mode fully buffered:

TAVWLA = TCYC − 100 ns − address latch delay − address buffer delay − chip select decode delay + write buffer delay (minimum)

Assuming inverting latches and buffers with 22 ns delay and an address decoder with 18 ns delay:

TAVWLA = 38 ns which is the time a 5 MHz 8086 system provides.

Multiple Communications Lines Example

Consider an interrupt drive procedure for handling multiple communication lines. On receiving an interrupt from one of the lines, the invoked procedure polls the lines (reading the status of each) to determine which line to service. The procedure does not enable lines but simply services input and output requests until the associated output buffer is empty (for output requests) or until an input line is terminated (for the example, only EOT is considered). On detection of the terminate condition, the routine will disable the line. It is assumed that other routines will fill a lines output buffer and enable the device to request output or empty the input buffer and enable the device to input additional characters.

The routine begins operation by loading CX with a count of the number of lines in the system and DX with the I/O address of the first line. The I/O addresses are designed with 8251's as the I/O devices (see Figure 6-57). The status of each line is read to determine if it needs service. If yes, the appropriate routine is called to input or output a character. After servicing the line or if no service is needed, CX is decremented and DX is incremented to test the next line. After all lines have been tested and serviced, the routine terminates. If all interrupts from the lines are OR'd together, only one interrupt is used for all lines. If the interrupt is input to the CPU through an 8259A interrupt controller, the 8259A should be programmed in the level triggered mode to guarantee all line interrupts are serviced.

To service either an input or an output request (see Figure 6-58), the called routine transfers DX to BX, and shifts BX to form the offset for this device into the table of input or output buffers. The first entry in the buffer is an index to the next character position in the buffer and is loaded into the SI register. By specifying the base address of the table of buffers as a displacement into the data segment, the base + index + displacement addressing mode allows direct access to the appropriate memory location.

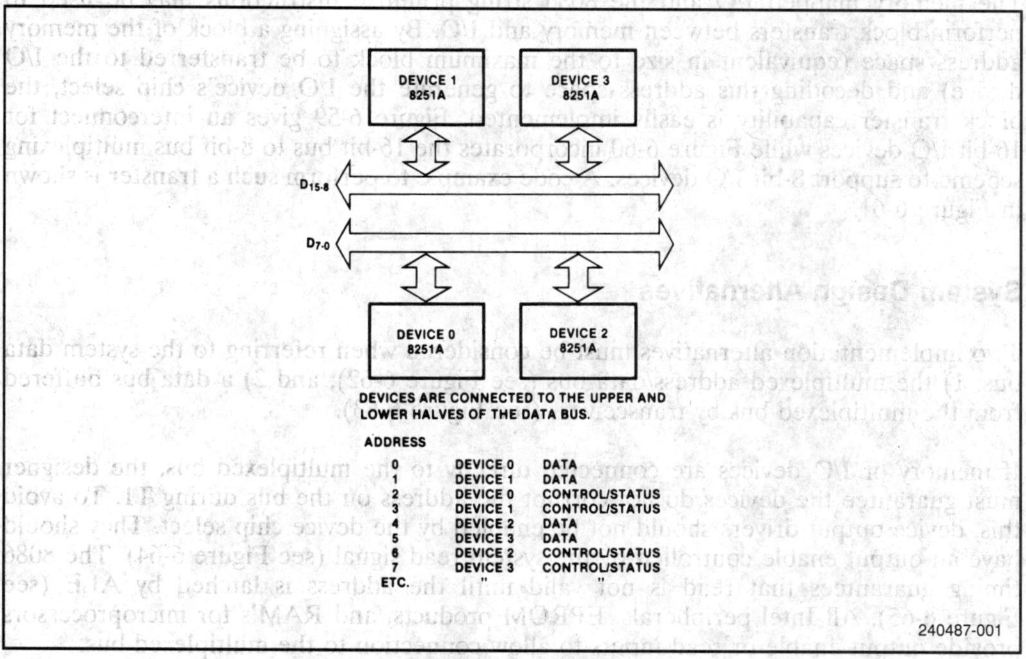

Figure 6-57. Device Assignment

```
; THIS CODE DEMONSTRATES TESTING DEVICE
; STATUS FOR SERVICE, CONSTRUCTING THE
; APPROPRIATE LINE BUFFER ADDRESS FOR INPUT
; AND OUTPUT AND SERVICING AN INPUT
; REQUEST

                MASK EQU OFFFDH
CHECK_STATUS:   INPUT   AL, DX                  ; GET 8251A STATUS.
                MOV     AH, AL
                TEST    AH, READ_OR_WRITE_STATUS
                JZ      NEXT_IO
                CALL    ADDRESS
                TEST    AH, READ STATUS
                JZ      WRITE_SERVICE
                CALL    READ
                TEST    AH, WRITE STATUS
                JZ      NEXT_IO
WRITE_SERVICE:  CALL    WRITE
NEXT_IO:        DEC     CX                      ; TEST IF DONE.
                JNC     EXIT                    ; YES, RESTORE & RETURN.
                AND     DX, MASK                ; REMOVE A1 AND
                ADD     DX, 3                   ; INCREMENT ADDRESS.
                OR      DX, 2                   ; SELECT STATUS FOR
                JMP     CHECK_STATUS            ; NEXT INPUT.

ADDRESS:        AND     DX, MASK                ; SELECT DATA.
                MOV     BH, DL                  ; CONSTRUCT BUFFER
                INC     BH                      ; DISPLACEMENT FOR
                SHR     BH                      ; THIS DEVICE.
                XOR     BL, BL                  ; BX IS THE DISPLACEMENT.
                RET

READ:           INPUT AL, DX                        ; READ CHARACTER.
                MOV SI, READ_BUFFERS [BX]           ; GET CHARACTER POINTER.
                MOV READ_BUFFERS [BX + SI], AL      ; STORE CHARACTER.
                INC READ_BUFFERS [BX]               ; INCR CHARACTER POINTER.
                CMP AL, EOT                         ; END OF TRANSMISSION?
                JNZ CONT_READ
                CALL DISABLE READ                   ; YES, DISABLE RECEIVER.
                CONT_READ:   RET                    ; SEND MESSAGE THAT INPUT
                                                    ; IS READY.
```

Figure 6-58. I/O Input Request Code Example

Memory — I/O Block Transfers Example

The memory mapped I/O and the 8086 string primitive instructions may be used to perform block transfers between memory and I/O. By assigning a block of the memory address space (equivalent in size to the maximum block to be transferred to the I/O device) and decoding this address space to generate the I/O device's chip select, the block transfer capability is easily implemented. Figure 6-59 gives an interconnect for 16-bit I/O devices while Figure 6-60 incorporates the 16-bit bus to 8-bit bus multiplexing scheme to support 8-bit I/O devices. A code example to perform such a transfer is shown in Figure 6-61.

System Design Alternatives

Two implementation alternatives must be considered when referring to the system data bus: 1) the multiplexed address/data bus (see Figure 6-62); and 2) a data bus buffered from the multiplexed bus by transceivers (see Figure 6-63).

If memory or I/O devices are connected directly to the multiplexed bus, the designer must guarantee the devices do not corrupt the address on the bus during T1. To avoid this, device output drivers should not be enabled by the device chip select. They should have an output enable controlled by the system read signal (see Figure 6-64). The 8086 timing guarantees that read is not valid until the address is latched by ALE (see Figure 6-65). All Intel peripherals, EPROM products, and RAM's for microprocessors provide output enable or read inputs to allow connection to the multiplexed bus.

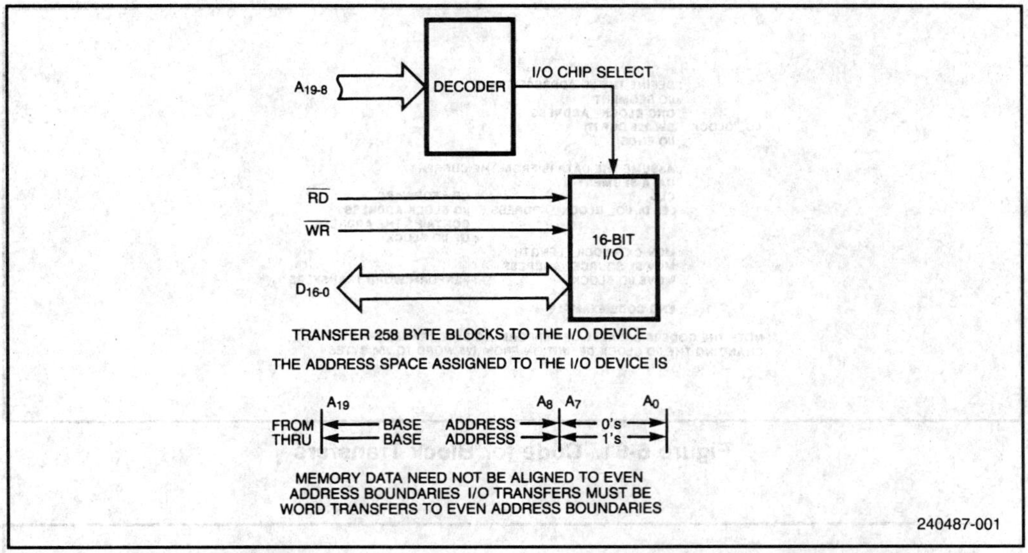

Figure 6-59. Block Transfer to 16-Bit I/O using 8086/8088 String Primitives

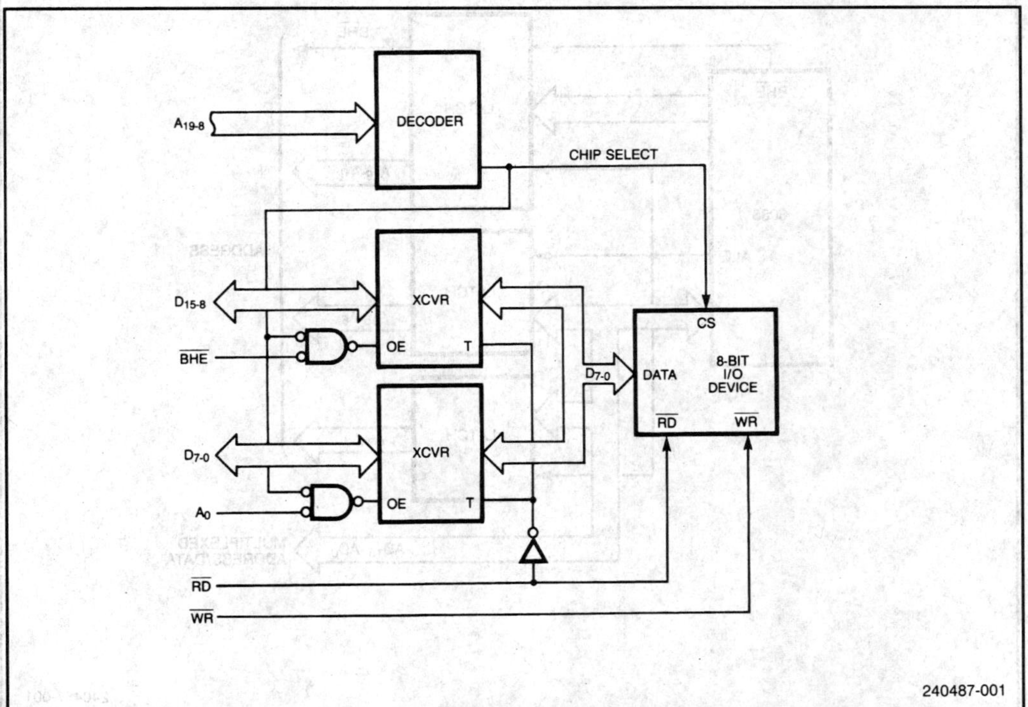

Figure 6-60. Block Transfer to 8-Bit I/O using 8086/8088 String Primitives

```
              ; DEFINE THE I/O ADDRESS SPACE
              I/O SEGMENT
              ORG BLOCK_ADDRESS
I/O_BLOCK:    DW 128 DUP (?)
              I/O ENDS

              ; ASSUME THE DATA IS FROM THE CURRENT
              ; DATA SEGMENT
              CLD                           ; DF = FORWARD
              LES DI, I/O_BLOCK_ADDRESS     ; I/O BLOCK ADDRESS
                                            ; CONTAINS THE ADDRESS
                                            ; OF I/O BLOCK
              MOV CX, BLOCK_LENGTH
              MOV SI, SOURCE_ADDRESS
              MOVS I/O BLOCK                ; PERFORM WORD TRANSFERS

              ; END CODE EXAMPLE

NOTE THE CODE IS CAPABLE OF PERFORMING BYTE TRANSFERS BY
CHANGING THE I/O BLOCK DEFINITION FROM 128 WORD TO 256 BYTES
```

Figure 6-61. Code for Block Transfers

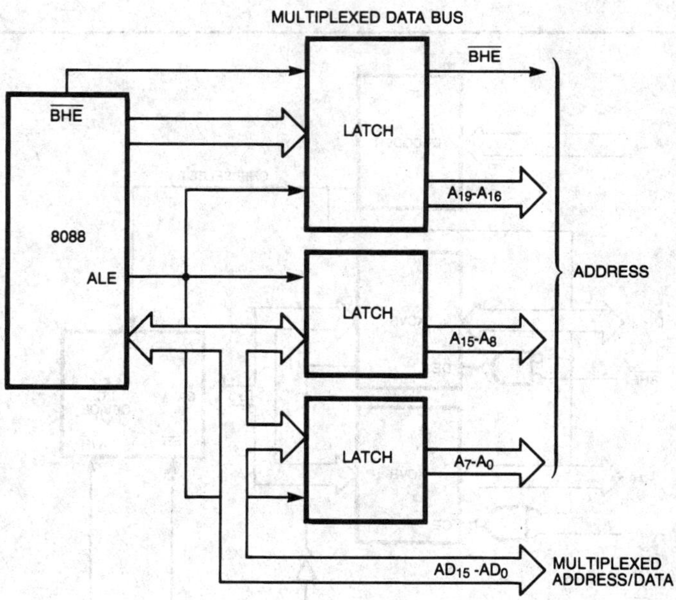

Figure 6-62. Multiplexed Data Bus

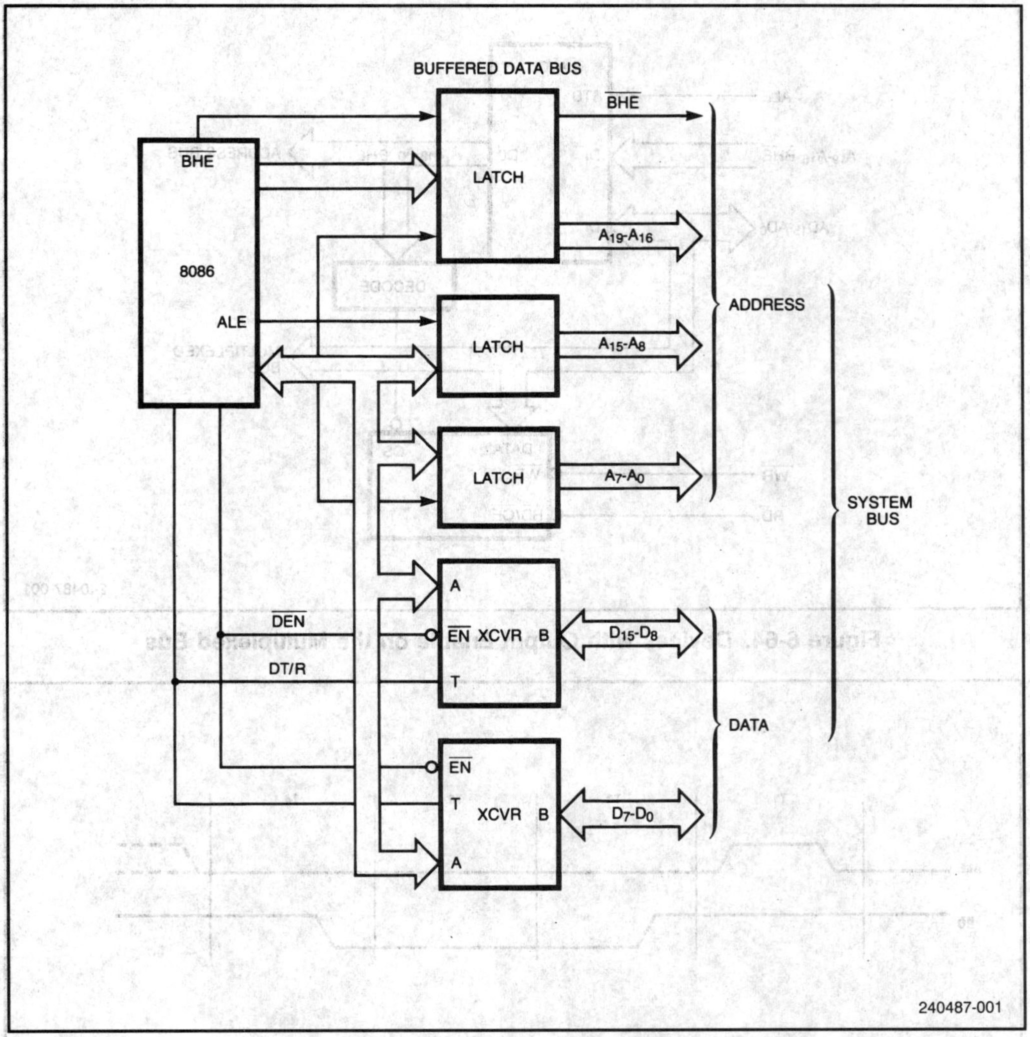

Figure 6-63. Buffered Data Bus

There are several techniques available for interfacing devices without output enables to the multiplexed bus. Note that each of these techniques introduces other restrictions or limitations. Consider the case of chip select gated with read and write (see Figure 6-66). Two problems exist with this technique. First, the chip select access time is reduced to the read access time, and may require a faster device if maximum system performance (i.e., no wait states) is to be achieved (see Figure 6-67). Second, the designer must verify that the chip select-to-write setup and hold times for the device are not violated (see Figure 6-68). Alternate techniques can be extracted from the bus interfacing techniques, also described in this chapter, but are subject to the associated restrictions. In general, for best results, use devices with output enables.

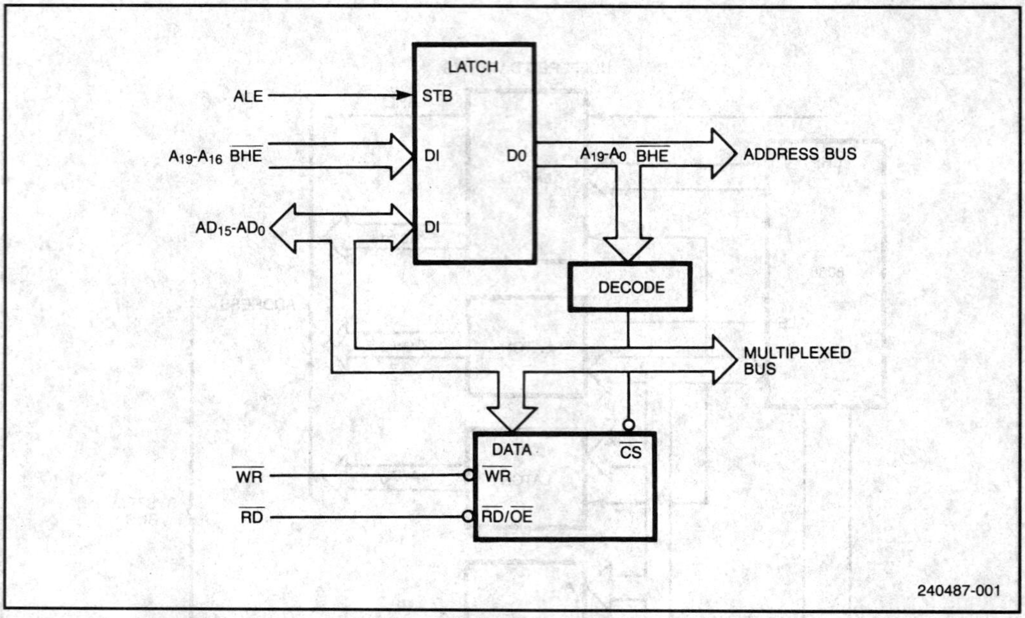

Figure 6-64. Devices with Output Enable on the Multiplexed Bus

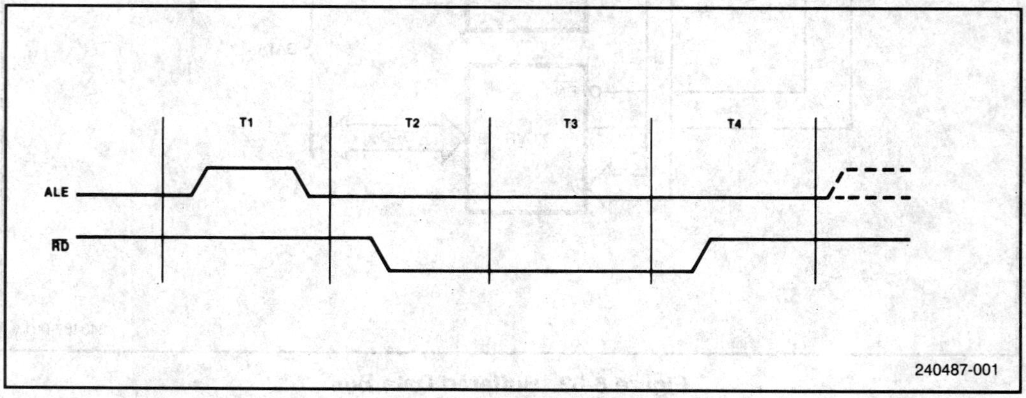

Figure 6-65. Relationship of ALE to READ

To guarantee the specified A.C. characteristics, the 8086's drive capability of 2.0 mA and capacitive loading of 100 pF subsequently limits the fan out of the multiplexed bus. Assuming capacitive loads of 20 pF per I/O device, 12 pF per address latch and 5-12 pF per memory device, a system mix of three peripherals and two to four memory devices (per bus line) approach the loading limit.

The data bus must be buffered using inverting or non-inverting octal buffers to satisfy the capacitive loading and drive requirements of larger systems. To enable and control the direction of the transceivers, the 8086 provides Data Enable (DEN) and Data

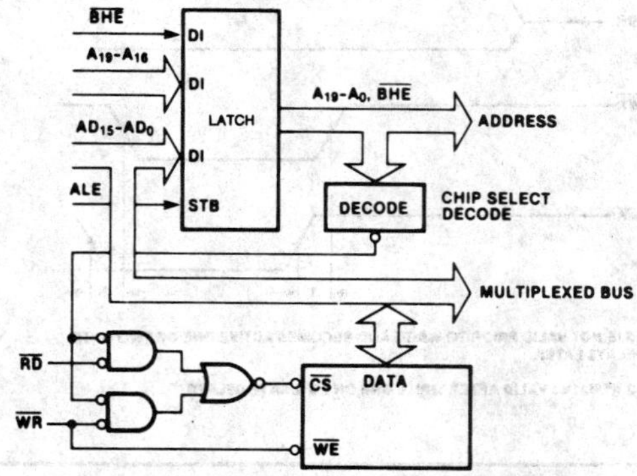

Figure 6-66. Devices without Output Enable on the Multiplexed Bus

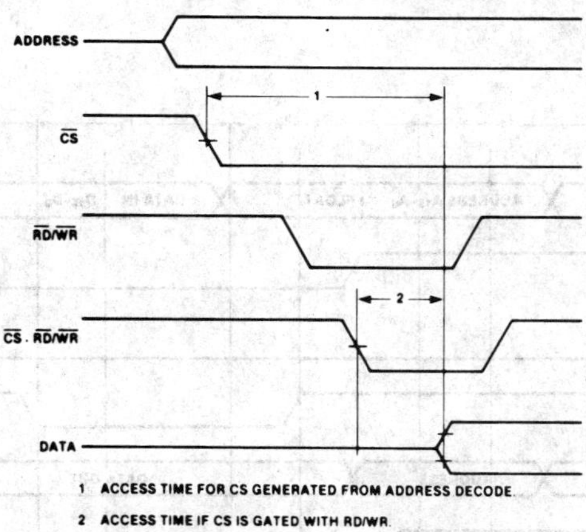

Figure 6-67. Access Time – CS Gated with AD*/WR*

Transmit/Receive (DT/R*) signals (see Figure 6-63). These signals provide the appropriate timing to guarantee isolation of the multiplexed bus from the system during T1 and elimination of bus contention with the CPU during read and write (see Figure 6-69). Although the memory and peripheral devices are isolated from the CPU (see Figure 6-70), bus contention may still exist in the system if the devices do not have an output enable control other than chip select. As an example, bus contention will exist during transition from one chip select to another (the newly selected device begins driving the bus before the previous device has disabled its drivers). Another, more severe case exists during a write cycle: from chip select to write active, a device whose outputs are controlled only by chip select, will drive the bus simultaneously with write data being driven through the transceivers by the CPU (see Figure 6-71). The same technique given for circumventing these problems on the multiplexed bus can be applied here with the same limitations.

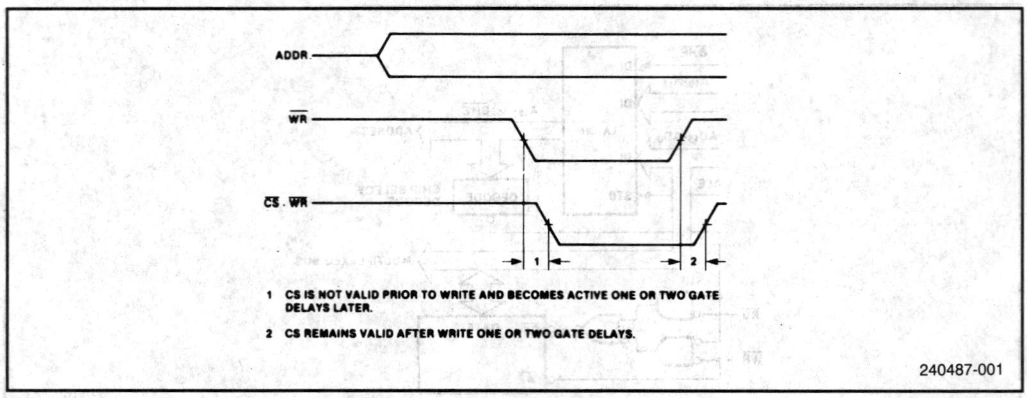

Figure 6-68. CE to WR* Setup and Hole

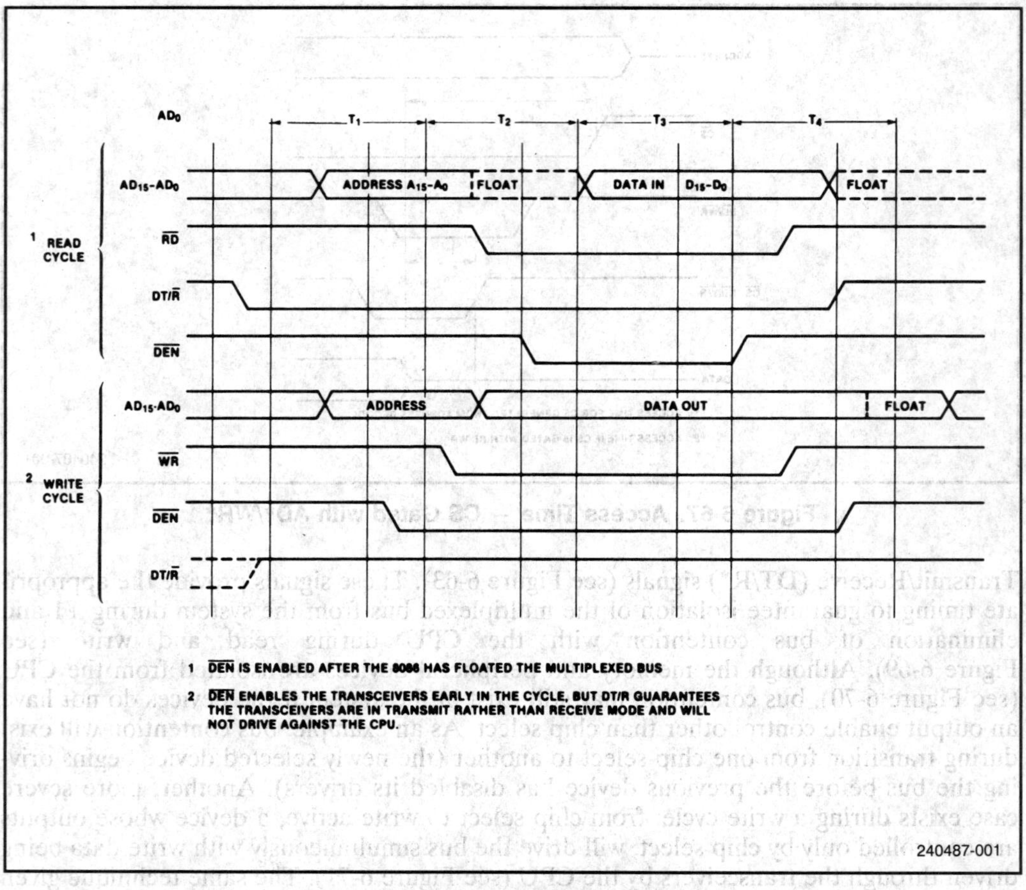

Figure 6-69. Bus Transceiver Control

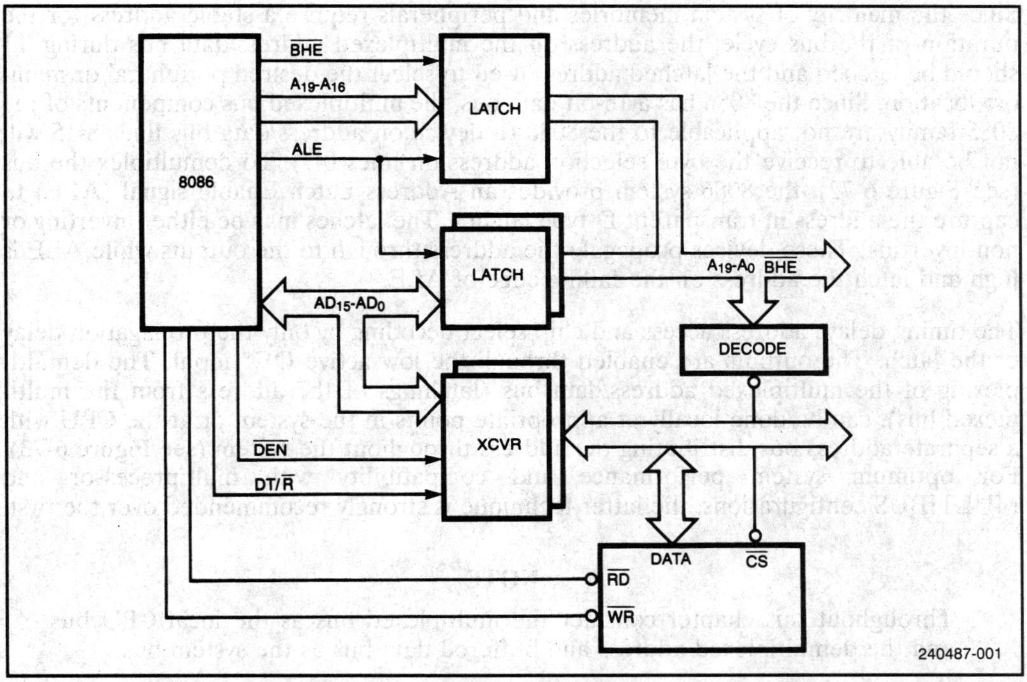

Figure 6-70. Devices with Output Enable on the System Bus

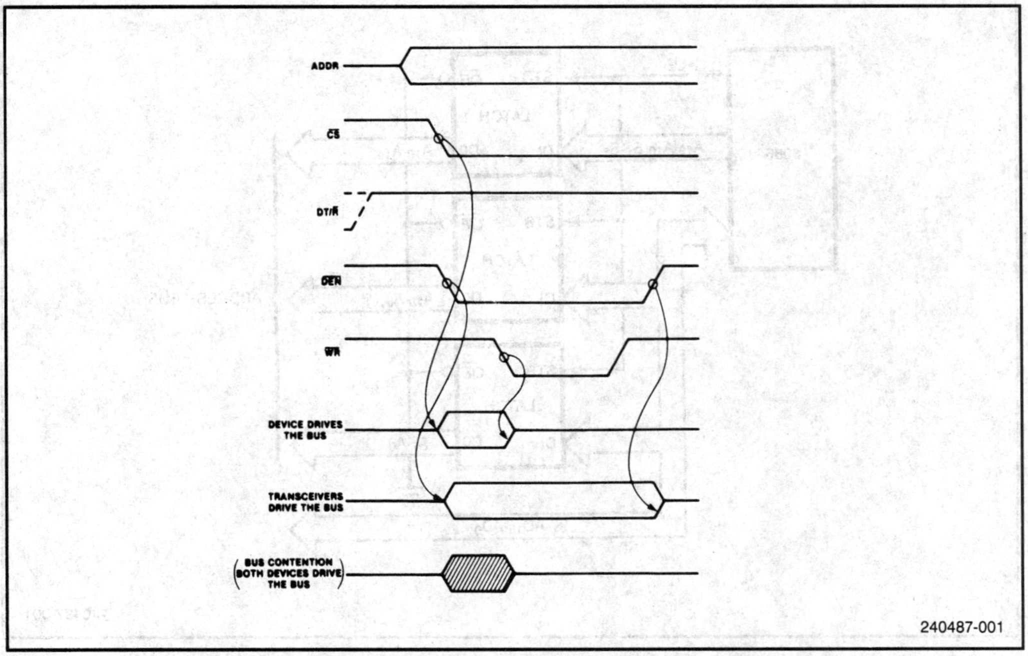

Figure 6-71. CS*/Bus Driving Device Timing

Since the majority of system memories and peripherals require a stable address for the duration of the bus cycle, the address on the multiplexed address/data bus during T1 should be latched and the latched address used to select the desired peripheral or memory location. Since the 8086 has a 16-bit data bus, the multiplexed bus components of the 8085 family are not applicable to the 8086 (a device on address/data bus lines 8-15 will not be able to receive the byte selection address on lines 0-7). To demultiplex the bus (see Figure 6-72), the 8086 system provides an Address Latch Enable signal (ALE) to capture the address in transparent D-type latches. The latches may be either inverting or non-inverting. These devices propagate the address through to the outputs while ALE is high and latch the address on the falling edge of ALE.

The timing delays address access and chip select decoding by only the propagation delay of the latch. The outputs are enabled through the low active OE* input. The demultiplexing of the multiplexed address/data bus (latchings of the address from the multiplexed bus), can be done locally at appropriate points in the system or at the CPU with a separate address bus distributing the address throughout the system (see Figure 6-73). For optimum system performance and compatibility with multiprocessor and MULTIBUS configurations, the latter technique is strongly recommended over the first.

NOTE

Throughout this chapter consider the multiplexed bus as the local CPU bus and the demultiplexed address and buffered data bus as the system bus.

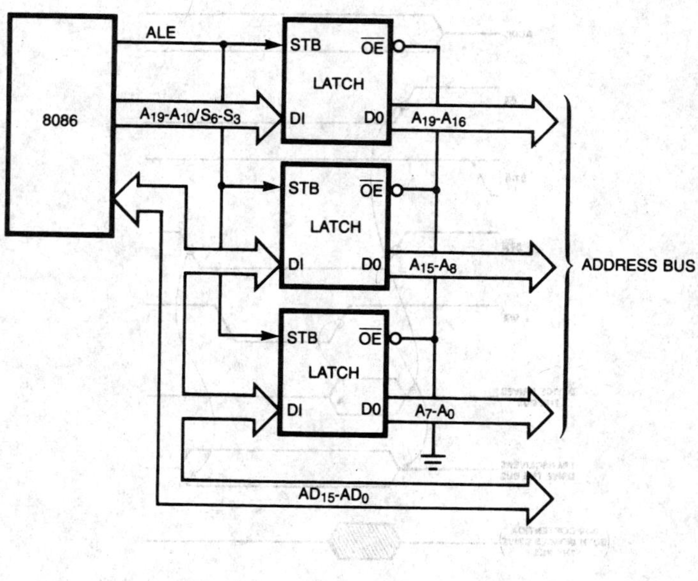

Figure 6-72. Demultiplexing Address and Data from the Processor Bus

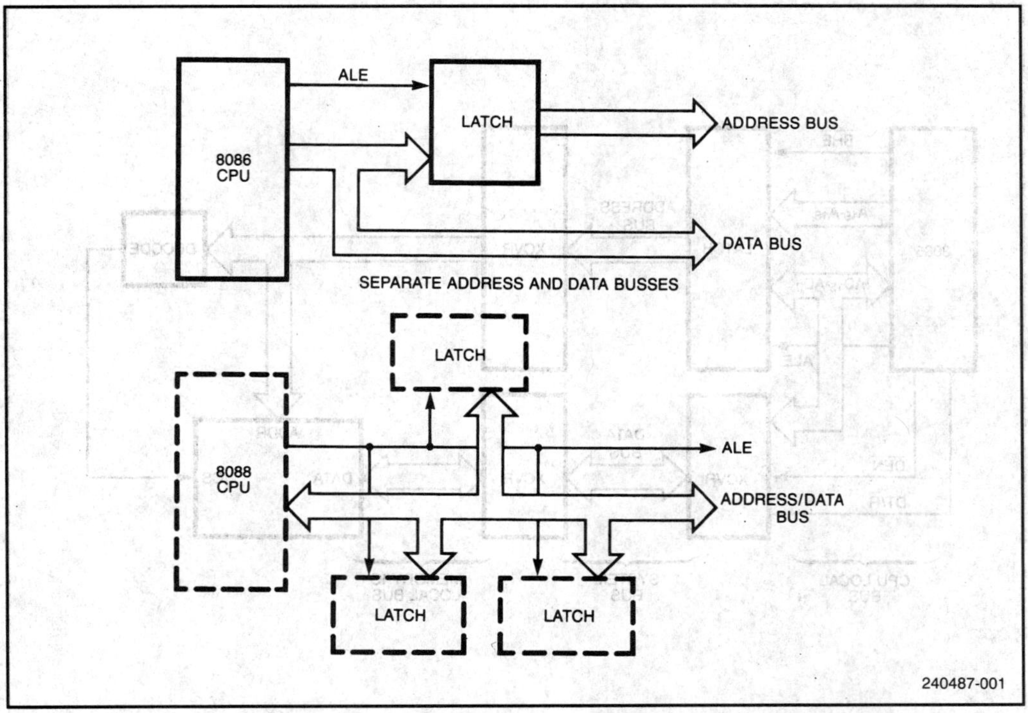

Figure 6-73. Multiplexed Bus with Local Address Demultiplexing

MULTIPLEXED ADDRESS AND DATA BUS

An additional extension to bus implementation is a second level of buffering to reduce the total load seen by devices on the system bus (see Figure 6-74). This technique is typically used for multiboard systems and for isolation of memory arrays. The concerns with this configuration are the additional delay for access and, more important, control of the second transceiver in relationship to the system bus and the device being interfaced to the system bus. One technique for controlling the transceiver (see Figure 6-75) simply distributes DEN and DT/R* throughout the system. DT/R* is inverted to provide proper direction control for the second level transceivers. Another technique (see Figure 6-76) provides control for devices with output enables. RD* is used to normally direct data from the system bus to the peripheral. The buffer is selected whenever a device on the local bus is chip selected. Bus contention is possible on the device's local bus during a read as the read simultaneously enables the device output and changes the transceiver direction. Contention may also occur as the read is terminated.

For devices without output enables, the same technique can be applied (see Figure 6-77) if the chip select to the device is conditioned by read or write. Controlling the chip select with read/write prevents the device from driving against the transceiver prior to the command being received. Using this technique, read/write time and CS-to-write setup and hold times limit access to the devices.

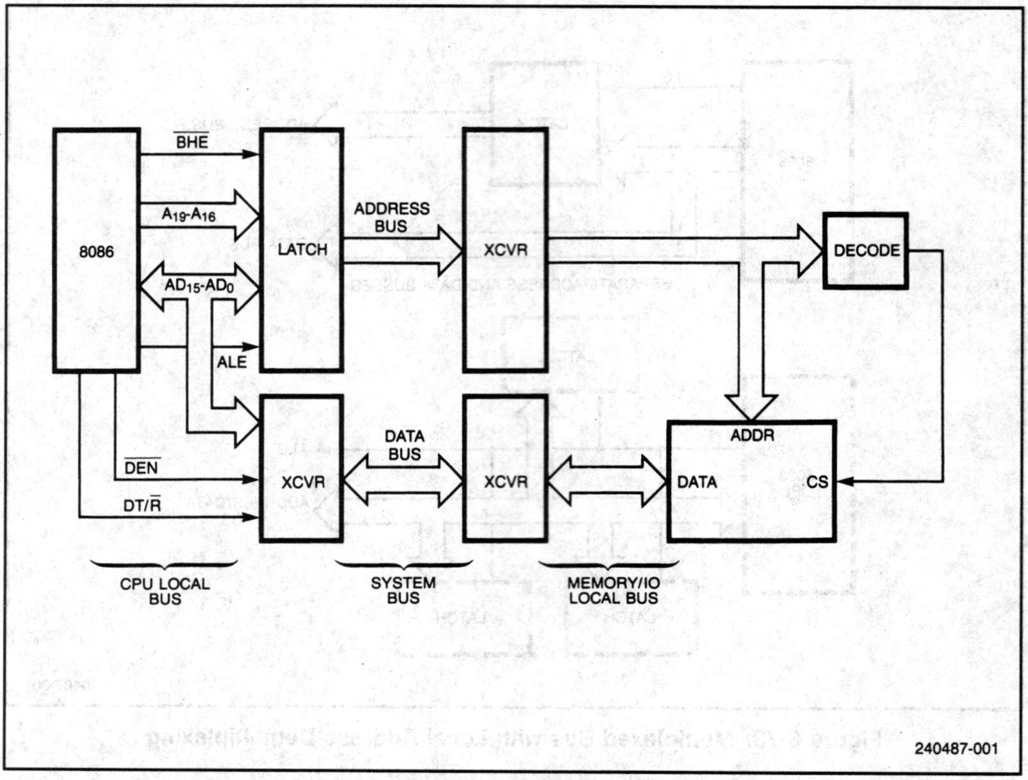

Figure 6-74. Fully Buffered System

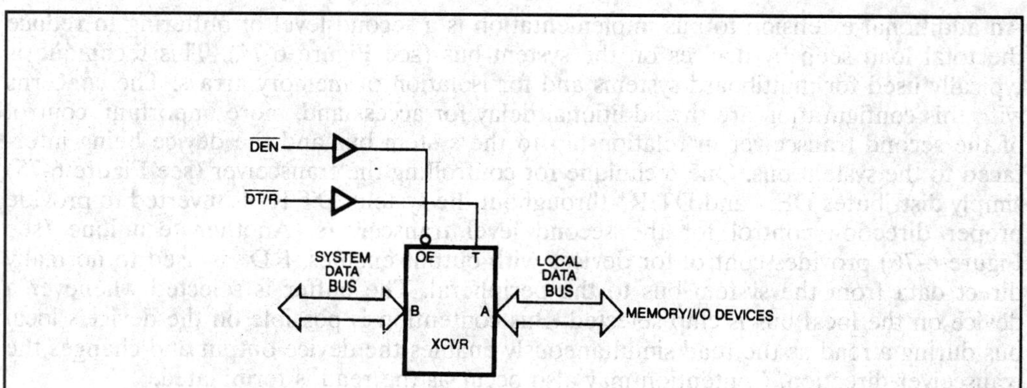

Figure 6-75. Controlling System Transceivers with DEN and DT/R*

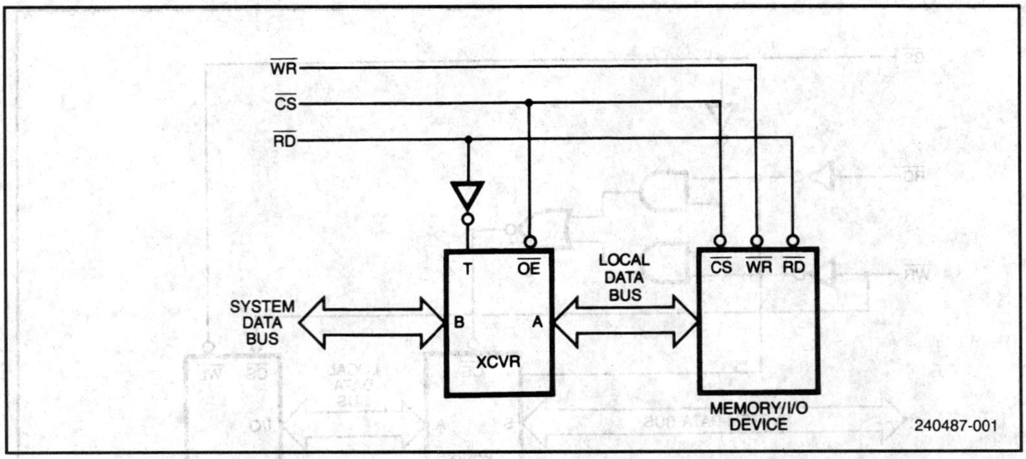

Figure 6-76. Buffering Devices with OE*/RD*

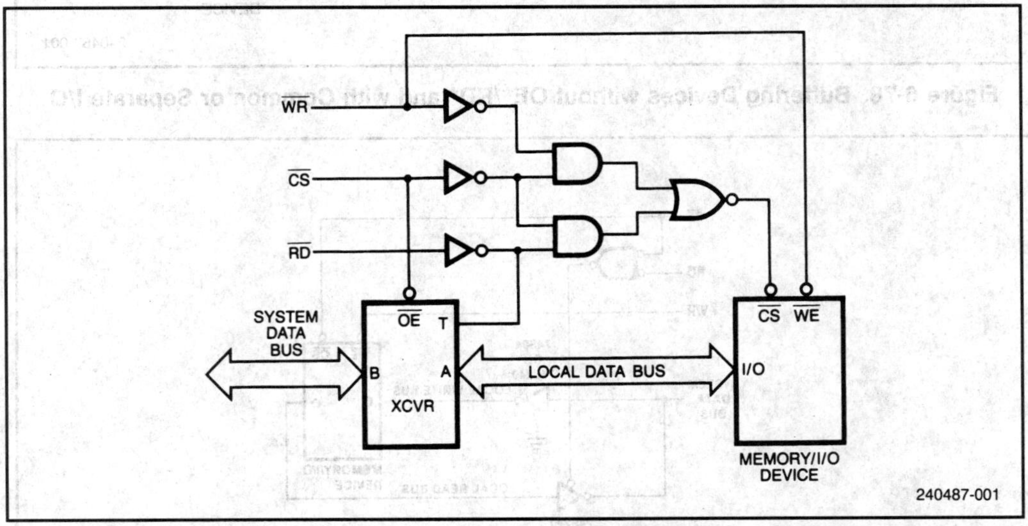

Figure 6-77. Buffering Devices without OE*/RD* and with Common or Separate I/O

Using an alternate technique applicable to devices with and without output enables, (see Figure 6-78). RD* controls the direction of the transceiver but it is not enabled until a command and chip select are active. The possibility for bus contention still exists but is reduced to variations in output enable versus direction change time for the transceiver. Full access time from chip select is now available, but data will not be valid prior to write and will only be held valid after write by the delay to disable the transceiver.

In the last example of a technique for devices with separate inputs and outputs (see Figure 6-79) separate bus receivers and drivers are provided rather than a single transceiver. The receiver is always enabled while the bus driver is controlled by RD* and chip

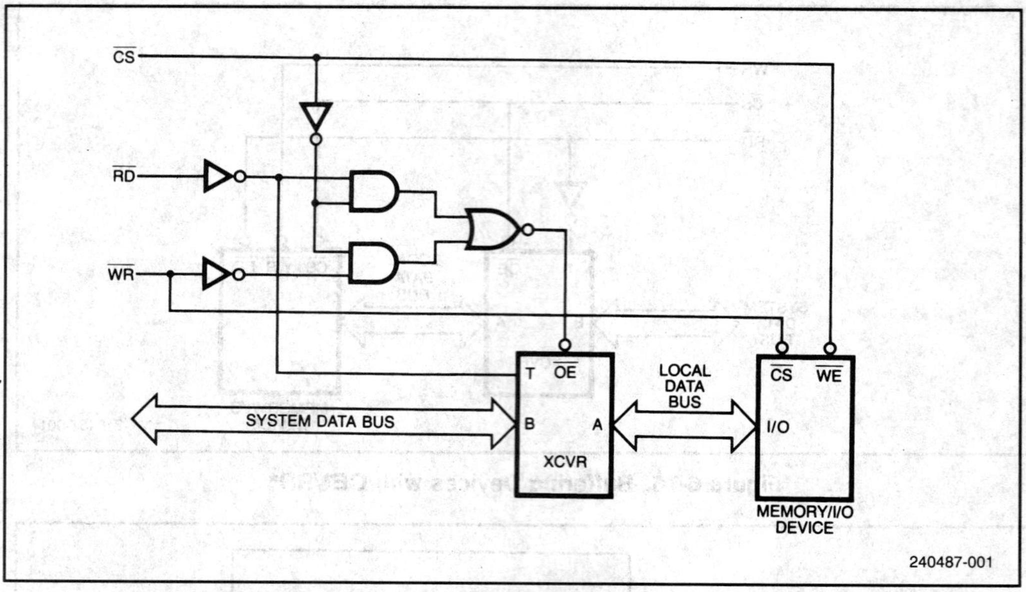

Figure 6-78. Buffering Devices without OE*/RD* and with Common or Separate I/O

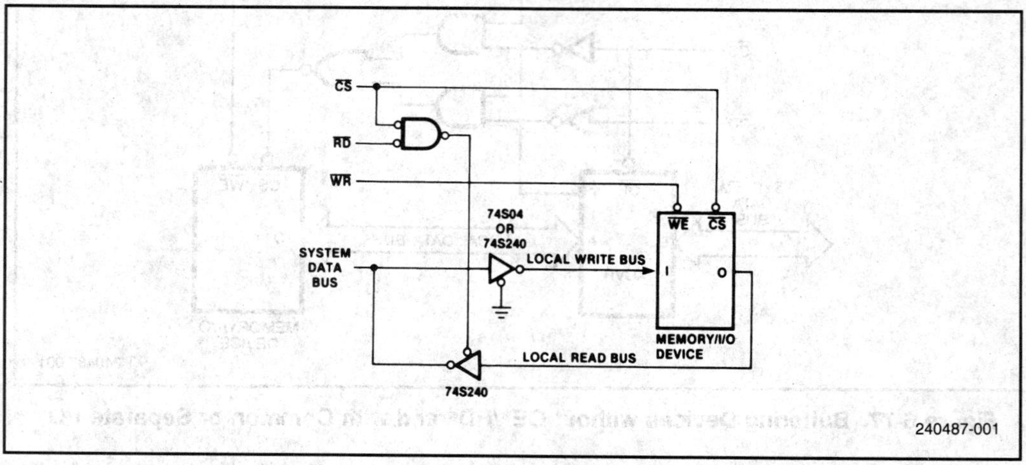

Figure 6-79. Buffering Devices without OE*/RD* and with Separate I/O

select. The only possibility for bus contention is in this system occurs as multiple devices during chip selection changes.

Interpreting the 8086/8088 Bus Timing Diagrams

The 8086/8088 bus timing diagrams are a powerful tool for determining system requirements. The timing diagrams for both the minimum and maximum modes (Figure 6-80 and 6-81) may be divided into six sections: (1) address and ALE; (2) read cycle timing;

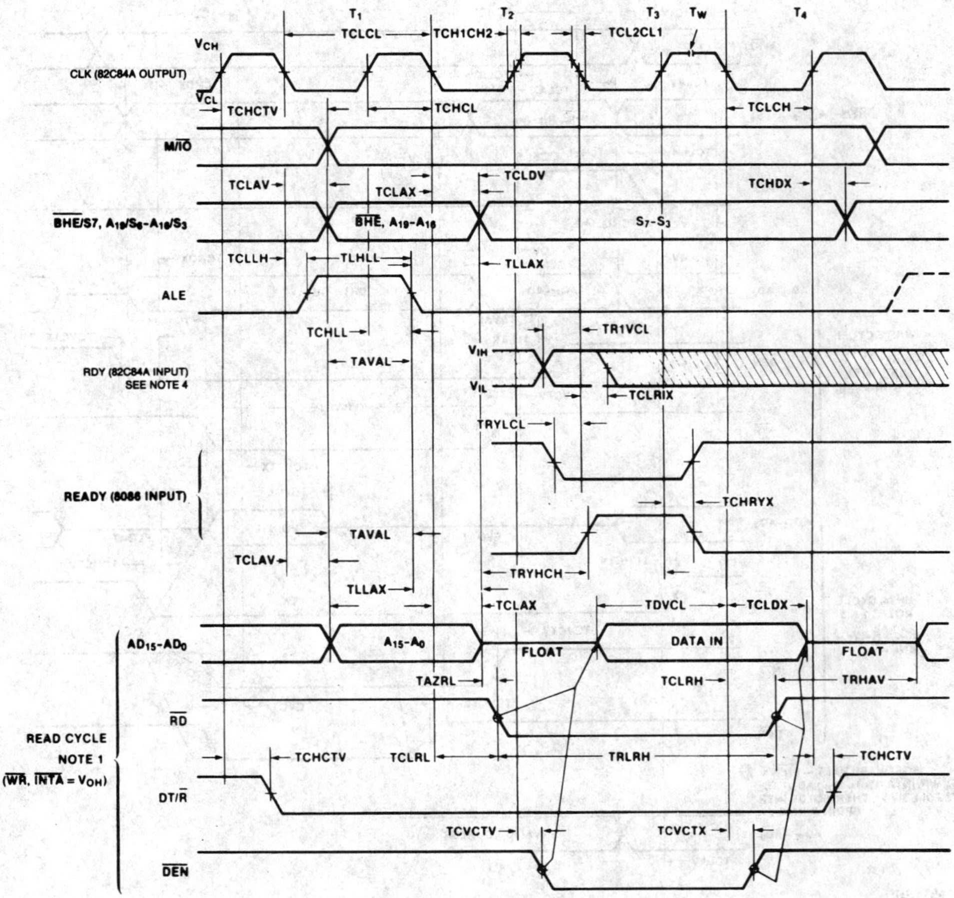

240487-001

Figure 6-80. 8086 Bus Timing – Minimum Mode System

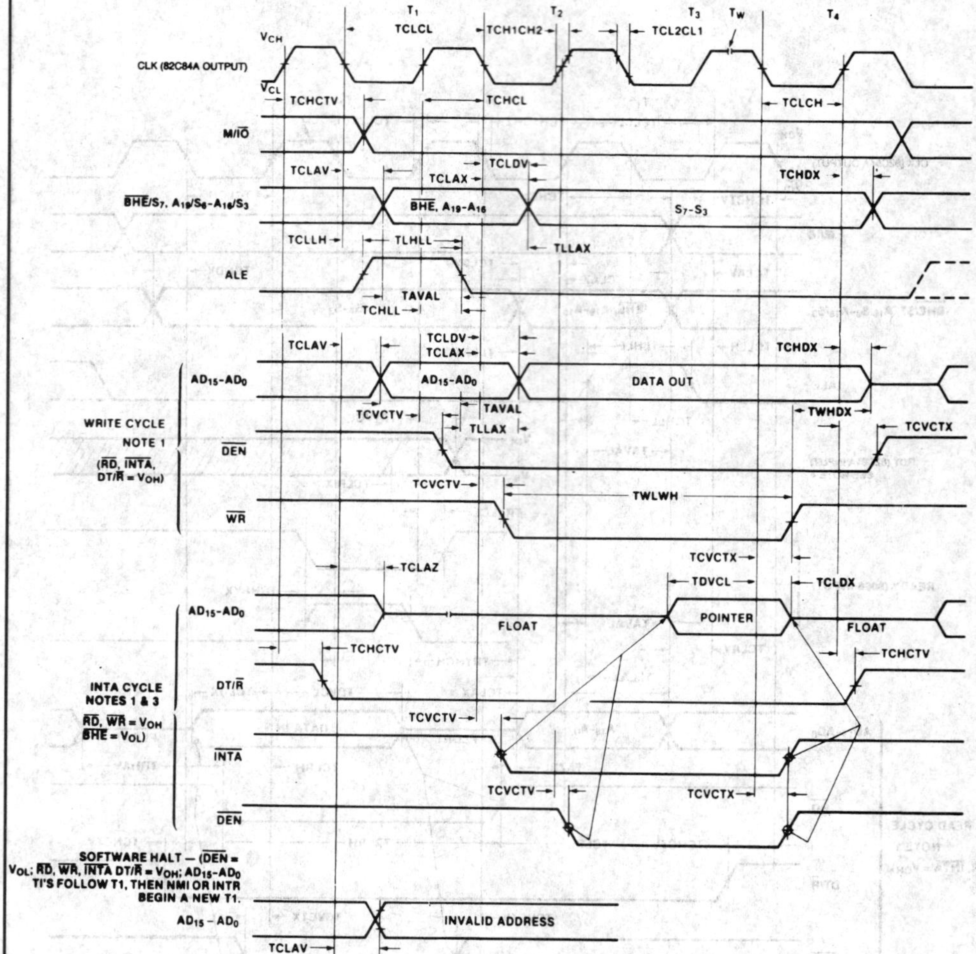

NOTES:

1. All signals switch between V_{OH} and V_{OI} unless otherwise specified.
2. RDY is sampled near the end of T_2, T_3, T_W to determine if T_W machines states are to be inserted.
3. Both INTA cycles run back-to-back. The 8088 local ADDR/DATA BUS is floating during the second INTA cycle. Control signals shown for second INTA cycle.
4. Signals at 82C84A are shown for reference only.
5. All timing measurements are made at 1.5V unless otherwise noted.

240487-001

Figure 6-80. 8086 Bus Timing — Minimum Mode System (Cont'd.)

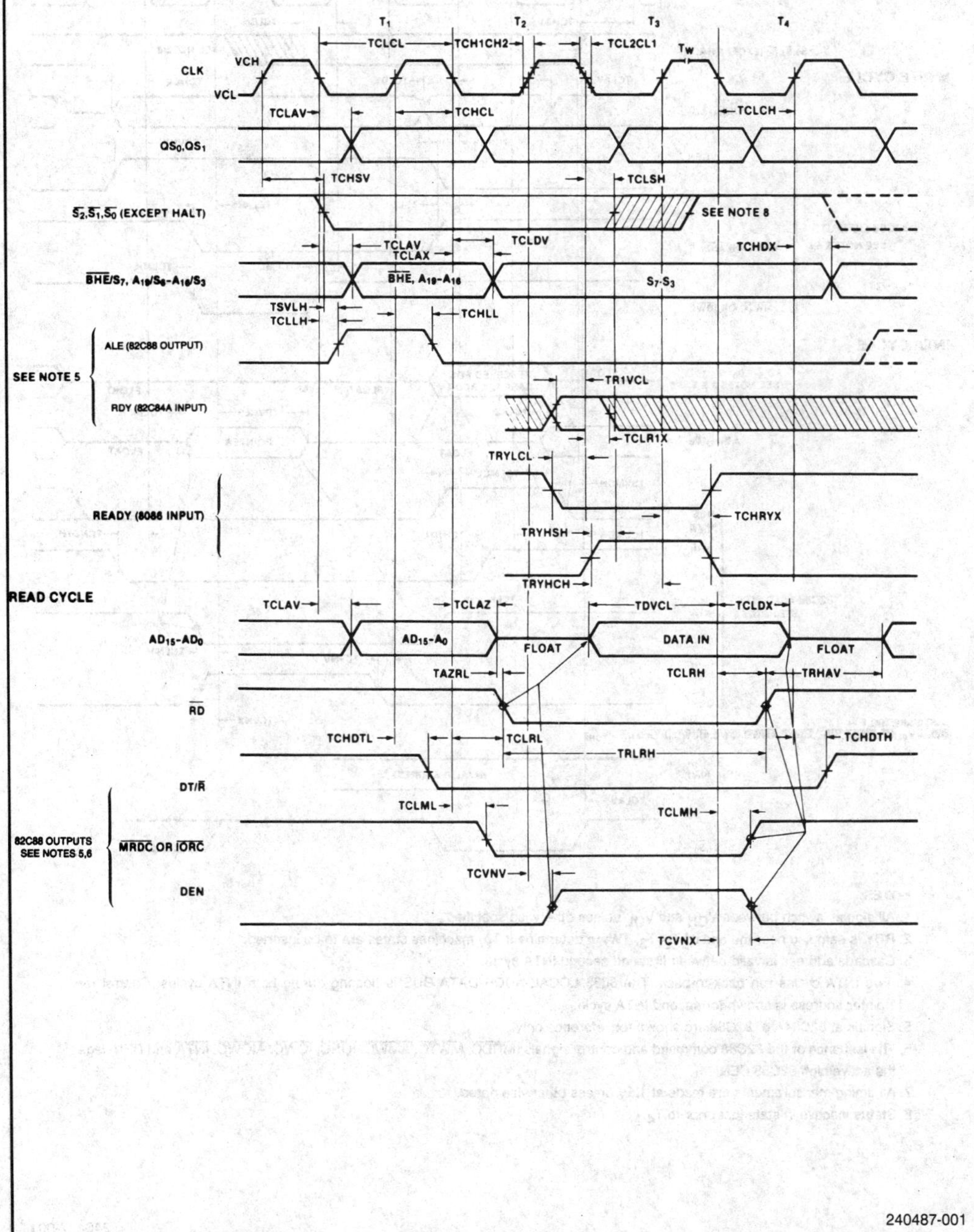

Figure 6-81. 8086 Bus Timing — Maximum Mode System (Using 82C88)

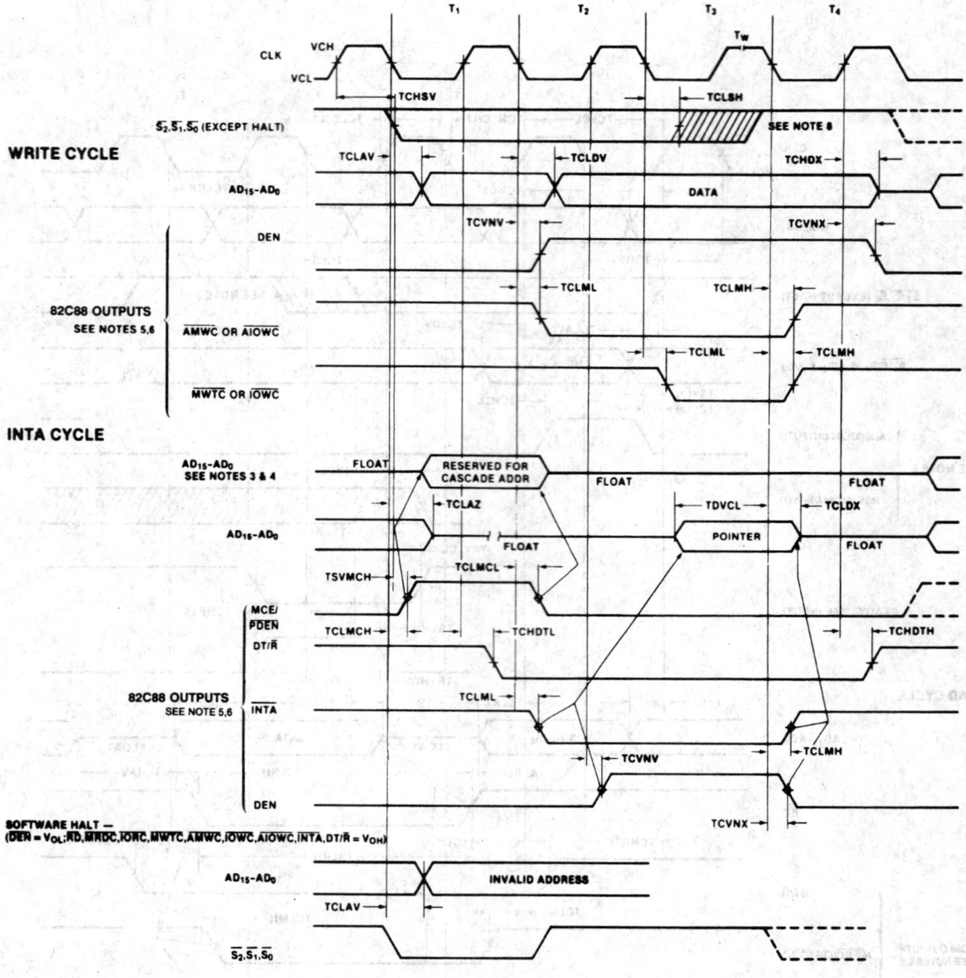

NOTES:

1. All signals switch between V_{OH} and V_{OL} unless otherwise specified.
2. RDY is sampled near the end of T_2, T_3, TW, to determine if T_W machines states are to be inserted.
3. Cascade address is valid between first and second INTA cycle.
4. Two INTA cycles run back-to-back. The 8086 LOCAL ADDR/DATA BUS is floating during both INTA cycles. Control for pointer address is shown for second INTA cycle.
5. Signals at 82C84A or 82C88 are shown for reference only.
6. The issuance of the 82C88 command and control signals ($\overline{MRDC}$, $\overline{MWTC}$, $\overline{AMWC}$, $\overline{IORC}$, $\overline{IOWC}$, $\overline{AIOWC}$, $\overline{INTA}$ and DEN) lags the active high 82C88 CEN.
7. All timing measurements are made at 1.5V unless otherwise noted.
8. Status inactive in state just prior to T_4.

240487-001

Figure 6-81. 8086 Bus Timing — Maximum Mode System (Using 82C88) (Cont'd.)

(3) write cycle timing; (4) interrupt acknowledge timing; (5) ready timing; and (6) HOLD/HLDA or RQ*/GT* timing. Since the A.C. characteristics of the signals are specified relative to the CPU clock, the relationship between the majority of the signals can be reduced by simply determining the clock cycles between the clock edges the signals are relative to and adding or subtracting the appropriate minimum or maximum parameter values. One aspect of system timing not compensated for in this approach is the worst case relationship between the minimum and maximum parameter values (also known as tracking relationships). As an example, consider a signal which has specified minimum and maximum turn on and turn off delays. Depending on device characteristics, it may not be possible for the component to simultaneously demonstrate a maximum turn on a minimum turn off delay even though worst case analysis might imply the possibility. This argument is characteristic of MOS devices and is therefore applicable to the 8086 A.C. characteristics. Therefore, the designer should assume that in worst case analysis mixing minimum and maximum delay parameters will typically exceed the worst case obtainable and should therefore receive further subjective degradation to obtain worst-worst case values. The following paragraphs provide guidelines for specific areas of 8086 timing sensitive to tracking relationships.

MINIMUM MODE BUS TIMING

The minimum mode address and ALE timing relationship determines the ability to capture a valid address from the multiplexed bus. Since the D-type latches capture the address on the trailing edge of ALE, the critical timing involves the state of the address lines when ALE terminates. If the address valid delay is assumed to be maximum TCLAV and ALE terminates at TCHLLmin, its earliest point (assuming zero minimum delay), the address would be valid only if TCLCHmin − TCLAVmax = 8 ns prior to ALE termination. This result is unrealistic in the assumption of maximum TCLAV and minimum TCHLL. To provide an accurate measure of the true worst case, a separate parameter specifies the minimum time for address valid prior to the end of ALE (TAVAL). TAVAL = TCLCH − 60 ns overrides the clock related timings and guarantees 58 ns of address setup to ALE termination for a 5 MHz 8086. The address is guaranteed to remain valid beyond the end of ALE by the TLLAX parameter. This specification overrides the relationship between TCHLL and TCLAX which might seem to imply the address may not be valid by the end of the latest possible ALE. TLLAX holds for the entire address bus. The TCLAXmin specification on the address indicates the earliest the bus will go invalid if not restrained by a slow ALE. TLLAX and TCLAX apply to the entire multiplexed bus for both read and write cycles. AD15-0 is tri-stated for read cycles and immediately switched to write data during write cycles. AD19-16 immediately switch from address to status for both read and write cycles. TLHLLmin, which takes precedence over the value obtained by relating TCLLHmax and TCHLLmin, guarantees the minimum ALE pulse width.

To determine the worst case delay-to-valid address on a demultiplexed address bus, two paths are considered: (1) delay of valid address and (2) delay to ALE. Since the D-type latches are flow through devices, a valid address is not transmitted to the address bus until ALE is active. A comparison of address valid delay TCLAVmax with ALE active, delay TCLLHmax indicates TCLAVmax is the worst case. Subtracting the latch propagation delay gives the worst case address bus valid delay from the start of the bus cycle.

Minimum Mode Read Cycle Timing

Read timing consists of conditioning the bus, activating the read command and establishing the data transceiver enable and direction controls. DT/R* is established early in the bus cycle and requires no further consideration. During read, the DEN* signal must allow the transceivers to propagate data to the CPU with the appropriate data setup time and continue to do so until the required data hold time. The DEN* turn on delay allows TCLCL + TCHCLmin − TCVCTV max − TDVCL = 127 ns transceiver enable time prior to valid data required by the CPU. Since the CPU data hold time TCLDXmin and minimum DEN* turnoff delay TCVCTXmin are both 10 ns relative to the same clock edge, the hold time is guaranteed. Additionally, DEN* must disable the transceivers prior to the CPU, redriving the bus with the address for the next bus cycle. The maximum DEN* turn off delay (TCVCTXmax), compared with the minimum delay for addresses out of the 8086 (TCLCL + TCLAVmin), indicates the transceivers are disabled at least 105 ns before the CPU drives the address onto the multiplexed bus.

If memory or I/O devices are connected directly to the multiplexed address and data bus, the TAZRL parameter guarantees the CPU will float the bus before activating read, allowing the selected device to drive the bus. At the end of the bus cycle, the TRHAV parameter specifies the bus float delay the device being deselected must satisfy to avoid contention with the CPU driving the address for the next bus cycle. The next bus cycle may start as soon as the cycle following T4 or any number of clock cycles later.

The minimum delay from read active to valid data at the CPU is 2TCLCL − TCLRLmax − TDVCL = 205 ns. The minimum pulse width is 2TCLCL − 75 ns = 325 ns. This specification (TRLRH) overrides the result which could be derived from the clock relative delays (2TCLCL − TCLRLmax + TCLRHmin).

Minimum Mode Write Cycle Timing

The write cycle provides write data to the system, generates the write command and controls data bus transceivers. The transceiver direction control signal DT/R* is conditioned to transmit at the end of each ready cycle and does not change during a write cycle. This process allows the transceiver enable signal DEN* to be active early in the cycle (while addresses are valid) without corrupting the address on the multiplexed bus. The leading edge of T2 enables both the write data and write command. A comparison of minimum WR* active delay TCVCTVmin with the maximum write data delay TCLDV indicates that write data may be not be valid until 100 ns after write is active. The devices in the system should capture data on the trailing edge of the write command rather than the leading edge to guarantee valid data. The data from the 8086 is valid a minimum of 2TCLCL − TCLDVmax + TCVCTXmin = 300 ns before the trailing edge of write. The minimum write pulse width is TWLWH = 2TCLCL − 60 ns = 340 ns. The CPU maintains valid write data TWHDX ns after write. The TWHDZ specification overrides the result derived by relating TCLCHmin and TCHDZmin which implies write data may only be valid 18 ns after WR*. Normally the CPU simply switches the output drivers from data to address at the beginning of the next bus cycle. If forced off the bus by a HOLD or RQ* input, the 8086 floats the bus after write. As with the read cycle, the next bus cycle may start in the clock cycle following T4 or any clock cycle later.

The CPU disables DEN* a minimum of TCLCHmin + TCVCTXmin − TCVCTXmax = 18 ns after write to guarantee data hold time to the selected device. Again comparing TCVCTXmin with TCVCTXmax, the real minimum delay from the end of write to transceiver disable equals approximately 60 ns.

Minimum Mode Interrupt Acknowledge Timing

The interrupt acknowledge sequence consists of two interrupt acknowledge timing cycles as previously described. The detailed timing of each cycle is identical to the read cycle timing with two exceptions: command timing and address/data bus timing.

The multiplexed address/data bus floats from the beginning (T1) of the INTA* cycle (within TCLAZ ns). The upper four multiplexed address/status lines do not three-state. The address value on A19-A16 is indeterminate, but the status information will be valid (S3=0, S4=0, S5=IF, S6=0, S7=BHE*=0). The multiplexed address/data lines will remain in three-state until the cycle after T4 of the INTA* cycle. This sequence occurs for each of the INTA* bus cycles. The interrupt type number read by the 8086 on the second INTA* bus cycle must satisfy the same setup and hold times required for data during a read cycle.

The DEN* and DT/R* signals are enabled for each INTA* cycle and do not remain active between the two cycles. Their timing for each cycle is identical to the read cycle.

The INTA* command has the same timing as the write command. It is active within 110 ns of the start of T2 providing 260 ns of access time from command to data valid at the 8086. The command is active a minimum of TCVCTXmin = 10 ns into T4 to satisfy the data hold time of the 8086. This provides minimum INTA* pulse width of 300 ns, however, taking signal delay tracking into consideration gives a minimum pulse width of 340 ns. Since the maximum inactive delay of INTA* is TCVCTXmax = 110 ns and the CPU will not drive the bus until 15 ns (TCLAVmin) into the next clock cycle, 105 ns are available for interrupt devices on the local bus to float their outputs. If the data bus is buffered, DEN* provides the same amount of time for local bus transceivers the three-state the outputs.

Minimum Mode Ready Timing

The CPU typically generates the system ready signal from either the address decode of the selected device or the address decode and the command (RD*, WR*, INTA*). For a system which is normally not ready, the time to generate ready from a valid address and not insert a wait state, requires 2TCLCL − TCLAVmax − TR1VCLmax = 255 ns. This time is available for buffered delays and address decoding to determine if the selected device does not require a wait state and drive the RDY line high. If wait cycles are required, the user hardware must provide the appropriate ready delay. Since the address will not change until the next ALE, RDY will remain valid throughout the cycle. If the system is normally ready, selected devices requiring wait states also have 255 ns to disable the RDY line. The user circuits must delay re-enabling RDY by the appropriate number of wait states.

If the RD* command is used to enable the RDY signal, TCLCL − TCLRLmax − TRIVCLmax = 15 ns are available for external logic. If the WR* command is used, TCLCL − TCVCTVmax − TRIVCLmax = 55 ns is available. Comparison of RDY control by address or command indicates that address decoding provides the best timing. If the system is normally not ready, address decode alone could be used to provide RDY for devices not requiring wait states while devices requiring wait states may use a combination of address decode and command to activate a wait state generator. If the system is normally ready, devices not requiring wait states do nothing to RDY while devices needing wait states should disable RDY via the address decode and use a combination of address decode and command to activate a delay to re-enable RDY.

If the system requires no wait states for memory and a fixed number of wait states for RD* and WR* to all I/O devices, the M/IO* signal can be used as an early indication of the need for wait cycles. This technique allows a common circuit to control ready timing for the entire system without feedback of address decodes.

Minimum Mode TEST* Timing

The TEST* input is sampled by the 8086 only during execution of the WAIT instruction. The TEST* signal should be active for a minimum of 6 clock cycles during the WAIT instruction to guarantee detection.

MAXIMUM MODE BUS TIMING

The maximum mode 8086 bus operations are logically equivalent to the minimum mode operation. Detailed timing analysis now involves signals generated by the CPU and the 82C88 bus controller. The 82C88 also provides additional control and command signals which expand the flexibility of the system.

Maximum Mode Address and ALE Timing

In the maximum mode, the address information continues to come from the CPU while the ALE strobe is generated by the 82C88. To determine the worst case relationships between ALE and the address, we first must determine 82C88 ALE activation relative to the S0*-S2* status from the CPU. The maximum mode timing diagram specifies two possible delay paths to generate ALE. The first is TCHSV + TSVLH measured from the rising edge of the clock cycle preceding T1. The second path is TCLLH measured from the start of T1. Since the 82C88 initiates a bus cycle from the states lines leaving the passive states (S0* − S2* = 1), if the 8086 is late in issuing the status (TCHSVmax) while the clock high time is a minimum (TCHCLmin), the status will not have changed by the start of T1 and ALE is issued TSVLH ns after the status changes. If the status changes prior to the beginning of T1, the 82C88 will not issue the ALE until TCLLH ns after the start of T1. The resulting worst case delay to enable ALE (relative to the start of T1) is TCHSVmax + TSVLHmax − TCHCLmin = 58 ns. Note, when calculating signal relationships, be sure to use the proper maximum mode values rather than equivalent minimum mode values.

The trailing edge of ALE is triggered in the 82C88 by the positive clock edge in T1 regardless of the delay to enable ALE. The resulting minimum ALE pulse width is TCLCHmax − 58 ns = 75 ns assuming the TCHLL = 0. TCLCHmax must be used since TCHCLmin was assumed to derive the 58 ns ALE enable delay. The addess is guaranteed to be valid TCLCHmin + TCHLLmin − TCLAVmax = 8 ns prior to the trailing edge of ALE to capture the address in the latches. Again we have assumed a very conservative TCHLL = 0. Note, since the address of ALE are driven by separate devices, no tracking of A.C. characteristics can be assumed.

The address hold time to the latches is guaranteed by the address remaining valid until the end of T1 while ALE is disabled a maximum of 15 ns from the positive clock transition in T1 (TCHCLmin − TCHLLmax = 52 ns address hold time). The multiplexed bus transitions from address to status and write data or tri-state (for read) are identical to the minimum mode timing. Also, since the address valid delay (TCLAV) remains the critical path in establishing a valid address, the address access times to valid data and ready are the same as the minimum mode system.

Maximum Mode Read Cycle Timing

The maximum mode system offers read signals generated by both the 8086 and the 82C88. The 8086 RD* output signal timing is identical to the minimum mode system. Since the A.C. characteristics of the read commands generated by the 82C88 are significantly better than the 8086 output, access to devices on the demultiplexed buffered system bus should use the 82C88 commands. The 8086 RD* signal is available for devices which reside directly on the multiplexed bus. The following evaluations for read, write and interrupt acknowledge only consider the 82C88 command timing.

The 82C88 provides separate memory and I/O read signals which conform to the same A.C. characteristics. The commands are issued TCLML ns after the start of T2 and terminate TCLMH ns after the start of T4. The minimum command length is 2TCLCL − TCLMLmax + TCLMLmin = 375 ns. The access time to valid data at the CPU is 2TCLCL − TCLMLmax − TDVCLmax = 335 ns. Since the 82C88 was designed for systems with buffered data busses, the commands are enabled before the CPU has tri-stated the multiplexed bus and should not be used with devices which reside directly on the multiplexed bus (to do so could result in bus contention during 8086 bus float and device turn-on).

The direction control for data bus transceivers is established in T1 while the transceivers are not enabled by DEN until the positive clock transition of T2. This provides TCLCH + TCVNVmin = 123 ns for 8086 bus float delay and TCHCLmin + TCLCL − TCVNVmax − TDVCLmax = 187 ns of transceiver active to data valid at the CPU. Since both DEN and command are valid a minimum of 10 ns into T4, the CPU data hold time TCLDX is guaranteed. A maximum DEN disable of 45 ns (TCVNXmax) guarantees the transceivers are disabled by the start of the next 8086 bus cycle (215 ns minimum from the same clock edge). On the positive clock transition of T4, DT/R* is returned to transmit in preparation for a possible write operation on the next bus cycle. Since the system memory and I/O devices reside on a buffered system bus, they must tri-state their outputs before the device for the next bus cycle is selected (approximately 2TCLCL) or the transceivers drive write data onto the bus (approximately 2TCLCL).

Maximum Mode Write Cycle Timing

In the maximum mode, the 82C88 provides normal and advanced write commands for memory and I/O. The advanced write commands are active a full clock cycle ahead of the normal write commands and have timing identical to the read commands. The advanced write pulse width is 2TCLCL − TCLMLmax + TCLMHmin = 375 ns while the normal write pulse width is TCLCL − TCLMLmax + TCLMHmin = 175 ns. Write data setup time to the selected device is a function of either the data valid delay from the 8086 (TCLDV) or the transceiver enable delay TCVNV. The worst case delay to valid write data is TCLDV= 110 ns minus transceiver propagation delays. This implies the data may not be valid until 100 ns after the advanced write command but will be valid approximately TCLCL − TCLDVmax + TCLMLmin 100 ns prior to the leading edge of the normal write command. Data will be valid 2TCLCL − TCLDVmax + TCLMHmin = 300 ns before the trailing edge of either write command. The data and command overlap for the advanced command is 300 ns while the overlap with the normal write command is 175 ns. The transceivers are disabled a minimum of TCLCHmin − TCLMHmax + TCVNXmin = 85 ns after the write command while the CPU provides valid data a minimum of TCLCHmin − TCLMHmax + TCHDZmin = 85 ns. This guarantees write data hold of 85 ns after the write command. The transceivers are disabled TCLCL − TCVNXmax + TCHDTLmin = 155 ns (assuming TCHDTL = 0) prior to transceiver direction change for a subsequent read cycle.

Maximum Mode Interrupt Acknowledge Timing

The maximum mode INTA* sequence is logically identical to the minimum mode sequence. The transceiver control (DEN and DT/R*) and INTA* command timing of each interrupt acknowledge cycle is identical to the read cycle. As in the minimum mode system, the multiplexed address/data bus will float from the leading edge of T1 for each INTA* bus cycle and not be driven by the CPU until after T4 of each INTA* cycle. The setup and hold times on the vector number for the second cycle are the same as data setup and hold for the read. If the device providing the interrupt vector number is connected to the local bus, TCLCL − TCLAZmax + TCLMLmin = 130 ns are available from 8086 bus float to INTA* command active. The selected device on the local bus must disable the system data bus transceivers since DEN is still generated by the 82C88.

If the 82C88 is not in the IOB (I/O Bus) mode, the 82C88 MCE/PDEN* output becomes the MCE output. This output is active during each INTA* cycle and overlaps the ALE signal during T1. The MCE is available for gating cascade addresses from a master 8259A onto three of the upper AD15-AD8 lines and allowing ALE to latch the cascade address into the address latches. The address lines may then be used to provide CAS and address selection to slave 8259A's located on the system bus (see Figure 6-82). MCE is active within 15 ns of status or the start of T1 for each INTA* cycle. MCE should not enable the CAS lines onto the multiplexed bus during the first cycle since the CPU does not guarantee to float the bus until 80 ns into the first INTA* cycle. The first MCE can be inhibited by gating MCE with LOCK*. The 8086 LOCK* output is activated during T2 of the first cycle and disabled during T2 of the first cycle and disabled during T2 of the second cycle. The overlap of LOCK* with MCE allows the first MCE to be masked and the second MCE to gate the cascade address onto the local bus. Since the 8259A will not provide a cascade address until the second cycle, no information is lost. As with

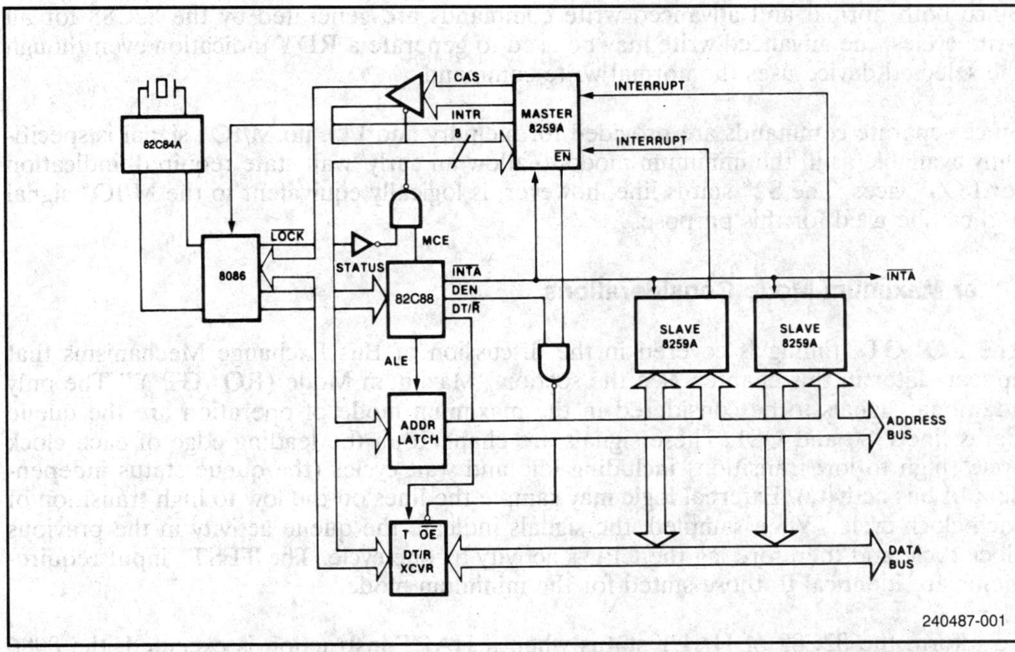

Figure 6-82. Max Mode 8086 with Master 8259A on the Local Bus and Slave 8259A's on the System Bus

ALE, MCE is guaranteed valid within 58 ns of the start of T1 to allow 75 ns CAS address setup to the trailing edge of ALE. MCE remains active TCHCLmin − TCHLLmax + TCLMCLmin = 52 ns after ALE to provide data hold time to the latches.

If the 82C88 is strapped in the IOB mode, the MCE output becomes PDEN* and all I/O references are assumed to be devices on the local bus rather than the demultiplexed system bus. Since INTA* cycles are considered I/O cycles, all interrupts are assumed to come from the local system and cascade addresses are not gated onto the system address bus. Additionally, the DEN signal is not enabled since no I/O transfers occur on the system bus. If the local I/O bus is also buffered by transceivers, the PDEN* signal is used to enable those transceivers. PDEN* A.C. characteristics are identical to DEN with PDEN* enabled for I/O references and DEN enabled for instruction or memory data references.

Maximum Mode Ready Timing

Ready timing based on address valid timing is the same for maximum and minimum mode systems. The delay from 82C88 command valid to RDY valid at the 82C84A is TCLCL − TCLMLmax − TRIVCLmin = 130 ns. This time is available for external circuits to determine the need to insert wait states and disable RDY or enable RDY to avoid wait states. INTA*, all read commands and advanced write commands provide this timing. The normal write command is not valid until after the RDY signal must be valid.

Since both normal and advanced write commands are generated by the 82C88 for all write cycles, the advanced write may be used to generate a RDY indication even though the selected device uses the normal write command.

Since separate commands are provided for memory and I/O, no M/IO* signal is specifically available as in the minimum mode to allow an early 'wait state required' indication for I/O devices. The S2* status line, however, is logically equivalent to the M/IO* signal and can be used for this purpose.

Other Maximum Mode Considerations

The RQ*/GT* timing is covered in the discussion of Bus Exchange Mechanisms that appears later in this chapter. See the section "Maximum Mode (RQ*/GT*)." The only additional signals to be considered in the maximum mode of operation are the queue status line QS0 and QS1. These signals are changed on the leading edge of each clock cycle (high to low transition) including idle and wait cycles (the queue status independent of bus activity). External logic may sample the lines on the low to high transition of each clock cycle. When sampled, the signals indicate the queue activity in the previous clock cycle and therefore lag the CPU's activity by one cycle. The TEST* input requirements are identical to those stated for the minimum mode.

To inform the 82C88 of HALT status when a HALT instruction is executed, the 8086 will initiate a status transition from passive to HALT status. The status change will cause the 82C88 to emit an ALE pulse with an indeterminate address. Since no bus cycle is initiated (no command is issued), the results of the address will not affect the CPU operation (i.e., no response such as READY is expected from the system). This external hardware to latch and decode all transitions in system status.

Wait State Insertion

The ready signal is used in the system to accommodate memory and I/O devices that cannot transfer information at the maximum CPU bus bandwidth. Ready is also used in multiprocessor systems to force the CPU to wait for access to the system bus or MULTIBUS system bus. To insert a wait state in the bus cycle, the READY signal to the CPU must be inactive (low) by the end of T2. To avoid insertion of a wait state, READY must be active (high) within a specified setup time prior to the positive transition during T3. Depending on the size and characteristics of the system, ready implementation may take one of two approaches.

The classical ready implementation is to have the system 'normally not ready.' When the selected device receives the command (RD*/WR*/INTA*) and has had sufficient time to complete the command, it activates READY to the CPU, allowing the CPU to terminate the bus cycle. This implementation is characteristic of large multiprocessor, MULTIBUS systems or systems where propagation delays, bus access delays and device characteristics inherently slow down the system. For maximum system performance, devices that can run with no wait states must return 'READY' within the previously described limit. Failure to respond in time will only result in the insertion of one or more wait cycles.

An alternate technique is to have the system 'normally ready.' All devices are assumed to operate at the maximum CPU bus bandwidth. Devices that do not meet the requirement must disable READY by the end of T2 to guarantee the insertion of wait cycles. This implementation is typically applied to small single CPU systems and reduces the logic required to control the ready signal. Since the failure of a device requiring wait states to disable READY by the end of T2 will result in premature termination of the bus cycle, the system timing must be carefully analyzed when using this approach.

The 8086 has two different timing requirements on READY depending on the system implementation. For a 'normally ready' system to insert a wait state, the READY must be disabled within 8 ns (TRYLCL) after the end of T2 (start of T3) (see Figure 6-83). To guarantee proper operation of the 8086, the READY input must not change from ready to not ready during the clock low time of T3. For a 'normally not ready' system to avoid wait states, READY must be active within 119 ns (TRYHCH) of the positive clock transition during T3 (see Figure 6-84). For both cases, READY must satisfy a hold time of 30 ns (TCHRYX) from the T3 or TW positive clock transition.

To generate a stable READY signal which satisfies the previous setup and hold times, the 82C84A provides two separate system ready inputs (RDY1, RDY2) and a single synchronized ready output (READY) for the CPU. The RDY inputs are qualified with separate access enables (AEN1*, AEN2*, low active) to allow selecting one of the two ready signals (see Figure 6-85). The gated signals are logically OR'ed and sampled at the beginning of each CLK cycle to generate READY to the CPU (see Figure 6-86). The sampled READY signal is valid within 8 ns (TRYLCL) after CLK to satisfy the CPU timing requirements on 'not ready' and ready. Since READY cannot change until the next CLK, the hold time requirements are also satisfied. The system ready inputs to the 82C84A (RDY1, RDY2) must be valid 35 ns (TRIVCL) before T3 and AEN* must be valid 60 ns before T3. For a system using only one RDY input, the associated AEN* is tied to ground while the other AEN* is connected to 5 volts through approximately 1K ohms (see Figure 6-87). If the system generates a low active ready signal, it can be connected to the 82C84A AEN* input if the additional setup time required by the 82C84A AEN* input is satisfied. In this case, the associated RDY input would be tied high (see Figure 6-88).

8086/8088 Instruction Sequence

Figure 6-89 illustrates the internal operation and bus activity that occur as an 8086 CPU executes a sequence of instruction. The figure presents the signals and timing relationships that help illustrate 886 operation. The following discussion interprets the figure.

Figure 6-89 shows the repeated execution of an instruction loop. This loop is defined in both machine code and assembly language by Figure 6-90. The loop demonstrates both the effects of a program jump on the queue and makes the instruction sequence easy to follow. The program sequence consists of seven instructions and 16 bytes, and is typical of the tight loops found in many application programs. This particular sequence contains several sort, fast-executing instructions that demonstrate both the effect of the queue on CPU performance and the interaction between the execution unit (EU) fetching code from the queue and the bus interface unit (BIU)

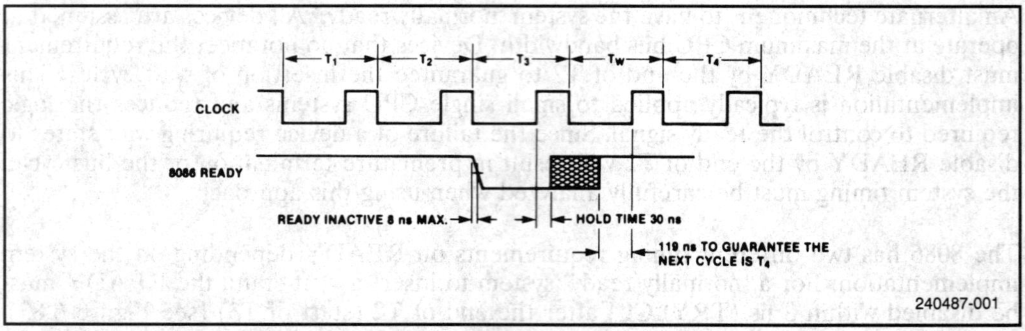

Figure 6-83. Normally Ready System Inserting a Wait State

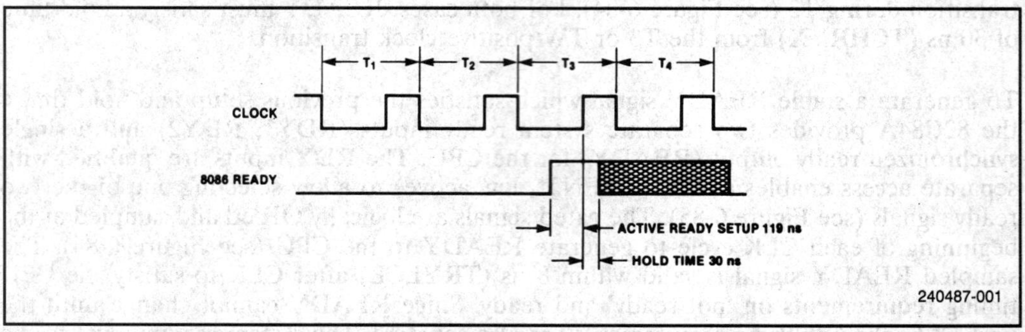

Figure 6-84. Normally Not Ready System Avoiding a Wait State

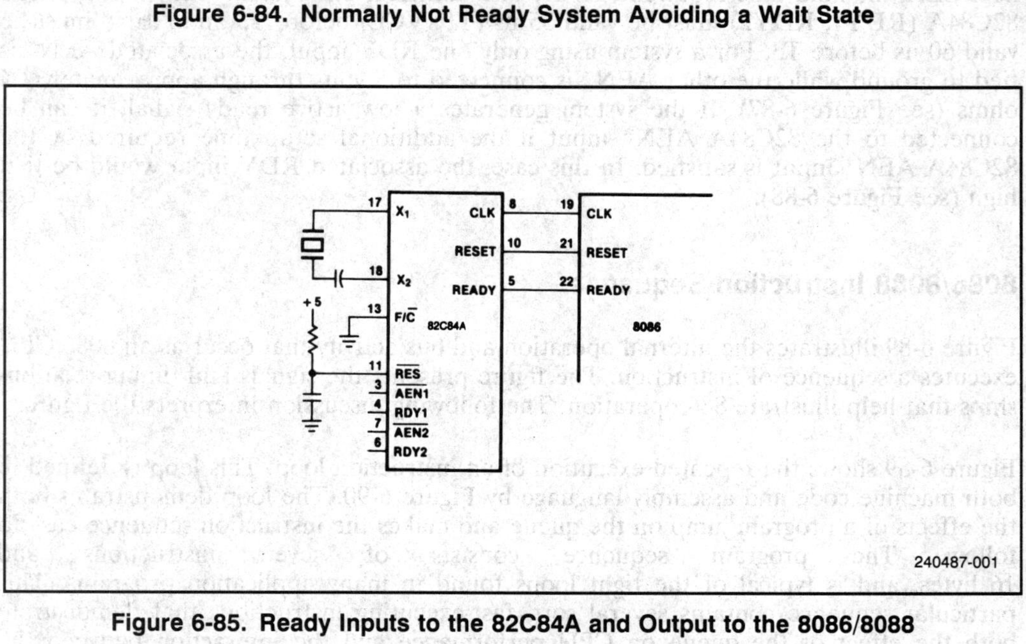

Figure 6-85. Ready Inputs to the 82C84A and Output to the 8086/8088

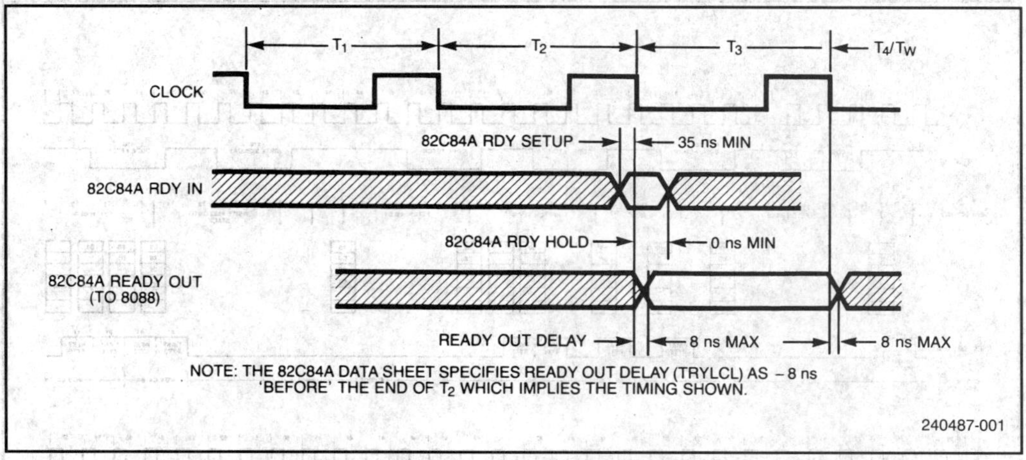

Figure 6-86. 82C84A with 8086/8088 Ready Timing

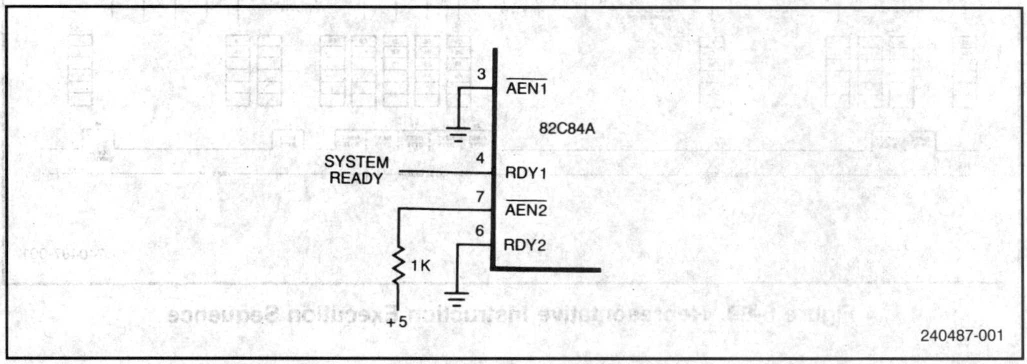

Figure 6-87. Using RDY1/RDY2 to Generate Ready

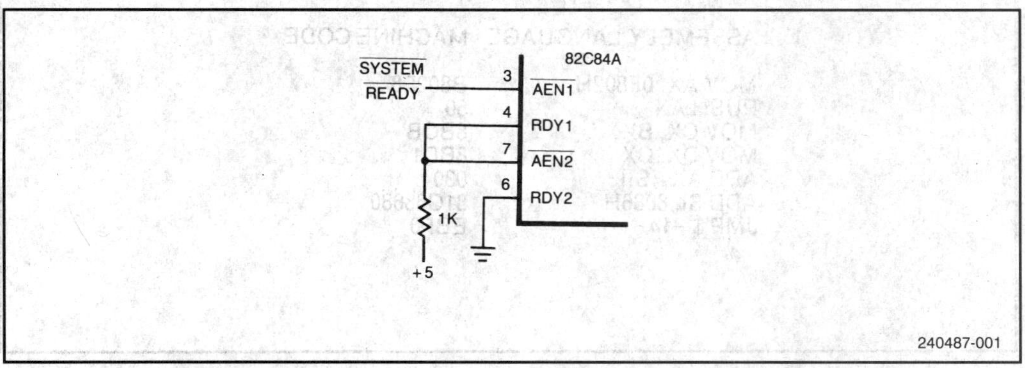

Figure 6-88. Using AEN1*/AEN2* to Generate Ready

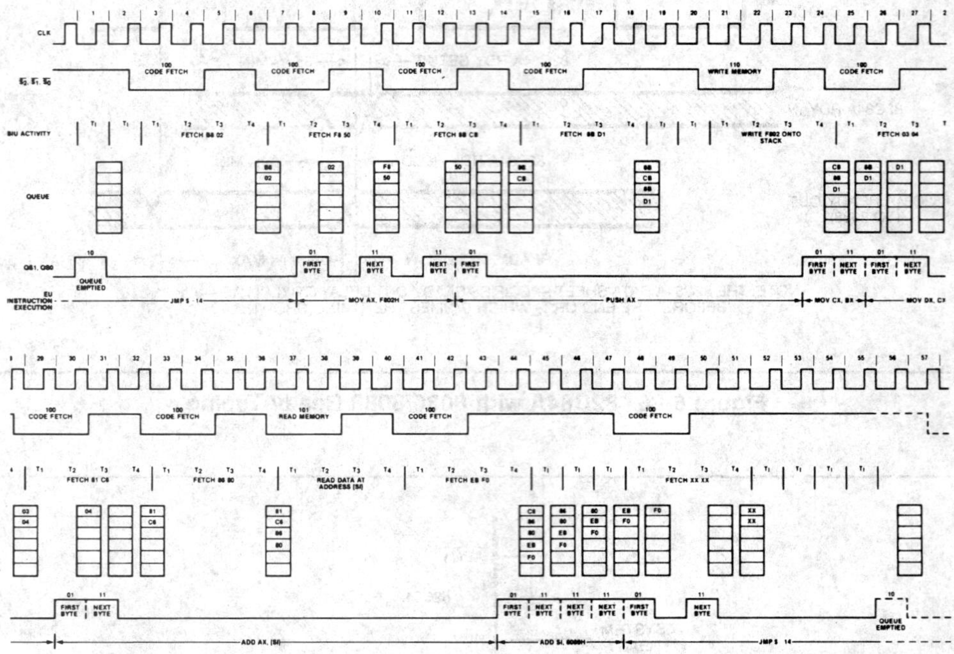

240487-001

Figure 6-89. Representative Instruction Execution Sequence

ASSEMBLY LANGUAGE	MACHINE CODE
MOV AX, 0F802H	B802F8
PUSH AX	50
MOV CX, BX	8BCB
MOV DX, CX	8BD1
ADD AX, [SI]	0304
ADD SI, 8086H	81C68680
JMP $ −14	EBF0

Figure 6-90. Instruction Loop Sequence

filling the queue and performing the requested bus cycles. For the purpose of this discussion, code, stack, and memory data references are aligned on even word boundaries. The entire sequence of instructions has taken 55 clock cycles. Eighteen opcode bytes were fetched, one word memory read occurred, and one word stack write was performed.

Consider that the loop starts in clock cycle 1 with the queue reinitialization that occurs as part of the JMP instruction. The EU completes JMP instruction execution. While the BIU performs an opcode fetch to begin refilling the queue.

In clock cycle 8, the queue status lines indicate that the first byte of the MOV immediate instruction has been removed from the queue (one clock cycle after it was placed there by the BIU fetch) and that execution of this instruction has begun. The second byte of this instruction is taken from the queue in clock cycle 10 and then, during clock cycle 12, the EU pauses to wait one clock cycle for the second BIU opcode fetch to complete and for the third byte of the MOV immediate instruction to become available for execution (recall that the queue status lines indicate queue activity that has occurred in the previous clock).

Clock cycle 13 begins the execution of the PUSH AX instruction, and during clock cycle 15, the BIU begins the fourth opcode fetch. The BIU finishes the fourth fetch in clock cycle 18 and prepares for another fetch when it receives a request from the EU for a memory write (the stack push). Instead of completing the opcode fetch and forcing the EU to wait for additional clock cycles, the BIU immediately aborts the fetch cycle (resulting in two idle clock cycles, TI, in clock cycles 19 and 20) and performs the required memory write. This interaction between the EU and BIU results in a single clock extension to the execution time of the PUSH AX instruction, the maximum delay that can occur in response to an EU bus cycle request.

Execution continues during clock cycle 24 with the execution of sequential registertoregister MOV instructions. The first of these instructions takes full advantage of the prefetched opcode to complete this operation in two clock cycles. The second MOV instruction, however, depletes the queue and requires two additional clock cycles (28 and 29).

During clock cycle 30, the ADD memory indirect to AX instruction begins. In the time required to execute this instruction, the BIU completes two opcode fetch cycles and a memory read, then begins a fourth opcode fetch cycle. Note that in the case of the memory read, the EU's request for a bus cycle occurs at a point in the BIU fetch cycle where it can be incorporate directly (idle states are not required and no EU delay is imposed).

During clock cycle 44, the EU begins the ADD immediate instruction, taking four bytes from the queue and completing instruction execution in four clock cycles. Also during this time, the BIU senses a full queue during clock cycle 45 and enters a series of bus idle states (five or six bytes constitute a full queue in the 8086; the BIU waits until it can fetch a full word or opcode before accessing the bus).

At clock cycle 47, the BIU again begins a bus cycle sequence, one that becomes an "overfetch" since the EU is executing a JMP instruction. As part of the JMP instruction, the queue reinitialization (which began the instruction sequence) occurs.

The example can be easily extended to incorporate wait states in the bus access cycles. In the case of a single wait state, each bus cycle would be lengthened to five clock cycles with a wait state (TW) inserted between every T3 and T4 state of the bus cycle. As a first approximation, the instruction sequence execution time would appear to be lengthened by 10 clock cycles, one cycle for each useful read or write bus cycle that occurs. Actually, this approximation for the number of wait states inserted is incorrect since the queue can compensate for wait states by making use of previously idle bus time. For the example code sequence, this compensation reduced the actual execution time by one wait state, and the sequence was completed in 64 clock cycles, one less than the approximated 65 clock cycles.

This example is, deliberately, partially bus limited and indicates the types of EU and BIU interaction that can occur in this type of situation. Most application code sequences, however, use a high proportion of more complex, longer-executing instructions and addressing modes, and therefore tend to be execution limited. In this case, less BIU-EU interaction is required, the queue more often is full, and more idle states occur on the bus.

BUS EXCHANGE MECHANISMS

The 8086 supports protocols for transferring control of the local bus between itself and other devices capable of acting as bus masters. The minimum mode configuration offers a signal level handshake similar to the 8080 and 8085 systems. The maximum mode provides an enhanced pulse sequence protocol designed to optimize utilization of CPU pins while extending the system configurations to two prioritized levels of alternate bus masters. These protocols are simply techniques for arbitration of control of the CPU's local bus and should not be confused with the need for arbitration of the system bus.

Minimum Mode (HOLD/HLDA)

The minimum mode 8086 system uses a hold request input (HOLD) to the CPU and a hold acknowledge (HLDA) output from the CPU. To gain control of the bus, a device must assert HOLD to the CPU and wait for the HLDA before driving the bus. When the 8086 can relinquish the bus, it floats the RD*, WR*, INTA* and M/IO* command lines, the DEN* and DT/R* bus control lines and the multiplexed address/data/status lines. The ALE signal is not tri-stated. The CPU acknowledges the request with HLDA to allow the requestor to take control of the bus. The requestor must maintain the HOLD request active until it no longer requires the bus. The HOLD request to the 8086 directly affects the execution unit. The CPU will continue to execute from its internal queue until either more instructions are needed or an operand transfer is required. This allows a high degree of overlap between CPU and auxiliary bus master operation. When the requestor drops the HOLD signal, the 8086 will respond by dropping HLDA. The CPU will not re-drive the bus, command and control signals from tri-state until it needs to perform a bus transfer. Since the 8086 may still be executing from its internal queue when HOLD device is driving the bus. To prevent the command lines from drifting below the minimum VIH level during the transition of bus control, 22K ohm pull up resistors should be connected to the bus command lines. The timing diagram in Figure 6-91 shows the handshake sequence and 8086 timing to sample HOLD, float the bus, and enable/disable HLDA relative to the CPU clock.

To guarantee valid system operation, the designer must assure that the requesting device does not assert control of the bus prior to the 8086 relinquishing control and that the device relinquishes control of the bus prior to the 8086 driving the bus. The HOLD request into the 8086 must be stable THVCH ns prior to the CPU's low to high clock transition. Since this input is not synchronized by the CPU, signals driving the HOLD input should be synchronized with the CPU clock to guarantee the setup time is not violated. Either clock edge may be used. The maximum delay between HLDA and the 8086 floating the bus is TCLAZmax − TCLHAVmin − 70 ns. If the system cannot tolerate the 70 ns overlap, HLDA active from the 8086 should be delayed to the device. The minimum delay for the CPU to drive the control bus from HOLD inactive is THVCHmin + 3TCLCL = 635 ns and THVCHmin + 3TCLCL + TCHCL = 701 ns to drive the multiplexed bus. If the device does not satisfy these requirements, HOLD inactive to the 8086 should be delayed. The delay from HLDA inactive to driving the busses is TCLCL + TCLCHmin − TCHAVmax = 158 ns for the control bus and 2TCLCL − TCLHAVmax = 240 ns for the data bus.

LATENCY OF HLDA TO HOLD

The decision to respond to a HOLD request is made in the bus interface unit. The major factors that influence the decision are the current bus activity, the state of the LOCK* signal internal to the CPU (d by the software LOCK prefix) and interrupts.

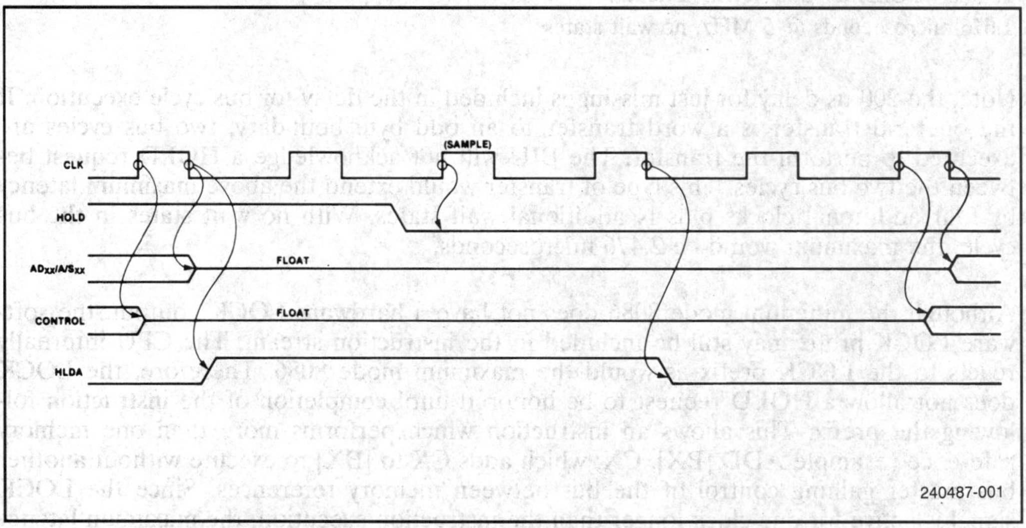

Figure 6-91. HOLD/HLDA Sequence Timing Diagram

If the LOCK* is not active, an interrupt acknowledge cycle is not in progress and the Bus Interface Unit (BIU) is executing a T4 or T1 when the HOLD request is received the minimum latency to HLDA is:

35ns THVCH min (Hold setup)
65 ns TCHCL min
200 nsTCLCL (bus float delay)
10 ns TCLHAV min (HLDA delay)
310 ns@ 5 MHz

The maximum delay under these conditions is:

34 ns (just missed setup time)
200 nsdelay to next sample
82 ns TCHCL max
200 nsTCLCL (bus float delay)
160 nsTCLHAV max (HLDA delay)
677 ns@ 5 MHz

If the BIU just initiated a bus cycle when the HOLD request was received, the worst case response time is:

34 ns THVCH (just missed)
82 ns TCHCL max
7*200 bus cycle execution
N*200 N wait states/bus cycle
160 ns TCLHAV max (HLDA delay)
1.676 microseconds @ 5 MHz, no wait states

Note, the 200 ns delay for just missing is included in the delay for bus cycle execution. If the operand transfer is a word transfer to an odd byte boundary, two bus cycles are executed to perform the transfer. The BIU will not acknowledge a HOLD request between the two bus cycles. This type of transfer would extend the above maximum latency by four additional clocks plus N additional wait states. With no wait states in the bus cycle, the maximum would be 2.476 microseconds.

Although the minimum mode 8086 does not have a hardware LOCK* output, the software LOCK prefix may still be included in the instruction stream. The CPU internally reacts to the LOCK prefix as would the maximum mode 8086. Therefore, the LOCK does not allow a HOLD request to be honored until completion of the instruction following the prefix. This allows an instruction which performs more than one memory reference (example ADD [BX], CX; which adds CX to [BX] to execute without another bus master gaining control of the bus between memory references. Since the LOCK signal is active for one clock longer than the instruction execution, the maximum latency to HLDA is:

34 ns THVC (just missed)
200 ns delay to next sample
82 ns TCHCL max
(M + 1)*200 ns LOCK instruction execution
200 ns set up HLDA (internal)
160 ns TCLHAV max (HLDA delay)
(M*200 ns) + 876 ns @ 5 MHz

If the HOLD request is made at the beginning of an interrupt acknowledge sequence, the maximum latency to HLDA is:

34 ns THVCH (just missed)
82 ns TCHCL max
2600 ns 13 clock cycles for INTA
160 ns TCLHAV max
2.876 microseconds @ 5 MHz

MINIMUM MODE DMA CONFIGURATION

A typical use of the HOLD/HLDA signals in the minimum mode 8086 system is bus control exchange with DMA devices like the Intel 8257-5 or 8237 DMA controllers. Figure 6-92 illustrates a general interconnect for this type of configuration using the 8237-2. The DMA controller resides on the upper half of the 8086's local bus and shares the A8-A15 demultiplexing address latch of the 8086. All registers in the 8237-2 must be assigned odd addresses to allow initialization and interrogation by the CPU over the upper half of the data bus. The 8086 RD*/WR* commands must be demultiplexed to provide separate I/O and memory commands which are compatible with the 8237-2 commands. The AEN control from the 8237-2 must disable the 8086 commands from the command bus, disable the address latches from the lower (A0-A7) and upper (A19-A16) address bus and select the 8237-2 address strobe (ADSTB) to the A8-A15 address latch. If the data bus is buffered, a pull-up resistor on the DEN line will keep the buffers disabled. The DMA controller will only transfer bytes between memory and I/O and requires the I/O devices to reside on an 8-bit bus derived from the 16-bit to 8-bit bus multiplex circuit given in Section 4. Address lines A7-A0 are driven directly by the 8237 and BHE* is generated by inverting A0. If A19-A16 are used, they must be provided by an additional port with either a fixed value or initialized by software and enabled onto the address bus by AEN.

Figure 6-93 gives an interconnection for placing the 8257 on the system bus. By using a separate latch to hold the upper address from the 8257-5 and connecting the outputs to the address bus as shown, 16-bit DMA transfers are provided. In this configuration, AEN simultaneously enables A0 and BHE* to allow word transfers. AEN still disables the CPU interface to the command and address busses.

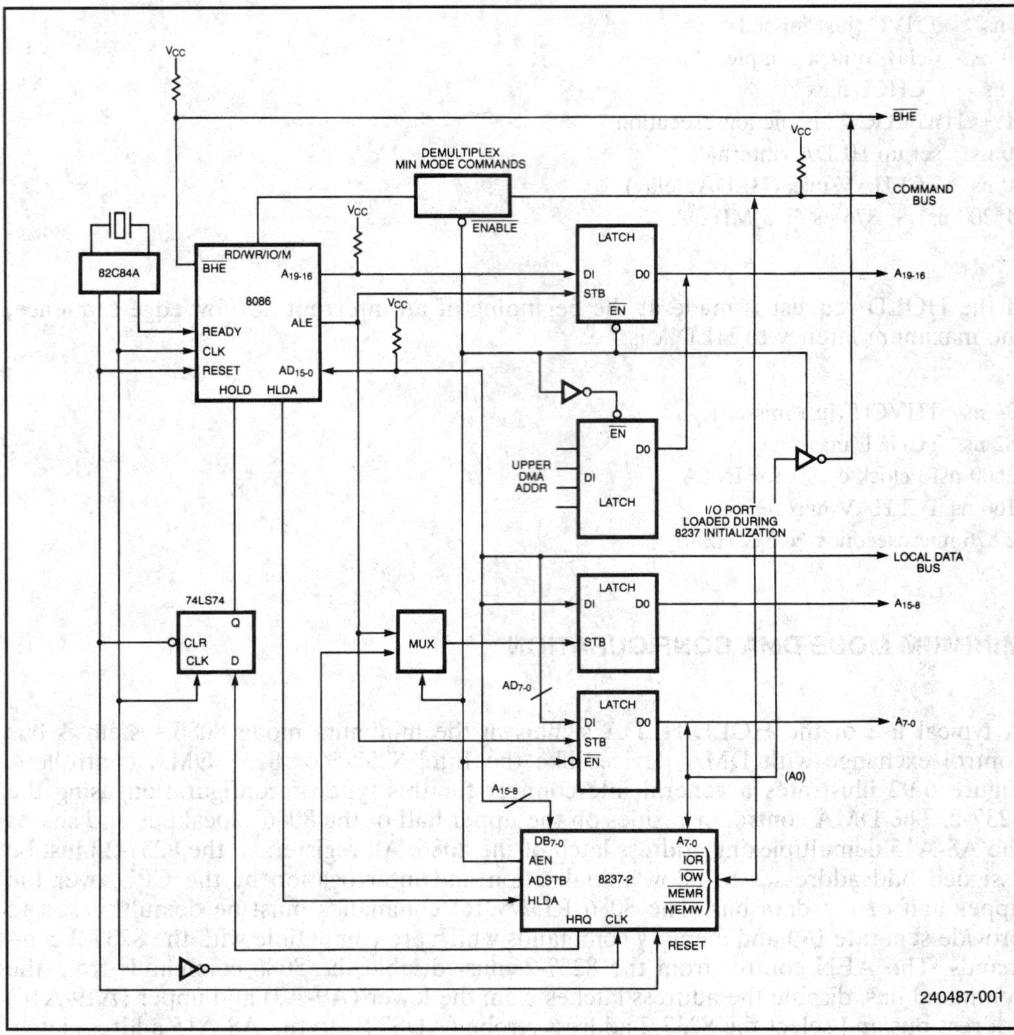

Figure 6-92. DMA using the 8237-2

RQ*/GT* TO HOLD/HLDA CONVERSION

Consider a circuit for translating a HOLD/HLDA handshake sequence into a RQ*/GT* pulse sequence (see Figure 6-94 and 6-95). After receiving the grant pulse, the HLDA is enabled TCHCLmin ns before the CPU has tri-stated the bus. If the requesting circuit drives the bus within 20 ns of HLDA, it may be desirable to delay the acknowledge one clock period. The HLDA is dropped not later than one clock period after HOLD is disabled. The HLDA also drops at the beginning of the release pulse to provide 2TCLCL + TCLCH for the requestor to relinquish control of the status lines and 3TCLCL to float the remaining signals.

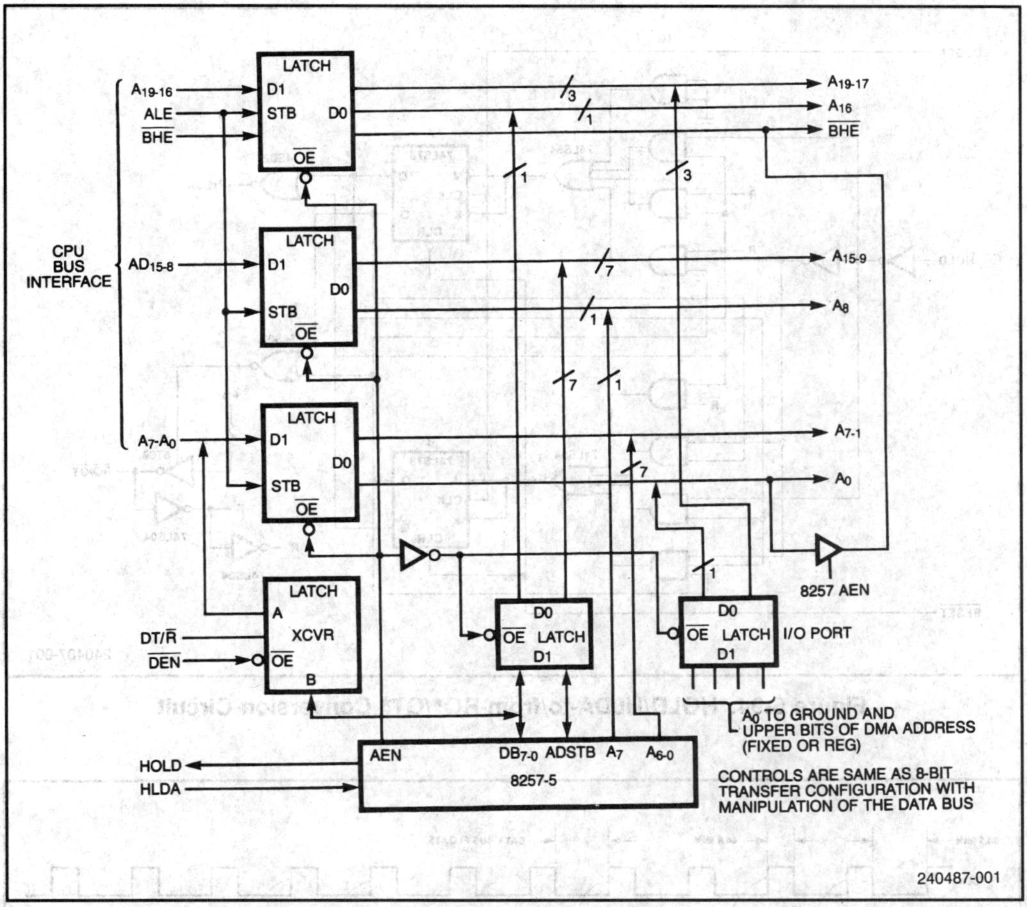

Figure 6-93. 8086/8088 Minimum System, 8257 on System Bus 16-Bit Transfers

Maximum Mode (RQ*/GT*)

The maximum mode 8086 configuration supports a significantly different protocol for transferring bus control. When viewed with respect to the HOLD/HLDA sequence of the minimum mode, the protocol appears difficult to implement externally. However, it is necessary to understand the intent of the protocol and its purpose within the system architecture.

The maximum mode RQ*/GT* sequence is intended to transfer control of the CPU local bus between the CPU and alternate bus masters which reside totally on the local bus and share the complete CPU interface to the system bus. The complete interface includes the address latches, data transceivers, 82C88 bus controller and multi-master bus arbiter. If the alternate bus masters in the system do not reside directly on the 8086 local bus, system bus arbitration is required rather than local CPU bus arbitration. To satisfy the need for multi-master system bus arbitration at each CPU's system interface, 8289 bus arbiter should be used rather than the CPU RQ*/GT* logic.

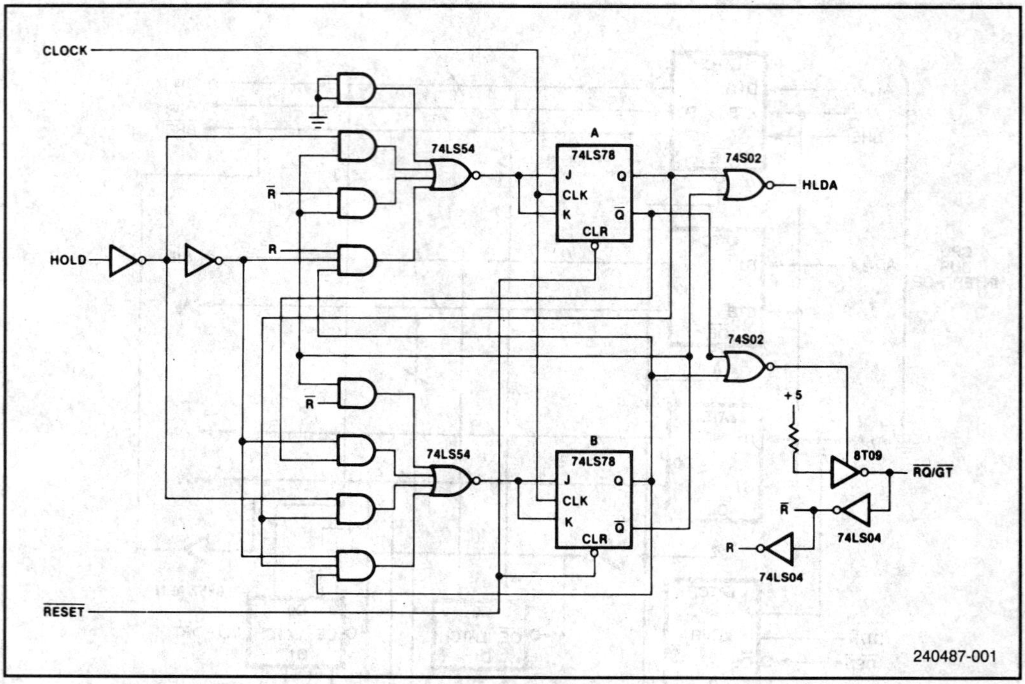

Figure 6-94. HOLD/HLDA-to/from-RQ*/GT* Conversion Circuit

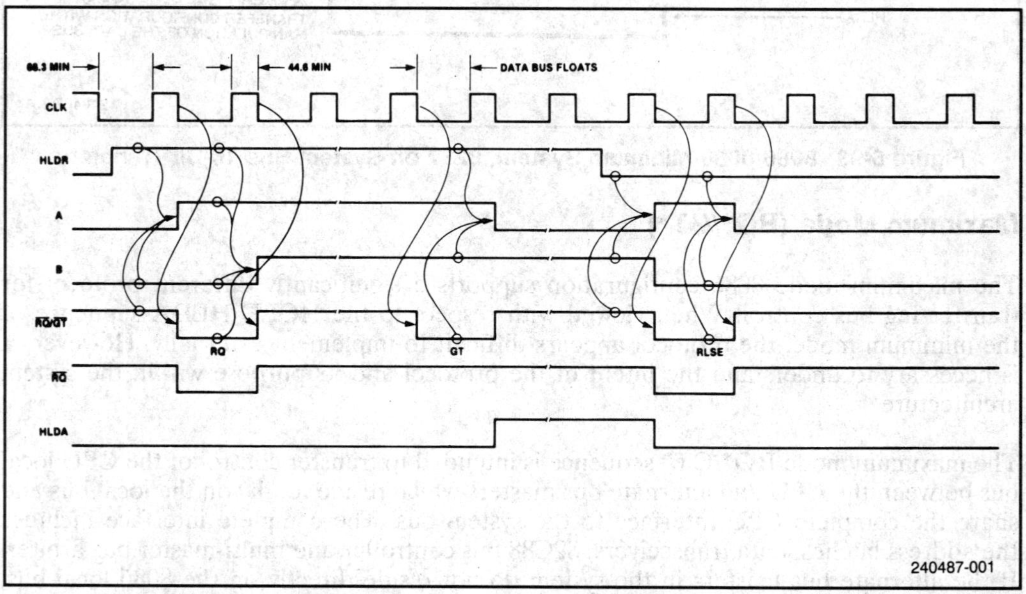

Figure 6-95. HOLD/HLDA-to/from-RQ*/GT* Conversion Timing

RQ*/GT* USAGE

The RQ*/GT* protocol was developed to allow up to two instruction set extension processor (co-processors) or other special function processors to reside directly on the 8086 local bus. Each RQ*/GT* pin of the 8086 supports the full protocol for exchange of bus control. The sequence consists of a request from the alternate bus master to gain control of the system bus, a grant from the CPU to indicate the bus has been relinquished and a release pulse from the alternate master when done. The two RQ*/GT* pins (RQ*/GT0* and RQ*/GT1*) are prioritized with RQ*/GT0* having the highest priority. The prioritization only occurs if requests have been received on both pins before a response has been given to either. For example, if a request is received on RQ*/GT1* followed by a request on RQ*/GT0* prior to a grant on RQ*/GT1*, RQ*/GT0* will gain priority over RQ*/GT1*. However, if RQ*/GT1* had already received a grant, a request on RQ*/GT0* must wait until a release pulse is received on RQ*/GT1*.

The request/grant sequence interaction with the bus interface unit is similar to HOLD/HLDA. The CPU continues to execute until a bus transfer for additional instructions or data is required. If the release pulse is received before the CPU needs the bus, it will not drive the bus until a transfer is required.

Upon receipt of a request pulse, the 8086 floats the multiplexed address, data and status bus, the S0*, S1*, and S2* status lines, the LOCK* pin and RD*. This action does not disable the 82C88 command outputs from driving the command bus and does not disable the address latches from driving the address bus. The 82C88 contains internal pull-up resistors on the S0*, S1*, and S2* status lines to maintain the passive state while the 8086 outputs are tri-state. The passive state prevents the 82C88 from initiating any commands or activating DEN to enable the transceivers buffering the data bus. If the device issuing the RQ* does not use the 82C88, it must disable the 82C88 command outputs by disabling the 82C88 AEN* input. Also, address latches not used by the requesting device must be disabled.

RQ*/GT* OPERATION

To request a transfer of bus control via the RQ*/GT* lines (see Figure 6-96), the device must drive the line low for no more than one CPU clock interval to generate a request pulse. The pulse must be synchronized with the CPU clock to guarantee the appropriate setup and hold times to the clock edge which samples the RQ*/GT* lines in the CPU. After issuing a request pulse, the device must begin sampling for a grant pulse with the next low to high clock edge. Since the 8086 can respond with a grant pulse in the clock cycle immediately following the request, the RQ*/GT* line may not return to the positive level between the request and grant pulses. Therefore edge triggered logic is not valid for capturing a grant pulse. It also implies the circuits which generate the request pulse must guarantee the request is removed in time to detect a grant from the CPU. After receiving the grant pulse, the requesting device may drive the local bus. Since the 8086 does not float the address and data bus, LOCK* or RD* until the high to low clock transition following the low to high clock transition the requestor uses to sample for the grant, the requestor should wait the float delay of the 8086 (TCLAZ) before driving the local bus. This precaution prevents bus contention during the access of bus control by the requestor.

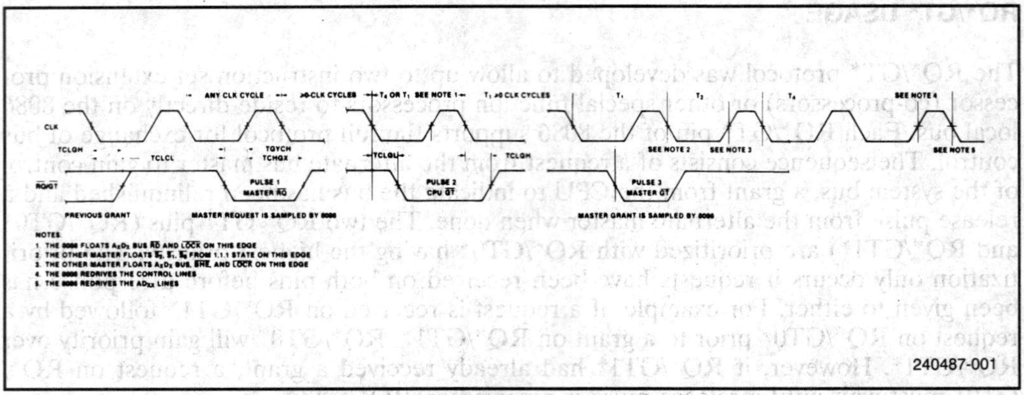

Figure 6-96. Request/Grant Sequence Timing

To return control of the bus to the 8086, the alternate bus master relinquishes bus control and issues a release pulse on the same RQ*/GT* line. The 8086 may drive the S0*-S2* status lines, RD* and LOCK*, three clock cycles after detecting the release pulse and the address/data bus TCHCLmin ns (clock high time) after the status lines. The alternate bus master should be tri-stated off the local bus and have other 8086 interface circuits 82C88 and address latches) re-enabled within the 8086 delay to regain control of the bus.

RQ*/GT* LATENCY

The RQ* to GT* latency for a single RQ*/GT* line is similar to the HOLD to HLDA latency. The cases given for the minimum mode 8086 also apply to the maximum mode. For each case the delay from RQ* detection by the CPU to GT* detection by the requestor is: (HOLD to HLDA delay) − (THVCH + TCHCL + TCLHAV).

This gives a clock cycle maximum delay for an idle bus interface. All other cases are the minimum mode result minus 476 ns. If the 8086 has previously issued a grant on one of the RQ*/GT* lines, a request on the other RQ*/GT* line will not receive a grant until the first device releases the interface with a release pulse on its RQ*/GT* line. The delay from release on one RQ*/GT* line to a grant on the other is typically one clock period (see Figure 6-97). Occasionally the delay from a release on RQ*/GT* to a grant on RQ*/GT* will take two clock cycles and is a function of a pending request for transfer of control from the execution unit. The latency from request to grant when the interface is under control of a bus master on the other RQ*/GT* line is a function of the other bus master. The protocol embodies no mechanism for the CPU to force an alternate bus master off the bus. A watchdog timer should be used to prevent an errant alternate bus master from 'hanging' the system.

HOLD/HLDA INTERFACE TO MAXIMUM MODE SYSTEMS

To allow a device with a simple HOLD/HLDA protocol to gain control of a single CPU system bus, the circuit in Figure 6-98 could be used. The design is effectively a simple

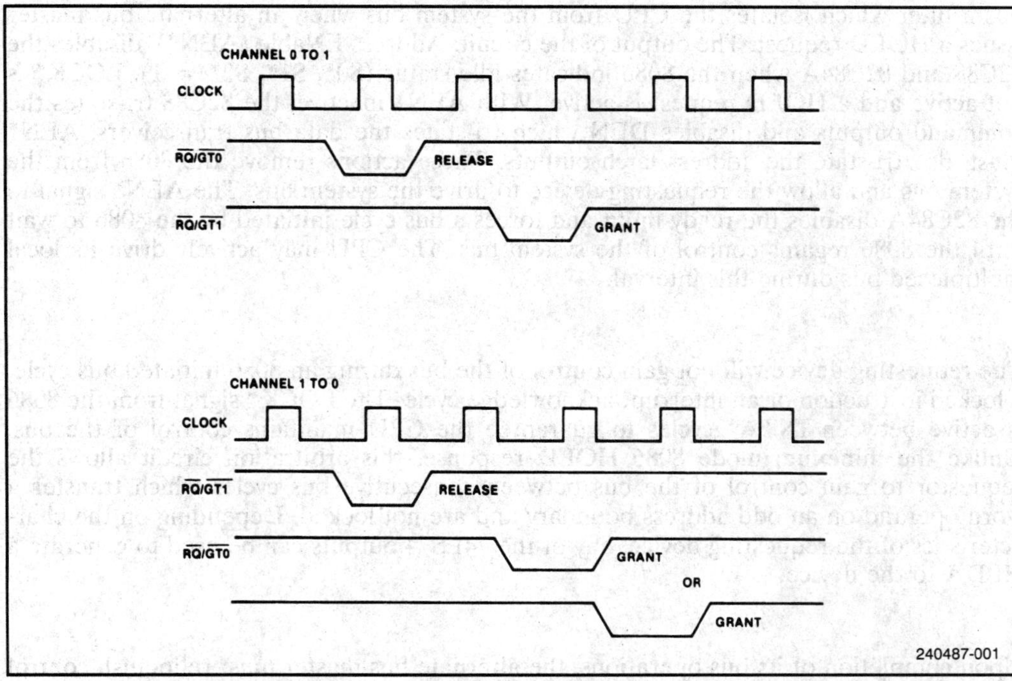

Figure 6-97. Channel Transfer Delay Timing

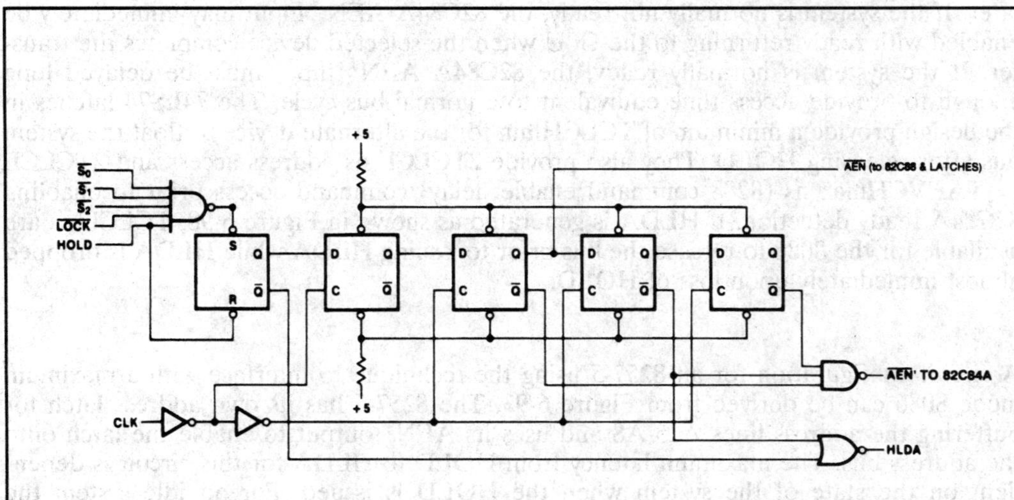

Figure 6-98. Circuit to Translate HOLD into AEN Disable for Maximum Mode 8086/8088

bus arbiter which isolates the CPU from the system bus when an alternate bus master issues a HOLD request. The output of the circuit, Address ENable (AEN*), disables the 82C88 and 82C84A when the 8086 indicates idle status (S0*, S1*, S2* = 1), LOCK* is not active and a HOLD request is active. With AEN* inactive, the 82C88 tri-states the command outputs and disables DEN which tri-states the data bus transceivers. AEN* must also tri-state the address latch outputs. These actions remove the 8086 from the system bus and allow the requesting device to drive the system bus. The AEN* signal to the 82C84A disables the ready input and forces a bus cycle initiated by the 8086 to wait until the 8086 regains control of the system bus. The CPU may actively drive its local multiplexed bus during this interval.

The requesting device will not gain control of the bus during an 8086 initiated bus cycle, a locked instruction or an interrupt acknowledge cycle. The LOCK* signal from the 8086 is active between INTA* cycles to guarantee the CPU maintains control of the bus. Unlike the minimum mode 8086 HOLD response, this arbitration circuit allows the requestor to gain control of the bus between consecutive bus cycles which transfer a word operand on an odd address boundary and are not locked. Depending on the characteristics of the requesting device, any of the 74LS74 outputs can be used to generate a HLDA to the device.

Upon completion of its bus operations, the alternate bus master must relinquish control of the system bus and drop the HOLD request. After AEN* goes inactive, the address latches and data transceivers are enabled but, if a CPU initiated bus cycle is pending, the 82C88 will not drive the command bus until a minimum of 105 ns or maximum of 275 ns later. If the system is normally not ready, the 82C84A AEN* input may immediately be enabled with ready returning to the CPU when the selected device completes the transfer. If the system is normally ready, the 82C84A AEN* input must be delayed long enough to provide access time equivalent to a normal bus cycle. The 74LS74 latches in the design provide a minimum of TCLCHmin for the alternate device to float the system bus after releasing HOLD. They also provide 2TCLCL ns address access and 2TCLCL − TAEVCHmax ns (8288 command enable delay) command access prior to enabling 82C84A ready detection. If HLDA is generated as shown in Figure 6-98, TCLCL ns are available for the 8086 to release the bus prior to issuing HLDA while HLDA is dropped almost immediately upon loss of HOLD.

A circuit configuration for an 8257-5 using the technique to interface with a maximum mode 8086 can be derived from Figure 6-93. The 8257-5 has its own address latch for buffering the address lines A15-A8 and uses its AEN* output to enable the latch onto the address bus. The maximum latency from HOLD to HLDA for this circuit is dependent on the state of the system when the HOLD is issued. For an idle system the maximum delay is propagtion delay through the NAND gate and R/S flip-flop (TD1) plus 2TCLCL plus TCLCHmax plus propagation delay of the 74LS74 and 74LS02 (TD2). For a locked instruction it becomes: TD1 + TD2 + (M + 2) *TCLCL + TCLCHmax where M is the number of clocks required for execution of the locked instruction. For the interrupt acknowledge cycle the latency is TD1 + TD2 + 9 *TCLCL + TCLCHmax.

RESET

The 8086/8088 RESET line provides an orderly way to start or restart an 8086/8088 system. When the processor detects the positive-going edge of a pulse on RESET, it terminates all activities until the signal goes LOW, at which time the internal CPU registers are initialized to the reset condition (see Figure 6-99).

Upon RESET, the code segment register and the instruction pointer are initialized to FFFFH and 0 respectively. Therefore, the 8086 executes its first instruction following system reset from absolute memory location FFFF0H. This location normally contains an intersegment direct JMP instruction whose target is the actual beginning of the system program.

As external (maskable) interrupts are disabled by system reset, the system software should re-enable interrupts as soon as the system is initialized.

The 8086/8088 requires a high active reset with minimum pulse width of four CPU clocks except after power on which requires a 50 microsecond reset pulse. Since the CPU internally synchronizes reset with the clock, the reset is internally active for up to one clock period after the external reset. Non-Maskable Interrupts (NMI) or hold requests on RQ*/GT* which occur during the internal reset, are not acknowledged. A minimum mode hold request or maximum mode RQ* pulses active immediately after the internal reset will be honored before the first instruction fetch.

Reset Bus Conditioning

From reset, the 8086/8088 will condition the bus (refer to Table 6-39). The multiplexed bus will tri-state upon detection of reset by the CPU. Other signals which tri-state will be driven to the inactive state for one clock low interval prior to entering tri-state (see Figure 6-99). In the minimum mode, ALE and HLDA are drive inactive and are not tri-stated. In the maximum mode, RQ*/GT* lines are held inactive and the queue status indicates no activity. The queue status will not indicate a reset of the queue so any user

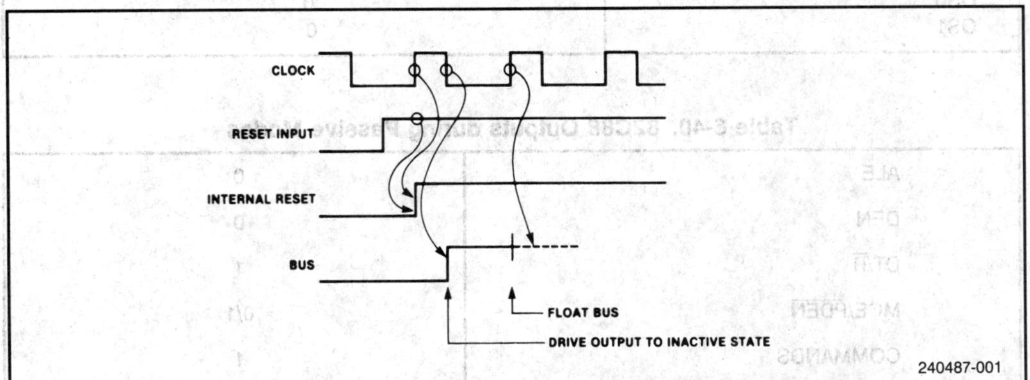

Figure 6-99. 8086/8088 Bus Conditioning on Reset Timing Diagram

defined external circuits monitoring the queue should also be reset by the system reset. 22K ohm pull-up resistors should be connected to the CPU command and bus control lines to guarantee the inactive state of these lines in systems where leakage currents or bus capacitance may cause the voltage levels to settle below the minimum high voltage of devices in the system. In maximum mode systems, the 82C88 contains internal pull-ups on the S0*-S2* inputs to maintain the inactive state for these lines when the CPU floats the bus. The high state of the status lines during reset causes the 82C88 to treat the reset sequence as a passive state (refer to Table 6-40). If the reset occurs during a bus cycle, the return of the status lines to the passive state will terminate the bus cycle and return the command lines to the inactive state.

NOTE

The 82C88 does not tri-state the command outputs based on the passive state of the status lines.

Table 6-39. Condition of 8086/8088 Bus and Output Signal Pins during Reset

Signals	Condition
AD_{15-0}	Three-State
A_{19-16}/S_{6-3}	Three-State
$\overline{BHE}/S_7$	Three-State
$\overline{S2}$/(M/$\overline{IO}$)	Driven to "1" then three-state
$\overline{S1}$/(DT/$\overline{R}$)	Driven to "1" then three-state
$\overline{S0}$/$\overline{DEN}$	Driven to "1" then three-state
$\overline{LOCK}$/$\overline{WR}$	Driven to "1" then three-state
$\overline{RD}$	Driven to "1" then three-state
$\overline{INTA}$	Driven to "1" then three-state
ALE	0
HLDA	0
$\overline{RQ}$/$\overline{GT0}$	1
$\overline{RQ}$/$\overline{GT1}$	1
QS0	0
QS1	0

Table 6-40. 82C88 Outputs during Passive Modes

ALE	0
DEN	0
DT/$\overline{R}$	1
MCE/$\overline{PDEN}$	0/1
COMMANDS	1

If the CPU needs to be tri-stated off the bus during reset in a single CPU system, connect the reset signal to the 82C88 AEN* input and output enable of the address latches (see Figure 6-100). This connection forces the command and address bus interface to tri-state while the inactive state of DEN from the 82C88 tri-states the transceivers on the data bus.

INTERRUPTS

CPU interrupts can be software or hardware initiated. Software interrupts originate directly from program execution (i.e., execution of a breakpointed instruction) or indirectly through program logic (i.e., attempting to divide by zero). Hardware interrupts originate from external logic and are classified as either non-maskable or maskable. All interrupts, whether software or hardware initiated, result in the transfer of control to a new program location. A 256-entry vector table (see Figure 6-101), which contains address pointers to the interrupt routines, resides in absolute locations 0 through 3FFH. Each entry in this table consists of two 16-bit address values (four bytes) that are loaded into the code segment (CS) and the instruction pointer (IP) registers as the interrupt routine address when an interrupt is accepted.

The first five interrupt vectors (see Figure 6-101) are associated with the software-initiated interrupts and the hardware non-maskable interrupt (NMI). The next 27 interrupt vectors are reserved by Intel and should not be used to ensure compatibility with future Intel products. The remaining interrupt vectors (vectors 32 through 255) are available for user interrupt routines.

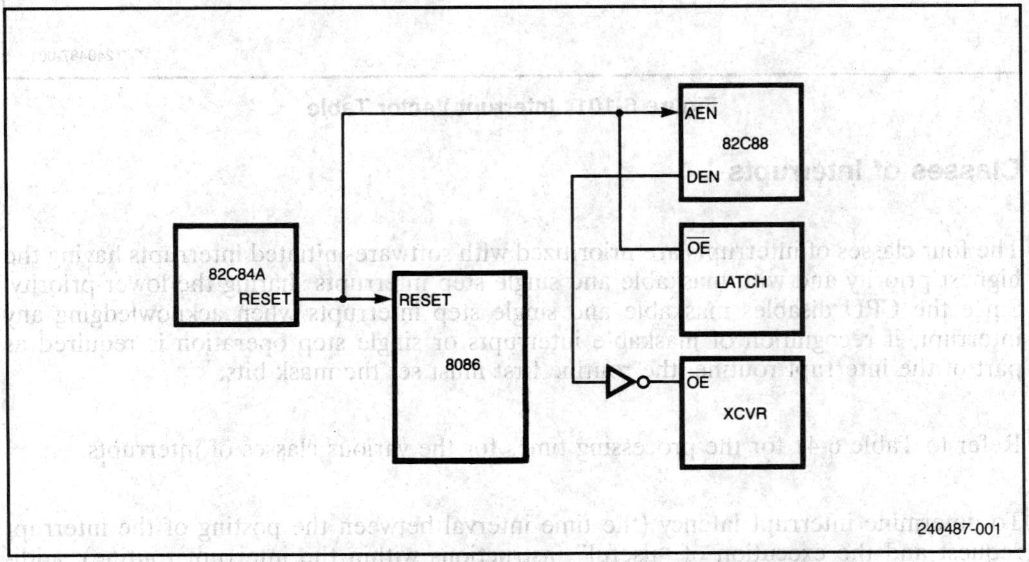

Figure 6-100. Reset Disable for Max Mode 8086/8088 Bus Interface

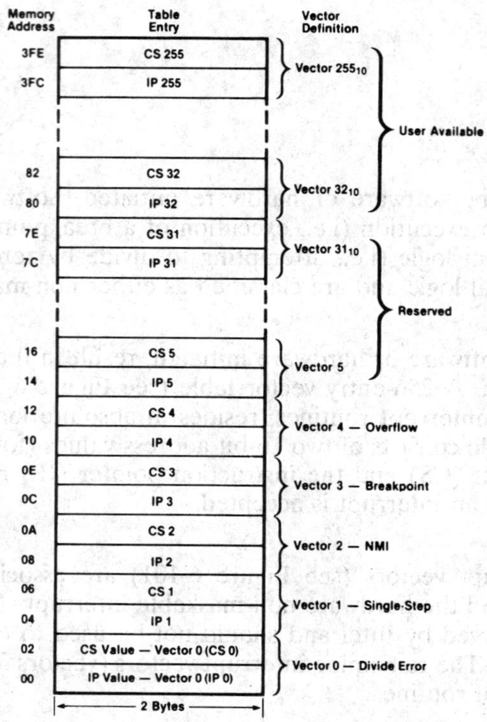

Figure 6-101. Interrupt Vector Table

Classes of Interrupts

The four classes of interrupts are prioritized with software-initiated interrupts having the highest priority and with maskable and single step interrupts sharing the lower priority. Since the CPU disables maskable and single step interrupts when acknowledging any interrupt, if recognition of maskable interrupts or single step operation is required as part of the interrupt routine, the routine first must set the mask bits.

Refer to Table 6-41 for the processing times for the various classes of interrupts.

To determine interrupt latency (the time interval between the posting of the interrupt request and the execution of "useful" instructions within the interrupt routine), additional time must be included for the completion on an instruction being executed when

Table 6-41. Interrupt Processing Timing

Interrupt Class	Processing Time
External Maskable Interrupt (INTR)	61 clocks
Non-Maskable Interrupt (NMI)	50 clocks
INT (with vector)	51 clocks
INT Type 3	52 clocks
INTO	53 clocks
Single Step	50 clocks

the interrupt is posted (interrupts are generally processed only at instruction boundaries), for saving the contents of any additional registers prior to interrupt processing (interrupts automatically save only CS, IP and Flags) and for any wait states that may be incurred during interrupt processing.

The predefined interrupt types in the 8086 are listed below and a brief description of how each is involved is included in this section. When invoked, the CPU will transfer control to the memory location specified by the vector associated with the specific type. The user must provide the interrupt service routine and initialize the interrupt vector table with the appropriate service routine address. The user may additionally invoke these interrupts through hardware or software. If the preassigned function is not used in the system, the user may assign some other function to the associated type. However, for compatibility with future Intel hardware and software products for the 8086 family, interrupt types 0-31 should not be assigned as user defined interrupts. Interrupt classes include the following:

Type 0 — Divide Error
Type 1 — Single Step
Type 2 — Non-Maskable Interrupt
Type 3 — One Byte Interrupt
Type 4 — Interrupt On Overflow
User Defined Software Interrupt
User Defined Hardware Interrupt

Divide Error — Type 0

Type 0 interrupts are invoked whenever a division operation is attempted during which the quotient exceeds the maximum value (e.g., division by zero). The interrupt is non-maskable and is entered as part of the execution of the divide instruction. If interrupts are not re-enabled by the divide error interrupt service routine, the service routine execution time should be included in the worst case divide instruction execution time (primarily when considering the longest instruction execution time and its effect on latency to servicing hardware interrupts).

Single Step — Type 1

This interrupt type occurs one instruction after the TF (Trap Flag) is set in the flag register. It is used to allow software single stepping through a sequence of code. Single stepping is initiated by copying the flags onto the stack, setting the TF bit on the stack and popping the flags. The interrupt routine should be the single step routine itself. The interrupt sequence saves the flag and program counter, then resets the TF flag to allow the single step routine to execute normally. To return to the routine under test, an interrupt return restores the IP, CS and flags with TF set. This allows the execution of the next instruction in the program under test before trapping back to the single step routine. Single Step is not masked by the IF (Interrupt Flag) bit in the flag register.

Non-Maskable Interrupt — Type 2

Interrupt Type 2 is the highest priority hardware interrupt and is non-maskable. The input is edge triggered but is synchronized with the CPU clock and must be active for two clock cycles to guarantee recognition. The interrupt signal may be removed prior to entry to the service routine. Since the input must make a low to high transition to generate an interrupt, spurious transitions on the input should be suppressed. If the input is normally high, the NMI must be two CPU clock times to guarantee triggering. This input is typically reserved for catastrophic failures like power failure or timeout of a system watchdog timer.

One-Byte Interrupt — Type 3

A special form of the software interrupt instruction which requires a single byte of code space involves Type 3 interrupts. It is primarily used as a breakpoint interrupt for software debug. With full representation within a single byte, the instruction can map into the smallest instruction for absolute resolution in setting breakpoints. This interrupt is not maskable.

Interrupt on Overflow — Type 4

This non-maskable interrupt occurs if the overflow flag (OF) is set in the flag register and the INTO instruction is executed. The instruction allows trapping to an overflow error service routine.

Interrupt types 0 and 2 can occur without specific action by the programmer (except for performing a divide for Type 0) while types 1, 3, and 4 require a conscious act by the programmer to generate these interrupt types. All but type 2 are invoked through software activity and are directly associated with a specific instruction.

User-Defined Software Interrupts

The user can generate an interrupt through the software with a two byte interrupt instruction INT nn. The first byte is the INT opcode while the second byte (nn) contains the top number of the interrupt to be performed. The INT instruction is not maskable by the interrupt enable flag. This instruction can be used to transfer control to routines that are dynamically relocatable and whose location in memory is not known by the calling program. This technique also saves the flags of the calling program on the stack prior to transferring control. The called procedure must return control with an interrupt return (IRET) instruction to remove the flags from the stack and fully restore the state of the calling program.

All interrupts invoked through software (all interrupts discussed thus far with the exception of NMI) are not maskable with the IF flag and initiate the transfer of control at the end of the instruction in which they occur. They do not initiate interrupt acknowledge bus cycles and will disable subsequent maskable interrupts by resetting the IF and TF flags. The interrupt vector for these interrupt types is either implied or specified in the instruction. Since the NMI is an asynchronous event to the CPU, the point of recognition and initiation of the transfer of control is similar to the maskable hardware interrupts.

User-Defined Hardware Interrupts

The maskable interrupts initiated by the system hardware are activated through the INTA pin of the 8086 and are masked by the IF bit of the status register (interrupt flag). During the last clock cycle of each instruction, the state of the INTA pin is sampled. The 8086 deviates from this rule when the instruction is MOV or POP to a segment register. For this case, the interrupts are not sampled until completion of the following instruction. This delay allows a 32-bit pointer to be loaded to the stack pointer registers SS and SP without the danger of an interrupt occurring between the two loads. An uninterruptable instruction sequence follows:

```
MOV SS, NEW$STACK$SEGMENT
MOV SP, NEW$STACK$POINTER
```

Another exception includes the WAIT instruction which waits for a low active input on the TEST* pin. This instruction also continuously samples the interrupt request during its execution and allows servicing interrupts during the wait. When an interrupt is detected, the WAIT instruction is again fetched prior to servicing the interrupt to guarantee the interrupt routine will return to the WAIT instruction.

Also, since prefixes are considered part of the instruction they precede, the 8086 will not sample the interrupt line until completion of the instruction the prefix(es) precede(s). Other than HALT or WAIT, the string primitives preceded by the repeat (REP) prefix deviate from this rule. The repeated string operations will sample the interrupt line at the completion of each repetition. This includes repeat string operations which include the lock prefix. If multiple prefixes precede a repeated string operation, and the instruction is interrupted, only the prefix immediately preceding the string primitive is restored. To allow correct resumption of the operation, use the following or a similar programming technique:

```
LOCKED$BLOCK$MOVE:
  LOCK REP MOVS DEST, CS:SOURCE
          AND CS,      CX
          JNZ LOCKED$BLOCK$MOVE
```

The code bytes generated by the 8086 assembler for the MOVS instruction are (in descending order): LOCK prefix, REP prefix, Segment Override prefix and MOVS. Upon return from the interrupt, the segment override prefix is restored to guarantee that one additional transfer is performed between the correct memory locations. The instructions following the Move operation test the repetition count value to determine if the move was completed and return if not.

If the INTR pin is high when sampled and the IF bit is set to enable interrupts, the 8086 executes an interrupt acknowledge sequence. To guarantee the interrupt will be acknowledged, the INTR input must be held active until the interrupt acknowledge is issued by the CPU. If the BIU is running a bus cycle when the interrupt condition is detected (as would occur if the BIU is fetching an instruction when the current instruction completes), the interrupt must be valid at the 8086 two clock cycles prior to T4 of the bus cycle if the next cycle is to be an interrupt acknowledge cycle. If the two clock setup is not satisfied, another pending bus cycle will be executed before the interrupt acknowledge is issued. If a hold request is also pending (this might occur if an interrupt and hold request are made during execution of locked instruction), the interrupt is serviced after the hold request is serviced.

Interrupt Acknowledge

The interrupt acknowledge sequence (see Figure 6-102) is only generated in response to an interrupt request (INTR) on the 8086 INTR input. The CPU provides a single INTR that can be software masked by clearing the interrupt enable bit in the flags register through the execution of a CLI instruction. The INTR input is level triggered and synchronized internally to the positive transition of the CLK signal. In order to be accepted before the next instruction, INTR must be active during the clock period preceding the end of the current instruction (and the interrupt enable bit must be set). When a maskable interrupt is acknowledged, the CPU executes two interrupt acknowledge (INTA*) bus cycles. The two INTA* bus cycles are typically separated by two idle clock cycles.

During the bus cycles the INTA* command is issued rather than read. No address is provided by the 8086 during either bus cycle (BHE* and status are valid). However, ALE is still generated and will load the address latches with indeterminate information. This condition requires that devices in the system do not drive their outputs without being qualified by the Read Command. The ALE is useful in maximum mode systems

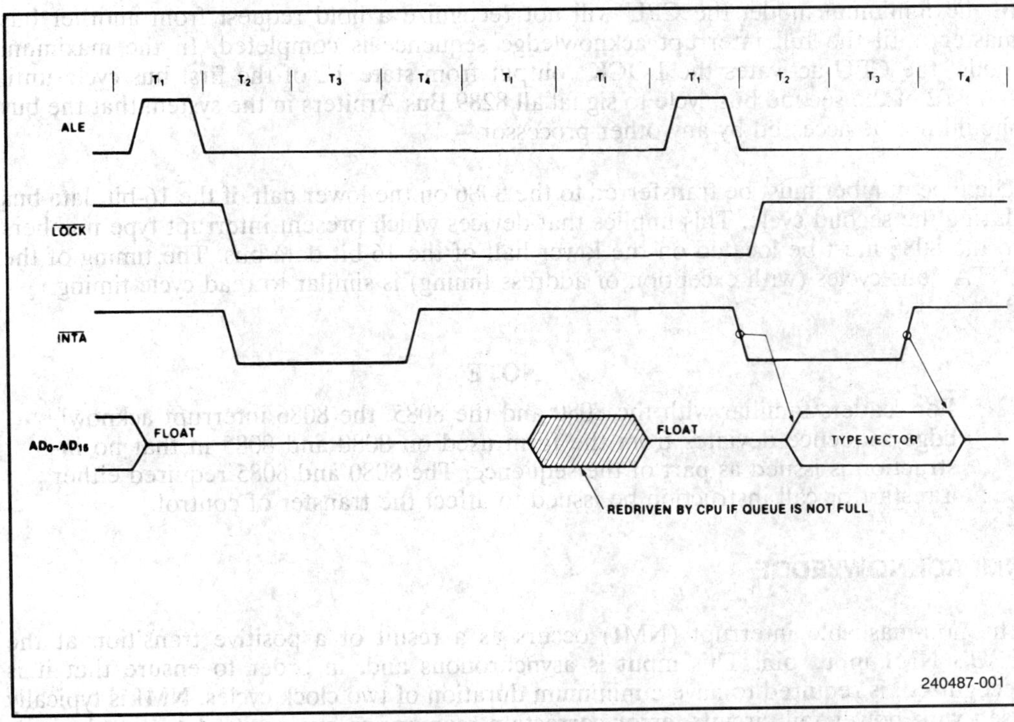

Figure 6-102. Interrupt Acknowledge Timing

with multiple 8259A priority interrupt controllers. During the INTA* bus cycle, DT/R* and DEN are conditioned to allow the 8086 to receive a one byte interrupt type number from the interrupt system.

The first INTA* bus cycle signals an interrupt acknowledge cycle is in progress and allows the system to prepare to present the interrupt type number on the next INTA* bus cycle. The CPU does not capture information on the bus during the first cycle. During the first bus cycle, the CPU floats the address/data bus and activates the INTA* (Interrupt Acknowledge) command output during states T2 and T4.

During the second bus cycle, the CPU again activates its INTA* command output. In response to the second INTA*, the external interrupt system (e.g., an Intel 8259A Programmable Interrupt Controller) places a byte on the data bus that identifies the source of the interrupt (the vector number or vector "type"). This byte is read by the CPU and then multiplied by four and the resultant value used as a pointer into the interrupt vector table. Before calling the corresponding interrupt routine, the CPU saves the machine status by pushing the current contents of the flags register onto the stack. The CU then clears the interrupt enable and trap bits in the flags register to prevent subsequent maskable and single step interrupts, and establishes the interrupt routine return linkage by pushing the current CS and IP register contents onto the stack before loading the new CS and IP register values from the vector table.

In the minimum mode, the CPU will not recognize a hold request from another bus master until the full interrupt acknowledge sequence is completed. In the maximum mode, the CPU activates the LOCK* output from state T2 of the first bus cycle until state T2 of the second bus cycle to signal all 8289 Bus Arbiters in the system that the bus should not be accessed by any other processor.

The type number must be transferred to the 8086 on the lower half of the 16-bit data bus during the second cycle. This implies that devices which present interrupt type numbers to the 8086 must be located on the lower half of the 16-bit data bus. The timing of the INTA* bus cycles (with exception of address timing) is similar to read cycle timing.

NOTE

> For readers familiar with the 8080 and the 8085, the 8086 interrupt acknowledge sequence deviates from the form used on 8080 and 8085 in that no instruction is issued as part of the sequence. The 8080 and 8085 required either a restart or call instruction be issued to affect the transfer of control.

NMI ACKNOWLEDGE

The non-maskable interrupt (NMI) occurs as a result of a positive transition at the CPU's NMI input pin. This input is asynchronous and, in order to ensure that it is recognized, is required to have a minimum duration of two clock cycles. NMI is typically used with power fail circuits, error correction memory or bus parity detection logic to allow fast response to these fault conditions. When NMI is activated, control is transferred to the interrupt service routine pointed to by vector 2 following execution of the current instruction. When a non-maskable interrupt is acknowledged, the current contents of the flags register are pushed onto the stack (the stack pointer is decremented by two), the interrupt enable and trap bits in the flags register are cleared (disabling maskable and single step interrupts), and the vector CS and IP address pointers are loaded into the CS and IP registers as the interrupt service routine address.

MINIMUM MODE SYSTEM INTERRUPT

In the minimum mode system, the M/IO* signal will be low indicating I/O during the INTA* bus cycles. The 8086 internal LOCK* signal will be active from T2 of the first bus cycle until T2 of the second to prevent the BIU from honoring a hold request between the two INTA* cycles.

MAXIMUM MODE SYSTEM INTERRUPT

In the maximum mode, the status lines S0*-S2* will request the 82C88 to activate the INTA* output for each cycle. The LOCK* output of the 8086 will be active from T2 of the first cycle until T2 of the second to prevent the 8086 from honoring a hold request on either RQ*/GT* input and to prevent bus arbitration logic from relinquishing the bus between INTA*'s in multi-master systems. The consequences of READY are identical to those for READ and WRITE cycles.

INTERRUPT TYPE PROCESSING

Once the 8086 has the interrupt type number (from the bus for hardware interrupts, from the instruction stream for software interrupts or from the predefined condition), the type number is multiplied by four to form the displacement to the corresponding interrupt vector in the interrupt vector table. The four bytes of the interrupt vector include:

1. Least significant byte of the instruction pointer.
2. Most significant byte of the instruction pointer.
3. Least significant byte of the code segment register.
4. Most significant byte of the code segment register.

   During the transfer of control, the CPU pushes the flags and current code segment register and instruction pointer onto the stack. The new code segment and instruction pointer values are loaded and the single step and interrupt flags are reset. Resetting the interrupt flag disables response to further hardware interrupts in the service routine unless the flags are specifically re-enabled by the service routine. The CS and IP values are read from the interrupt vector table with data read cycles. No segment registers are used when referring to the vector table during the interrupt context switch. The vector displacement is added to zero to form the 20-bit address and S4, S3 = 10 indicating no segment register selection.

BUS ACTIVITY DURING A HARDWARE INTERRUPT

The hardware interrupt acknowledge sequence bus activity includes: Two interrupt acknowledge bus cycles, read new IP from the interrupt vector table, read new CS from the interrupt vector table, Push flags, Push old CS, Opcode fetch of the first instruction of the interrupt service routine, and Push old IP. After saving the old IP, the BIU will resume normal operation of prefetching instructions into the queue and servicing EU requests for operands. S5 (interrupt enable flag status) will go inactive in the second clock cycle following reading the new CS.

The elapsed time from the end of the instruction during which the interrupt occurred to the start of interrupt routine execution consists of 61 clock cycles. For software generated interrupts, the sequence of bus cycles is the same except no interrupt acknowledge bus cycles are executed. This reduces the delay to service routine execution to 51 clocks for INT nn and single step, to 52 clock for INT3 and to 53 clocks for INTO. The same interrupt setup requirements with respect to the BIU that were stated for the hardware interrupts also apply to the software interrupts. If wait states are inserted by either the memories or the device supplying the interrupt type number, the given clock times will increase accordingly.

INTERRUPT PRECEDENCE

When considering the precedence of interrupts for multiple simultaneous interrupts, the following guidelines apply:

1. INTR is the only maskable interrupt and if detected simultaneously with other interrupts, resetting of IF by the other interrupts will mask INTR. This causes INTR to be the lowest priority interrupt serviced after all other interrupts unless the other interrupt service routines re-enable interrupts.
2. Of the non-maskable interrupts (NMI, single step and software generated), in general single step has the highest priority (will be serviced first) followed by NMI, followed by the software interrupts.

This priority implies that a simultaneous NMI and single step trap will cause the MMI service routine to follow single step; a simultaneous software trap and single step trap will cause the software interrupt service routine to follow single step and simultaneous NMI and software trap will cause the NMI service routine to be executed followed by the software interrupt service routine. An exception to this priority structure occurs if all three interrupts are pending. For this case, transfer of control to the software interrupt service routine followed by the NMI trap will cause both the NMI and software interrupt service routines to be executed without single stepping. Single stepping resumes upon execution of the instruction following the instruction causing the software interrupt (the next instruction in the routine being single stepped).

If the user does not wish to single step before INTR service routines, the single step routine need only disable interrupts during execution of the program being single stepped and re-enable interrupts on entry to the single step routine. Disabling the interrupts during the program under test prevents entry into the interrupt service routine while single step (TF = 1) is active. To prevent single stepping before NMI service routines, the single step routine must check the return address on the stack for the NMI service routines address and return control to that routine without single step enabled. As examples, consider Figure 6-103 and 6-104. In Figure 6-103 single step and NMI occur simultaneously while in Figure 6-104, NMI, INTR and a divide error all occur during a divide instruction being single stepped.

SUPPORT COMPONENTS

The following paragraphs provide descriptions of the various unique support components used in systems to support the 8086/8088 CPU's. These components include the 82C84A Clock Generator/Driver, the 82C88 Bus Controller, the 8259A Programmable DMA Controller. These components may be used when designing both minimum and maximum mode applications for the 8086/8088 Microprocessors. The following paragraphs present detailed design information on the various support circuits and describe the benefits of each. The circuit designer should also refer to the *Intel® Microprocessor and Peripheral Handbook* (Order No. 230843) for detailed data sheets on each of the devices.

82C84A Clock Generator and Driver

The 82C84A Clock Generator/Driver is an integral part of the 8086 family that Intel offers to satisfy the 8086 requirement for an external clock signal. In addition to providing the primary (system) clock signal, this device provides both the hardware reset interface and the mechanism for the insertion of wait states in the bus cycle. An optimum

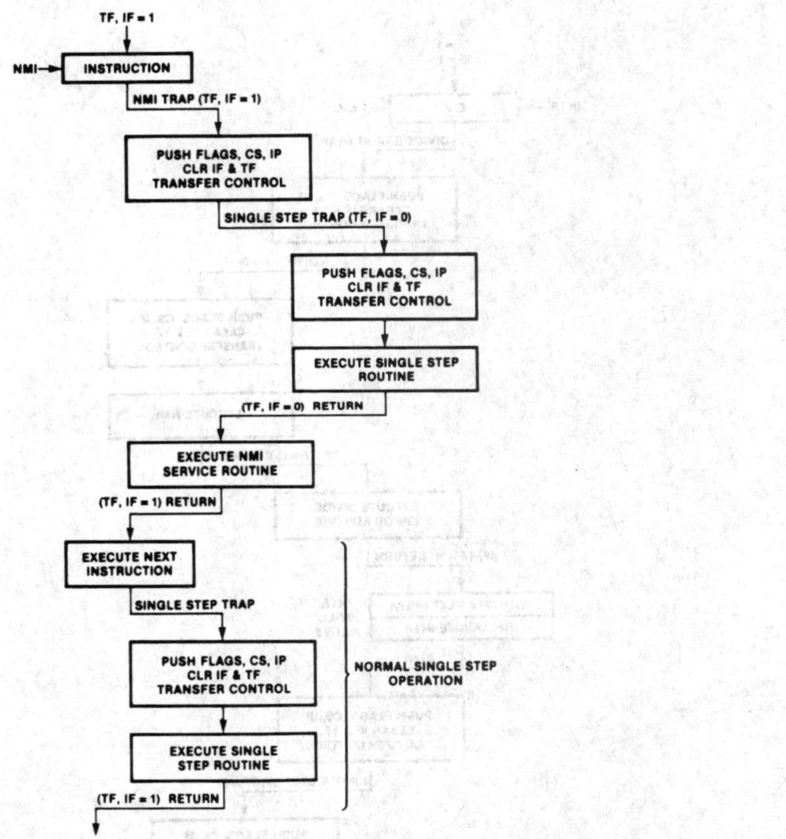

Figure 6-103. NMI during Single Stepping and Normal Single Step Operation

33% duty cycle clock with the required voltage levels and transition times can be obtained with the 82C84A clock generator (see Figure 6-105). Either an external frequency source or a series resonant crystal may drive the 82C84A.

CLOCK GENERATION

The 8086 requires a clock signal with fast rise and fall times (10 ns max) between low and high voltages of −0.5 to +0.6 low and 3.9 to VCC + 1.0 high (see Figure 6-106). The maximum clock frequency of the 8086 is 5 MHz, 8 MHz for the 8086-2 and 10 MHz for the 8086-1.

Since the design of the 8086 incorporates dynamic cells, a minimum frequency of 2 MHz is required to retain the state of the machine. Due to the minimum frequency requirement, single stepping or cycling of the CPU may not be accomplished by disabling the

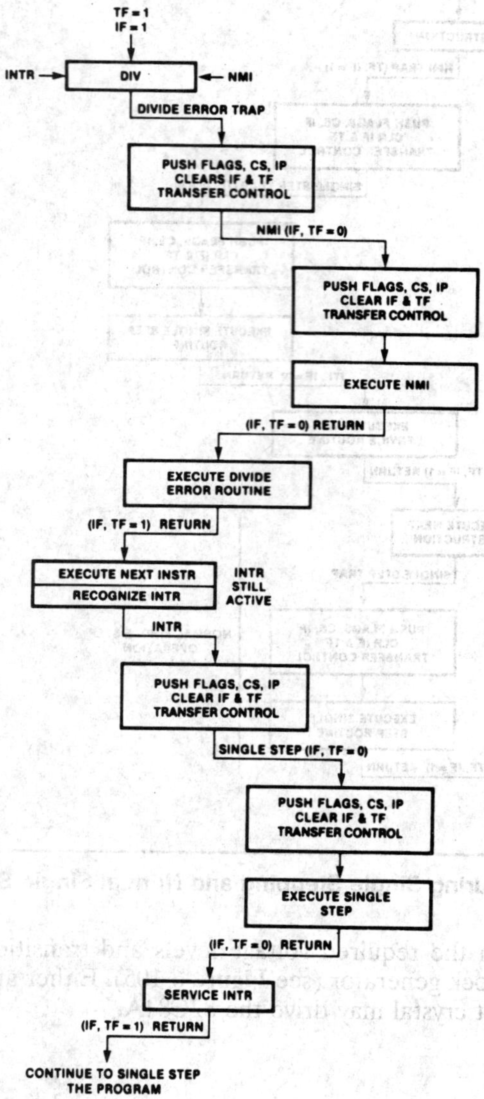

Figure 6-104. NMI, INTR, Single Step, and Divide Error Simultaneous Interrupts

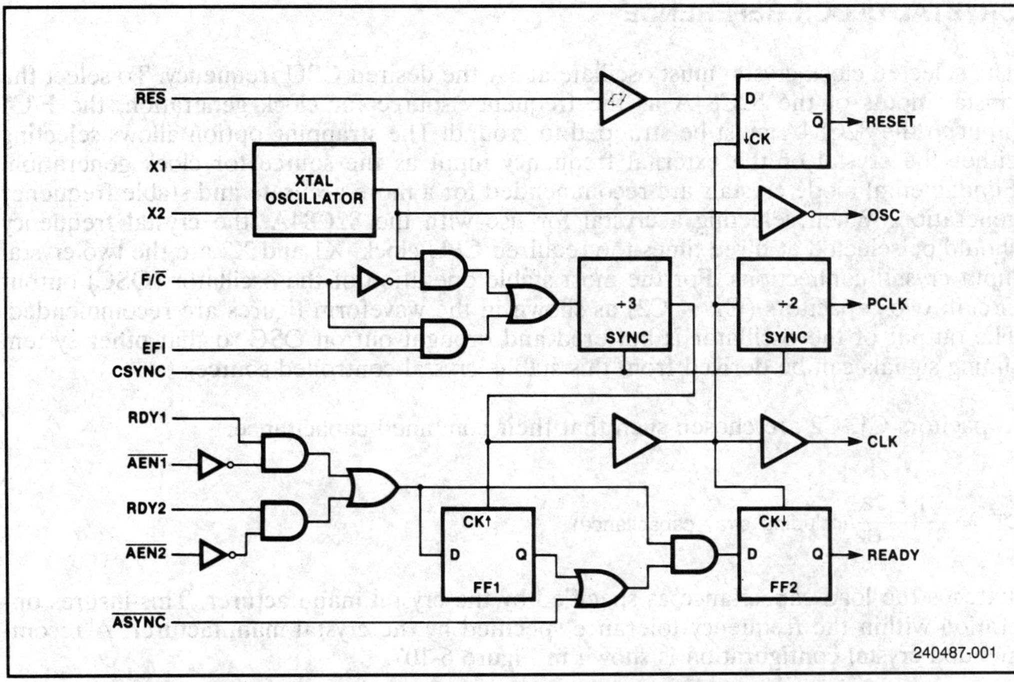

Figure 6-105. 82C84A Clock Generator/Driver Block Diagram

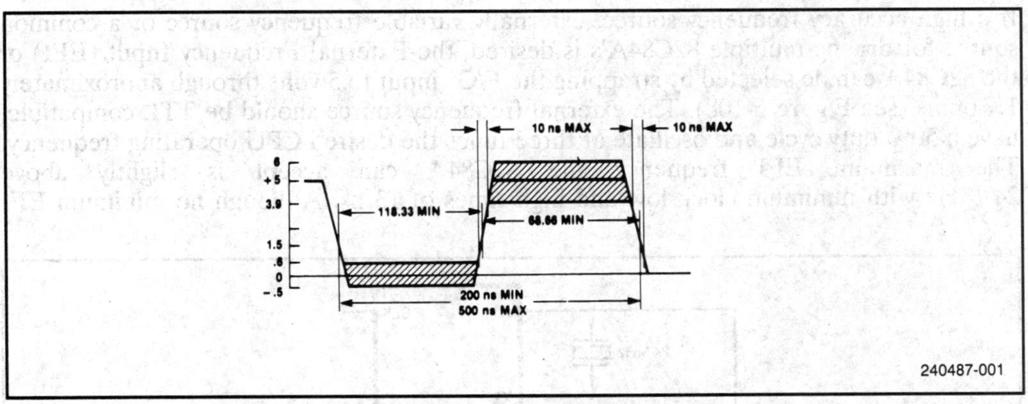

Figure 6-106. 5 MHz 8086/8088 Clock Waveform

clock. In general, for frequencies below the maximum, the CPU clock need not satisfy the frequency dependent pulse width limitations stated in the 8086 data sheet. The values specified only reflect the minimum values which must be satisfied and are stated in terms of the maximum clock frequency. As the clock frequency approaches the maximum frequency of the CPU, the clock must conform to a 33% duty cycle to satisfy the CPU minimum clock low and high time specifications.

CRYSTAL CLOCK REFERENCE

The selected clock crystal must oscillate at 3X the desired CPU frequency. To select the crystal inputs of the 82C84A as the frequency source for clock generation, the F/C* input to the 82C84A must be strapped to ground. The strapping option allows selecting either the crystal or the external frequency input as the source for clock generation. Fundamental mode crystals are recommended for a more accurate and stable frequency generation. When selecting a crystal for use with the 82C84A, the crystal frequency should be selected at three times the required CPU clock. X1 and X2 are the two crystal input crystal connections. For the most stable operation of the oscillator (OSC) output circuit, two capacitors (C1 = C2) as shown in the waveform figures are recommended. The output of the oscillator is buffered and brought out on OSC so that other system timing signals can be derived from this stable, crystal-controlled source.

Capacitors C1, C2 are chosen such that their combined capacitance:

$$CT = \frac{C1 \cdot C2}{C1 + C2} \text{(including stray capacitance)}$$

matches the load capacitance as specified by the crystal manufacturer. This insures operation within the frequency tolerance specified by the crystal manufacturer. A recommended crystal configuration is shown in Figure 6-107.

EXTERNAL FREQUENCY CLOCK REFERENCE

If a high accuracy frequency source, externally variable frequency source or a common source for driving multiple 82C84A's is desired, the External Frequency Input (EFI) of the 82C84A can be selected by strapping the F/C* input to 5 volts through approximately 1K ohms (see Figure 6-108). The external frequency source should be TTL compatible, have a 50% duty cycle and oscillate at three times the desired CPU operating frequency. The maximum EFI frequency the 82C84A can accept is slightly above 24 MHz with minimum clock low and high times of 13 ns. Although no minimum EFI

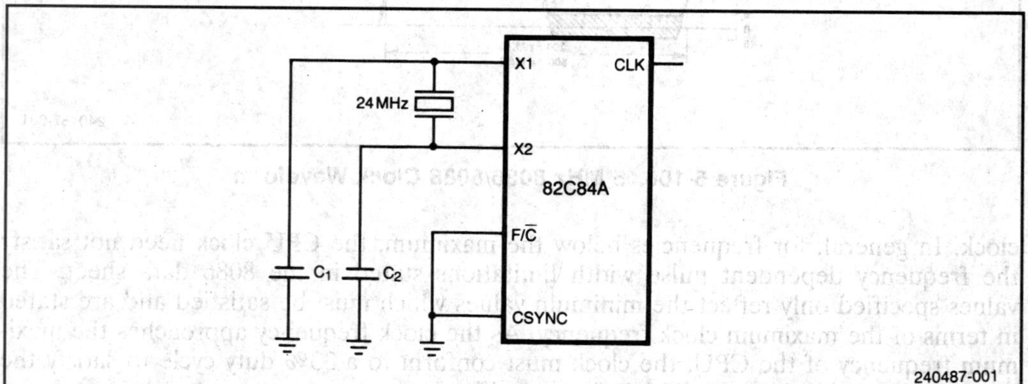

Figure 6-107. Recommended Crystal Clock Configuration

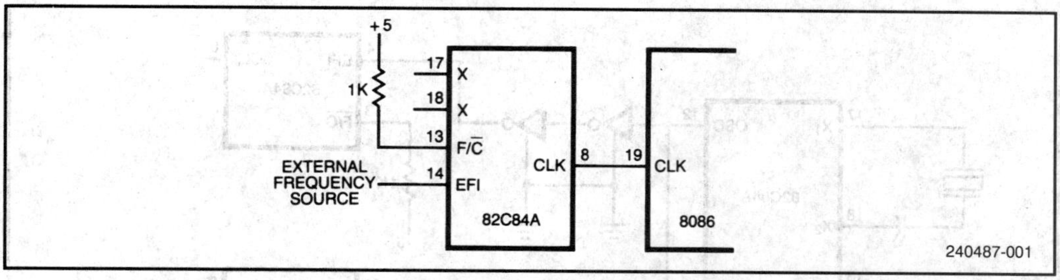

Figure 6-108. 82C84A Interfaced to an 8086/8088

frequency is specified, it should not violate the CPU minimum clock rate. If a common frequency source is used to drive multiple 82C84A's distributed throughout the system, each 82C84A should be driven by its own line from the source. To minimize noise in the system, each line should be a twisted pair driven by a buffer like the 74LS04 with the ground of the twisted pair connecting the ground of the source and receiver. To minimize clock skew, the lines to all 82C84A's should be equal length. A simple technique for generating a master frequency source for additional 82C84A is shown in Figure 6-109 where an 82C84A with a crystal is used to generate the desired frequency. The oscillator output of the 82C84A (OSC) equals the crystal frequency and is used to drive the external frequency to all other 82C84A's in the system.

The oscillator output is inverted from the oscillator signal used to drive the CPU clock generator circuit. Because of this inversion, the oscillator output of one 82C84A should not drive the EFI input of a second 82C84A if both are driving clock inputs of separate CPU's that are to be synchronized. The variation on EFI to CLK delay over a range of 82C84A's may approach 35 to 45 ns. If, however, all 82C84A's are the same package type, have the same relative supply voltage and operate in the same temperative environment, the variation will be reduced to between 15 and 25 ns.

82C84A OUTPUTS

There are three frequency outputs from the 82C84A, the oscillator (OSC) mentioned above, the system clock (CLK) which drives the CPU, and a peripheral clock (PCLK) that runs at one half the CPU clock frequency (see Figure 6-110). The oscillator output is only driven by the crystal and is not affected by the F/C* strapping option. If a crystal is not connected to the 82C84A when the external frequency input is used, the oscillator output is indeterminate. The CPU clock is derived from the selected frequency source by an internal divide by three counter. The counter generates the 33% duty cycle clock which is optimum for the CPU at maximum frequency. The peripheral clock has a 50% duty cycle and is derived from the CPU clock. The maximum skew is 20 ns between OSC and CLK, and 22 ns between CLK and PCLK.

Since the state of the 82C84A divide by three counter is indeterminate at system initialization (power on), an external sync to the counter (CSYNC) provides synchronization of the CPU clock to an external event. When CSYNC is brought high, the CLK and PCLK outputs are forced high. When CSYNC returns low, the next positive clock from the frequency source starts clock generation. CSYNC must be active for a minimum of

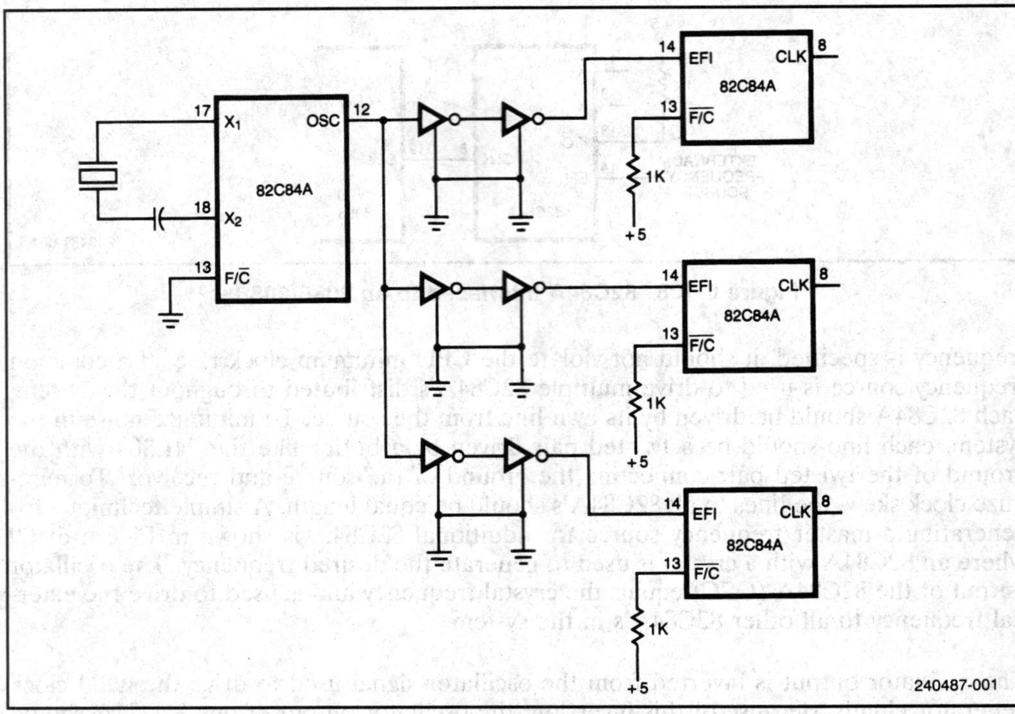

Figure 6-109. External Frequency for Multiple 82C84A

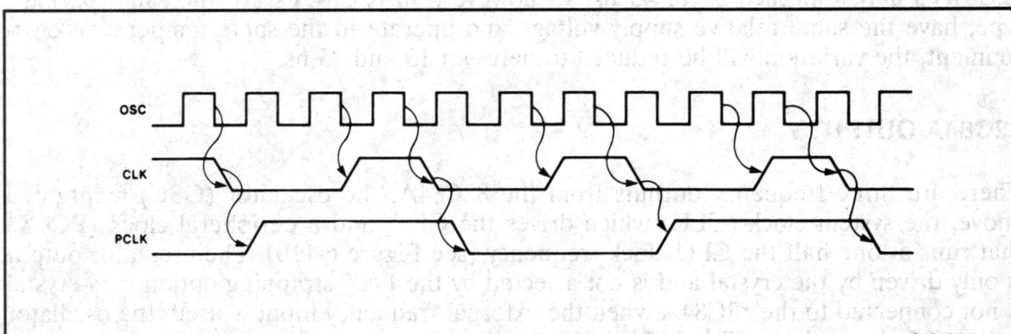

Figure 6-110. Oscillator to CLK and CLK to PCLK Timing Relationships

two periods of the frequency source. If CSYNC is asynchronous to the frequency source, use the circuit in Figure 6-111 for synchronization. The two latches minimize the probability of a meta-stable state in the latch driving CSYNC. The latches are clocked with the inverse of the frequency source to guarantee the 82C84A setup and hold time of CSYNC to the frequency source (see Figure 6-112). If a single 82C84A is to be synchronized to an external event and an external frequency source is not used, the oscillator output of the 82C84A may be used to synchronize CSYNC (see Figure 6-113). Since the

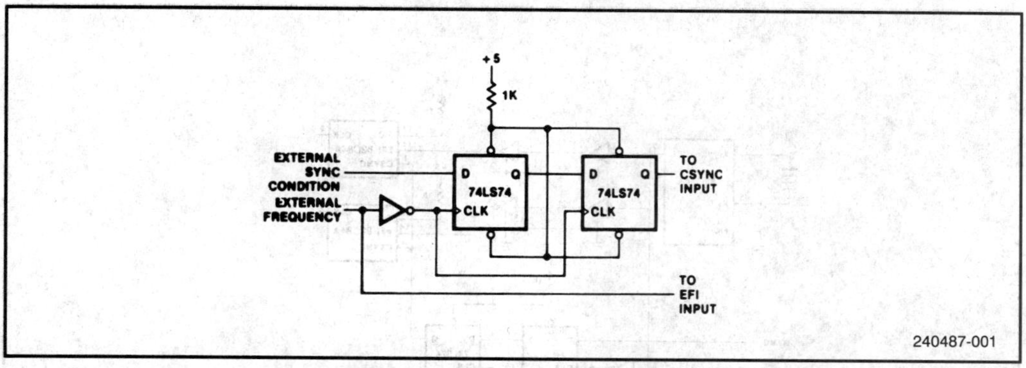

Figure 6-111. Synchronizing CSYNC with EFI

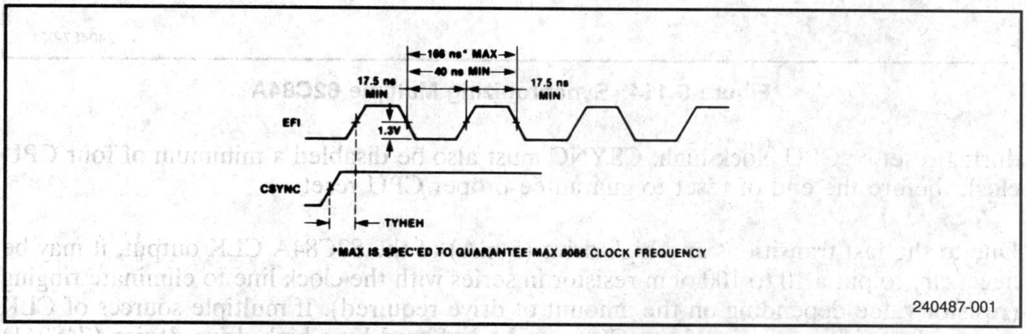

Figure 6-112. CSYNC Setup and HOLD to EFI

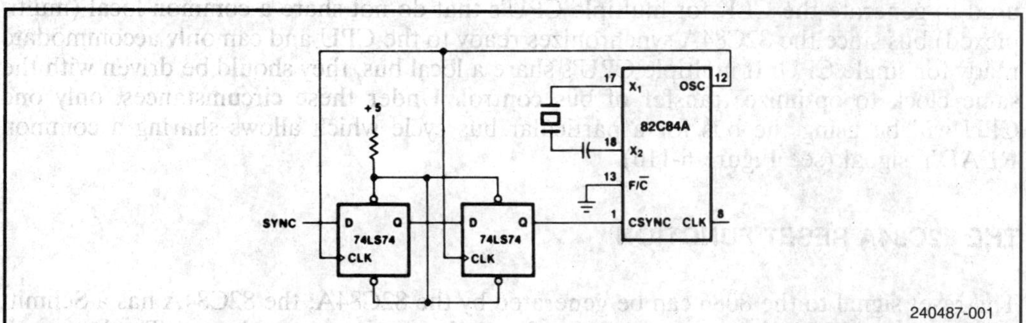

Figure 6-113. EFI from Oscillator

oscillator output is inverted from the internal oscillator signal, the inverter in the previous example is not required. If multiple 82C84A's are to be synchronized, an external frequency source must drive all 82C84A's and a single CSYNC synchronization circuit must drive the CSYNC input of all 82C84A's (see Figure 6-114). Since activation of CSYNC may cause violation of CPU minimum clock low time, it should only be enabled

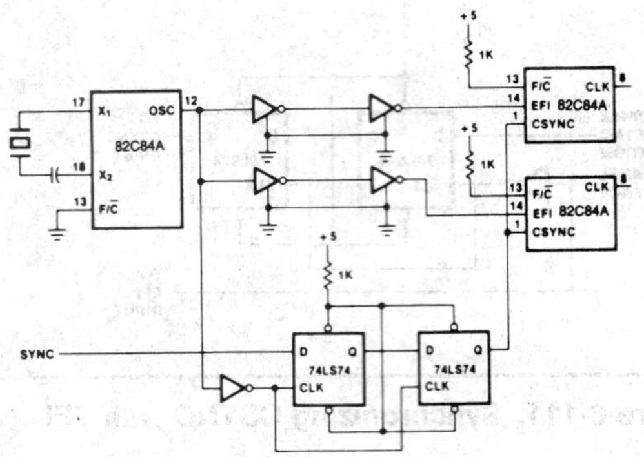

Figure 6-114. Synchronizing Multiple 82C84A

during reset or CPU clock high. CSYNC must also be disabled a minimum of four CPU clocks before the end of reset to guarantee proper CPU reset.

Due to the fast transitions and high drive (5 mA) of the 82C84A CLK output, it may be necessary to put a 10 to 100 ohm resistor in series with the clock line to eliminate ringing (resistor value depending on the amount of drive required). If multiple sources of CLK are needed with minimum skew, CLK can be buffered by a high drive device (74S241) with outputs tied to 5 volts through 100 ohms to guarantee VOH = 3.9 min (8086 minimum clock input high voltage) (see Figure 6-115). A single 82C84A should not be used to generate the CLK for multiple CPU's that do not share a common local (multiplexed) bus since the 82C84A synchronizes ready to the CPU and can only accommodate ready for single CPU. If multiple CPU's share a local bus, they should be driven with the same clock to optimize transfer of bus control. Under these circumstances, only one CPU will be using the bus for a particular bus cycle which allows sharing a common READY signal (see Figure 6-116).

THE 82C84A RESET FUNCTION

The reset signal to the 8086 can be generated by the 82C84A; the 82C84A has a Schmitt trigger input (RES*) for generating reset from a low active external reset. The hysteresis specified in the 82C84A data sheet implies that at least 0.25 volts will separate the 0 and 1 switching point of the 82C84A reset input. Inputs without hysteresis will switch from low to high and high to low at approximately the same voltage threshold. The inputs are guaranteed to switch at specified low and high voltages (VIL and VIH) but the actual switching point is anywhere inbetween. Since VIL min is specified at 0.8 volts, the hysteresis guarantees that the reset will be active until the input reaches at least 1.05 volts. A reset will not be recognized until the input drops at least 0.25 volts below the reset inputs VIH of 2.6 volts.

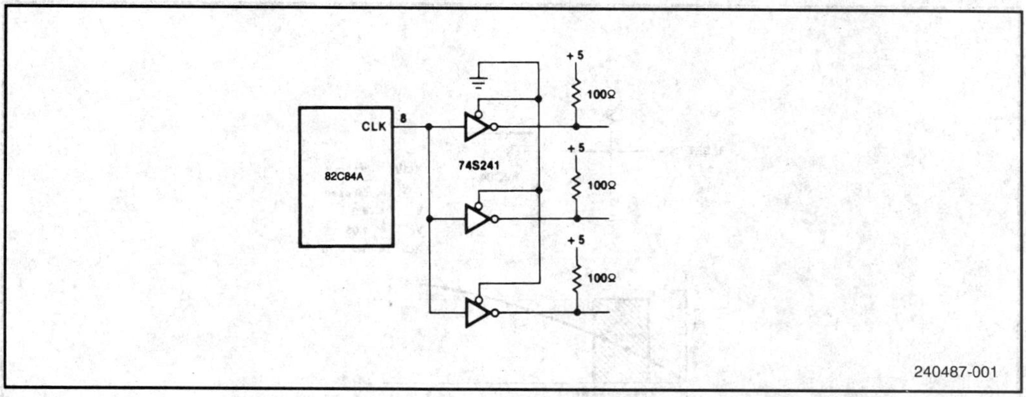

Figure 6-115. Buffering the 82C84A CLK Output

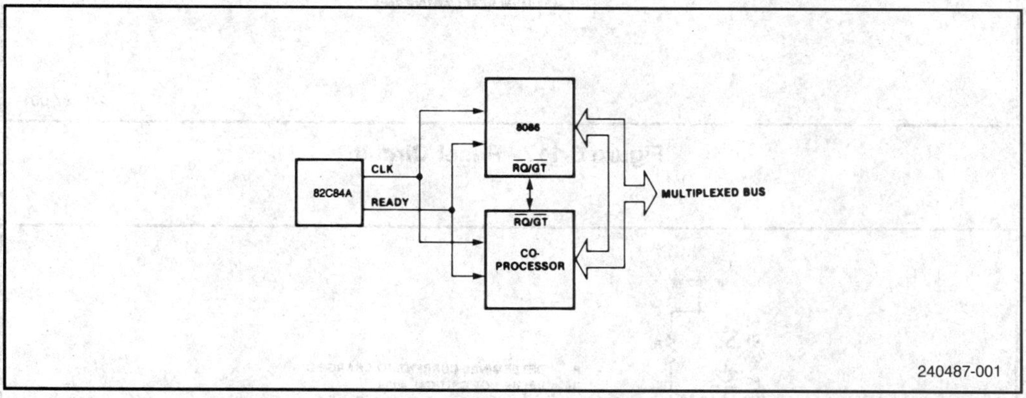

Figure 6-116. 8086 and Coprocessor on the Local Bus Share One Common 82C84A

POWER UP RESET

To guarantee reset from power up, the reset input must remain below 1.05 volts for 50 microseconds after V_{CC} has reached the minimum supply voltage of 4.5 volts. The hysteresis allows the reset input to be driven by a simple RC circuit (see Figure 6-117). The calculated RC value does not include time for the power supply to reach 4.5 volts or the charge accumulated during this interval. Without the hysteresis, the reset output might oscillate as the input voltage passes through the switching voltage of the input. The calculated RC value provides the minimum required reset period of 50 microseconds for 82C84A's that switch at the 1.05 volt level and a reset period of approximately 162 microseconds of 82C84A's that switch at the 2.6 volt level. If tighter tolerance between the minimum and maximum reset times is necessary, the reset circuit shown in Figure 6-118 might be used rather than the simple RC circuit. This circuit provides a constant current source and a linear charge rate on the capacitor rather than the inverse exponential charge rate of the RC circuit. This implementation generates a maximum reset period of 124 microseconds.

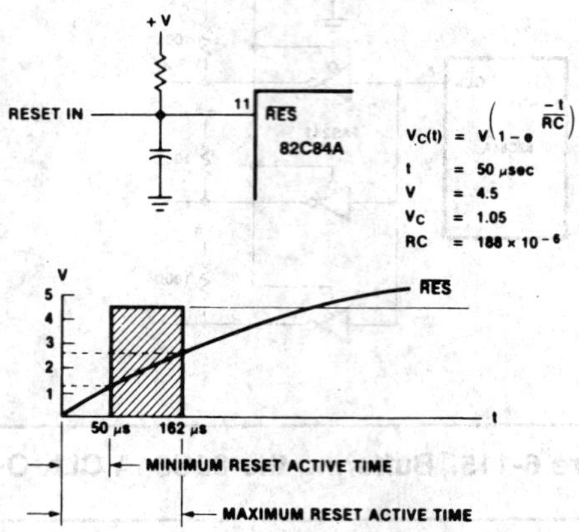

Figure 6-117. Reset Circuit

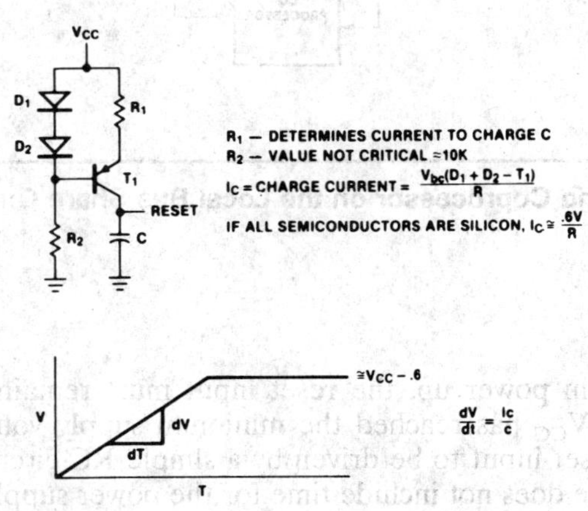

Figure 6-118. Constant Current Power Up Reset Circuit

The 82C84A synchronizes the reset input with the CPU clock to generate the RESET signal to the CPU (see Figure 6-119). The output is also available as a general reset to the entire system. The reset has no effect on any clock circuits in the 82C84A.

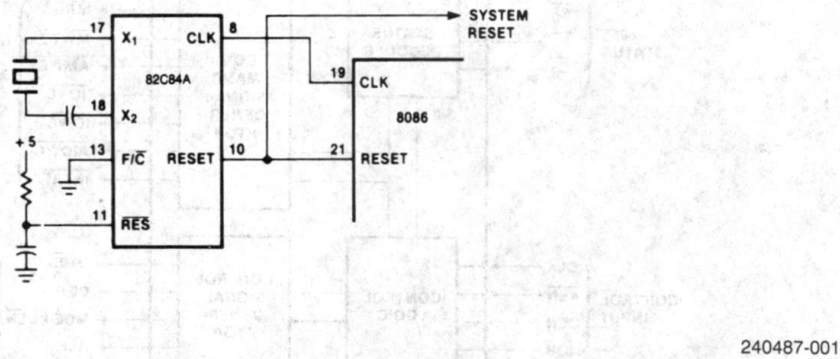

Figure 6-119. 8086/8088 Reset and System Reset

82C88 Bus Controller

The 82C88 Bus Controller (Figure 6-120) uses the S2*, S1* and S0* status bit outputs from the CPU to generate all bus control and command output signals required for a bus cycle. The status bit outputs are decoded as outlined in Table 6-42. For a detailed description of the operation of the 82C88 Bus Controller, refer to the *Microprocessor and Peripheral Handbook* (Intel Order No. 230843).

The three status lines (S0*, S1*, S2*) are defined to provide communications with the 82C88. The status lines tell the 82C88 when to initiate a bus cycle, what type of command to issue and when to terminate the bus cycle. The 82C88 samples the status lines at the beginning of each CPU clock (CLK). To initiate a bus cycle, the CPU drives the status lines from the passive state (S0*, S1*, S2* = 1) to one of the seven possible command codes (see Table 6-42). This occurs on the rising edge of the clock during T4 of the previous bus cycle or a TI (idle cycle, no current bus activity). The 82C88 detects the status change by sampling the status lines on the high to low transition of each clock cycle. The 82C88 starts a bus cycle by generating ALE and appropriate buffer direction control of the clock cycle immediately following detection of the status change (T1). The bus transceivers and the selected command are enabled in the next clock cycle (T2) (or T3 for normal write commands). When the status returns to the passive state, the 82C88 will terminate the command (see Figure 6-121). Since the CPU will not return the status to the passive state until the 'ready' indication is received, the 82C88 maintains active command and bus control for any number of wait cycles. The status lines may also be used by other processors on the 8086's local bus to monitor bus activity and control the 82C88 if they gain control of the local bus.

The 82C88 provides the bus control (DEN, DT/R*, ALE) and commands (INTA*, MRDC*, IORC*, MWTC*, AMWC*, IOWC*, AIOWC*) removed from the CPU. The command structure has separate read and write commands for memory and I/O to provide compatibility with the MULTIBUS command structure.

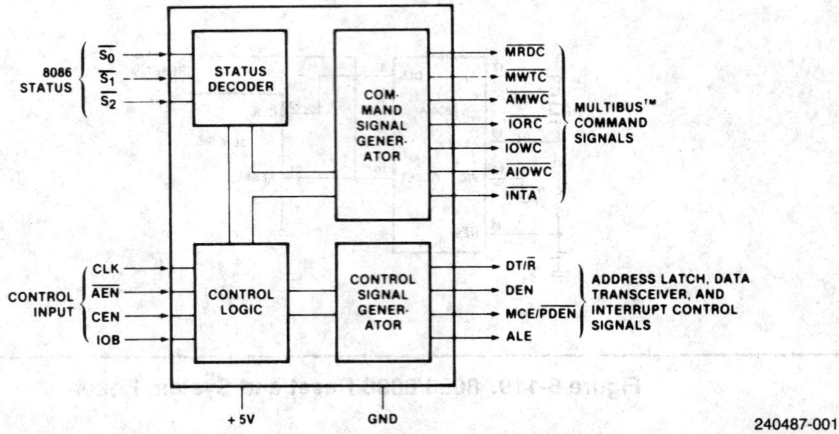

Figure 6-120. 82C88 Bus Controller Block Diagram

Table 6-42. Status Line Decode Chart

$\overline{S_2}$	$\overline{S_1}$	$\overline{S_0}$	Processor State	82C88 Command
0	0	0	Interrupt Aknowledge	$\overline{\text{INTA}}$
0	0	1	Read I/O Port	$\overline{\text{IORC}}$
0	1	0	Write I/O Port	$\overline{\text{IOWC}}$,$\overline{\text{AIOWC}}$
0	1	1	Halt	None
1	0	0	Code Access	$\overline{\text{MRDC}}$
1	0	1	Read Memory	$\overline{\text{MRDC}}$
1	1	0	Write Memory	$\overline{\text{MWTC}}$,$\overline{\text{AMWC}}$
1	1	1	Passive	None

The advanced write commands are enabled one clock period earlier than the normal write to accommodate the wider write pulse widths often required by peripherals and static RAMs. The normal write provides data setup prior to write to accommodate dynamic RAM memories and I/O devices which strobe data on the leading edge of write. The advanced write commands do not guarantee that data is valid prior to the leading edge of the command. The DEN signal in the maximum mode is inverted from the minimum mode to extend transceiver control by allowing logical conjunction of DEN with other signals. While not appearing to be a significant benefit of interrupt control

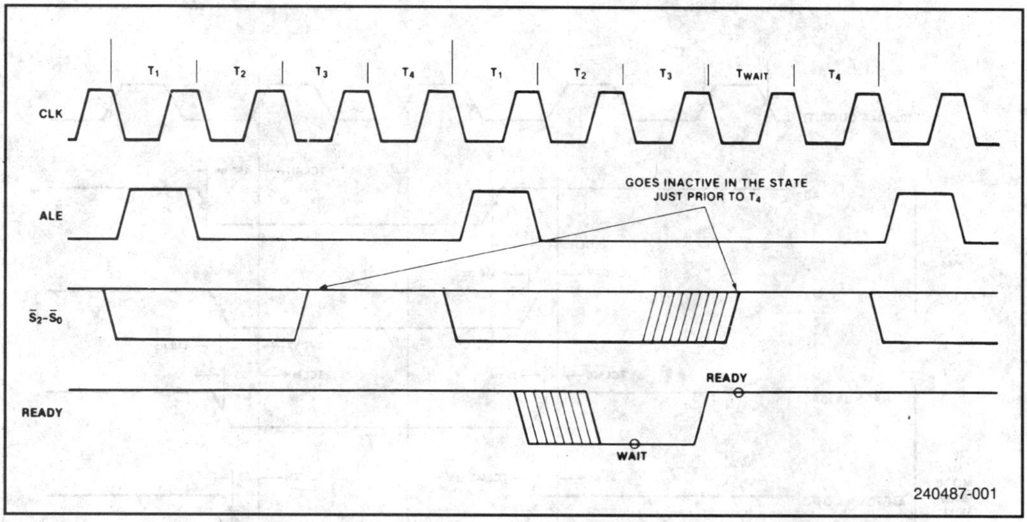

Figure 6-121. Status Line Activation and Termination

and various system configurations will demonstrate the usefulness of qualifying DEN. Figure 6-122 compares the timing of the minimum and maximum mode bus transfer commands. Although the maximum mode configuration is designed for multiprocessor environments, large single CPU designs (either MULTIBUS systems or greater than two PC boards) should also use the maximum mode. Since the 82C88 is a bipolar dedicated controller device, its output drive for the commands (32 mA) and tolerances on A.C. characteristics (timing parameters and worst case delays) provide better large system performance than the minimum mode 8086.

In addition to assuming the functions removed from the CPU, the 82C88 provides additional strapping options and controls to support multiprocessor configurations and peripheral devices on the CPU local bus. These capabilities allow assigning resources (memory or I/O) as shared (available on the MULTIBUS system bus) or private (accessible only by this CPU) to reduce contention for access to the MULTIBUS system bus and improve multi-CPU system performance. The following paragraphs describe these strapping options.

I/O BUS MODE

Strapping the IOB pin HIGH puts the 82C88 in the I/O Bus mode of operation. In the I/O Bus mode all command lines (IORC*, IOWC*, AIOWC*, INTA*) are always enabled and not dependent on AEN*. When an I/O command is issued by the processor, the 82C88 immediately activates the command lines using PDEN* and DT/R* to control the I/O bus transceiver. In this configuration the I/O command lines should not be used to control the system bus because there is no arbitration present. In this mode one 82C88 can handle two external busses. No waiting is involved when the CPU wants to

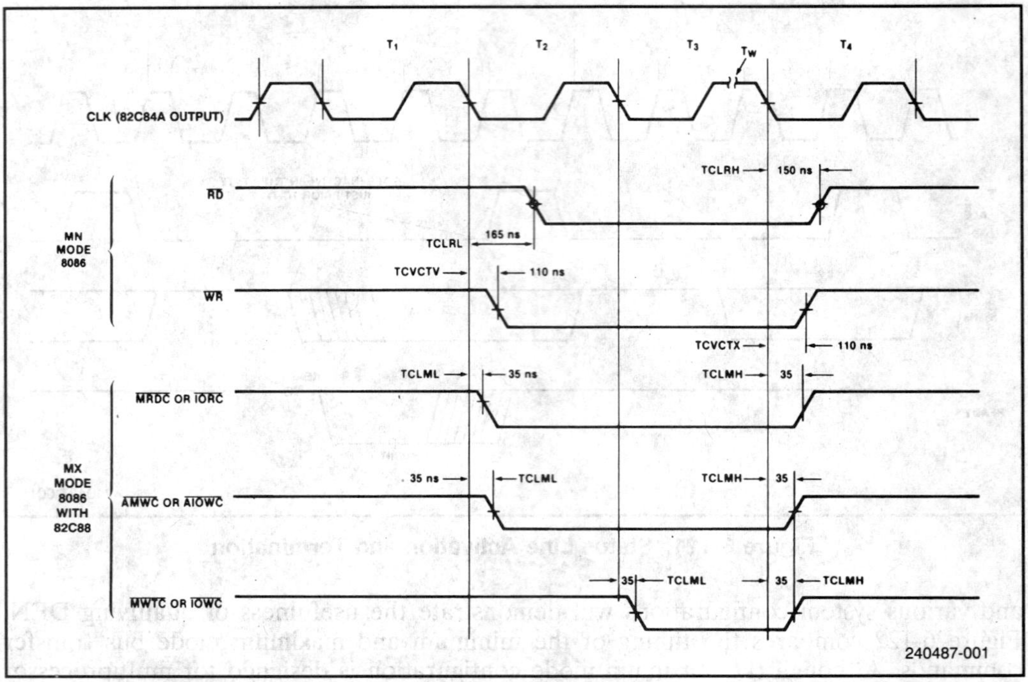

Figure 6-122. Maximum and Minimum Mode Command Timing

gain access to the I/O bus. Normal memory access requires a "Bus Ready" signal (AEN* LOW) before it will proceed. The IOB mode of operation is especially advantageous in a multi-processor system where there are I/O or peripherals are dedicated to only one processor.

SYSTEM BUS MODE

When the IOB pin is strapped LOW the 82C88 is in the System Bus Mode of operation. No commands are issued in this mode until 115 ns after the AEN* line is activated (LOW). The System Bus Mode assumes arbitration logic will inform the bus controller (on the AEN* line) when the bus is free for use. Both memory and I/O commands wait for arbitration. This mode is used when only one bus exists. In this case, both I/O and memory are shared by more than one processor.

8259A Programmable Interrupt Controller

The 8259A is a programmable interrupt controller (PIC) designed to accommodate the INTA* protocol of maskable hardware interrupts. This component is programmable to operate in both 8080/8085 systems and 8086 systems. The 8259A manages eight levels of interrupts and has built-in features for expansion. The devices are cascadable in master/slave arrangements to allow up to 64 interrupt levels in the system with additional 8259A's.

Figure 6-123 and 6-124 are examples of 8259A's in minimum and maximum mode 8086 systems. The minimum mode configuration (a) shows an 8259A connected to the CPU's multiplexed bus. Configuration (b) illustrates an 8259A connected to a demultiplexed bus system. These interconnects are also applicable to maximum mode systems. The configuration given for a maximum mode system shows a master 8259A on the CPU's multiplexed bus witave 8259A's out on the buffered system bus. This configuration demonstrates several unique features of the maximum mode system interface. If the master 8259A receives interrupts from a mix of slave 8259A's and regular devices, the slaves must provide the type number for devices connected to them while the master provides the type number for devices directly attached to its interrupt inputs. The master 8259A is programmable to determine if an interrupt is from a direct input or a slave 8259A and will use this information to enable or disable the data bus transceivers (via the NAND function of DEN and EN*). If the master must provide the type number, it will disable the data bus transceivers. If the slave provides the type number, the master will enable the data bus transceivers. The EN* output is normally high to allow the 8086/82C88 to control the bus transceivers. To select the proper slave when servicing a slave interrupt, the master must provide a cascade address to the slave. If the 82C88 is not strapped in the I/O bus mode (the 82C88 IOB input connected to ground), the MCE/PDEN* output becomes an MCE or Master Cascade Enable output. This signal is only active during INTA* cycles (see Figure 6-125) and enables the master 8259A's cascade address onto the 8086's local bus during ALE. This allows the address latches to capture the cascade address with ALE and allows use of the dress bus for selecting the proper slave 8259A. The MCE is gated with LOCK* to minimize local bus contention between the 8086 tri-stating its bus outputs and the cascade address being enabled onto the bus. The first INTA* bus cycle allows the master to resolve internal priorities and output a cascade address to be transmitted to the slaves on the subsequent INTA* bus cycle.

The following paragraphs provide a more detailed description of interrupt vectoring, the interrupt priority scheme, the edge and level triggering modes and interrupt cascading. For additional information on the 8259A, refer to Intel Application Note AP-59.

INTERRUPT VECTORING

Each IR input of the 8259A has an individual interrupt vector address in memory associated with it. Designation of each address depends upon the initial programming of the 8259A. The 8259A must be programmed in the MCS-86/88 mode of operation to insure correct interrupt vectoring when used in an 8086/8088 system.

When programmed in the MCS-86/88 mode, the 8259A should only be used with an MCS-86 or MCS-88 system. In this mode, the 8086/8088 will handle interrupts in the format described in the 8259A – 8086/8088 Overview.

Upon interrupt in the MCS-86/88 mode, the 8259A will output a single interrupt-vector byte to the data bus. This is in response to only two INTA* pulses issued by the 8086/8088 after the 8259A has raised INT high.

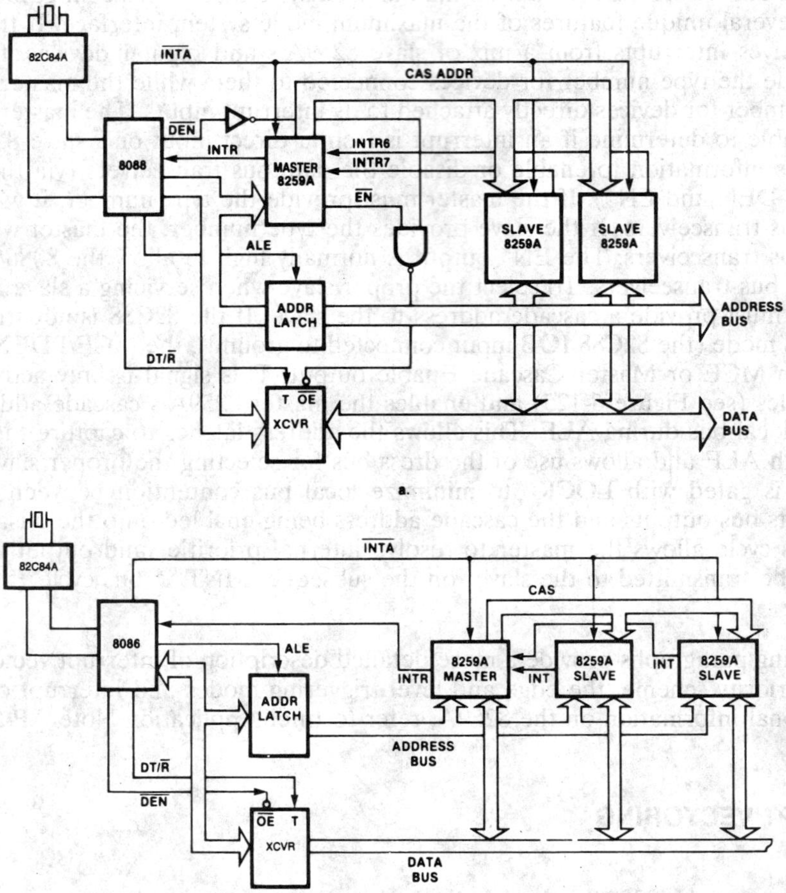

240487-001

Figure 6-123. Min Mode 8086 with Master 8259A on the Local Bus, and Slave 8259A's on the System Bus

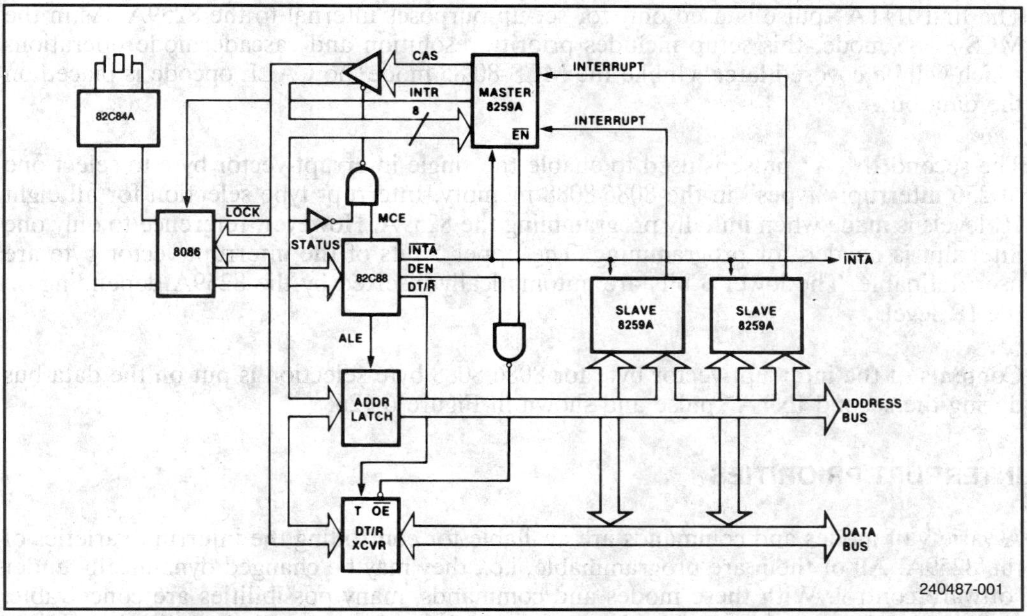

Figure 6-124. Max Mode 8086 with Master 8259A on the Local Bus, and Slave 8259A's on the System Bus

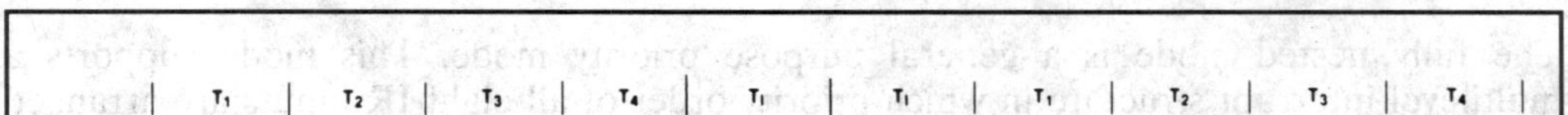

Figure 6-125. MCE Timing to Gate 8259A CAS Address onto the 8086 Local Bus

The first INTA* pulse is used only for set-up purposes internal to the 8259A. As in the MCS-80/85 mode, this setup includes priority resolution and cascade mode operations which will be covered later. Unlike the MCS-80/85 mode, no CALL opcode is placed on the data bus.

The second INTA* pulse is used to enable the single interrupt-vector byte to select one of 256 interrupt "types" in the 8086/8088 memory. Interrupt type selection for all eight IR levels is made when initially programming the 8259A. However, reference to only one interrupt is needed for programming. The upper 5 bits of the interrupt vector byte are user definable. The lower 3 bits are automatically inserted by the 8259A depending on the IR level.

Contents of the interrupt-vector byte for 8086/8088 byte selection is put on the data bus during the second INTA* pulse and shown in Figure 6-126.

INTERRUPT PRIORITIES

A variety of modes and commands are available for controlling the interrupt varieties of the 8259A. All of them are programmable, i.e., they may be changed dynamically under software control. With these modes and commands, many possibilities are conceivable, giving the user enough versatility for almost any interrupt controlled application.

Fully Nested Mode

The fully nested mode is a general purpose priority mode. This mode supports a multilevel-interrupt structure in which priority order of all eight IR inputs are arranged from highest to lowest.

Unless otherwise programmed, the fully nested mode is entered by default upon initialization. At this time, IR0 is assigned the highest priority through IR7 the lowest. The fully nested mode, however, is not confined to this IR structure alone. Once past initialization, other IR inputs can be assigned highest priority also, keeping the multilevel-interrupt structure of the fully nested mode. Figure 6-127 shows some variations of the priority structures in the fully nested mode.

IR	D7	D6	D5	D4	D3	D2	D1	D0
7	T7	T6	T5	T4	T3	1	1	1
6	T7	T6	T5	T4	T3	1	1	0
5	T7	T6	T5	T4	T3	1	0	1
4	T7	T6	T5	T4	T3	1	0	0
3	T7	T6	T5	T4	T3	0	1	1
2	T7	T6	T5	T4	T3	0	1	0
1	T7	T6	T5	T4	T3	0	0	1
0	T7	T6	T5	T4	T3	0	0	0

240487-001

Figure 6-126. Interrupt Vector Byte

IR LEVELS	IR7	IR6	IR5	IR4	IR3	IR2	IR1	IR0
PRIORITY	7	6	5	4	3	2	1	0

A

IR LEVELS	IR7	IR6	IR5	IR4	IR3	IR2	IR1	IR0
PRIORITY	4	3	2	1	0	7	6	5

B

IR LEVELS	IR7	IR6	IR5	IR4	IR3	IR2	IR1	IR0
PRIORITY	1	0	7	6	5	4	3	2

C

240487-001

Figure 6-127. Priority Structure Variations – Fully Nested Mode

In general, when an interrupt is acknowledged, the highest priority request is determined from the IRR (Interrupt Request Register). The interrupt vector is then placed on the data bus. In addition, the corresponding bit in the ISR (In-Service Register) is set to designate the routine in service. This ISR bit remains set until an EOI (End-Of-Interrupt) command is issued to the 8259A. EOI's will be explained in greater detail shortly.

In the fully nested mode, while an ISR bit is set, all further requests of the same or lower priority are inhibited from generating an interrupt to the microprocessor. A higher priority request, though, can generate an interrupt, thus vectoring program execution to its service routines. Interrupts are only acknowledged, however, if the microprocessor has previously executed an "Enable Interrupts" instruction. This is because the interrupt request pin on the microprocessor gets disabled automatically after acknowledgement of any interrupt. The assembly language instruction used to enable interrupts is "STI." Interrupts can be disabled by using the instruction "CLI." When a routine is completed a "return" instruction "IRET" is executed.

A single 8259A is essentially always in the fully nested mode unless certain programming conditions disturb it.

The following programming conditions can cause the 8259A to go out of the high to low priority structure of the fully nested mode.

- The automatic EOI mode
- The special mask mode
- A slave with a master not in the special fully nested mode

Additional details on these interrupt modes can be found in Intel Application Note AP-59. These modes are mentioned here so that the designer will be aware of them. As long as these program conditions are not enacted, the fully nested mode remains undisturbed.

End of Interrupt (EOI)

Upon completion of an interrupt service the 8259A must be informed so that its ISR can be updated. This is done to keep track of which interrupt levels are in the process of being serviced and their relative priorities. Three different End-Of-Interrupt (EOI) formats are available to the designer. These are: 1) non-specific EOI command; 2) specific EOI command; and, 3) automatic EOI command. Selection of which EOI to use is dependent on the interrupt operation the designer wishes to perform.

a. Non-Specific EOI Command

   The microprocessor sends a non-specific EOI command to let the 8259A know when a service routine has been completed. This command does not specify the exact interrupt level. The 8259A automatically determines the interrupt level and resets the correct bit in the ISR.

   To use the non-specific EOI command the 8259A must be in a mode of operation where it can predetermine in-service routine levels. For this reason the non-specific EOI command should only be used when the most recent level acknowledged and serviced is always the highest priority level. When the 8259A receives a non-specific EOI command, it resets the highest priority ISR bit. This confirms to the 8259A that the highest priority routine of the routines in service is finished.

b. Specific EOI Command

   A specific EOI command is sent from the microprocessor to let the 8259A know when a service routine of a particular interrupt level is completed. Unlike the non-specific EOI command which automatically resets the highest priority ISR bit, a specific EOI command specifies an exact ISR bit to be reset. One of the eight IR levels of the 8259A can be specified in this command. The purpose of the specific EOI command is to reset the ISR bit of a completed service routine whenever the 8259A cannot automatically determine the completion.

c. Automatic EOI Mode

   When programmed in the automatic EOI mode the microprocessor does not need to issue a command to notify the 8259A of a completed interrupt routine. The 8259A accomplishes this by performing a non-specific EOI automatically at the trailing edge of the last INTA* pulse (second pulse). The advantage of automatic EOI over the other EOI commands is that no command has to be issued. This simplifies programming and lowers code requirements within interrupt routines. However, special consideration must be taken when deciding to use the automatic EOI mode because it disturbs the fully nested mode.

NOTE

Automatic EOI cannot be used when the 8259A is programmed in slave mode.

Automatic Rotation — Equal Priority

Automatic rotation of priorities is used in applications where interrupting devices are of equal priority, such as communications channels. The concept is that once a peripheral is serviced, all other equal priority peripherals should be given a chance to be serviced before the original peripheral is serviced again. This is accomplished by automatically assigning a peripheral the lowest priority after it has been serviced. Therefore, worst case, the device would have to wait until all other devices have been serviced before being serviced again.

There are two methods of accomplishing automatic rotation. One is the "rotate on non-specific EOI command" which is used with the non-specific EOI command. The other is the "rotate in automatic EOI mode" which is used with the automatic EOI mode.

a. Rotate on Non-Specific EOI Command

   When the rotate on non-specific EOI command is issued, the highest ISR bit is reset as in a normal non-specific EOI command. However, after the ISR bit is reset the corresponding IR level is assigned the lowest priority. Other IR priorities rotate to conform to the fully nested mode based on the newly assigned low priority.

b. Rotate on Automatic EOI Mode

   The rotate in automatic EOI mode operates similar to the non-specific EOI command. The main difference is that priority is done automatically after the last INTA* pulse of an interrupt request. To enter or exit this mode a rotate-in-automatic-EOI set command and a rotate-in-automatic-EOI clear command is provided. After these two commands, no other commands are needed, as in the automatic EOI mode. However, when using any form of the automatic EOI mode, special consideration since the guideline for the automatic EOI mode also stands for the rotate in automatic EOI mode.

Specific Rotation — Specific Priority

The specific rotation mode provides the designer with versatile capabilities in interrupt controlled operations. This priority mode is very useful in applications where a specific device's interrupt priority must be altered. Unlike automatic rotation, which automatically sets priorities, specific rotation is completely user controlled. The user selects which interrupt level is to receive lowest or highest priority. This can be done during the main program or within interrupt routines. Two specific rotation commands are available to the user, the "set priority command" and the "rotate on specific EOI command."

a. Set Priority Command

   The set priority command allows the programmer to assign an IR level to the lowest priority. All other interrupt levels will conform to the fully nested mode based on the newly assigned low priority.

b. Rotate on Specific EOI Command

   The rotate on specific EOI command is a combination of the set priority and the specific EOI command. As in the set priority command, a specified IR level is assigned lowest priority. As in the specific EOI command, a specified level will be reset in the ISR. Therefore, the rotate on specific EOI command accomplishes both tasks in only one command.

INTERRUPT TRIGGERING

There are two basic ways of sensing an active interrupt request. One is a level sensitive input and the other is an edge sensitive input. The 8259A provides the edge triggered mode and the level triggered mode to allow the user the capability of either method. Selection of one of these methods is done during the programmed initialization of the 8259A.

Level Triggered Mode

When the 8259A is in the level triggered mode it will recognize any active (high) level on the IR input as an interrupt request. If the IR input remains active after an EOI command has been issued, resetting its ISR bit, another interrupt will be generated. This assumes the processor INT pin is enabled. Unless repetitious interrupt generation is desired, the IR input must be brought to an inactive state before an EOI command is issued in its service routine. However, necessary timing requirements must be obeyed (see Figure 6-128). Note that the request on the IR line must remain until after the falling edge of the first INTA* pulse. On any IR input, if the request goes inactive before the first INTA* pulse, the 8259A will respond as if IR7 was active. In any design where there is a possibility of this happening, the IR7 default feature can be used as a safeguard. This can be accomplished by using the IR7 routine as a "cleanup routine" which might check the 8259A status or merely return program execution to its pre-interrupt location.

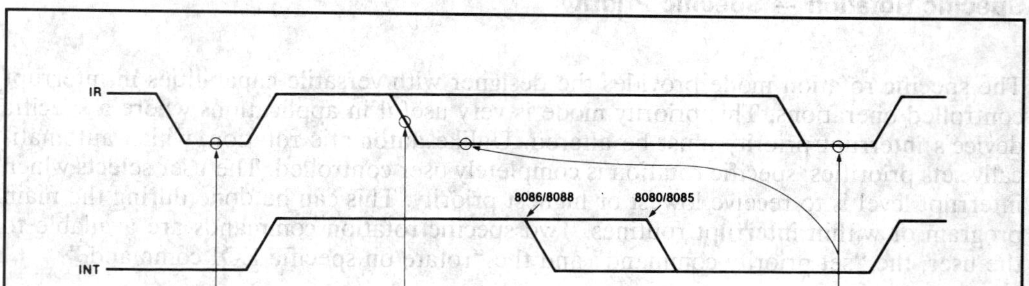

Figure 6-128. IR Triggering Timing Requirements

Edge Triggered Mode

In the edge triggered mode the 8259A will only recognize interrupts if generated by an inactive (low) to active (high) transition on the IR input. The edge triggered mode incorporates an edge lockout method of operation. This means that after the rising edge of an interrupt request and the acknowledge of the request, the positive level of the IR input will not generate further interrupts on this level. The user does not need to worry about quickly removing the request to avoid generating further interrupts. Before another interrupt can be generated the IR input must return to the inactive state.

Timing requirements for the edge triggered mode are shown in Figure 6-128. As in the level triggered mode, the request on the IR input must remain active until after the falling edge of the first INTA* pulse in the edge triggered mode. Unlike the level triggered mode, after the interrupt request is acknowledged its IRR latch is disarmed. Only after the IR input goes inactive will the IRR latch again become armed making it ready to receive another interrupt request (in the level triggered mode the IR latch is always armed). Note that the IR7 default discussed in the level triggered mode also works in the edge triggered mode.

INTERRUPT CASCADING

More than one 8259A can be used to expand the priority interrupt scheme to up to 64 levels without additional hardware. This method for expanded interrupt capability is called cascading. The 8259A supports cascading operations with the cascade mode. Additionally, the specially fully nested mode and the buffered mode are available for increased flexibility when cascading 8259A's under certain applications.

Cascade Mode

In the cascade mode, basic operation consists of one 8259A acting as a master to the others which are acting as slaves. A specific hardware set-up is required to establish operation in the cascade mode (see Figure 6-129). Figure 6-129 shows a typical system containing a master and two slaves, providing 22 interrupt levels. Note that the master is designated by a high on the SP*/EN* pin, while the SP*/EN* pins on the slaves are grounded (this can also be done by software, see the buffered mode). Also the INT output pin of each slave is connected to an IR input pin on the master. The CAS0-2 pins on all 8259A's are paralleled. These pins, which act as outputs when the 8259A is a master and inputs for the slaves, serve as a private 8259A bus. They control which slave has control of the system bus for interrupt vectoring operation with the processor. All other pins are connected as in normal operation (each receives an INTA pulse).

In addition to the hardware set-up requirements, all 8259A's must be software programmed to work in the cascade mode. Programming the cascade mode is done during the initialization of each 8259A. The 8259A that is selected as master must receive specification during its initialization as to which of its IR inputs are connected to a slave's INT pin. Each slave must be designated during its initialization with an ID (0-7) corresponding to which of the master's IR inputs its INT pin is connected to. This is

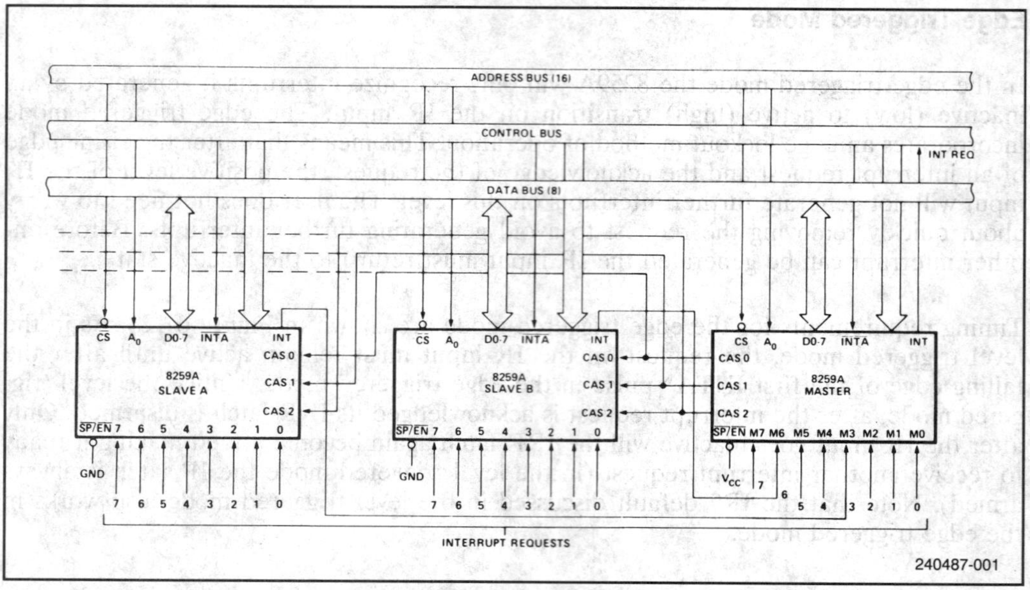

Figure 6-129. Cascaded 8259A's 22 Interrupt Levels

necessary so the master's CAS0-2 pins will be able to address each individual slave. Note that as in normal operation, each 8259A must also be initialized to give its IR inputs a unique interrupt vector.

Specially Fully Nested Mode

Depending on the application, changes in the nested structure of the cascade mode may be desired. This is because the nested structure of a slave 8259A differs from that of the normal fully nested mode. In the cascade mode, if a slave receives a higher priority interrupt request than the one in service (through the same slave), it will not be recognized by the master. This is because the master's ISR bit is set, ignoring all requests of equal or lower priority. In this case, the higher priority slave interrupt will not be serviced until after the master's ISR bit is reset by an EOI command. This will normally be after completion of the lower priority routine.

If the user wishes to have a truly fully nested structure within a slave 8259A, the specially fully nested mode should be used. The specially fully nested mode is programmed in the master only. This is done the master's initialization. In this mode the master will ignore only those interrupt requests of lower priority than the set ISR bit and will respond to all requests of equal or higher priority. Therefore, if a slave receives a higher priority request than the one in service, it will be recognized. To ensure proper interrupt operation when using the special fully nested mode, the software must determine if any other slave interrupts are still in service before issuing an EOI command to the master. This is done by resetting the appropriate slave ISR bit with an EOI and then reading its ISR. If the ISR contains all zeros, there aren't any other interrupts from the slave in service and an EOI command can be sent to the master. If the ISR isn't all zeros, an EOI command should not be sent to the master. Clearing the master's ISR bit with an EOI command while there are still slave interrupts in service would allow lower priority interrupts to be recognized at the master.

Buffered Mode

The buffered mode is useful in large systems where buffering is required on the data bus. Although not limited to cascading, the buffered mode is most pertinent for this use. In the buffered mode, whenever the 8259A's data bus output is enabled, its SP*/EN* pin will go low. This signal can be used to enable data transfer through a buffer transceiver in the required direction.

A conceptual diagram of three 8259A's in cascade is shown in Figure 6-130. Each slave is controlling an individual 8-bit bidirectional transceiver by means of the buffered mode. Note the pull-up on the SP*/EN* line. This pull-up is used to enable data transfer to the 8259A for its initial programming. When data transfer is to go from the 8259A to the processor, SP*/EN* will go low, otherwise it will be high.

8237A Programmable DMA Controller

When configured in minimum mode, the 8086 and 8088 provide HOLD (hold) and HLDA (hold acknowledge) signals that are compatible with the 8237A DMA controller. The 8237A can request use of the bus for direct transfer of data between an I/O device

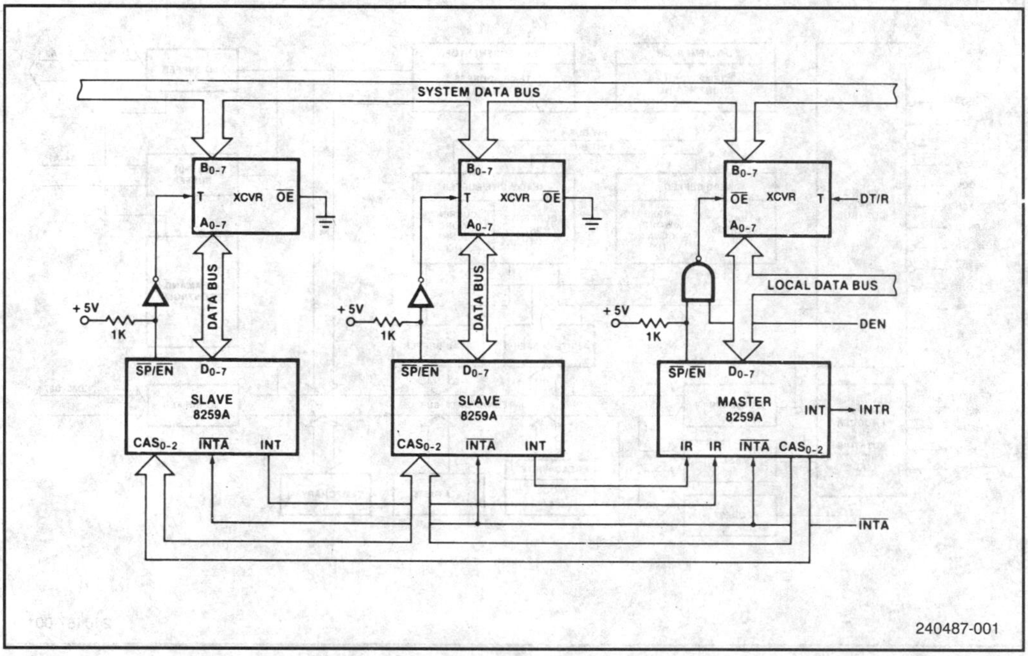

Figure 6-130. Cascade-Buffered Mode Example

and memory be activating HOLD. The CPU will complete the current bus cycle, if one is in progress, and the issue HLDA, granting the bus to the DMA controller. The CPU will not attempt to use the bus until HOLD goes inactive.

The 8086 addresses memory that is physically organized in two separate banks, one containing even-addressed bytes and one containing odd-addressed bytes. An 8-bit DMA controller must alternately select these banks to access logically adjacent bytes in memory. Used as a maximum mode DMA controller, the 8089 provides a simple way to interface a high-speed 8-bit device to an 8086-based system.

The 8237A Multimode Direct Memory Access (DMA) Controller (see Figure 6-131) is a peripheral interface circuit designed to improve system performance by allowing external devices to directly transfer information from the system memory. Memory-to-memory transfer capability is also provided. The 8237A offers a wide variety of programmable control features to enhance data throughput and system optimization and to allow dynamic reconfiguration under program control. The 8237A is designed to be used in conjunction with an external 8-bit address latch. It contains four independent channels and may be expanded to any number of channels by cascading additional controller chips. The three basic transfer modes allow programmability of the types of DMA service by the user. Each channel can be individually programmed to Autoinitialize to its original condition following an End of Process (EOP).

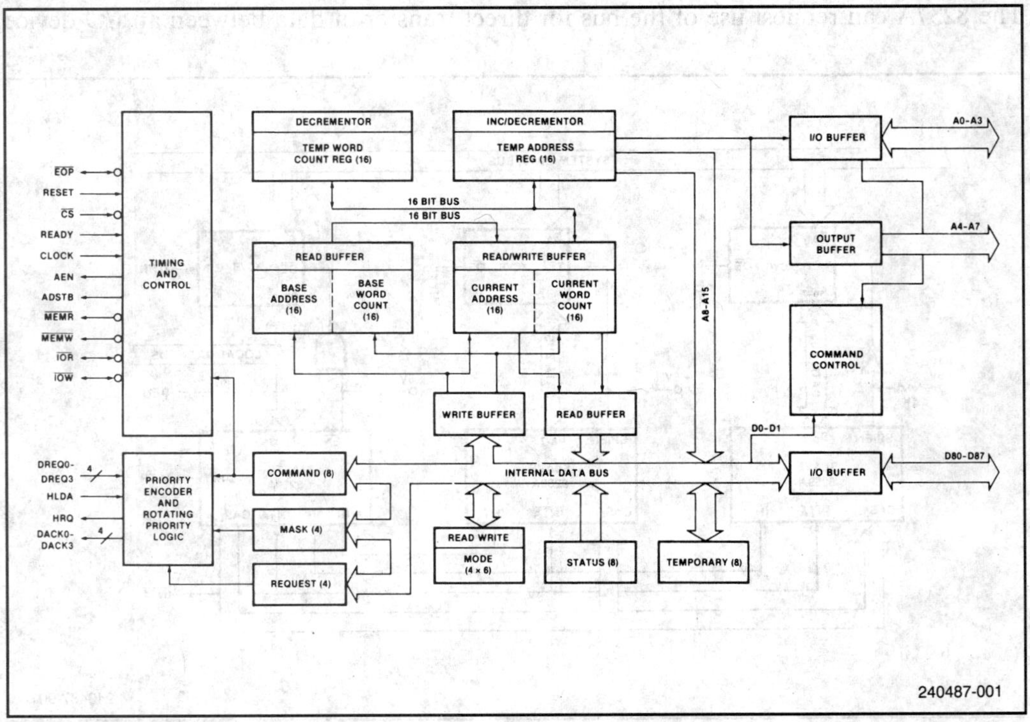

Figure 6-131. 8237A DMA Controller Block Diagram

DMA OPERATION

The 8237A operates in two major cycles, the Idle cycle and the Active cycle. Both device cycles are made up of several states. The 8237A can assume seven different states, each composed of one or more complete clock cycles. State I (SI) is the inactive state. This state is entered when the 8237A has no valid DMA requests pending. In the SI state, the DMA controller is inactive, but may be in the Program Condition, being programmed by the processor. State S0 (S0) is the first state of a DMA service. At this point the 8237A has requested a hold, but the processor has not yet returned an acknowledge. The 8237 may still be programmed until it receives HLDA from the CPU. An acknowledge from the CPU signals that DMA transfers can begin. S1, S2, S3 and S4 are working the states of the DMA service. If more time is needed to complete a transfer than is available with normal timing, wait states (SW) can be inserted between S2 or S3 and S4 by use of the Ready line on the 8237A. Note that the data transferred directly from the I/O device-to-memory (or vice versa) with IOR* and MEMW* (or MEMR* and IOW*) begin active at the same time. The data is not read into or driven out of the 8237A in I/O-to-memory or memory-to-I/O DMA transfers.

Memory-to-memory transfers require a read-from and a write-to-memory to complete each transfer. The states, which resemble the normal working states, use two digit numbers for identification. Eight states are required for a single transfer. The first four states (S11, S12, S13, S14) are used for the read-from-memory half and the last four states (S21, S22, S23, S24) for the write-to-memory half of the transfer.

Idle Cycle

When no channel is requesting service, the 8237A will enter the Idle cycle and perform SI states. In this cycle the 8237A will sample the DREQ lines every clock cycle to determine if any channel is requesting a DMA service. The device will also sample CS*, looking for an attempt by the microprocessor to write or read the internal registers. When CS* is low and HLDA is low, the 8237A enters the Program condition. The CPU can now establish, change or inspect the internal definition of the part by reading from or writing to the internal registers. Address lines A0-A3 are inputs to the device and select which registers will be read or written. The IOR* and IOW* lines are used to select and time reads or writes. An internal flip-flop is used to generate an additional bit of address due to the number and size of the internal registers. This bit is used to determine the upper or lower byte of the 16-bit Address and Word Count registers. The flip-flop is reset by Master Clear or Reset. A separate software command can also reset this flip-flop.

Special software commands can be executed by the 8237A in the Program Condition. These commands are decoded as sets of addresses with the CS* and IOW*. The commands do not make use of the data bus. Instructions include Clear First/Last Flip-Flop and Master Clear.

Active Cycle

When the 8237A is in the Idle cycle and a non-masked channel requests a DMA service, the device will output an HRQ to the microprocessor and enter the Active cycle. In this cycle the DMA service will take place. The DMA service takes place in one of four modes: 1) single transfer mode; 2) block transfer mode; 3) demand transfer mode; and 4) cascade mode.

a. Single Transfer Mode

   In the Single Transfer mode the 8237A is programmed to make one transfer only. The word count will be decremented and the address decremented or incremented following each transfer. When the word count "rolls over" from zero to FFFFH, a Terminal Count (TC) will cause an Autoinitialization if the channel has been programmed to do so.

   DREQ must be held active until DACK becomes active in order to be recognized. If DREQ is held active throughout the single transfer, HRQ will go inactive and release the bus to the system. HRQ will again go active and another single transfer will occur upon receipt of a new HLDA. This ensures one full machine cycle execution between DMA transfers.

b. Block Transfer Mode

   In the Block Transfer Mode the device is activated by DREQ to continue making transfers during service until a TC, caused by word count going to FFFFH, or an external End of Process (EOP*) is encountered. DREQ should be held active until DACK becomes active. Autoinitialization will occur at the end of the service if the channel is programmed for it.

c. Demand Transfer Mode

   In this mode the device is programmed to continue making transfers until a TC of external EOP* is encountered, or until DREQ goes inactive. Therefore, transfers may continue until the I/O device has exhausted its data capacity. After the I/O device has had a chance to catch up, the DMA service is re-established by means of a DREQ. During the time between services when the microprocessor is allowed to operate, the intermediate values of address and word count are stored in the 8237A Current Address and Current Word Count registers. Only EOP* can cause an Autoinitialize at the end of the service. EOP* is generated by TC or by an external signal.

d. Cascade Mode

   This mode is used to cascade more than one 8237A together for simple system expansion. The HRQ and HLDA signals from the additional 8237A are connected to the DREQ and DACK signals of a channel of the initial 8237A. This allows the DMA requests of the additional device to propagate through the priority chain network circuits of the preceding device. The priority is preserved and the new device must wait for its turn to acknowledge requests. Since the cascade channel of the initial 8237A is used only for prioritizing the additional device, it does not output any address or control signals of its own. The 8237A will respond to DREQ and DACK but all other outputs except HRQ will be disabled.

Two additional 8237A devices cascaded into an initial device using two of the previous channels are shown in Figure 6-132. This forms a two level DMA system. More 8237A's could be added at the second level by using the remaining channels of the first level. Additional devices can also be added by cascading into the channels of the second level devices, forming a third level.

TRANSFER TYPES

Each of the three active transfer modes can perform three different types of transfers. These are Read, Write, and Verify. Write transfers move data from an I/O device to the memory by activating MEMW* and IOR*. Read transfers move data from memory to an I/O device by activating MEMR* and IOW*. Verify transfers are pseudo transfers. The 8237A operates as in Read or Write transfers generating addresses, and responding to EOP, however, the memory and I/O control lines all remain inactive. Verify mode is not permitted during memory to memory operation.

Memory-to-Memory Transfers

The 8237A includes a memory-to-memory transfer feature to perform block moves of data from one memory address space to another with a minimum of program space and effort. (See Figure 6-133 for timing.) Channels 0 and 1 are selected to operate in the memory-to-memory mode by programming a bit in the Command register. A transfer is initiated by setting the software DREQ for channel 0. The 8237A requests a DMA service in the normal manner. After HLDA is true, the device reads data from the memory using eight-state transfers in the Block Transfer mode. The channel 0 Current Address register is the source for the address used and is decremented or incremented in the normal manner. The data byte read from the memory is stored in the 8237A

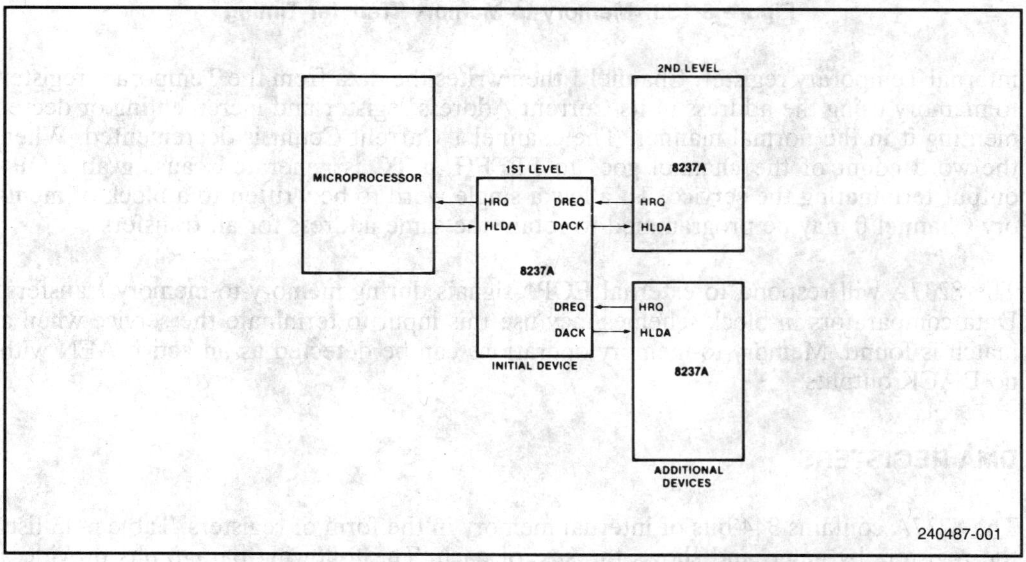

Figure 6-132. Cascaded 8237A's

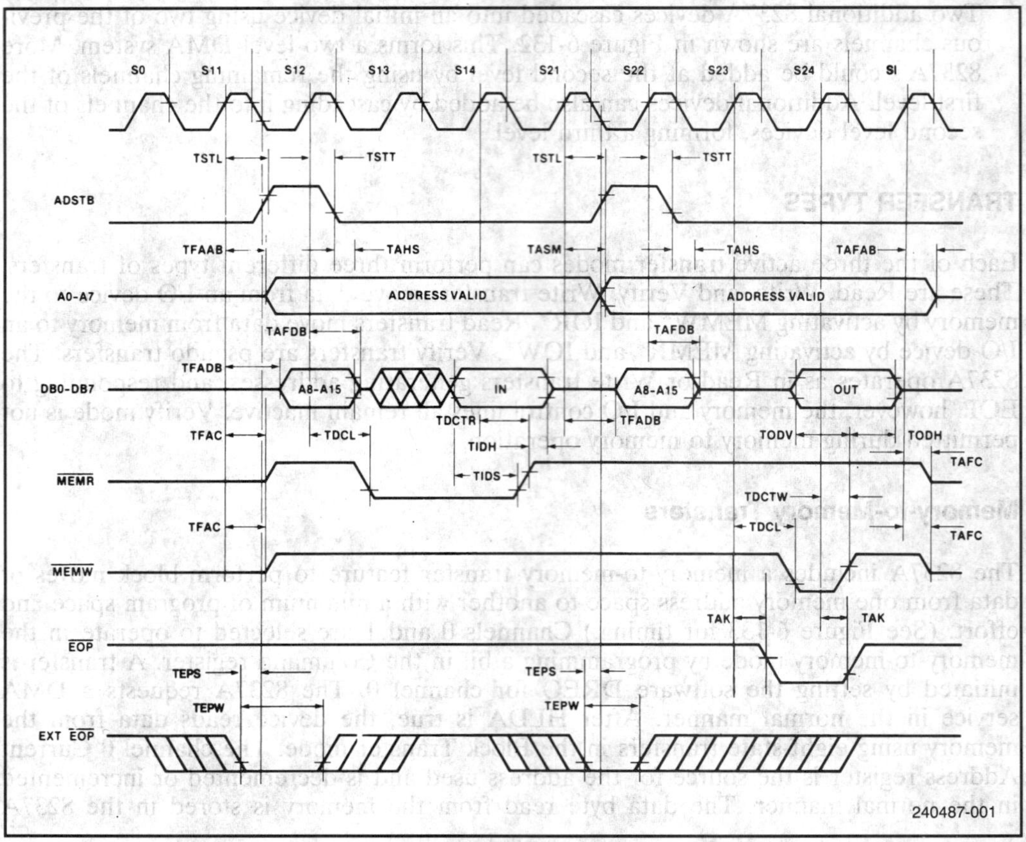

Figure 6-133. Memory-to-Memory Transfer Timing

internal Temporary register. Channel 1 then writes the data from the Temporary register to memory using the address in its Current Address register and incrementing or decrementing it in the normal manner. The channel 1 Current Count is decremented. When the word count of the channel goes to FFFFH, a TC is generated causing an EOP* output terminating the service. To allow a single word to be written to a block of memory Channel 0 may be programmed to retain the same address for all transfers.

The 8237A will respond to external EOP* signals during memory-to-memory transfers. Data comparators in block schemes may use this input to terminate the service when a match is found. Memory-to-memory operations can be detected as an active AEN with no DACK outputs.

DMA REGISTERS

The 8237A contains 344 bits of internal memory in the form of registers. Table 6-43 lists the registers by name and shows the size of each. The following paragraphs provide a detailed description of each register and their functions.

Table 6-43. 8237A Internal Registers

Name	Size	Number
Base Address Registers	16 bits	4
Base Word Count Registers	16 bits	4
Current Address Registers	16 bits	4
Current Word Count Registers	16 bits	4
Temporary Address Register	16 bits	1
Temporary Word Count Register	16 bits	1
Status REgister	8 bits	1
Command Register	8 bits	1
Temporary Register	8 bits	1
Mode Registers	6 bits	4
Mask REgister	4 bits	1
Request Register	4 bits	1

Current Address Register

Each channel has a 16-bit Current Address register. This register holds the value of the address used during DMA transfers. The address is automatically incremented or decremented after each transfer and the intermediate values of the address are stored in the Current Address register during the transfer. This register is written or read by the microprocessor in successive 8-bit bytes. The register may also be reintialized back to its original value by an Autoinitialize. Autoinitialize takes place after EOP*.

Current Word Register

Each channel has a 16-bit Current Word Register. This register determines the number of transfers to be performed. The actual number of transfers will be one more than the number programmed in the Current Word register (programming a count of 100 will result in 101 transfers, etc.). The word count is decremented after each transfer. The immediate value of the word count is stored in the register during the transfer. When the value in the register goes from zero to FFFFH, a TC will be generated. This register is loaded or read in successive 8-bit bytes by the microprocessor in the Program Condition. Following the end of a DMA service it may also be reinitialized by an Autoinitialization back to its original value. Autoinitialize can occur only when EOP* occurs. If it is not Autoinitialized, this register will have a count of FFFFH after TC.

Base Address and Base Word Count Registers

Each channel has a pair of Base Address and Base Word Count Registers. These 16-bit registers store the original value of their associated current registers. During Autoinitialize these values are used to restore the current registers to their original values. The base registers are written simultaneously with their corresponding current register in 8-bit bytes in the Program Condition by the microprocessor. These registers cannot be read by the microprocessor.

Command Register

The 8-bit Command register controls the operation of the 8237A (see Figure 6-134). This register is programmed by the microprocessor in the Program Condition and is cleared by Reset or a Master Clear instruction. Figure 6-134 lists the function of each of the command bits. Figure 6-135 shows the address coding.

Mode Register

Each channel has a 6-bit Mode register associated with it (see Figure 6-136). When the register is being written to by the microprocessor in the Program condition, bits 0 and 1 determine which channel Mode register is to be written.

Request Register

The 8237A can respond to requests for DMA service which are initialized by software as well as by a DREQ. Each channel has a request bit associated with it in the 4-bit Request register (see Figure 6-137). These are non-maskable and subject to prioritization by the Priority Encoder network. Each register bit is set or reset separately under software control or is cleared upon generation of a TC or external EOP*. The entire register is cleared by a Reset. To set or reset a bit, the software loads the proper form of the word. See Table 6-44 for register address coding. In order to make a software request, the channel must be in Block Mode.

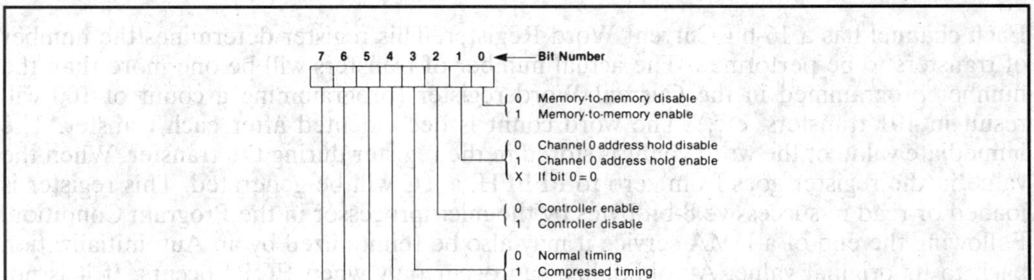

Figure 6-134. Command Register

Signals						
A3	A2	A1	A0	$\overline{IOR}$	$\overline{IOW}$	Operation
1	0	0	0	0	1	Read Status Register
1	0	0	0	1	0	Write Command Register
1	0	0	1	0	1	Illegal
1	0	0	1	1	0	Write Request Register
1	0	1	0	0	1	Illegal
1	0	1	0	1	0	Write Single Mask Register Bit
1	0	1	1	0	1	Illegal
1	0	1	1	1	0	Write Mode Register
1	1	0	0	0	1	Illegal
1	1	0	0	1	0	Clear Byte Pointer Flip/Flop
1	1	0	1	0	1	Read Temporary Register
1	1	0	1	1	0	Master Clear
1	1	1	0	0	1	Illegal
1	1	1	0	1	0	Clear Mask Register
1	1	1	1	0	1	Illegal
1	1	1	1	1	0	Write All Mask Register Bits

240487-001

Figure 6-135. Software Command Codes

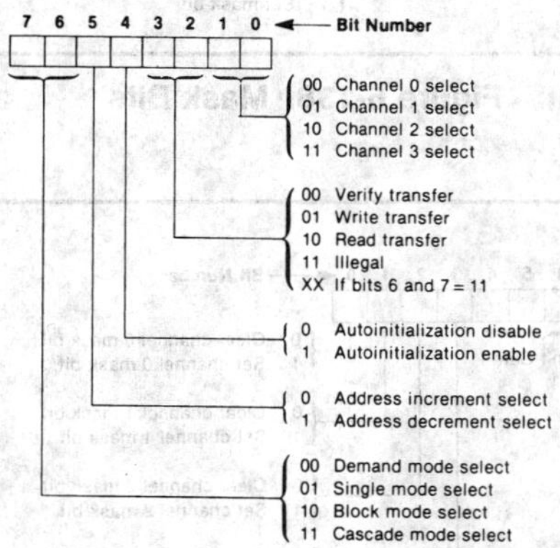

240487-001

Figure 6-136. Mode Register

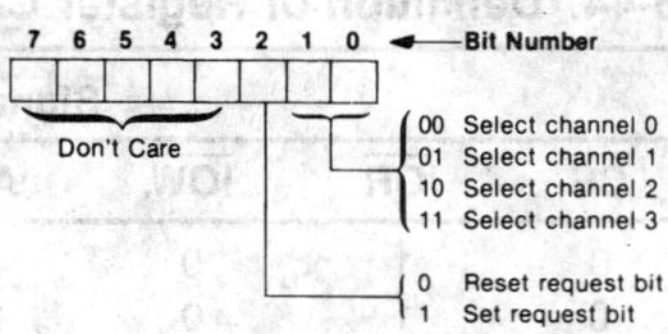

240487-001

Figure 6-137. Request Register

Mask Register

Each channel has a mask bit (see Figure 6-138) which can be set to disable the incoming DREQ. Each mask bit is set when its associated channel produces an EOP* if the channel is not programmed for Autoinitialize. Each bit of the 4-bit Mask register (see Figure 6-139) may also be set or cleared separately under software control. The entire register is also set by a Reset. This disables all DMA requests until a clear Mask register instruction allows them to occur. The instruction to separately set or clear the mask bits is similar in form to that used with the Request register. See Table 6-44 for instruction addressing.

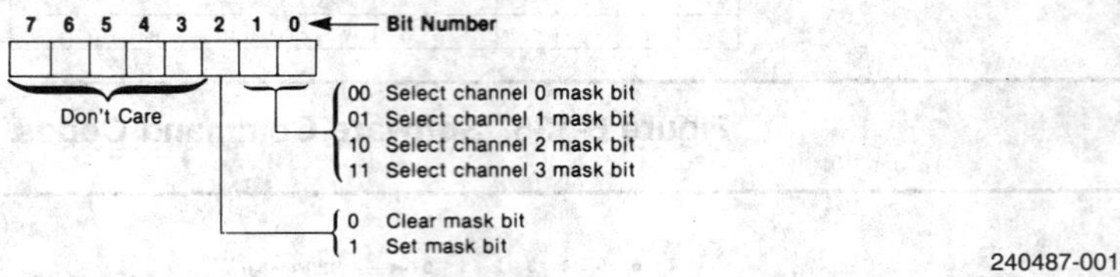

Figure 6-138. Mask Bits

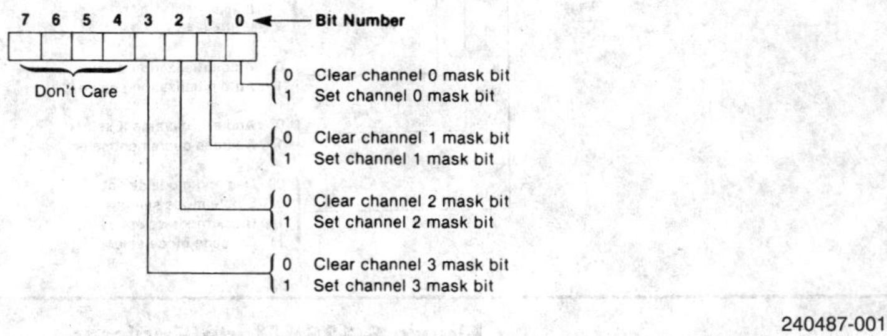

Figure 6-139. Mask Register

Table 6-44. Definition of Register Codes

Register	Operation	Signals						
		$\overline{CS}$	$\overline{IOR}$	$\overline{IOW}$	A3	A2	A1	A0
Command	Write	0	1	0	1	0	0	0
Mode	Write	0	1	0	1	0	1	1
Request	Write	0	1	0	1	0	0	1
Mask	Set/Reset	0	1	0	1	0	1	0
Mask	Write	0	1	0	1	1	1	1
Temporary	Read	0	0	1	1	1	0	1
Status	Read	0	0	1	1	0	0	0

Status Register

The Status register (see Figure 6-140) is available to be read out of the 8237A by the microprocessor. This register contains information about the status of the devices at this point. This information includes which channels have reached a terminal count and which channels have pending DMA requests. Bits 0-3 are set every time a TC is reached by that channel or an external EOP* is applied. These bits are cleared upon Reset and on each Status Read. Bits 4-7 are set whenever their corresponding channel is requesting service.

Temporary Register

The Temporary register is used to hold data during memory-to-memory transfers. Following the completion of the transfers, the last word moved can be read by the microprocessor in the Program Condition. The Temporary register always contains the last byte transferred in the last memory-to-memory operation, unless cleared by a Reset.

Software Commands

The software commands are additional special software commands which can be executed in the Program Condition (see Figure 6-135). The commands do not depend on any specific bit pattern on the data bus. The software command are Clear First/Last Flip-Flop, Master Clear and Clear Mask Register. Figure 6-135 lists the address codes for the software commands.

a. Clear First/Last Flip-Flop

This command is executed prior to writing or reading new address or word count information to the 8237A. This initializes the flip-flop to a known state so that subsequent acccesses to register contents by the microprocessor will address upper and lower bytes in the correct sequence.

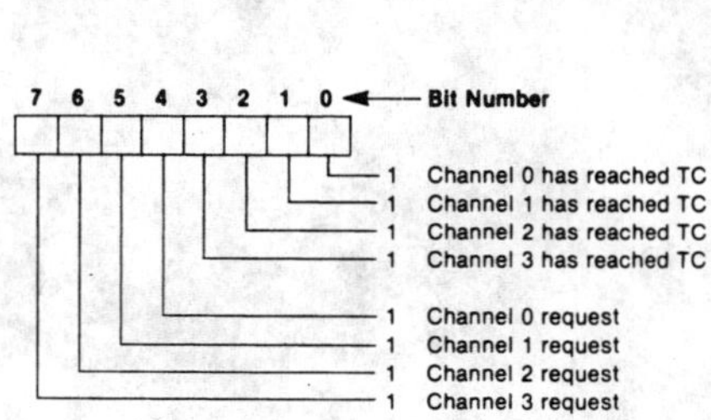

Figure 6-140. Status Register

b. Master Clear

This software instruction has the same effect as the hardware Reset. The Command, Status, Request, Temporary, and Internal First/Last Flip-Flop registers are cleared and the Mask register is set. The 8237A will enter the Idle cycle.

c. Clear Mask Register

This command clears the mask bits of all four channels, enabling them to accept DMA requests.

8087 NPX Hardware Design 7

CHAPTER 7
8087 NUMERIC PROCESSOR EXTENSION (NPX) HARDWARE DESIGN

INTRODUCTION

This chapter provides specific hardware design information on the operation and functions of Intel®'s 8087 Numeric Processor Extension (NPX). General information on the NPX coprocessor and its applications is presented, along with a component overview of the architectural and software considerations, and individual device pin functional signal definitions. Detailed descriptions of the NPX operating modes, general operation with the 8086/8088 host CPU's, and bus operation and timing are also presented. In addition, an explanation of the protocols supporting local bus transfers to the host CPU's, and a description of interrupt operation are also provided. For more specific information of any of the 8086 family support circuits, refer to the *Microprocessor and Peripheral Handbook* (Order Number: 230843).

8086/8088 Base

The 8087 Numeric Processor Extension (NPX) is based on the 8086/8088 family of microprocessors. These microprocessors are general purpose devices, designed for general data processing applications that require fast, efficient data movement and control instructions. The actual arithmetic performed on data values is fairly simple in data applications. The 8086/8088 family of microprocessors fills this need in an effective, low cost manner. However, some applications require more powerful arithmetic instructions and data types than provided by a general purpose data processor. Since the real world deals in fractional values and requires arithmetic operations like square root, sine and logarithms, integer data types and their operations may not meet the needed accuracy, speed, and ease of use requirements.

These advanced functions are not simple to implement and are not inexpensive. General data processors do not provide these features because of their cost to other less-complex applications that do not require such sophisticated features. Therefore a special, easy to use processor which has a high level of hardware and software support is required to implement these functions.

The 8087 (NPX) provides these features and supports the data types and operations needed. The NPX allows use of all of the current hardware and software support that is availble for the 8086/8088 family microprocessors. The following paragraphs present some typical applications for microprocessors using the NPX. In addition, a discussion of the use of the special hardware component, the 8087 NPX, and its software based 8087 emulator is also included. Both the component and the software emulator add extra data types and operations to the 8086/8088 family of microprocessors. The hardware component and the software emulator are completely compatible.

NUMERIC PROCESSOR EXTENSION APPLICATIONS

The versatility and performance of the 8087 NPX make it appropriate for a broad array of numerically-oriented applications. Generally, any application that exhibits the following characteristics will benefit by implementing numeric processing on the 8087:

1. Numeric data vary over a wide range of values or include non-integral values;
2. Algorithms produce very large or very small intermediate results;
3. Computations must be very precise, i.e., a large number of significant digits must be maintained;
4. Performance requirements exceed the capacity of traditional microprocessors;
5. Consistently safe, reliable results must be delivered using a programming staff that is not expert in numeric techniques.

The 8087 can also reduce software development costs and improve the performance of systems that do not use real numbers, but operate on multi-precision binary or decimal integer values.

A few examples, which show how the 8087 might be used in specific numerics applications, are described in the following list. In the past, these types of systems have typically been implemented with minicomputers. The advent of the 8087 brings the size and cost savings of microprocessor technology to these applications for the first time.

1. Business data processing – the NPX's ability to accept decimal operands and produce exact decimal results up to 18 digits greatly simplifies accounting programming. Financial calculations which use power functions can take advantage of the 8087's exponentiation and logarithmic instructions.
2. Process control – the 8087 solves dynamic range problems automatically, and its extended precision allows control functions to be finite-tuned for more accurate and efficient performance. Control algorithms implemented with the NPX also contribute to improved reliability and safety, while the 8087's speed can be exploited to real-time operations.
3. Numeric control – The 8087 can move and position machine tool heads with extreme accuracy. Axis positioning also benefits from the hardware trigonometric support provided by the 8087.
4. Robotics – Coupling small size and modest power requirements with powerful computational abilities, the NPX is ideal for on-board six-axis positioning.
5. Navigation – Very small, light weight, and accurate inertial guidance systems can be implemented with the 8087. Its built-in trigonometric functions can speed and simplify the calculation of position from bearing data.
6. Graphics terminals – The 8087 can be used in graphics terminals to locally perform many functions which normally demand the attention of a main computer; these include rotation, scaling, and interpolation. Very powerful and highly self-sufficient terminals can be built from a relatively small number of 8086/8088 family components.

7. Data acquisition – The 8087 can be used to scan, scale and reduce large quantities of data as it is collected. This lowers the storage requirements as well as the time required to process the data for analysis.

These examples are all oriented toward the "traditional" numerics applications. There are, however, many other types of systems that do not appear to the end user as "computational," but can employ the 8087 to advantage. The 8087 presents the imaginative system designer with an opportunity similar to that created by the introduction of the microprocessor itself. Many applications can be viewed as numerically-based if sufficient computational power is available to support this view. This is analogous to the thousands of successful products that have been built around "buried" microprocessors, even though the products themselves bear little resemblance to computers.

8087 EMULATOR VERSUS COMPONENT USE

Two basic implementations of the Numeric Data Processor Extension (NPX) are available. One is using the 8087 component and the other is with its software emulator (E8087). Whether the emulator or the component is used has no effect on programs at the source level. All instructions, data types and features are used in the same way at the source level.

All numeric instruction opcodes must be replaced with an interrupt instruction when the emulator is used. This replacement is performed by the LINK86 program. Interrupt vectors in the hosts interrupt vector table will point to numeric instruction emulation routines in the 8087 software emulator.

When the emulator is used, the linker changes all the 2-byte wait-escape, nop-escape, wait-segment override, or nop-segment override sequences generated by an assembler or compiler for the 8087 component with a 2-byte interrupt instruction. Any remaining bytes of the numeric instruction are left unchanged.

The host executes software interrupt instructions formed by the linker when it encounters numeric and emulated instructions. The interrupt vector table directs the host to the proper entry point in the 8087 emulator. The host then decodes any remaining part of the numeric instruction using the interrupt return address and CPU register set, performs the indicated operation, and returns to the next instruction following the emulated numeric instruction. One copy of the 8087 emulator can be shared by all programs in the host.

The decision to use the 8087 or the software emulator is made at link time, when all software modules are brought together. Depending on whether an 8087 or its software emulator is used, a different group of library modules are included for linking with the program.

If the 8087 component is used, the libraries do not add any code to the program, they just satisfy external references made by the assembler or compiler. Using the emulator will not increase the size of individual modules, however, other modules requiring about 16K bytes that implement the emulator will be automatically added.

Selecting between the emulator or the 8087 can be very easy. Different versions of submit files performing the link operation can be used to specify the different set of library modules needed. See Figure 7-1 for an example of the two different submit files for the same program using the NPX with an 8087 or the 8087 emulator.

8087 Mobility in any 8086/8088 Design

The design of any maximum mode 8086 or 8088 system can be easily upgraded with an 8087. Such a system would be an 8086/8087. See Figure 7-2 for 8087 DIP pin assignments, Figure 7-3 for local bus interconnections of a typical 8086/8087 (or 8088/8087) system. The 8087 shares the maximum mode host's multiplexed address/data bus, status signals, queue status signals, ready status signals, clock and reset signal. Two dedicated signals, BUSY and INT, are used to inform the host of the 8087's status. To ensure that the host will always see a "not busy" status if an 8087 is not installed, a 10K pull-down resistor should be installed on the BUSY signal line.

```
8087 BASED LINK/LOCATE COMMANDS

LINK86 :F1:PROG.OBJ, IO.LIB, 8087.LIB TO
       :F1:PROG.LNK
LOC86  :F1:PROG.LNK TO :F1:PROG

SOFTWARE EMULATOR BASED
LINK/LOCATE COMMANDS

LINK86 :F1:PROG.OBJ,  IO.LIB, E8087.LIB,
        E8087 TO :F1:PROG.LNK
LOC86  :F1:PROG.LNK TO :F1:PROG
```

Figure 7-1. Submit File Example

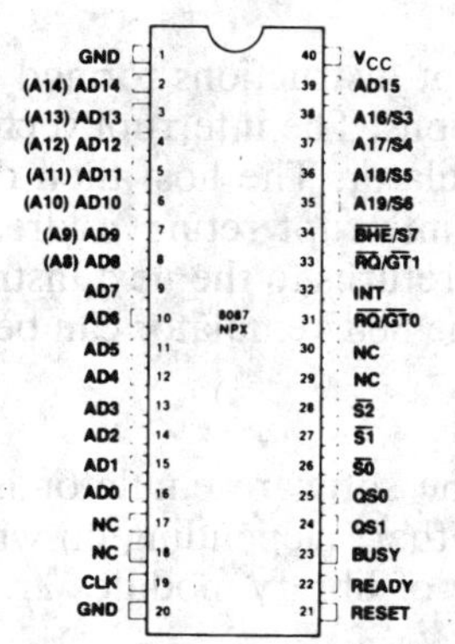

240487-001

Figure 7-2. 8087 Numeric Data Processor Pin Diagram

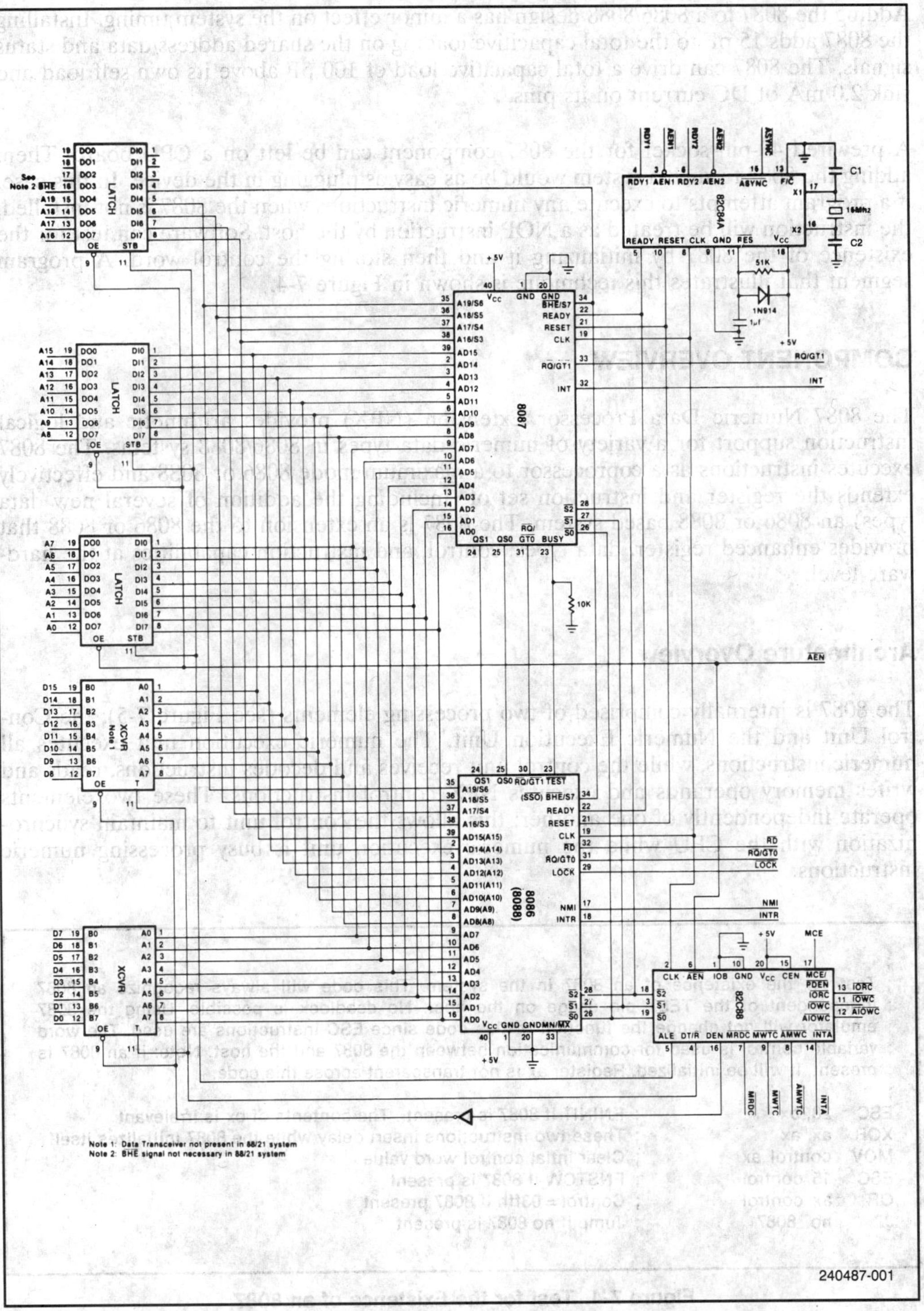

Figure 7-3. Typical 8086/8087 Family System Diagram

Adding the 8087 to a 8086/8088 design has a minor effect on the system timing. Installing the 8087 adds 15 pF to the total capacitive loading on the shared address/data and status signals. The 8087 can drive a total capacitive load of 100 pF above its own self load and sink 2.0 mA of DC current on its pins.

A prewired 40-pin socket for the 8087 component can be left on a CPU board. Then, adding the 8087 to such a system would be as easy as plugging in the device. In this case, if a program attempts to execute any numeric instructions when the 8087 is not installed, the instruction will be treated as a NOP instruction by the host. Software can test for the existence of the 8087 by initializing it and then storing the control word. A program segment that illustrates this technique is shown in Figure 7-4.

COMPONENT OVERVIEW

The 8087 Numeric Data Processor Extension (NPX) provides arithmetic and logical instruction support for a variety of numeric data types in 8086/8088 systems. The 8087 executes instructions as a coprocessor to a maximum mode 8086 or 8088 and effectively extends the register and instruction set of (including the addition of several new data types) an 8086 or 8088 based system. The 8087 is an extension to the 8086 or 8088 that provides enhanced register, data types, control, and instruction capabilities at the hardware level.

Architecture Overview

The 8087 is internally comprised of two processing elements (see Figure 7-5), the Control Unit and the Numeric Execution Unit. The numeric execution unit executes all numeric instructions, while the control unit receives and decodes instructions, reads and writes memory operands and executes NPX control instructions. These two elements operate independently of one another; this allows the control unit to maintain synchronization with the CPU while the numeric execution unit is busy processing numeric instructions.

```
;
; Test for the existence of an 8087 in the system. This code will always recognize an 8087
; independent of the TEST pin usage on the host. No deadlock is possible. Using the 8087
; emulator will not change the function of this code since ESC instructions are used. The word
; variable control is used for communication between the 8087 and the host. Note: if an 8087 is
; present, it will be initialized. Register ax is not transparent across this code.
;
ESC   28, bx          ; FNINIT if 8087 is present . The contents of bx is irrelevant
XOR   ax, ax          ; These two instructions insert delay while the 8087 initializes itself
MOV   control, ax     ; Clear intial control word value
ESC   15, control     ; FNSTCW if 8087 is present
OR    ax, control     ; Control = 03ffh if 8087 present
JZ    no_8087         ; Jump if no 8087 is present
```

Figure 7-4. Test for the Existence of an 8087

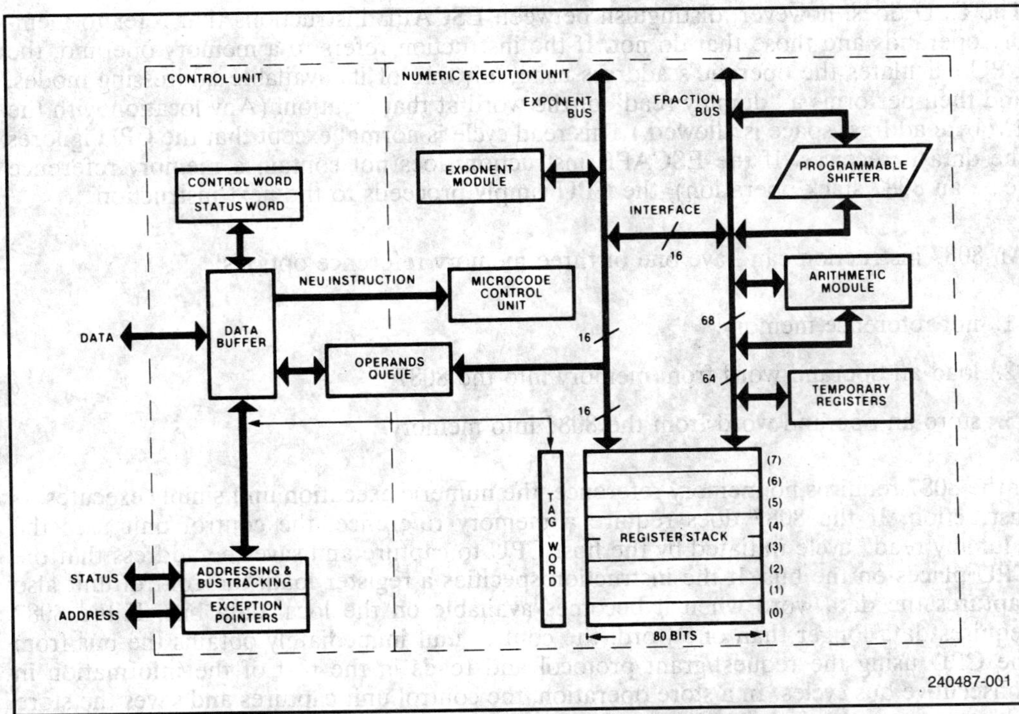

Figure 7-5. 8087 Numeric Processor Extension Block Diagram

CONTROL UNIT

The control unit keeps the 8087 synchronized with its host CPU. 8087 instructions intermix with host CPU instructions in a single instruction stream (the CPU fetches all instructions from memory). By monitoring the status signals (S0*-S2*, S6) of the CPU, the NPX control unit determines when an 8086 instruction is being fetched. At the same time, the control unit monitors the Data bus in parallel with the host CPU to obtain instruction that pertain to the 8087.

The CPU maintains an instruction queue that is identical to the queue in the host CPU. By monitoring the BHE*/S7 line, the control unit automatically determines if the CPU is an 8086 or an 8088 immediately after reset and matches its queue length accordingly. Also, by monitoring the CPU's queue status lines (QS0, QS1), the control unit obtains and decodes instructions from the queue synchronously with the CPU.

A numeric instruction for the 8087 appears as an ESCAPE instruction to the 8086 or 8088 CPU; both the CPU and the NPX decode and execute the ESCAPE instruction together. Only the 8087, however, recognizes the numeric instructions. The start of a numeric operation begins when the CPU executes the ESCAPE instruction (the instruction may or may not identify a memory operand).

The CPU does, however, distinguish between ESCAPE instructions that refer to memory operands and those that do not. If the instruction refers to a memory operand, the CPU calculates the operand's address using any one of its available addressing modes, and then performs a "dummy read" of the word at that location. (Any location with the 1M byte address space is allowed.) This read cycle is normal except that the CPU ignores the data it receives. If the ESCAPE instruction does not contain a memory reference (e.g., an 8087 stack operation), the CPU simply proceeds to the next instruction.

An 8087 instruction can have one of three memory reference options:

1. not reference memory;
2. load an operand word from memory into the 8087;
3. store an operand word from the 8087 into memory.

If the 8087 requires no memory reference, the numeric execution unit simply executes its instruction. If the 8087 does require a memory reference, the control unit uses the "dummy read" cycle initiated by the host CPU to capture and save the address that the CPU places on the bus. If the instruction specifies a register load, the control unit also captures the data word when it becomes available on the local data bus. If the 8087 requires data longer than one word, the control unit immediately obtains the bus from the CPU using the request/grant protocol and reads in the rest of the information in consecutive bus cycles. In a store operation, the control unit captures and saves the store address as in a register load operation, and ignores the data word that follows in the "dummy read" cycle. When the 8087 is ready to perform the store, the control unit obtains the bus from the CPU and writes the operand starting at the specified address.

NUMERIC EXECUTION UNIT

The 8087 executes all instructions that involve the numeric register stack. These instructions include arithmetic, logical, transcendental, constant and data transfer operations. The numeric execution unit in the NPX has an 80-bit wide data path (64 fraction bits, 15 exponent bits and a sign bit) that allows internal operand transfers to be performed at very high speeds.

When the numeric execution unit begins executing an instruction, it activates the 8087 BUSY signal. This signal can be used in conjunction with the CPU WAIT instruction to resynchronize both processors when the numeric execution unit has completed its current instruction.

Software Overview

The following paragraphs discuss the ESCAPE instruction format and discuss the use of the ESCAPE instruction with customer coprocessors. The constraints which the designer must exercise when designing this type of circuit are also discussed.

ESCAPE INSTRUCTION FORMAT

There are two basic forms of the ESCAPE instructions. These are non-memory form (see Figure 7-6) and the memory reference form (see Figure 7-7). All ESCAPE instructions start with the high order 5-bits of the instruction being 11011. The non-memory form of the ESCAPE instruction initiates some activity in the coprocessor using the nine available bits of the ESCAPE instruction to indicate which action to perform.

The memory reference forms of the ESCAPE instruction allow the host to point out a memory operand to the coprocessor using any host memory addressing mode. Six bits are available in this form to identify what to do with the memory operand. Note that the coprocessor may not recognize all possible ESCAPE instructions. In this case the coprocessor ignores the unrecognized ESCAPE instructions.

In the memory reference forms of the ESCAPE instructions bits 7 and 6 of the byte follow the ESCAPE opcode. These two bits are the MOD field of the 8086 or 8088 effective address calculation. Together with R/M field bits 2 through 0, bits 7 and 6 determine the addressing mode and how many subsequent bytes still remain in the instruction.

The 8086 or 8088 ESCAPE instructions provide 64 memory reference opcodes and 512 non-memory reference opcodes. The 8087 only uses 57 of the memory reference opcodes and 406 of the non-memory reference opcodes. Refer to Figure 7-8 for a list of the ESCAPE instructions not used by the 8087.

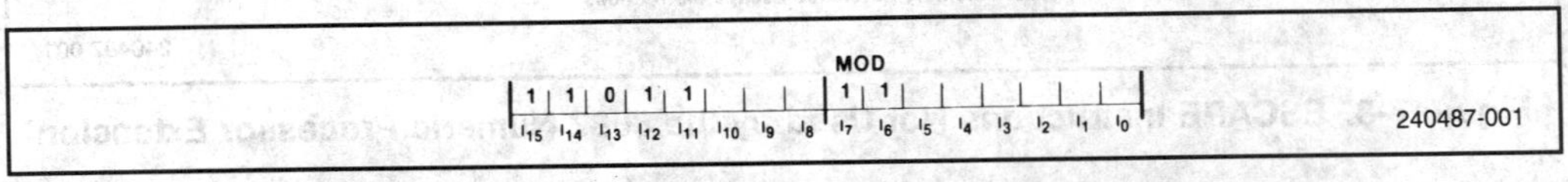

Figure 7-6. Non-Memory Reference Escape Instruction Form

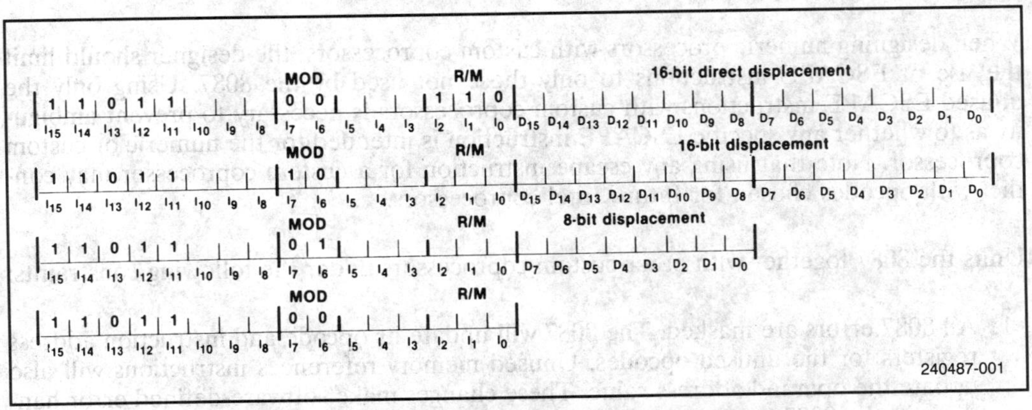

Figure 7-7. Memory Reference Escape Instruction Form

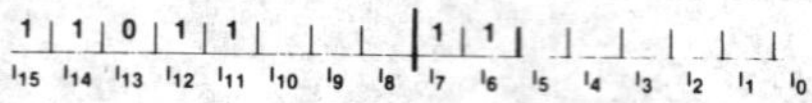

I_{10}	I_9	I_8	I_5	I_4	I_3	I_2	I_1	I_0	Available codes
0	0	1	0	1	0	0	0	1	1
0	0	1	0	1	0	0	1	—	2
0	0	1	0	1	0	1	—	—	4
0	0	1	1	0	0	0	1	—	2
0	0	1	1	0	0	1	1	—	2
0	0	1	1	0	1	1	1	1	1
0	0	1	1	1	0	1	0	1	1
0	0	1	1	1	1	0	1	1	1
0	0	1	1	1	1	1	1	—	2
0	1	1	1	0	0	1	0	1	1
0	1	1	1	0	0	1	1	—	2
0	1	1	1	0	1	—	—	—	8
0	1	1	1	1	—	—	—	—	16
1	0	1	1	—	—	—	—	—	32
1	1	1	1	0	0	0	0	1	1
1	1	1	1	0	0	0	1	0	1
1	1	1	1	0	0	1	—	—	4
1	1	1	1	0	1	—	—	—	8
1	1	1	1	1	—	—	—	—	16
									105 total

Available Non-Memory Reference Escape Instructions

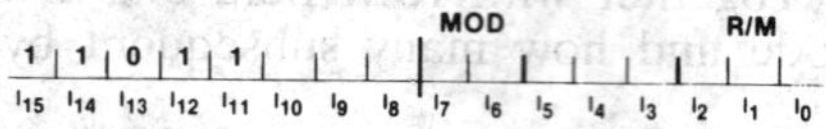

I_{10}	I_9	I_8	I_5	I_4	I_3
0	0	1	0	0	1
0	1	1	0	0	1
0	1	1	1	0	0
0	1	1	1	1	0
1	0	1	0	0	1
1	0	1	1	0	1
1	1	1	0	0	1

Available Memory Reference Escape Instructions

240487-001

Figure 7-8. ESCAPE Instructions Not Used by the 8087 Numeric Processor Extension

USING THE 8087 WITH CUSTOM COPROCESSORS

When designing numeric processors with custom coprocessors, the designer should limit the use of ESCAPE instructions to only those not used by the 8087. Using only the unused ESCAPE instructions with custom coprocessors is necessary to prevent ambiguity as to whether any specific ESCAPE instruction is intended for the numeric or custom coprocessor. Note that using any escape instruction for a custom coprocessor may conflict with opcodes chosen for future Intel coprocessors.

Units the 8087 together with other custom coprocessors under the following constraints:

1. All 8087 errors are masked. The 8087 will update its opcode and instruction address registers for the unused opcodes. Unused memory references instructions will also update the operand address value. These changes make software-defined error handling in the 8087 impossible.

2. If the coprocessors provide a BUSY signal, they must be ORed together for connection to the host TEST pin. When the host executes a WAIT instruction, it does not know which coprocessor will be effected by the following ESCAPE instruction. Typically, all coprocessors must be idle before executing the ESCAPE instruction.

DEVICE PIN ASSIGNMENTS

A complete functional description of each device pin signal is provided in Table 7-1. This table correlates the description to the pin number and associated signal symbol.

OPERATING MODES

The following paragraphs describe the operation of the 8087 NPX in conjunction with the 8086(88) microprocessors, describe the overall electrical interface and present design considerations relate to the interface.

8087/8086(88) Interface

When installed as a coprocessor to the 8086 or 8088, the 8087 connects in parallel with the CPU. The CPU's status lines (S0*-S2*) and queue status lines (QS0-QS1) allow the 8087 to monitor and decode instructions in synchronization with the CPU and without any CPU overhead. The 8087 can process instructions in parallel with and independent of the host CPU. For resynchronization, the NPX's BUSY signal informs the CPU that the 8087 is executing an instruction; the CPU WAIT instruction tests this signal to insure that the NPX is ready to execute subsequent instructions. The NPX can interrupt the CPU when it detects an error or exception. The 8087's interrupt request line is typically routed to the CPU through an 8259A Programmable Interrupt Controller (see Figure 7-2) for 8087 pinout information.

The 8087 uses one of the request/grant lines of the 8086 architecture to obtain control of the local bus for data transfers. The other request/grant line is available for general system use (e.g., an I/O processor in LOCAL mode). A bus master can also be connected to the 8087's RQ*/GT1* line. In this configuration the 8087 will pass the request/grant handshake signals between the CPU and the attached master when the 8087 is in control. Therefore, two additional masters can be configured in an 8086/8087 or an 8088/8087 system; one master will share the 8086 bus with the 8087 on a first come first serve basis, and the second master will be guaranteed to be higher in priority than the 8087. All processors use the same clock generator and system bus interface components (bus controller, latches and transceivers).

8086/8087 OPERATION

The following paragraphs describe 8087 NPX escape sequence (ESCAPE) operation, and also describe the operational sequence where 8087 controls the bus.

Table 7-1. 8087 Device Pin Descriptions

Symbol	Type	Name and Function
AD15-AD0	I/O	**Address Data**: These lines constitute the time multiplexed memory address (T_1) and data (T_2, T_3, T_W, T_4) bus. A0 is analogous to $\overline{BHE}$ for the lower byte of the data bus, pins D7-D0. It is LOW during T_1 when a byte is to be transferred on the lower portion of the bus in memory operations. Eight-bit oriented devices tied to the lower half of the bus would normally use A0 to condition chip select functions. These lines are active HIGH. They are input/output lines for 8087 driven bus cycles and are inputs which the 8087 monitors when the 8086/8088 is in control of the bus. A15-A8 do not require an address latch in an 8088/8087 system. The 8087 will supply an address for the T_1-T_4 period.
A19/S6, A18/S5, A17/S4, A16/S3	I/O	**Address Memory**: During T_1 these are the four most significant address lines for memory operations. During memory operations, status information is available on these lines during T_2, T_3, T_W, and T_4. For 8087 controlled bus cycles, S6, S4, and S3 are reserved and currently one (HIGH), while S5 is always LOW. These lines are inputs which the 8087 monitors when the 8086/8088 is in control of the bus.
BHE/S7	I/O	**Bus High Enable**: During T_1 the bus high enable signal ($\overline{BHE}$) should be used to enable data onto the most significant half of the data bus, pins D15-D8. Eight-bit oriented devices tied to the upper half of the bus would normally use $\overline{BHE}$ to condition chip select functions. $\overline{BHE}$ is LOW during T_1 for read and write cycles when a byte is to be transferred on the high portion of the bus. The S7 status information is available during T_2, T_3, T_W, and T_4. The signal is active LOW. S7 is an input which the 8087 monitors during 8086/8088 controlled bus cycles.
$\overline{S2}$, $\overline{S1}$, $\overline{S0}$	I/O	**Status**: For 8087 driven bus cycles, these status lines are encoded as follows: **$\overline{S2}$ $\overline{S1}$ $\overline{S0}$** 0(LOW) X X Unused 1(HIGH) 0 0 Unused 1 0 1 Read Memory 1 1 0 Write Memory 1 1 1 Passive Status is driven active during T_4, remains valid during T_1 and T_2, and is returned to the passive state (1, 1, 1) during T_3 or during T_W when READY is HIGH. This status is used by the 82C88 Bus Controller to generate all memory access control signals. Any change in $\overline{S2}$, $\overline{S1}$, or $\overline{S0}$ during T_4 is used to indicate the beginning of a bus cycle, and the return to the passive state in T_3 or T_W is used to indicate the end of a bus cycle. These signals are monitored by the 8087 when the 8086/8088 is in control of the bus.

Table 7-1. 8087 Device Pin Descriptions

Symbol	Type	Name and Function
$\overline{\text{RQ}}/\overline{\text{GT0}}$	I/O	**Request/Grant**: This request/grant pin is used by the NPX to gain control of the local bus from the CPU for operand transfers or on behalf of another bus master. It must be connected to one of the two processor request/grant pins. The request grant sequence on this pin is as follows: 1. A pulse one clock wide is passed to the CPU to indicate a local bus request by either the 8087 or the master connected to the 8087 $\overline{\text{RQ}}/\overline{\text{GT1}}$ pin. 2. The 8087 waits for the grant pulse and when it is received will either initiate bus transfer activity in the clock cycle following the grant or pass the grant out on the $\overline{\text{RQ}}/\overline{\text{GT1}}$ pin in this clock if the initial request was for another bus master. 3. The 8087 will generate a release pulse to the CPU one clock cycle after the completion of the last 8087 bus cycle or on receipt of the release pulse from the bus master on $\overline{\text{RQ}}/\overline{\text{GT1}}$.
$\overline{\text{RQ}}/\overline{\text{GT1}}$	I/O	**Request/Grant**: This request/grant pin is used by another local bus master to force the 8087 to request the local bus. If the 8087 is not in control of the bus when the request is made the request/grant sequence is passed through the 8087 on the $\overline{\text{RQ}}/\overline{\text{GT0}}$ pin one cycle later. Subsequent grant and release pulses are also passed through the 8087 with a two and one clock delay, respectively, for resynchronization. $\overline{\text{RQ}}/\overline{\text{GT1}}$ has an internal pull-up resistor, and so may be left unconnected. If the 8087 has control of the bus the request/grant sequence is as follows: 1. A pulse 1 CLK wide from another local bus master indicates a local bus request to the 8087 (pulse 1). 2. During the 8087's next T_4 or T_1 a pulse 1 CLK wide from the 8087 to the requesting master (pulse 2) indicates that the 8087 has allowed the local bus to float and that it will enter the "RQ/GT acknowledge" state at the next CLK. The 8087's control unit is disconnected logically from the local bus during "RQ/GT acknowledge." 3. A pulse 1 CLK wide from the requesting master indicates to the 8087 (pulse 3) that the "RQ/GT" request is about to end and that the 8087 can reclaim the local bus at the next CLK.f Each master-master exchange of the local bus is a sequence of 3 pulses. There must be one dead CLK cycle after each bus exchange. Pulses are active LOW.

Table 7-1. 8087 Device Pin Descriptions

Symbol	Type	Name and Function
QS1,QS2	I	**QS1, QS0**: QS1 and QS0 provide the 8087 with status to allow tracking of the CPU instruction queue. **QS1** **QS0** 0(LOW) 0 No Operation 0 1 First Byte of Op Code from Queue 1(HIGH) 0 Empty the Queue 1 1 Subsequent Byte from Queue
INT	O	**Interrupt**: This line is used to indicate that an unmasked exception has occurred during numeric instruction execution when 8087 interrupts are enabled. This signal is typically routed to an 8259A. INT is active HIGH.
BUSY	O	**BUSY**: This signal indicates that the 8087 NEU is executing a numeric instruction. It is connected to the CPU's $\overline{TEST}$ pin to provide synchronization. In the case of an unmasked exception BUSY remains active until the exception is cleared. BUSY is active HIGH.
READY	I	**READY**: READY is the acknowledgment from the addressed memory device that it will complete the data transfer. The RDY signal from memory is synchronized by the 82C84A Clock Generator to form READY. This signal is active HIGH.
RESET	I	**Reset**: RESET causes the processor to immediately terminate its present activity. The signal must be active HIGH for at least four clock cycles. RESET is internally synchronized.
CLK	I	**Clock**: The clock provides the basic timing for the processor and bus controller. It is asymmetric with a 33% duty cycle to provide optimized internal timing.
V_{CC}		**Power**: V_{CC} is the +5V power supply pin.
GND		**Ground**: GND are the ground pins.

NOTE: For the pin descriptions of the 8086 and 8088 CPU's reference those respective data sheets.

Decoding Escape Instructions

The coprocessor must examine all instructions executed by the host to recognize ESCAPE instructions. When the host fetches an instruction byte from its internal queue, the coprocessor must also fetch an instruction byte.

The queue status state, fetch opcode byte, identifies when an opcode byte is being examined by the host. At the same time, the coprocessor will check if the byte fetched from its internal instruction queue is an ESCAPE opcode. If the instruction is not an ESCAPE, the coprocessor will ignore it. The queue status signals for fetch subsequent byte and flush queue let the coprocessor track the host's queue without knowledge of the length and function of host instructions and addressing modes.

HOST ESCAPE INSTRUCTION PROCESSING

The host performs one of two possible actions when an ESCAPE instruction occurs. The host may either do nothing or read a word value beginning at that address. The host ignores the value of the word read. ESCAPE instructions change none of the registers in the host except for advancing IP. Therefore, the ESCAPE instruction will effectively be a NOP to the host if no coprocessor exists, or the coprocessor ignores the ESCAPE instruction. Except for calculating a memory address and reading a word of memory, the host makes no other assumptions regarding coprocessor activity.

Many reference ESCAPE instructions have two purposes. One identifies a memory operand and the other is, for certain instructions, to transfer a word from memory to the coprocessor.

COPROCESSOR INTERFACE TO MEMORY

Coprocessor design is greatly simplified if only the reading of memory values of 16 bits or less is required. the host can perform all the reads with the coprocessor latching the value as it appears on the data bus at the end of T3 during the memory read cycle. The coprocessor does not need to become a local bus master to read or write additional information.

If the coprocessor must write information to memory, or deal with data values longer than one word, it must save the memory address and be able to become the local bus master. The read operation performed by the host when executing the ESCAPE instruction places the 20-bit physical address of the operand on the address/data pins during T1 of the memory cycle. The coprocessor can latch the address at this time. If the coprocessor instruction also requires reading a value, it will appear on the data bus during T3 of the memory read. All other memory bytes are addressed relative to this starting physical address.

Whether the coprocessor becomes a bus master or not, it must be able to identify the memory read performed by the host in the course of executing an ESCAPE instruction if it has memory reference instruction forms. Identifying the memory read requires the following conditions be met:

1. A MOD value of 00, 01 or 10 in the second byte of the ESCAPE instruction executed by the host.
2. This action must be the first data read memory cycle performed by the host after it encountered the ESCAPE instruction (i.e., S2-S0 will be 101 and S6 will be 0).

The coprocessor must continue to track the host's instruction queue while it calculates the memory address and reads the memory value. This simply requires following the fetch subsequent byte status commands that occur on the queue status pins.

The coprocessor must be aware of the host bus characteristics that determine how the host will read the word operand of a memory refernce ESCAPE instruction. An 8088 host will always perform two byte reads at sequential addresses, but an 8086 can perform either single word read or two byte reads to sequential addresses. The 8086 places no restrictions on the alignment of word operands in memory. It will automatically perform two byte operations for word operands at an odd address. These two operations are necessary because the two bytes of operand exist in two different memory words. The coprocessor must be able to accept the two possible methods of reading a word value on the 8086.

The coprocessor determines whether an 8086 performs one or two memory cycles as a part of the current ESCAPE instruction execution. During T1 of the first memory read by the host, the AD0 pin tells the coprocessor if this is the only read to be performed as part of the ESCAPE instruction. If AD0 is a 1 during T1 of the memory cycle, the 8086 immediately follows this memory read cycle with another one at the next byte address.

Concurrent Execution of Host and Coprocessor

After the coprocessor has started its operation, the host may continue on with the program, executing it in parallel while the coprocessor performs the function started earlier. The parallel operation of the coprocessor does not normally affect that of the host unless the coprocessor must reference memory or I/O-based operands. When the host releases the local bus to the coprocessor, the host may continue to execute from its internal instruction queue. However, the host must stop when it also needs the local bus currently in use by the coprocessor. Except for the stolen memory cycle, the operation of the coprocessor is transparent to the host.

This parallel operation of the host and coprocessor is called concurrent execution. Concurrent execution of instructions requires less total time than a strictly sequential execution would. System performance will be higher with concurrent execution of instructions between the host and coprocessor.

SYNCHRONIZATION

In exchange for the higher system performance made available by concurrent execution, programs must synchronize the coprocessor with the host. Synchronization is necessary whenever the host and coprocessor must use information available from the other. Synchronization involves either the host or coprocessor waiting for the other to finish an operation currently in progress. Since the host executes the program, and has program control instructions like jumps, it is given the responsibility for synchronization. To meet this need, a special host instruction exists to synchronization host operation with a coprocessor.

A more detailed discussion of the effects of instruction execution synchronization between the host CPU and the 8087 coprocessor is contained in the following paragraphs in the section "Instruction Synchronization."

COPROCESSOR CONTROL

The host has the responsibility for overall program control. Coprocessor operation is initiated by special "ESCAPE" instructions encountered by the host. When the host encounters an ESCAPE instruction, the coprocessor is expected to perform the action indicated by the instruction.

The host's coprocessor interface requires the coprocessor to recognize when the host has encountered an ESCAPE instruction. Whenever the host begins executing a new instruction, the coprocessor must look to see if it is an ESCAPE instruction. Since only the host fetches instructions and executes them, the coprocessor must monitor the instructions being executed by the host.

Instruction Synchronization

Instruction synchronization is required because the 8087 can only perform one numeric operation at a time. Before any numeric operation is started, the 8087 must have completed all activity from previous instructions. When executing a typical NPX instruction, the CPU will complete the ESC long before the 8087 finishes interpretation of the same machine instruction. Upon completion of the ESC, the CPU will decode and execute the next instruction, and the NPX's control unit, tracking the CPU, will do the same. (The NPX "executes" a CPU instruction by ignoring it.) If the CPU has work to do that does not effect the NPX, it can proceed with a series of instructions while the NPX is executing in parallel. The NPX's control unit will ignore these CPU-only instructions as they do not contain the 8087 escape code. This asynchronous execution of the processors can substantially improve the performance of systems that can be designed to exploit it.

Two cases, however, make it necessary to synchronize the execution of the CPU to NPX:

1. An NPX instruction that is executed by the numeric execution unit must not be started if the execution unit is still busy executing a previous instruction.
2. The CPU should not execute an instruction that accesses a memory operand being referenced by the NPX until the NPX has actually accessed the location.

The host coprocessor synchronization instruction (WAIT) uses the TEST pin of the host. The coprocessor can signal that it is still busy to the host via this pin. Whenever the host executes a wait instruction, it will stop program execution while the TEST input is active. When the TEST pin becomes inactive, the host will resume program execution with the next instruction following the WAIT. While waiting on the TEST pin, the host can be interrupted at 5 clock intervals; however, after the TEST pin becomes inactive, the host will immediately execute the next instruction, ignoring any pending interrupts between the WAIT and the following instruction.

The WAIT instruction allows software to synchronize the CPU to the NPX so that the CPU will not execute the following instruction until the NPX is finished with its current (if any) instruction.

Whenever the 8087 is executing an instruction, it activates its BUSY line. This signal is wired to the CPU's TEST* input as shown in Figure 7-8. The NPX ignores the WAIT instruction, and the CPU executes it. The CPU interprets the WAIT instruction as "wait while TEST* is active." The CPU examines the TEST* pin every 5 clocks. If TEST* is inactive, execution proceds with the instruction following the WAIT. If TEST* is active, the CPU examines the pin again. Therefore, the effective execution time of a WAIT can stretch from 3 clocks (3 clocks are required for decoding and setup) to infinity, as long as TEST* remains active. The purpose of the WAIT instruction is to prevent the CPU from decoding the next instruction until the 8087 is not busy. The instruction following a WAIT is decoded simultaneously by both processors.

To satisfy the first synchronization case, every 8087 instruction that affects the numeric execution unit should be preceded by a WAIT to ensure that the execution unit is ready. All instructions except the processor control class affect the numeric execution unit. To simplify programming, the 8086 family language translators provide the WAIT automatically, therefore, when an assembly language programmer codes:

```
FMUL     ;(multiply)
FDIV     ;(divide)
```

The assembler produces *four* machine instructions, as if the programmer had written:

```
WAIT
FMUL     ;(multiply)
WAIT
FDIV     ;(divide)
```

This ensures that the multiply runs to completion before the CPU and the 8087 control unit decode the divide.

To satisfy the second synchronization case, the programmer must explicitly code the FWAIT instruction immediately before a CPU instruction that accesses a memory operand read or written by a previous 8087 instruction. This will ensure that the 8087 has read or written the memory operand before the CPU attempts to use it. (The FWAIT mnemonic causes the assembler to create a CPU WAIT instruction that can be eliminated at link time if the program is run on an 8087 emulator.)

A typical sequence of instructions that illustrates the effect of the WAIT instruction and parallel execution of the NPX with a CPU is shown in Figure 7-9. The first two instructions in the sequence (FMUL and FSQRT) are 8087 instructions that illustrate the ASM-86 assembler's automatic generation of a proceding WAIT, and the effect of the WAIT when the NPX is, and is not, busy.

Since the NPX is not busy when the first WAIT is encountered, the CPU executes it and immediately proceeds to the next instruction, and the NPX ignores the WAIT. The next instruction is decoded simultaneously by both processors. The NPX starts the multiplication and raises its BUSY line. The CPU executes the ESC and then the second WAIT.

```
             ;ASSUME 8087 REGISTER STACK IS LOADED WITH OPERANDS,
             ;       NEU IS NOT BUSY,
             ;       AND THAT 'ALPHA' AND 'BETA' ARE WORD
             ;       INTEGERS.
             FMUL                         ;MULTIPLY TOP STACK
                                          ;ELEMENTS
             FSQRT                        ;SQUARE ROOT OF PRODUCT
             CMP       ALPHA,100          ;ALPHA > 100?
             JG        CONTINUE           ;YES, LEAVE UNALTERED
             MOV       ALPHA,100          ;NO, SET TO 100
   CONTINUE: FIST      BETA               ;STORE ROOT AS INTEGER WORD
             FWAIT                        ;WAIT FOR 8087 TO COMPLETE
                                          ;STORE OF BETA
             MOV       AX,BETA            ;PROCEED TO PROCESS BETA
```

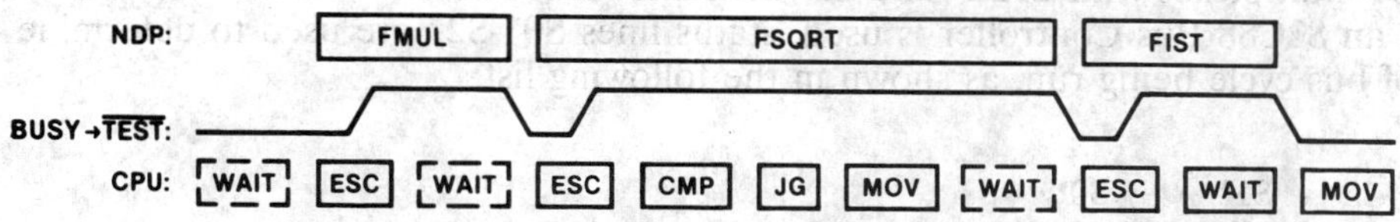

NOTES:
- WAIT (dashed box) = Assembler-generated instruction.
- Instruction execution times are not drawn to scale.

Figure 7-9. Synchronizing Execution with WAIT

Since TEST* is active (it is tied to BUSY), the CPU effectively stretches execution of the multiply by lowering BUSY. The next instruction is interpreted as a square root by the NPX and another escape by the CPU. The CPU finishes the ESC well before the NPX completes the FSQRT. This time, instead of waiting, the CPU executes three instructions (CMP, JG and MOV) while the 8087 is working on the FSQRT. The 8087 ignores these CPU-only instructions. The CPU then encounters the third WAIT, generated by the assembler immediately preceding the FIST (store stack top into integer word). When the NPX finished the FSQRT, both processors proceed to the next instruction. FIST to the NPX and ESC to the CPU. The CPU completes the escape quickly and then executes an explicit programmer-coded FWAIT to ensure that the 8087 has updated BETA before it moves BETA's new value to the register AX (refer to Figure 7-9).

The 8087 control unit can execute most processor control instructions by itself regardless of what the numeric execution unit is doing. Therefore, in these cases the 8087 can potentially execute two instruction at once. The ASM-86 assembler provides separate "wait" and "no wait" mnemonics for these instructions. For example, the instruction that sets the 8087 interrupt enable mask, and therefore disables interrupts, can be coded as FDISI or FNDISI. The assembler does not generate a WAIT if the second form is coded, so that the interrupts can be disabled while the numeric execution unit is busy with a previous instruction. The no-wait forms are principally used in exception handlers and operating systems.

8086/8087 Bus Operation

Operation and timing for the 8087 bus structure are identical to all 8086/8088 family processors in the maximum mode configuration. The address time-multiplexes with the data on the first 16/8 lines of the address/data bus. A16 through A19 are time-multiplex with four status lines S3-S6. Lines S3, S4, and S6 are always high (logical 1) for 8087 driven bus cycles while S5 is always low (logical 0). When the 8087 is monitoring CPU bus cycles (passive mode), the 8087 monitors S6 to discriminate between 8086/8088 activity and that of a local I/O processor or any other local bus master.

NOTE

The 8086/8088 must be the only processor on the local bus to drive S6 low.

Line S7 multiplexes with BHE* and has the same value as BHE* for all 8087 bus cycles. When an 82C88 Bus Controller is used, status lines S0*-S2* are used to determine the type of bus cycle being run, as shown in the following list:

S2*	S1*	S0*	
0	X	X	Unused
1	0	0	Unused
1	0	1	Memory Data Read
1	1	0	Memory Data Write
1	1	1	Passive (no bus cycle)

System Configuration

As a coprocessor to an 8086 or 8088, the 8087 is wired in parallel with the CPU as shown in Figure 7-10. The CPU's status (S0-S2) and queue status lines (QS0-QS1) enable the 8087 to monitor and decode instructions in synchronization with the CPU and without any CPU overhead. Once started, the 8087 can process in parallel with, and independent

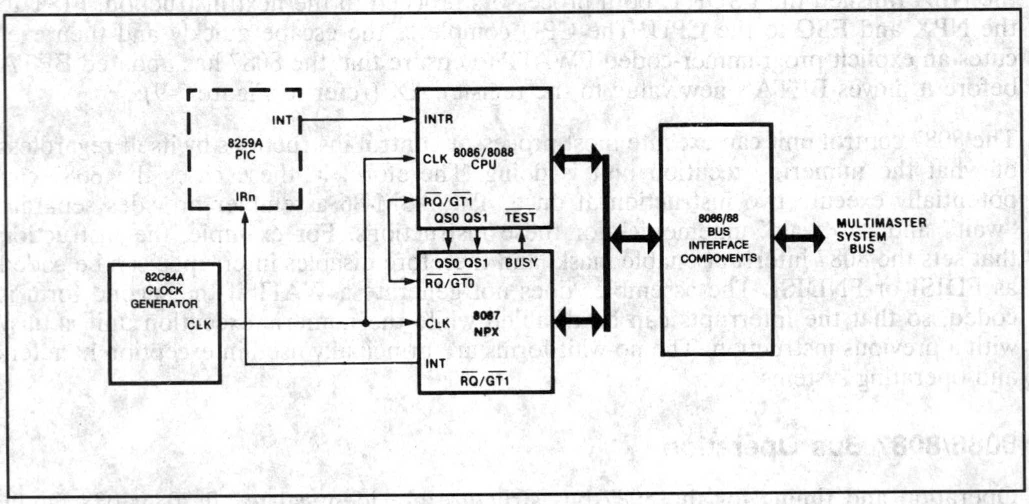

Figure 7-10. 8086/8087, 8088/8087 System Configuration

of, the host CPU. For resynchronization, the 8087's BUSY signal informs the CPU that the 8087 is executing an instruction and the CPU WAIT instruction tests this signal to insure that the 8087 is ready to execute subsequent instructions. The 8087 can interrupt the CPU when it detects an error or exception. The 8087's interrupt request line is typically routed to the CPU through an 8259A Programmable Interrupt Controller for 8086, 8088 systems.

The 8087 uses one of the request/grant lines of the 8086/8088 architecture (typically $\overline{\text{RQ}}/\overline{\text{GT0}}$) to obtain control of the local bus for data transfers. The other request/grant line is available for general system use (for instance by an I/O processor in LOCAL mode). A bus master can also be connected to the 8087's $\overline{\text{RQ}}/\overline{\text{GT1}}$ line. In this configuration the 8087 will pass the request/grant handshake signals between the CPU and the attached master when the 8087 is not in control of the bus and will relinquish the bus to the master directly when the 8087 is in control. In this way two additional masters can be configured in an 8086/8088 system; one will share the 8086/8088 bus with the 8087 on a first-come first-served basis, and the second will be guaranteed to be higher in priority than the 8087.